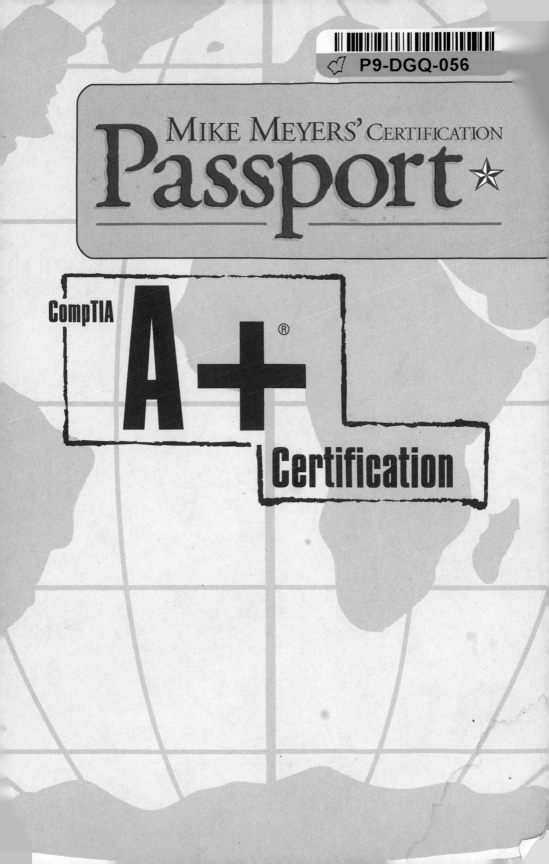

P9-DGQ-056

MIKE MEYERS' CERTIFICATION

Passport ★

CompTIA

A+®

Certification

MIKE MEYERS' CERTIFICATION
Passport ★

CompTIA **A+** ®

Certification

Fifth Edition

MIKE MEYERS

SCOTT JERNIGAN

New York • Chicago • San Francisco
Lisbon • London • Madrid • Mexico City
Milan • New Delhi • San Juan
Seoul • Singapore • Sydney • Toronto

(Exams 220-801 & 220-802)

The McGraw·Hill Companies

Cataloging-in-Publication Data is on file with the Library of Congress

McGraw-Hill books are available at special quantity discounts to use as premiums and sales promotions, or for use in corporate training programs. To contact a representative, please e-mail us at bulksales@ mcgraw-hill.com.

Mike Meyers' CompTIA A+° Certification Passport, Fifth Edition
(Exams 220-801 & 220-802)

234567890 DOC/DOC 109876543

ISBN: Book p/n 978-0-07-179564-7 and CD p/n 978-0-07-179566-1
of set 978-0-07-179567-8

MHID: Book p/n 0-07-179564-2 and CD p/n 0-07-179566-9
of set 0-07-179567-7

Sponsoring Editor	**Technical Editor**	**Production Supervisor**
Tim Green	Christopher Crayton	Jean Bodeaux
Editorial Supervisor	**Copy Editor**	**Composition**
Janet Walden	Lisa McCoy	Cenveo Publisher Services
Project Editor	**Proofreader**	**Illustration**
Howie Severson, Fortuitous	Paul Tyler	Cenveo Publisher Services
Publishing Services	**Indexer**	**Art Director, Cover**
Acquisitions Coordinator	Jack Lewis	Jeff Weeks
Stephanie Evans		

We dedicate this book to our students, past, present, and future.
You're why we do what we do!

About the Authors

Mike Meyers, lovingly called the "AlphaGeek" by those who know him, is the industry's leading authority on CompTIA A+ certification. He is the president and co-founder of Total Seminars, LLC, a provider of PC and network repair seminars, books, videos, and courseware for thousands of organizations throughout the world. Mike has been involved in the computer and network repair industry since 1977 as a technician, instructor, author, consultant, and speaker.

Author of numerous popular PC books and videos, including the best-selling *CompTIA A+ Certification All-in-One Exam Guide*, Mike is also the series editor for the highly successful *Mike Meyers' Certification Passport* series, the *Mike Meyers' Computer Skills* series, and the *Mike Meyers' Guide To* series, all published by McGraw-Hill.

As well as writing, Mike has personally taught (and continues to teach) thousands of students, including U.S. senators, U.S. Supreme Court justices, members of the United Nations, every branch of the U.S. Armed Forces, most branches of the U.S. Department of Justice, and hundreds of corporate clients, academic students at every level, prisoners, and pensioners.

<div align="right">

E-mail: michaelm@totalsem.com
Facebook: Mike Meyers (Houston, TX)
Twitter/Skype/Most IMs: desweds
Web Forums: www.totalsem.com/forums

</div>

Scott Jernigan wields a mighty red pen as Editor in Chief for Total Seminars. With a Master of Arts degree in medieval history, Scott feels as much at home in the musty archives of London as he does in the warm computer glow of Total Seminars' Houston headquarters. After fleeing a purely academic life, he dove headfirst into IT, working as an instructor, editor, and writer. Scott has written, edited, and contributed to dozens of books on computer literacy, hardware, operating systems, networking, and certification. His latest book (aside from the one in your hands) is *Computer Literacy: Your Ticket to IC³ Certification*. Scott co-authored the best-selling *CompTIA A+ Certification All-in-One Exam Guide*, the *Mike Meyers' A+ Guide to Managing and Troubleshooting PCs*, and the *CompTIA Strata IT Fundamentals All-in-One Exam Guide* (all with Mike Meyers). He has taught computer classes all over the United States, including stints at the United Nations in New York and the FBI Academy in Quantico, Virginia.

About the Technical Editor

Christopher A. Crayton (MCSE, MCP+I, CompTIA A+, CompTIA Network+) is an author, technical editor, technical consultant, security consultant, and trainer. Formerly a computer and networking instructor at Keiser College (2001 Teacher of the Year), Chris has also worked as network administrator for Protocol and at Eastman Kodak Headquarters as a computer and network specialist. Chris has authored several print and online books on topics ranging from CompTIA A+ and CompTIA Security+ to Microsoft Windows Vista. Chris has provided technical edits and reviews for many publishers, including McGraw-Hill, Pearson Education, Charles River Media, Cengage Learning, Wiley, O'Reilly, Syngress, and Apress.

About Total Seminars

Total Seminars provides certification training services to thousands of schools, corporations, and government agencies. Total Seminars produces the #1 selling CompTIA A+ and best-selling CompTIA Network+ certification books, and develops training materials such as the Total Tester for superior exam preparation. You can find Total Seminars on the Web at www.totalsem.com.

Contents at a Glance

Contents

Acknowledgments

As with every book, a lot of work from a lot of people went into making this happen.

Our managing editor, Tim Green, provided his special brand of motivation and wisdom throughout the project. Thanks for only yelling at us when we deserved it.

Howie Severson, our project editor, did an outstanding job coordinating every piece of this book, leaving no stone unturned.

Our acquisitions coordinator, Stephanie Evans, kept us organized and efficient, as usual. Your ability to find any e-mail message we've ever sent is unmatched. Thank you.

Aaron Verber, our trusty in-house editor, was his usual charming self (and smoothed out some last-minute rough edges, too).

Michael Smyer provided great photographs for the book, and Ford Pierson added his incredible illustrations. Thanks guys!

Lisa McCoy did great work as our copy editor. She transformed every awkward stumble of language into a grammatical gem.

Our technical editor, Chris Crayton, took what some would describe as gleeful delight in pointing out every technical error he found. But since he helped us fix every error, too, we won't hold it against him. Thanks, once again, for your technical expertise.

The layout team at Cenveo Publisher Services did a remarkable job, putting the prose and pictures into printable form, that you get to enjoy now!

Finally, thanks proofreader to, Paul Tyler, for catching every error last There's no error too big or smell—he'll find them all. Thank you.

Great work, team!

CompTIA Approved Quality Curriculum

It Pays to Get Certified

In a digital world, digital literacy is an essential survival skill. Certification proves you have the knowledge and skill to solve business problems in virtually any business environment. Certifications are highly valued credentials that qualify you for jobs, increased compensation, and promotion.

IT is Everywhere	IT Knowledge and Skills Get Jobs	Job Retention	New Opportunities	High Pay-High Growth Jobs
IT is mission critical to almost all organizations and its importance is increasing. • 79% of U.S. businesses report IT is either important or very important to the success of their company	Certifications verify your knowledge and skills that qualifies you for: • Jobs in the high growth IT career field • Increased compensation • Challenging assignments and promotions • 60% report that being certified is an employer or job requirement	Competence is noticed and valued in organizations. • Increased knowledge of new or complex technologies • Enhanced productivity • More insightful problem solving • Better project management and communication skills • 47% report being certified helped improve their problem solving skills	Certifications qualify you for new opportunities in your current job or when you want to change careers. • 31% report certification improved their career advancement opportunities	Hiring managers demand the strongest skill set. • There is a widening IT skills gap with over 300,000 jobs open • 88% report being certified enhanced their resume

CompTIA A+ Certification Advances Your Career

- **The CompTIA A+ credential**—provides foundation-level knowledge and skills necessary for a career in PC repair and support.
- **Starting Salary**—CompTIA A+ Certified individuals can earn as much as $65,000 per year.
- **Career Pathway**—CompTIA A+ is a building block for other CompTIA certifications such as Network+, Security+, and vendor-specific technologies.
- **More than 850,000**—individuals worldwide are CompTIA A+ certified.
- **Mandated/Recommended by organizations worldwide**—such as Cisco and HP and Ricoh, the U.S. State Department, and U.S. government contractors such as EDS, General Dynamics, and Northrop Grumman.
- **Some of the primary benefits individuals report from becoming CompTIA A+ certified are**
 - More efficient troubleshooting
 - Improved career advancement
 - More insightful problem solving
- Target audience for both the CompTIA A+ certification and the Mike Meyers' *Passport to CompTIA A+* book:
 - People who want to build and fix computers and networks professionally
 - People who want industry certifications to advance their careers
- **Prerequisites for taking the CompTIA A+ exams**—CompTIA recommends at least 12 months of hands-on lab or field experience. We recommend you read this book and practice on hardware and operating systems to get started on the path to becoming CompTIA A+ certified!

CompTIA Career Pathway

CompTIA offers a number of credentials that form a foundation for your career in technology and that allow you to pursue specific areas of concentration. Depending on the path you choose to take, CompTIA certifications help you build upon your skills and knowledge, supporting learning throughout your entire career.

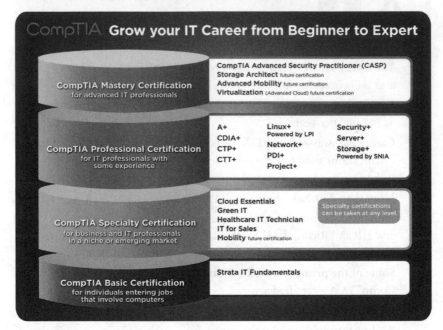

Steps to Getting Certified and Staying Certified

1. **Review exam objectives.** Review the certification objectives to make sure you know what is covered in the exam:
 www.comptia.org/certifications/testprep/examobjectives.aspx

2. **Practice for the exam.** After you have studied for the certification, take a free assessment and sample test to get an idea what type of questions might be on the exam:
 www.comptia.org/certifications/testprep/practicetests.aspx

3. **Purchase an exam voucher.** Purchase your exam voucher on the CompTIA Marketplace, which is located at: www.comptiastore.com

4. **Take the test!** Select a certification exam provider and schedule a time to take your exam. You can find exam providers at the following link: www.comptia.org/certifications/testprep/testingcenters.aspx

5. **Stay certified!** Continuing education is required. Effective January 1, 2011, CompTIA A+ certifications are valid for three years from the date of certification. There are a number of ways the certification can be renewed. For more information go to:

 http://certification.comptia.org/getCertified/steps_to_certification/stayCertified.aspx

Join the Professional Community

The free online IT Pro Community provides valuable content to students and professionals. Join the IT Pro Community:

http://itpro.comptia.org

Career IT job resources include

- Where to start in IT
- Career assessments
- Salary trends
- U.S. job board

Join the IT Pro Community and get access to

- Forums on networking, security, computing, and cutting-edge technologies
- Access to blogs written by industry experts
- Current information on cutting-edge technologies
- Access to various industry resource links and articles related to IT and IT careers

Content Seal of Quality

AUTHORIZED

This courseware bears the seal of CompTIA Approved Quality Content. This seal signifies this content covers 100 percent of the exam objectives and implements important instructional design principles. CompTIA recommends multiple learning tools to help increase coverage of the learning objectives.

Why CompTIA?

- **Global recognition**—CompTIA is recognized globally as the leading IT nonprofit trade association and has enormous credibility. Plus, CompTIA's certifications are vendor-neutral and offer proof of foundational knowledge that translates across technologies.

- **Valued by hiring managers**—Hiring managers value CompTIA certification because it is vendor- and technology-independent validation of your technical skills.

- **Recommended or required by government and businesses**—Many government organizations and corporations (for example, Dell, Sharp, Ricoh, the U.S. Department of Defense, and many more) either recommend or require technical staff to be CompTIA certified.

- **Three CompTIA certifications ranked in the top 10**—In a study by DICE of 17,000 technology professionals, certifications helped command higher salaries at all experience levels.

How to Obtain More Information

Visit CompTIA online Go to www.comptia.org to learn more about getting CompTIA certified.

Contact CompTIA Please call 866-835-8020, ext. 5 or e-mail questions@comptia.org.

Join the IT Pro Community Go to http://itpro.comptia.org to join the IT community to get relevant career information.

Connect with CompTIA Find us on Facebook, LinkedIn, Twitter, and YouTube.

CAQC Disclaimer

The logo of the CompTIA Approved Quality Curriculum (CAQC) program and the status of this or other training material as "Approved" under the CompTIA Approved Quality Curriculum program signifies that, in CompTIA's opinion, such training material covers the content of CompTIA's related certification exam.

The contents of this training material were created for the CompTIA A+ exams covering CompTIA certification objectives that were current as of the date of publication.

CompTIA has not reviewed or approved the accuracy of the contents of this training material and specifically disclaims any warranties of merchantability or fitness for a particular purpose. CompTIA makes no guarantee concerning the success of persons using any such "Approved" or other training material in order to prepare for any CompTIA certification exam.

Check-In

May I See Your Passport?

What do you mean you don't have a passport? Why, it's sitting right in your hands, even as you read! This book is your passport to a very special place. You're about to begin a journey, my friend—a journey toward certification! It's magical, isn't it? You don't need a ticket, you don't need a suitcase—just snuggle up and read this passport, because it's all you need to get there. Are you ready? Let's go!

Your Travel Agent: Mike Meyers

Hello! I'm Mike Meyers, president of Total Seminars and author of a number of popular certification books. On any given day, you'll find me replacing a hard drive, setting up a Web site, or writing code. I love every aspect of this book you hold in your hands. It's part of a powerful book series called the *Mike Meyers' Certification Passports*. Every book in this series combines easy readability with a condensed format—in other words, it's the kind of book I always wanted when I went for my certifications. Putting a huge amount of information in an accessible format is an enormous challenge, but I think we have achieved our goal and I am confident you'll agree.

I designed this series to do one thing and only one thing—to get you the information you need to achieve your certification. You won't find any fluff in here. Scott and I packed every page with nothing but the real nitty-gritty of the CompTIA A+ certification exams. Every page has 100 percent pure concentrate of certification knowledge! But we didn't forget to make the book readable, so I hope you enjoy the casual, friendly style.

My personal e-mail address is mikem@totalsem.com; Scott's e-mail is scottj@totalsem.com. Please feel free to contact either of us directly if you have any questions, complaints, or compliments.

Your Destination: CompTIA A+ Certification

This book is your passport to CompTIA A+ certification, the vendor-neutral industry standard certification for PC hardware technicians, the folks who build and fix PCs. To get CompTIA A+ certified, you need to pass two exams, 220-801 and 220-802. Past CompTIA A+ exams used friendly names like "Essentials" and "Practical Application," but these terms don't apply anymore.

The 220-801 exam concentrates on five areas: Hardware, Networking, Laptops, Printers, and Operational Procedures. This exam focuses on your understanding of the terminology and technology used in each of the five subject areas, as well as appropriate workplace safety practices.

The 220-802 exam works the same way, covering Operating Systems, Security, Mobile Devices (think smartphones and tablets), and Troubleshooting. That last one is big—expect fewer technology identification questions, and a lot more "What is the process to fix [insert problem here]" questions.

Both of the exams are extremely practical, with little or no interest in theory. When you take the exams, you will see four types of questions: multiple-choice, fill-in-the-blank, picture-matching, and simulation.

The following is an example of a multiple-choice question you will see on the exams:

An impact printer is printing blank pages. Which item should you check first?

A. Printer drivers

B. Platen

C. Print head

D. Ribbon

The correct answer is D, the ribbon. You can make an argument for any of the others, but common sense (and skill as a PC technician) tells you to check the simplest possibility first.

Fill-in-the-blank questions work a lot like the multiple-choice questions, but instead of being provided with possible answers, you will need to type the answer into an empty box. For example:

An impact printer is printing blank pages. To troubleshoot this problem, first check the _____.

To answer the question, you would type "ribbon."

Picture-matching questions involve dragging and dropping a picture onto the relevant text. For example, you might see the words "Inkjet" and "Laser," and then two printer diagrams next to them. You would need to drag the inkjet printer diagram onto the word "Inkjet," then drag the other diagram onto the word "Laser."

Simulation questions ask you to re-create a real process used by techs when working on PCs. You might be asked to copy a file or change a setting in Control Panel, but instead of picking a multiple-choice answer, your screen will look like a Windows desktop and you will follow the provided instructions, just like you were using the real thing.

Always read the questions very carefully, especially when dealing with fill-in-the-blank and simulation questions. Remember to look for the *best* answer, not just the right answer.

CompTIA A+ certification can be your ticket to a career in IT or simply an excellent step in your certification pathway. This book is your passport to success on the CompTIA A+ certification exams.

Your Guides: Mike Meyers and Scott Jernigan

You get a pair of tour guides for this book—both me and Scott Jernigan. I've written numerous computer certification books—including the best-selling *All-in-One CompTIA A+ Certification Exam Guide* and the *All-in-One CompTIA Network+ Certification Exam Guide*. More to the point, I've been working on PCs and teaching others how to make and fix them for a very long time, and I love it! When I'm not lecturing or writing about PCs, I'm working on PCs or spanking Scott in *Counter-Strike: Source*—on the PC, naturally!

Scott has been playing with and working on PCs since before the Web went graphical (that's the mid-1990s for you youngsters) and teaching CompTIA A+ certification classes for nearly as long. When not doing the tech thing, you'll find him building Web sites, making videos, or manipulating digital photographs in Adobe Photoshop...and whiling away the hours with any number of computer games. Scott is the author of *Computer Literacy: Your Ticket to IC³ Certification*. Plus, this is the eighth book we have co-authored, and Scott has been deeply involved in nearly every book I've written that doesn't have his name on the cover.

Why the Travel Theme?

The steps to gaining a certification parallel closely the steps to planning and taking a trip. All the elements are the same: preparation, an itinerary, a route—even mishaps along the way. Let me show you how it all works.

This book is divided into 22 chapters. Each chapter begins with an itinerary that provides objectives covered in each chapter, and an ETA to give you an idea of the time involved learning the skills in that chapter. Each chapter is broken down by objectives, either those officially stated by the certifying body or our expert take on the best way to approach the topics. Windows troubleshooting appears in several CompTIA A+ competencies, for example, but the topic works best in book form when covered in a single chapter. Also, each chapter contains a number of helpful items to call out points of interest:

Exam Tip
Points out critical topics you're likely to see on the actual exam.

Travel Assistance
Shows you additional sources, such as books and Web sites, to give you more information.

Local Lingo
Describes special terms, in detail and in a way you can easily understand.

Travel Advisory
Warns you of common pitfalls, misconceptions, and downright physical peril!

The end of the chapter gives you two handy tools. The checkpoint reviews each objective covered in the chapter with a handy synopsis—a great way to review quickly. Plus, you'll find end-of-chapter questions to test your newly acquired skills.

CHECKPOINT

But the fun doesn't stop there! After you've read the book, pull out the CD and take advantage of the free practice questions! Use the full practice exam to hone your skills and keep the book handy to check answers.

When you're acing the practice questions, you're ready to take the exam.

Go get certified!

The End of the Trail

The IT industry changes and grows constantly, and so should you. Finishing one certification is just a step in an ongoing process of gaining more and more certifications to match your constantly changing and growing skills. Read the Career Flight Path at the end of the book to see where this certification fits into your personal certification goals. Remember, in the IT business, if you're not moving forward, you are way behind!

Good luck on your certification! Stay in touch.

Mike Meyers, Series Editor
Mike Meyers' Certification Passport

The Art
of the Tech

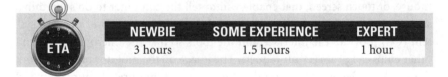

ETA	NEWBIE	SOME EXPERIENCE	EXPERT
	3 hours	1.5 hours	1 hour

When a mission-critical computer goes down, regardless of the industry, people get upset. Workers can't work, so they feel guilty. Employers can't get product out on time, so they feel anxious. Supervisors blame employees for fouling things up, or at least the employees fear such blame, even if they did not break the machine.

Into this charged atmosphere comes the tech, ready to fix the computer and move on to the next challenge. To accomplish this task, the tech requires three things. First, a good tech must know the broken machine inside and out, how it's *supposed* to work when it's working properly. Second, the tech has to calm the workers and supervisors and get answers to questions to gain relevant information about the problem. Finally, the tech must troubleshoot the problem and fix the machine.

This chapter starts with an overview of how computers work and then dives into a section on dealing with customers, including how to get them to tell you what you need to know. The chapter wraps up with a proven troubleshooting methodology to help you figure out the source of problems and point you to the quickest fixes.

Objective 1.01 How Computers Work

Computers work through a three-stage process: input, processing, and output (Figure 1.1). Input requires specific devices, such as the keyboard, mouse, or touch screen, that enable you to tell the computer to do something, such as open a program or display a word that you just typed. The operating system (OS) provides the interface and the tools so that the microprocessor and other chips can process your request. The image on the monitor or sound from the speakers effectively tells you that the computer interpreted your command and has spit out the result.

Making this process work requires the complex interaction of many components, including multiple pieces of hardware and layers of software. As a tech, you need to understand all the components and how they work together so that when something doesn't work properly, you can track down the source and fix it. A look at a modern program reveals that even a relatively simple-seeming action or change on the screen requires many things to happen within the computer.

FIGURE 1.1 Input, processing, and output

Huge games such as *Second Life* (Figure 1.2) take up multiple gigabytes of space on a hard drive. They simply won't fit into the random access memory (RAM) in most computers, so developers have figured out ways to minimize RAM usage.

FIGURE 1.2 *Second Life*

Players move through the *Second Life* online world in a series of connected areas. A player crossing a bridge from one island to another, for example, triggers the game to update information quickly on the new island, so the player won't be left out of the action and the illusion of the game world remains intact.

Local Lingo

MMORPG *Second Life* is a massively multiplayer online role-playing game (MMORPG) that offers a unique twist on the genre. You can create just about anything you can imagine, as far as your time and talent can take you. *Second Life* has a functioning economy that spills out into the real world, meaning you can buy and sell things within the game and turn that into real US dollars—although the more common scenario is to spend real money to get virtual possessions.

Here's what happens when a player presses the W key on the keyboard and the character steps across the invisible zone line: The keyboard controller reads the grid of the keyboard and, on discovering the input, sends the information to the central processing unit (CPU) through the wires of the motherboard (Figure 1.3). The CPU understands the keyboard controller because it loaded a

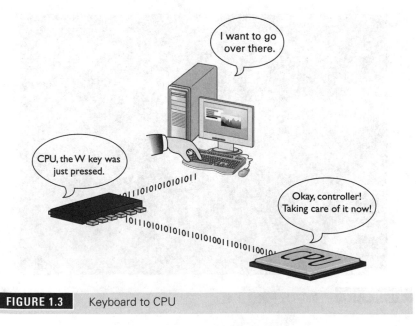

FIGURE 1.3 Keyboard to CPU

small program into RAM from the system basic input-output system (BIOS) stored on the system read-only memory (ROM) chip on the motherboard when the computer was first booted.

The CPU and the application determine what should happen in the game, and on discovering that the character is about to cross the zone line, they trigger a series of actions. The application sends a signal to the OS that it needs a specific area loaded into RAM. The OS sends a signal to the CPU that it needs data stored on the hard drive plus information stored on the *Second Life* servers. The CPU then sends the commands to the hard drive controller so it can grab the desired stored data and send it to RAM, while at the same time sending a command to the network interface card (NIC) to download the updated information (Figure 1.4).

The hard drive controller tells the hard drive to cough up the data—megabytes' worth—and then sends that data through the motherboard to the memory controller, which puts it into RAM and communicates with the CPU when it's finished. The network card and network operating system communicate with the *Second Life* servers and download the necessary updated information. The CPU then uses the application and OS to process the new data, sending video data to the video card and sound data to the sound card, again through the motherboard (Figure 1.5).

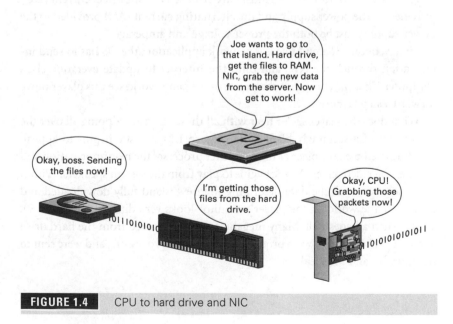

FIGURE 1.4 CPU to hard drive and NIC

FIGURE 1.5 CPU to video card and sound card

The video card processor—called the *graphics processing unit (GPU)*—puts the incoming data into its RAM, processes the data, and then sends out commands to the monitor to update the screen. The sound card processor likewise processes the data and sends out commands to the speakers to play a new sound (Figure 1.6).

For all of this to work, the PC must have electricity, so the direct current (DC) provided by the power supply and the alternating current (AC) provided to the power supply must be both the proper voltage and amperage.

Finally, because *Second Life* is a network application, the OS has to send information through the NIC and onto the Internet to update everyone else's computer. That way, the other characters in the game world see this player move forward a step (Figure 1.7).

What does the player see or hear with all these electrons zipping all over the place? Out of a seemingly blank vista (Figure 1.8), a castle begins to appear, building itself piece by piece as the computer processes the new information and updates the video screen. Music begins to play from the system speakers. Within a few seconds, with the data describing the new island fully downloaded and processed, the world on the player's monitor looks very different (Figure 1.9). That's when all goes well. Many megabytes of data flowed from the hard drive and across the Internet, were processed by multiple processors, and were sent to the monitor and the speakers.

FIGURE 1.6 Updating the screen and speakers

FIGURE 1.7 PC to *Second Life* servers

FIGURE 1.8 New area loading

FIGURE 1.9 Castle completed

Good techs understand the components involved in inputting, processing, and outputting data, including devices that store data, such as hard drives. That's because if something doesn't work properly, a good tech can start answering the ultimate troubleshooting question—what can it be?—accurately. If your screen freezes or the sound goes "wonky," where in the process could the problem be?

As you go into any troubleshooting scenario, always keep the computing process in mind. This helps you sort through possibilities quickly and accurately. If you know all the stages, you won't miss a simple step—such as figuring out that a user can't print because the cleaning service accidentally turned off the print server the night before—and you won't waste time reinstalling printer drivers when the real issue was a stalled print job in the print queue.

Travel Assistance

This book outlines the processes involved with each facet of computing in the appropriate chapter. Chapter 11, for example, details the printing process. Chapter 19 covers the essentials of the networking process.

Objective 1.02 # Dealing with Customers

When you work with users, managers, and owners who are frustrated and upset because a computer or network is down and they can't work, your job takes on the role of detective and psychologist rolled into one. It takes skill to talk with distraught people and get answers to questions about how a PC got into the state it's in. You need to maintain a positive attitude while following the basic rules of "tech-person decorum," with personal integrity and respect for the customer. You should also be culturally sensitive—have respect for the diverse customs, attire, living situations, and disabilities that you may encounter. Finally, use assertive communication to empathize with and educate the user. Great techs spend the time to develop these essential skills.

Exam Tip
Be sure you are familiar with the appropriate use of communication skills and professionalism in the workplace for both the CompTIA A+ exams and real-world application.

Eliciting Answers

Although each person is different, most users with a malfunctioning computer or peripheral will be afraid and automatically defensive about the problem. To help users overcome this initial attitude, you need to ask the right questions *and* listen to the customer's answers. Then ask the proper follow-up questions.

Always avoid accusatory questions, because they won't help you in the least. "What did you do?" generally gets a surly "Nothing" in reply and doesn't help you get closer to solving the problem. Better to ask oblique questions: "When did it last work?" "Has it ever worked in this way?" "Has any software changed recently?" "Any new hardware?"

By taking the user explicitly out of the questions initially, you show the person that you won't accuse him or her or judge his or her actions. You show that you're offering to help. After the initial tension eases, you'll often get more information, such as a recitation of something the user might have tried or changed. These clues can help lead to a quick resolution of the problem.

You know the technology, but most users do not. This means you'll often hear jargon used incorrectly and the wrong words used to describe a particular computer component or function. Don't bother to correct the user. Don't be judgmental at his or her lack of knowledge. Definitely don't add any jargon, acronyms, or abbreviations specific to computers. They can confuse the user and make most people think you're talking down to them. Just ask direct questions in simple, non-jargon language to zero in on what precisely the user is trying to explain. Point at the machine or go to a working PC and ask the user to show what went wrong or what he or she was trying to accomplish.

Integrity

A computer tech must bring integrity to the job, just as with any other service profession. Treat anything said to you as a personal confidence, not to be repeated to coworkers or bosses. Respect the user's privacy and property.

You wield a lot of power when you sit in front of someone's computer. You can readily read private e-mail, discover visited Web sites, and more. With a click of the Start button, you can know the last five programs the user ran, including Word and Solitaire, and the last few documents he or she worked on. Don't do this. You really don't want to know! Plus, if you get caught, your credibility will go through the floor and you might as well hand in your letter of resignation.

It's funny, but people assume ownership of things they use at work. John in accounting doesn't call the computer he uses anything but "my PC." The phone on Susie's desk isn't the company phone, it's "Susie's phone." Regardless of the logic or illogic involved with this sense of ownership, a tech needs to respect that feeling. Just as you would have other people behave with your things, treat their things the same way. Don't use or touch anything—keyboard, printer, laptop, monitor, mouse, phone, pen, paper, cube toy—without asking permission. Follow this rule even when the customer isn't looking!

Respect

The final key in communicating with the user is respect. You don't do his or her job, but you should respect that job and person as an essential component in your organization. Communicate with the user the way you would like him or her to communicate with you were the roles reversed.

Engage the user with the standard rules of civil conversation. Take the time to listen. Don't interrupt a story, but let it play out. You might hear something that leads to problem resolution. Use a level, nonaccusatory tone, and never argue with the user. Remain positive in the face of adversity. Don't get defensive if you can't figure something out quickly and the user starts complaining. Take it in stride; smile and assure him or her that computer troubleshooting sometimes takes a while.

If you're going to be late for a job, call ahead of time to inform the customer and give the customer the opportunity to reschedule if necessary. They might be in such a rush that they will need to select someone else to do the work instead, but you will have saved them quite a bit in terms of lost productivity.

Avoid letting outside interruptions take your focus away from the user's computer problem or from the user. Things that break your concentration slow down the troubleshooting process, and customers will feel insulted if you start

chatting on your cell with your significant other about a movie date later that night when you're supposed to be fixing their computers. Set your cell phones and pagers to vibrate. Even taking a call from one of your coworkers can be distracting. If you receive a call from a coworker that you must take, politely excuse yourself and speak briefly in a place where the customer cannot overhear the conversation. Remember, you do have voicemail.

If you discover that the user caused the problem, either through ignorance or accident, don't be judgmental or insulting. Don't minimize the importance of the problem. *You get paid because people make mistakes and machines break.* Chances are, you'll be back at that workstation six months or a year later, fixing something else. By becoming the user's advocate and go-to person, you create a better work environment. If a user's action caused the problem, explain how to perform the task properly, and then have the user go through the process to reinforce what you said.

Assertiveness

In many cases, PC problems result from a user's error or neglectfulness. As a technician, you must show users the error of their ways without creating anger or conflict. You do this by using assertive communication. *Assertive communication* is a technique that isn't pushy or bossy, but it's also not the language of a pushover. Assertive communication first requires you show the other person that you understand and appreciate the importance of his or her feelings. Use statements such as, "I know how frustrating it feels to lose data," or "I understand how infuriating it is when the network goes out and you can't get your job done." Such statements cool off the situation and let the customer know you are on his or her side.

The second part of assertive communication is making sure the problem is clearly stated without accusing the user directly: "Not keeping up with defragmenting your hard drive slows it down," or "Help me understand how the network cable keeps getting unplugged during your lunch hour." Last, tell the user what you need from him or her to prevent this error in the future. "Please call me whenever you hear that buzzing sound," or "Please check the company's approved software list before installing anything." Always use "I" and "me," and never make judgments. "I can't promise the keyboard will work well if it's always getting dirty" is much better than "Stop eating cookies over the keyboard, you slob!"

Troubleshooting Methodology

Following a sound troubleshooting methodology helps you figure out and fix problems quickly. But because troubleshooting is as much an art as a science, no detailed step-by-step list of things to try in a particular order will suffice. You've got to be flexible. But following are some general steps.

First, you need to secure the proper tools for the job. Second, you should back up everything important before you start doing repair work. And third, analyze, test, and complete your troubleshooting.

Tech Toolkit

A tech toolkit should include a few basic tools and some spare parts for testing. The basic technician toolkit consists of a Phillips-head screwdriver and not much else—seriously—but a half-dozen tools round out a fully functional toolkit. Most kits have a star-headed torx wrench, a nut driver or two, a pair of tweezers, a little grabber tool, and a hemostat to go along with Phillips-head and straight-slot screwdrivers (Figure 1.10). An extension magnet can help you reach and grab any stray screws or other metal parts. If you'll be working with a lot of networking equipment, cable testers and loopback plugs can make your job easier. You might also carry a flashlight, a magnifying glass, and an antistatic wrist strap for highly charged environments.

Always carry several *field replaceable units* (FRUs)—a fancy way to say *spare parts*—when going to a job site or workstation. Having several known-good components on hand lets you swap out a potentially bad piece of hardware to

FIGURE 1.10 Typical technician toolkit

test whether that's the problem. I generally carry a couple of RAM sticks (DDR, DDR2, and DDR3), a PCIe video card, a NIC, and a 500-watt power supply.

Backup

In many troubleshooting situations, you should back up critical files before making changes to a system. This is partly a maintenance issue. If you're in charge of a set of machines for your company, for example, make sure they're set up to back up critical files automatically on a regular basis.

Travel Assistance
Chapter 17 goes into detail on the tools in Windows 7, Windows Vista, and Windows XP used for backup, including System Restore, the Backup and Restore Wizard, the Backup Files and Folders tool (Vista), Automated System Recovery, the Recovery Console, and more.

If you run into a partially functional system, for which you might have to re-install the OS but can access the hard drive, you should definitely back up essential data. Back up e-mail, favorites, personal documents, and any data not stored on a regularly backed up server. Because you can always boot to a copy of Windows and go to a recovery environment, such as the Recovery Console in Windows XP or System Recovery Options in Windows 7, you should never lose essential data, barring anything short of a full-blown hard drive death.

Travel Advisory
Dead hard drives retain their data, so you can recover it—if you're willing to pay a lot of money. Having a good backup in place makes a lot more economic sense.

Exam Tip
The CompTIA A+ certification exams assume that techs should *always* back up systems before working on them, even though that's not how it works in the real world.

Steps

Troubleshooting a computer problem can create a great day for a computer tech—if the tech goes about solving the problem systematically and logically. Too many techs get into a rut, thinking that when symptom A occurs, the

problem must be caused by problem A and must require solution A. This assumption might even be right nine times out of ten, but if you think this way, and the problem is really problem Z and requires a completely different solution, you're in trouble. What do you do when the fix doesn't work and you're sure it's got to be problem A? Your customer won't be happy, you'll end up frustrated or embarrassed, and you still won't have the problem fixed. Follow the right methodology and analyze, test, and complete your task. During this process, communicate with the user to manage his or her expectations.

Analyze

Everything starts with analyzing the problem. Because you know how everything *should* work, when you run into a computer problem, the first question you should ask is, "What can it be?" Don't limit yourself in the initial analysis, but examine all possibilities.

Make sure you understand the nature of the problem first. A big portion of the initial fact-finding involves talking to the user with your newly honed customer communication skills. Practice those oblique questions to get the results you want.

Once you have an idea of the scope of the problem, communicate with the user. Set expectations about how long it will take for you to troubleshoot and fix the computer. If you run into problems that will make the troubleshooting process longer than initially thought, let the user know as soon as possible.

When you run into big problems, such as a completely dead PC or some weird issue that involves networking as well as a local machine, break them down into smaller parts. For a dead PC, for example, organize your inquiry into categories, like this:

- **Power** Check the AC connections and power switches on the power supply and uninterruptible power supply (UPS) or surge suppressor.
- **Connectivity** Check inside the box to make sure nothing was unplugged.
- **CMOS** If you've got power (you see an LED lit up, for example), check CMOS to see if the hard drive shows up.
- **Operating system** If you see some life in the PC but you get no boot option, try booting to the installation media of your operating system to access a recovery environment. Check to see whether you can access the hard drive. If you have a boot option, try booting to Safe Mode or Last Known Good Configuration.

By breaking the problem into discrete chunks, you make a big problem more manageable. You can determine whether the problem lies in hardware failure or disconnection or in an OS or other software error.

Test

Once you determine what might have caused the problem, test your theories. The testing procedure follows a simple set of rules:

1. Check the easy stuff. Is the failed device plugged in? Is it turned on? Does the printer have paper?

2. Use a process of elimination to narrow down the possible problems. Use a notepad to write down what you've tried and what effect that effort had. Do one thing at a time. If you go into CMOS and make a whole series of changes to various settings, for example, and the computer suddenly works, you won't be able to identify what was wrong. You can't know when you make multiple changes. What if you made other things break while fixing the first problem?

3. Swap out parts with known good parts from your stash of FRUs. With a dead or dying piece of hardware, you can generally get quick results. A fried stick of RAM, for example, can create a dead PC. Pop in a good stick and you'll have a functional machine.

The power supply provides the only exception to the instant gratification of part swapping. If you have a wonky computer that has intermittent problems, swap out the power supply and leave your FRU in the computer for a half day or longer. You need the user to road test the PC and report if he or she has the same problems.

If you discover during the testing process the customer has options in the repair or replacement process, let him or her know. If the built-in Hi-Speed Universal Serial Bus (USB) controller has gone south, for example, the customer could replace it with a PCIe Hi-Speed controller expansion card or jump to a SuperSpeed USB 3.0 version. The customer might find paying the extra money for the better part offers greater value in the long run.

Complete

Once you finish the testing phase, you can complete the troubleshooting process with three more steps.

First, evaluate the results of your actions. Run the system through its paces; don't just get it working and walk away. Make certain that the user can accomplish his or her primary tasks before you consider a job complete.

If you can't get the computer or peripheral working in a fairly short period of time, take the second step and call for help. In other words, escalate the problem. Because you've taken notes on the symptoms and each troubleshooting step

you've tried, you can quickly get a more senior tech up to speed on the problem and get suggestions about where you might go next.

Finally, document your results. Many companies have set forms for you to use to describe the problem and its resolution. If not, make some for yourself and other techs in your workplace. The document should provide a space for a description of the problem, a summary of the solution, and an area where the work performed can be itemized.

Depending on the situation, the document may also include the hours of work spent resolving the problem and a list of all the parts that were replaced. If the customer owns the removed parts, offer them to the customer (this is especially true if you replace any storage media). If applicable, your charges can be listed on this document as well.

Documenting problems helps keep track of machines over time so you can make longer-term determinations about retiring a machine or changing out more parts. If you and fellow techs fix a specific problem with Mary's machine several times, for example, you might decide to swap out her whole system rather than fix it a fourth time.

Documenting also helps fellow techs if they have to follow up on a task you didn't finish or work with a machine that you've worked on previously. The reverse is also true. If you get a call about Frank's computer, for example, and check the records to find other service calls on his computer, you might find that the fix for a particular problem is already documented. This is especially true if the problem is user generated.

Last, it is helpful to follow up on the work you performed by giving the customer a courtesy phone call. This gives the customer a chance to detail any special issues that may have arisen and also gives that final extra touch that ensures they will come to you again.

Exam Tip

The CompTIA A+ Exam Objectives define the "Troubleshooting Theory" as a six-step process that you must know (in order):
1. Identify the problem.
2. Establish a theory of probable cause (question the obvious).
3. Test the theory to determine the cause.
4. Establish a plan of action to resolve the problem and implement the solution.
5. Verify full system functionality and implement preventive measures.
6. Document findings, actions, and outcomes.

CHECKPOINT

✔ **Objective 1.01: How Computers Work** Computers work in a three-stage process: input, processing, and output. Almost every process requires the complex interaction of many devices, including multiple pieces of hardware and layers of software. Good techs understand each process to facilitate their troubleshooting.

✔ **Objective 1.02: Dealing with Customers** A tech's job takes on the role of psychologist as well as detective when users get into the mix. Asking the right questions—and avoiding the wrong ones—helps elicit answers for your troubleshooting. Avoid accusatory questions and focus on indirect ones. Treat customers properly, respecting their privacy and the sanctity of their possessions. Use a level, nonaccusatory tone when conversing with customers, and practice assertive communication.

✔ **Objective 1.03: Troubleshooting Methodology** You need to have the right tools to accomplish your job. At the least, carry a Phillips-head screwdriver; also carry some FRUs for part swapping. Back up critical files before making changes to a computer. Analyze, test, and complete your troubleshooting. Use the Troubleshooting Theory to help resolve issues: identify the problem, establish a theory of probable cause, test the theory to determine the cause, establish a plan of action, verify full system functionality, and document your findings.

REVIEW QUESTIONS

1. While troubleshooting a fairly routine printing problem, the customer explains in great detail precisely what he was trying to do, what happened when he tried to print, and what he had attempted as a fix for the problem. At what point should you interrupt him?

 A. After he describes the first problem

 B. As soon as you understand the problem

 C. As soon as you have a solution

 D. Never

2. What are the first two steps (in order) of the Troubleshooting Theory?

 A. Establish a theory of probable cause; test the theory to determine the cause.

 B. Document findings, actions, and outcomes; verify full system functionality.

 C. Identify the problem; establish a theory of probable cause.

 D. Test the theory to determine the cause; identify the problem.

3. While manning the help desk, you get a call from Sharon in accounting. She's lost a file that she knows she saved to her hard drive. Which of the following statements would direct Sharon to open her My Documents folder in the most efficient and professional manner?

 A. Sharon, check My Documents.

 B. Sharon, a lot of programs save files to a default folder, often to a folder called My Documents. Let's look there first. Click the Start button and move the mouse until the cursor hovers over My Documents. Click the left mouse button and tell me what you see when My Documents opens.

 C. Probably just defaulted to My Docs. Why don't you open Excel or whatever program you used to make the file, and then open a document and point it to My Documents?

 D. Look Sharon, I know you're a clueless noob when it comes to computers, but how could somebody lose a file? Just open up My Documents and look there for the file.

4. What tool should be in every technician's toolkit?

 A. Pliers

 B. Hammer

 C. Straight-slot screwdriver

 D. Phillips-head screwdriver

5. When is it appropriate to yell at a user?

 A. When he screws up the second time

 B. When he interrupts your troubleshooting

 C. When he screws up the fifth time

 D. Never

6. Al in marketing calls in for tech support, complaining that he has a dead PC. What is a good first question or questions to begin troubleshooting the problem?

 A. Did the computer ever work?

 B. When did the computer last work?

 C. When you say "dead," what do you mean? What happens when you press the power button?

 D. What did you do?

7. While manning the help desk, you get a call from Bryce in sales complaining that he can't print, and every time he clicks the network shared drive, his computer stops. He says he thinks it's his "hard driver." What would be a good follow-up question or statement?

 A. Bryce, you're an idiot. Don't touch anything. I'll be there in five minutes.

 B. Okay, let's take this one step at a time. You seem to have two problems, one with printing and the second with the network shared drive, right?

 C. First, it's not a hard *driver*, but a hard *drive*. It doesn't have anything to do with the network share or printing, so that's just not right.

 D. When could you last print?

8. When troubleshooting a software problem on Phoebe's computer and listening to her describe the problem, your beeper goes off. It's your boss. What would be an acceptable action for you to take?

 A. Excuse yourself, walk out of the cube, and use a cell phone to call your boss.

 B. Pick up Phoebe's phone and dial your boss's number.

 C. Wait until Phoebe finishes her description and then ask to use her phone to call your boss.

 D. Wait until Phoebe finishes her description and run through any simple fixes; then explain that you need to call your boss on your cell phone.

9. You've just installed new printer drivers into Roland's computer for the big networked laser printer and verified that everything works. Using the Troubleshooting Theory, how should you complete the repair?

 A. Document that you installed new printer drivers.

 B. Tell Roland to print a test page.

C. Print a test page and go to the printer to verify the results. Assuming everything works, you're done.

D. Print a test page and go to the printer to verify the results. Document that you installed new printer drivers successfully.

10. What's an FRU?

A. Foreign replacement unit—a cheaper part to replace an expensive, American-made part

B. Field replaceable unit—a known-good computer part to swap in or out in the troubleshooting process

C. Free repair unit—a gimmick used by some companies to provide free tech support for the first-time customer

D. Short for FRU Linux, a Linux distribution

REVIEW ANSWERS

1. **D** Don't interrupt the customer when he or she is explaining the problem!

2. **C** Always begin by identifying the problem and establishing a theory of probable cause.

3. **B** The better explanation tells about the probable location of the file—in this case, in My Documents—and does so without slang or jargon. It also doesn't assume knowledge on the part of the user. Finally, never call a user a "clueless noob"!

4. **D** The minimum tool every computer tech needs is a Phillips-head screwdriver.

5. **D** Never yell at users.

6. **C** It's always a good idea to ask follow-up questions that clarify the situation. Both A and B are questions that you'll ask during the questioning of the user, but C is the better first question.

7. **B** Taking a nonaccusatory approach with a question or questions that help clarify the problems is a good initial follow-up. Answer D would come up probably as a second or third question.

8. **D** This is a tough one, but because the user is in the midst of explanation, you shouldn't interrupt her. You should use your own cell phone, not the user's equipment, if at all possible.

9. **A** Always document your findings, actions, and outcomes.

10. **B** An FRU is a field replaceable unit.

Ports and Connectors

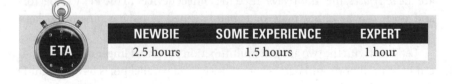

	NEWBIE	SOME EXPERIENCE	EXPERT
ETA	2.5 hours	1.5 hours	1 hour

Mastering the craft of the PC technician requires that you learn a lot of details about what sometimes seem to be thousands of individual parts, connections, and settings. Even the most basic PC contains many hardware components, each with its own set of characteristics, shapes, sizes, and colors. Fortunately, it's much simpler than it seems! Computer makers use only a few types of connectors for most devices, so once you learn one type of connector, you'll know how to use it on any type of PC.

This chapter describes *integrated I/O devices*—the major connectors, plugs, and sockets that you'll find on a typical PC—and spells out many of the acronyms and abbreviations used by techs. The CompTIA A+ certification exams expect you to recognize a particular part simply by seeing what type of connector attaches to that part, so pay attention, folks!

Objective 2.01 Legacy Multifunction Ports

Good techs don't go around saying, "Just plug that *doohickey* into the *whatchamacallit* on the back of the PC," and you shouldn't either. These things have names, after all, so you should get into the habit of using them. Every cable has a *connector* at the end that plugs into a corresponding *port* on a PC. Connectors carry data and sometimes power between devices attached to the PC. Ports are the *interfaces,* the "doorways" used to connect devices to the PC. Connectors and ports can be either male or female, defined as having pins or sockets, respectively.

Let's start with the two ancient multifunction ports that linger on some modern PCs: serial ports and parallel ports. Serial and parallel ports have a slight D shape, which allows only one proper way to insert a plug into the socket and makes it easier to remember what they're called. Technically, they're known as *D-sub* or *D-subminiature* connectors, but most techs call them *DB*.

Exam Tip

The CompTIA A+ exams refer to D-subminiature connectors as *D-shell* connectors.

FIGURE 2.1	A 25-pin serial port and a 9-pin serial port

Serial Ports

Serial ports come in 9-pin and 25-pin varieties (Figure 2.1). Of the two, the 9-pin (five pins on the top row, four on the bottom) variety is much more common, although even these are rapidly disappearing from modern PCs.

Serial ports transfer data one *bit* (the smallest unit of data in the PC world) at a time. The Electronic Industries Association (EIA) defines a maximum transmission speed of 115 *kilobits per second* (Kbps) for serial ports. The standard setting for serial ports still in use is 9600 bps. Devices that traditionally connected to the PC via the serial ports included mice, external modems, label printers, personal digital assistants (PDAs), and digital cameras.

Exam Tip
Remember that serial ports transfer data one bit at a time.

All devices in a PC get assigned certain *system resources,* and serial ports are no exception. The central processing unit (CPU) uses input/output (I/O) addresses to give commands to devices; some devices use an interrupt request (IRQ) to contact the CPU. This process is completely automatic today and requires no tech intervention.

Although manufacturers produce few motherboards with serial ports today, many motherboards in service possess at least one serial port—appropriately called Serial Port 1. By default, this port gets assigned the I/O address 3F8 and IRQ 4 (COM1). The rare Serial Port 2 on a PC gets I/O address 2F8 and IRQ 3 (COM2) by default.

If you find yourself in need of a legacy port on a modern system that doesn't have one built in, they can usually be added to the system by means of an expansion card or universal serial bus (USB) adapter. Legacy port expansion cards and USB adapters are equally handy when you need more ports than are built into the motherboard.

You can use the CMOS setup utility to change the resources assigned to devices built into the motherboard—such as serial ports. Further, you can enable or disable the serial port(s) in the CMOS setup utility. Chapter 7 covers the CMOS setup utility in great detail.

Local Lingo

System Setup Utility Many techs refer to the CMOS program as the *system setup utility.* The latter term happens to be more accurate because no modern PC uses a *complementary metal-oxide semiconductor* chip to store CMOS information, but the older term has stuck. As one old tech said, looking me straight in the eye, "CMOS is CMOS, son."

Parallel Ports

Parallel ports are the 25-pin (13 on the top row, 12 on the bottom) female ports on the back of older PCs, as shown in Figure 2.2. Folks often incorrectly refer to parallel ports simply as "printer ports," but many other devices have used parallel ports, such as external CD-ROM drives, Zip drives, and scanners.

Exam Tip

Parallel ports transfer data eight bits, or one byte, at a time.

Printers that connect to parallel ports on the PC have a *centronics* port rather than a parallel port. Centronics connectors have a central tongue with contacts rather than pins, and they come in two varieties. The more common is the 36-pin IEEE 1284B connector (Figure 2.3); the rarely used variety is the mini centronics IEEE 1284C connector (Figure 2.4).

 A 25-pin parallel port

FIGURE 2.3 IEEE 1284B centronics port and connector

Local Lingo

IEEE IEEE stands for the *Institute of Electrical and Electronics Engineers*, the international organization that creates standards for electrical things, such as ports, cables, and connectors. You'll see them mentioned again later in this chapter.

FIGURE 2.4 IEEE 1284C mini centronics connector

Parallel ports traditionally get I/O address 378 and IRQ 7 (LPT1), but as with the serial port assignments, modern motherboards give you the option of changing this setting. Technological advances, such as the Extended Capability Port (ECP) and the Enhanced Parallel Port (EPP), offer improved throughput of about ten times faster than a standard parallel port.

Objective 2.02 Standard Single-Function Ports

Every PC sports several single-function ports for connecting peripherals such as keyboards, monitors, and the like. With only a couple of exceptions, these standard ports support only a single type of device.

The Keyboard Port

Keyboards come in a variety of styles, from the plain-Jane, rectangular typewriter substitute, to the exotically curved, multifunction gadget that's bristling with special function *hotkeys* and equipped with ports of its own. Regardless of their appearance, however, all keyboards enable you to do one thing: enter commands into your PC.

Many PCs have a purple 6-pin mini-DIN port (commonly called a *PS/2 port*) (Figure 2.5). The mini-DIN port is keyed so you can insert the keyboard connector only one way.

Exam Tip
The CompTIA A+ objectives refer to the mini-DIN port as a Din-6 connector.

The Mouse Port

Like keyboards, mice come in an array of sizes and shapes, and they have used a couple of connectors to attach to the PC (see Figure 2.6). All mice enable you to manipulate the operating system (OS) and applications.

FIGURE 2.5 A six-pin mini-DIN (PS/2) connector

FIGURE 2.6 An ancient serial mouse port (left) and a PS/2 mouse port

Most motherboards have a dedicated mini-DIN mouse port. Aside from color, the green mouse port appears identical to the purple PS/2 keyboard port, but they're not interchangeable.

You can plug a PS/2 mouse connector into a PS/2 keyboard port, and vice versa, but they won't work. Mice go into mouse ports; keyboards go into keyboard ports. Some portable computers have a single black, gray, or multicolored purple and green mini-DIN port that can handle both a mouse and a keyboard (though obviously not at the same time!). A PC that lacks PS/2 connectors requires USB input devices.

Video Ports

Most monitors and projectors connect to one of three video ports, Video Graphics Array (VGA), Digital Visual Interface (DVI), or DisplayPort. The oldest of these connector types, VGA, is an analog connector, meaning that it sends video information to the monitor as a modulated frequency wave. Digital signals send video information to the monitor as a series of ones and zeroes. DVI offers analog and digital varieties. DisplayPort is digital.

FIGURE 2.7 A female 15-pin DB connector

Almost all cathode ray tube (CRT) monitors, and many flat-panel liquid crystal display (LCD) monitors and projectors, connect to your PC using a 15-pin D-subminiature connector arranged in three rows of five pins each. The corresponding VGA port on the PC, shown in Figure 2.7, accommodates only that connector. No other port on your PC looks like the VGA port.

Many LCD monitors and projectors can use a DVI connector that plugs into a DVI port on the back of your video adapter card. DVI is actually three different connectors that look very much alike: DVI-D is for digital and has 18 pins, DVI-A is for analog (for backward compatibility if the monitor maker so desires), and DVI-A/D or DVI-I (interchangeable) accepts either DVI-D or DVI-A (see Figure 2.8). DVI-D and DVI-A are keyed differently and are not interchangeable.

DVI-I and DVI-D also support a configuration called Dual-Link DVI, which uses a 24-pin connector. Dual-Link DVI supports higher resolutions and features a similar connector that simply has extra pins. This clever arrangement allows a regular Single-Link DVI display to be driven by a Dual-Link connection. Chapter 10 covers monitors and projectors in more detail.

Local Lingo

Thin-film transistor The most common LCD monitors use a technology called *thin-film transistor (TFT)*. Many techs erroneously refer to all LCD monitors as TFTs.

FIGURE 2.8 DVI-I connector

RGB connectors Component connectors

| **FIGURE 2.9** | RGB and component connectors |

Some high-end CRT monitors used in video production attach to computers using three RCA connectors that split the video signal into its primary colors—red, green, and blue—or into a light or luminance channel combined with two color-only channels. These connectors are called *RGB* and *component* video, respectively (Figure 2.9). You can attach one type of device to the other using a simple converter box.

DisplayPort features a compact 20-pin connector that is slightly larger than a USB port, as well as a smaller Mini DisplayPort connector that is less than a centimeter wide (Figure 2.10). DisplayPort is a direct-drive display technology, which means that monitors do not need special scaling circuitry when being driven by the interface.

DisplayPort supports the transmission of resolutions of up to 2560×1600 and refresh rates of up to 120 Hz (though not at the same time). When coupled with supporting monitors, up to four displays can be driven simultaneously by a single port. DisplayPort is optionally capable of encryption and the transmission of audio; these features allow DisplayPort to be a multimedia interface similar to HDMI, which is discussed later in this chapter.

| **FIGURE 2.10** | DisplayPort and Mini DisplayPort connectors |

Sound card 3.5-mm mini-audio connectors

Audio Ports

Most audio ports take the form of the popular 3.5-mm mini-audio connectors commonly seen on an iPod or other MP3 players. A PC typically has at least three color-coded sound ports: a green speaker output port, a pink microphone input port, and a blue auxiliary input port, as shown in Figure 2.11 (if the picture wasn't in black and white). Better audio systems offer more jacks for rear speakers, center speaker, and subwoofer.

Travel Advisory

Some sound cards have audio ports that are all the same color. If you run into one of those, you can try to figure out what the obscure symbols mean or get the information from a user manual or the manufacturer's Web site.

You will occasionally see variations, particularly on systems with high-performance sound cards. Some have separate outputs for each audio channel, or they may incorporate one or two connectors called *Sony/Philips Digital Interface (S/PDIF)* ports, as shown in Figure 2.12. S/PDIF ports come in two flavors: electrical and optical. The electrical port uses an RCA connector on a coaxial cable; the optical port uses a fiber connector. Some sound cards from Creative Labs use a 3.5-mm mini-audio jack for electrical S/PDIF.

Multimedia Ports

The convergence of television, music, and the computer has many newer PCs sporting various multimedia connectors. Some of these connectors, such as the *RG-6 coaxial* connector, have been around for a long time. The RG-6 connector sits on the video card or a dedicated TV tuner card and enables your PC to receive video and audio signals from a cable company or antenna. Other older connectors include *S-Video*—for sending video content from the PC to the

FIGURE 2.12 S/PDIF connectors: electrical (left) and optical (right)

TV—and *composite* connectors—for connecting left- and right-channel audio and a single video source to the PC. Figure 2.13 shows an ATI All-in-Wonder card with the many multimedia connectors it offers.

The latest media-center PCs, designed to fit into your living room décor rather than your office space, come with High Definition Multimedia Interface (HDMI) ports (Figure 2.14) for connecting the PC to a high-definition television (HDTV). The HDMI interface handles both the high-definition video signal and multichannel digital audio streams. Unlike VGA ports, HDMI ports are purely digital.

FIGURE 2.13 Video card with multimedia ports

FIGURE 2.14 HDMI connector

Some portable computers and mobile devices use smaller versions of HDMI called Mini HDMI and Micro HDMI. Figure 2.15 shows a Micro HDMI port on an ASUS tablet.

MIDI/Joystick Ports

Very old PCs have an integrated female DB-15 port for connecting joysticks or other game controllers. These ports also support MIDI devices, such as a music synthesizer keyboard, although you need a special breakout box to make the MIDI connection. Unlike DB-15 video connectors, MIDI/joystick connectors have pins arrayed in two rows, with eight on the top and seven on the bottom, as shown in Figure 2.16.

FIGURE 2.15 Micro HDMI port

FIGURE 2.16 MIDI/joystick port

Exam Tip

Make sure you know that the 15-pin DB connector can be used for both MIDI devices and joysticks.

Modem Ports

PC modem ports look identical to female telephone jacks and use standard, two-wire RJ-11 telephone cables and connectors (Figure 2.17). The locking clips on the male RJ-11 connectors secure the cable into the port. Most modems also have an output port for a telephone.

FIGURE 2.17 RJ-11 connectors on a modem

Network Interface Ports

Network interfaces come in several varieties. Most network interface cards (NICs) and motherboards have an eight-wire RJ-45 port (Figure 2.18). RJ-45 connectors look like wider-than-normal RJ-11 telephone connectors and plug into the female RJ-45 ports in the same manner that RJ-11 telephone cables plug into a modem.

Exam Tip

Make sure you know the difference between RJ-11 connectors and RJ-45 connectors, and that you can easily tell the difference between the two at a glance.

High-end NICs have two fiber connections (in/out) of one variety or another. The most common fiber connectors are the ST, the SC, and the LC (Figure 2.19). Other fiber connectors that you might see are FDDI, MT-RJ, and FC.

Local Lingo

NIC A network interface card enables a PC to connect to a network. Techs call them NICs even when the network adapter is built into a motherboard and thus is distinctly lacking in "card-ness."

| FIGURE 2.18 | An RJ-45 connecter and port |

FIGURE 2.19 ST, SC, and LC fiber connectors

> **Exam Tip**
>
> Very old NICs might have a bayonet-style coax connector called a BNC connector, used for 10Base2 or Thinnet networking. You won't see these on working systems, but you might on the exams!

eSATA Ports

Most modern motherboards sport one or two eSATA ports (Figure 2.20), enabling you to connect external mass storage devices such as an optical drive or

FIGURE 2.20 eSATA connector

back-up hard drive. You'll learn more about eSATA (and its internal brother, SATA) in Chapter 8.

Travel Advisory
You'll only find eSATA on PCs, not on Macs.

Objective 2.03 Modern Multifunction Ports

Modern PCs use one or more multifunction ports to supplement or replace the aged serial and parallel ports. All newer machines have *universal serial bus (USB)* ports, some have *IEEE 1394 (FireWire)* ports, and a few have a *small computer systems interface (SCSI)* port. All three come in at least two varieties and can be used to connect everything from printers to digital cameras.

USB

USB comes in three flavors: USB, Hi-Speed USB, and SuperSpeed USB. Regular USB—often called USB 1.1—devices transfer data at speeds of either 1.5 or 12 megabits per second (Mbps) depending on the device, making them much faster than parallel or serial communications. These are commonly referred to as Low-Speed USB and Full-Speed USB, though these are not terms used in the official standard. Hi-Speed USB (USB 2.0) is faster still, capable of bursts up to 480 Mbps. SuperSpeed USB (USB 3.0) devices run at up to 5 Gbps.

If you think all of those names and numbers are confusing, you're right. Table 2.1 provides a quick reference to help you sort it all out.

TABLE 2.1	USB Standards		
Name	**Standard**	**Maximum Speed**	**Cable Length**
Low-Speed USB	USB 1.1	1.5 Mbps	3 meters
Full-Speed USB	USB 1.1	12 Mbps	3 meters
Hi-Speed USB	USB 2.0	480 Mbps	5 meters
SuperSpeed USB	USB 3.0	5 Gbps	3 meters

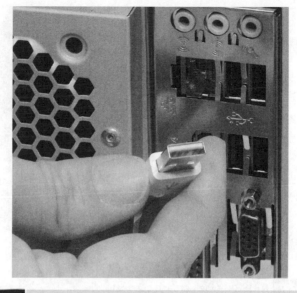

FIGURE 2.21 USB A-type ports and connector

USB 1.1 and 2.0 ports come in multiple varieties, but the most common are A, B, Mini A, Mini B, Micro A, and Micro B. All are female and rectangular shaped. The contact pins are mounted on a plastic protrusion that keeps you from inserting the USB cable improperly. You plug the flat USB A connector into the corresponding port on a PC or *USB hub*—a generic term for a device with multiple USB ports (Figure 2.21).

Most bigger peripherals, such as printers and scanners, have a B port into which you'd plug a B connector (Figure 2.22). Small USB devices, such as digital cameras and music players, use a Mini B (older) or Micro B (newer) port. Figure 2.23 shows a Micro B USB port and connector.

USB 3.0, on the other hand, is different enough from USB 1.1 and 2.0 that it uses separate and clearly marked ports and connectors. The USB 3.0 standard suggests that the ports should be colored blue to differentiate them. You can still plug older USB devices into a USB 3.0 port, but they will run at the slower speeds. The only ports that work at 5 Gbps are the blue USB 3.0 ports (see Figure 2.24).

Many current devices, such as keyboards, mice, joysticks, microphones, scanners, printers, modems, tablets, digital cameras, lap warmers, cup heaters, personal fans, lamps, personal cube-based missile launchers, and more, connect to the PC via USB.

FIGURE 2.22 USB B-type port and connector

Since so many devices use USB, it is not uncommon to run out of built-in ports. To gain additional ports, a USB expansion card can be added to a system, or a device known as a USB hub can be used. A USB hub is nothing more than a USB device that has ports for more USB devices. USB hubs come in powered and bus-powered varieties. Powered USB devices have their own power plug, while bus-powered USB devices do not and instead draw their power from the

FIGURE 2.23 USB Micro B port and connector

FIGURE 2.24 USB 3.0 ports

USB bus itself. Too many bus-powered devices on a bus-powered hub can be problematic, so it's best to use powered hubs in such situations.

Travel Assistance

For more information about USB, visit www.usb.org.

USB devices are *hot-swappable*, which means that you can connect or disconnect them at any time without powering down your PC. USB technology lets you connect up to 127 devices together in a series called a *daisy chain*.

Travel Advisory

For the purposes of the CompTIA A+ certification exams, you need to know that you can connect 127 devices to a single USB port. But for real-life, on-the-job situations, it's a bad idea to hit this maximum. Some applications reserve bandwidth, and you could wind up with quite a mess. Too much of a good thing isn't good!

IEEE 1394

Different manufacturers market IEEE 1394 technology under different trade names, such as *FireWire* (Apple), *iLink* (Sony), or *Lynx* (Texas Instruments), but they all refer to the same thing. Of these terms, *FireWire* is the most popular term among techs.

Local Lingo
FireWire, iLink, and Lynx These terms all refer to the IEEE 1394 interface.

The original specification for FireWire—*1394a*—calls for data transfers of up to 400 Mbps. The current generation of FireWire—*1394b*—is capable of speeds up to a blinding 800 Mbps. What's even more impressive is that the design spec for FireWire states that speeds of up to 1600 Mbps are possible. FireWire technology is a very good match for video, external hard drives, backup storage devices, and other hardware that needs real-time data access.

Connecting FireWire devices together enables them to communicate. Running a FireWire cable between two Windows XP PCs, for example, creates an instant point-to-point network for sharing files. (You cannot network two Windows Vista/7 PCs using FireWire.)

You can connect up to 63 FireWire devices together in a daisy chain, although you would need devices that came with their own power supplies to use that many. One cool feature of FireWire chains is that you can use a device somewhere down the chain even if one or more devices in between the port and device are powered down.

The 6-pin standard FireWire 400 ports are slightly taller than USB ports and rounded on one end. The connector plugs are, of course, shaped to fit, as shown in Figure 2.25. Some devices, such as digital camcorders, use a 4-pin mini-FireWire connector, similar to the mini-USB connector, although they are certainly not interchangeable (Figure 2.26). FireWire 800 devices use a square 9-pin connector (Figure 2.27). You can get adapters and two-headed cables to connect a FireWire 400 device into a FireWire 800 port.

Travel Assistance
For more information regarding FireWire and the IEEE 1394 standard, visit www.ieee.org.

FIGURE 2.25 FireWire 400 (IEEE 1394a) port and connector

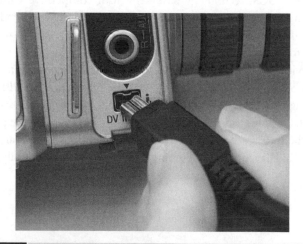

FIGURE 2.26 Mini-FireWire port and connector

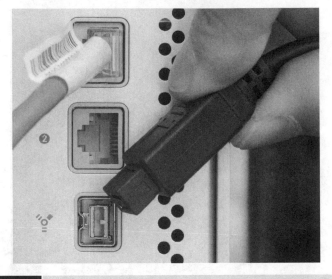

FIGURE 2.27 FireWire 800 (IEEE 1394b) port and connector

SCSI

SCSI—amusingly pronounced "skuzzy"—has been around for a long time. Innovations in SCSI technology have kept SCSI competitive with other enhanced technologies such as USB and FireWire. Many high-end PCs have built-in SCSI connectors, and SCSI controller cards are widely available to add SCSI ports to your system.

SCSI devices have a variety of interfaces—*SCSI-1, SCSI-2, Ultra SCSI,* and *Wide Ultra SCSI,* just to name a few—but the 68-pin female Ultra-320 port shown in Figure 2.28 is the most common today. You may also see 50-pin or 25-pin ports on some older devices or PCs. Note that the very fine port sockets shown in the figure are matched to fine contact pins on the male Ultra-320 connector. Take it from me, these tiny pins bend and break easily, so handle with care!

FIGURE 2.28 Ultra-320 port

Data throughput on SCSI varies from around 5 to 80 megabytes per second (MBps) for early incarnations, and up to 320 MBps for many current versions.

> **Travel Assistance**
>
> For more information on SCSI, check out the SCSI Trade Organization at www.scsita.org.

Thunderbolt

Intel developed the *Thunderbolt* interface to connect peripherals to the internal PCIe bus. Thunderbolt also integrates DisplayPort and devices that use DisplayPort connectors. This combines the PCIe bus with the excellent DisplayPort connector and technology. As of this writing, you'll find Thunderbolt primarily on Apple MacBook Pro portable computers, though the technology should spread to PCs soon enough. You will *not* find Thunderbolt on the CompTIA A+ exams. The only way to tell the difference between a standard DisplayPort and a Thunderbolt port is the latter has a little lightning bolt symbol next to it.

CHECKPOINT

✔**Objective 2.01: Legacy Multifunction Ports** The 9-pin and 25-pin serial ports and the 25-pin parallel port are used for connecting serial and parallel devices, respectively, to the PC. Serial devices transfer data one bit a time, whereas parallel devices transfer data eight bits at a time.

✔**Objective 2.02: Standard Single-Function Ports** Keyboards connect to the motherboard with 6-pin mini-DIN (PS/2) or USB connectors. Mice connect to the 9-pin serial bus in older systems, and PS/2 or USB in newer systems. Make sure you remember that the 15-pin, three-row D-sub port is for video, whereas the 15-pin, two-row D-sub port is for MIDI devices or joysticks. Finally, know the difference between the RJ-11 connectors for modems and the RJ-45 connectors for NICs. Most modern motherboards sport one or two eSATA ports, enabling you to connect external mass storage devices such as an optical drive or back-up hard drive.

✔**Objective 2.03: Modern Multifunction Ports** USB enables you to hot-swap devices and daisy-chain up to 127 devices to a single USB port. The Type A connector goes into the USB port; the Type B or mini connector goes into the USB device. USB (aka normal USB 1.1) is capable of throughput speeds up to 12 Mbps, while Hi-Speed USB is good for up to 480 Mbps. SuperSpeed USB (USB 3.0) devices run at up to 5 Gbps.

IEEE 1394 is also known as FireWire, iLink, and Lynx. The 1394a version is capable of speeds up to 400 Mbps, and 1394b runs at up to 800 Mbps. Either version of IEEE 1394 enables you to connect up to 63 devices to a single IEEE 1394 port. Finally, the 68-pin ports used by Ultra-320 devices are the most common ones seen on the many SCSI technologies available today, but you might also see 50-pin, 25-pin, or other varieties.

REVIEW QUESTIONS

1. Which of these connectors can you use to connect a keyboard to a PC? (Select all that apply.)

 A. Mini-DIN

 B. 9-pin serial

 C. 25-pin parallel

 D. USB

2. Which of these connectors can you use to connect a CRT monitor to a PC?

 A. 25-pin serial

 B. 9-pin serial

 C. 15-pin D-sub in two rows

 D. 15-pin D-sub in three rows

3. Which of the following ports can be found on network cards?

 A. HDMI

 B. Parallel

 C. RJ-45

 D. USB

4. How many pins does a parallel (printer) port have?

 A. 10

 B. 25

 C. 34

 D. 36

5. How is data transferred in serial communications?

 A. 10 bits at a time

 B. 1 bit at a time

 C. 1 byte at a time

 D. 16 bits at a time

6. In theory, how many USB devices can you daisy-chain together?

 A. 1

 B. 2

 C. 63

 D. 127

7. Which connector provides high-quality video *and* audio?

 A. HDMI

 B. S/PDIF

 C. S-Video

 D. VGA

8. To what does a Type A USB connector connect?

 A. To a USB port on the PC

 B. To a USB device

 C. To a serial port on the back of your PC

 D. To a USB modem

9. What is the top data transfer speed possible under the USB 3.0 standard?

 A. 50 megabits per second

 B. 480 megabits per second

 C. 400 megabytes per second

 D. 5 gigabits per second

10. How many devices can you daisy-chain on a single FireWire connection?

 A. 63

 B. 65

 C. 127

 D. 1023

REVIEW ANSWERS

1. **A** **D** Keyboards can use a mini-DIN or USB connector.

2. **D** A CRT monitor cable has a 15-pin D-sub connector in three rows.

3. **C** Most network cards have RJ-45 ports.

4. **B** Parallel ports have 25 pins or contacts.

5. **B** Serial communications transfer data one bit at a time.

6. **D** You can, in theory, daisy-chain 127 USB devices together.

7. **A** The HDMI connector can handle high-definition video and multiple digital audio signals.

8. **A** The Type A connector on a USB cable connects to a USB port on a PC. USB devices have a Type B port.

9. **D** The USB 3.0 SuperSpeed standard enables data transfers of up to 5 gigabits per second.

10. **A** You can daisy-chain up to 63 devices on a single FireWire port.

Maintenance and Safety Precautions

CHAPTER 3

	NEWBIE	SOME EXPERIENCE	EXPERT
ETA	3 hours	2 hours	1 hour

49

There's more to keeping a PC running smoothly than launching an occasional **chkdsk** or deleting some temporary Internet files. PCs are machines, and all machines need regular maintenance. This doesn't include changing the oil every 3000 miles, but it does include cleaning and dusting, among other things. Yes, *dusting!* Being a PC tech doesn't get you out of housework!

Don't be fooled by the benign appearance of a typical PC, monitor, or printer. Underneath that unassuming exterior lurk dozens of voltage-carrying wires and circuits. Any one of these can reach out and bite an unwary tech—sometimes with deadly effect.

Finally, you should appreciate that all PCs and PC components have a finite service life. Where do old monitors, batteries, and toner cartridges go to die?

This chapter covers the important cleaning and maintenance routines that you should follow to keep your system in optimal running condition. These routines take you into the very guts of your PC, so to prevent damage to your PC and to you, it's vital that you use the appropriate tools and follow proper safety precautions. This chapter wraps up with a discussion on how to dispose of dead or obsolete PC equipment properly.

Objective 3.01 Cleaning and Maintenance Procedures

To prolong the life of your PC, you must inspect and clean it regularly. Inspecting your PC alerts you to any dangerous or damaging conditions that exist, such as rust and corrosion, damaged connectors, damaged and improperly installed components, frayed cables, loose connections, and heat damage. Cleaning your PC rids it of the dirt, dust, and grime that build up from normal use. This does more than simply maintain a neat appearance; it helps you prevent two of the most damaging conditions: overheating and electrostatic discharge (ESD).

> **Local Lingo**
>
> **ESD** ESD is a quick electrical charge that occurs when two objects with different electrical potentials come into contact with each other. For more on this subject, see the section "Electrostatic Discharge Precautions and Procedures" later in this chapter.

Your cleaning routine should include the PC and monitor case, the monitor screen, the keyboard and mouse, and any printer, switch, scanner, and other devices connected to the PC. Don't forget the inside of the PC case, the motherboard, adapter cards, drives, and power supply.

Following is a look at the safest cleaning compounds and tools you can use to keep your PC looking and running its best, plus steps for properly cleaning and maintaining your PC, monitor, and peripherals.

> **Exam Tip**
>
> Regular cleaning of the PC will prolong the life of your components, help to prevent ESD, and help to prevent overheating.

Liquid Cleaning Compounds

You can safely use several kinds of liquid cleaners on the PC, from plain water to specially formulated commercial compounds.

Clean or Soapy Water

Many cleaning chores require nothing more than a cloth dampened with some clean water. Common tap water is usually fine, but some local water is heavy with minerals and may leave a residue. If this is the case in your area, use filtered or distilled water instead.

If water alone cannot do the job, use a mild soap solution. Dish soap is best, but make certain that you dilute it thoroughly.

Denatured Alcohol

Use denatured alcohol to clean electrical contacts and components such as the drive heads on removable media drives. Make certain, however, that you never use alcohol on mechanisms such as motors or rubber drive belts. The alcohol dissolves the lubricants in motor bearings, and rubber belts may stretch or become brittle when exposed to alcohol.

> **Local Lingo**
>
> **Denatured alcohol** Denatured alcohol is alcohol with stuff added to make it poisonous if consumed. That way, manufacturers can sell it to anyone rather than only to people old enough to drink alcohol. Standard rubbing alcohol, mineral spirits, or isopropyl alcohol with a high percentage of alcohol (think 95 percent) work well for computer components.

Glass Cleaner

Glass cleaners such as Windex are usually safe to use on most metal and plastic surfaces on PCs. Ironically, they're not always recommended for use on a PC's glass surfaces, such as the monitor screen. Some monitor screens have special coatings that can be damaged by commercial glass cleaners. In particular, you should never use glass cleaner on older liquid crystal display (LCD) screens. You will melt the screens! Instead, use either clean water or a vinegar and water solution. For modern LCD screens, check the user's manual or the manufacturer's Web site for best practices. Each company has different recommendations for its LCDs.

Vinegar and Water Solution

A solution of one part vinegar to four parts water is great for removing dirt, grime, and fingerprints from surfaces such as your monitor screen, LCD screen, or scanner bed. Use plain white vinegar, not the fancier balsamic or red wine vinegar. Save those for your salads!

Commercial Computer Cleaning Solutions

If you want to save yourself the trouble of custom-brewing your own cleaning solution, try commercial products from 3M and Belkin. These come in spray form and as premoistened towelettes (minus the lemon scent). These work just fine, although it's debatable if they work any better than homemade solutions. Still, if you don't want to lug a jug of white vinegar from job to job, commercial cleaners are a good alternative.

As a general rule, remember to read the labels of any commercial cleaning product before applying it to your PC. If you have any doubts about its safety, contact the manufacturer before using it.

Cleaning Tools

Along with your trusty Phillips-head screwdriver and multimeter, a complete PC toolkit should contain the following cleaning tools: canned air, lint-free cloths, a small soft-bristled brush and swabs, and a non-static vacuum. Some techs recommend used fabric softening sheets from your dryer to pick up dust, but avoid using the scratchy ones on LCD screens.

Canned Air

Use canned air to loosen dirt and dust from delicate PC components. Canned air comes in a couple of forms: the liquid propellant kind and the kind that uses small cartridges of compressed CO_2. You can find both at computer stores, office supply stores, camera shops, and big-box stores that sell electronics.

Follow three rules when using canned air:

- Never breathe this stuff in. It's not *that* kind of air, and inhaling it can, quite literally, kill you!
- With regard to the liquid propellant type of canned air, always keep the can upright. Tilting or turning the can upside down causes the liquid inside to come squirting out. This liquid can cause frostbite to the tech and irreparable damage to any PC components that it touches.
- Don't shake canned air cans. They don't need to be shaken to work, and you run a small but real risk of the can exploding in your hand.

Lint-Free Cloths

Lint-free cloths such as the type used for cleaning eyeglasses or cameras work well for general PC cleaning. These cloths are better than plain paper towels because they don't leave residue and won't scratch plastic surfaces.

> **Travel Advisory**
>
> Make sure you never use "dry dusting" cleaning products in or on your computer. Products such as the Swiffer Sweeper use statically charged cloths to collect the dust. Static electricity and computers don't mix!

Brushes and Swabs

Try using soft-bristled brushes and lint-free swabs to clean dust and dirt from hard-to-reach areas and to wipe grime from electrical contacts.

| **FIGURE 3.1** | A non-static vacuum |

Some technicians use rubber pencil erasers to clean contacts, but I don't recommend this practice because some erasers contain acids that can leave a residue or destroy your contacts. Plus, they may rub the metal coating completely off the contacts—a bad thing.

Non-static Vacuums

Small, hand-held vacuums designed specifically for use on PCs (shown in Figure 3.1) suck up dirt and dust loosened by a brush or canned air. Note that you should definitely *not* use a common household vacuum cleaner. These create static electricity and can toast your PC! Some computer vacuums can also act as blowers. Some stand-alone blower products go by names such as "electric dusters." They can be used as alternatives to canned air and do not create condensation or contain harmful liquid propellants.

Cleaning the Outside of the PC, Monitor, and Peripherals

For regular cleaning, wipe down the exterior of your PC, monitor, and peripherals with a lint-free cloth dampened, not soaked, with clean water. Take care not to drip water or anything else onto or into your PC components.

If you're dealing with a buildup of grime, use a mild soap solution. For harder cleaning chores, such as ink, crayon, and tape adhesive, try using a vinegar and water solution, denatured alcohol diluted with water, or commercial cleaners.

Travel Assistance	
Chapter 11 covers printer-specific cleaning and maintenance.	

Use canned air to blast dust and hair from air vents and other openings. This helps keep the hot air flowing out and cool air flowing in to maintain the appropriate temperature inside the PC or peripheral. This will extend the life of

your computer. When you're using canned air, remember the words of Cpl. Hicks from the *Aliens* movie, and use "short, controlled bursts." If you haven't dusted the computer or peripheral in a while, take it outside before spraying. Otherwise, you'll spread dust everywhere.

Travel Advisory

Read the label on any commercial cleaning solution before using it on your PC. If you have any doubts, contact the manufacturer before using it.

You can use one or more of these solutions to clean your PC and the majority of your peripherals safely and effectively. Because they get the majority of the grime, mice, keyboards, and monitor screens warrant a little more discussion.

Mice

For older mice, use a damp cloth to clean the mouse cover, buttons, and ball. Use a swab dipped in denatured alcohol to loosen any dirt, lint, and hair wrapped around the tracking rollers. Tweezers are handy for picking the rollers clean, but avoid scratching the rollers. A quick blast of canned air is a good finishing touch.

An optical mouse has no ball to clean, but it does have an optical sensor behind a recessed lens. It's important that you keep this lens clean for optimal tracking. A lint-free swab dipped in denatured alcohol diluted with water does a good job.

Keyboards

Out of any PC component, the keyboard tends to accumulate the most grunge. Use canned air and a soft-bristled brush to lift out dirt, crumbs, hair, and other unmentionables from between the keys. Wipe down the exterior thoroughly with a dampened lint-free cloth. If necessary, use soapy water or one of the other cleaning solutions to remove stickier messes, but make sure that you disconnect the keyboard from the computer first. Be careful to avoid dripping cleaning liquids onto or into your keyboard. As a general rule, let your keyboard air-dry for 48 hours before plugging it back into the PC.

Monitor Screens

Monitor screens sometimes take a little extra effort to get clean and streak-free. The vinegar and water solution works quite well on both CRT and LCD monitors, as do commercial cleaners (on CRTs, but not LCDs). Make certain that you never spray cleaners directly onto the screen; always put the cleaner onto a lint-free cloth first. Dripping fluid into a monitor is a bad thing.

Cleaning Contacts, Connectors, Motherboard, and Components

Once you've got the exterior of your PC and components in tip-top shape, it's time to do the same for your computer's contacts, connectors, motherboard, and components. Before you go tugging on cables and removing the cover of your computer, read the "Electrostatic Discharge Precautions and Procedures" and "Safety and Environmental Issues" sections of this chapter to protect you and your PC from electrical hazard.

Contacts and Connectors

Start by unplugging and inspecting the cables from the back of the PC. Look for signs of dirt, rust, or corrosion on the contact pins or sockets. Believe it or not, the main culprit in dirty contacts is you! Your skin contains natural oils, and touching the contacts while handling components leaves behind a small amount of oily residue. Given time, this residue leads to dirt and dust buildup, corrosion, and electrical interference.

The best way to protect your electrical components from becoming dirty is to avoid touching the contact pins, connectors, and sockets. If you must touch the contacts or pins, clean them immediately afterward with a lint-free swab dipped in denatured alcohol.

If you see signs of dirt on the contacts, use a lint-free swab dipped in denatured alcohol to loosen and remove it. You can also use a soft-bristled brush. If you see signs of rust or corrosion, you should replace the cable or component.

Motherboards and Components

Next, remove the PC cover to clean accumulated dust, dirt, and hair off the motherboard and adapter cards. Use canned air to loosen the dust and dirt from the delicate electrical components, and use a non-static vacuum to suck it up. Pay particular attention to the case air vents and the power supply intake and exhaust vents. Note also that dust tends to collect in the door openings of the floppy disk drive (if present) and optical drives, and inside the central processing unit (CPU) heat sink.

Thoroughly clean any fans you can touch. The fans draw cool air into the computer or push hot air away from components, protecting your computer from overheating. Heat kills electrical components, so it's important to do this right. Don't open the power supply to clean the fan inside! Use the tiny straw that comes with canned air to blow out as much dust as possible.

After you've cleaned out the dust and dirt, check to make sure that the adapter cards and drive cables are properly seated. Follow all of the precautions listed in Objective 3.03 to prevent ESD damage while working inside the PC case. When you've finished your inspection and maintenance, replace the cover on the computer and reattach the cables. Plug in the computer as the last step.

Turn on the computer and listen. If you placed the fans and plugged in the cables properly, the computer should sound right and boot nicely. If all does not go well, shut down the computer, open the case, and start with a visual inspection to determine whatever is not properly connected.

Objective 3.02 Component Protection and Storage

Computers need electricity to work, as you know, but that same juice can kill a PC or its data if it doesn't flow correctly. This section discusses the causes of power disturbances and covers steps and tools you can use to protect working equipment. Components not currently in use also run risks, so this section wraps up with a bit about properly storing PC components.

Power Problems

Your computer needs power to run properly, but various factors can turn what should be a steady stream of electricity from the wall socket into either a trickle

or a fire hose. It's important that you know how to protect your computing environment from electrical power sags and power losses, power spikes, lightning strikes, and electromagnetic interference. Let's start with a look at the causes of these power problems.

A *brownout* occurs when the supply of electricity drops dramatically but does not go out completely. During a brownout, you'll notice lights flickering or growing dim. When the power rises back up to its original level, your computer might not be able to handle the drastic change, and damage may occur.

Blackouts occur when power goes out completely. The danger of a blackout is twofold. First, you may have data loss or corruption when the power goes out. Second, the power surge when the electricity comes back on may damage your PC's electronics.

Power spikes or *power surges* occur when the voltage on your power line rises suddenly to above-normal levels. Power spikes are extremely dangerous and can destroy PCs, monitors, and any other component plugged in to the affected power line.

Lightning storms are an underrated hazard. Using a computer or even leaving it plugged in during a lightning storm is asking for trouble. Keep in mind that no accessory can completely protect your PC from the damage caused by a lightning strike.

All electrical equipment puts out a certain amount of electrical noise caused by the signal running through wires, cables, and circuits. *Electromagnetic interference (EMI)* occurs when two signals get too close together and the noise of one is picked up by the other. In computers and networking, this can cause problems such as wavy screens or slow or corrupted data transfers. Long cable runs tend to pick up EMI, especially if a power cable is running alongside a data cable.

Local Lingo

EMI Electromagnetic interference occurs when two signals are close enough to each other to interfere with each other.

Saving Your PC from Electrical Problems

Many products help protect a computer from power problems, such as a UPS and a surge protector. You can also prevent certain problems by optimizing the computing space.

Uninterruptible Power Supplies

An *uninterruptible power supply (UPS)* protects your PC from brownouts and blackouts. A UPS has built-in batteries that supply power to your PC when the electricity traveling through the power line drops below a certain level. Most UPS devices have an integrated alarm that tells you when your PC is running on battery power. Many techs call a UPS a *battery backup*. Note that a UPS does not provide unlimited power so you can keep working while the city lights are out! A UPS gives you a short window of opportunity to save your data and shut down the PC properly.

Local Lingo

Battery backup An uninterruptible power supply is sometimes called a *battery backup*.

UPSs come in two main varieties: *standby power systems (SPSs)* and *online* UPSs. Both of these protect your system in the event of a brownout or blackout, but they work differently and provide different levels of protection. A subvariety of UPS that you might encounter is called a *line-interactive* UPS.

Standby Power Systems

An SPS actively monitors the electricity traveling through the power line and begins supplying power as soon as the unit detects a sag. It takes a split second for the SPS to come online, however, and therein lies the main disadvantage. The brief lapse of time can result in data loss or damage before the SPS has kicked in.

Online UPS

An online UPS, in contrast, acts as a power source to the PC, using the electricity from the alternating current (AC) outlet simply to recharge its internal batteries. If an electrical brownout or blackout occurs, your PC doesn't even flinch! Of course, as mentioned earlier, you don't have a tremendous amount of time to work, but you certainly have a safe window in which to save your work and shut down properly before the UPS runs out of juice.

As an added bonus, most online UPS boxes act as power conditioners—that is, they regulate the flow of electricity to your PC to even out any fluctuations your power line might experience. An online UPS costs more than an SPS, but in the long run its benefits justify the expense.

> **Exam Tip**
>
> Don't plug a laser printer into a UPS. Laser printers draw massive amounts of electricity and may interfere with the function of the UPS and prevent you from shutting down safely.

Line-Interactive UPS

A line-interactive UPS is similar to a standby UPS but has special electronic inverter/converter circuitry that can handle moderate AC sags and surges without the need to switch to battery power. This allows for faster response to a power loss than a standby UPS. Due to the circuitry that adapts to undervoltage and overvoltage conditions, a line-interactive UPS may draw more or less electrical current for a device than is normally needed. As a result, when using a line-interactive UPS, be aware of the impact an increase in current consumption might have on any fuses or circuit breakers in the electric supply.

Surge Suppressors

Surge suppressors help to absorb power surges so that your computer does not feel their effects. They come as either separate modules or are integrated into the UPS. Good surge suppressors come with long-term or lifetime guarantees against damage to your PC. Avoid purchasing or using cheap surge suppressors. These are usually little more than power strips and provide virtually no protection against power spikes.

Unplug Your PC

Even if you have any or all of the layers of protection mentioned so far, the only sure protection against severe threats such as lightning is to shut down and

unplug your PC and peripherals. Leave no stone unturned: make sure that you unplug even your modem, because lightning can travel up the telephone line to give your system a shock. (I've seen it happen, folks!)

Exam Tip
Remember that in the event of an electrical storm, the only way to protect a system is to unplug it completely, plus unplug all peripherals with external power cords.

EMI Noise Filters

EMI can be controlled by using cables with a Mylar coating and through the use of special EMI noise filters. Noise filters can be purchased as stand-alone products or are sometimes integrated into a UPS. You can also minimize EMI by moving data cables away from power cables and by shortening the cables you use.

Power fluctuations can wreak havoc on an unprotected PC, and not just in the obvious ways. Surges and sags can damage power supplies and components and cause file corruption. The cost of a good UPS or surge suppressor is nothing compared to the cost in time and money caused by lost components or corrupted files that you may have to endure if you don't use either one.

Storing Components for Future Use

If you plan on storing computer components for future use, you need to protect them from ESD, corrosion, and other damage.

Storage Environment

Even when your PC is not in use, heat, moisture, and dirt are still hazards. Heat causes plastics to fade and become brittle, moisture encourages rust and corrosion, and dirt is, well, *dirty*. For these reasons, PC components and peripherals should be stored indoors in a climate-controlled environment.

Electrical Precautions

Take precautions to prevent electrical damage when storing PCs and components. Always store PC equipment away from high-voltage devices, and never store batteries of any kind for long periods of time. Old batteries leak or corrode, so if you are not planning on reusing them during their recommended lifetime, recycle them and purchase new ones as needed.

The safest way to store your components for future use and to protect them from ESD is to put them in antistatic bags (discussed in the section "

Electrostatic Discharge Precautions and Procedures"). For the ultimate in component safety, store the components in their manufacturers' original boxes and packaging. That should be encouraging news to the packrats among you!

Exam Tip
The safest way to store components for future use is in their original packaging or in antistatic bags.

Moisture

Moisture and PCs don't mix. You must control moisture to keep rust and corrosion at bay and ensure that your components are still functional when you return them to service. *Silica-gel* packets are available from electronics stores and shipping supply companies. Place one or more small packets inside your component's antistatic bags and inside your PC case. Heed the manufacturers' warnings when using this stuff! It is poisonous, so don't eat it, and don't get any in your eyes.

Objective 3.03 # Electrostatic Discharge Precautions and Procedures

ESD is one of the main enemies of your computer. To maintain your computer and prolong the life of components, you need to learn about the effects of ESD and how to protect your computer from those effects.

A prime example of ESD is the small shock you receive when you walk across a carpeted floor and then touch a metal doorknob. *Zap!* The small discharge doesn't cause any lasting damage to your body, but such a seemingly harmless shock will destroy computer components. In fact, even discharges well below the level that you can feel can damage or destroy PC components.

Types of ESD

The types of ESDs that affect computers can be placed into three broad categories: catastrophic damage, hidden damage, and gradual degradation.

Catastrophic ESD Damage

Catastrophic ESD causes a computer component to fail immediately. When catastrophic ESD occurs, it will be obvious to you, because, in all likelihood, you will be the one who caused it! Picture the scenario described a few paragraphs ago with you walking across a carpeted floor. This time, instead of the doorknob, picture an expensive RAID (redundant array of independent disks) controller, video card, or hard disk full of vital data. Are you concerned yet?

Hidden ESD Damage

Dust buildup on PC components causes *hidden ESD* damage. Over time, this buildup creates a small electrical charge. This charge is not enough to cause obvious damage, and in most cases you will not even be aware that a problem exists until a component begins to behave erratically. By that point, it is extremely difficult or impossible to pinpoint the original source of the problem. Hidden ESD is a good reason to clean your computer regularly.

ESD Degradation

ESD degradation occurs when the effects of ESD are cumulative. This is caused by situations in which low levels of ESD occur repeatedly. Damage caused by ESD degradation is not immediately apparent in full force; instead, the effects gradually get more and more noticeable. Like hidden ESD, degradation will cause your components to behave erratically, and it can make the original problem hard to recognize.

Exam Tip

Make sure that you understand what ESD is, how it can damage your PC, and what you can do to protect against it.

Common ESD Protection Devices

ESD protection devices help to ensure a longer and more productive life for your PC components. These devices include antistatic wrist and ankle straps, antistatic mats, antistatic floor mats, and antistatic bags. Antistatic devices make your body's electrical potential the same as the electrical potential of your PC or component.

Local Lingo

Electrical potential Everything has a certain *electrical potential,* or how charged it is relative to the *zero ground* of the Earth. Note the term *relative.* If your body has a +3000-volt charge and you touch a component that also has a +3000-volt charge (working in the International Space Station, perhaps?), no damage will occur. As far as you and the component are concerned, you're at the same electrical potential. Touch a component that has a −3000-volt charge, on the other hand, and watch the sparks fly!

One of the most important steps you can take to prevent the effects of ESD is to ground yourself before you handle PC components. Do this *self-grounding* by touching a metal surface such as the exterior of the PC power supply before touching any of your system components.

Exam Tip

Enclosures, such as the case of a PC or the shell that holds an external hard drive, provide protection from ESD. You don't have to worry about picking up that backup drive and transporting it from place to place. (Don't drop it, of course!)

Antistatic Wrist and Ankle Straps

Antistatic wrist and ankle straps, fondly called "nerd bracelets" by many techs, keep you at the same relative electrical ground level as the computer components on which you're working. Antistatic straps wrap around your wrist or ankle with an elastic strap attached to a long grounding wire. On some models, the grounding wire attaches to a metal clip that you attach to a metal device to ground yourself. Figure 3.2 shows an antistatic wrist strap grounded to a computer chassis. Others have a prong that you plug into the ground wire of an electrical wall outlet.

Travel Advisory

Antistatic wrist and ankle straps use a 1-megohm resistor that is suitable for protection against only very low-level static electricity. They are unsuitable as protection against high voltage and can even make high-voltage shocks more dangerous! Make sure that you always remove your antistatic strap before you work on or near high-voltage components.

FIGURE 3.2 An antistatic wrist strap grounded to a computer

By the way, don't forget to remove your antistatic strap before walking away from your work area! Or, if you forget frequently, try to leave a camcorder running so you'll have something funny to show at your next family reunion.

Antistatic Mats

Portable antistatic mats provide a work surface that dissipates ESD. They look like large place mats or those baby-changing mats that come with diaper bags. They are distinguished by a small metal clip that you can attach to an antistatic strap to ground out ESD. In addition to helping prevent ESD, these mats help keep your work area organized by giving you a place to put your tools and components while you work.

Antistatic Floor Mats

Antistatic floor mats are basically the same as portable antistatic mats, except much larger. Instead of placing them on top of your work area, you place them on the floor and stand on them while you work.

Antistatic Bags

Antistatic bags have a special coating or contain small filaments that help dissipate any static charge. Always store adapter cards and drives in antistatic bags when they're not in use and when transporting them—even if you're just going down the hall or across the room. Antistatic bags dissipate charge most effectively when they're closed, so it's a good idea to fold the end over and tape it down with an antistatic sticker if possible. Do not place components on top of antistatic bags, as charge is directed from the inside of the bag to the outside. Note that regular plastic or paper bags will *not* protect your components. In fact, plastic baggies conduct static electricity rather than preventing it, so don't use them!

Travel Advisory

Special antistatic sprays dissipate static charges built up in your clothing. Commonly used to prevent unsightly static "cling," they are also good to use before you start working on PCs. Some folks also use these sprays to try to protect their work areas from the effects of ESD, but this is not an effective or recommended procedure. Never use these sprays directly on your components!

 Objective 3.04 # Safety and Environmental Issues

Certain factors increase the risk of injury, both to the computer and to the tech. Some factors can be controlled, such as what you wear when working on PCs, and some can't, such as the weather. You simply need to know and avoid other issues to stay safe.

Tech-Controlled Factors

Take control of the computing environment to minimize the risk of damage to you or to any computers around you. You make all the difference when it comes to what you wear and how orderly or disorderly the computer space is kept. Plus, you need to use the proper tool for the job at hand and, if anything goes wrong, report it properly.

What to Wear

What you wear, including your hairdo (I'm serious!), affects both the risk of electrostatic discharge and electrical shorts. Different fabrics have different electrical potentials. Wear natural-fiber clothing, such as cotton or linen, when working on computers. Don't wear silk, though, because it picks up static electricity. Definitely avoid synthetic fabrics. They have a tendency to *produce* static electricity. If you needed an excuse to give the double-knit polyester leisure suit to charity, now you have one! Finally, wear rubber-soled shoes rather than leather-soled shoes.

Keep your hair short or pulled back away from the computer. I've seen techs with long hair shock a computer by brushing it with their hair. That's never fun!

Rings, bracelets, necklaces, watches, and other metal adornments can short out devices if touched on the wrong part of a PC. They can also scratch (or be scratched) by scraping against the PC's surfaces. Remove jewelry and watches before working on or inside of a PC. Just remember to put your wedding ring back on before you head home to the spouse!

Control Those Cords!

A disorderly computing environment invites problems, so successful techs keep it neat. People place computers or peripherals in crazy places: on rickety desks, cardboard boxes, and other places where they could easily fall (Figure 3.3). Arrange your computer and peripherals safely on the floor or on a sturdy desk. Tape or cover cords (using cable raceways or trays) running along the ground to avoid people tripping on them or accidentally ripping a computer off a desk—two very not-funny options. If you see a potential hazard at a work site—even one that's not yours—report it or fix it. You're the expert, so take charge!

Use the Right Tool for the Job

Whenever possible, use the tool designed to do the job at hand. This might seem obvious to most of you, but don't use a knife when you need a screwdriver. Don't use a screwdriver designed for large heads on small-head screws. Using the wrong tool for a job can cost you, both in time and equipment. Bleeding all over a motherboard you just sliced into would just add insult to injury, so avoid it!

FIGURE 3.3 Don't do this!

Heavy Devices

It seems that everything we use—computers, printers, monitors—comes to us in heavy boxes. Remember never to lift with your back; lift with your legs, and always use a hand truck if available. You are never paid enough to risk your own health.

Exam Tip

Carry a cathode ray tube (CRT) monitor with the screen against your body. That puts the heaviest part of the monitor closest to your center and reduces the risk of back strain.

Also pay attention to weight limitations when wall-mounting monitors. Even relatively light LCD monitors require a mounting arm strong enough to support them.

Incident Reports

When accidents happen—and they will—at the workplace, always provide an *incident report* that details the accident, conditions that contributed to the accident, and, if you know, the cost to replace the equipment damaged. A small company might accept a verbal report; larger companies most likely prefer a formal, written report. Be sure always to follow company procedures concerning incident reporting.

Environmental Factors

Proper environmental controls help secure servers and workstations from the environmental impact of excessive heat, dust, and humidity. Such *environmental controls* include air conditioning, proper ventilation, air filtration, and monitors for temperature and humidity. A CompTIA A+ technician maintains an awareness of temperature, humidity level, and ventilation so that he or she can tell very quickly when proper levels or settings are out of whack.

Dust and debris aren't good for any electronic components. Equipment closets filled with racks of servers need proper airflow to keep things cool and to control dusty air. Make sure that the room is ventilated and air-conditioned and that the air filters are changed regularly. This provides protection from airborne particles as well as heat and humidity.

Good techs keep up with weather conditions. Believe it or not, the temperature and humidity level *outside* can dramatically affect the risk of ESD *inside*. If the weather is cold and dry, the potential for a PC-killing zap is greatly increased. Take extra precautions to prevent ESD when the weather calls for it.

High-Voltage Equipment

The capacitors in PC power supplies, monitors, and laser printers carry very high voltages that can cause severe injury or death if you touch them. Fortunately, manufacturers mark high-voltage equipment with a bright yellow warning sticker, making it easy to identify. Watch for these labels and heed them!

Further, any time you work with a piece of high-voltage equipment, make sure the device is unplugged and that you have *removed* your antistatic wrist strap.

Power Supplies

In the old days, the conventional thinking was that you should leave the PC plugged in while working inside it to ensure electrical grounding. The opposite is true for modern PCs, because modern motherboards always have a small

amount of voltage running anytime the PC is plugged in, even if it's not running. Therefore, you should completely unplug the PC before servicing or you'll likely toast something!

Unplugging power supplies does not make them safe enough to work on. The capacitors inside can hold a dangerous charge even when the unit is unplugged, making them extremely risky to open. As the label says, "No serviceable components inside." With that in mind, the safest method of repairing power supplies is not to repair them at all. It's better to dispose of them properly (as discussed in the "Special Disposal Procedures and Environmental Protection Guidelines" section of this chapter) and install a brand-new power supply.

Travel Advisory

As electricians will tell you, it's amperage (the amount of electricity) that's dangerous, not voltage. Power supplies have relatively low voltages, but high amperage. It's not worth the risk for you to attempt to service a power supply.

Monitors

Let's keep this section short and to the point—*never* open the case of a CRT monitor! As with power supplies, they are not designed to be serviced by field techs. CRT monitors have extremely high voltages that must be drained away through a special tap before servicing. Return damaged or malfunctioning monitors to the manufacturer for servicing or to a qualified monitor repair shop.

Take care when moving CRT monitors. Watch for cords and other tripping factors. Every CRT has a vacuum tube inside that will implode if cracked. Implode or explode, you're still going to be showered with glass if you drop one.

Fires

Thankfully, the risk of fire occurring inside your PC is relatively low. If, however, you do experience a computer fire, or any electrical fire for that matter, never try

to extinguish it with water. This can cause the electrical current to travel up and straight into you! Instead, use a fire extinguisher certified for fighting electrical fires. These are type C and type ABC fire extinguishers.

Exam Tip

Make sure that you know that you need to use a type C or type ABC fire extinguisher to put out a fire in a computer.

 Objective 3.05

Special Disposal Procedures and Environmental Protection Guidelines

Many computer components, such as batteries, CRTs, chemical solvents, and toner kits, contain harmful ingredients. Don't throw these items in the garbage, as this is wasteful and possibly illegal. Recycle, recycle, recycle! If you can't recycle an item, dispose of it properly. We all share the same planet.

Different cities and counties have different requirements for safe disposal of materials such as PC components. Always check with the appropriate authorities before tossing that old Pentium on the curb! Visit your city's official Web site for more information.

Exam Tip
Make sure you know the proper disposal procedures for each of the following items prior to taking the exam.

Batteries

Batteries often contain lithium, mercury, nickel-cadmium, and other hazardous materials. If they are thrown in the garbage and carried off to a landfill, they will contaminate the water and soil. Take batteries to a recycling center or send them back to the manufacturer. Most batteries have disposal instructions printed on them. Familiarize yourself with these instructions and follow them.

CRTs

Many CRT monitors contain lead and mercury. Both materials are poisonous, so CRTs must be disposed of properly to avoid contamination. To dispose of nonfunctional CRTs, send them to a commercial recycler or contact your city's hazardous waste management department. They will give you the proper procedure for disposing of them.

Toner and Inkjet Cartridges

You have a couple of options when dealing with depleted toner and inkjet cartridges. You can refill them yourself, which saves on environmental wear, but this can wreak havoc on your printer if it is not done properly. You can also search the Web to see if commercial toner recyclers service your area. Alternatively, many toner cartridge manufacturers have a recycling program. Check with your vendor and see if this is an option for you.

Travel Assistance

Most cities in the United States have one or more *environmental services centers* that you can use to recycle electronic components. For your city, try a Google (or other search engine) search on the term "environmental services" and you'll almost certainly find a convenient place for e-waste disposal. Use these centers to comply with local governmental regulations on disposal.

Chemical Solvents and Cans

Chemical solvents or canned products for PC use (such as canned air mentioned earlier) contain harmful chemicals that should not be loosed in the environment. Instead, dispose of these through your city's hazardous waste program.

Material Safety Data Sheet

All batteries, chemicals, and other hazardous materials come with a *Material Safety Data Sheet* (MSDS) that documents any safety warnings about the product, safe methods of transportation, and safe disposal requirements. If you have any doubts or questions about how to handle and dispose of chemicals or compounds, check the MSDS. If an item comes without an MSDS, you can obtain one from the manufacturer, or you can locate one on the Internet.

Travel Assistance
For more information about MSDSs, or to search for an MSDS, visit www.msdssearch.com.

CHECKPOINT

✔**Objective 3.01: Cleaning and Maintenance Procedures** You should regularly inspect and clean your PC and peripherals. Plain water or a solution of mild soap and water does a great job of cleaning most PC surfaces. Canned air, non-static vacuums, and soft-bristled brushes help maintain a clean PC. Electrical contacts get dirty from the oily residue from your fingers, so you should exercise care when handling components. Denatured alcohol is the best solution to use for cleaning drive heads and contacts. Keep fans and vents clean and dust free to protect a computer from overheating.

✔**Objective 3.02: Component Protection and Storage** A UPS protects your system against power sags, and a surge suppressor protects your system from power surges. Noise filters help prevent electromagnetic interference. In the event of a lightning storm, make sure you completely unplug the PC and any peripherals with external power cords. When storing components for future use, make sure to store them in a cool, dry place in antistatic bags or in their original packaging.

✔**Objective 3.03: Electrostatic Discharge Precautions and Procedures** To help protect your system from the effects of ESD, always use an antistatic wrist strap or ankle strap while working on the system, unless you're working around high-voltage devices such as power supplies and CRTs. Antistatic mats, floor mats, and sprays can also protect your work area from ESD.

✔**Objective 3.04: Safety and Environmental Issues** Wear natural-fiber clothing and rubber-soled shoes when working on computers. Keep your hair pulled back and remove excess jewelry. Keep the computing environment neat, but if accidents happen, file an incident report. The capacitors in power supplies, monitors, and laser printers carry very high voltages that can cause

severe bodily injuries. Don't touch them! This is especially true for CRT monitors, which carry *deadly* levels of electricity even after being unplugged.

✔ **Objective 3.05: Special Disposal Procedures and Environmental Protection Guidelines** Batteries contain nasty chemicals, CRTs contain lead and mercury, and even innocuous-seeming toner cartridges contain environmentally unfriendly chemicals. Always be sure to recycle batteries, monitors, and toner cartridges, or have them picked up as hazardous waste.

REVIEW QUESTIONS

1. Steve in accounting was rearranging his cubicle and knocked his new monitor off the side of the desk, breaking the frame and cracking the screen. As the tech on site, what should you do?

 A. Clean up and quietly replace the monitor so Steve can get back to work.

 B. Prepare an incident report to send to your supervisor.

 C. Prepare an accident report to send to your supervisor.

 D. Start yelling at Steve so everyone knows it wasn't your fault.

2. After wiping down your keyboard with a mild cleaning solution, what should you do?

 A. Use canned air to dry it out.

 B. Use antistatic spray to give it a protective coating.

 C. Use a pencil eraser to clean the contact pins.

 D. Let it air-dry for 48 hours.

3. Which of the following products will do the best job of completely removing the dust from your computer? (Select two.)

 A. Lint-free cloths

 B. Canned air

 C. Non-static vacuums

 D. Paint brushes

4. What type of fire extinguisher should you use to put out a PC fire?

 A. Type A

 B. Type B

 C. Type C

 D. Type D

5. When should you always remove your antistatic wrist strap?

 A. When working around high-voltage devices such as power supplies and CRTs.

 B. When cleaning your PC.

 C. When changing a toner cartridge in your printer.

 D. You should never remove your antistatic wrist strap.

6. If you use an antistatic wrist strap with a prong, where do you attach the prong?

 A. To the grounding wire of a wall outlet

 B. In the slot of a wall outlet

 C. In a special hole that is incorporated into every PC case

 D. Into the back of the power supply

7. If you do not receive an MSDS with a product, where can you obtain one? (Select two.)

 A. The Internet

 B. The outside of the box the product came in

 C. The manufacturer

 D. Any good technical book

8. Which of the following should you avoid using on LCD displays?

 A. Distilled water

 B. Commercial glass cleaners

 C. Mild soap solution

 D. Vinegar and water solution

9. What are two proper ways to dispose of CRTs?

 A. Throw them in the garbage.

 B. Recycle them.

 C. Have them picked up by a hazardous waste program.

 D. There is no proper way to dispose of a CRT.

10. What should the conditions be like in the area where you store computer components? (Select two.)

 A. Cool

 B. Warm

 C. Humid

 D. Dry

11. What weather conditions are most likely to be associated with ESD? (Select two.)

 A. When it is cold

 B. When it is dry

 C. When it is hot

 D. When it is humid

12. How can you completely protect your PC in the event of a lightning storm?

 A. With a UPS

 B. With a suppressor

 C. By unplugging the PC and all of its components

 D. By turning off the PC

REVIEW ANSWERS

1. **B** Although it might be fun to yell at Steve, it's best to prepare an incident report for your supervisor.

2. **D** Let the keyboard air-dry for 48 hours before plugging it back into the computer.

3. **B C** Canned air loosens dirt and dust. Non-static vacuums remove the dust from your system.

4. **C** You would use a type C fire extinguisher to put out a PC or other electrical fire. If a choice on the exam is type ABC, that type of fire extinguisher can also be used.

5. **A** You should always remove your antistatic wrist strap when working around CRTs and power supplies. The wrist strap provides a connection from the PC to your body, and wearing a wrist strap while working on either of these components could cause your body to absorb extremely high electrical charges, which could harm or kill you.

6. **A** If you are using an antistatic wrist strap with a prong, the prong should be attached in the wire ground of a wall outlet. The wire ground is the round hole—*never* place the prong in one of the slots because they contain electricity.

7. **A C** If you do not receive an MSDS with a product, you can obtain one from the manufacturer or you can find one on the Internet. Technical books won't have MSDS information, and you won't find it on the outside of the box.

8. **B** Commercial glass cleaners such as Windex will melt LCD display screens. Use plain or mildly soapy water or a vinegar and water solution to clean LCDs.

9. **B C** The proper way to dispose of CRTs is either to recycle them or have them picked up by a hazardous waste program. CRTs often contain lead, so you can't throw them in a landfill because they could contaminate the water supply.

10. **A D** The area where you store computer components should be kept cool and dry. PC components do not like extreme heat, and condensation could cause corrosion.

11. **A B** ESD is most likely to occur when it is cold and dry.

12. **C** The only way to protect your system completely in the event of an electrical storm is to unplug it and all of its components. Simply turning off the machine or using a suppressor will not fully protect your system.

Motherboards, Power Supplies, and Cases

	NEWBIE	SOME EXPERIENCE	EXPERT
ETA	5 hours	3 hours	2 hours

At the heart of all personal computers live certain core components. The *motherboard* provides the framework upon which every other component builds. The *power supply* provides direct current (DC) to feed the hungry motherboard and components and makes everything chug along happily. The *case* or *system unit* holds it all together. Don't think that all cases are created equal, however, as subtle differences between identical-looking cases can influence how difficult it is to upgrade and service the PC. Every good tech needs to understand these basic ingredients of the PC, including their common variants.

Objective 4.01 Motherboards

Every device in your computer system connects either directly or indirectly to the motherboard. The motherboard, in essence, defines the type of computer you have.

Local Lingo
System boards, mobos Many PC techs call motherboards *system boards* or *mobos*.

Manufacturers decide three things when creating a new motherboard. First, they select the set of chips—appropriately called the *chipset*—that provide support for everything that plugs into the motherboard. Second, they select a style of motherboard, the *form factor*, that defines the size and shape, among other things. Finally, manufacturers decide which connectors to include for both internal and external devices.

This section looks at chipsets, form factors, and connections available on motherboards. It wraps up with notes on installation and troubleshooting.

Chipsets

Every motherboard has a chipset that determines the type of processor the motherboard accepts and what sort of internal and external devices the motherboard supports. For older systems, the chipset determines how much and what kind of random access memory (RAM) a system can accept. The system

read-only memory (ROM) chip provides part of the basic input-output system (BIOS) for the chipset, but only a bare-bones, generic level of support. The chipset still needs support for the rest of the things it can do, so it requires drivers loaded from a CD or downloaded from the manufacturer's Web site. Three companies make the vast majority of chipsets for PCs: Intel, NVIDIA, and AMD.

Travel Assistance

Chapter 7 covers the system BIOS and system ROM chip in detail.

Travel Advisory

Like most devices, motherboards ship with dated drivers. Smart techs download updated drivers from the manufacturer's Web site.

In today's marketplace, PC chipsets come in three distinct configurations: traditional, modern, and post-modern.

Traditional Chipsets

The oldest, traditional configuration of the chipset contains two chips called the northbridge and the southbridge (Figure 4.1). The terms come from a theoretical map of the computer architecture: the central processing unit (CPU) is at the north pole and the slowest device is at the south pole. The northbridge connects the CPU to the fastest devices. The northbridge is connected to the southbridge, which, in turn, connects to the slowest devices. Intel likes to call the northbridge the Memory Controller Hub (MCH) and the southbridge the I/O Controller Hub (ICH), but different vendors use different terms for the chips.

The function of the northbridge is to help the CPU work with RAM and the video card. The northbridge does a lot of work and thus gets pretty hot, so it has its own heat sink and fan assembly (Figure 4.2).

Travel Assistance

Chapter 5 covers CPUs in detail.

Northbridge Southbridge

FIGURE 4.1 Northbridge and southbridge

 Heat sink and fan on a northbridge

FIGURE 4.2 Heat sink and fan on a northbridge

FIGURE 4.3 An Intel southbridge chip on a motherboard

The southbridge handles some expansion devices and mass storage drives, such as hard drives. Most southbridge chips don't need extra cooling, leaving the chip exposed or passively cooled with only a heat sink. This makes the southbridge a great place to see the manufacturer of the chipset, such as Intel Corporation (Figure 4.3).

Most motherboards support old technologies such as floppy drives, parallel ports, and serial ports. Although supporting these old devices was once part of the southbridge's job, hardly any modern chipsets still support these devices. Motherboard manufacturers add a third chip called the *Super I/O chip* to handle these chores. Figure 4.4 shows a typical Super I/O chip.

FIGURE 4.4 Super I/O chip on ASUS motherboard

Travel Advisory
Super I/O chips work with chipsets but are not part of the chipset. Motherboard makers purchase them separately from chipsets.

Modern Chipsets

In 2003, chipsets saw a new revision with the launch of the Athlon 64 micropro-cessor. Since the Athlon 64 contains the memory controller on the CPU, the northbridge no longer had to handle communication with RAM. Its duties changed to communicating with the video card(s) and the southbridge. Intel switched to this configuration in 2008 with the release of the Core i7 processor and the X58 Express Chipset.

With the X58 Express Chipset, Intel further refined its terminology, calling the northbridge simply the *I/O Hub (IOH),* since the memory controller is no longer located on the chip. With the IOH, Intel refers to the southbridge as the *Legacy I/O Controller Hub.*

Post-Modern Chipsets

The latest iterations of the chipset were spearheaded by Intel's P55 Express Chipset, released in 2009. In this configuration, the CPU incorporates both the memory controller and the video interface, eliminating the need for a north-bridge chip altogether. Intel does not use the term *southbridge* for the lone re-maining chip that makes up the chipset, instead calling it the *Platform Controller Hub (PCH).* AMD has also switched to a chipset configuration that no longer requires a discrete northbridge with the launch of its Fusion platform.

Exam Tip
For some reason, CompTIA doesn't follow chipset development closely. Be sure that you can identify and explain the function of various chipsets on both older and more current motherboards.

Motherboard Form Factors

Most motherboards come in one of two form factors, ATX or ITX, plus you'll see a sprinkling of proprietary and other form factor motherboards out there as well. Each form factor has several varieties.

The form factor defines the motherboard's size, its orientation, the location of built-in sockets and expansion slots, and so on. The motherboard's form

factor determines the type of power supply and case a PC can use. Form factors are not interchangeable. That means, for example, that ATX motherboards fit into ATX cases, and ITX motherboards fit into ITX cases.

ATX

In 1995, Intel introduced the ATX motherboard form factor (Figure 4.5) to replace the aging AT form factor originally developed by IBM. The ATX form factor possesses many improvements over the AT form factor. Most notably, the expansion slots, CPU, and RAM have been rearranged to enable easier access and enhanced performance, and to prevent long expansion cards from colliding with the CPU, which was a common problem in AT systems.

ATX motherboards sport a rear I/O area that makes the ports for built-in peripherals accessible on the back of a case. A sheet metal cutout that matches the ports, called the *I/O shield,* typically covers this space.

There have been several revisions of the ATX standards over the years. Two of the more notable changes are the inclusion of new power connectors for modern, power-hungry motherboards and various changes to the recommendations concerning power supply fans and airflow.

Two popular variations of the ATX form factor are *microATX* and *FlexATX.* These use the same power connections and have the same basic layout as ATX but are scaled to fit into much smaller ATX cases. Full-sized ATX motherboards will not fit into microATX or FlexATX cases, although most full-size cases support the smaller motherboards.

FIGURE 4.5 ATX motherboard

Mini-ITX (photo courtesy of VIA Technologies, Inc.)

ITX

VIA Technologies created the standard for the current leader in *small form factor (SFF)* motherboards with ITX. Although the full-sized ITX design wasn't a success, VIA created several smaller form factors that today populate the SFF market: Mini-ITX, Nano-ITX, and Pico-ITX.

Mini-ITX is the largest and the most popular of the three ITX form factors. At a miniscule 6.7 by 6.7 inches, Mini-ITX competes with the much larger microATX (see Figure 4.6). For comparison, microATX motherboards are 9.6 inches square.

If you think that's small, *Nano-ITX* at 4.7 by 4.7 inches and *Pico-ITX* at 3.8 by 2.8 inches are even smaller. These tiny motherboard form factors are commonly used for embedded systems and highly specialized devices such as routers.

NLX

The NLX form factor is an older slimline form factor for desktop computers. The NLX form factor met the demands of the slimline market by providing a central riser slot to enable the insertion of a special *riser card* (Figure 4.7), or, as it's sometimes called, a *daughterboard*. Expansion cards then fit into the riser card horizontally. Combining built-in connections with a riser card enabled manufacturers to produce PCs shorter than 4 inches. NLX has been superseded by the microATX, FlexATX, and Mini-ITX form factors.

FIGURE 4.7 Riser card on an older motherboard

Proprietary Form Factors

Several major PC makers, including Dell and Sony, make motherboards that
work only with their cases. These *proprietary* motherboards enable these com-
panies to create systems that stand out from the generic ones and, not
coincidently, push you to get service and upgrades from their authorized deal-
ers. Some of the features you'll see in proprietary systems are riser boards like
you see with the NLX form factor—part of a motherboard separate from the
main one, but connected by a cable of some sort—and unique power connec-
tions. Proprietary motherboards drive techs crazy because replacement parts
tend to cost more and are not readily available.

Motherboard Connections

Motherboards today come with connectors to support literally dozens of de-
vices, from the core components of CPU and memory, to sophisticated
high-speed networking. You've already seen the most common integrated I/O
ports in Chapter 2, which covered serial, parallel, keyboard, mouse, video, audio,
multimedia, MIDI/joystick, modem, network, eSATA, USB, FireWire, and SCSI
ports. Six of the next seven chapters of this book cover the rest: CPU, RAM, hard
drives, removable drives, and expansion slots. (There's no reason to go through
any of these in any detail in this chapter.)

Exam Tip

In the late 1990s, Intel created a special slot called the *audio modem riser* (AMR), which was later followed by the *communications and networking riser* (CNR). These slots allowed motherboard manufacturers to avoid Federal Communications Commission (FCC) certification (required for all electronic communication devices) by creating a separate card and slot for audio, modem, and network devices.

When you upgrade or recommend an upgrade, you must address one question: Can the hardware do the job desired by your client? If your client wants to play the latest and greatest games, for example, you need to look at his or her machine and determine its capability. Can it handle a powerful enough CPU? How much RAM does the processor or chipset support? Is the motherboard capable of supporting NVIDIA SLI or AMD CrossFireX to use more than one graphics card to produce a single output (Figure 4.8)? All such factors must be weighed in order to deliver the greatest value to the client. The client should be informed of the various upgrade paths available, their costs, and, to your best estimation, their benefits.

If your client wants to get a new, fast external hard drive—a more mundane example—you need to weigh several factors. If the motherboard has an eSATA port, just recommend an eSATA-capable hard drive enclosure, and the client is set. If the motherboard has Hi-Speed USB but not eSATA, on the other hand, you need to determine which route provides the best experience for the client.

FIGURE 4.8 A motherboard supporting multiple graphics cards

He or she can get a USB-only enclosure or get an eSATA enclosure and an eSATA controller card. The latter option will cost more and require more installation, but also offer much faster performance. By examining the capabilities and limitations of specific motherboards, you can provide the right experience for your clients.

Installing a Motherboard

Installing or replacing a motherboard requires a couple of simple steps. If your motherboard has tiny *jumpers* or switches, you may need to set them before you get started. These jumpers adjust different settings, depending on the specific motherboard. They might control the motherboard bus speed, the multiplier, or the voltage. Once that is settled, install the motherboard into a case designed for the motherboard.

> ## Exam Tip
> Using jumpers to control the system bus speed used to be a common chore for techs and might show up as an answer choice on the 801 exam. (Most motherboards today handle everything through the CMOS setup utility that you'll learn about in Chapter 7.)

Most system boards come with an I/O shield that matches the external I/O connectors on the motherboard, so you might have to replace the one that's in the case before you can insert the new motherboard. Second, adjust the standouts on the case to align with the mounting holes in the motherboard. Third, angle the motherboard into the I/O shield (Figure 4.9) and screw it down snugly. Assuming the CPU and RAM are already installed, you're now ready to plug in the power connections, storage devices, expansion cards, any fans that need to connect to the motherboard, and the front panel connections for the case. The next section of this chapter covers power supply connections, and later chapters will cover storage and expansion, so let's take a moment here to discuss fans and the front panel connections.

Motherboard Fan Connections

Most motherboards support one or more case fans that plug directly into three- or four-wire standouts (Figure 4.10). These provide good 12-volt power for spinning fans and have the added benefit of enabling the motherboard to monitor the fans. That way, you'll get a warning if one of the fans stops spinning and know to shut down your system before overheating causes problems. Use the motherboard connectors if you can.

FIGURE 4.9 Installing a motherboard (note spare I/O shield)

FIGURE 4.10 Three-wire chassis fan standout

Front Panel Connections

Connecting the wires for the light-emitting diodes (LEDs), buttons, and front-mounted ports on the front of the box to the motherboard completes the installation process. These usually include the following: soft power switch, reset button, internal PC speaker, hard drive activity LED, power LED, front or top mount USB ports, and audio ports.

These wires have specific pin connections to the motherboard. Although you can refer to the motherboard manual to determine their location, a quick inspection of the motherboard will usually suffice for an experienced tech (Figure 4.11).

You need to follow a few rules when installing these wires. First, the lights are LEDs, not light bulbs—they have a positive and negative side. If they don't work one way, turn the connector around and try the other. Second, when in doubt, guess. Incorrect installation results only in the device not working; it won't damage the computer. Refer to the motherboard manual for the correct installation. The third and last rule is that with the exception of the soft power switch on an ATX system, you do not need any of these wires for the computer to run! Many techs often ignore these wires, although this would not be something I'd do to any system but my own.

FIGURE 4.11 Wire connections labeled on the motherboard

Troubleshooting Motherboards

Motherboards can go bad over time because of external factors such as power spikes and sags, electrostatic discharge, or excessive heat. A motherboard can be faulty right out of the box, too, so if you run into a new system that you have trouble getting to work, you can add the new motherboard to the list as a possible culprit.

Troubleshooting motherboards—even in a new installation—can drive a tech to distraction, because the symptoms of a failing motherboard range from devices not working to intermittent lockups. What would you suspect first if a network card that worked before a storm didn't work after a storm? The card seems like the logical suspect, and that's what you'd check first, but the motherboard could have taken a hit from the storm and have a few electrons jangling loose. This is especially true in motherboards with built-in network interface cards (NICs).

Travel Advisory

You can update a motherboard's internal drivers through a process called *flashing the BIOS.* You can also turn a motherboard into an inert piece of wall art by flashing the BIOS incorrectly or having an error occur during the flashing process. *There's no recovery* from a flashing failure, so be careful! See Chapter 7 for the scoop on flashing the BIOS.

When you suspect a motherboard has gone or is going bad, replace it. A computer must have a rock-solid foundation, and a buggy motherboard is simply not acceptable.

Objective 4.02 Power Supplies

The PC's power supply (Figure 4.12) converts high-voltage AC power into the lower-voltage DC power that your motherboard and drives need. Its internal fan also provides essential cooling for the PC components and drives. When connected to a properly grounded outlet, the power supply also provides grounding for all the other equipment inside the case.

FIGURE 4.12 Power supply

In the United States, standard AC comes in somewhere between 110 and 120 volts, often written as ~115 VAC. Most of the rest of the world uses 220–240 VAC, so many power supplies offer a dual-voltage option through a little switch in the back that enables you to use them anywhere. Power supplies that can handle different voltages are called *switched-mode power supplies* (though the "switch" in this case refers to the internal components and not the little switch on the back).

Exam Tip

The power connector for the AC plug on the back of a power supply is called an *IEC 320* connector.

Power supplies come in various form factors that determine the physical size and shape, as well as the types of connectors you'll find. Power supplies vary in output and efficiency.

Exam Tip

Look for the acronym *PSU,* for *power supply unit,* on the CompTIA A+ exams. Most techs refer to power supplies using the full words rather than the acronym.

Power Supply Form Factors

The ATX power supply form factor is by far the most popular PSU form factor available. Full-size ATX cases use ATX power supplies. Smaller cases that house smaller form factor motherboards such as microATX, FlexATX, and Mini-ITX may use smaller form factor PSUs. Note that many manufacturers have created proprietary power supplies that come in all sorts of shapes and sizes (such as the one shown in Figure 4.13). They might not exactly conform to the ATX power standards, so watch out! Using one of these proprietary power supplies in a regular system can damage the motherboard and other components.

Power Supply Connectors

Power supplies offer several connectors for the motherboard and drives. All have four-wire *mini* and Molex connectors for floppy, parallel ATA (PATA), and SCSI drives, and most have serial ATA (SATA) connectors for SATA drives (Figure 4.14). Better power supplies have a dedicated six- or eight-wire *PCIe* connector for PCI Express video cards (Figure 4.15).

> ### Exam Tip
> The 801 objectives use the term *PCIe 6/8-pin* to refer to the six- and eight-wire connectors for PCIe video cards.

FIGURE 4.13 Proprietary power supply

FIGURE 4.14 Mini, Molex, and SATA power connectors

Power supplies connect to the motherboard with up to four connectors: the 20- or 24-wire *P1* connector, the primary power circuit; a four-wire *P4* secondary power connector, which typically supplies power to the CPU; and a six-wire auxiliary connector (referred to as an *AUX* connector) that very few motherboards use (Figure 4.16).

Exam Tip
The 5-volt orange wire on the P1 connector is called *power good* and is used in the initial boot sequence. See Chapter 7 for the boot sequence.

Many modern ATX motherboards use an 8-pin CPU power connector. This connector is referred to by several names, including EPS12V, EATX12V, and ATX12V 2x4. One half of this connector will be pin compatible with the P4 power connector and the other half may be under a protective cap.

Be sure to check the motherboard installation manual for recommendations on if and when the full 8 pins need to be used. For backward compatibility, some power supplies provide an 8-pin power connector that can split into two, 4-pin sets, one of which is the P4 connector. Although they look similar, the 8-pin CPU power connector is not compatible with the 8-pin PCIe power connector. Table 4.1 lists the common connectors of the *ATX12V* power supplies—the current standard—with their voltages and uses.

FIGURE 4.15 PCIe power connector

FIGURE 4.16 P1, P4, and AUX connectors (left to right)

Exam Tip

The 801 objectives refer to the secondary motherboard power connector as a *4/8-pin 12v* connector.

Travel Advisory

All power connectors are keyed so you can't easily plug them in backward. The mini socket keying on floppy drives is often flimsy, however, so you need to take care with them. Reversing the power on a device will destroy that device, because you're plugging a 12-volt wire into a 5-volt circuit. That's a bad thing!

TABLE 4.1 Power Connectors and Voltages

Connector	Voltages	Common Use
Molex	5 V, 12 V	PATA and SCSI hard drives and optical drives; some PCIe video cards; some PCIe motherboards
Mini	5 V, 12 V	Floppy drives
SATA	5 V, 12 V	SATA drives
PCIe	12 V	PCIe video cards
P1 (20-wire)	3.3 V, 5 V, 12 V	Primary power for older ATX motherboards
P1 (24-wire)	3.3 V, 5 V, 12 V	Primary power for current ATX motherboards
P4 and 8-pin CPU power connector	12 V	Secondary power for current ATX motherboards
AUX	3.3 V, 5 V, 12 V	Auxiliary power for motherboards

Output: Wattage and Harmonics

Power supplies provide a certain amount of *wattage* that the motherboard, drives, and fans draw on to run. That's the desired output. Power supplies also produce *harmonics,* the hum you hear when the power supply runs, that can cause problems if not controlled.

Local Lingo
Wattage Wattage is the amount of amperage flowing at a specific voltage, usually written as W = VA.

A PC requires sufficient wattage to run properly. Every device in a PC also requires a certain amount of wattage in order to function. A typical hard drive draws 15 watts of power when accessed, for example, whereas some Athlon 64 X2 CPUs draw a whopping 110 watts at peak usage—with average usage around 70 watts. The total wattage of all devices combined is the minimum you need the power supply to provide.

If the power supply cannot produce the wattage needed by a system, that PC won't work properly. Because most devices in the PC require maximum wattage when first starting, the most common result of insufficient wattage is a paperweight that looks like a PC. The only fixes for this problem are to remove a device from the PC—such as the new hard drive you just plugged in—or get a power supply with more wattage. Today's PCs require 500+ watt power supplies to function.

Good PC power supplies come with *active power factor correction (active PFC),* extra circuitry that smoothes out the way the power supply takes power from the power company and eliminates harmonics. Older and poorer power supplies don't have this circuitry and should not be used if at all possible.

Most active PFC power supplies are *auto-switching,* meaning they can detect the voltage coming from the wall and adjust accordingly. You can use an auto-switching power supply anywhere in the world, from the ~115 VAC in New York City to the ~230 in Hong Kong. This is especially important with portable computers!

Installation Notes

Installing a power supply means properly connecting cables to the motherboard and devices and mounting it in the case. Mounting in almost every case consists of attaching with four standard case screws (Figure 4.17). This has been true for more than a decade. The only time you'll run into some different procedure is with some SFF cases or proprietary cases.

FIGURE 4.17 Power supply secured in case

Troubleshooting Power Supplies

Power supplies fail in two ways: sudden death and slowly over time. When they die suddenly, the computer will not start and the fan in the power supply will not turn. In this case, verify that electricity is getting to the power supply before you do anything else.

Assuming that the system has electricity, the best way to verify that a power supply is working or not working is to check the voltages coming out of the power supply with a multimeter (Figure 4.18).

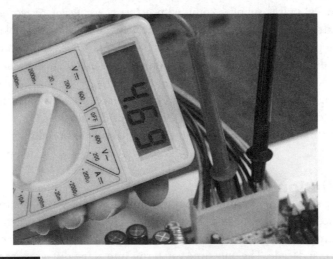

FIGURE 4.18 Testing one of the 5-volt DC connections

The voltages supplied by most PC power supplies can safely vary by as much as ±10 percent of their stated values. This means that the 12-volt line can vary from roughly 10.5 to 12.9 volts without exceeding the tolerance of the various systems in the PC. The 5.0- and 3.3-volt lines offer similar tolerances.

If the power supply provides no power, throw it into the recycling bin and get a new one. Do *not* open a power supply and try to service it yourself, because it contains dangerous high-voltage capacitors.

Power supplies that die suddenly are often accompanied by some telltale signs. You might see smoke, for example, or get a whiff of a burning electronics smell. You might hear a loud noise. You'll definitely get a dead PC.

Power supplies require some kind of load, like being connected to a motherboard, before they'll start. If you don't have a motherboard handy and want to test a power supply, you can use a dedicated power supply tester. Many companies make these devices. Look for one that supports both 20- and 24-pin motherboard connectors as well as all of the other connectors on your motherboard. Figure 4.19 shows a power supply tester.

When power supplies die slowly, bad things begin to happen to the computer intermittently. The computer locks up every once in a while, for example, or it takes two tries before it boots up in the morning. You might get intermittent device failure. Because a Blue Screen of Death (BSoD) in Windows can be caused by a lot of things, diagnosing a lockup as a power supply problem is tough. The key is the word *intermittent*. If you run into phantom problems, switch out the power supply to see if that makes a difference. Every tech should have a known-good power supply as a *field replaceable unit (FRU)*.

One common power-related issue happens when you first build a system. You'll press the power button and the fans spin and the indicator lights flip on, but nothing else happens. You're staring at a blank screen when the system should be booting. This happens when you forget to install the 4/8-pin secondary power connector to the motherboard. Oops! Power down, plug it in, and then power up the system. (And hope no one noticed.)

FIGURE 4.19 Power supply tester

FIGURE 4.20 AC adapter

Many devices in the computing world use an AC adapter (Figure 4.20) rather than an internal power supply. Even though it sits outside a device, an AC adapter converts AC current to DC, just like a power supply. Unlike power supplies, AC adapters are rarely interchangeable. Although manufacturers of different devices often use the same kind of plug on the end of the AC adapter cable, these adapters are not necessarily interchangeable. Just because you can plug an AC adapter from your friend's laptop into your laptop does not mean it's going to work!

You need to make sure that three things match before you plug an AC adapter into a device: voltage, amperage, and polarity. If the voltage or amperage output is too low, the device won't run. If the polarity is reversed, it won't work—just like putting a battery backward in a flashlight. If the voltage or amperage—especially the latter—is too high, on the other hand, you can quickly toast your device. Don't do it! Always check the voltage, amperage, and polarity of a replacement AC adapter before you plug it into a device.

Objective 4.03 Cases

Cases come in six basic sizes: slimline, desktop, mini-tower, mid-tower, tower, and cube. Slimline and desktop models generally sit on the desk, beneath the monitor. The various tower cases usually occupy a bit of floor space next to the desk. The mini-tower and mid-tower cases are the most popular choices. Make sure you get a case that will fit your motherboard—many microATX and all FlexATX cases are too small for a regular ATX motherboard. Cube cases generally require a specific motherboard, so be prepared to buy both pieces at once. A quick test fit before you buy saves a lot of return trips to the supplier.

Exam Tip

The six case sizes listed here apply only to consumer or workstation PCs. Server PCs come in several different varieties, such as huge dual-power supply behemoths and rack-mounted systems too svelte to handle a normal expansion card. The CompTIA A+ certification exams test you only on the consumer or workstation models.

The typical case has four screws on the back, two of which you remove with a Phillips-head screwdriver. This releases the side panel and enables access to the interior of the case. Panels slide into a slot, so they should fit snugly.

Vendors such as Alienware offer many colors and exotic body styles. More important, these cases are outfitted with detailing that enhances the PC's function, such as additional cooling fans or liquid cooling systems, high-output power supplies, cable management systems, roomier interiors, screwless body panels (these require no tools to remove), and such welcome touches as front-mounted USB and audio ports.

CHECKPOINT

✔**Objective 4.01: Motherboards** All motherboards have a chipset. Traditional chipsets are composed of two chips: a northbridge and a southbridge. The northbridge communicates with the fastest devices, namely the RAM and the video card, and the southbridge communicates with slower devices such as the lower-throughput expansion busses, I/O ports, and integrated peripherals. Communication with legacy devices, such as the floppy disk drive or the serial port, is usually delegated out to a circuit called the Super I/O chip. In many recent system architectures, the CPU communicates with RAM directly, instead of relying on the northbridge—and in the latest architectures, the northbridge has been eliminated since the CPU possesses all of its functionality. The ATX form factor—including full-sized, microATX, and FlexATX—dominates the PC market. Motherboards support literally dozens of device types through integrated I/O and expansion slots. Installation is a matter of placing standouts properly and screwing down the motherboard. Troubleshooting is tough, though, because of all the variables in the computer, but the fix for a bad motherboard is simple: replace it.

✔**Objective 4.02: Power Supplies** The PSU converts AC power into the DC power that your motherboard and drives need. Its internal fan also provides essential cooling for the PC components and drives. ATX power supplies dominate the market and plug into all ATX form-factor motherboards. You'll find up to seven connectors on power supplies—Molex, mini, SATA, PCIe, P1, P4 (or ATX12V 2x4), and AUX—for drives, video cards, and motherboards, respectively. Power supplies are rated in wattage, such as 400-watt or 1-kilowatt; plus better PSUs employ active PFC to stop harmonics. Power supplies die either suddenly or slowly over time. With the latter, the clue is intermittent problems. Replace, and don't try to fix, a dead or dying power supply.

✔**Objective 4.03: Cases** PC cases come in six basic sizes: slimline, desktop, mini-tower, mid-tower, tower, and cube. Make sure you get a case that will fit your motherboard—microATX and FlexATX cases are too small for a regular ATX motherboard. Cube cases generally require a specific motherboard, so be prepared to buy both pieces at once.

REVIEW QUESTIONS

1. What part of the PC is the framework on which everything is built?
 A. I/O busses
 B. Expansion slots
 C. CPU
 D. Motherboard

2. Which of the following motherboards are you most likely to see in modern PCs? (Select two.)
 A. AT
 B. ATX
 C. Baby ATX
 D. MicroATX

3. If you have a PC with an ATX motherboard and case and you decide you would like to upgrade the motherboard, can you replace it with an ITX motherboard?
 A. No
 B. Yes, if you reset the jumpers
 C. Yes, if you add more screw holes
 D. Yes, if you remove the integrated ports

4. If you have a PC with a full-sized ATX motherboard and case and you decide you would like to upgrade the motherboard, can you replace it with a microATX motherboard? (Select the best answer.)

 A. No

 B. Yes, if you reset the jumpers

 C. Yes, if you add more screw holes

 D. Most likely, if you move the standouts

5. What types of connectors attach the ATX power supply to a modern ATX motherboard? (Select two.)

 A. P1

 B. PDC

 C. P4

 D. P9

6. Which part of the chipset traditionally helps the CPU work with the RAM and video card?

 A. IDE controller

 B. Northbridge

 C. Southbridge

 D. RAID controller

7. Mario bought a PCI Express video card. What type of connector might he need to plug into the card? (Select two.)

 A. Molex

 B. P1

 C. P4

 D. PCIe

8. Which motherboard type uses a riser card?

 A. ATX

 B. BTX

 C. MicroATX

 D. NLX

9. Molex connectors supply electricity to which devices? (Select two.)

 A. Floppy drives

 B. Hard drives

 C. Optical drives

 D. Thumb drives

10. A client notices the 115/230 switch on the back of a power supply you're installing. What's the switch used for?

A. Powering computers in countries that run at a higher standard voltage than that used in the United States

B. Powering computers in countries that run at a lower standard voltage than that used in the United States

C. Powering server computers that need double the normal voltage

D. Overclocking

11. In what circumstance should you open a power supply?

A. You open a power supply for routine cleaning.

B. If the computer suddenly won't start up, you can check and replace the fuse inside the power supply.

C. If you see a flash of light or see smoke coming out, you should open the power supply.

D. Never open a power supply. It's not safe.

12. Which voltages does a power supply provide through a mini connector?

A. 3.3 V, 5 V

B. 5 V, 12 V

C. 3.3 V, 12 V

D. 115 V, 230 V

13. After installing an additional drive into a working computer, the computer won't power up at all—no lights, no spinning drives, nothing. What's most likely the problem?

A. Dead hard drive

B. Dead power supply

C. Insufficient DC wattage provided by the power supply

D. Insufficient AC wattage provided by the electrical outlet

14. ATX PSUs can be used with which form factors?

A. ATX

B. ITX

C. NLX

D. SFX

15. What feature do you find on better power supplies that eliminates harmonics?

 A. Active PFC

 B. Active scan

 C. Passive PFC

 D. Passive scan

REVIEW ANSWERS

1. **D** The motherboard can be considered the cornerstone of the PC. All your system devices are either directly or indirectly attached to the motherboard, making it the most important part of your PC.

2. **B D** You'll find primarily ATX and microATX motherboards in modern systems. AT motherboards are old, and baby ATX motherboards don't exist.

3. **A** You cannot replace an ATX motherboard with an ITX motherboard using the same case. ATX motherboards go into ATX cases, and ITX motherboards go into ITX cases.

4. **D** Most full-sized ATX cases support microATX motherboards.

5. **A C** Modern ATX motherboards use P1 for primary power and P4 for secondary power.

6. **B** The northbridge helps the CPU work with the RAM and video card.

7. **A D** Some PCIe video cards use a Molex connector, although most require a PCIe connector.

8. **D** NLX motherboards use a riser card.

9. **B C** Molex connectors supply power for hard drives and optical drives.

10. **A** When powering up computers in countries that use ~230 VAC, you simply flip the switch from ~115 to ~230.

11. **D** Don't open that power supply because the capacitors can bite. Hard.

12. **B** Mini connectors provide 5 V and 12 V.

13. **C** If a power supply does not have enough DC wattage to power up the computer, you'll get a completely inert computer.

14. **A** ATX PSUs can be used with the ATX form factor.

15. **A** Active power factor correction (PFC) helps smooth out those nasty harmonics.

CPUs

	NEWBIE	SOME EXPERIENCE	EXPERT
ETA	3 hours	2 hours	1 hour

The microprocessor, or as most techs call it, the *central processing unit (CPU)*, is the thing that enables a computer to compute. Everything else on the computer can be considered part of the CPU's life-support system. So what does the CPU do? If you believe the hyperbole of popular culture, the CPU is some sort of machine brain that's always on the verge of declaring, "I think, therefore I am" and trying to take over the world. Don't let them kid you—computers don't think! What the CPU does, and does amazingly well, is add numbers. The CPU is really just a super-fast, super-powerful calculator.

As simple as that may sound, keep in mind that a CPU churns out *billions* of calculations every second. These calculations make possible everything that your PC does: displaying your operating system (OS) desktop, processing print jobs, grabbing Web pages, and doing everything else that you ask it to do. Of all the whiz-bang pieces of engineering that go into the PC, the CPU is by far the most impressive. The CPU has gone through many evolutions since its introduction more than 30 years ago, but even the most advanced CPUs still operate in much the same manner as the old Intel 8088 that powered the first IBM PC.

Today's desktop CPU market is dominated by two vendors: Intel and Advanced Micro Devices (AMD). Intel's CPU offerings include the Pentium, Celeron, Atom, Core, Core 2, Core i5, Core i7, Xeon, and Itanium processor lines. AMD gives us the Sempron, Turion, Athlon 64, Athlon II, Phenom, Phenom II, FX, and A product families, and the server-oriented Opteron processors.

Travel Advisory

Over the years, other companies have tried to get into the CPU business. Companies such as Cyrix, IDT, VIA, and Transmeta have all developed CPUs, but they met with limited success and minor market share. Motorola made the CPU for Apple Macintosh computers for many years, though now Macs have Intel inside. The only other big player in CPUs is ARM, a British company that designs the CPUs used in many mobile devices, such as the Apple iPad.

The CompTIA A+ certification exams concentrate on the aspects of the CPU that a tech has to know to service PCs in today's business world. First, you need to understand the basic internal components of a CPU and what they do so that you can make informed decisions and recommendations on CPUs. Second, you need to know how to install a CPU and its cooling system. Finally, you need to handle the relatively simple troubleshooting that CPUs require.

Objective 5.01 CPU Technology

Modern CPUs are composed of multiple distinct components, from processing to memory, and the variations among them can give you pause when you look at the price. Why is one Intel processor so much more expensive than another? How do you compare AMD and Intel CPUs? This section looks at components shared by all CPUs and variations in computing processes, and then it finishes with a discussion of technology innovations.

Inside the CPU

Ancient CPUs operated pretty much like simple calculators that were able to do basic arithmetic, but modern CPUs have dedicated circuitry to process amazingly complex things. Here's a brief look at those circuits (Figure 5.1). You can't fix any of this stuff, but it's good to know how processors work, because the knowledge enables you to see differences among CPUs.

Arithmetic Logic Unit

The *arithmetic logic unit (ALU)* processes data and is the primary processing component of the CPU. The ALU takes data from the CPU registers, processes it, and copies it back into the registers before moving on to the next batch of data.

FIGURE 5.1 Inside the CPU

Registers

Registers are memory circuits located inside the CPU that hold data before and after processing. In essence, the registers are the ALU's workbenches. Early Intel Pentium CPUs (the original Pentium up through most Pentium 4 variants) used 32-bit, general-purpose registers; modern CPUs use 64-bit, general-purpose registers.

Floating-Point Unit

The *floating-point unit (FPU)* handles complex calculations for applications that require it, such as graphics programs and 3-D games. The FPU on today's PCs is integrated with the CPU. Ancient, pre-Pentium CPUs relied on a separate FPU chip, sometimes called the *math coprocessor*, to handle FPU mathematics.

Cache Memory

Modern CPUs have two sets of ultra-fast *static RAM (SRAM)* memory built in, called *cache*. Normal system RAM is called *dynamic RAM (DRAM)*, because it can hold data only for a very short duration before it needs to be *refreshed*—that is, so a *1* stays a *1* rather than draining to become a *0*. (It's all just binary, after all!) SRAM, in contrast, never needs to be refreshed and is therefore much faster than DRAM. The *Level 1 (L1)* cache memory is the first and fastest, and is built into the processor. *Level 2 (L2)* cache memory is the second cache. Some processors prior to the Pentium 4 placed the L2 cache separately on the CPU package (or cartridge) with a special bus connecting it to the processor core, called the *backside bus*. Most modern processors now integrate the L2 cache onto the processor die directly. The L2 cache is larger than the L1 cache and is usually slower.

Local Lingo

Package and die The ceramic casing that holds the CPU is called the *package*. The silicon wafer that has all the transistors is called the *die*. Components that are incorporated into the silicon, such as L2 cache memory, are referred to as being *on-die*.

Cache design is very important in multicore processors. Each core has its own L1 cache. In some configurations, the L2 cache is shared by all cores; in other configurations, each core also has its own L2 cache and an L3 cache is shared among cores (Figure 5.2).

Since SRAM is so much faster, why don't PCs use it for system RAM instead of SDRAM? The answer is simple: cost. SRAM is roughly ten times more expensive than SDRAM.

FIGURE 5.2 Multicore cache configuration

Exam Tip

Remember that SDRAM is fast, cheap, and must be refreshed; SRAM is much faster, very expensive, and requires no refreshing.

Address Space

The number of wires on the address bus defines the maximum amount of RAM a CPU can theoretically address. This is called the *address space*. With a 32-bit address bus, for example, the maximum amount of memory the CPU can address is 2^{32}, or 4,294,967,296 bytes (4 GB). Modern CPUs have address busses larger than 32-bit, so can support substantially more than 4 GB of RAM. (See "64-Bit Processors" later in this chapter for details.)

Concepts

Techs use certain concepts and terms to differentiate among CPUs, so you can judge pretty quickly which specific make and model fits your client's needs. Specifically, the pipeline, clock speed, and clock multipliers give you a good indication of the caliber of the CPU.

Pipeline

The term *pipeline* refers to the discrete series of steps that the CPU follows to process commands. You can think of a pipeline in terms of doing laundry, which follows an ordered series of steps: wash, dry, iron, and hang up. You don't have to wait until the first load of laundry is done to start the second—you only have to wait for the washer to become available; this is the basic concept behind pipelining. Just as multiple loads of laundry can be "in flight" at once, so can multiple instructions be in flight at once in a pipelined processor.

Early, pre-Pentium CPUs had only a single pipeline and thus could process only a single stream of commands at a time. When the CPU was working on a complex mathematical command, for example, the FPU might have been working hard while the ALU sat idle. The Pentium introduced dual pipelines that enabled the CPU to break down the instructions into two separate streams that could be processed simultaneously. Current CPUs have many more pipelines and can thus process more commands at once.

Don't confuse pipelining with simultaneous multithreading or multicore processing. Although pipelined processors can process multiple instructions at once, they can handle instructions originating from only a single stream, or *thread,* at a time. Special circuitry is needed to be able to process multiple threads at once, and this is discussed later in this chapter.

Clock Speed

The CPU clock speed, or *frequency,* tells you how many calculation cycles a CPU can (in theory) execute per second. One calculation cycle per second is equal to 1 hertz (Hz). Of course, nobody measures clock cycles in hertz, but rather in millions of calculation cycles per second, or megahertz (MHz). These days, it's more common to see clock speed measured in billions of cycles per second, or gigahertz (GHz).

Two things determine clock speed: the maximum speed of the CPU itself and the maximum speed that the motherboard can handle. The CPU speed is determined by the manufacturer and is set at the factory. The *system crystal*—a quartz crystal circuit that oscillates at a fixed frequency when fed current—sets the motherboard's clock speed.

Multipliers

Early CPUs took the beat set by the clock and simply doubled it, thus enabling the CPU to run internally at twice the speed of the motherboard. Modern CPUs multiply the signal many times. A CPU running at 2 GHz on a 200-MHz system bus, for example, uses a ×10 clock multiplier. Because CPUs do so much more work processing than any other component, it makes sense for them to do ten things while some other processor—such as a sound card processor—does a single thing.

The system bus speed and the multiplier on the CPU had to be manually configured via jumpers on the motherboard in the old days. Today's CPUs actually report to the motherboard through a function called *CPUID (CPU identifier),* and the system bus speed and multiplier are often set automatically. Many motherboards offer manual configuration, but this is primarily for tweaking systems. See the section "Overclocking" later in this chapter for more details.

Performance Ratings

Intel has traditionally been able to produce CPUs that run at higher frequencies than CPUs from AMD, and its marketing reflected this aspect of CPUs. AMD, in contrast, has argued that raw clock speed is less important than processing efficiency and has concentrated on the latter for its CPUs. Unfortunately for AMD, Intel has a great marketing force, and most consumers bought the erroneous line that raw speed is the most important aspect of a CPU.

To overcome this marketing, AMD marked its CPUs with a *performance rating* in addition to a clock speed to advertise that a slower AMD CPU performed on par with a faster Intel CPU. An AMD Athlon XP 3200+ might run at only 2.2 GHz, for example, but according to AMD it can compete head to head with a 3.2-GHz Intel CPU. With the Pentium M and the more recent Core 2 and Core i7 processors, Intel conceded the point and removed raw speed as the primary factor in CPU quality and performance.

CPU Packages

All current CPUs come in a square package called a *pin grid array (PGA)*, like that shown in Figure 5.3, but variations exist within and among manufacturers. Collectively, Intel and AMD have used close to 100 variations of the PGA package over the years for hundreds of different CPU models with names such as staggered-PGA, micro-PGA, *ball grid array*, or *BGA* (which uses tiny balls instead of pins), and land grid array (which uses flat pads instead of pins).

Many different varieties of PGA CPUs are based on the number of pins sticking out of the CPU. These CPUs snap into special sockets on the motherboard, with each socket designed to match the pins (or balls or pads) on the CPU.

FIGURE 5.3 Typical PGA CPU

To make CPU insertion and removal easier, these sockets—officially called *zero insertion force (ZIF) sockets*—use a small arm on the side of the socket (Figure 5.4) or a cage that fits over the socket to hold the CPU in place. ZIF sockets are easily identified by their squarish shape. Most modern Intel sockets have official names such as "Socket T," but they are usually referred to by names such as "Socket LGA 775" to reflect the number of pins in the CPU socket. AMD's latest sockets go by names such as "Socket AM3" and are generally not referred to by the number of pins on the CPU or in the socket.

Exam Tip

For a short time, Intel and AMD produced large, rectangular-shaped CPU packages called *single edge cartridges (SECs)* that fit into a slot, kind of like an expansion card. The first was the Intel Pentium II. The SEC is long dead, but might show up as an incorrect answer on the 801 exam.

FIGURE 5.4 ZIF socket (arm up)

Voltage Regulator Modules

CPUs vary greatly in the amount of voltage they need to run. With the many variations among CPUs you can install into a single motherboard, motherboards need to have some mechanism to accommodate the different voltages. Older motherboards used an add-on device called a *voltage regulator module* that you could replace or adjust via jumpers or switches to handle CPU varieties. Modern motherboards do this automatically.

Variations

Several innovations have created a great divide between CPUs on the high end and all the rest. Technology innovations include enhanced registers, Hyper-Threading, 64-bit processors, multicore CPUs, and mobile CPU varieties.

Enhanced Registers

Starting with later versions of the Intel Pentium, manufacturers have improved some of the registers inside the CPU, adding specific-use and general-use registers along with special CPU instructions to use them. The first, developed by Intel, were called *multimedia extensions (MMX)*; they were 64-bit and borrowed the FPU's registers while in use.

Later Intel options were the 128-bit *streaming SIMD extensions (SSE)*, SSE2, SSE3, and SSE4. Over the years AMD developed 3DNow!, which was compatible with MMX, and 3DNow! Professional, which added SSE, SSE2, and SSE3 compatibility. AMD's latest processors also include support for some SSE4 instructions in a standard AMD calls SSE4a.

Hyper-Threading

Most desktop CPUs handle multiple *processes*—opening a file, playing an MP3, and so on—nearly simultaneously by switching rapidly back and forth between the subunits, called *threads*, that make up processes. Many processes are made up of only one thread, but some processes comprise numerous threads.

Intel introduced *Hyper-Threading Technology* with the Pentium 4 processor. Hyper-Threading is Intel's brand name for its implementation of simultaneous multithreading, which is a way of executing multiple threads simultaneously on a single processor core. For instance, a single-core Intel Pentium 4 with Hyper-Threading looks like two CPUs to the OS (Figure 5.5). Currently, Intel offers Hyper-Threading Technology on its Pentium 4, Core i7, and Xeon processor lines. As of this writing, AMD has not released a processor that uses simultaneous multithreading technology.

FIGURE 5.5 Pentium 4 showing up as two processors

Exam Tip

Know that Hyper-Threading is a form of simultaneous multithreading used in Intel chips to increase performance on a single processor core.

64-Bit Processors

Typically, a 64-bit CPU has address and general-purpose registers that are 64 bits wide and can access much, much more memory than a 32-bit CPU. Both AMD and Intel currently produce 64-bit CPUs.

Since the introduction of the Pentium Pro, most 32-bit processors have come with a 36-bit physical address bus that allows the CPU to address a maximum of 2^{36} (64 GB) of memory. On a 32-bit CPU, however, each individual process is limited to accessing a memory space of only 2^{32} (4 GB). The AMD64 and Intel 64 architectures define a 52-bit physical address bus for 2^{52} (4 PB—petabytes) of memory, but current implementations use only 40 or 48 bits, making 2^{40} (1 TB) or 2^{48} (256 TB) the maximum amount of memory addressable by the CPU. In 64-bit mode, most current implementations allow each process up to 48 bits of virtual address space, thus eliminating the restriction put on applications by 32-bit CPUs.

AMD64 was originally called x86-64, and Intel 64 was originally named EM64T. The term "x64" is a generic term that applies to either of them. Both may run either 32-bit or 64-bit operating systems, so they support 64-bit versions of Windows out of the box. Current consumer-oriented 64-bit CPUs include AMD's Athlon 64 (Figure 5.6), Athlon II, Phenom, Phenom II, A, and FX series of CPUs, and Intel's Core 2, Core i3, Core i5, and Core i7 CPUs, as well as some Atom-, Celeron-, and Pentium-branded processors.

Exam Tip

Processors come in both 32-bit (x86) and 64-bit (x64) varieties. 64-bit processors can access more memory (RAM) than 32-bit processors and, when used in conjunction with 64-bit software, they can improve performance.

Multicore CPUs

CPU clock speeds hit a practical limit of roughly 4 GHz around the years 2002–2003, motivating the CPU makers to find new ways to get more processing power for CPUs. Although Intel and AMD had different opinions about 64-bit CPUs, both decided at virtually the same time to combine multiple CPUs onto the same physical processor die. CPUs with more than one processor core are known as *multicore* CPUs.

FIGURE 5.6 AMD Athlon 64

INTEL®©'06 E7400
INTEL® CORE™2 DUO
SLB9Y COSTA RICA
2.80GHZ/3M/1066/06
3847A448 ⓔ④

2L84419
2B0168

FIGURE 5.7 Intel Core 2 Duo

The first batch of multicore processors combined two CPU cores onto a single chip, creating a *dual-core* architecture (Figure 5.7). Unlike Hyper-Threading, where a single processor core shares execution resources among threads, a true dual-core CPU has two discrete processor cores, each possessing its own execution machinery.

Intel and AMD followed up with *quad-core* CPUs. AMD also produces a *triple-core* CPU by disabling one core of a quad-core CPU (presumably because it's defective). With its Core i7 processor, Intel has combined a quad-core processor with Hyper-Threading Technology, allowing each CPU core to handle two threads simultaneously, resulting in the CPU having a net capability of handling up to eight simultaneous threads. In its server-oriented Opteron processor line, AMD produces a six-core version of the chip that is capable of handling six threads simultaneously.

Mobile CPUs

The inside of a laptop PC is a cramped, hot environment, where no self-respecting CPU should ever need to operate. Since the mid-1980s, CPU manufacturers have endeavored to make specialized versions of their processors to function in the rugged world of laptops. These are called *mobile processors*. Over the years, a number

of CPU laptop solutions have appeared. Virtually every CPU made by Intel or AMD is available in a mobile version. You can usually tell a mobile version by the word *mobile* or the letter *M* in its name. Several mobile processor lines produced by Intel, however, share brand names with their desktop counterparts without many extra identifiers. In these cases, the mobile versions can be identified by their model numbers. Here are a few examples of mobile processors:

- Intel Pentium M
- Mobile AMD Athlon 64
- AMD Turion 64 X2 (All Turions are mobile processors but don't use *mobile* or *M* in their name. AMD usually adds *mobile technology* as part of the Turion description.)
- Intel Core 2 Duo Mobile
- Intel Core i7 Mobile
- Intel Celeron
- Intel Atom

A mobile processor uses less power than an equivalent desktop model. This provides two advantages. First, it enables the battery in the laptop to last longer. Second, it makes the CPU run cooler, and the cooler the CPU, the fewer cooling devices you need.

Almost every mobile processor today runs at a lower voltage than the desktop version of the same CPU. As a result, most mobile CPUs also run at lower speeds—it takes juice if you want the speed! Mobile CPU performance usually tops out at about 75 percent of the speed of the same CPU's desktop version.

Throttling

Modern CPUs can reduce their processing cycles and lower their clock speeds when they reach a certain temperature, a feature called *throttling*. This is incredibly important with mobile processors, because the heat dissipation methods for portable PCs are wimpy compared with those of desktop PCs. It's also essential when you have a catastrophic fan failure—either through animal hair gunking up the works or technician error when installing a fan. Rather than overheating and destroying the CPU, and most likely the motherboard—the way it worked in the old days—modern CPUs simply throttle down to the point where they can survive. You'll recognize serious throttling by the amazingly slow response times when trying to do anything on the PC.

Virtualization Support

Intel and AMD have built-in support for running more than one operating system at a time, a process called *virtualization*. The key issue from a CPU standpoint is that virtualization used to work entirely through software. Programmers had to write a ton of code to enable a CPU that was designed to run one OS at a time to run more than one OS at the same time. Think about the issues involved. How does the memory get allocated, for example, or how does the CPU know which OS to update when you type something or click an icon? With hardware-based virtualization support, CPUs took a lot of the burden off the programmers and made virtualization a whole lot easier.

Integrated Memory Controller

Almost all current microprocessors have an *integrated memory controller (IMC)*, moved from the motherboard chip into the CPU to optimize the flow of information into and out from the CPU. An IMC enables faster control over things like the large L3 cache shared among multiple cores.

Just like in so many other areas of computing, manufacturers implement a variety of IMCs in their CPUs. In practice, this means that different CPUs handle different types and capacities of RAM. I'll save the details on those RAM variations for Chapter 6. For now, add "different RAM support" to your list of things to look at when making a CPU recommendation for a client (see "Recommending a CPU").

Integrated Graphics Processing Unit

The video-processing portion of the computer—made up of the parts that put a changing image on the monitor—traditionally has a discrete microprocessor that differs in both function and architecture from the CPUs designed for general-purpose computing. The generic term for the video processor is a *graphics processing unit (GPU)*. Because graphics processors can handle certain tasks much more efficiently than the standard CPU, integrating a GPU into the CPU enhances the overall performance of the computer while at the same time reducing energy use, size, and cost. With the proliferation of mobile devices and portable computers today, all of these benefits have obvious merit.

Both major CPU manufacturers have released CPUs with integrated GPUs. The architecture differs in some ways, such as how they use the cache on the chip. The *Intel HD Graphics* integrated into many Core i3/i5/i7 processors, for example, has the CPU cores and the GPU core sharing the "last level cache," which is either L2 or L3, depending on the processor. With the AMD *accelerated processing unit (APU)*, such as the AMD Fusion, the GPU has access to all levels of cache on the CPU.

Recommending a CPU

The CPU that's right for a specific situation depends entirely on the computing needs of your client. For a workstation that does primarily documents, e-mail, and the Web, *any* modern processor will do. In fact, slapping in the latest quad-core CPU isn't going to provide much of a different experience at all from its dual-core little brother running the same low-end applications. Save your clients some money and recommend a lower-end CPU in such a situation.

Where you see the great benefits of high-end processors is in 3-D modeling programs, high-end photograph and video editing, and 3-D games. Plus you provide a bit of future-proofing for the client, so he or she can upgrade software but not have to worry about hardware for a few years. Aside from raw computing power providing a little burst, though, few applications take full advantage of multicore CPUs, so ask your clients what kind of applications they use and then do some research online at the application makers' Web sites. If the applications kick into overdrive on multicore CPUs, then recommend multicore CPUs to your clients.

Objective 5.02 Installing CPUs

Installing a CPU successfully requires three steps. First, do your homework so you know what CPU works with your motherboard. Second, practice proper electrostatic discharge (ESD) avoidance techniques during the install. Third, install a cooling solution, generally a heat sink and fan assembly.

Compatibility Issues

The key to a successful CPU installation is making sure that the processor and motherboard are compatible. The motherboard's documentation is the best source for compatibility information. The motherboard manual should contain some sort of chart listing the CPUs that it supports. You can also check the motherboard manufacturer's Web site for details.

Because Intel and AMD CPUs are not pin-compatible, all motherboards made since the mid-1990s support *either* Intel CPUs *or* AMD CPUs—not both. Once you know which brand of processor your motherboard takes, the next step is to match the model. The type of CPU socket that the motherboard uses (such as PGA) determines which model of Intel or AMD CPU you can install.

Many motherboards accept more than one model of CPU into a compatible socket; for example, motherboards supporting LGA 1156 may accept either an Intel Core i5 or an Intel Core i7.

Remember that some CPU models use more than one socket type. For instance, the Athlon 64 CPU comes in three socket varieties: Socket 754, Socket 939, and Socket AM2. Make certain that you know which one you need before you make a decision! Also note that Socket AM3 processors may work with Socket AM2+, and Socket AM2+ processors may work with Socket AM2, but in both cases a performance penalty can be incurred due to limitations of the previous generation of socket. Tables 5.1 and 5.2 show the processors and their socket types that you'll find on the CompTIA A+ exams.

Exam Tip

The Table 5.1 list of Intel CPUs covers only those included on the CompTIA A+ 801 exam objectives. The CompTIA A+ 701/702 exams mentioned a couple of other processors, such as the *Pentium Pro* (very old, 32-bit) and the *Itanium* (also old; used for servers exclusively). You might see them as incorrect answer choices on the 801 exam.

Travel Advisory

Tables 5.1 and 5.2 leave out a lot of the older or less mainstream products, so they are by no means a complete listing of what you'll find in the field.

TABLE 5.1	Intel-based Sockets and Processors
Socket	**CPU**
LGA 775[1]	Pentium 4, Celeron, Pentium 4 Extreme Edition, Core 2 Duo, Core 2 Quad, Xeon, and many others
LGA 1155[2]	Core i3/i5/i7, Pentium, Celeron, Xeon
LGA 1156[3]	Core i3/i5/i7, Pentium, Celeron, Xeon
LGA 1366[4]	Core i7, Xeon, Celeron

[1] The LGA 775 socket was the only desktop or server socket used for many years by Intel, and thus just about every branded Intel CPU used it at one time or another.
[2] Socket LGA 1155 CPUs are based on Sandy Bridge or Ivy Bridge architecture.
[3] Socket LGA 1156 CPUs are based on the pre–Sandy Bridge architecture.
[4] The very first Core i7 processors used LGA 1366.

TABLE 5.2		AMD-based Sockets and Processors
Socket	**Pins**	**CPU**
940[1]	940	Opteron, Athlon 64 FX
AM2[2]	940	Athlon 64, Athlon 64 X2, Athlon 64 FX, Opteron, Sempron, Phenom
AM2+[2]	940	Athlon 64, Athlon 64 X2, Athlon II, Opteron, Phenom, Phenom II
AM3[3]	941	Phenom II, Athlon II, Sempron, Opteron
AM3+[4]	942	FX
FM1	905	A[5]
F	1207	Opteron, Athlon FX

[1] You would usually find only an Opteron server–based CPU in a socket 940. The Athlon 64 FX was a super-high-end CPU for the day and is very unlikely to be on the exams.

[2] AMD says that CPUs designed for AM2 sockets will work in a Socket AM2+ and vice versa, though at the slower memory movement speeds of the AM2 component (socket or CPU). Many manufacturers have not released motherboard updates that would enable support for a Socket AM2+ CPU on a Socket AM2 motherboard, thus making it impossible to upgrade just the CPU.

[3] Though the names of some of the processors designed for Socket AM3 match the names of CPUs designed for earlier sockets, they're *not* the same CPUs. They are specific to AM3 because they support different types of RAM (see Chapter 6). Just to make things even crazier, though, AM3 CPUs work just fine in Socket AM2/2+ motherboards.

[4] AMD had only released the FX-branded CPUs that use the Bulldozer core at the time of this writing. Motherboards with AM3+ sockets already out tout support for Phenom II, Athlon II, and Sempron CPUs, in addition to the FX series.

[5] The A series features integrated GPUs and other chips.

Once you've narrowed down your choices to a particular brand and model, you need to determine which CPU speed your system can support. The maximum speed of a particular CPU that a motherboard can handle is determined by the chipset and basic input/output system (BIOS) and is listed along with the other information in the motherboard documentation. Sometimes you can upgrade the speed of CPU that a motherboard can handle by updating (flashing) the BIOS. Your motherboard maker's Web site is the best place to find out whether this is an option for you.

CPU Physical Installation

After you have the preliminaries out of the way, you can install the CPU. First, power down the PC and unplug the power cable. Put the PC case on your antistatic mat, if you have one. Make sure you've got enough room and light to work and remove the cover from the case.

If you plan to upgrade the CPU, strap on your nerd bracelet and ground yourself, and then skip to "Installing the Cooling System" for steps on removing the heat sink and fan assembly. Then come back here. If you plan to install a CPU onto an uninstalled motherboard, just leave the motherboard on an antistatic mat. Different socket designs have different steps for CPU installation, so be sure to read the documentation for the exact procedure, but the steps should follow this general pattern:

1. Lift the CPU release lever arm (Figure 5.8).

2. Locate the orientation mark on the corner of the CPU and socket. They are usually marked with an arrow or raised dot. Double-check the orientation by looking at the pin configuration—the CPU and socket should be oriented so that the corner (or corners) with missing pins align (Figure 5.9).

FIGURE 5.8 Lifting the arm

FIGURE 5.9 CPU orientation marks

3. Holding the CPU by its edges, position it over the socket and gently set it in place. If the pins and socket holes are oriented correctly, the CPU should drop right in without any force (*zero* insertion force—get it?). If the CPU doesn't fit easily into the socket, you're doing it wrong! Make certain that it's oriented correctly and try again. When seated, the CPU package should sit flush with the socket mount with no pins showing.

4. Lower and lock the release lever into place.

If you install CPUs on a motherboard designed for multiple microprocessors, you should install them in the proper order. A single CPU goes into the socket for CPU 0, for example. Add a second CPU and you'd put it in the socket for CPU 1. Note that this applies only to motherboards that support multiple physical CPUs, what's called *symmetric multiprocessing*, not multiple-core single CPUs.

That's all there is to it. Your next step is to install the cooling system.

Installing the Cooling System

CPUs have no moving parts (that you can see with the naked eye), but they nonetheless generate considerable heat. Excessive heat to the CPU leads to system instability, lockups, and dead CPUs. CPU packages are made from high-tech thermal plastics and ceramics that dissipate heat, but they still can't provide enough relief without help. This help comes in the form of heat sink and fan assemblies (Figure 5.10) and from liquid cooling systems.

Heat sink and fan assemblies take a bit of force and finesse to mount properly—more than you might think! A small, straight-slot screwdriver will help.

Heat sink and fan assemblies for PGA-packaged CPUs usually come as a unit, but if not, you should attach the fan to the heat sink before installing them onto the CPU. Again, different CPUs, socket designs, and heat sinks require different installation procedures, so be sure to read the documentation. The general steps for installation are as follows:

1. If your CPU has thermal paste preapplied, remove and discard the protective tape. If not, apply a thin film of thermal paste to the raised center of the CPU package (Figure 5.11).

FIGURE 5.10 Retail heat sink and fan assembly

FIGURE 5.11 Applying thermal compound

2. Align the mounting bracket hardware on the heat sink and fan assembly with the mounting notches on the CPU socket.

3. With Intel stock fans, push the mounting pins in until they click in place. It's fairly easy to do if you have the motherboard outside the case. Support the motherboard with one hand and push with the other so the motherboard does not flex.

4. AMD fans take a little more effort. Attach the mounting bracket to one side of the CPU socket.

5. Using your screwdriver as a lever, press down on the mounting bracket on the other side of the CPU socket and snap the bracket into place (Figure 5.12). If this makes you nervous, don't worry—that's normal. Most techs are surprised by the amount of force needed to mount the heat sink and fan assembly into place.

6. The last step is to plug the fan's power cable into the appropriate socket or header on the motherboard. Check your motherboard documentation for information.

FIGURE 5.12 Using a straight-slot screwdriver to move the mounting bracket

Installing a Liquid Cooling System

Despite all the differences between traditional heat sink and fan assemblies and the more modern liquid cooling systems, the essential installation steps are similar:

1. Follow the manufacturer's instructions to attach the hoses from the coolant reservoir tank to the CPU cooling element and the heat exchanger unit. Make certain that all hoses are secure and crimped properly.

2. Fill the coolant reservoir with the recommended amount of distilled water.

3. Apply a small amount of thermal compound to the CPU.

4. If your liquid cooling system uses a separate CPU temperature sensor on the cooling element, attach it to the appropriate slot or groove and secure it with the supplied metal tape. Mount the cooling element to the CPU with the attached bracket and secure it in place with the tension screw (Figure 5.13). Be careful not to overtighten the screw. You're ready to go!

Exam Tip

You don't have to know how to install a liquid cooling system in a PC for the CompTIA A+ certification exams. You simply need to know that the option is available. This information has been added here for a quick reference.

FIGURE 5.13 Cooling element mounted on CPU

FIGURE 5.14 CMOS clear jumper, marked JCMOS1 JCI1

Overclocking

Most modern systems use the CPUID to set the clock speed and clock multiplier automatically for any CPU you install, so all but true enthusiasts are done with installation at this point. Boot up the PC and watch the screen. Assuming you've done everything correctly, your system will start without any undue alarms or errors. If, however, something has gone wrong, you need to turn to troubleshooting.

Some motherboards enable you to adjust CPU settings manually by moving a jumper, changing a CMOS setting, or using software. Many enthusiasts deliberately change these settings to enhance performance; this is called *overclocking*. You can make a couple of adjustments to overclock successfully. First, increase the bus speed for the system. Next, you often have to increase the voltage going into the CPU just a little to provide stability. You do that by changing a jumper or CMOS setting. Always do only one thing at a time, document your change, and then reboot.

Overriding the defaults can completely lock up your system to the point where even removing and reinstalling the CPU doesn't bring the motherboard back to life. (There's also a slight risk of toasting the processor, although all modern processors have circuitry that quickly shuts them down before they overheat.) Most motherboards have a jumper setting called *CMOS clear* (Figure 5.14) that makes the CMOS go back to default settings. Before you try overclocking on a modern system, find the CMOS clear jumper and make sure you know how to use it.

Objective 5.03 Troubleshooting CPUs

CPUs are pretty robust beasts and rarely have problems after they're installed. You're most likely to encounter problems with installation, although heat issues can become a big deal at a later time.

Installation Problems

Look (and listen) for the following signs of installation problems:

- It's normal for the CPU fan speed to fluctuate, but if the fan doesn't spin at all for more than five seconds or so, turn the system off and make sure that the fan is plugged in correctly.
- If the fan is spinning but the PC doesn't boot, make certain that any jumpers governing speed or voltage are set correctly.
- If, after a few minutes, you hear a loud alarm, this is an indication that the system is overheating. Turn it off immediately and check your fan installation to make sure you've got good CPU/heat sink contact and that the fan is functioning properly.
- If the system does not boot and the fan does not spin, check to ensure that the CPU is seated properly and that no other components or cables have been unseated or disturbed.

Heat Issues

Excessive heat can cause serious damage to your CPU and to any other components inside your computer. The fan on the CPU pushes hot air away from the CPU and into the case; case fans and power supply fans push hot air out the back of the case. Front case fans pull cool air into the case.

The problems start with ribbon cables that impede airflow and clogged or dying fans. Incautious drive installation can leave ribbon cables strewn all over the case (Figure 5.15). Dirt, dust, hair, and age can slow down fans to the point where they can't do the job.

The warning signs will be there: spontaneous reboots, especially on warmer days or with the heat blasting in winter time; occasional alarms from the tinny PC speaker; lockups; excessively loud fans. The fix is easy. Check the fans and replace when necessary.

Travel Assistance

Installing good fans in a case can make a world of difference to the user experience. No one wants to use a new or upgraded PC that sounds like a helicopter! I always install the quietest fans I can get, generally as big as I can get into a case. If you have a case with options for 80 mm or 120 mm fans, for example, go for the latter. Bigger fans move more air at lower speeds. Check out the "quiet fans" at one of my favorite online retailers, Directron: www .directron.com/quietfans.html. I recommend Papst, but all the top brands listed (Zalman, Cooler Master, Antec, Panaflo) produce excellent products.

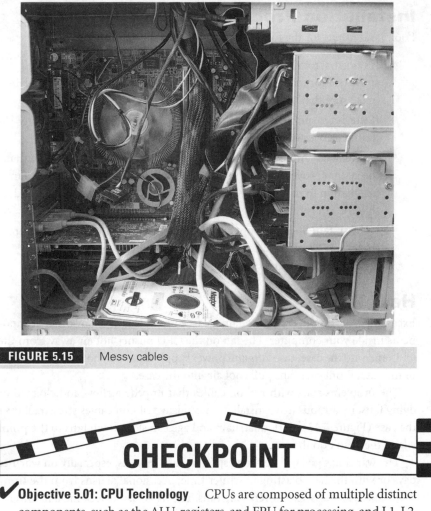

FIGURE 5.15 Messy cables

CHECKPOINT

✔**Objective 5.01: CPU Technology** CPUs are composed of multiple distinct components, such as the ALU, registers, and FPU for processing, and L1, L2, and L3 cache of SRAM for quick data access. Modern CPUs use multiple processing pipelines and run at a clock speed that is some multiple of the system bus speed. Every current processor comes in some form of PGA package. Advances in CPUs include enhanced registers; Hyper-Threading; 64-bit processing; dual-core and multicore processors; cool, energy-sipping mobile processors; virtualization support; and integrated memory controllers and GPUs.

✔**Objective 5.02: Installing CPUs** Motherboards are made to accommodate a narrow range of CPU types. The CPU's form factor must be compatible with the socket on the motherboard. Installing a CPU is simple, but you must be careful not to damage the CPU pins or package. Proper cooling is absolutely essential. Use thermal compound between the CPU and the heat sink and fan assembly, or between the CPU and cooling element if using a liquid cooling system. You can deliberately push the CPU to run faster than recommended through overclocking.

✔**Objective 5.03: Troubleshooting CPUs** Installation errors and heat buildup over time are the two biggest problem areas for CPUs. Look and listen for erratic fan noise, no fan noise, or alarms. Crashing PCs and lockups on warm days are also good clues. Check your installation; clean or replace your fans to fix the problem.

REVIEW QUESTIONS

1. Which component inside the CPU holds data before and after processing?
 A. ALU
 B. FPU
 C. Pipeline
 D. Registers

2. Which component inside the CPU is the primary processing component?
 A. ALU
 B. FPU
 C. Pipeline
 D. Registers

3. What type of memory is an L1 cache?
 A. DRAM
 B. ROM
 C. SRAM
 D. VRAM

4. Which component sets the clock speed of the motherboard?
 A. Cache
 B. CPU
 C. System crystal
 D. ZIF crystal

5. What form factor do modern CPUs use?

 A. EGA

 B. SVGA

 C. PGA

 D. VGA

6. What function enables motherboards to set up BIOS for CPUs automatically?

 A. BIOS

 B. CPUID

 C. CPUNow!

 D. Processor ID

7. What technology enables a single-core CPU to appear as two CPUs?

 A. Dual-core

 B. Hyper-Threading

 C. Multicore

 D. Z-core

8. The Intel Core i7 is an example of what sort of processor? (Select two.)

 A. Quad-core

 B. Hyper-Threading

 C. BGA

 D. SEC

9. Which of the following must you do to install a CPU successfully?

 A. Align the orientation marks on the CPU with the marks on the socket.

 B. Push hard to seat the CPU properly.

 C. Lift the socket arm to lock the CPU into place.

 D. Plug in the power cable.

10. Intentionally increasing the clock speed of a CPU beyond the manufacturer's recommendation is called _____.

 A. CMOS clear

 B. Overclocking

 C. SpeedStep

 D. Underclocking

11. John installed a new CPU. When he boots the system, it comes up for a few seconds and then shuts down. What could be the problem?

 A. John forgot to plug in the fan and the CPU is overheating.

 B. John installed an AMD CPU in an Intel motherboard.

 C. John installed an Intel CPU in an AMD motherboard.

 D. John failed to raise the arm on the socket to lock down the CPU.

12. What should be placed between the processor and the heat sink or cooling element?

 A. Thermal compound/paste

 B. Fan

 C. Denatured alcohol

 D. Power supply

REVIEW ANSWERS

1. **D** The registers hold data before and after processing.

2. **A** The arithmetic logic unit (ALU) handles the primary processing duties.

3. **C** The L1 cache uses SRAM.

4. **C** The system crystal sets the motherboard clock speed.

5. **C** Modern CPUs use the pin grid array (PGA) form factor.

6. **B** The motherboard scans the CPUID to set up BIOS automatically.

7. **B** Hyper-Threading makes a single CPU appear to be a dual-core CPU.

8. **A B** The Intel Core i7 is a quad-core CPU with Hyper-Threading Technology.

9. **A** To install a CPU, align the orientation marks on the CPU with the marks on the socket.

10. **B** Although you might need to use the CMOS clear jumper in case it fails, *overclocking* is the term for cranking up your CPU speed.

11. **A** Starting and closing down at boot is a classic sign of overheating. Plug in that fan!

12. **A** Thermal compound/paste should be applied to the processor before installing the heat sink or cooling element.

RAM

CHAPTER 6

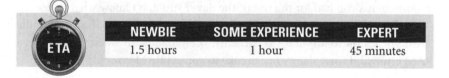

	NEWBIE	SOME EXPERIENCE	EXPERT
ETA	1.5 hours	1 hour	45 minutes

PC users are curious people, and before long one of them is going to ask you, the learned PC tech, "Where are programs stored as they run?" Without hesitation, you might answer, "In your system RAM, of course!" If you're like most techs, you might continue to talk about how random access memory (RAM) works until her eyes glaze over and she asks you to go away.

Many PC users falsely believe that programs run directly off of the PC's hard drive. This is, of course, impossible, because even the fastest hard drive simply can't keep up with even the slowest central processing unit (CPU). Instead, programs must be copied to a super-fast medium that can supply the CPU with the data it needs to run an application at a speed it can use: this is the function of RAM. Launching an application loads the necessary files from the hard disk into RAM, where the CPU can grab the specific data that it needs to run the program.

Not long ago, RAM was a precious commodity in the PC world, and even a small upgrade would set you back hundreds of dollars. Things have changed dramatically for the better, so nowadays adding more RAM is often the best upgrade option for a sluggish PC. This doesn't mean that you can just grab any type of RAM that you can get your hands on and stick it in your system. You've got to match the motherboard with the right type of RAM, running at the right speed.

In most cases, installing RAM is literally a snap, but don't take the installation procedure for granted. RAM is perhaps the most sensitive component on the system when it comes to the dreaded electrostatic discharge (ESD). Safe handling is absolutely vital. Once you've successfully installed RAM, you may find that your work isn't done. Memory errors come in many shapes and sizes, and when things go wrong with RAM, you can pretty much plan on canceling any appointments you had for the rest of the day if you don't know what to do.

In this chapter, you'll learn how to identify types of RAM, how to handle RAM safely, how to install RAM correctly, what to look for when you suspect a RAM error, and what steps you can take to correct RAM errors.

Objective 6.01 RAM Overview

Manufacturers have produced RAM in a wide variety of physical form factors (sometimes called *packages*) and technologies over the years. This section looks at several types of RAM, including those covered on the CompTIA A+ certification exams.

RAM Form Factors

RAM form factors have gone through several evolutionary steps since the introduction of the first PC. Manufacturers originally installed RAM directly onto the motherboard, as shown in Figure 6.1, but this took up too much room and made upgrading difficult.

The next step was to put RAM memory chips onto special removable circuit boards, called RAM *sticks,* that fit into sockets on the motherboard. These RAM sticks are what we use today: the SIMM, the DIMM, and the RIMM.

SIMM

Single inline memory modules (SIMMs) used to be the most common form of memory, but you won't see them on any PCs manufactured in the last decade. SIMM RAM sticks come in either 30-pin or 72-pin layouts. There's no real significance to the number of pins as far as PC techs are concerned. You might occasionally find an older printer that needs 72-pin SIMMs, but that's about it today. Figure 6.2 shows two SIMMs.

FIGURE 6.1 RAM soldered onto an ancient motherboard, now part of the Total Seminars Tech Museum

FIGURE 6.2 72-pin and 30-pin SIMMs

DIMM

Dual inline memory modules (DIMMs) are the sticks you're most likely to run into these days, including two popular variants used in laptops, *MicroDIMMs* and *small outline DIMMs (SO-DIMMs)*. DIMMs for desktop PCs look similar to SIMMs but are wider and longer. DIMMs have 168, 184, or 240 pins; are 64-bits wide; and have a capacity of up to 32 GB at this writing. Figure 6.3 shows 184-pin and 240-pin DIMMs.

MicroDIMM RAM comes in 144-pin, 172-pin, and 214-pin packages. The SO-DIMM variant comes in 72-pin, 144-pin, 200-pin, and 204-pin configurations. Generally, you can find MicroDIMMs and SO-DIMMs with capacities comparable to those of their full-sized counterparts.

FIGURE 6.3 184-pin (top) and 240-pin DIMMs

> **Exam Tip**
>
> You should know the most common memory module sizes: 168-, 184-, and 240-pin DIMMs; and 200-pin SO-DIMMs. Note also that you see the latter written with or without the hyphen.

RIMM

The other RAM package you might see is the *RIMM*. Technically, the term RIMM doesn't stand for anything, but most techs use it as an acronym for *Rambus inline memory module*. RIMMs come in capacities of up to 512 MB. RIMM sticks look like DIMMs and come in 184-pin and 232-pin packages. Figure 6.4 shows a typical 184-pin RIMM stick. Note that the memory chips themselves are covered by a thin metal shield called a *heat spreader*. This shield helps dissipate heat generated by the RIMM memory chips.

RAM Packaging

RAM manufacturers produce an amazing variety of RAM packages. You'll find sticks that offer the same capacity, for example, but vary in number or location of memory chips. One 256-MB stick, for example, might have four chips on the front and four on the back—a double-sided stick—whereas another might have eight chips on the front only—a single-sided stick. A third one might be single-sided with only four chips, and a fourth, double-sided with sixteen chips!

Individual memory chips come in different capacities and in how many bits they can put on the bus at one time. A ×32 chip, for example, puts four bytes on the bus at once, whereas a ×16 chip does two, and a ×8 only one. Manufacturers use different combinations to make their sticks.

The general rule on memory packaging is *never mix packages* if you can help it. It leads to overall system instability in enough cases that a prudent tech sticks with uniform RAM sticks.

FIGURE 6.4 184-pin RIMM

Exam Tip

I know that many techs will shake their heads about this and say they've been mixing RAM packages for years and never had any problems. CompTIA's subject matter experts (SMEs) think it's a problem to mix RAM packages, however, so look for a question on the topic and get it right.

Memory Banks

A *bank* of memory is a module, or group of modules, that provides enough data for the CPU's data bus. For instance, Intel's 486 processor had a 32-bit data bus, and, as a result, either *four* 8-bit, 30-pin SIMMs or *one* 32-bit, 72-pin SIMM could be used to fill a single memory bank. In the same vein, Intel's Pentium processor had a 64-bit data bus requiring either two 32-bit, 72-pin SIMMs or one 64-bit, 168-pin DIMM per bank. Most modern processors have a minimum bank size of 64 bits, requiring one 64-bit DIMM.

Memory Channels

Current motherboards use multichannel memory configurations to increase memory performance. With only a 64-bit data bus, DIMMs can deliver only 64 bits of data at a time. That's pretty logical! This data path is known as a *single memory channel*. Memory controllers can be designed to use two channels simultaneously, creating a *dual-channel* configuration, or three channels simultaneously, creating a *triple-channel* configuration.

In dual-channel mode, the memory controller has a 128-bit-wide data path, thus necessitating two DIMMs per bank. In triple-channel mode, the memory controller has a data path that is 192 bits wide, requiring three DIMMs per bank. Typically, for multichannel systems, all the DIMM slots for a particular bank are the same color on the motherboard. When populating a bank for a multichannel memory mode, use identical RAM sticks. Always check the motherboard book to see specific details about a motherboard.

Motherboards that can run in dual- or triple-channel mode can also run in single-channel mode—they're just not as snappy. Triple-channel boards run in dual-channel mode with only a pair of sticks.

As a rule, you'll get the best performance using the highest mode the motherboard can handle. The only exception to this rule is when the need for a quantity of RAM outstrips the need for speed, such as when dealing with huge files. (Think video editing here.)

RAM Types

RAM comes in two forms: static RAM (SRAM) and dynamic RAM (DRAM). SRAM is faster than DRAM, because it never needs to be refreshed; however, it is also much more expensive. SRAM is, therefore, reserved for special purposes, such as L1, L2, and L3 system cache memory. DRAM is used for system memory and needs to be refreshed every few nanoseconds (ns). During this time it is inaccessible to the CPU. This interval is called a *wait state*. Faster RAM has a shorter wait state. The paragraphs that follow describe the various types of DRAM that have been developed for the PC over the years.

Asynchronous RAM

Very old computers used *asynchronous RAM,* memory types that ran at a speed independent of the system clock speed. Two types saw extensive use: fast page mode (FPM) and extended data out (EDO). You could find both types on 72-pin SIMMs, and you could find (rarely) EDO on 168-pin DIMMs.

Exam Tip
You might see FPM or EDO RAM as incorrect answer choices on the CompTIA A+ exams.

SDRAM

Synchronous dynamic RAM (SDRAM) delivers data in high-speed bursts. SDRAM runs at the speed of the system bus (thus, *synchronously*) and is rated according to the highest speed data bus it runs on, such as 66, 100, or 133 MHz. Hence, we have PC66, PC100, and PC133 SDRAM. SDRAM (and more advanced) DIMMs have a *serial presence detect (SPD)* chip that identifies a DIMM's capacity, speed, and *latency*—the latter being a measurement of how long the RAM takes to respond to the memory controller.

Exam Tip
SDRAM transfers data in high-speed bursts and is measured in megahertz.

The most common form of SDRAM uses a 168-pin DIMM (Figure 6.5). SDRAM for laptops comes in two reduced-size varieties, 72-pin and 144-pin SO-DIMMs, and MicroDIMMs.

FIGURE 6.5 SDRAM DIMM

RDRAM

When Intel developers were working on the Pentium 4 chip, they knew that regular SDRAM just wasn't going to be fast enough to handle the quad-pumped 400-MHz frontside bus. Intel announced plans to replace SDRAM with a faster, new type of RAM developed by Rambus, Inc., called *Rambus DRAM,* or simply *RDRAM.* Hailed by Intel as the next great leap in DRAM technology, RDRAM could handle speeds up to 800 MHz, which gave Intel plenty of room to improve the Pentium 4.

RDRAM was greatly anticipated by the industry for years, but industry support for RDRAM proved less than enthusiastic due to significant delays in development plus a price many times that of SDRAM. Rambus DRAM was available only in the RIMM form factor.

RDRAM memory controllers required dual-channel memory, meaning that all RDRAM had to be installed in pairs. Because RDRAM was significantly more expensive than SDRAM, the fact that you had to buy two RIMMs at a time made adoption even slower.

Exam Tip

The CompTIA A+ exams refer to RDRAM and RIMMs by the manufacturer's name in all caps: RAMBUS memory. Don't be thrown off by this mislabeling.

Even quirkier, RDRAM motherboards required that all RIMM slots be populated. Unused slots needed a passive device called a *continuity RIMM* (CRIMM) installed in each slot to enable the RDRAM system to terminate properly. Figure 6.6 shows a CRIMM.

RDRAM offered dramatic possibilities for high-speed PCs, but it is effectively dead in today's market. You'll see it still on some game consoles.

CRIMM

DDR SDRAM

Many motherboards support *double data rate (DDR) SDRAM,* usually referred to as simply *DDR*. DDR operates by performing data operations on both the rising and falling edge of the clock signal, effectively doubling it. DDR ranges from 266 MHz (PC2100) to 400 MHz (PC3200)—the top end of the official standard—to well beyond (see Table 6.1). DDR comes in a 184-pin DIMM package for desktops and either a 200-pin SO-DIMM or a 172-pin MicroDIMM for laptops.

Travel Advisory

The *PC####* that often follows the name of a DDR stick—such as *DDR 333 (PC2700)*—refers to the data throughput possible with that particular stick. A DDR 333 stick, therefore, has a bandwidth of 2.7 GB per second (GBps). PC2 refers to DDR2, and PC3 refers to DDR3.

TABLE 6.1 DDR Speeds

Clock Speed	DDR Speed Rating	PC Speed Rating
100 MHz	DDR200	PC1600
133 MHz	DDR266	PC2100
166 MHz	DDR333	PC2700
200 MHz	DDR400	PC3200
217 MHz	DDR433	PC3500
233 MHz	DDR466	PC3700
250 MHz	DDR500	PC4000
275 MHz	DDR550	PC4400
300 MHz	DDR600	PC4800

DDR2

DDR2 succeeded the DDR SDRAM standard. Improvements in DDR2's electrical characteristics enable it to run even faster than DDR while using less power. The big speed increase from DDR2 comes by clock doubling the input/output circuits on the chips. This does not speed up the core RAM—the part that holds the data—but speeding up the input/output and adding special buffers (sort of like a cache) makes DDR2 run much faster than regular DDR.

DDR2 uses a 240-pin DIMM as well as a 200-pin SO-DIMM or 214-pin MicroDIMM for portable systems. DDR2 modules and systems are not compatible with DDR memory. You'll find motherboards running both single-channel and dual-channel DDR2. DDR2 modules come in official speeds between DDR2-400 and DDR2-1000 (see Table 6.2). Some frequency grades may come in more than one PC2 speed rating. For instance, DDR2-667 yields a transfer speed of 5333 MBps, and manufacturers may choose to rate it as either PC2-5300 or PC2-5400.

DDR3

DDR2 was the standard for several years, but *DDR3* boasts higher speeds, more efficient architecture, and around 30 percent lower power consumption than DDR2 RAM. DDR3 uses a 240-pin DIMM, but one that is slotted differently than DDR2 modules. DDR3 SO-DIMMs for portable computers have 204 pins. Neither will fit into a DDR2 socket.

DDR3 doubles the size of the prefetch buffers of DDR2, giving it a huge boost in bandwidth over older RAM when reading contiguous data. DDR3 modules also use higher-density memory chips, which means that we may eventually see DDR3 modules beyond the 32-GB high end today. DDR3 is available in speeds

TABLE 6.2	DDR2 Speeds		
Core RAM Clock Speed	DDR I/O Speed	DDR2 Speed Rating	PC Speed Rating
100 MHz	200 MHz	DDR2-400	PC2-3200
133 MHz	266 MHz	DDR2-533	PC2-4200
166 MHz	333 MHz	DDR2-667	PC2-5300
200 MHz	400 MHz	DDR2-800	PC2-6400
250 MHz	500 MHz	DDR2-1000	PC2-8000

TABLE 6.3	DDR3 Speeds		
Core RAM Clock Speed	**DDR I/O Speed**	**DDR3 Speed Rating**	**PC Speed Rating**
100 MHz	400 MHz	DDR3-800	PC3-6400
133 MHz	533 MHz	DDR3-1066	PC3-8500
166 MHz	667 MHz	DDR3-1333	PC3-10667
200 MHz	800 MHz	DDR3-1600	PC3-12800
233 MHz	933 MHz	DDR3-1866	PC3-14900
266 MHz	1066 MHz	DDR3-2133	PC3-17000

between DDR3-800 (PC3-6400) and DDR3-2133 (PC3-17000) (see Table 6.3). Many DDR3 systems support dual- and triple-channel memory configurations.

Exam Tip
You should be familiar with the various RAM speeds.

To familiarize yourself with the many RAM standards and specifications for both desktops and laptops, visit www.crucial.com. Pay special attention to descriptions such as Module Size, Package, and Features. Be sure to check out the Crucial Memory Advisory Tool while you're there.

Error-Checking RAM: Parity and ECC

High-end, mission-critical systems often use special *parity* or *error-correcting code (ECC)* RAM. These types of RAM use special circuitry to detect and, in some cases, correct errors in data. Parity RAM, the older technology, used a dedicated parity chip mounted on the RAM stick that added an extra bit—the parity bit—to each byte of data. Parity checking was useful in the early days of desktop computers when DRAM had a relatively high failure rate, but today's DRAM is so dependable that few PCs still support parity.

ECC RAM contains circuitry that not only detects errors, but corrects them on the fly without causing interruption to system processes. ECC RAM is common on performance-enhanced workstations and server systems.

Note that the PC's motherboard and basic input/output system (BIOS) must be designed to support either parity or ECC RAM. Most motherboards that are designed for parity or ECC RAM can be configured in BIOS to disable error checking, thus enabling you to install RAM that is not parity or ECC RAM.

Objective 6.02	# Handling and Installing RAM

It's important that you follow the proper RAM handling and installation procedures to prevent damage to your PC. In this section, you will learn the proper way to handle RAM, how to install RAM, and how to confirm RAM installation.

Handling RAM

RAM is extremely sensitive to ESD, so take precautions while transporting, handling, and installing RAM. Always store RAM in antistatic bags or sleeves when it's not installed on a PC. If you have spare RAM lying around, always keep it labeled with the type, size, and speed so that you can identify it later. Don't take a RAM stick out of its bag before you actually need to install it. Handle RAM by the edges, and avoid touching the contacts or circuits.

Installing RAM Modules

DIMM and RIMM sticks need to go into their sockets vertically. You'll note on the motherboard that the guide notches on the sockets match up to the notches on the RAM to prevent you from inserting it the wrong way. Glance back at Figures 6.3 and 6.4. All three RAM sticks pictured are the same size—roughly five inches wide—but the notches enable you to install each in only the proper slot.

Before you install a DIMM or RIMM into a slot, power down the computer and unplug it from the AC outlet. Make sure that the RAM retention clips at either end of the socket are pushed completely outward. Holding your RAM stick by the edges, position it above the RAM socket and press it straight down into the slot with gentle pressure. When the RAM is fully inserted, the retention clips will swing up and engage the retention notches in the outside edges of the RAM. Snap the clips firmly into place, and you're done. Figure 6.7 shows a properly seated DIMM RAM stick.

Travel Advisory

Don't just turn off the PC before installing memory. Unplug it from the AC outlet. Modern PCs always have a current on the motherboard when plugged in, even when turned off.

FIGURE 6.7 Properly seated DIMM

Barring ESD, not a lot can go wrong with installing DIMMs or RIMMs. The main thing to look for is improper seating. If the retention clip doesn't engage fully, your RAM stick isn't inserted completely. Double-check your positioning, and insert the RAM again. If it doesn't go in easily, it's not in the right position.

To remove a DIMM or RIMM, push the retention clips on the socket outward. These clips act as levers to raise the RAM stick out of the socket so that you can then pull it all the way out.

Confirm RAM Installation

Once you've installed your RAM, confirm that your PC recognizes it by booting up and checking the RAM count message (see Figure 6.8). Modern systems automatically detect the RAM size and configure the system accordingly. You rarely need to reconfigure BIOS RAM settings. You can also verify the amount of installed RAM from within the operating system (OS)—in any version of Windows, simultaneously press the WINDOWS LOGO and PAUSE keys to bring up the System Properties applet.

```
Award Modular BIOS v6.00PG, An Energy Star Ally
Copyright (C) 1984-2005, Award Software, Inc.

GA-K8NP F13

Processor : AMD Athlon(tm) 64 Processor 3200+
<CPUID:0000F4A Patch ID:003A>
Memory Testing : 1048576K OK
CPU clock frequency : 200 Mhz

Detecting IDE drives ...
```

FIGURE 6.8 Confirm RAM installation by checking RAM count at startup

Objective 6.03 Troubleshooting RAM Errors

Y our first task is to determine whether or not the error is, indeed, RAM re- lated. Once you've done that, you can begin the process of pinpointing the cause and taking corrective measures. The following sections list symptoms of false and genuine RAM errors, causes of errors, and corrective measures that you should take.

False Memory Errors

A lot of system errors get blamed on memory when they don't really have any- thing to do with RAM. Several errors that mimic RAM errors are page faults, ex- ception errors, the dreaded Blue Screen of Death, the system slowdown or freeze, and the ever-popular spontaneous reboot. These are often tied to other factors, such as a badly fragmented hard disk, an overtaxed CPU, or a faulty ap- plication or driver. Overheating as a result of dust and dirt accumulated inside the PC case or a failed cooling fan is also a common culprit. Finally, a dying power supply can cause any or all of these random types of errors.

Common Symptoms of RAM Errors

The majority of genuine memory errors happen after you've made a change to your PC's hardware and restart the system, at which time it goes through the *power-on self test* (POST) routine. Common startup errors include the following:

- System won't boot, accompanied by a loud, continuously repeating beep
- System boots, but the display screen is blank
- System boots, misreports RAM size
- System boots, reports memory or address error
- Continuous reboots after installing new RAM

Once you've determined that the error you're getting is a genuine RAM error, you can determine the cause and take corrective measures.

Common Causes of RAM Errors

Genuine RAM-related system errors are generally the result of one of three things: a RAM installation error, RAM stick incompatibility, or a faulty RAM component.

Improper installation is pretty common, though most techs don't like to admit it! This can mean you didn't fully seat or snap a RAM stick into its socket, or it can mean that some other related factor, such as dirt, dust, or corrosion on the RAM contact pins or socket, is causing a problem. Installation errors may also mean that while you were installing RAM, you accidentally unseated another hardware component or cable. Remove and inspect the RAM and RAM sockets for dirt or corrosion, and clean as necessary. Then reinstall the RAM and test the system again.

If you install multiple RAM sticks of differing speeds or configurations (single-sided vs. double-sided), you can create instability in a system. Some motherboards can handle the differences in RAM sticks. Others will give you all kinds of problems (like frequent crashes, system lockups, or unexpected shutdowns). It's easy enough to test. Pull out any nonhomogeneous sticks and see if the problems go away. If so, then install matching RAM to add to capacity.

Faulty RAM is less common, but it does happen. Sometimes it comes out of the factory that way, but it's more likely that the RAM was damaged somehow during transport or storage. Don't forget that our old enemy, ESD, can cause good RAM to go bad in no time flat.

To test for bad RAM, remove and replace the RAM. Try to use RAM that you know is good, such as RAM taken from another working system of the same configuration. If the error recurs after you've installed known good RAM, you know that it's unlikely that the RAM is at fault. If the error goes away after you swap RAM sticks, you've probably got bad RAM.

The Windows Vista/7 DVD enables you to access the System Recovery Options menu that contains the Windows Memory Diagnostic tool. You can use this tool to check your system for memory hardware errors. To run the tester, boot to the DVD and let the start-up program run. You'll get a screen with options to install, repair, restore, and so on.

CHECKPOINT

✔**Objective 6.01: RAM Overview**　DRAM requires periodic refreshing, unlike SRAM, but it costs substantially less. SRAM is used mainly for the L1, L2, and L3 cache. SDRAM improves on EDO RAM by running at the speed of the data bus and moving data in high-speed bursts. Current systems sport DDR2 and DDR3 RAM using differently keyed 240-pin DIMMs. To increase throughput, memory may be organized in dual-channel or triple-channel configurations. The two most common styles of error-checking RAM are parity and ECC.

✔**Objective 6.02: Handling and Installing RAM**　RAM is very sensitive to ESD, so always keep it in an antistatic bag or package until you're ready to install it. Make certain that you orient the RAM sticks properly using the motherboard socket's guide notches, and be sure to lock the RAM into place. Following installation, confirm the RAM count during bootup.

✔**Objective 6.03: Troubleshooting RAM Errors**　Many errors that are not directly related to memory mimic RAM errors. Genuine RAM errors are caused by improper RAM installation or faulty or damaged RAM. Make certain that RAM is properly seated and banked, and that you don't accidentally unseat other components or cables during RAM installation. If you suspect faulty or damaged RAM, swap it out with known good RAM of the same type and speed.

REVIEW QUESTIONS

1. Which type of RAM never needs periodic refreshing?
 A. SRAM
 B. DRAM
 C. FPM RAM
 D. EDO RAM

2. How many pins does a stick of DDR3 RAM for the desktop use?
 A. 108 pins
 B. 186 pins

C. 205 pins

D. 240 pins

3. Which type of RAM is used mainly for cache memory?

 A. SRAM

 B. DRAM

 C. EDO RAM

 D. SDRAM

4. What is stored in RAM?

 A. Currently running programs

 B. Programs that aren't running

 C. Nothing is stored in RAM

 D. Hardware information

5. Which type of RAM must be installed in pairs?

 A. SRAM

 B. DRAM

 C. SDRAM

 D. RDRAM

6. What were parity chips used for?

 A. Error checking for RAM

 B. To increase the speed of RAM

 C. To increase the capacity of RAM

 D. To speed up Windows

7. What is a CRIMM used for?

 A. Error-checking

 B. Termination

 C. To synchronize RAM with the system clock

 D. To identify the RAM to the system BIOS

8. How many pins does a DDR2 SO-DIMM module have?

 A. 168

 B. 184

 C. 200

 D. 240

9. What's a simple way to test for faulty RAM that applies to all versions of Windows?

 A. Open all programs to see if the system will lock up.

 B. Watch the startup screen for memory error reports.

 C. Swap out the suspect RAM module with a known good module and see if the problem goes away.

 D. RAM doesn't go bad, so it's not a legitimate question.

10. What feature of modern memory modules enables motherboards to support memory at the proper speed and latency?

 A. CPUID

 B. MEMTEST86

 C. MEMMGR

 D. SPD

REVIEW ANSWERS

1. **A** SRAM requires no refreshing and, thus, incurs no CPU wait states.

2. **D** DDR3 DIMMs use 240 pins.

3. **A** SRAM is used mainly for cache memory because it's extremely expensive, but it doesn't need to be refreshed.

4. **A** Currently running programs are stored in RAM. When you start a program, part of the program is taken from the hard drive and placed into RAM to make access speeds quicker.

5. **D** RDRAM must be installed in pairs.

6. **A** Parity chips were used to check RAM for errors.

7. **B** CRIMMs are used to terminate RDRAM.

8. **C** DDR2 SO-DIMM modules have 200 pins.

9. **C** The best way to check for faulty RAM is to swap out for a known good stick. Windows Vista/7 come with a memory tester in the DVD startup environment.

10. **D** The serial presence detect (SPD) chip on memory modules enables proper motherboard support for the RAM.

BIOS and CMOS

	NEWBIE	SOME EXPERIENCE	EXPERT
ETA	2 hours	1.5 hours	1 hour

In the seconds between the time that you press the power button and the desktop appears on your monitor, your PC goes through a series of ordered steps called the *boot process*. The vital components that drive the boot process are the system ROM, the system *basic input/output system (BIOS)*, and the *complementary metal-oxide semiconductor (CMOS)* memory chip and setup utility. The system ROM—for *read-only memory*—is the special memory chip that stores the BIOS programs. System BIOS is the collective name for the hundreds of tiny programs that tell your computer everything from what time it is to what *kind* of computer it is. The CMOS memory chip and the setup utility enable you to control important aspects of your PC configuration such as the boot device sequence.

All PCs have these components in common and follow the same process when booting up. Understanding the boot process on one computer enables you to troubleshoot the boot process on any computer. Likewise, with only slight variations, BIOS and CMOS work the same on practically any PC. You will find yourself entering CMOS many times in your career as a PC technician, and the CompTIA A+ certification exams expect you to demonstrate an understanding of the system ROM, system BIOS, and CMOS setup utility functions.

Objective 7.01 Boot Process and POST

The three main stages of the boot process are the power-on, *power-on self test (POST)*, and operating system (OS) loading steps.

Power-on/CPU Wakes

You start the process by powering the system on, sending current to the motherboard and drives. Assuming your power supply is in good working order, a special wire on the central processing unit (CPU) called the *power good* wire is charged, telling it to wake up. The CPU then communicates with the system ROM chip and starts the BIOS programs.

POST

Unlike a person who wakes up knowing who she is and how many fingers she has, a computer literally rediscovers itself every time it powers up. This is done via the POST process. During POST, the system BIOS communicates with all

essential hardware and, in essence, tells them all to identify themselves. The devices—the keyboard, mouse, drives, RAM, display adapter, and so on—then run internal diagnostic routines and report back to the BIOS. If one of the devices reports an error condition back to the BIOS, the BIOS reports this to the user by using special POST *error codes.*

POST Error Codes

As you may have guessed, the POST process is the most vital of the steps in the boot process. It's during POST that any serious low-level hardware errors come to light. The way that the PC communicates POST errors is through special sound codes called *beep codes* and through text or numeric messages displayed on your monitor.

Beep Codes

Beep codes vary according to the PC's BIOS manufacturer, although you'll find certain codes are common on most PCs. A single, happy-sounding chirp at bootup signals that all is well. A long, repeating beep signals a problem with RAM. A series of beeps—one long and three short—usually points to a problem with the video card.

Numeric and Text Codes

POST may also display numeric or text errors indicating the nature of a hardware problem. Numeric error codes are somewhat standardized into certain code *ranges.* For instance, an error code in the range 100–199 indicates a motherboard error, and an error code in the 200–299 range indicates a RAM error.

Text errors tend to be fairly direct statements, such as "Floppy drive failure" or "Keyboard error or no keyboard present," that display on your monitor and usually require you to press a key such as F1 to continue.

Some hardware problems prevent any POST errors from properly appearing on the display screen or coming through the system speaker. In these cases, a special hardware tool called a *POST card* comes in handy.

POST Cards

POST cards aren't the kind you use to send snail-mail holiday greetings. A POST card, shown in Figure 7.1, is a dedicated hardware component that plugs into a PCI slot and displays POST codes coming from the system BIOS.

The POST card uses a light-emitting diode (LED) display to present special POST code listings that the technician then interprets. Most POST cards come

FIGURE 7.1 POST card error code readout

with documentation explaining the various error codes in general, but different BIOS manufacturers use different codes. Visit the motherboard manufacturer's Web site for information on the specific motherboard you're testing. You can also check the BIOS maker's Web site for error code explanations.

> **Exam Tip**
>
> You can use a POST card to check a PC that won't boot to see how dead it really is. If you see POST readings on the card when you press the power button, you'll know at least the CPU, RAM, and BIOS are functional and can look at other settings or devices for the boot problem.

OS Loads

During POST, the BIOS also locates the system boot device—such as the floppy disk, optical media, USB device, or hard drive—that contains the OS. Once the POST process completes successfully, the BIOS then passes control of the boot

process over to the PC's OS. The exact loading process differs from one OS to the next, but in general, one or more vital system files loads into memory and starts the ball rolling. Things move fast from there, as the OS loads its core files, drivers, and services into RAM. The next thing you know, you're looking at your desktop and hearing the soothing strains of the Windows logon sound file.

Objective 7.02 System ROM

The system ROM chip stores the system BIOS routines and CMOS setup utility. System ROM is often distinctively labeled with the BIOS maker's name, but can also appear as a very small chip near the southbridge, as shown in Figure 7.2. On older PCs, the BIOS routines were hard-coded onto the system ROM chip, meaning that the BIOSs were unchangeable without replacing the entire ROM chip. Current motherboards use writable ROM chips such as *flash ROM*, or, more technically, *electrically erasable programmable read-only memory (EEPROM)*. (Now you know why most writers and techs prefer the common term of flash ROM!) Writable ROM chips enable you to install updated BIOS information without physically replacing the chip.

Exam Tip
Many techs refer to the system BIOS as the *ROM BIOS*, and the CompTIA A+ certification exams may use either term.

FIGURE 7.2 System ROM chips

There's a big difference between system ROM chips and RAM that you need to appreciate. RAM is called *volatile* memory because RAM stores data only while the PC is powered on. System ROM memory, on the other hand, is *non-volatile* memory and retains data even when the system is powered off.

From a technician's standpoint, you don't need to do much to maintain the system ROM. System ROM requires no servicing beyond the usual blowing-out-the-dust type of PC case maintenance that should be a part of your routine. Nor does the system ROM itself ever need to be updated, although the BIOS programs residing on it sometimes do. The only type of maintenance that you'll ever undertake on the system ROM is replacing the CMOS battery (described in the next section). Let's take a closer look at the system BIOS and CMOS setup utility.

Objective 7.03 System BIOS and CMOS Setup Utility

You never deal directly with the many BIOS routines but instead interact with them peripherally through the CMOS setup utility. Motherboard manufacturers don't actually write their own BIOS routines. Instead, they buy BIOS from third-party BIOS makers; among the largest makers are American Megatrends (AMI) and Phoenix Technologies. The latter produces BIOS under both the Phoenix and Award brands. A great deal of uniformity exists among brands of BIOS software, however, so from a technician's point of view, there's not all that much of a difference between them.

System BIOS

The system BIOS contains many routines—called *services*—to initialize and support the many devices that make up a modern PC. Services control things as mundane as whether the NUM LOCK key is engaged at startup, to things as exotic-sounding as the *SDRAM precharge control*, and beyond.

Unlike most types of PC software, BIOS routines rarely change. BIOS makers update BIOS routines only to fix known bugs (thus enhancing stability) and to add important functions such as compatibility with new hardware or hardware standards.

Updating the System BIOS

Techs refer to updating system BIOS as *flashing the BIOS*. It's a simple procedure, but you must take care to ensure that it's done correctly and without interruption. A BIOS flash procedure that gets interrupted usually results in a PC that won't boot and a motherboard that's rendered completely useless! Before flashing your BIOS, back up your important documents and update any system repair discs or emergency rescue diskettes. Do your best to make certain that the process isn't disturbed once you start.

BIOS makers provide updating utilities for their BIOSs on their Web sites. Some motherboards come with a Windows-based utility that will go to the Web, download an updated BIOS, and enable you to flash the BIOS from within Windows. When it works, it's sweet.

CMOS Setup Utility

The CMOS setup utility, stored in the system ROM, enables you to configure important system BIOS settings stored in the CMOS chip, which is a part of the southbridge on most PCs. These settings include CPU setup, boot device sequence, power management, and a number of others, as described here. Every motherboard has a CMOS battery that enables the motherboard to retain CMOS settings when powered off and disconnected from external power.

```
  Award Modular BIOS v6.00PG, An Energy Star Ally
  Copyright (C) 1984-2005, Award Software, Inc

GA-K8NP F13

Processor : AMD Athlon(tm) 64 Processor 3200+
<CPUID:00000F4A Patch ID:003A>
Memory Testing : 3145728K OK
CPU clock frequency : 200Mhz

  Primary Master   : WDC WD400BB-00JHA0 05.01C05
  Primary Slave    : None
Secondary Master   : None
  Secondary Slave  : LTN403 DQ19
```

EPA POLLUTION PREVENTER

Instructions to Enter CMOS

```
<DEL>:BIOS Setup/Dual BIOS, <F9>:Xpress Recovery
09/08/2005-nForce-6A61CG0AC-00
```

FIGURE 7.3 Each BIOS maker provides instructions for entering CMOS at bootup.

Entering the CMOS Setup Utility

You can't enter the CMOS setup utility from within your OS; you must do it during the early stages of the boot process. Different BIOS makers specify different methods for entering CMOS. The instructions for entering CMOS appear on your monitor during bootup (Figure 7.3). Watch the messages carefully and press the proper key when prompted. Typically, AMI and Award BIOSs have you press the DEL key when prompted. Phoenix might have you press the CTRL-ALT-ESC combination or possibly F2. Check your motherboard documentation for the exact method on your PC.

Once you enter CMOS, navigate with the keyboard (AMI provides mouse support). Use the TAB and ARROW keys to move around and the ENTER key to make selections. This also varies according to which BIOS is installed on your PC. Navigation instructions should be prominent in the display somewhere. If you get stuck, press the F1 key to bring up a Help menu.

Let's take a look at some of the more important CMOS settings.

Standard CMOS Features The Standard CMOS Features screen (Figure 7.4) enables you to change floppy drive and hard drive settings, as well as the system's date and time. Most systems display automatically set BIOS component information here, such as the channels used by the hard drives and optical drives and the amount of RAM.

CMOS Setup Utility - Copyright (C) 1984-2009 Award Software
Standard CMOS Features

		Item Help
Date (mm:dd:yy)	Wed, Mar 7 2012	
Time (hh:mm:ss)	16 : 2 : 30	
		Menu Level ▶
▶ IDE Channel 0 Master	[None]	
▶ IDE Channel 0 Slave	[None]	Change the day, month,
▶ IDE Channel 1 Master	[WDC WD2500YS-01SHB1]	year
▶ IDE Channel 1 Slave	[WDC WD800AAJS-00PSA0	
▶ IDE Channel 2 Master	[WDC WD5000AAKS-00A7B	<Week>
▶ IDE Channel 2 Slave	[SONY DVD RW AW-G1	Sun. to Sat.
▶ IDE Channel 3 Master	[None]	
▶ IDE Channel 3 Slave	[None]	<Month>
▶ IDE Channel 4 Master	[None]	Jan. to Dec.
▶ IDE Channel 4 Slave	[None]	
		<Day>
Drive A	[1.44M, 3.5"]	1 to 31 (or maximum
Floppy 3 Mode Support	[Disabled]	allowed in the month)
Halt On	[All , But Keyboard]	<Year>
		2000 to 2099

↑↓→←:Move Enter:Select +/-/PU/PD:Value F10:Save ESC:Exit F1:General Help
F5:Previous Values F6:Fail-Safe Defaults F7:Optimized Defaults

FIGURE 7.4 Standard CMOS Features screen

MB Intelligent Tweaker You can use MB Intelligent Tweaker (M.I.T.) to change the voltage and multiplier settings on the motherboard for the CPU from the defaults. Motherboards that cater to overclockers tend to have this option. Usually you just set this to Auto or Default and stay away from this screen (see Figure 7.5).

CMOS Setup Utility - Copyright (C) 1984-2009 Award Software
MB Intelligent Tweaker (M.I.T.)

			Item Help
▶ Advanced Clock Calibration	[Press Enter]		
CPU Clock Ratio	[Auto]	2600Mhz	
CPU NorthBridge Freq.	[Auto]	2000Mhz	Menu Level ▶
CPU Host Clock Control	[Auto]		
x CPU Frequency(MHz)	200		
PCIE Clock(MHz)	[Auto]		
HT Link Width	[Auto]		
HT Link Frequency	[Auto]	2000Mhz	
Set Memory Clock	[Auto]		
x Memory Clock	x5.33	1066Mhz	
▶ DRAM Configuration	[Press Enter]		
******** System Voltage Optimized ********			
System Voltage Control	[Auto]		
x DDR3 Voltage Control	Auto		
x SB/HT Voltage Control	Auto		
x NB/PCIe/PLL Voltage Contro	Auto		
x CPU PLL Voltage Control	Auto		
x DDR VTT Voltage Control	Auto		
x NB Voltage Control	Auto		

↑↓→←:Move Enter:Select +/-/PU/PD:Value F10:Save ESC:Exit F1:General Help
F5:Previous Values F6:Fail-Safe Defaults F7:Optimized Defaults

FIGURE 7.5 MB Intelligent Tweaker (M.I.T.)

Advanced BIOS Features The Advanced BIOS Features screen is the dumping ground for all the settings that aren't covered in the Standard screen but don't fit nicely under any other screen. This screen varies wildly from one system to the next. You most often use this screen to select the boot options, the boot sequence, turn virtualization support on or off, and more (Figure 7.6).

Travel Advisory

Advanced BIOS Features is the first place to check if you have a computer that attempts to boot to an incorrect device. The computer might have always booted fine, for example, but then gives you a boot error, like *invalid boot device*. If you have a USB thumb drive inserted and this CMOS setting has removable devices ahead of hard drives in the boot order, the computer will dutifully try to boot from the thumb drive.

Advanced Chipset Features The Advanced Chipset Features screen strikes fear into most everyone because it deals with extremely low-level chipset functions. Avoid this screen unless a high-level tech (such as a motherboard maker's support tech) explicitly tells you to do something in here (Figure 7.7).

```
          CMOS Setup Utility - Copyright (C) 1984-2009 Award Software
                          Advanced BIOS Features

     Virtualization              [Disabled]              Item Help
     AMD K8 Cool&Quite control   [Auto]
  ▶  Hard Disk Book Priority     [Press Enter]        Menu Level  ▶
     First Boot Device           [CDROM]
     Second Boot Device          [Hard Disk]          Hardware assisted
     Third Boot Device           [CDROM]              Virtualization
     Password Check              [Setup]              Technology which help
     HDD S.M.A.R.T. Capability   [Enabled]            improve performance of
     Away Mode                   [Disabled]           system running
     Full Screen LOGO Show       [Enabled]            Virtual Machine
     Init Display First          [PEG]                Softwares.

                                                      Virtual Machine
                                                      allows multiple OS
                                                      on one computer
                                                      simultaneously.

  ↑↓←:Move  Enter:Select  +/-/PU/PD:Value  F10:Save  ESC:Exit  F1:General Help
         F5:Previous Values  F6:Fail-Safe Defaults  F7:Optimized Defaults
```

FIGURE 7.6 Advanced BIOS Features screen

FIGURE 7.7 Advanced Chipset Features screen

Integrated Peripherals On the Integrated Peripherals screen you configure, enable, or disable the onboard ports, such as the serial and parallel ports (Figure 7.8).

FIGURE 7.8 Integrated Peripherals screen

```
         CMOS Setup Utility - Copyright (C) 1984-2009 Award Software
                          Power Management Setup

   ACPI Suspend Type          [S3(STR)]                    Item Help
   Soft-Off by Power button   [Instant-Off]
   USB Wake Up from S3        [Enabled]          Menu Level    ▶
   Modem Ring Resume          [Disabled]
   PME Event Wake Up          [Enabled]          [S1(POS)]
   HPET Support               [Enabled]          Set suspend type to
   Power On By Mouse          [Disabled]         Power On Suspend under
   Power On By Keyboard       [Disabled]         ACPI OS
 x KB Power ON Password       Enter
   AC Back Function           [Soft-Off]         [S3(STR)]
   Power-On by Alarm          [Disabled]         Set suspend type to
 x Date (of Month)            Everyday           Suspend to RAM under
 x Resume Time (hh:mm:ss)      0 :  0 :  0       ACPI OS

 ↑↓→←:Move  Enter:Select  +/-/PU/PD:Value  F10:Save  ESC:Exit  F1:General Help
      F5:Previous Values  F6:Fail-Safe Defaults  F7:Optimized Defaults
```

FIGURE 7.9 Power Management Setup screen

Power Management Setup As the name implies, you can use the Power Management Setup screen to set up the power management settings for the system. These settings work in concert (sometimes in conflict) with Windows's power management settings to control how and when devices turn off and back on to conserve power (Figure 7.9). These built-in diagnostic tools can be very helpful if you're having trouble with a particular motherboard.

Travel Assistance

For more information on power management, check out Chapter 12.

PnP/PCI Configurations All CMOS setup utilities come with menu items that are, for the most part, no longer needed, but no one wants to remove them. PnP/PCI is a perfect example. Plug and Play (PnP) is how devices automatically work when you snap them into your PC. Peripheral Component Interconnect (PCI) is a type of slot used for cards. Odds are very good you'll never deal with this screen (Figure 7.10).

```
              Phoenix - Award BIOS CMOS Setup Utility
                      PnP/PCI Configurations

   Resources Controlled By    Auto(ESCD)              Item Help
 x IRQ Resources              Press Enter
                                                Menu Level    ▶
   PCI/VGA Palette Snoop      Disabled
   PIRQ_0 Use IRQ No.         Auto           BIOS can automatically
   PIRQ_1 Use IRQ No.         Auto           configure all the
   PIRQ_2 Use IRQ No.         Auto           boot and Plug and Play
   PIRQ_3 Use IRQ No.         Auto           compatible devices.
                                             If you choose Auto,
   ** PCI Express relative items **          you cannot select IRQ
   Maximum Payload Size       4096           DMA and memory base
                                             address fields, since
                                             BIOS automatically
                                             assigns them

 ↑↓→←:Move  Enter:Select  +/-/PU/PD:Value  F10:Save  ESC:Exit  F1:General Help
    F5:Previous Values   F6:Fail-Safe Defaults   F7:Optimized Defaults
```

FIGURE 7.10 PnP/PCI

Other Options Some of the other options you'll find in CMOS, such as the PC Health Status, enable you to monitor the active temperature of the computer or how fast the fans are spinning. This generally involves loading motherboard software so you can view and change settings in Windows rather than having to reboot each time (Figure 7.11).

FIGURE 7.11 Monitoring software on an Alienware system

Other options don't even have their own screens. They simply use small dialog boxes that pop up, usually asking, "Are you sure?" The Load Fail-Safe/ Optimized default options keep you from having to memorize all those weird settings you'll never touch. Fail-Safe sets everything to simple settings—you might occasionally use this setting when low-level problems such as freeze-ups occur and you've checked more obvious areas first. Optimized sets the CMOS to the best possible speed/stability for the system. You might use this option after tampering with the CMOS so much so that you need to put it back like it was!

- **Set Password** A user-CMOS password enables you to set a degree of low-level security on the PC. With this setting configured, the user is required to enter a password during the early stages of the boot process. The PC will not boot without the correct password. In most CMOS utilities, you can also set supervisor passwords that prevent unauthorized persons from accessing the CMOS. This is especially important if the PC is accessible by the public, such as at a trade show or in a library. Remember, however, that if you forget or lose the password, you'll be unable to access the CMOS, though you will still be able to boot the system.

Exam Tip

Most CMOS setup utilities enable you to set both a user-level and a supervisor-level password for protection. A CMOS password provides decent security for a computer that multiple people might access.

Should you wind up locking yourself out of your PC by losing the user CMOS password, or if you need to access the CMOS and don't have the supervisor CMOS password, you can gain access in a couple of ways. You can use the CMOS clear jumper, as discussed in Chapter 5. Check the motherboard's documentation for the exact instructions for your particular motherboard. The other method is to disconnect the AC power cable (remember that ATX systems always have a 5-V trickle charge on the motherboard when plugged in) and unplug the CMOS battery for a few seconds. This clears your CMOS of all settings, including the offending password.

Exam Tip

Remember that in many cases setting a jumper on the motherboard or removing and replacing the CMOS battery can clear CMOS passwords.

- **Intrusion Detection/Notification** Most new systems have an option in CMOS that tattles when the side of the case is opened. This is a very nice tool for warning techs of any tampering or attempts to tamper with public systems.

- **DriveLock** *DriveLock* uses two passwords (master and user) to control access to a system's hard drive. In high-security mode, both passwords can be used to access the drive, but in max security mode, only the user password can gain access to the drive. The master password can be used to reset the user password, but all data on the protected drive will be lost. The passwords are stored in the hard disk's control circuitry and cannot be reset by clearing CMOS.

- **Trusted Platform Module** The *Trusted Platform Module (TPM)* acts as a secure cryptoprocessor, which is to say that it is a hardware platform for the acceleration of cryptographic functions and the secure storage of associated information. It can be a small circuit board plugged into the motherboard, or it can be built directly into the chipset. TPMs can be used in a wide array of cryptographic operations, but one of the most common uses of TPMs is hard disk encryption. For example, the BitLocker Drive Encryption feature of Microsoft's Windows Vista and Windows 7 can be accelerated by a TPM, which is more secure because the encryption key is stored in the tamper-resistant TPM hardware instead of on an external flash drive.

Exam Tip

Some PC manufacturers also include *LoJack* security features in their BIOS—this way, if your PC or laptop is stolen, you can track its location, install a key logger, or even remotely shut down your computer.

- **Save & Exit Setup** This option will make any changes you've configured in CMOS setup permanent. Use it with caution! Typically, selecting this option brings up a confirmation prompt along the lines of "Are you really, really sure you want to make these changes? Y/N." Don't make any changes unless you're absolutely certain what the effect will be.

- **Exit Without Saving** Of all the options on the CMOS setup menu, this one is your best friend. Exit Without Saving undoes any changes you've made. Choosing this option brings up another "Are you sure? Y/N" type of confirmation prompt. Press *Y* to take your leave of CMOS setup without doing any damage.

Replacing the CMOS Battery

When CMOS batteries fail, they do so gradually. The first and best indicator that a PC's CMOS battery is dying is that the PC starts to lose time or the settings reset. If you notice that your PC's clock is running slowly, or if you're consistently prompted to enter the date and time when you boot the PC, it's time to replace the CMOS battery.

Replacing the CMOS battery is as simple as sliding the old one out of the bracket and slipping the new one in its place. Be sure to use a new battery that matches the voltage of the old battery. Figure 7.12 shows a CMOS battery.

FIGURE 7.12 CMOS battery

CHECKPOINT

✔**Objective 7.01: Boot Process and POST** After the CPU powers up, the system BIOS loads and runs the POST to test all the built-in and common devices in the PC. The POST sounds a beep code or displays numeric or text error messages in the event of hardware failure. POST cards let you interpret POST error codes and troubleshoot a dead PC. At the end of the POST, the operating system loads.

✔**Objective 7.02: System ROM** The system ROM chip stores the system BIOS programs and CMOS setup utility. System ROM is flash ROM memory that maintains data even while the PC is turned off through the use of a CMOS battery.

✔**Objective 7.03: System BIOS and CMOS Setup Utility** The system BIOS includes hundreds of small programs that establish communication between your PC hardware and the OS. System BIOS can be updated (*flashed*) to fix bugs or add new functions. The CMOS setup utility enables you to modify settings for built-in and common devices, such as hard drives. You access CMOS by entering a key combination that's specific to the manufacturer of the BIOS on your OS. You should write down your CMOS settings before making any changes. The CMOS setup utility also includes settings and features for securing your system, such as intrusion detection, DriveLock, LoJack, and the Trusted Platform Module.

REVIEW QUESTIONS

1. Which of the following can you configure in the CMOS? (Select three.)

 A. Parallel ports

 B. Serial ports

 C. Hard drive

 D. Video resolution

2. When should you update your system BIOS?

 A. When you upgrade your OS

 B. Every time you boot your computer

 C. Every time you defragment your computer

 D. To add functionality or fix known bugs

3. What should you do before making any changes to your CMOS settings?

 A. Reboot your computer.

 B. Write down the current settings.

 C. Remove all the cables from your PC.

 D. Replace the BIOS.

4. What do you need to do if the clock on your PC starts losing time?

 A. Replace your BIOS.

 B. Replace the CMOS battery.

 C. Replace your hard drive.

 D. Reinstall Windows.

5. If a user password has been set in the CMOS, what will happen?

 A. An unauthorized person will be unable to enter the CMOS settings program.

 B. The user must enter the correct password to boot the system.

 C. Nothing will happen.

 D. Only certain settings in the CMOS will be available to unauthorized users.

6. If you've set and forgotten a supervisor password for your CMOS, how can you get into the CMOS settings program in many systems? (Select two.)

 A. Reboot the PC and press F1.

 B. Set a jumper on your motherboard to clear the password.

 C. Reinstall Windows.

 D. Remove and reinstall the CMOS battery.

7. At startup, where does your PC receive its first set of instructions?

 A. Operating system

 B. RAM BIOS

 C. ROM BIOS

 D. CMOS

8. If you're using Windows and set your Plug and Play BIOS so the BIOS configures your PnP devices, what will happen?

 A. Your BIOS will configure the devices.

 B. Windows will configure the devices.

 C. The devices will need to be configured manually.

 D. None of the above.

9. How can you access a hard drive if DriveLock is enabled and set to max security mode, but you have forgotten or lost the user password?

 A. Reinstall Windows; your data will be unaffected.

 B. Without the user password, you can never access the hard drive again; your hard drive is permanently useless.

 C. Use a jumper to clear the password; your data will be unaffected.

 D. Use the master password to reset the user password; your data will be destroyed.

10. Which Windows Vista/7 feature uses a Trusted Platform Module (TPM)?

 A. Windows Update

 B. Windows Easy Transfer

 C. BitLocker Drive Encryption

 D. Windows Defender

REVIEW ANSWERS

1. **A** **B** **C** Parallel ports, serial ports, and your hard drive are all configurable in the CMOS settings program.

2. **D** System BIOS should be updated only when a new BIOS version will fix a problem or add new functions.

3. **B** Before making any changes in the CMOS, you should write down the current CMOS settings. Taking the time to do this can save you from having to retrace your steps later.

4. **B** If the clock on your PC starts losing time, this is a good indication that you need to change the CMOS battery.

5. **B** If a user password is set in the CMOS, the computer won't fully boot until the correct password is entered by the user.

6. **B** **D** If you've set and forgotten a supervisor password in the CMOS, you can still enter the CMOS by setting a jumper on the motherboard to clear the password or by removing and reinstalling the CMOS battery.

7. **C** At startup, your PC receives its first set of instructions from the system BIOS, also called ROM BIOS. There's no such thing as RAM BIOS, a fact you should remember for the exam.

8. **B** If you're using a PnP operating system, regardless of the settings made for the PnP BIOS, the operating system will override the settings.

9. **D** The best course of action would be to use the master password to reset the user password, although your data would be lost.

10. **C** Windows Vista/7 BitLocker Drive Encryption uses a Trusted Platform Module (TPM).

Hard Drives

	NEWBIE	SOME EXPERIENCE	EXPERT
ETA	4 hours	3 hours	1.5 hours

Hard drives store operating systems (OSs), applications, and data so that they're available when the PC powers up. Because they store data, hard drives hold a central place in the computer. If the drive dies, all the data dies, too, and that's not a good thing!

This chapter looks at five aspects of hard drives in the PC: various hard drive technologies so you can make excellent recommendations for your clients; installation steps for ATA and SCSI drives; preparing a drive to hold data; setting up drives for data redundancy; and essential tools and practices to maintain and troubleshoot hard drives.

Objective 8.01 Hard Drive Technologies

Traditional *hard disk drives* (*HDDs*) store data magnetically onto spinning platters, using a fast-moving actuator arm with read-write heads. Figure 8.1 shows the inside of a traditional hard drive.

> **Exam Tip**
>
> You'll see the platter-reading component of an HDD mentioned on the exams as a *head actuator.*

Solid-state drives (SSDs) use memory chips to store data, speeding up load times and reducing the possibility of damage. Solid-state technology is commonly used in desktop and laptop hard drives, memory cards, cameras, Universal Serial Bus (USB) thumb drives, and other handheld devices.

SSDs use the same connectors as HDDs and come in similar form factors, but use a lot less electricity because they have no moving parts.

Although almost all hard drives look similar on the outside, their mechanical nature reveals wide variations in three categories: capacity, seek time, and bandwidth. The key for recommending a drive is to understand that a 200-GB drive is smaller than a 2-TB drive; a 5400-rpm drive is slower than a 7200-rpm drive (but perhaps a little quieter) and will have a correspondingly slower seek time; and a drive with a 2-MB cache won't have the sustained throughput of a drive with a 16-MB cache. Table 8.1 shows common HDD spindle speeds with typical use.

FIGURE 8.1 Inside a hard drive

TABLE 8.1 Typical HDD Spindle Speeds

Spindle Speed	Typical Purpose
3600 rpm	Older portable computers
5400 rpm	Standard for portable computers
7200 rpm	Standard for desktop computers
10000 rpm	Enthusiast and server computers
15000 rpm	Enthusiast and server computers

All hard drives connect to a hard drive controller of some sort with a cable. All drives need 5 V and 12 V power from the power supply, although connectors differ among the various technologies. Traditionally, desktop hard drives have the same 3.5-inch rectangular shape. As SSDs have become more common, however, a lot of 2.5-inch drives have started appearing in desktop PCs.

Exam Tip

HDDs use mechanical spinning parts; SSDs have no moving parts.

For all the similarities, two distinctly different hard drive technologies have been used in PCs: ATA and SCSI. They connect to their own type of controller and use cabling unique to themselves. Both technologies have been around for many years, so you'll find lots of variation in the hardware out in the field and in the marketplace.

ATA

Advanced Technologies Attachment (ATA) drives have been around since the beginning of the PC, though they've advanced a lot since the early days. Two styles exist in modern PCs, *parallel ATA (PATA)* and *serial ATA (SATA)*, with the latter replacing the former as the hard drive of choice in most systems. Techs often refer to ATA drives as *integrated drive electronics (IDE)* or *Enhanced IDE (EIDE)*, and CompTIA has adopted the use of the terms specifically for PATA drives.

PATA

The last PATA standard, called ATA/ATAPI-7, provides support for very large hard drives (144 petabytes [PB], a number greater than 144 million GB) at speeds up to 133 MB per second (MBps). All PATA drives use a standard Molex power connector (Figure 8.2). Slower PATA drives (33 MBps and slower) can get

FIGURE 8.2 Molex connector

FIGURE 8.3 40-pin and 80-wire PATA cables

by with a 40-pin ribbon cable. Drives that go 66 MBps or faster require an 80-wire cable. Figure 8.3 shows both types of cables, and Table 8.2 shows the types of PATA drives you might see.

Exam Tip

The 801 objectives refer to PATA cables and connectors as IDE and EIDE cables and connectors, possibly meaning 40-wire and 80-wire, respectively. If so, it's an error in the objectives. The terms are interchangeable today.

You can connect up to two PATA drives—including hard drives, optical drives, and tape drives—to a single ATA controller. You set jumpers on the drives to make one master and the other slave. (See the discussion on installation later in this chapter for the full scoop.)

Exam Tip

You should know that the technologies that enabled steadily larger drive size are Logical Block Addressing (LBA) (up to 8 GB), interrupt 13 (INT 13) extensions (up to 137 GB), and ATA/ATAPI-7 (up to 144 PB).

TABLE 8.2 Common PATA Drive Types

Name	Transfer Mode	Speed	Cable Type
ATA/33	Ultra DMA mode 2	33 MBps	40-pin
ATA/66	Ultra DMA mode 3	66 MBps	80-wire
ATA/100	Ultra DMA mode 4	100 MBps	80-wire
ATA/133	Ultra DMA mode 5	133 MBps	80-wire

SATA

For all its longevity as the mass storage interface of choice for the PC, PATA has problems. First, the flat ribbon cables impede airflow and can be a pain to insert properly. Second, the cables have a limited length, only 18 inches. Third, you can't hot-swap PATA drives. You have to shut down completely before installing or replacing a drive. Finally, the technology has simply reached the limits of what it can do in terms of throughput.

Serial ATA addresses these issues. SATA creates a point-to-point connection between the SATA device—hard disk or optical-media drive—and the SATA controller. At a glance, SATA devices look identical to standard PATA devices. Take a closer look at the cable and power connectors, however, and you'll see significant differences (Figure 8.4).

Because SATA devices send data serially instead of in parallel, the SATA interface needs far fewer physical wires—7 instead of the 80 wires typical of PATA—resulting in much thinner cabling. This might not seem significant, but the benefit is that thinner cabling means better cable control and better airflow through the PC case, resulting in better cooling.

Further, the maximum SATA device cable length is more than twice that of a PATA cable—1 meter (~39 inches) instead of 18 inches. Again, this might not seem like a big deal, unless you've struggled to connect a PATA hard disk installed into the top bay of a full-tower case to a PATA connector located all the way at the bottom of the motherboard.

FIGURE 8.4 SATA power and data connectors

SATA does away with the entire master/slave concept. Each drive connects to one port, creating a point-to-point connection. Further, there's no maximum number of drives—many motherboards support eight or more SATA drives. Want more? Snap in a SATA host card and load 'em up.

The big news, however, is in data throughput. As the name implies, SATA devices transfer data in serial bursts instead of parallel, as PATA devices do. A SATA device's single stream of data moves much faster than the multiple streams of data coming from a PATA device—theoretically up to 30 times faster. SATA drives come in three varieties—1.0 (1.5Gb/s), 2.0 (3Gb/s), and 3.0 (6Gb/s)—that have an actual maximum throughput of 150 MBps, 300 MBps, and 715 MBps, respectively.

SATA's ease of use has made it the choice for desktop system storage, and its success is already showing in the fact that more than 90 percent of all hard drives sold today are SATA drives.

eSATA

External SATA (eSATA) extends the SATA bus to external devices, as the name implies. The eSATA drives use similar connectors to internal SATA, but they're keyed differently so you can't mistake one for the other. Figure 8.5 shows eSATA connectors on the back of a motherboard. eSATA adapter cards are also available if you run out of SATA ports on your motherboard. eSATA uses shielded cable lengths up to two meters (about six feet) outside the PC and is hot-pluggable. The beauty of eSATA is that it extends the SATA bus at the same speeds as the internal SATA bus (up to 715 MB/s), so you're not limited to the meager 50 or 60 MBps of FireWire or Hi-Speed USB.

FIGURE 8.5 eSATA connectors

Exam Tip
You should know the various IDE speeds, including PATA (specifically ATA-100), SATA 1, SATA 2, SATA 3, and eSATA.

SCSI

Many specialized server machines and enthusiasts' systems use the *small computer system interface (SCSI)* technologies for various pieces of core hardware and peripherals, from hard drives, to printers, to high-end tape backup machines. SCSI differs from ATA in that SCSI devices connect together in a string of devices called a chain. Each device in the chain gets a unique SCSI ID to distinguish it from other devices on the chain. Last, the ends of a SCSI chain must be terminated. Let's dive into SCSI now and see how SCSI chains, SCSI IDs, and termination all work.

SCSI is an old technology dating from the late 1970s, but it has been continually updated. SCSI is faster than ATA (though the gap is closing fast), and until SATA arrived, SCSI was the only choice for anyone using RAID (see the "Protecting Data with RAID" section later in this chapter). SCSI is arguably fading away, but it still deserves some mention.

SCSI Chains

SCSI manifests itself through a SCSI chain, a series of SCSI devices working together through a host adapter. The host adapter provides the interface between the SCSI chain and the PC. Figure 8.6 shows a typical SCSI host adapter.

FIGURE 8.6 SCSI host adapter

FIGURE 8.7 Internal SCSI CD-ROM drive

Many techs refer to the host adapter as the *SCSI controller,* so you should be comfortable with both terms.

All SCSI devices can be divided into two groups: internal and external. Internal SCSI devices are attached inside the PC and connect to the host adapter through the latter's internal connector. Figure 8.7 shows an internal SCSI device— in this case, a CD-ROM drive. External devices hook to the external connector of the host adapter. Figure 8.8 is an example of an external SCSI device.

FIGURE 8.8 Back of external SCSI device

FIGURE 8.9 Typical 68-pin ribbon cable

Internal SCSI devices connect to the host adapter with a 68-pin ribbon cable (Figure 8.9). This flat, flexible cable functions precisely like a PATA cable. Many external devices connect to the host adapter with a 50-pin, high-density (HD) connector. Figure 8.10 shows a host adapter external port. Higher-end SCSI devices use a 68-pin HD connector.

Multiple internal devices can be connected together simply by using a cable with enough connectors. The 68-pin ribbon cable in Figure 8.9, for example, can take up to four SCSI devices, including the host adapter.

Assuming the SCSI host adapter has a standard external port (some controllers don't have external connections at all), plugging in an external SCSI device is as simple as running a cable from device to controller. The external SCSI

FIGURE 8.10 50-pin HD port on SCSI host adapter

FIGURE 8.11 Internal SCSI chain with two devices and the host adapter

connectors are D-shaped, so you can't plug them in backward. As an added bonus, some external SCSI devices have two ports, one to connect to the host adapter and a second to connect to another SCSI device. The process of connecting a device directly to another device is called *daisy-chaining*. You can daisy-chain up to 15 devices to one host adapter. SCSI chains can be internal, external, or both. Figure 8.11 shows an internal SCSI chain. Figure 8.12 shows both internal and external chains using a single controller.

FIGURE 8.12 Internal and external devices on one SCSI chain

SCSI IDs

If you're going to connect a number of devices on the same SCSI chain, you must provide some way for the host adapter to tell one device from another. To differentiate devices, SCSI uses a unique identifier called the *SCSI ID*. The SCSI ID number can range from 0 to 15. SCSI IDs are similar to many other PC hardware settings in that a SCSI device can theoretically have any SCSI ID, as long as that ID is not already taken by another device connected to the same host adapter.

SCSI IDs follow some conventions, but nothing is set in stone. Typically, most people set the host adapter to 7 or 15, but you can change this setting. Aside from the host adapter, it does not matter which device gets which number, and you can skip numbers. Many folks give ID 0 to a bootable hard drive, but in reality, the ID simply has to match what the controller has as the ID for a bootable drive. Restrictions on IDs apply only within a single chain. Two devices can have the same ID, in other words, as long as they are on different chains (Figure 8.13).

Every SCSI device has some method of setting its SCSI ID. The trick is to figure out how to set the SCSI ID when you're holding the device in your hand. A SCSI device may use jumpers, dip switches, or even tiny dials; every new SCSI device is a new adventure as you try to determine how to set its SCSI ID.

Termination

Whenever you send a signal down a wire, some of that signal reflects back up the wire, creating an echo and causing electronic chaos. SCSI chains use *termination*

FIGURE 8.13 IDs don't conflict between separate SCSI chains.

to prevent this problem. Termination simply means putting something on the ends of the wire to prevent this echo. Terminators are usually pull-down resistors and can manifest themselves in many different ways. Most of the devices within a PC have the appropriate termination built in. On other devices, including SCSI chains and some network cables, you have to set termination during installation.

The rule with SCSI is that you *must* terminate *only* the ends of the SCSI chain. You have to terminate the ends of the cable, which usually means that you need to terminate the two devices at the ends of the cable. Do *not* terminate devices that are not on the ends of the cable. Figure 8.14 shows some examples of where to terminate SCSI devices.

Because any SCSI device might be on the end of a chain, most manufacturers build SCSI devices that can self-terminate. Some devices will detect that they are on the end of the SCSI chain and will automatically terminate themselves. Most devices, however, require that you set a jumper or switch to enable termination (Figure 8.15).

FIGURE 8.14 Location of the terminated devices

FIGURE 8.15 Termination settings

Objective 8.02 Installing Hard Drives

Installing a drive is a fairly simple process if you take the time to make sure you've got the right drive for your system, you've configured the drive properly, and you've made a few quick tests to make sure it's running properly. Since PATA, SATA, and SCSI have different cabling requirements, we'll look at each of these separately.

Choosing Your Drive

First, decide where you're going to put the drive. Look for an open ATA connection. Is it PATA or SATA? Is it a dedicated RAID controller? (See "Protecting Data with RAID," later in the chapter.) Many motherboards with built-in RAID controllers have a CMOS setting that enables you to turn the RAID on or off (Figure 8.16). Do you have the right controller for a SCSI drive?

Next, make sure you have room for the drive in the case. Where will you place it? Do you have a spare power connector? Will the data and power cables reach the drive? A quick test fit is always a good idea.

Jumpers and Cabling on PATA Drives

If you have only one hard drive, set the drive's jumpers to master or standalone. If you have two drives, set one to master and the other to slave. Figure 8.17 shows a close-up of a PATA hard drive showing the jumpers.

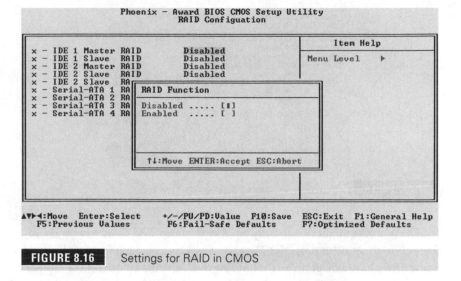

```
          Phoenix - Award BIOS CMOS Setup Utility
                    RAID Configuation

                                                    Item Help
 x - IDE 1 Master RAID       Disabled
 x - IDE 1 Slave  RAID       Disabled         Menu Level  ▶
 x - IDE 2 Master RAID       Disabled
 x - IDE 2 Slave  RAID       Disabled
 x - IDE 2 Slave  RA ┌─────────────────────────────────┐
 x - Serial-ATA 1 RA │ RAID Function                   │
 x - Serial-ATA 2 RA │                                 │
 x - Serial-ATA 3 RA │ Disabled ..... [■]              │
 x - Serial-ATA 4 RA │ Enabled  ..... [ ]              │
                     │                                 │
                     │                                 │
                     │ ↑↓:Move  ENTER:Accept  ESC:Abort│
                     └─────────────────────────────────┘

▲▼►◄:Move  Enter:Select    +/-/PU/PD:Value  F10:Save   ESC:Exit  F1:General Help
   F5:Previous Values         F6:Fail-Safe Defaults    F7:Optimized Defaults
```

FIGURE 8.16 Settings for RAID in CMOS

FIGURE 8.17 Master/slave jumpers on a hard drive

FIGURE 8.18 Drive label showing master/slave settings

The jumpers might not actually be labeled *master* and *slave,* so how do you know how to set them properly? The easiest way is to read the front of the drive; most drives have a diagram on the housing that explains how to set the jumpers properly. Figure 8.18 shows the front of one of these drives, so you can see how to set the drive to master or slave.

Hard drives may have other jumpers that may or may not concern you during installation. One common set of jumpers is used for diagnostics at the manufacturing plant or for special settings in other kinds of devices that use hard drives. Ignore them. They have no bearing in the PC world. Many drives provide a third setting, which is used if only one drive connects to a controller. Often, master and single drive are the same setting on the hard drive, although some hard drives require separate settings.

> **Travel Advisory**
>
> The name for the single drive setting varies among manufacturers. Some use *Single;* others use *1 Drive* or *Standalone.*

Many current PATA hard drives use a jumper setting called *cable select* rather than master or slave. As the name implies, the position on the cable determines which drive will be master or slave: master on the end, slave in the middle. For cable select to work properly with two drives, both drives should be set as cable select.

If you don't see a label on the drive that tells you how to set the jumpers, you can also check the drive maker's Web site. Every drive manufacturer lists its drive jumper settings on the Web, although it can take a while to find the information you want. Try phoning the hard drive maker directly. Unlike many other PC parts manufacturers, hard drive producers tend to stay in business for a long period of time and offer great technical support.

Hard drive cables have a colored stripe that corresponds to the number-one pin—called *Pin 1*—on the connector. You need to make certain that Pin 1 on the controller is on the same wire as Pin 1 on the hard drive. Failing to plug in the drive properly will also prevent the PC from recognizing the drive. If you incorrectly set the master/slave jumpers or cable to the hard drives, you won't break anything; it just won't work.

Finally, you need to plug a Molex connector from the power supply into the drive. All modern PATA drives use a Molex connector.

Cabling SATA Drives

Installing SATA hard disk drives is even easier than installing PATA devices because there's no master, slave, or cable select configuration to mess with. In fact, there are no jumper settings to worry about at all, because SATA supports only a single device per controller channel. Simply connect the power and plug in the controller cable as shown in Figure 8.19—the OS automatically detects the drive and it's ready to go. The keying on the SATA controller and power cables makes it impossible to install either incorrectly.

The biggest problem with SATA drives is that many motherboards come with four or more SATA connectors. Sure, the cabling is easy enough, but what do you

FIGURE 8.19 Properly connected SATA cable

do when it comes time to start the computer and the system is trying to find the right hard drive to boot up? That's where CMOS comes into play. By default, boot order and drive letter priority follow SATA controller ID, so SATA 0 in a single drive system would be C:, SATA 1 would be D:, and so on.

Travel Advisory
Most CMOS setup utilities let you change the boot order easily, which is great for multiple-OS computers. Just put one OS on one drive and the other OS on the other. A simple reboot and quick trip to CMOS, and you can switch from one drive to the other.

Connecting SCSI Drives

Connecting SCSI drives requires three things: You must use a controller that works with your drive. You need to set unique SCSI IDs on the controller and the drive. Finally, you need to connect the ribbon cable and power connections properly. With SCSI, you need to attach the data cable correctly. You can reverse a PATA cable, for example, and nothing happens except the drive doesn't work. If you reverse a SCSI cable, however, you can seriously damage the drive. Just as with PATA cables, Pin 1 on the SCSI data cable must go to Pin 1 on both the drive and the host adapter.

Objective 8.03 Partitioning and Formatting

After installing a hard drive of any sort, you need to prepare the drive for holding data. *Partitioning* establishes the framework upon which your file system is built. *Formatting* creates the file system.

Partitioning

Windows supports two different partitioning methods: the older but more universal master boot record (MBR) partitioning scheme and the newer (but proprietary to Microsoft) dynamic storage partitioning scheme. Microsoft calls a hard drive that uses the MBR partitioning scheme a *basic disk* and a drive using the dynamic storage partitioning scheme a *dynamic disk*. A single Windows

system with two hard drives may have one of the drives partitioned as a basic disk and the other as a dynamic disk, and the system will run perfectly well.

> **Exam Tip**
>
> Your forefathers used a command-line tool for partitioning a Microsoft OS called *fdisk*. Current versions of Windows don't use fdisk, but it might show up as an incorrect answer on the 802 exam.

Basic Disks

Basic disk partitioning creates two very small data structures on a drive, the MBR and a partition table, and stores them on the first sector of the hard drive, called the *boot sector*. The MBR is nothing more than a tiny bit of code that takes control of the boot process from the system basic input/output system (BIOS). When the computer boots to a hard drive, the BIOS automatically looks for MBR code on the boot sector. The MBR has only one job: to look in the partition table for a partition with a valid OS (Figure 8.20).

> **Travel Advisory**
>
> Only one MBR and one partition table exist per basic disk.

All basic disk partition tables support up to four partitions. The partition table supports two types of partitions: primary partitions and extended partitions. *Primary partitions* are designed to support bootable operating systems. *Extended partitions* are not bootable. A single basic disk may have up to three primary partitions and one extended partition. If your disk does not have an extended partition, it may have up to four primary partitions.

FIGURE 8.20 Functions of the MBR and partition table

Partitioning enables multiple OSs. You can install up to four different OSs, each installed on its own primary partition, and boot to your choice each time you fire up the computer.

Every primary partition on a single drive has a special setting called *active* stored in the partition table. This setting is either on or off on each primary partition. At boot, the MBR uses the active setting in the partition table to determine which primary partition to choose to try to load an OS.

Each partition must have some unique identifier to enable users to recognize it as an individual partition. Microsoft operating systems (DOS and Windows) traditionally assign primary partitions a drive letter from C: to Z:. Extended partitions do not get drive letters.

After you create an extended partition, you must create logical drives within that extended partition. A logical drive traditionally gets a drive letter from D: to Z:.

Note that when you create partitions and logical drives in Windows Vista/7, the OS prompts you to create *volumes*. Further, Vista/7 create logical drives automatically when you exceed four volumes on a single drive.

Windows partitions are not limited to drive letters. With the exception of the partition that stores the boot files for Windows (which will always be C:), any other primary partitions or logical drives may get either a drive letter or a folder on a primary partition.

Instead of assigning drive letters, you can mount partitions as folders on an existing drive. A *volume mount point* (or simply mount point) is a place in the directory structure of an existing volume that you can point to a volume or partition. The mounted volume then functions just like a folder, but all files stored in that segment of the directory structure will go to the mounted volume. After partitioning and formatting the drive, you don't give it a drive letter; instead, you *mount* the volume to a folder on the C: drive and make it nothing more than just another folder.

Local Lingo

GPT partitioning MBR-partitioned disks have limits, specifically on size (no larger than 2.2 TB) and number of partitions (no more than four). The GUID partition table (GPT) partitioning scheme overcomes these limits. GPT drives function similarly to basic drives. The only quirk you might run into is the need for a Unified Extensible Firmware Interface (UEFI) motherboard and the 64-bit versions of Windows Vista/7/8 if you want to boot to a GPT drive. (UEFI is like a souped-up version of the traditional BIOS that you learned about in Chapter 7.) Neither GPT nor UEFI is on the current CompTIA A+ exams.

Dynamic Disks

With the introduction of Windows 2000, Microsoft defined an entirely new type of partitioning called *dynamic storage partitioning*, better known as *dynamic disks*. Dynamic disks drop the word *partition* and instead use the term *volume*. There is no dynamic disk equivalent to primary versus extended partitions. A volume is still technically a partition, but it can do things a regular partition cannot do, such as spanning. A *spanned volume* goes across more than one drive. Windows allows you to span up to 32 drives under a single volume. Dynamic disks also support RAID 0, 1, and 5, though support differs among the various editions and versions of Windows (see Table 8.3).

Exam Tip
Only the high-end editions of each version of Windows support dynamic disks. This includes Windows XP Professional; Windows Vista Business, Ultimate, and Enterprise; and Windows 7 Professional, Ultimate, and Enterprise.

How to Partition Using Disk Management

Follow these steps to create a new partition:

1. To access the Disk Management console, open the Control Panel, and then open Administrative Tools. Double-click Computer Management.

2. Expand the Storage branch in the left pane to access the storage management tools, and then click Disk Management.

TABLE 8.3	Dynamic Disk Compatibility			
Volume	Windows XP Professional	Windows Vista Business/ Ultimate/ Enterprise	Windows 7 Professional/ Ultimate/ Enterprise	Windows Server 2008/ Server 2008 R2
Simple	X	X	X	X
Spanned	X	X	X	X
Striped	X	X	X	X
Mirrored		X		X
RAID 5				X

3. Right-click an unallocated section of the disk, and select New Simple Volume (Create Partition in Windows XP) to start the New Simple Volume Wizard (see Figure 8.21). Then follow the prompts from the wizard to specify partition size, assign a drive letter or path (mount the partition to a folder), and format the partition with a file system.

Exam Tip

The CompTIA A+ 802 exam objectives mention "splitting" partitions. To be clear, you never actually split a partition. If you want to turn one partition into two, you need to remove the existing partition and create two new ones, or shrink the existing partition and add a new one to the unallocated space. If you see it on the exam, know that this is what CompTIA means.

Formatting

Formatting creates a file system for the drive—essentially a big spreadsheet that tracks what piece of data is stored in which location. As described earlier,

FIGURE 8.21 The New Simple Volume Wizard in Windows Disk Management

Windows supports three different file systems—FAT, FAT32, and NTFS. Each of these file systems has its own benefits and drawbacks. Windows 7 (and earlier operating systems with specific patches) supports a fourth file system, called FAT64, that's not for hard drives. I'll discuss it last.

FAT

Formatting a drive with the oldest of the file systems still used by windows, FAT, creates a 16-bit *file allocation table (FAT)*—that's the big spreadsheet. FAT's strength is that it is supported by all operating systems, but aside from that, FAT has some considerable limitations. For instance, FAT does not support disk partitions larger than 2.1 GB, and it offers no local file-level security. The main reason to keep FAT around is for backward compatibility with older operating systems. FAT is often referred to as FAT16, the label used in the Windows 9*x* versions.

FAT32

FAT32 is the 32-bit version of FAT that was introduced with Windows 95 OSR2. FAT32 supports partitions as large as 2 terabytes (TB). FAT32 is also more efficient than FAT16 at storing data. Like FAT16, however, FAT32 has no mechanism for controlling local security.

NTFS

Older versions of Windows operated well on FAT- and FAT32-formatted disks, but to get the full benefits of these as well as newer operating systems, you need New Technology File System (NTFS). Put simply, NTFS is the way to go in Windows. Why? How about the fact that NTFS supports partitions as large as 16 TB? How about built-in compression and encryption capabilities that let you conserve disk space and secure files against prying eyes? How about support for *disk quotas*—a method of limiting the amount of disk space a user can use—and dynamic disk configurations that enable you to add space to existing partitions on the fly? Oh, and the last three big reasons to use NTFS:

1. Security
2. Security!
3. *Security!!!*

NTFS supports local security, and without that, you have no true control over your resources. That reason alone is worth the price of admission!

> ### Exam Tip
> By default, NTFS supports partitions of up to 16 TB minus 4 KB. If using MBR-based drives, the limit is 2.2 TB, but that's a factor of MBR, not NTFS. To support larger partitions, use GPT and NTFS.

NTFS uses an enhanced file allocation table called the *master file table (MFT)* to keep track of the locations of files and folders. An NTFS partition keeps a backup copy of the most critical parts of the MFT in the middle of the disk, thus reducing the chance that a serious drive error can wipe out both the MFT and the MFT partial copy.

Compression NTFS enables you to compress individual files and folders to save space on a hard drive. Compression makes access time to the data slower, because the OS has to uncompress files every time you use them, but in a space-limited environment, sometimes that's what you have to do.

Encrypting File System One of the big draws with NTFS is file encryption, the black art of making files unreadable to anybody who doesn't have the right key. You can encrypt a single file, a folder, and a folder full of files. Microsoft calls the encryption utility in NTFS the *encrypting file system (EFS)*, but it's simply an aspect of NTFS, not a stand-alone file system.

> ### Exam Tip
> The CompTIA A+ exams in the past have referred to EFS as if it is a stand-alone file system. Don't be surprised if you see that on the exams.

To encrypt a file or folder, right-click it in My Computer/Computer and select Properties to open the folder's Properties dialog box (Figure 8.22). Click the Advanced button to open the Advanced Attributes dialog box. As you can see in Figure 8.23, the options for encryption (and compression) are simply selectable check boxes. Click the check box next to Encrypt Contents To Secure Data and then click the OK button—instantly, your file is safe from prying eyes! Keep in mind that encryption does not hide files; it simply makes them unreadable to other users.

January 10 Properties — ☒ ✕

| General | Security | Custom | Details | Previous Versions |

 January 10

Type of file: Microsoft Office Excel 97-2003 Worksheet (.xls)

Opens with: 📊 Microsoft Office Excel Change...

Location: C:\Users\michaels\Desktop

Size: 51.5 KB (52,736 bytes)

Size on disk: 52.0 KB (53,248 bytes)

Created: Tuesday, January 05, 2010, 8:29:40 AM

Modified: Wednesday, January 20, 2010, 9:51:36 AM

Accessed: Wednesday, January 20, 2010, 9:51:36 AM

Attributes: ☐ Read-only ☐ Hidden Advanced...

 OK Cancel Apply

FIGURE 8.22 Folder Properties dialog box

Travel Advisory

Windows home editions (Windows XP Home and Media Center, Windows Vista Home Basic and Home Premium, and Windows 7 Home Premium) do not support EFS.

Travel Advisory

Windows ties file encryption with EFS to specific user accounts and passwords. If an administrator resets a password for an account with encrypted files, those files will not be recoverable unless the user created an EFS recovery agent.

FIGURE 8.23 Options for compression and encryption

Disk Quotas

NTFS supports *disk quotas* that enable administrators to set limits on drive space usage for users. To set quotas, you must log in as an Administrator, right-click the hard drive name, and select Properties. In the Local Disk Properties dialog box, select the Quota tab and make changes. Figure 8.24 shows configured quotas for a hard drive. While rarely used on single-user systems, setting disk quotas on multi-user systems prevents any individual user from monopolizing the hard disk space.

FAT64

Everyone loves USB thumb drives. Their ease of use and convenience make them indispensible for those of us who enjoy sharing a program, some photos, or a playlist. But people today want to share more than just a few small files, and they can do so with larger thumb drives. As thumb drives grow bigger in capacity, however, the file system becomes a problem.

More Space (E:) Properties

| General | Tools | Hardware | Sharing |
| Security | Previous Versions | Quota | Customize |

Status: Disk quotas are disabled

☑ Enable quota management

☑ Deny disk space to users exceeding quota limit

Select the default quota limit for new users on this volume:

○ Do not limit disk usage

● Limit disk space to 500 MB ▼

Set warning level to 5 MB ▼

Select the quota logging options for this volume:

☑ Log event when a user exceeds their quota limit

☐ Log event when a user exceeds their warning level

Quota Entries...

OK Cancel Apply

FIGURE 8.24 Hard drive quotas

Travel Assistance

Chapter 9 discusses thumb drives and other removable media in detail.

The file system we have used for years on thumb drives, FAT32, does not work on drives larger than 2 TB. Worse, FAT32 limits *file* size to 4 GB. Now that you can find many thumb drives larger than 2 GB, Microsoft wisely developed a replacement for FAT32.

Exam Tip

FAT32 only supports drives up to 2 TB and only supports files up to 4 GB.

The newer file system, called *exFAT* or *FAT64*, breaks the 4-GB file size barrier, supporting files up to 16 exabytes (EB) and a theoretical partition limit of 64 zettabytes (ZB). Microsoft recommends a partition size of up to 512 TB on today's USB flash drives, which should be enough for a while. The exFAT file system extends FAT32 from 32-bit cluster entries to 64-bit cluster entries in the file table. Like FAT32, on the other hand, exFAT still lacks all of NTFS's extra features such as permissions, compression, and encryption.

Local Lingo

Exabytes and Zettabytes An *exabyte* is 2^{60} bytes; a *zettabyte* is 2^{70} bytes. For comparison, a terabyte is 2^{40} bytes. Remember from your binary practice that each superscript number doubles the overall number, so $2^{41} = 2$ TB, $2^{42} = 4$ TB, and so on. That means a zettabyte is really, really big!

How to Format a Partition

You can format partitions from the command line, using the **format** command, or from within the OS using My Computer/Computer. You can also use the Disk Management console.

Using format Syntax for **format** is as follows: **format** *drive* [/**v**:*label*]. For example, to format a hard drive with the letter D:, open a command-line window and type **format d:**. You are warned that all data will be lost; press the Y key to proceed or press N to cancel (see Figure 8.25). Note that the label parameter

```
Administrator: C:\Windows\system32\cmd.exe

C:\>format f: /fs:ntfs
The type of the file system is RAW.
The new file system is NTFS.

WARNING, ALL DATA ON NON-REMOVABLE DISK
DRIVE F: WILL BE LOST!
Proceed with Format (Y/N)? y
Verifying 2047M
Volume label (ENTER for none)?
Creating file system structures.
Format complete.
    2096482 KB total disk space.
    2083612 KB are available.

C:\>_
```

FIGURE 8.25 Using the **format** command from a Windows command-line window

switch is optional but useful if you want to assign the drive a distinct, user-friendly name in addition to its drive letter. Windows also offers the /fs: *file system* parameter switch, with which you can specify whether to format the partition with FAT or NTFS.

Using My Computer/Computer All versions of Windows enable you to right-click a partition or volume in My Computer/Computer or Windows Explorer and choose Format from the drop-down menu to open a Format dialog box (see Figure 8.26).

Using Disk Management Windows XP, Vista, and 7 offer a third way to format a partition—the Disk Management utility. Access the Disk Management console as described earlier and right-click an unformatted partition. Then select Format from the pop-up menu to open the Format dialog box (shown in Figure 8.27). Type a volume label (optional), select a file system from the drop-down menu, and specify any other options. Then click OK.

FIGURE 8.26 Using Computer to format a flash drive volume

FIGURE 8.27 Windows Vista Disk Management Format dialog box

Travel Advisory

If a drive has been previously formatted, you can save a lot of time when reformatting it by selecting *quick format* from the Disk Management options. This simply replaces the FAT or MFT with a blank one. A *full format* checks the drive clusters for read/write integrity.

Partitioning and Formatting During Installation

Windows includes a partitioning and formatting tool for the installation process. You can create one or more partitions on a blank drive, delete partitions on a drive already partitioned, and format partitions. The process is pretty straightforward. Just read the screen.

You should know about two potential quirks in the process. First, the installer tool will not delete a dynamic volume in Windows Vista or Windows 7. You need to use Disk Management for that process.

Second, if you're installing onto a drive that's plugged into an expansion card rather than the motherboard, you will need drivers. Each version of Windows has some support for third-party controllers, but if yours is not one of those, you need to press F6 (Windows XP) or click the Load driver option (Windows Vista/7) early in the installation process to signal Windows that you have drivers. After you've loaded drivers you can get into or continue with the partitioning tool and go from there.

Objective 8.04 # Protecting Data with RAID

A few sharp guys in Berkeley back in the 1980s organized the many techniques for using multiple drives for data protection and increasing speeds as the *redundant array of independent (or inexpensive) disks (RAID)*. They outlined seven levels of RAID, numbered 0 through 6.

Local Lingo

Array An *array* in the context of RAID refers to a collection of two or more hard drives.

- **RAID 0—Disk Striping** Disk striping requires at least two drives. It does not provide redundancy to data. If any one drive fails, all data is lost.

- **RAID 1—Disk Mirroring/Duplexing** RAID 1 arrays require at least two hard drives, although they also work with any even number of drives. RAID 1 is the ultimate in safety, but you lose storage space since the data is duplicated—you need two 100-GB drives to store 100 GB of data.

- **RAID 2—Disk Striping with Multiple Parity Drives** RAID 2 was a weird RAID idea that never saw practical use. Unused, ignore it.

- **RAID 3 and RAID 4—Disk Striping with Dedicated Parity** RAID 3 and RAID 4 combined dedicated data drives with dedicated parity drives. The differences between the two are trivial. Unlike RAID 2, these versions did see some use in the real world but were quickly replaced by RAID 5.

- **RAID 5—Disk Striping with Distributed Parity** Instead of dedicated data and parity drives, RAID 5 distributes data and parity information evenly across all drives. This is the fastest way to provide data redundancy. RAID 5 is by far the most common RAID implementation and requires at least three drives. RAID 5 arrays effectively use one drive's worth of space for parity. If, for example, you have three 2-TB drives, your total storage capacity is 4 TB. If you have four 2-TB drives, your total capacity is 6 GB.

Exam Tip

The CompTIA A+ certification exams expect you to be familiar with RAID levels 0, 1, 5, and 10 (see the upcoming Travel Advisory for the so-called RAID 10). If you see a question on "disk striping with parity," always assume the question is asking about RAID 5.

- **RAID 6—Disk Striping with Extra Parity** If you lose a hard drive in a RAID 5 array, your data is at great risk until you replace the bad hard drive and rebuild the array. RAID 6 is RAID 5 with extra parity information. RAID 6 needs at least five drives, but in exchange you can lose up to two drives at the same time. RAID 6 is gaining in popularity for those willing to use larger arrays.

Travel Advisory

After the first RAID levels were defined, some manufacturers came up with ways to combine different RAID arrays. For example, if you mirror two pairs of striped drives, you get what is called *RAID 0+1*. Or (read this carefully now) if you take two pairs of mirrored drives and stripe the pairs, you then get *RAID 1+0*, or what is often called *RAID 10*. Combinations of different types of single RAID are called *multiple RAID solutions* or *nested RAID*. Multiple RAID solutions, while enjoying some support in the real world, are quite rare when compared to single RAID solutions RAID 0, RAID 1, and RAID 5.

Local Lingo

JBOD *JBOD* stands for Just a Bunch of Disks (or Drives). It's a term used for a storage system composed of multiple independent disks, rather than disks organized using RAID.

Implementing RAID

All RAID implementations break down into either hardware or software methods. Software is often used when price takes priority over performance. Hardware is used when you need speed along with data redundancy. Software RAID does not require special controllers—you can use the regular ATA controllers or SCSI host adapters to make a software RAID array. But you do need "smart" software. The most common software implementation of RAID is the built-in RAID software that comes with Windows Professional, Business, and Ultimate editions. The Disk Management program in Windows Server editions can configure drives for RAID 0, RAID 1, or RAID 5, and it works with ATA and/or SCSI (Figure 8.28). Disk Management in Windows XP and Windows Vista can only do RAID 0, while Windows 7's Disk Management can do RAID 0 and 1.

Exam Tip

You need to know which level of RAID each OS can implement.

Computer Management										
File	Action	View	Window	Help						
Volume	Layout	Type	File System	Status	Capacity	Free Space	% Free	Fault Tolerance	Overhead	
(C:)	Partition	Basic	NTFS	Healthy (System)	74.52 GB	65.50 GB	87 %	No	0%	
Shares	RAID-5	Dynamic	NTFS	Healthy	931.52 GB	246.33 GB	26 %	Yes	33%	

Disk 0
Dynamic
465.76 GB
Online

Shares
465.76 GB NTFS
Healthy

Disk 1
Dynamic
465.76 GB
Online

Shares
465.76 GB NTFS
Healthy

1 N
Un

Disk 2
Basic
74.52 GB
Online

(C:)
74.52 GB NTFS
Healthy (System)

Disk 3
Dynamic
465.76 GB
Online

Shares
465.76 GB NTFS
Healthy

■ Unallocated ■ Primary partition □ RAID-5 volume

FIGURE 8.28 Disk management in Windows Server

Software RAID means the OS is in charge of all RAID functions. It works for small RAID solutions but tends to overwork your OS easily, creating slowdowns. When you *really* need to keep going, when you need RAID that doesn't even let the users know that a problem has occurred, hardware RAID is the answer.

Hardware RAID centers around an *intelligent* controller—either a SCSI host adapter or an ATA controller that handles all the RAID functions (Figure 8.29). Unlike a regular ATA controller or SCSI host adapter, these controllers have chips that know how to "talk RAID."

FIGURE 8.29 Serial ATA RAID controller

```
FastBuild <tm> Utility <c> 2004-2005 Promise Technology, Inc.
============================[ View Drives Assignments ]============================

    Channel:ID         Drive Model         Capacity <MB>   Assignment
         1:Mas  HDT722525DLA380                250059
                Extent 1                       249992        LD  1-1
         2:Mas  HDT722525DLA380                250059
                Extent 2                       249992        LD  1-2
         3:Mas  HDT722525DLA380                250059
                Extent 3                       249992        LD  1-3
         4:Mas  HDT722525DLA380                250059
                Extent 4                       249992        LD  1-4

==============================[ Keys Available ]==============================

   [↑] Up    [↓] Down   [ESC] Exit
```

FIGURE 8.30 RAID configuration utility

Most RAID setups in the real world are hardware based. Almost all of the many hardware RAID solutions provide *hot-swapping*—the ability to replace a bad drive without disturbing the OS. Hot-swapping is common in hardware RAID.

Hardware-based RAID is invisible to the OS and is configured in several ways, depending on the specific chips involved. Most RAID systems have a special configuration utility in flash ROM that you access after CMOS but before the OS loads. Figure 8.30 shows a typical firmware program used to configure a hardware RAID solution.

Objective 8.05 Maintaining and Troubleshooting Hard Drives

Hard drives are complex mechanical and electrical devices. HDDs have platters spinning at thousands of rotations per minute; they also generate heat and vibration. All of these factors make HDDs susceptible to failure. (With their lack of moving parts, SSDs don't fail like HDDs.) In this section, you will learn some basic maintenance tasks that will keep your hard drives healthy. For those inevitable instances when a hard drive fails, you will learn what you can do to repair them.

Maintenance

Hard drive maintenance can be broken down into two distinct functions: checking the disk occasionally for failed clusters, and keeping data organized on the drive so that it can be accessed quickly.

Error-Checking

Individual clusters on hard drives sometimes go bad. There's nothing you can do to prevent this from happening, so it's important that you check occasionally for bad clusters on the drives. The tools used to perform this checking are generically called *error-checking utilities,* although the terms for two older Microsoft tools—ScanDisk and chkdsk (pronounced "check disk")—are often used. Microsoft calls the tool Error-checking in current versions of Windows. Whatever the name of the utility, each does the same job: when the tool finds bad clusters, it puts the electronic equivalent of orange cones around them so that the system won't try to place data in those clusters.

Most error-checking tools do far more than just check for bad clusters. They go through all the drive's filenames, looking for invalid names and attempting to fix them. They look for clusters that have no filenames associated with them (we call these *lost chains*) and erase them. From time to time, the underlying links between parent and child folders are lost, so a good error-checking tool checks every parent and child folder. With a folder such as C:\TEST\DATA, for example, they make sure that the folder DATA is properly associated with its parent folder, C:\TEST, and that C:\TEST is properly associated with its child folder, C:\TEST\DATA.

To access Error-checking, open My Computer/Computer, right-click the drive you want to check, and choose Properties to open the drive's Properties dialog box. Select the Tools tab and click the Check Now button (Figure 8.31) to display the Check Disk dialog box, which has two options (Figure 8.32). Check the box next to Automatically fix file system errors, but save the option to Scan for and attempt recovery of bad sectors for times when you actually suspect a problem, because it takes a while on bigger hard drives.

Many techs run Error-checking from the command line using the chkdsk /f command. The /f tells the program to fix any problems discovered.

Now that you know how to run Error-checking, your next question should be, "How often do I run it?" A reasonable maintenance plan would include running it about once a week. Error-checking is fast (unless you use the Scan for and attempt recovery of bad sectors option), and it's a great tool for keeping your system in top shape.

The Tools tab in the Local Disk Properties dialog box in Windows XP

Check Disk Local Disk dialog box options

Exam Tip

The CompTIA 802 objectives mention "best practices" for scheduled check disks. That would imply running Error-checking on a regular basis using the Task Scheduler/Scheduled Tasks utility, but we don't really do that task. What it means in practice is that when you try to run Error-checking on the primary hard drive—the one with the in-use OS files—the utility will balk and *schedule* chkdsk to run automatically on reboot.

Defragmentation

Fragmentation of clusters can make your drive-access times increase dramatically. It's a good idea to defragment—or *defrag*—your drives as part of your monthly maintenance. You access the defrag tool, called Disk Defragmenter, the same way you access Error-checking—right-click a drive in My Computer/Computer and choose Properties—except you click the Defragment Now button on the Tools tab to open the Disk Defragmenter (Figure 8.33).

SSDs don't fragment like HDDs, so you don't need to defragment them at all. The tools in Windows Vista/7 detect SSDs and won't run on them. Be careful in Windows XP.

FIGURE 8.33 Disk Defragmenter in Windows XP

Defragmentation is interesting to watch—once. From then on, schedule it to run late at night. You should defragment your drives about once a month, although you could run it every week. If you run it every night, it takes only a few minutes. The longer you go between defrags, the longer it takes. If you don't run Disk Defragmenter, your system will run slower. If you don't run Error-checking, you may lose data.

Note
Windows Vista/7/8 run Disk Defragmenter automatically by default.

Exam Tip
Best practice for scheduled defragmentation is to let Windows (Vista/7/8) run it automatically. That means leaving the PC turned on but in sleep mode on Wednesday nights. That's when Disk Defragmenter runs by default.

Disk Cleanup

Did you know that the average hard drive is full of trash? Not the junk you intentionally put in your hard drive, like the 23,000 e-mail messages that you refuse to delete from your e-mail program. This kind of trash is all the files that you never see that Windows keeps for you. Here are a few examples:

- **Files in the Recycle Bin** When you delete a file, it isn't really deleted. It's placed in the Recycle Bin in case you decide you need the file later. I just checked my Recycle Bin and found 3 GB worth of files (Figure 8.34). That's a lot of trash!

- **Temporary Internet files** When you go to a Web site, Windows keeps copies of the graphics and other items on the page so that the page will load more quickly the next time you access it. You can see these files by opening the Internet Options applet on the Control Panel. Figure 8.35 shows my temporary Internet files.

- **Downloaded program files** Your system always keeps a copy of any Java or ActiveX applets that it downloads. You can see these in the Internet Options applet. You'll generally find only a few tiny files here.

FIGURE 8.34 Mike's Recycle Bin

FIGURE 8.35 Lots of temporary Internet files

- **Temporary files** Many applications create temporary files that are supposed to be deleted when the application is closed. For one reason or another, these temporary files sometimes aren't deleted. The location of these files varies with the version of Windows, but they always reside in a folder called Temp.

Every hard drive will eventually become filled with lots of unnecessary trash. All versions of Windows tend to act erratically when the drives run out of unused space. Fortunately, all versions of Windows have a powerful tool called Disk Cleanup (Figure 8.36). You can access Disk Cleanup in all versions of Windows by choosing Start | All Programs | Accessories | System Tools | Disk Cleanup.

Disk Cleanup gets rid of the four types of files just described (and a few others). Run Disk Cleanup once a month or so to keep plenty of space available on your hard drive.

Disk Management

Disk Management shows you the status of every drive in your system. Hopefully, most of the drives listed will be Healthy, meaning that nothing is happening to them and things are going along swimmingly. You're also already familiar with

FIGURE 8.36 Disk Cleanup dialog box

the Unallocated and Active status, but here are a few more to be familiar with for the CompTIA A+ exams:

- **Foreign Drive** You see this when you move a dynamic disk into another computer.
- **Formatting** As you might have guessed, you see this when you're formatting a drive.
- **Failed** Pray you never see this status, because it means that the disk is damaged or corrupt and you've probably lost some data.
- **Online** This is what you see if a disk is healthy and communicating properly with the computer.
- **Offline** The disk is either corrupted or having communication problems.

Troubleshooting

There's no scarier computer problem than an error that points to trouble with a hard drive. This section looks at some of the more common problems that occur with hard drives and how to fix them. These issues fall into three broad categories: installation, data corruption, and dying hard drives.

Installation Errors

Installing a drive and getting to the point at which it can hold data require four distinct steps: connectivity, CMOS, partitioning, and formatting. If you make a mistake at any point during any of these steps, the drive won't work. The beauty is that if you make an error, you can walk back through each step and check for problems.

Connectivity A connectivity error means something isn't plugged in correctly or something has managed to unplug itself. These problems virtually always show themselves at boot time. Here are some classics:

- Hard drive error
- No fixed disks present
- HDD controller failure
- No boot device available
- Drive not found

If you plug the data cable in backward for a PATA drive, for example, the computer simply won't see the drive—it's a famous error, and everyone who has ever installed a PATA hard drive has done it. Just reinsert the cable properly and

turn the machine back on. The power connectors aren't nearly as forgiving. If you install the power cable backward, you will destroy the drive in a dazzling display of sparks and smoke. Fortunately, the chamfers on Molex connectors make this mistake difficult to do.

You can usually conquer connectivity errors by carefully inspecting the entire connection system (including electricity) and finding the silly mistake (welcome to the club). Always remove and reseat the controller (if it's on an expansion card) if you get an HDD controller failure, as the controllers are prone to static buildup. Cables can go bad, but it is rare unless the cable is obviously ripped or pinched. The BIOS autodetection function will not detect a drive unless everything is installed correctly. It's a great, quick connectivity verifier.

If you've just installed the drive, check the jumper settings. You can't have two masters or two slaves on a single controller. And don't forget the 1 Drive or Standalone setting on some drives.

Installing two drives on the same controller dramatically increases the chances of errors. For example, adding a slave drive to an existing single drive requires that you check the first drive to see if its jumper needs to change from single to master. You need to make sure to install the slave drive properly or neither drive will work, causing the system to fail on boot. I've worked on many systems where I had to add a second drive to the secondary controller since it would not work with the existing drive.

CMOS Modern systems rarely get CMOS errors, because the autodetection feature handles most drives. The errors occur on older systems and generally fall into two groups: forgetting to run Autodetect and selecting the wrong sector translation in Autodetect. Two rules apply here: Always run Autodetect and *always* select LBA.

Older systems could lose CMOS data for a variety of reasons, including static electricity, inserting an expansion card, and blinking with too much force. It takes nothing to do a quick CMOS check to verify that the drive's geometry is correct using autodetection. Here are some of the more common errors that might point to CMOS problems:

- CMOS configuration mismatch
- No boot device available
- Drive not found
- Missing OS

If Autodetect fails to see the drive in question, it's probably a connectivity problem. Grab a screwdriver and look inside the system. This is also the one time where your hard drive's S.M.A.R.T. (Self-Monitoring, Analysis, and Reporting

Technology) functions may help. Unplug the drive and make it an extra drive on a working system. Go to the hard drive manufacturer's Web site and download its diagnostic tool and run it. If you get a failure, the drive is dead and there's nothing you can do except be really happy that you back up your data all the time.

Partitioning Partitioning errors generally fall into two groups: failing to partition at all and making the wrong size or type of partition. You'll recognize the former type of error the first time you open My Computer/Computer after installing a drive. If you forgot to partition it, the drive won't even show up in My Computer/Computer. If you made the partition too small, that will become painfully obvious when you start filling it up with files.

The fix for partitioning errors is simply to open Disk Management and do the partitioning correctly. If you've added files to a drive you're going to repartition, don't forget to back them up before you repartition.

Formatting Failing to format a drive makes the drive unable to hold data. Accessing the drive in Windows will result in a drive "is not accessible" error, and from a C:\ prompt, you'll get the famous "Invalid media" type error. Format the drive, unless you're certain that the drive is already formatted. Corrupted files can create the "Invalid media" type error. Check the sections on data corruption later in this chapter for the fix.

Most of the time, formatting is a slow, boring process. But sometimes the drive makes "bad sounds" and you start seeing errors like the one shown in Figure 8.37 at the bottom of the screen.

An *allocation unit* is Windows' term for a cluster. The drive has run across a bad cluster and is trying to fix it. For years, I've told techs that seeing this error a few (610) times doesn't mean anything, because every drive comes with a few bad spots. This is no longer true. Modern ATA drives actually hide a significant number of extra sectors that they use to replace bad sectors automatically. If a new drive gets a lot of "Trying to recover lost allocation unit" errors, you can bet that the drive is dying and needs to be replaced. Get the hard drive maker's diagnostic to be sure. Bad clusters are reported by S.M.A.R.T.

```
A:\>format C:/s

WARNING:   ALL DATA ON NON-REMOVABLE DISK
DRIVE C:   WILL BE LOST!
Proceed with Format   (Y/N)?y

Formatting  30709.65M

Trying to recover lost allocation unit 37,925
```

FIGURE 8.37 The "Trying to recover lost allocation unit" error

Mental Reinstall Focus on the fact that all of these errors share a common thread—you just installed a drive! Installation errors don't show up on a system that has been running correctly for three weeks; they show up the moment you try to do something with the drive you just installed. If a newly installed drive fails to work, do a "mental reinstall." Does the drive show up in the CMOS Autodetect? No? Then recheck the cables, master/slave settings, and power. If it does show up, did you remember to partition and format the drive? Did it need to be set to active? These are common-sense questions that come to mind as you march through your mental reinstall. Even if you've installed thousands of drives over the years, you'll be amazed at how often you do things such as forget to plug in power to a drive, forget CMOS, or install a cable backward. Do the mental reinstall—it really works!

Data Corruption

All hard drives occasionally get corrupted data in individual sectors. Power surges, accidental shutdowns, corrupted installation media, and viruses, along with hundreds of other problems, can cause this corruption. In most cases, this type of error shows up while Windows is running. Figure 8.38 shows a classic example.

You may also see Windows error messages saying one of the following:

* The following file is missing or corrupt
* The download location information is damaged
* Unable to load file

If core boot files become corrupted, you may see text errors at boot, such as the following:

* Cannot find COMMAND.COM
* Error loading operating system
* Invalid BOOT.INI
* BOOTMGR is missing

Winamp: winamp.exe - Unable To Locate Component ✕

This application has failed to start because libsndfile.dll was not found. Re-installing the application may fix this problem.

OK

FIGURE 8.38 A corrupted data error

On older programs, you may see a command prompt open with errors such as this one:

```
Sector not found reading drive C: Abort, Retry, Fail?
```

The first fix for any of these problems is to run the Error-checking utility. Error-checking will go through and mark bad clusters and hopefully move your data to a good cluster.

Extract/Expand If Error-checking fails to move a critically important file, such as a file Windows needs in order to load, you can always resort to the command line and try to extract the file from the Windows cabinet files. Most Windows programs store all files in a compressed format called CAB (short for cabinet file). One CAB file contains many files, and most installation disks have lots of CAB files (see Figure 8.39).

To replace a single corrupt file this way, you need to know two things: the location of the CAB file that contains the file you need, and how to get the file out so you can copy it back to its original spot.

In most cases, all the CAB files for a program are piled into some folder, as shown in Figure 8.39. Let's say you need a file called OLEPRO32.DLL. (I have no idea what this file does. I only know that Windows can't find it and you need to put it back!) Get to a command prompt within Windows and tell the expand

FIGURE 8.39 CAB files

command to check *all* the CAB files on your installation disc (drive E: in this example) with this command:

```
expand e:\i386\*.cab -f:olepro32.dll
```

The expand command goes through all the CAB files and finds the file. If you want to see details on the expand command, use Windows Help or type **expand** /? at a command prompt.

Corrupted Data on Bad Sectors If the same errors continue to appear after running the Error-checking utility, there's a chance that the drive has bad sectors.

Almost all drives today take advantage of built-in error correction code (ECC) that constantly checks the drive for bad sectors. If the ECC detects a bad sector, it marks the sector as bad in the drive's internal error map. Don't confuse this error map with a FAT. The partitioning program creates the FAT. The drive's internal error map was created at the factory on reserved drive heads and is invisible to the system. If the ECC finds a bad sector, you will get a corrupted data error as the computer attempts to read the bad sector. Error-checking utilities fix this problem most of the time.

Dying Hard Drive

Physical problems are rare, but they're devastating when they happen. If a hard drive is truly damaged physically, there is nothing that you or any service technician can do to fix it. Fortunately, hard drives are designed to take a phenomenal amount of punishment without failing. Physical problems manifest themselves in two ways: either the drive works properly but makes a lot of noise, or the drive seems to disappear.

Windows will give you error messages with read/write failures. Good hard drives don't fail to read or write. Only dying ones have these problems.

All hard drives make noise—the hum as the platters spin and the occasional slight scratching noise as the read/write heads access sectors are normal. If your drive begins to make any of the following sounds, however, it is about to die:

- Continuous high-pitched squeal
- Series of clacks or clicks, a short pause, and then another series of clacks or clicks
- Continuous grinding or rumbling

Back up your critical data and replace the drive. Windows comes with great tools for backing up data. Chapter 17 covers this in more detail.

You'll know when a drive simply disappears. If it's the drive that contains your OS, the system will lock up. You might get a Blue Screen of Death (BSoD), a Windows Stop error. When you try to restart the computer, you'll get a failure to boot and see this error message:

```
No Boot Device Present
```

If it's a second drive, it will simply stop showing up in My Computer/Computer. The first thing to do in this case is to fire up the System Setup program and see if Autodetect sees the drive. If it does, you do not have a physical problem with the drive. If Autodetect fails, shut off the system and remove the ribbon cable, but leave the power cable attached. Restart the system and listen to the drive. If the drive spins up, you know that the drive is getting good power. In most cases, this is a clue that the drive is probably good. In that case, you need to look for more mundane problems such as an unplugged power cord or jumpers incorrectly set. If the drive doesn't spin up, try another power connector. If it still doesn't spin up and you've triple-checked the jumpers and ribbon cable, you have a problem with the onboard electronics, and the drive is dead.

Travel Advisory

Most hard drives have three-year warranties. Before you throw away a dead drive, check the hard-drive maker's Web site or call the manufacturer to see if the drive is still under warranty. Ask for a return material authorization (RMA). You'll be amazed how many times you get a newer, usually larger, hard drive for free! It never hurts to check!

Troubleshooting RAID

For the most part, drive problems in a RAID array are identical to those seen on individual drives. There are a couple of errors unique to RAID, however, that need their own separate discussion.

Drives Not Recognized If you're using hardware RAID and the configuration firmware doesn't recognize one of the drives, first check to make sure the drives are powered and that they are connected to the proper connections. This is especially true of motherboards with onboard RAID that require you to use only certain special RAID connectors.

RAID Stops Working When one of the drives in a RAID array fails, several things can happen depending on the type of array and the RAID controller. With RAID 0, the effect is dramatic. Many enthusiasts use RAID 0 for their OS

drive to make it snappier. If you're running such a rig that then loses a drive, you'll most likely get a critical stop error, a BSoD. On reboot, the computer will fail to boot or you'll get a message that the OS can't be found. You lose all your data because there's no redundancy on a stripe set.

All the other levels of RAID tend to do nothing extraordinary when one drive in the array fails. When you reboot the system, that's when the RAID controller—if hardware—or Windows—if you've used the built-in tools—will squeal and tell you that a drive has failed.

Often, the failure of a drive will cause access to the contents of the drive to slow to a crawl, and that *slow performance* is your clue to check Device Manager or the RAID controller firmware. Some drive failures will cause the computer to crash. Others will show no effects until you get the error messages at reboot.

Regardless of the reason a RAID stops working or the effects, the fix is simple. Replace the failed drive and let the RAID rebuild itself. Life is good.

RAID Not Found The CompTIA A+ 220-802 exam objectives use the term "RAID not found," which doesn't really exist as an error but instead implies a series of errors where an existing RAID array suddenly fails to appear. The problem with these errors is that they vary greatly depending on the make and model of hardware RAID or (heaven forbid) if you used software RAID.

A properly functioning hardware RAID array will always show up in the configuration utility. If an existing array stops working and you enter the configuration utility only to find the array is gone, you have big trouble. This points to either dead drives or faulty controllers. In either case they must be replaced.

CHECKPOINT

✔**Objective 8.01: Hard Drive Technologies** You'll find three types of hard drives in personal computers today: PATA, SATA, and SCSI. PATA drives use either a 40-wire or 80-wire ribbon cable and a Molex power connector. SATA drives use a seven-wire ribbon cable and SATA power. SCSI drives differ according to the type of SCSI used, but most require a 68-pin ribbon cable and a Molex connector. A hard drive can be the traditional magnetic hard disk drive that stores data on platters or a solid-state drive that stores data on memory chips.

✔**Objective 8.02: Installing Hard Drives** PATA controllers can handle up to two drives on each cable. Set the jumpers on the drives as master, slave, or standalone, depending on the configuration of the system. SATA drives are point to point, whereas SCSI drives differ by technology. You can have up to 16 SCSI drives connected to a single controller as long as all the drives have unique SCSI IDs.

✔**Objective 8.03: Partitioning and Formatting** Partitioning and formatting establish the framework upon which your file system is built. Formatting creates the file system. Use NTFS whenever possible. You can use Disk Management to do both partitioning and formatting.

✔**Objective 8.04: Protecting Data with RAID** The many techniques for using multiple drives for data protection and increasing speeds are called the redundant array of independent disks (RAID). In the field, you're likely to run into three types of RAID. RAID 0 is called disk striping, using two drives as a single unit. RAID 1 is mirroring, where two drives contain matching content for data redundancy. RAID 5 is disk striping with parity. Three drives provide data redundancy, but this requires the equivalent of one drive's capacity. If you take two pairs of mirrored drives and stripe the pairs, you then get *RAID 1+0,* or what is often called *RAID 10.*

✔**Objective 8.05: Maintaining and Troubleshooting Hard Drives** Maintaining hard drives requires three pieces of software. Error-checking, or chkdsk, checks the physical disk for problems. Disk Defragmenter does exactly what it sounds like, taking files and folders fragmented on the drive and putting them back together. Disk Cleanup completes the triumvirate, enabling you to empty temporary files and other debris from your drive quickly and easily.

REVIEW QUESTIONS

1. What kind of cable fully supports a PATA drive running at 100 MBps?
 A. 7-wire
 B. 40-pin
 C. 68-pin
 D. 80-wire

2. What is the maximum data cable length for an internal SATA drive?

 A. 18 inches

 B. 36 inches

 C. 1 meter

 D. 2 meters

3. Which hard drive technology offers the best airflow?

 A. EATA

 B. PATA

 C. SATA

 D. SCSI

4. How does the controller differentiate among devices on a SCSI chain?

 A. Cable select

 B. Master/slave

 C. RAID number

 D. SCSI ID

5. Where do you terminate the SCSI chain? (Select the best answer.)

 A. Only at the ends

 B. Always at the controller

 C. Only on external devices

 D. Never on the controller

6. John has two hard drives set to cable select. Where should he place the drive he wants to be the C: drive?

 A. In the center of the cable, closest to the controller.

 B. At the end of the cable.

 C. It doesn't matter.

 D. This does not apply. He needs to jumper the drive's master and slave.

7. What partitioning method creates an MBR?

 A. Dynamic storage

 B. Master boot record

 C. Volume boot record

 D. Dynamic volume

8. What must a partition be to be bootable?

 A. Basic disk, active

 B. Dynamic disk, active

 C. Primary partition, active

 D. Extended partition, active

9. When do you format extended partitions?

 A. Immediately after you create them.

 B. After you create a primary partition.

 C. After you create a dynamic partition.

 D. You don't format extended partitions; you create logical drives in the extended partition and then format those.

10. Eileen has been called in to look at a client's machine and discovers that the computer has a second hard drive, but it doesn't have a drive letter. Instead, to access that drive she clicks a drive icon that says "My Stuff." What kind of partition is the "My Stuff" drive?

 A. Basic disk

 B. Extended partition

 C. Mounted volume

 D. Primary partition

11. What advantage does FAT have over FAT32?

 A. Larger partition size

 B. Better security

 C. Better compression

 D. None

12. Which format offers local file security?

 A. FAT

 B. FAT32

 C. NTFS

 D. NTFS32

13. What is the minimum number of drives required for disk striping with parity?

 A. One

 B. Two

 C. Three

 D. Four

14. What tool enables you to create a RAID 0 array in Professional and Business versions of Windows?

 A. Disk Management

 B. FDISK

 C. RAID Management

 D. SCSI configuration utility

15. What tool scans and corrects hard drive problems?

 A. Disk Management

 B. Disk Defragmenter

 C. Error-checking

 D. File Checker

REVIEW ANSWERS

1. **D** PATA drives running at 100 MBps need an 80-wire cable.

2. **C** SATA cables can be up to 1 meter long.

3. **C** The thin and narrow SATA cables offer the best airflow of the technologies mentioned.

4. **D** The controller uses the SCSI IDs to differentiate among different devices on the SCSI chain.

5. **A** Only terminate SCSI chains at the ends of the chain.

6. **B** With cable select, the drive at the end of the cable will get a drive letter before the one in the middle. Since C: is the first possible drive letter, he's got to place that drive at the end of the cable.

7. **B** A master boot record partitioning method creates an MBR.

8. **C** You need a primary, active partition to be bootable.

9. **D** Format the logical drives in an extended partition.

10. **C** "My Stuff" is a mounted volume.

11. **D** FAT32 pretty much blows FAT away.

12. **C** NTFS supports local file security.

13. **C** You need at least three drives to support a RAID 5 array.

14. **A** Disk Management is the tool for creating a software striped (RAID 0) array.

15. **C** Error-checking is the official name for the tool that scans and fixes hard drive problems.

Removable Media

CHAPTER 9

	NEWBIE	SOME EXPERIENCE	EXPERT
ETA	3 hours	2 hours	1 hour

Removable media refers to any type of mass-storage device that you can use in one system and then physically remove from that system and use in another. As a PC technician, you'll need to install, maintain, and troubleshoot removable media on users' systems, but you'll also use removable media to store and run software tools to perform all types of PC support.

This chapter covers the most common types of removable media used today. For the sake of organization, all removable media fall into these groups:

- **Floppy drives** The traditional floppy drive
- **Flash memory** From USB thumb drives to flash memory cards
- **Optical media** Any shiny disc technology from CD-ROMs to Blu-ray Discs
- **Tape media** Magnetic storage on flimsy ribbon inside a cartridge
- **External drives** Any hard drive, optical drive, or tape drive that connects to a PC via an external cable

Objective 9.01 Floppy Drives

When you insert a *floppy disk* into a *floppy drive*, the protective slide on the disk opens, revealing the magnetic media inside the plastic casing. A motor-driven spindle snaps into the center of the drive to make it spin. A set of read/write heads then moves back and forth across the disk, reading or writing tracks on the disk as needed. The few floppy disks in use today are 3.5 inches wide and store 1.44 MB of data (Figure 9.1). You use a 3.5-inch floppy drive to access the contents of the disk.

Whenever a system accesses a floppy disk in a floppy drive, a read/write LED on the outside front of the drive flashes on. You should not try to remove the floppy disk from the drive when this light is lit. That light means that the read/write heads are accessing the floppy disk, so pulling the disk out while the light is on can damage it. When the light is off, you can push in the small release button on the front of the drive to eject the disk.

Installing Floppy Drives

All Windows systems reserve the drive letters A: and B: for floppy drives. You cannot name them anything other than A: or B:, but you can configure a floppy drive to get either drive letter. Convention dictates that if you have only one

FIGURE 9.1 Internal floppy drive and floppy disk

floppy drive, however, you should call it A:. The second floppy drive will then be called B:.

Floppy drives connect to the computer via a *34-pin ribbon cable*. If the cable supports two floppy drives, it will have a seven-wire twist in the middle, used to differentiate electronically between the A: and B: drives (Figure 9.2). Because most users do not want two floppy drives, many system makers have dropped the twist and saved a couple of pennies on a simpler cable.

Exam Tip

Although floppy drives have disappeared from modern PCs, CompTIA continues to ask questions about them. Look for something on the ribbon cable, such as number of wires/pins (34) or distinctive twist, and the capacity of the disk (1.44 MB).

Inserting Ribbon Cables

Look at the ribbon cable shown in Figure 9.2 and notice the connector on the left side. This connector, identical to the other connectors on the same cable, plugs into the floppy controller on the motherboard, as shown in Figure 9.3. Be sure to orient the cable so that the colored stripe is aligned with Pin 1. Not all motherboards clearly label Pin 1's location—the motherboard shown in Figure 9.3 does not. Keep in mind that the connector is keyed so that it can be inserted in only one way.

Floppy B

Floppy A

Floppy Controller Plug

FIGURE 9.2 Floppy cable that supports two drives

After you insert the floppy ribbon cable into the floppy controller, you need to insert the ribbon cable into the floppy drive, also properly orienting Pin 1.

If the floppy drive is installed on the end connector, it becomes the A: drive; if the drive is installed on the middle connector, it is the B: drive. If you're installing only one floppy drive, make sure you install it in the A: drive position.

If you install the ribbon cable incorrectly, the floppy drive won't work. If you reverse one end of the cable, the floppy drive LED will come on and stay on, a classic signal. You won't hurt anything by doing this, so you can just put the cable on correctly and then check that the drive works.

FIGURE 9.3 Plugging a ribbon cable into a controller

Power

Floppy drives, just like every other device in the PC, need electricity to work. The 3.5-inch floppy drives use a mini power connector. Be careful! It is easy to insert a mini connector incorrectly, and if you install it incorrectly, you'll destroy the floppy drive and experience what we call "The Nasty Smell." In Figure 9.4, note the bottom view of a properly installed mini connector—note the chamfers (beveled edges) that show correct orientation. The problem lies in the plastic used to make the connector. The plastic connector bends easily, giving even the least brawny techs the ability to plug in a mini connector backward or to hit only three of the four pins.

CMOS

After the floppy drive is installed, you can configure the CMOS settings, which must correspond to the capacities of the drives. Look in your CMOS for a menu called "Standard CMOS Features" (or something similar to that) to see your floppy settings. Most CMOS setups configure the A: drive by default as a 3.5-inch, 1.44-MB drive, so in most cases the floppy drive is already configured. Simply double-check the setting in CMOS; if it's okay, exit without changing anything.

FIGURE 9.4 Properly installed mini connector

Objective 9.02 Flash Memory

Flash memory, the same flash memory that replaced CMOS technology for your system BIOS, found another home in PCs in the form of removable mass storage devices. Flash memory comes in two different families: USB thumb drives and memory cards. *USB thumb drives* contain a standard USB connection. *Memory card* is a generic term for a number of different tiny cards that are used in cameras, tablets, and other devices. Both of these families can manifest themselves as drives in Windows, but they usually perform different jobs. USB thumb drives have replaced virtually all other rewritable removable media as the way people transfer files or keep copies of important programs.

USB Thumb Drives

Moving data between computers is always a pain, and even more so since digital photography and multimedia storage has littered hard drives with huge files that won't fit on a single floppy disk. The USB flash memory drive— also known as the USB thumb drive, jump drive, or flash drive—has almost completely replaced the floppy disk. These tiny drives (Figure 9.5) are incredibly popular. For a low price, you can get an 8-GB thumb drive that holds as much data as 9800 standard 3.5-inch floppy disks—and it's much faster.

The smallest thumb drives are slightly larger than an adult thumbnail, whereas others are larger and more rounded. The drives are hot-swappable in Windows XP/Vista/7/8.

FIGURE 9.5 USB thumb drives

Flash Cards

Flash cards are used to store data on small appliances. Every digital camera and many cell phones come with slots for some type of memory card. Memory cards come in a number of different incompatible formats, such as CompactFlash (CF) and Extreme Digital (xD) Picture Card. The most popular types of card are Secure Digital (SD) and its two smaller siblings, Mini-SD and Micro-SD. Figure 9.6 shows typical cards. Keep in mind that most devices use only a single format, and with few exceptions, the cards are not interchangeable.

Card Readers

Whatever type of flash memory you use, your PC must have a *card reader* to access the data on the card directly. A number of inexpensive USB card readers are available (Figure 9.7), and some PCs, especially those tuned to home theater use, often come with built-in readers—handy to have when someone pulls out an SD card and says "Let's look at the pictures I just took!"

Of course, if the person just happened to bring along his or her camera and the usually proprietary USB cable, you could connect the camera to the PC and pull pictures in that way. Just make sure you have spare batteries. Wouldn't a card reader be a more elegant solution?

Whichever type of flash memory you have, understand that it acts exactly like a hard drive. If you want, you can format a memory card as well as copy, paste, and rename files stored on the card.

Travel Advisory

Most flash memory removable media is formatted with FAT32 (which does not have many of the powers of NTFS). If you copy, paste, or move files from an NTFS volume to a FAT32 USB thumb drive, those files will lose all NTFS attributes.

FIGURE 9.6 Typical flash memory cards

FIGURE 9.7 USB card reader

Maintaining and Troubleshooting Flash Media

Other than keeping the media clean, there's not much maintenance needed with flash media. Don't send it through the wash in your jeans (I've done this more than once), and don't touch the contacts on flash memory cards with your fingers. When flash media dies, there's no fix, so you have to replace it.

Objective 9.03 Optical Drives

C D, DVD, and Blu-ray Discs and drives come in a variety of flavors and standards, enabling you to back up data, record music, master a home video, and much, much more. Generically, we call them *optical discs* and the drives that support them *optical drives*. Optical drives that enable you to write to optical discs are called *burners*.

Optical discs come in three standards—*compact disc (CD)*, *digital versatile disc (DVD)*, and *Blu-ray Disc*—and three main styles: read-only, write-once, and rewritable.

Optical drives can read and write specific standards and styles—that is, a CD-ROM drive can read CD-ROM, CD-R, and CD-RW discs, but it can't write to any type of disc. Many optical drives support multiple media types. Most modern DVD drives, for example, are known as *combo drives* and can read and write to any optical media, including all of the CD styles. Here's a list of the common optical standards and styles:

- CD-ROM
- CD-R
- CD-RW
- DVD-ROM
- DVD-Video
- DVD-R

- DVD-R DL
- DVD-RW
- DVD-RW DL
- DVD+R
- DVD+R DL
- DVD+RW

- DVD+RW DL
- DVD-RAM
- BD-ROM
- BD-R
- BD-RE

Travel Advisory

Manufacturers label DVD drives that can read and write multiple DVD disc types as *DVD±RW*. There's no ± type, just − and +.

The types that end in *ROM* are read-only. The types that end in *R* are recordable once. *RW* and *RE* discs are rewritable many times. The DVD-Video is a DVD-ROM movie, such as the copy of *Star Trek* you got for your birthday. Blu-ray Discs are also used for movies and can use high-definition resolutions and include more extra features on a single disc. DVD-RAM is just different— an RW type that requires a special cartridge. *DL* stands for *dual-layer* and requires a bit more explanation about capacity.

Local Lingo

ISO 9660 Optical discs use a unique format, generally called *Compact Disc File System (CDFS)*, but more accurately the *ISO 9660 file system*.

Capacity

Optical discs vary considerably in capacity among CDs, DVDs, and Blu-ray Discs, and even more among various DVD and Blu-ray Disc types. CDs come in either 650-MB or 700-MB capacity. DVDs and Blu-ray Discs vary according to how many layers manufacturers use—single or dual—and whether they're single- or double-sided (the latter meaning you have to flip the disc over to get

the second half of the data). Blu-ray Discs do not yet come in a double-sided variety. Table 9.1 shows the various capacities.

Exam Tip

The CompTIA A+ certification exams use the DVD-industry term *GB* to denote the capacity of a DVD disc. According to the exams, therefore, a single-sided, single-layer DVD has a capacity of 4.7 GB. Also, expect the abbreviations for single-layer and dual-layer discs, such as *SL DVD* or *DL DVD*.

Note two things about DVD capacity: First, unlike CD media, DVD capacity is rated in billions of bytes, not the binary number you'd think. So a 4.7-GB disc holds 4,700,000,000 bytes of data, which translates to a mere 4.38 gigabytes. You don't need to know this for the CompTIA A+ certification exams, but a client might query you about the discrepancy. Second, you need a special dual-layer–capable DVD drive to burn a dual-layer disc.

Local Lingo

Gigabyte and **gigibyte** The computer industry has always used the term *gigabyte* (GB) with an *a* to refer to the binary number 2^{30}, or 1,073,741,824 bytes. The DVD industry has chucked that consensus, claiming that the term *gigabyte* specifically refers to the decimal number 10^9, or 1,000,000,000, and that the binary number 2^{30} is 1 *gigibyte* (GiB). Outside of Wikipedia and the DVD industry, nobody in the PC industry uses the term *gigibyte* and you won't find it on the CompTIA A+ certification exams.

TABLE 9.1	Standard DVD/Blu-ray Capacities	
	Single Layer	**Dual Layer**
Single-sided DVD	4.7 GB	8.5 GB
Double-sided DVD	9.4 GB	17.1 GB
Blu-ray Disc	25 GB	50 GB
Mini Blu-ray Disc	7.8 GB	15.6 GB

Speed

Though woefully slow compared with hard drive speeds, optical drive through-put has improved through the years from the 150-KBps speed of the original CD-ROM drive. Modern drives have up to three speeds listed for each action—read, write, and rewrite, listed in that order. Optical-media drives use a "number times" designation, such as 40×, to denote the speeds. It's simple math, so if you see 40×, think (40 × 150), and you'll come up with 6000-KBps throughput. A CD-RW will have three speeds, such as 48×32×52× for the write, rewrite, and read, respectively.

DVD drives read, write, and rewrite DVDs nine times faster than CD drives, so a 1× DVD drive and disc has a throughput of 1.32 MBps. They read and write CDs faster than that, though, so they often have multiple speeds listed, just like CD-R and CD-RW drives.

Blu-ray Disc burners can write to BD-R media at speeds up to 54 MBps (12×). They can rewrite BD-RE discs at speeds up to 9 MBps (2×) and read BD-ROM discs as fast as 36 MBps (8×). Blu-ray Disc burners can also burn to other media, such as DVD+/-RW discs and CD-R discs.

Installing Optical Drives

Most optical drives use parallel ATA (PATA) or serial ATA (SATA) connections and support the ATAPI (AT Attachment Packet Interface) standard. (Other con-nections, such as SCSI, are possible but less common. You'll definitely find USB external optical drives. See "External Drives" later in this chapter for details.) ATAPI treats an optical drive exactly as though it were an ATA drive. PATA opti-cal drives have regular 40-pin ATA connectors and master/slave jumpers. SATA optical drives use standard SATA cables. You install them the same way you would install any ATA hard drive. Figure 9.8 shows a typical DVD drive installa-tion using PATA. The DVD drive is configured as the slave with a master hard drive on a system's primary ATA controller. Optical drives require no CMOS changes as part of the install process.

A regular CD-ROM drive installation involves no applications. You install it, Windows sees it, and you're done. CD-R and CD-RW drives, in contrast, require that you install applications to enable their burning features. DVD-media drives need software to enable you to watch movies, burn DVDs, and so on, as do Blu-ray Disc drives. As of this writing, Nero Burning ROM (www.nero.com) and Roxio Creator (www.roxio.com) program suites share the crown as the most popular optical-media burning software applications.

FIGURE 9.8 Typical PATA DVD drive installation

Blu-ray Disc Drive Considerations

Physically installing, attaching, and maintaining optical drives are pretty straightforward, but a Blu-ray Disc drive (Figure 9.9) installation requires some special considerations. If you plan to use your Blu-ray Disc drive primarily for storage purposes, for example, system requirements are minimal. If you plan to watch Blu-ray Disc movies in HD resolution (720p, 1080i, or 1080p), on the other hand, the requirements are quite hefty.

FIGURE 9.9 Blu-ray Disc drive

Here's a list of recommended minimum specs:

- **Processor** At least a Pentium 4, Pentium D, or dual or multicore processor; or an AMD Athlon 64 X2 or Phenom multicore processor.
- **System Memory** At least 1 GB RAM for Windows XP; 2 GB RAM for Windows Vista/7/8.
- **Video** You need an HDCP-compliant (either DVI or HDMI) video card and drivers. That's a lot of initials in one sentence! Here's the scoop: The High-Bandwidth Digital Content Protection (HDCP) is a standard developed by Intel to ensure copyright protection. You learned about DVI and HDMI in Chapter 2.

CyberLink provides an awesome tool called BD and 3D Advisor that will tell you if your system meets the requirements to play Blu-ray Discs. You can get it at www.cyberlink.com/prog/bd-support/diagnosis.do.

Travel Advisory

Blu-ray Discs are considered high definition, whereas DVDs aren't. If you want HD video, go with Blu-ray Disc.

ISO Files

Ever wanted to make a perfect copy of an optical-media disc so that you can keep your original in a safe place? You can do so using a special file type called an ISO file. An *ISO file* is a complete copy—an ISO image as we say—of an optical-media disc. As you might imagine, they are huge files, but they are also very important to techs. Techs use ISO images to send each other copies of bootable utility CDs. For example, if you want a copy of the Ultimate Boot CD (an excellent utility for techs), you go to the Ultimate Boot Web site and download an ISO image. You then take your third-party burning program (the built-in burning software included with Windows XP and Vista can't do this, although Windows 7's can) and go through a special process called *burning an ISO image*. Learn how to burn ISO images with your burning program, because you'll use it all the time.

Troubleshooting Optical Drives and Discs

Optical drives are extremely reliable and durable PC components. At times, however, a reliable and durable device decides to turn into an unreliable, nondurable pile of plastic and metal frustration.

The single biggest problem with optical drives, especially in a new installation, is the connection. Your first guess should be that the drive has not been properly installed in some way. A few of the common culprits are forgetting to plug in a power connector, inserting a cable backward, and misconfiguring jumpers/switches. Although you need to know the type of drive, the test for an improper physical connection is always the same: using BIOS to see whether the system can see the optical drive.

The way in which a BIOS detects an optical drive depends on the system. Most BIOS makers have created intelligent BIOS software that can see an installed optical-media drive. Figure 9.10 shows an Award Software BIOS recognizing an optical drive during startup.

If the device is detected in BIOS, Windows will recognize the drive and you'll see it in My Computer/Computer and Device Manager.

If the drive won't read a CD-R or CD-RW disc, first try a commercial CD-ROM disc that is in good condition. CD-R and CD-RW discs sometimes have compatibility issues with CD-ROM drives. The same goes for a DVD-RW or any other writable DVD disc in your DVD drive. As mentioned, DVD drives have issues with media incompatibility. Also, no optical drive will read badly scratched discs.

If the drive still does not see a disc, try cleaning the drive. Most modern optical drives have built-in cleaning mechanisms, but from time to time, you need to use a commercial optical-drive cleaning kit (see Figure 9.11).

Optical drives are not cleaned too often, but the discs are. Although a number of fine optical-disc cleaning kits are available, most discs can be cleaned quite well with nothing more than a damp, soft cloth, sometimes with a mild

```
●Award Modular BIOS v6.00PG, An Energy Star Ally
🏵Copyright (C) 1984-2003 Phonix Technologies, LTD

Main Processor : AMD Athlon(tm) 64 Processor 3200+
Memory Testing : 1048576K OK
CPU0 Memory Information: DDR 400 CL:3 ,1T Dual Channel, 128-bit

IDE Channel 1 Master : WDC WD1200JB-75CRA0 16.06V16
IDE Channel 1 Slave  : None
IDE Channel 2 Master : TOSHIBA CD=DVDW SDR5372V TV11
IDE Channel 2 Slave  : None
```

FIGURE 9.10　BIOS recognizing an optical drive at boot

FIGURE 9.11 Optical-drive cleaning kit

detergent. Always wipe from the center of the optical disc to the edge—never clean an optical-media disc using a circular motion.

Travel Advisory

A common old tech's tale about cleaning optical discs is that they can be washed in a dishwasher! Although this may seem laughable, the tale has become so common that it requires a serious response. This is *not true* for two reasons: First, the water in most dishwashers is too hot and can cause the discs to warp. Second, the water pushes the discs around, causing them to hit other objects and get scratched. Don't do it!

The final problem with optical drives—stuck discs—comes from *technician* error and is not actually the fault of the drives. I can't tell you the number of times I've pulled an optical drive out of a system to replace it, only to discover that I or my customer left an essential disc inside the now-powerless drive. Luckily, most optical drives have a small hole in the front, usually just below the drive opening, into which you can insert a wire—an unbent paper clip is the standard tool for this purpose—and push on an internal release lever that will eject the disc.

Objective 9.04 Tape Drives

Tape drives connect to the ATA or SCSI bus, just like optical drives, but rather than using a shiny CD-R or DVD+R disc, you store data on magnetic tape (see Figure 9.12). Tape drives were used for many years as primary backup drives because tape was cheap in comparison to hard drives.

There are a large number of different tape formats, but CompTIA lists only one technology, Digital Linear Tape (DLT), in the CompTIA A+ Acronyms list. DLT was a popular tape format from the 1980s up to the early 2000s, with capacities from 10 MB in the early versions up to (arguably) around 800 GB. DLT is rarely used anymore, and CompTIA should have removed this from the CompTIA A+ exam competencies.

FIGURE 9.12 Backup tapes

Tape drive manufacturers have done pretty much everything they can to make tape backups as fast as possible, but the technology suffers from two huge drawbacks. First, it's tape, which means all data must be stored and restored in sequential access. The drive has to go through Files 1 and 2 before reaching File 3, in other words. Second, tape is painfully slow in comparison to hard drives, optical drives, or flash-media drives. With plenty of cheap online, hard drive, and recordable optical-media options available for backup, though, tape's days are numbered.

Objective 9.05 External Drives

External drives enable you to add functions and storage to your system without opening the case. If you want to add the capability to play Blu-ray Disc movies to your PC, for example, you could simply add an external Blu-ray Disc drive. *Enclosures* enable you to connect internal hard drives—both can find external versions of all the optical drive types and external hard drive enclosures for 3.5" desktop hard drives and 2.5" portable hard drives—without using a screwdriver at all. Figure 9.13 shows a typical external hard drive enclosure.

FIGURE 9.13 External hard drive enclosure

Connection Types

All PCs have one or more external expansion busses, enabling you to add an external drive to any system. Hi-Speed USB (USB 2.0) is the most common today, but you'll also see FireWire 400, FireWire 800, SuperSpeed USB (USB 3.0), and eSATA.

Performance-wise, SuperSpeed USB is the fastest, with eSATA close behind. The two FireWire standards offer excellent sustained data transfers, though they're much rarer than Hi-Speed USB. The least expensive option, as you might suspect, is USB 2.0; it's the most common and the slowest performer. Choose wisely when picking an external drive type.

Exam Tip

CompTIA likes to mix things up on removable media questions. You might get a question on a removable drive that connects via 50- or 68-pin SCSI. These devices exist, but are not commonly used. The same is true about external tape drives.

Finally, you should know about external storage devices connecting via Ethernet. Such devices, called *network attached storage (NAS)* boxes, are purpose-built computers that have a narrow set of functions, namely to enable you to store data in a central location over a network. Check out www.drobo.com for the flagship consumer-oriented NAS boxes.

Uses for External Drives

External drives have three basic functions: installing software, backup, and troubleshooting. Many smaller portable computers, such as Ultrabooks, don't have optical drives at all. One common way to add software is to use an external optical drive. You can leave it at home when travelling to keep the weight down in your pack, but have it handy for upgrades and new apps.

Although tape is the traditional backup media for computers, it's slow, painfully slow. Plus, if you want to recover something from the tape, you must access it sequentially.

External drives have become the go-to choice for small office/home office (SOHO) backup solutions for a couple of reasons. First, they're much faster than any other backup solution. Second, hard drive prices have collapsed at the same time that capacity has skyrocketed. You can get a lot of storage for just a little cash these days.

FIGURE 9.14 Hard drive dock

As troubleshooting tools, hard drive enclosures enable you to run diagnostic tests on many hard drives quickly, all without worrying about installing the drives into a case. When clients bring in dead PCs, for example, we can pop their hard drive out and slip it into one of the slots in a hard drive dock (Figure 9.14)—connected via eSATA or USB 3.0—and run chkdsk in a matter of seconds.

CHECKPOINT

✔**Objective 9.01: Floppy Drives** The most common type of floppy disks stores 1.44 MB of data and requires a properly installed floppy disk drive. Internal floppy drives connect to a floppy drive controller using a 34-pin ribbon cable with a twist to distinguish drive A: (end of cable) from drive B: (middle of cable). Orient the cable pin 1 to pin 1. Floppy drives use a mini power connector.

✔**Objective 9.02: Flash Memory** Flash memory comes in two different families: USB thumb drives and memory cards. USB thumb drives are flash devices that contain a standard USB connection. Memory card is a generic term for a number of different tiny cards that are used in cameras, tablets, smartphones, and other devices.

✔**Objective 9.03: Optical Drives** Optical discs and drives come in several formats—CD, DVD, and Blu-ray Disc—and three main styles: read-only, write-once, and rewritable. The different media offer dramatically different capacities, with the typical CD holding 650 MB, whereas the lowest-capacity DVD holds 4.7 GB of data, and a dual-layer Blu-ray Disc can hold 50 GB of data. Optical drives connect the same way as hard drives, following the rules of PATA, SATA, SCSI, and so on.

✔**Objective 9.04: Tape Drives** Tape drives store data sequentially on magnetic tapes. The technology was widely used as backup, though it's rare today because hard drive capacity is plentiful and cheap and hard drives are much faster than tape drives.

✔**Objective 9.05: External Drives** External drives are standard drives that connect to one of four busses: FireWire, USB, eSATA, or SCSI. Of the four, FireWire and Hi-Speed USB are the most common. You'll also find NAS boxes that enable external data storage over an Ethernet network. Typical uses for external drives are installing programs, backups, and troubleshooting.

REVIEW QUESTIONS

1. You installed a floppy drive that you want to function as the A: drive, but your system won't boot to it. What is the most likely cause of this problem?

 A. You attached the drive to the middle connector on the cable.

 B. You attached the drive to the end connector on the cable.

 C. You forgot to configure the CMOS settings for drive A:.

 D. You forgot to configure the CMOS settings for a single floppy drive.

2. You just installed a floppy drive and you notice that the drive LED stays on. What is most likely the problem?

 A. You attached the floppy drive to the wrong connector on the ribbon cable.

 B. You forgot to configure the floppy drive through the CMOS setup.

C. You did not attach the colored stripe on the ribbon cable to Pin 1 at the drive or at the controller.

D. You forgot to attach the power cable to the floppy drive.

3. What is the minimum capacity of a Blu-ray Disc?

A. 650 MB

B. 4.7 GB

C. 25 GB

D. 50 GB

4. What type of device must be installed on your system in order to access data on a flash memory card?

A. Scanner

B. Card reader

C. Floppy drive

D. Zip drive

5. A copy of an optical-media disc can be saved as what type of file?

A. ISO

B. ISO-9660

C. INF

D. CDDA

6. Both CD and DVD drive speeds are based on multiples of the original CD-ROM drive speed. What is that speed?

A. 100 KBps

B. 150 KBps

C. 100 MBps

D. 150 MBps

7. A CD-RW has a speed rating of 48×32×52×. What do the three numbers refer to, in order?

A. Write, rewrite, read

B. Read, write, rewrite

C. Rewrite, read, write

D. Write, read, rewrite

8. What settings in the CMOS setup must you change to install an optical drive?

A. Number of heads and cylinders in the drive

B. Whether the drive is installed on the primary or secondary IDE channel

 C. Whether the jumpers on the drive are set to master or slave

 D. None, because an optical drive is not configured through the CMOS setup

9. What type of DVD can store 17.1 GB of data or more than eight hours of video?

 A. Double-sided, single-layered

 B. Single-sided, single-layered

 C. Single-sided, dual-layered

 D. Double-sided, dual-layered

10. What type of video card must you have to watch Blu-ray Discs on your computer?

 A. AGP

 B. HDCP-compliant

 C. HDMI-compliant

 D. ISA

REVIEW ANSWERS

1. **A** When you install a floppy drive that you want to function as the A: drive, you should attach it to the end connector, not the middle connector.

2. **C** If you just installed a floppy drive and you notice that the drive LED stays on, you most likely reversed the cable on one end, so the colored stripe on the ribbon cable did not go to Pin 1.

3. **C** A single-layer Blu-ray Disc holds 25 GB of data.

4. **B** A card reader must be installed on your system in order to access data on a flash memory card.

5. **A** CDs and DVDs can be copied as ISO files.

6. **B** Both CD and DVD drive speeds are based on multiples of 150 KBps, the speed of the original CD-ROM drives.

7. **A** If a CD-RW has a speed rating of 48×32×52×, the three numbers refer, in order, to the write, rewrite, and read speeds.

8. **D** You do not have to change any CMOS settings when you install an optical drive because it is not configured through the CMOS setup.

9. **D** For a DVD to store 17.1 GB of data or over eight hours of video, the disc must be double-sided, dual-layered.

10. **B** To watch Blu-ray Discs on your computer, your video card must be HDCP-compliant.

Peripherals and Specialty PCs

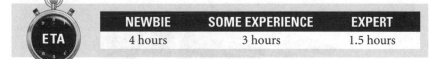

	NEWBIE	SOME EXPERIENCE	EXPERT
ETA	4 hours	3 hours	1.5 hours

At this point in the book, you know about ports, processing, and storage; now it's time for you to learn about the final step in the computing process—input/ output (I/O)—and put it all together. Most input devices plug into ports built into the motherboard, as do some of the common output devices, notably speakers. Other output devices plug into expansion cards that you need to add and configure. This chapter looks at input devices, expansion cards, and output devices, and then finishes up with recommended configurations for specialty PCs.

Objective 10.01 Input Devices

Input devices enable you to interact with the computer and give it commands through typing, clicking, speaking, and touching. Windows supports common devices, such as a basic keyboard, straight out of the box, but some fancier or specialty input devices require drivers and configuration. This section looks at the input devices you're likely to see in the field and run into on the 801 exam.

Keyboards

The keyboard continues to be the primary input device for the PC, as it has been since the original IBM PC several decades ago. Keyboards come in wired (PS/2 and USB) and wireless (radio frequency, or RF, and Bluetooth) versions. Windows supports standard QWERTY keyboards completely; extra features, like the multimedia controls on the fancy keyboard in Figure 10.1, require drivers.

| **FIGURE 10.1** | Fancy multimedia keyboard |

You can adjust keyboard settings, such as the repeat rate when you hold down a key, in the Keyboard Control Panel applet.

The primary issue with keyboards for techs is keeping them dry and not sticky. This means educating users who require a replacement keyboard to use common sense—don't eat or drink over a keyboard if you want it to last!

Pointing Devices

Moving a cursor across the screen and clicking or double-clicking a screen element requires some kind of pointing device. Most PCs have a mouse attached (same connection options as keyboards) with two buttons and a scroll wheel (see Figure 10.2). The buttons enable the left and right clicks; the wheel scrolls the page (in whatever application) up and down. Modern *optical mice* use LEDs or lasers to track movement around a mouse pad.

Local Lingo

Ball mouse Early mice used with PCs had a small ceramic ball that rolled around under the mouse. Sensors tracked the motion, and the cursor on the screen would move. These types of mice collected dust and grime over time and had to be cleaned regularly. Accordingly, we love optical mice—no moving parts!

FIGURE 10.2 Optical mouse

FIGURE 10.3	Trackball

Some PC users prefer a *trackball* (see Figure 10.3) to a mouse. Trackballs can provide welcome relief for people with damaged wrists or arms. Movement is controlled by a thumb or finger moving a ball around, with the movement tracked by sensors in the trackball. The key maintenance issue with trackballs is to keep them clean. If necessary, you can pop the ball out and use a cotton swab and denatured alcohol to clean the sensors. The Mouse applet in the Control Panel enables you to change settings for both mice and trackballs.

A touchpad (see Figure 10.4) offers a static cursor control surface, where the movement of your finger or fingers on the pad moves the cursor around the screen. Although you'll find these primarily on portable computers and not desktops at the time of this writing, Windows 8 will most likely change that in a big way over the next few years. Current stand-alone touchpads connect via USB

FIGURE 10.4	Wacom touchpad

or Bluetooth, although other technologies may be in use by the time you read this book. We'll revisit touchpads in Chapter 12 when we talk about portable computers.

> **Travel Advisory**
>
> Windows 8 uses an interface that functions very much like a tablet or smartphone interface, where you use your fingers to scroll up and down and swipe right and left. Use a touchpad or scroll wheel on a mouse to use the interface properly.

Imaging Tools

Four peripheral types enable you to capture a static or moving image from life, digitize it, and save it on the computer to view again: scanners, cameras, camcorders, and webcams. Almost every modern imaging device plugs into USB, so no real issues there on troubleshooting for a tech. Let's look at each device type.

Scanners

You use a scanner to make digital copies of existing paper photos, documents, drawings, and other items. Better scanners give you the option of copying directly from a photographic negative or slide, providing images of stunning visual quality—assuming the original photo was halfway decent, of course.

All consumer-level scanners—called *flatbed scanners*—work the same way. You place a photo or another object face-down on the glass, close the lid, and then use software to initiate the scan. The scanner runs a bright light along the length of the glass tray one or more times to capture the image. Figure 10.5 shows an open scanner.

The scanning software that controls the hardware can be manifested in a variety of ways. Nearly every manufacturer includes some sort of drivers and other software to create an interface between your computer and the scanner. When you push the front button on an Epson Perfection scanner, for example, the Epson software opens the Photoshop program as well as its own interface (Figure 10.6).

You can also open your favorite image-editing software first and choose to acquire a file from a scanner. Figure 10.7 shows the process of acquiring an image from a scanner in the popular shareware image-editing software Paint Shop Pro. As in most such software, you choose File | Import and then select a source. In this case, the scanner uses the traditional TWAIN drivers. *TWAIN* stands for *Technology Without an Interesting Name* and has been the default driver type for scanners for a long time.

| FIGURE 10.5 | Scanner open with photograph face-down |

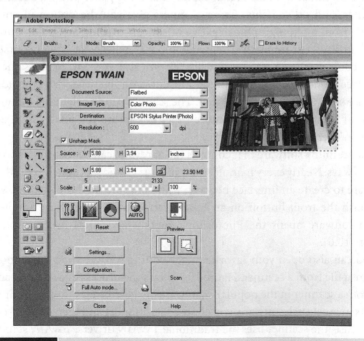

| FIGURE 10.6 | Epson software interface with Photoshop open in the background |

FIGURE 10.7 Acquiring an image in Paint Shop Pro

Travel Advisory

If you travel a lot, you'll want to make sure to use the locking mechanism for the scanner light assembly. Just be sure to unlock it before you try to use it, or the light will be stuck in one position. That won't make for very good scans!

Digital Cameras

Another input option available for those not-yet-taken pictures is to put away your point-and-shoot film camera and use a digital camera (Figure 10.8). Digital cameras are a wonderful tool for capturing a moment and then sending it to friends and relatives. Most current digital cameras enable you to take both still photos and video.

FIGURE 10.8 Typical digital camera

Digital cameras use flash memory—such as Secure Digital (SD)—to store pictures and connect to PCs via a USB cable. Another common option, though, is to connect only the camera's storage media to the computer, using one of the many digital media readers available.

Windows has limited photo-editing options built in; Macs have iPhoto. Do yourself a favor and download Picasa from Google if you want to do image editing on the inexpensive side. Otherwise, both Paint Shop Pro and Photoshop offer superb editing tools.

Camcorders

Camcorders (see Figure 10.9) enable you to capture full-motion video of that wonderful moment (so you can watch Junior poop explosively every time an unwelcome girl visits the house many years later). Camcorder capture has evolved from analog film and tape of various sorts to full digital. Storage media today vary from built-in hard drives and SSDs to flash media (permanent or on a removable card). You can spend $200 on a camcorder that can record in full 1080p HD, with vibrant color and stereo sound, so what are you waiting for? Junior's growing up quickly!

FIGURE 10.9 Typical camcorder

You need specialized applications to work with the stored output of camcorders. Windows comes with Windows Live Movie Maker; Macs offer iMovie; either program enables you to edit recorded footage. Better programs, such as Final Cut Pro and Premier, offer more features, though at a cost.

Web Cameras

PC cameras, often called *webcams,* enable you to chat over the Internet with video. Webcams measure their resolution in pixels. You can find webcams with resolutions of as few as 100,000 pixels and webcams with millions of pixels. Most people who use webcams agree that 1.3 million pixels (1 megapixel) is pretty much the highest resolution you can use before your video becomes so large it will bog down a broadband connection.

Most people who use online video will also want a microphone. Many cameras come with microphones, or you can use a separately purchased device. Those who do a lot of video chatting may prefer to get a camera without a microphone, and instead buy a good quality headset with which to speak and listen.

Windows comes with a limited set of webcam drivers, so always make sure that you install the drivers supplied with the camera before you plug it in.

The biggest challenge to using webcams is getting your webcam applications to recognize that your webcam is available and configured for use. Every program does this differently, but conceptually the steps are the same (with plenty of exceptions):

1. Tell the program you want to use a camera.
2. Tell the program whether you want the camera to turn on automatically when you chat.
3. Configure the image quality.
4. Test the camera.

If you're having problems with a camera, always go through the general I/O problems first, as this will clear up most problems. If you're still having problems getting the camera to work in a program, be sure to turn off all other programs that may also be using the camera. Windows allows only one program at a time to use a webcam.

Multimedia Devices

Various peripherals fall into the category of multimedia, most notably sound input devices. The PC is a great platform for recording and editing sound and music. Two types of devices are microphones and MIDI devices.

Plug a *microphone* into a sound card or microphone port if you want to input audio into a PC (see Figure 10.10). A microphone records sound by detecting vibrations and turning them into an electronic signal. Microphones are most commonly used for recording voices and for video chatting, such as through Skype.

Travel Advisory

You can also buy microphones that connect via USB instead of the microphone port.

MIDI-enabled devices, also known as *MIDI controllers,* come in several form factors, but most look and feel like standard music keyboards (see Figure 10.11).

FIGURE 10.10 A standard microphone

FIGURE 10.11 A MIDI keyboard

Others use a grid or row of square buttons—the best ones light up, too! In the past, MIDI devices used MIDI-to-serial or MIDI-to-joystick-port adapters, but almost all modern MIDI controllers use USB connections.

> **Exam Tip**
>
> A MIDI/joystick port on a PC was a 15-pin, two-row, female DB (or D-shell) port. These are long gone from PCs, but might show up on the 801 exam.

Many MIDI controllers can do more than just play music. More elaborate models include extra knobs, sliders, and buttons for controlling the digital audio workstation software. Your audio software should include options and instructions for configuring the MIDI device, but for many applications, you can just plug it in and start playing.

Game Controllers

Whether you're flying a state-of-the-art jet fighter or racing through tight turns at top speeds, having the right controller for the job is important for an enjoyable gaming experience. Two peripherals are commonly used for controlling PC games: joysticks and gamepads.

Over the past decade, flight simulator programs have declined in popularity, and so have joysticks (see Figure 10.12). Once a required component of a gamer's arsenal, you only need joysticks now if you are a serious flight simulator fan. Most modern PC games are controlled by mouse and keyboard.

FIGURE 10.12 A joystick

Some PC games, especially those that were designed to be played on consoles like the Microsoft Xbox 360 or Sony PlayStation 3 are best enjoyed when using a gamepad. A *gamepad* looks more like your standard video game controller, usually covered in an array of buttons and triggers (see Figure 10.13).

Joysticks and gamepads have used plenty of connectors over the years, including the eponymous joystick connector. These days, they all connect to your PC via USB. Depending on the complexity of the controller, you may need to install drivers to get a joystick or gamepad working. Simpler controllers, however, can probably get by using the default gamepad drivers included in Windows.

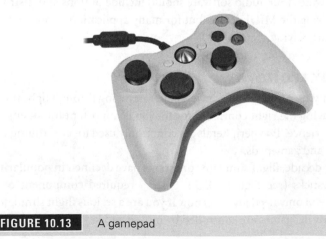

FIGURE 10.13 A gamepad

You'll need to configure your joystick or gamepad to make sure all the buttons and controls work properly. In Windows XP and Vista, open the Game Controllers Control Panel applet. In Windows 7, open the Start menu and select Devices and Printers. Right-click the controller and select *Game controller settings*. Select your device from the list of controllers and click Properties. Depending on your gamepad or joystick, you'll be able to configure the buttons, sticks, triggers, and more (see Figure 10.14). You can calibrate the analog sticks so they accurately register your movements. You can even adjust the amount of vibration used by the controller's force feedback (if available).

FIGURE 10.14 Game controller properties

Travel Advisory

You might also need to configure your controller from within the game you want to play. Most games are set to use keyboard and mouse controls by default. You'll need to play around with the settings to enable your game controller.

Once you've set up your controller, you should be ready to take to the skies, or the streets, or wherever else you go to game.

Specialty Input Devices

The CompTIA A+ certification exams want to make sure you're aware of four other types of I/O devices: biometric scanners and bar code readers; touch screens; graphics tablets; and keyboard, video, mouse (KVM) switches. Let's look at these specialized devices.

Biometric Devices

PCs use biometrics for security. Biometric security devices scan and remember unique aspects of various body parts, such as your retina, iris, head image, or fingerprint, using some form of sensing device, such as a retinal scanner. This information is used as a key to prevent unauthorized people from accessing whatever the biometric device is securing. The USB thumb drive in Figure 10.15 has a tiny fingerprint scanner. You slide your finger (any finger you choose) over the drive to unlock the contents of the thumb drive.

FIGURE 10.15 USB thumb drive with fingerprint scanner (courtesy of Lexar Media, Inc.)

Less common are biometric security devices that secure entire computers. The Microsoft fingerprint scanner is a USB device that replaces standard user name and password security. Figure 10.16 shows the scanner built into a keyboard. When a program or Web site asks for a user name and password, you simply press your finger against the fingerprint scanner. It will confirm your identity (assuming your fingerprint matches), and then special software that comes with the scanner will supply the program or Web site with your stored user name and password.

No matter what biometric device you use, you follow the same steps to make it work.

1. Install the device.

2. Register your identity with the device by sticking your eye, finger, or other unique body part (why are you snickering?) into the device so it can scan you.

3. Configure its software to tell the device what to do when it recognizes your scanned identity.

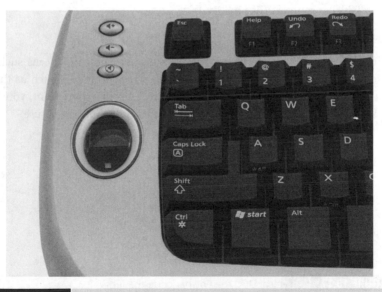

FIGURE 10.16 Microsoft fingerprint scanner on a keyboard

Bar Code Readers

Bar code readers are designed to read standard Universal Product Code (UPC) bar codes (Figure 10.17). You would want to read bar codes for only one reason—to track inventory. Bar code readers enable easy updating of inventory databases stored on PCs. These readers are just about the oldest "specialty" I/O device used with PCs. Older bar code readers used serial ports, but all newer readers use USB ports. No configuration is usually necessary, other than making sure that the particular reader works with the database/point-of-sale software you use.

Touch Screens

A *touch screen* is a monitor with some type of sensing device across its face that detects the location and duration of contact, usually by a finger or stylus. All touch screens then supply this contact information to the PC as though it were a click event from a mouse. Here are a few places you'll see touch screens at work:

- Information kiosks
- Smartphones
- Point-of-sale systems
- Tablet PCs
- Tablet computers (like the iPad)
- Windows 8 desktop PCs

Touch screens can be separated into two groups: built-in screens such as those in smartphones, and stand-alone touch screen monitors such as those used in many point-of-sale systems. From a technician's standpoint, you can think of a stand-alone touch screen as a monitor with a built-in mouse.

FIGURE 10.17 Typical UPC read by bar code readers

Graphics Tablets

PCs and Macs have quickly become the most powerful and flexible tools available for visual artists. Given the number of applications dedicated to producing various visual styles, including painting, sketching, animation, and more, digital art stands toe-to-toe with its more traditional counterpart. It's only reasonable that a category of hardware would appear to help users take advantage of these tools.

A *graphics tablet* or *digitizer* (also known as a *pen tablet*) enables users to paint, ink, pencil, or otherwise draw on a computer (see Figure 10.18). Now, don't get carried away and start taking watercolors to your monitor. The digitizer receives input using a special surface. When a user presses against the surface, usually using a stylus, the surface transforms (or digitizes) the analog movements into digital information. The drawing application receives the information from the digitizer and turns it into an image on screen (see Figure 10.19). If you draw a line on the digitizer, for example, that line should appear on screen.

Travel Advisory

Not all digitizers are designed for digital art. Some are used for handwriting, technical drawings, writing complex characters, or even as a replacement mouse.

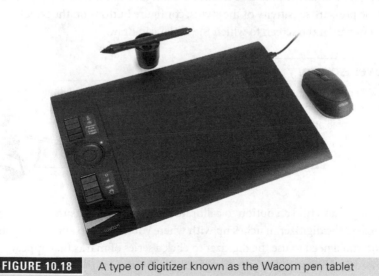

FIGURE 10.18 A type of digitizer known as the Wacom pen tablet

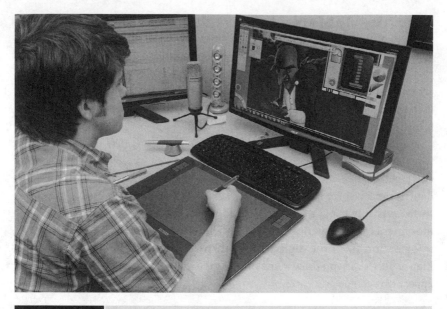

FIGURE 10.19	Drawing with a digitizer

Most digitizers connect to your PC via a USB connection. You'll usually install drivers before you connect the device, although they should be included in the box. The digitizer should also include a configuration utility. Here you can adjust the pressure sensitivity of the stylus, configure buttons on the tablet, and set the portion of the screen to which the tablet can draw.

Travel Advisory

In addition to drivers, most digitizers require specific software to use their advanced functions. With digital art digitizers, for example, you'll need a graphic arts program like Adobe Illustrator or Autodesk SketchBook, which knows how to use several brands and varieties of pen tablets.

You might also find an option to calibrate the digitizer. To ensure that where you press on the digitizer matches up with where you want it to appear on your monitor, you'll need to use the digitizer to click a series of marks that appear on your monitor. If your digitizer is incorrectly calibrated, your inputs won't appear correctly when you are drawing.

KVM Switches

A *keyboard, video, mouse (KVM) switch* is a hardware device that enables multiple computers to be viewed and controlled by a single mouse, keyboard, and monitor. Some KVMs reverse this, allowing a single computer to be controlled by multiple mice and keyboards. KVMs are useful in data centers where multiple servers are rack-mounted and space is limited. An administrator can use a single KVM to control multiple server systems from a single keyboard, mouse, and monitor.

To use a KVM, simply connect a keyboard, mouse, and monitor to the KVM and then connect the KVM to the desired computers. Once properly configured, you can use keyboard hotkeys (a combination of keys typically assigned by the KVM manufacturer) to toggle between the computers connected to the KVM. In most cases, you simply press the SCROLL LOCK key twice to switch between sessions.

Objective 10.02 Adapter Cards

A *dapter cards* let you add functions to the PC and, in the case of video cards, install and configure an essential output signal, video. Also called *expansion cards,* these fit into expansion slots in the expansion bus, the wires that connect those cards to the CPU and chipset. Modern motherboards offer two general-purpose internal expansion busses: peripheral component interconnect (PCI) and PCI Express (PCIe). Older motherboards have an accelerated graphics port (AGP) slot dedicated to video.

PCI

Intel introduced the PCI bus architecture (Figure 10.20) in the early 1990s. Intel made many smart moves with PCI, not the least of which was releasing PCI to the public domain to make it attractive to manufacturers. PCI provided a wider, faster, more flexible alternative than any previous expansion bus. The exceptional technology of the new bus, combined with the lack of a price tag, made manufacturers quickly drop earlier busses and adopt PCI.

PCI really shook up the PC world with its capabilities. The original PCI bus was 32 bits wide and ran at 33 MHz, which was superb, but these features were expected and not Earth-shattering. PCI devices were (and still are) self-configuring, a feature that led to the industry standard that became known as Plug and Play (PnP).

FIGURE 10.20 PCI expansion bus slots

> **Travel Advisory**
>
> Before PCI, it was rare to see more than one type of expansion slot on a motherboard. Today, this is not only common—it's expected!

AGP

Shortly after Intel invented PCI, the company presented a specialized, video-only version of PCI called the *accelerated graphics port (AGP)*. An AGP slot is a modified PCI slot with a direct connection to the northbridge. AGP cards and slots come in three common flavors: 2×, 4×, and 8×, essentially reflecting how efficiently the card and slot combination use the system clock.

AGP slots are only for video cards—don't try to snap a sound card or modem into one. Figure 10.21 shows a typical AGP slot. Most are brown in color, making them easy to spot.

FIGURE 10.21 AGP slot

FIGURE 10.22 PCI-X slot

PCI-X

PCI-X enhanced PCI technology and offered backward compatibility. PCI-X is a 64-bit–wide bus (see Figure 10.22). Its slots will accept regular PCI cards. The real bonus of PCI-X is its much enhanced speed. The PCI-X 2.0 standard features four speed grades (measured in MHz): PCI-X 66, PCI-X 133, PCI-X 266, and PCI-X 533. You'll find PCI-X in a few high-end systems today, but it has been eclipsed by newer technologies.

Mini-PCI

PCI has even made it into laptops in the specialty Mini-PCI format (Figure 10.23). Mini-PCI is designed to use low power and to lie flat—both good features for a laptop expansion slot. Mini-PCI is common on older portable computers, though not on modern ones.

PCI Express

PCI Express (PCIe) is the latest, fastest, and most popular expansion bus in use today. As its name implies, PCI Express is still PCI, but it uses a point-to-point serial connection instead of PCI's shared parallel communication. Consider a single 32-bit chunk of data moving from a device to the CPU. In PCI parallel

FIGURE 10.23 Mini-PCI

communication, 32 wires each carry one bit of that chunk of data. In serial communication, only one wire carries those 32 bits.

Moving to a serial interface reduces transfer overhead and enables developers to greatly increase the speeds without causing interference with other parts. It's relatively easy to shield a couple of wires rather than 32 or 64. Plus, a PCIe device has its own direct connection (a point-to-point connection) to the northbridge, so it does not wait for other devices. PCIe doesn't share the bus.

And is PCIe fast! A PCIe connection uses one wire for sending and one for receiving. Each of these pairs of wires between a PCIe controller and a device is called a *lane*. Each lane runs at 2.5 Gbps. Better yet, each point-to-point connection can use 1, 2, 4, 8, 12, 16, or 32 lanes to achieve a maximum bandwidth of 160 Gbps. The effective data rate drops a little bit because of the *encoding scheme*—the way the data is broken down and reassembled—but full-duplex data throughput can go up to a whopping 12.8 GBps on a ×32 connection.

The most common PCIe slot is the 16-lane (×16) version most commonly used for video cards, as shown in Figure 10.24. The first versions of PCIe motherboards used a combination of a single PCIe ×16 slot and a number of standard PCI slots.

FIGURE 10.24 PCIe ×16 slot (black) with PCI slots (white)

Travel Advisory

When you talk about the lanes, such as ×1 or ×8, say "by" rather than "ex" for the multiplication mark. So "by 1" and "by 8" are the correct pronunciations. You'll probably hear it referred to as "ex 8" and "8 ex" for the next few years until the technology has become a household term.

The bandwidth generated by a ×16 slot is far more than anything other than a video card would need, so most PCIe motherboards also contain slots with fewer lanes. Currently, ×1 (Figure 10.25) and ×4 are the most common general-purpose PCIe slots.

Travel Advisory

You'll find a smaller version of PCI Express in portable computers, called *Mini PCIe*. It offers the same speeds as its desktop brother.

FIGURE 10.25 PCIe ×1 slots

Installing Expansion Cards

Installing an expansion card successfully—another one of those bread-and-butter tasks for the PC tech—requires at least four steps. First, you need to know that the card works with your motherboard and your operating system. Second, you have to insert the card in an expansion slot properly and without damaging that card or the motherboard. Third, you need to provide drivers for the operating system—that's *proper* drivers for the *specific* OS. Finally, you should always verify that the card functions properly before you walk away from the PC.

Exam Tip

The four steps involved in installing expansion cards apply to *all* types of expansion cards. The CompTIA A+ 801 exam will ask you about cards ranging from the common—sound, video, and networking—to the legacy—serial, parallel, and modem. It will ask about wireless networking cards, cellular cards, riser cards, TV tuner cards, and video capture cards. The 801 exam might question how to install a USB, FireWire, or storage card.

The specific card type doesn't matter. You install any of them using the same four steps: knowledge, physical installation, device drivers and other software, and verification.

Step 1: Knowledge

Learn about the device you plan to install. For Windows systems, your best resource for this knowledge is the Microsoft Web site. The specific list of supported hardware has changed names many times. Currently for Windows 7 it's called the *Windows 7 Compatibility Center*. Earlier operating systems called it the Hardware Compatibility List (HCL) or Windows Logo'd Product List, and you'll still hear lots of people refer to it by one of those names, especially the former. You can check out the Web site at www.microsoft.com/windows/compatibility/windows-7/en-us/default.aspx. This might list your product, but most people just look on the box of the device in question (see Figure 10.26)—all Windows-certified devices proudly display that they work with Windows.

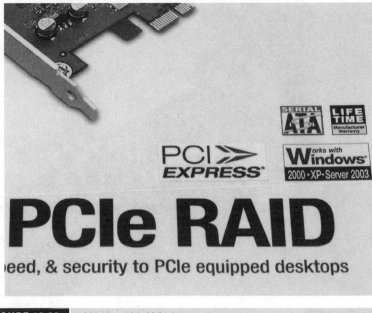

FIGURE 10.26 Works with Windows

Step 2: Physical Installation

To install an expansion card successfully, you need to take steps to avoid damaging the card, the motherboard, or both. This means knowing how to handle a card and avoiding electrostatic discharge (ESD) or any other electrical issue. You also need to place the card firmly and completely into an available expansion slot.

Optimally, a card should always be in one of two places: in a computer or in an antistatic bag. When inserting or removing a card, be careful to hold the card only by its edges. Do not hold the card by the slot connectors or touch any components on the board (Figure 10.27).

Use an antistatic wrist strap if possible, properly attached to the PC, as noted in Chapter 3. If you don't have a wrist strap, you can use the tech way of avoiding ESD by touching the power supply after you remove the expansion card from its antistatic bag. This puts you, the card, and the PC at the same electrical potential and thus minimizes the risk of ESD.

Modern systems have a trickle of voltage on the motherboard at all times when the computer is plugged into a power outlet. Chapter 4 covers power for the PC and how to deal with it in detail, but here's the short version: *Always unplug the PC before inserting an expansion card! Failure to do so can destroy the card, the motherboard, or both.* It's not worth the risk!

FIGURE 10.27 Where to handle a card

Never insert or remove a card at an extreme angle. This may damage the card. A slight angle is acceptable and even necessary when removing a card. Always screw the card to the case with a connection screw. This prevents the card from slipping out and potentially shorting out against other cards. Also, many cards use the screw connection to ground the card to the case (Figure 10.28).

Step 3: Device Drivers and Other Software

Installing device drivers is fairly straightforward. You should use the correct drivers—kind of obvious, but you'd be surprised by how many techs mess this up—and, if you're upgrading, you might have to unload current drivers before loading new ones. Finally, if you have a problem, you may need to uninstall the drivers you just loaded or roll back to earlier, more stable drivers.

To be sure you have the best possible driver you can get for your device, you should always check the manufacturer's Web site. The drivers that come with a device may work well, but odds are good that you'll find a newer and better driver on the Web site. How do you know that the drivers on the Web site are newer? First, take the easy route: look on the disc. Often the version is printed right on the optical media itself. If it's not printed there, you're going to have to load the disc in your optical-media drive and poke around. Many driver discs have an Autorun screen that advertises the version. If there's nothing on the pop-up screen, look for a Readme file (Figure 10.29).

FIGURE 10.28 Always screw down all cards.

Not all driver makers use the Windows Certification program. When Windows runs into such a driver, it brings up a scary-looking screen (Figure 10.30) that says you're about to install an unsigned driver.

The fact that a company refuses to use the Windows Certification doesn't mean that its drivers are bad—it simply means that they haven't gone through Microsoft's exhaustive quality-assurance certification procedure. If I run into this, I usually check the driver's version to make sure I'm not installing something

```
README.txt - Notepad                                      [ – ][ □ ][ X ]
File  Edit  Format  View  Help
       Realtek Semiconductor Corp. AC'97 Sound System Software    ver:A3.72
                      Installation and Setup

Driver & Application Installation/Removal Procedure For Realtek AC'97 Codec:
==============================================================================
<<< For Win2000/WinME/WinXP (WDM driver)/Win98 Gold(First Edition)/Win98SE >>>

-----------------------------------------
Setup Driver/Application at first time:
-----------------------------------------
Step 1. Before installing the Realtek AC'97 Drivers & Applications, Press the
        [Cancel] button if windows detect the PCI Multimedia Audio device.

Step 2. Insert the "Realtek AC'97 Drivers & Applications" CD into the CD-ROM
        drive and run the setup.exe program to finish the installation.

Step 3. Click on [Next/OK/Go] to continue the procedure. If the Windows popup
        "Digital Signature Not Found" message, press [Yes] to continue the
        installation.
```

FIGURE 10.29 Part of a Readme file showing the driver version

FIGURE 10.30 Unsigned driver warning

outdated, and then I just take my chances and install it. (I've yet to encounter a problem with an unsigned driver that I haven't also seen with Windows Certified drivers.)

Travel Advisory

With the 64-bit versions of Windows Vista and Windows 7, Microsoft tightened the rules to try to provide the most stable platform possible. You simply cannot install unsigned drivers without clunky workarounds. Microsoft must approve each 64-bit driver.

Windows offers the nifty feature of rolling back to previous drivers after an installation or driver upgrade. If you decide to live on the edge and install beta drivers for your video card, for example, and your system becomes frightfully unstable, you can back up to the drivers that worked before you installed the betas. (Not that I've ever had to use that feature, of course!) To access the roll-back feature, simply open the Device Manager and access the properties for the device you want to adjust. On the Drivers tab (Figure 10.31), you'll find the Roll Back Driver button.

Some devices—most notably video cards—offer support software beyond drivers. These include Control Panel or notification area icons that enable you to configure the cards in specific ways or for specific games. Support software used to be a separate installation from the drivers, but most card manufacturers bundle them all into a single executable.

Driver rollback feature

Step 4: Verification

As a last step in the installation process, inspect the results of the installation and verify that the device works properly. Immediately after installing, you should open Device Manager and verify that Windows sees the device (Figure 10.32). Assuming that Device Manager shows the device working properly, your next check is to put the device to work by making it do whatever it is supposed to do. If you installed a printer, print something; if you installed a scanner, scan something. If it works, you're done!

Troubleshooting Expansion Cards

A properly installed expansion card rarely makes trouble—it's the botched installations that produce headaches. Chances are you'll have to troubleshoot an expansion card installation at some point, usually from an installation that you botched personally.

FIGURE 10.32 Device Manager shows the device working properly

The first sign of an improperly installed card usually shows up the moment you try to get that card to do whatever it's supposed to do and it doesn't do it. When this happens, your primary troubleshooting process—after checking in with Device Manager—is a reinstallation.

Device Manager

Device Manager provides the first diagnostic and troubleshooting tool in Windows. After you install a new device, Device Manager gives you many clues if something has gone wrong.

Occasionally, Device Manager may not even show the new device. If that happens, verify that you inserted the device properly and, if needed, that the device has power. Run the Add Hardware Wizard and see if Windows recognizes the device. If Device Manager doesn't recognize the device at this point, you have one of two problems: either the device is physically damaged and you must replace it, or the device is an onboard device, not a card, and is turned off in the CMOS setup utility.

Device Manager rarely completely fails to see a device. More commonly, device problems manifest themselves in Device Manager via error icons:

- A black "!" on a yellow circle (Windows XP) or triangle (Windows Vista/7) indicates that a device is missing (see Figure 10.33), that Windows does not recognize a device, or that there's a device driver problem. A device may still work even while producing this error.

- A black downward-pointing arrow on a white field in Windows Vista and Windows 7 indicates a disabled device. This usually points to a device that's been manually turned off or a damaged device. A device producing this error will not work. Windows XP uses a red "X" for the same status indicator.

The "!" symbol is the most common error symbol and is usually the easiest to fix. First, double-check the device's connections. Second, try reinstalling the driver with the Update Driver button. To get to the Update Driver button,

FIGURE 10.33 An "!" in Device Manager, indicating a problem with the selected device

right-click the device in Device Manager and select Properties. In the Properties dialog box, select the Driver tab. On the Driver tab, click the Update Driver button to launch the Hardware Update Wizard (Figure 10.34).

If you get a downward-pointing arrow or a red "X" error, first check that the device isn't disabled. Right-click the device and select Enable. If that doesn't work (it often does not), try rolling back the driver (if you updated the driver) or uninstalling (if it's a new install). Shut the system down and make triple-sure you have the card physically installed. Then redo the entire driver installation procedure, making sure you have the most current driver for that device. If none of these procedures works, return the card—it's almost certainly bad.

FIGURE 10.34 Updating the driver

Objective 10.03 Output Devices

O utput devices enable you to see or hear feedback from the computer. You've done your input; the computer processes that information and then provides output. Output devices come in three main categories: sound, video, and hard copy. Printing gets its own chapter (see Chapter 11), so this section concentrates on sound and video.

Sound

Sound output in the PC has two basic components: the sound card and the speakers. Most PCs use sound cards built into the motherboard, but these are not as good as stand-alone cards. Most built-in sound lacks a dedicated sound processor, relying on the CPU for the processing power. This eats into CPU time and reduces overall performance. Built-in sound usually picks up interference from the rest of the motherboard, thus leading to a noticeable hiss, especially when you're listening through headphones.

A dedicated sound card—particularly in Windows XP—offers an inexpensive performance-enhancing upgrade that should be done for most systems. Windows Vista and Windows 7 offer a different story, though, because they don't support dedicated sound processors. Vista and 7 require sound processing through the OS and thus through the CPU.

Speakers make a huge difference in customer satisfaction, much more than the sound card or built-in sound circuits. This won't show up on the CompTIA A+ certification exams, but it is useful information nonetheless. Spend the extra small amount of money to get better speakers. If you can fit only a 2.1 set, then go for the big subwoofer and nice satellites, like those shown in Figure 10.35.

Sound cards install and configure similar to every other expansion device. Install the card, and then install updated drivers. Plug things into the correct ports, and they'll work fine.

Video

The video card and the monitor make up the video system in a PC. The video card handles the commands from the CPU and OS and then sends commands to the monitor to update and change what it displays.

FIGURE 10.35 Klipsch 2.1 speaker set

Video Cards

As far as the CompTIA A+ certification exams go, you can treat a video card—whether stand-alone or built into the motherboard—like any other expansion card. It goes into the PCIe slot and you install drivers. Use Device Manager when you set it up to make sure everything works right. You can make changes to the function of the video card (or *display adapter*) in the Display Control Panel applet or in the software that came with your video adapter, as shown in Figure 10.36.

Just giving you the CompTIA A+ certification line on video cards would be a disservice, even in a cram-style book, because a properly chosen and set up video card can make an amazing difference in the performance of a computer, especially when it comes to gaming, image editing, and 3-D modeling. Plus, Windows Vista and Windows 7 use 3-D video card processing extensively, so you need to know about video cards in the real world.

The video card has two major pieces: the video RAM and the video processor circuitry. The video RAM stores the video image. On the first video cards, this RAM was good old dynamic RAM (DRAM), just like the RAM on the motherboard. Today's video cards often have better RAM than your system has. The video-processing circuitry takes the information on the video RAM and shoots it out to the monitor. While early video-processing circuitry was little more than an intermediary between the CPU and the video RAM, modern video processors are more powerful than all but the latest CPUs! Most video cards need fans to cool their onboard processors (see Figure 10.37).

SyncMaster T220/T220G,SyncMaster Magic T220/T220G(Digit...

| Adapter | Monitor | Troubleshoot |
| Color Management | | Catalyst(TM) Control Center |

ATI Catalyst™ Control Center

The ATI Catalyst Control Center is used to configure displays and settings for all your ATI GPUs.

ATI Catalyst Control Center

To open the ATI Catalyst Control Center, click on this button:

ATI Catalyst Control Center

OK Cancel Apply

FIGURE 10.36 Monitor and display adapter properties

FIGURE 10.37 Video card with a cooling fan

Video card discussion, at least among techs, almost always revolves around the *graphics processing unit (GPU)* the video card uses and the amount of RAM on board. A typical video card might be called an XFX Radeon HD7970 3-GB 384-bit GDDR5 PCI Express 3.0, so let's break that down. XFX is the manufacturer of the video card; Radeon HD7970 is the graphics processor; 3-GB 384-bit GDDR5 describes the dedicated video RAM and the connection between the video RAM and the graphics processor; and PCI Express 3.0 describes the motherboard expansion slot the card requires.

The choice of GPU is your single most important decision in buying a video card. Low-end graphics processors will usually work fine for the run-of-the-mill user who wants to write letters or run a Web browser. High-end graphics processors are designed to support the beautiful 3-D games that are so popular today.

The two major GPU makers, NVIDIA and AMD, compete vigorously, and both companies introduce multiple models of GPUs (and therefore new models of cards) every year. Unless you're using the Windows Aero glass desktop, however, all of these extra features you see in video cards are really only for the true driving force in video cards: 3-D gaming. Your PC can provide you with hours of incredible entertainment via a huge number of popular games that immerse you in 3-D environments full of light, shadows, explosions, and other amazing effects that create a fun and beautiful gaming experience.

Drivers Because of the complexity of modern video cards, manufacturers constantly tweak their drivers to make them work better with Windows. With almost no exception, when you take a video card out of the box, the drivers on the optical media bundled with the card are outdated. Always hit the manufacturer's Web site as soon as possible and download the latest non-beta drivers. You and your clients will be much better served than if you installed the bundled drivers.

DirectX and Video Cards In the old days, many applications communicated directly with much of the PC hardware and, as a result, could crash your computer if not written well enough. Microsoft tried to fix this problem by placing all hardware under the control of Windows, but programmers balked because Windows added too much work for the video process and slowed down everything. For the most demanding programs, such as games, only direct access to the hardware would work.

This need to "get around Windows" motivated Microsoft to unveil a new set of protocols called *DirectX*. Programmers use DirectX to take control of certain pieces of hardware and to talk directly to that hardware; it provides the speed

necessary to play more of today's advanced games. The primary impetus for DirectX was to build a series of products to enable Windows to run 3-D games. That's not to say that you couldn't run 3-D games in Windows *before* DirectX; rather, it's just that Microsoft wasn't involved in the API rat race at the time and wanted to be. Microsoft's goal in developing DirectX was to create a 100-percent stable environment, with direct hardware access, for running 3-D applications and games within Windows.

DirectX is not only for video; it also supports sound, network connections, input devices, and other parts of your PC. Each of these subsets of DirectX has a name such as DirectDraw, Direct3D, or DirectSound:

- **DirectDraw** Supports direct access to the hardware for 2-D graphics
- **Direct3D** Supports direct access to the hardware for 3-D graphics—the most important part of DirectX
- **DirectInput** Supports direct access to the hardware for joysticks and other game controllers
- **DirectSound** Supports direct access to the hardware for waveforms in Windows XP (though not in Vista/7)
- **DirectMusic** Supports direct access to the hardware for MIDI devices
- **DirectPlay** Supports direct access to network devices for multiplayer games
- **DirectShow** Supports direct access to video and presentation devices

Microsoft constantly adds and tweaks this list. Because almost all games need DirectX and all video cards have drivers to support DirectX, you need to verify that DirectX is installed and working properly on your system. To do this in Windows XP, use the DirectX Diagnostic Tool in the System Information program. After you open System Information (it usually lives in the Accessories | System Tools area of the Start menu), click the Tools menu and select DirectX Diagnostic Tool. The easiest way to access the DirectX Diagnostic Tool in Windows Vista/7 is to use the Start Search bar in the Start menu. Type **dxdiag** and press ENTER to display the tool (Figure 10.38).

Monitors

Video displays for PCs come in three varieties: CRT, LCD, and projectors. CRT monitors are pretty much gone, and were restricted to the desktop. LCD monitors can be found on laptops and connected to desktops. You'll find projectors in boardrooms, classrooms, and media rooms, splashing a picture onto a screen. Figure 10.39 shows an LCD and a CRT.

FIGURE 10.38 The DirectX Diagnostic Tool

LCD CRT

FIGURE 10.39 LCD and CRT

Exam Tip

The 801 competencies mention three other monitor types: LED, plasma, and OLED. An *LED monitor* is a marketing term, as you'll see shortly. Plasma screens make lovely televisions, but are completely horrid as computer monitors because of problems with permanent ghosting if a screen element displays in one spot for a certain length of time. You'll find the organic light-emitting diode (OLED) screens on a few mobile phones, but not as computer screens. They're way too expensive at this time.

CRT Monitors

Cathode ray tube (CRT) monitors contain a large, airtight vacuum tube. One end of this tube is a slender cylinder that contains three electron guns. The other end of the tube, which is fatter and wider, is the display screen.

The inside of the display screen has a phosphor coating. The monitor displays video data as the electron guns make a series of horizontal sweeps across the screen, energizing the appropriate areas of the phosphor coating. The sweeps start at the upper-left corner of the monitor and move across and down to the lower-right corner.

The speed at which the electron beam moves across the screen is known as the *horizontal refresh rate (HRR)*. The monitor draws a number of lines across the screen, eventually covering the screen with glowing phosphors. The number of lines is not fixed, unlike television screens, which have a set number of lines. After the guns reach the lower-right corner of the screen, they turn off and point back to the upper-left corner. The amount of time it takes to draw the entire screen and get the electron guns back to the upper-left corner is called the *vertical refresh rate (VRR)*.

If the video card is set to push at too low a VRR, the monitor produces a noticeable flicker, causing eyestrain and headaches for users. Pushing the monitor at too high of a VRR, however, causes a definite distortion of the screen image and will damage the circuitry of the monitor and eventually destroy it. Set the VRR on the Advanced tab of the Display/Display Settings Control Panel applet.

Resolution

Monitor *resolution* is always shown as the number of horizontal pixels times the number of vertical pixels. A resolution of 640×480, therefore, indicates a horizontal resolution of 640 pixels and a vertical resolution of 480 pixels. Figure 10.40 shows the relationship between resolution and pixels.

Lower resolution

Higher resolution

| FIGURE 10.40 | Resolution and pixels |

Some common resolutions are 640×480, 800×600, 1024×768, 1280×960, 1280×1024, and 1600×1200. Notice that most of these resolutions match a 4:3 ratio. This is called the *aspect ratio*. Most CRT monitors are shaped like older television screens, with a 4:3 aspect ratio, so most resolutions are designed to match—or at least be close to—that shape. Other monitors, generically called *widescreen monitors,* have a 16:9 or 16:10 ratio. (Widescreen CRTs are rare. See the discussion on LCDs next for today's more typical widescreen monitors.)

LCD Monitors

Liquid crystal displays (LCDs) are the most common type of display technology for PCs. LCD monitors have many advantages over CRTs. They are thinner and lighter, use much less power, are virtually flicker free, and don't emit potentially harmful radiation.

Exam Tip

LCD monitors are fully digital devices, but some offer the analog VGA connector instead of or in addition to one of the digital connectors (DVI, DisplayPort, and HDMI). When they first debuted, the analog vs. digital debate raged, but in practice the extra conversion step doesn't seem to matter in terms of performance.

A color LCD screen is composed of a large number of tiny liquid-crystal molecules (called *sub-pixels*) arranged in rows and columns between polarizing filters. A translucent sheet above the sub-pixels is colored red, green, or blue. Each tiny distinct group of three sub-pixels—one red, one green, and one blue—forms a physical pixel, as shown in Figure 10.41.

LCD Resolution

All LCD monitors have a *native resolution,* such as 1680×1050, that enables them to display the sharpest picture possible. As mentioned earlier, the pixels are fixed. You simply cannot run an LCD monitor at a resolution higher than the native one. Worse, because LCDs have no equivalent to a shadow mask, they can't run at a lower-than-native resolution without severely degrading image quality. A CRT can simply use more dots and the filtering and smoothing of the shadow mask to make a picture at a lower resolution look as good and crisp as the same picture at a higher resolution, but an LCD cannot. The LCD has to use an edge-blurring technique called *anti-aliasing* to soften the jagged corners of the pixels when running at lower than native resolution, which simply does not look as good. The bottom line? Always set the LCD at native resolution.

Travel Advisory

Two LCD panels that have the same physical size may have different native resolutions.

FIGURE 10.41 LCD pixels and resolution

LCD Technologies

Two technologies dominate the LCD market. PC monitors and portable computers use active matrix or thin film transistor (TFT) technology to provide a responsive, color-saturated display. You'll find passive matrix technology in use on little monochrome screens such as point-of-sale machines and automated teller machines (ATMs).

LCD Components

The typical LCD projector has three main components: the LCD panel, the backlight(s), and the inverters. The LCD panel creates the image, the backlights illuminate the image so you can see it, and the inverters send power to backlights. Figure 10.42 shows a typical layout for the internal components of an LCD monitor.

LCDs traditionally use *cold cathode fluorescent lamp (CCFL)* technology for the backlights, but manufacturers currently use several types of *light-emitting diode (LED)* light for backlighting, either directly illuminating pixels from behind or flooding the panel from the edges of the bezel. The former produces outstanding contrast and color, but costs a lot more than the edge types. The edge types function similarly to a CCFL-style display, so they produce similar contrast and colors to the older technology. Manufacturers have rebranded LCD monitors that use LEDs for backlighting as *LED monitors*.

FIGURE 10.42 LCD internals

Exam Tip
The CompTIA A+ 801 exam refers to LEDs as a display type, but such displays don't exist aside from marketing terms. LEDs manifest only as one form of backlighting for LCD monitors.

Contrast Ratio

A big drawback of LCD monitors is that they don't have nearly the color satura-tion or richness of contrast of a good CRT monitor—although LCD technology continues to improve every year. A good contrast ratio—the difference between the darkest and lightest spots that the monitor can display—is 450:1, although a quick trip to a computer store will reveal LCDs with lower levels (250:1) and higher levels (1000:1).

Add-on Filters

Two types of add-on filters can enhance the user experience with monitors: anti-glare and privacy. Anti-glare filters correct some overly reflective screens. Privacy filters limit the viewing range of a monitor to the spot directly in front of it. This helps shield the monitor's contents from prying eyes, a feature very use-ful if you're working in a café or other public space.

Projectors

Projectors shoot the image out the front and count on you to put up a screen at the proper distance. Front-view projectors connected to PCs running Microsoft PowerPoint have been the cornerstone of every meeting almost everywhere for years (Figure 10.43).

The bane of every projector is the lamp. Lamps work hard in your projector, as they must generate a tremendous amount of light. As a result, they generate quite a bit of heat, and all projectors come with a fan to keep the lamp from over-heating. When you turn off a projector, the fan will continue to run until the lamp is fully cooled. Lamps are also very expensive, which comes as a nasty shock to someone who's not prepared for the price when their lamp dies.

The brightness of a projector is measured in lumens. A *lumen* is the amount of light emitted by a light source from a certain angle that is perceived by the human eye. The greater the lumen rating, the brighter the projector will be.

A projector's *throw* is the size of the image at a certain distance from the screen. All projectors have a recommended minimum and maximum throw distance. For instance, a projector with a 16:9 image-aspect ratio needs to be 11 to 12 feet away from the screen to create a 100-inch diagonal image.

FIGURE 10.43 Front-view projector (photo courtesy of Dell, Inc.)

Common Features

For all the radical differences among monitor technologies, they have several aspects in common. They're the classic visual output device, of course, but you can make adjustments to how they appear and apply techniques to minimize their power consumption.

Adjustments

Most adjustments to the monitor take place at installation, but for now, let's just make sure you know what they are and where they are located. Clearly, all monitors have an On/Off button or switch. Also, they should have Brightness and Contrast buttons. Beyond that, most monitors (at least the ones you should buy) have an onboard menu system, enabling a number of adjustments. Every monitor maker provides a different way to access these menus, but they all provide two main functions: physical screen adjustment (bigger, smaller; move to the left, right, up, or down; and others) and color adjustment. The color adjustment lets you adjust the red, green, and blue guns to give you the best color tones. All these settings are a matter of personal taste. Make sure the person who will use the computer understands how to adjust these settings (see Figure 10.44).

Power Conservation

CRT and LCD monitors differ greatly in the amount of electricity they require. The bottom line is that CRTs use a lot and LCDs use a lot less. Here's the scoop.

FIGURE 10.44 Typical menu controls

Approximately half the power required to run a desktop PC is consumed by the CRT monitor. Monitors that meet the Video Electronics Standards Association (VESA) specification for *display power-management signaling (DPMS)* can reduce monitor power consumption by roughly 75 percent. This is accomplished by reducing or eliminating the signals sent by the video card to the monitor during idle periods. By eliminating these pulses, the monitor essentially takes catnaps. The advantage over simply shutting off the monitor is in the time it takes to restore the display.

A typical CRT monitor consumes approximately 120 watts. During a catnap or power-down mode, the energy consumption is reduced to less than 25 watts, while enabling the screen to return to use in less than 10 seconds. A typical LCD monitor, in contrast, uses less than half the electricity that a CRT uses. A 19-inch, 4:3 aspect-ratio flat panel, for example, uses around 33 watts at peak usage and less than 2 watts in DPMS mode. Larger LCDs use more power at peak usage than smaller ones. A 21-inch widescreen model, for example, might draw about 75 watts at peak, but still drop down to less than 2 watts in DPMS mode. Swapping out CRTs with LCDs is a great way to save on your electric bill.

Display Settings

The Display applet in Control Panel enables you to adjust monitor resolution and other monitor settings. The way to change settings differs among all three operating systems, although in each case the options are fairly obvious because

you know you *can* make these changes. In Windows 7, for example, click the Adjust resolution link on Display, then click the arrow in the the Resolution drop down (Figure 10.45). Manually slide the marker to change resolution.

The Monitor tab of the Display Settings applet in Windows Vista and the Settings tab of the Display Properties applet (Figure 10.46) provide similar options. Windows displays only resolutions and color depths that your video card/monitor combination can accept and that are suitable for most situations. Everyone has a favorite resolution, and higher isn't always better. For those with trouble seeing small screen elements, higher resolutions can present a difficulty—already small icons are *much* smaller at 1280×1024 than at 800×600. Try all of the resolutions to see which you like—just remember that LCD monitors look sharpest at their native resolution (usually the highest listed). Table 10.1 shows some common resolutions.

FIGURE 10.45 Screen Resolution options in Windows 7 Display applet

TABLE 10.1	Typical Display Modes		
Video Mode	**Resolution**	**Aspect Ratio**	**Typical Device**
HDTV 720p	1280×720	16:9	Lowest resolution that can be called HDTV
SXGA	1280×1024	5:4	Native resolution for many desktop LCD monitors
WSXGA	1440×900	16:10	Widescreen laptops
SXGA+	1400×1050	4:3	Laptop monitors and high-end projectors
UXGA	1600×1200	4:3	Larger CRT monitors
WSXGA+	1680×1050	16:10	For medium-sized widescreen monitors
HDTV 1080p	1920×1080	16:9	Full HDTV resolution
WUXGA	1920×1200	16:10	For large-sized widescreen monitors

FIGURE 10.46	Display Settings in Windows Vista (left) and Display Properties in Windows XP (right)

The color quality is the number of colors displayed on the screen. You can change the screen resolution with a simple slider, adjusting the color depth from 4-bit all the way up to 32-bit color. Unless you have an older video card or a significant video speed issue, you'll probably set your system for 32-bit color and never touch this setting again.

Another option you may see is dual monitors. Windows supports the use of two (or more) monitors. These monitors may work together like two halves of one large monitor, or the second monitor might simply show a duplicate of what's happening on the first monitor. Dual monitors are handy if you need lots of screen space but don't want to buy a really large, expensive monitor (Figure 10.47). Microsoft calls this feature *DualView*.

Exam Tip

Windows supports *DualView* technology, enabling you to use multiple monitors.

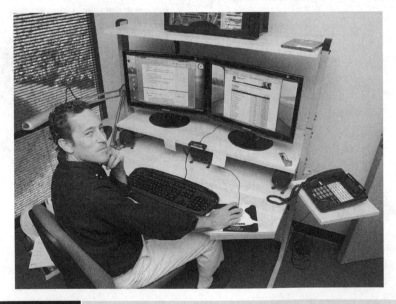

FIGURE 10.47 Scott hard at work with dual monitors

You can set up dual monitors in two ways: plug in two video cards or use a single video card that supports two monitors (a "dual-head" video card). Both methods are quite common and work well. Dual monitors are easy to configure: Just plug in the monitors and Windows should detect them. Windows will show both monitors in the Display settings, as shown in Figure 10.48. By default, the second monitor is not enabled. To use the second monitor, just select the *Extend the desktop onto this monitor* check box.

If you need to see more advanced settings, click the cleverly labeled Advanced or Advanced Settings button. The title of this dialog box reflects the monitor and video card. As you can see in Figure 10.49, this particular monitor is a Samsung SyncMaster T220 running off of an ATI Radeon 3800-series video card.

Troubleshooting Video

Video problems fall into several categories: video cards, drivers, monitors, OS settings, and application settings. Any of these issues can create a less-than-optimal screen output, something that no user can tolerate for any length of time.

FIGURE 10.48 Enabling dual monitors

FIGURE 10.49 Advanced video settings

Every tech, therefore, needs to recognize common video and display issues and to know how to fix them. The CompTIA A+ 802 exam is surprisingly uninterested in OS and app problems, focusing instead on hardware and drivers. Let's take a look.

Troubleshooting Video Cards/Drivers

Video cards rarely go bad, so the vast majority of video card/driver problems are bad or incompatible drivers or incorrect settings. Always make sure you have the correct driver installed. If you're using an incompatible driver, Windows defaults to good old 640×480, 16-color VGA mode, or you might get a Blue Screen of Death (BSoD) as soon as Windows starts to load. A driver that is suddenly corrupted usually doesn't show the problem until the next reboot. If you reboot a system with a corrupted driver, Windows will do one of the following: go into VGA mode, display no image on the screen, lock up, or display a garbled screen with weird or incorrect color patterns or a very distorted image. Whatever the output, reboot into Safe Mode and roll back or delete the driver. Keep in mind

that more advanced video cards tend to show their drivers as installed programs under Add or Remove Programs in Windows XP or Programs and Features in Windows Vista/7, so always check there first before you try deleting a driver by using Device Manager. Download the latest driver and reinstall.

Video cards are pretty durable, but they have two components that do go bad: the fan and the RAM. Lucky for you, if either of these goes out, it tends to show the same error—bizarre screen outputs followed shortly by a screen lockup. Usually Windows keeps running; you may see your mouse pointer moving around and windows refreshing, but the screen turns into a huge mess.

Bad drivers sometimes also make this error, so always first try going into Safe Mode to see if the problem suddenly clears up. If it does, you do not have a problem with the video card!

Excessive heat inside the case, even with the video card fan running at full blast, can create some interesting effects. The computer could simply shut down due to overheating. You'll recognize this possible cause because the computer will come back up in a minute or two, but then shut down again as you use it hard and it heats up again. Sometimes the screen will get bizarre artifacts or start distorting. Check your case fans and make sure nothing is too close to the video card. You might need to blow out (outdoors!) the dust from filters, vents, and fans.

The last and probably most common problem is nothing more than improperly configured video settings. Identifying the problem is just common sense—if your monitor is showing everything sideways, someone messed with your rotation settings; if your gorgeous wallpaper of a mountain pass looks like an ugly four-color cartoon, someone lowered the color depth. You'll need to reset the color depth to a more appropriate setting. In Windows XP, open the Display Properties. In Windows Vista, go to Personalization | Display Settings. In Windows 7, go to Display | Change display settings | Advanced settings, then open the Monitor tab.

Troubleshooting Monitors

Because of the inherent dangers of the high-frequency and high-voltage power required by monitors, and because proper adjustment requires specialized training, this section concentrates on giving a support person the information necessary to decide whether a trouble call is warranted. Virtually no monitor manufacturers make schematics of their monitors available to the public because of liability issues regarding possible electrocution.

Common Problems Specific to CRTs The complexity of CRTs compared to LCDs requires us to look at a number of monitor problems unique to CRTs. Most of these problems require opening the monitor, so be careful! When in doubt, take it to a repair shop.

- Big color blotches or discoloration on the display are an easy and cheap repair. Find the Degauss button and use it. If your monitor doesn't have a Degauss button, you can purchase a special tool called a degaussing coil at any electronics store.
- Suppose you got a good deal on a used 19-inch monitor, but the display is kind of dark, even though you have the brightness turned up all the way. This dim image points to a dying CRT. So, how about replacing the CRT? Forget it. Even if the monitor was free, it just isn't worth it; a replacement tube runs into the hundreds of dollars. Nobody ever sold a monitor because it was too bright and too sharp. Save your money and buy a new monitor.

Troubleshooting LCDs With the proliferation of LCD panels in the computing world, PC techs need to have some understanding of what to do when they break. Some of the components you can fix, including replacing some of the internal components. I tend to use monitor repair shops for most LCD issues, but let's take a look.

An LCD monitor may have dead pixels. A dead pixel is any single pixel that does not react the way it should. A pixel that never lights up is a *dead pixel,* a pixel that is stuck on pure white is a lit pixel, and a pixel on a certain color is a stuck pixel. You cannot repair bad pixels; the panel must be replaced. All LCD panel makers allow a certain number of bad pixels, even on a brand-new LCD monitor! You need to check the warranty for your monitor and see how many they allow before you may return the monitor.

- If your LCD monitor cracks, it is not repairable and must be replaced.
- A flickering image with an LCD usually points to either a very inexpensive panel with too much light bleed from the backlight or a dying CCFL backlight. LEDs don't flicker, so you won't see this issue with those types of LCDs. Replace the backlight if necessary.
- A dim image, especially on only the top or bottom half of the screen, points to a dead or dying backlight in a multibacklight system. Replace as necessary.

- If the LCD goes dark but you can still barely see the image under bright lights, you lost either the backlight or the inverter. In many cases, especially with super-thin panels, you'll replace the entire panel and backlight as a unit. On the other hand, an inverter can be on a separate circuit board that you can replace.
- If your LCD makes a distinct hissing noise, an inverter is about to fail. Again, you can replace the inverter if need be.

Be careful if you open an LCD to work on the inside. The inverter can bite you in several ways. First, it's powered by a high-voltage electrical circuit that can give you a nasty shock. Worse, the inverter will retain a charge for a few minutes after you unplug it, so unplug and wait for a bit. Second, inverters get very hot and present a very real danger of burning you at a touch. Again, wait for a while after you unplug it to try to replace it. Finally, if you shock an inverter, you might irreparably damage it. So use proper ESD-avoidance techniques.

Bottom line on fixing LCD monitors? You can find companies that sell replacement parts for LCDs, but repairing an LCD is difficult, and there are folks who will do it for you faster and cheaper than you can. Search for a specialty LCD repair company. Hundreds of these companies exist all over the world.

Objective 10.04 Specialty PCs

Techs need to understand components needed to create PCs for special purposes and be able to evaluate and select the best components for the job. You know from previous chapters how to differentiate among specific components. This section lists eight types of PCs and their typical components:

- **Standard thick client** CompTIA's term for a standard desktop computer. It meets the recommended requirements for running Windows and can handle standard desktop applications.
- **Thin client** CompTIA uses this term to refer to a PC that meets the minimum requirements for running Windows and can run basic applications. The industry uses the term a little differently, generally referring to thin clients as computers that run applications and even an operating system housed on a server, using the power of that server to accomplish tasks.

- **Virtualization workstation** Essentially the opposite of a classic thin client, this workstation runs multiple instances of operating systems at the same time through virtual machines. Correspondingly, the machine needs maximum RAM and a multicore CPU just to keep juggling all those machines.

- **Audio/video editing workstation** CompTIA lists a need for specialized audio and video cards, a large and fast hard drive, and dual monitors. I would add tons of RAM and a very fast CPU.

- **Graphic/CAD/CAM design workstation** This mouthful refers to a computer that a person can use to design products using specialized computer-aided design (CAD) software, such as AutoCAD, and also run the robots and other machines at a factory to build those products. Such a machine needs a powerful processor, high-end video, and maximum RAM.

- **Gaming PC** Similar in needs to a graphics workstation, though the video card should use a game-oriented GPU rather than a workstation GPU. CompTIA lists a powerful processor, better sound card, and high-end cooling as well. Don't forget to add neon lights and lots of shiny brass....

- **Home server PC** A home server today has several roles, such as central file storage, print server, and streaming media machine. As such, a home server PC needs to have processing power, robust networking capability, and solid and redundant storage. CompTIA specifically lists the following requirements:

 - Media streaming
 - File sharing
 - Print sharing
 - Gigabit NIC
 - RAID array

Local Lingo

Media Center Although the 801 competencies don't specify the need for specific software, to make a truly excellent home server today, you should employ some kind of media center software. The Home and Ultimate editions of Windows have Media Center; Macs have Front Row. You can also do better with one of two free programs: the wildly customizable XBMC (see Figure 10.50) or the solidly performing Plex.

FIGURE 10.50 XBMC

- **Home theater PC** Of all the specialty PCs mentioned in the 801 objectives, the home theater PC (HTPC) offers the most variation from the standard thick client. First, most home theater PCs look like a piece of stereo equipment, not a desktop PC. CompTIA calls this case form factor an HTPC compact form factor (Figure 10.51).

FIGURE 10.51 HTPC

Second, home theater PCs usually have a TV tuner that enables it to display and record standard cable or broadcast television signals. Third, home theater PCs have surround-sound audio, usually with four satellites, a center speaker, and a subwoofer (5.1 audio). Finally, the HTPC needs to connect to a big monitor via an HDMI cable that carries both audio and high-definition video.

CHECKPOINT

✔**Objective 10.01: Input Devices** Input devices enable you to interact with the computer and give it commands through typing, clicking, speaking, and more. Windows supports common devices, such as a keyboard or mouse, straight out of the box, but some fancier or specialty input devices require drivers and configuration. Other common input devices include scanners, digital cameras, camcorders, and webcams. Multimedia peripherals include microphones and MIDI devices. Game controllers run riot, but the two most common are joysticks and game pads. Specialty input devices include biometric scanners, bar code readers, and touch screens. A graphics tablet or digitizer enables you to use a special pen to draw directly into the computer. A KVM switch, a device that has both input and output, enables you to connect a single keyboard, mouse, and monitor to multiple systems.

✔**Objective 10.02: Adapter Cards** Adapter or expansion cards come in several varieties, such as PCI, AGP, PCI-X, Mini-PCI, PCI Express, and Mini PCIe. Installing an expansion card successfully requires at least four steps: knowledge of the proper device, physical installation, device driver installation, and verification of success.

✔**Objective 10.03: Output Devices** Output devices enable you to see or hear feedback from the computer and come in three main categories: sound, video, and printing. Sound manifests as a sound card and speakers. Video manifests as a video card or display adapter and monitor. Monitors come in three types: CRT, LCD, and projectors.

✔**Objective 10.04: Specialty PCs** The CompTIA 801 competencies outline the need for techs to evaluate and recommend hardware for specialized PCs. These PCs include thick and thin clients; virtualization, audio/video editing, and graphics/CAD/CAM workstations; gaming PCs; home server PCs; and home theater PCs.

REVIEW QUESTIONS

1. Which of the following devices enables you to input a picture into a computer easily?

 A. Keyboard

 B. Mouse

 C. Printer

 D. Scanner

 E. KVM

2. Which of the following devices enables voice and video connection over the Internet?

 A. Digital camera

 B. Printer

 C. Scanner

 D. Webcam

3. Which of the following is an example of a biometric device?

 A. Digital camera

 B. Flatbed scanner

 C. Retinal scanner

 D. Webcam

4. What device enables you to enter data directly into a computer using only your fingers?

 A. Bar code reader

 B. Flatbed scanner

 C. Touch screen

 D. Webcam

5. A "32-bit parallel expansion bus" describes which of the following technologies?

 A. AGP

 B. PCI

 C. PCI Express

 D. PCI-X

6. With which expansion bus can you add devices to a portable computer?

 A. Micro-PCI

 B. Mini-PCI

 C. PCI

 D. PCI Express

7. Which of the following technologies provides a serial expansion bus?

 A. AGP

 B. PCI

 C. PCI Express

 D. PCI-X

8. Mary wants to add a new sound card to a client's system. What should she do before inserting the card into the motherboard? (Select two.)

 A. Isolate the card.

 B. Install the drivers.

 C. Ground herself.

 D. Unplug the PC.

9. After installing an updated sound card driver, Tiffany's Windows system boots but now no sound comes out of the speakers. She has the speakers plugged in properly and powered up. What can she do to get the sound working again?

 A. Roll back the drivers.

 B. Reinstall the drivers.

 C. Reload Windows.

 D. Unsign the drivers.

10. Which of the following devices are examples of output devices? (Select two.)

 A. Keyboard

 B. Mouse

 C. Monitor

 D. Speaker

11. Which monitor technology offers the least power consumption?

 A. AMD

 B. CRT

 C. DirectX

 D. LCD

12. Akili gets a tech call about a new LCD that's "fuzzy." What might he check first?

 A. Check the resolution and set it at the native resolution.

 B. Check the refresh rate and increase the vertical refresh rate.

 C. Check the refresh rate and increase the horizontal refresh rate.

 D. Check the lamp and replace it if necessary.

13. What's a typical adjustment you can make on a monitor?

 A. Increase the brightness.

 B. Increase the inverter.

 C. Increase the lamp.

 D. Increase the response rate.

14. What do you use in Windows Vista to adjust the resolution of a monitor?

 A. Display Settings applet

 B. Monitor applet

 C. Resolution applet

 D. Video applet

15. What type of workstation would you recommend to a client who needs to run multiple instances of operating systems at the same time?

 A. Thin client

 B. Virtualization workstation

 C. Standard thick client

 D. Audio/video editing workstation

REVIEW ANSWERS

1. **D** You can import or input pictures easily into a computer using a scanner.

2. **D** A webcam enables you to chat with both voice and video over the Internet.

3. **C** A retinal scanner is an example of a biometric device.

4. **C** A touch screen enables direct input of data using your fingers or a stylus.

5. **B** PCI is a 32-bit, parallel expansion bus.

6. **B** Many portable computers have a Mini-PCI slot where you can add a device.

7. **C** PCI Express (PCIe) provides a serial, rather than parallel, expansion bus.

8. **C** **D** Mary should both ground herself to the PC and unplug the PC to turn off the trickle charge on the motherboard before inserting the card.

9. **A** The quickest fix here would be to reinstall the old card and do a driver rollback.

10. **C** **D** Monitors and speakers are the two most common output devices on the PC, with the printer (not an option here) being the third.

11. **D** LCDs have far lower power demands than CRTs.

12. **A** A fuzzy LCD often is just running in a resolution that's not its native resolution. That's the first thing to check in such a situation.

13. **A** All monitors have some option to increase or decrease the brightness.

14. **A** You can use the Display Settings applet in Windows Vista to adjust the resolution of a monitor.

15. **B** A virtualization workstation can run multiple instances of operating systems at the same time through virtual machines.

Printers

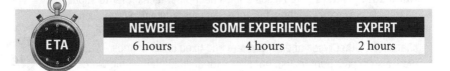

ETA	NEWBIE	SOME EXPERIENCE	EXPERT
	6 hours	4 hours	2 hours

A good tech understands the various types of printers and printer connections and can diagnose and troubleshoot printing problems to keep users up and running with all those paper documents. In most office and repair situations, you (as a tech) almost always get tagged, not as the PC repair person, but as the *computer person,* and *everyone* knows that printers are included in that description!

Objective 11.01 Types of Printers

Printers create print output—usually on paper, but also on other materials such as transparencies and cloth. This chapter helps you identify the different printer types, connections, configurations, and common troubleshooting issues.

Impact Printers

Impact printers use a series or matrix of pins to create printed dots arranged to form characters on paper, what's called a *dot-matrix pattern.* The speed at which an impact printer prints is measured in the number of characters it can produce per second. The print head mechanism pushes each pin into the ribbon, which then strikes the paper. The original dot-matrix print heads had 7 pins, while newer, letter-quality print heads use 24 pins to produce near letter quality (NLQ) documents. Figure 11.1 shows a typical impact printer.

Local Lingo

Dot-matrix printers You'll sometimes hear older techs refer to impact printers as dot-matrix printers, because that was a common term used during the heyday of impact printers that used a set of pins to draw characters. Other types of early printers had fixed letter stamps. These were also impact printers, but not useful for anything but typing words and numbers.

With impact printers, the printing mechanism physically strikes the page. The continual motion of the pins through the print head creates a ton of heat, so you should avoid touching the print head after printing a handful of pages or more. A hot print head can give you a nasty burn.

FIGURE 11.1 Impact printer

> **Exam Tip**
>
> Impact printers are the only style of printer that physically strike the paper.

Paper moves through an impact printer using a *tractor-feed* mechanism, as shown in Figure 11.2. Spoked wheels located on each side of the paper feed mechanism move the paper. The spokes on the outer edges of the wheels fit into holes on the sides of specially designed continuous-form paper. As the wheels turn, they pull the paper through the printer.

Because impact printers physically strike the page, you can use them to create multipart forms with ease using special, multilayer *impact paper*. Many offices and government agencies use them for that very reason. Although impact printers have been replaced in most homes and offices by newer, sexier inkjet and laser printers (discussed in the sections that follow), they are still popular in some settings.

FIGURE 11.2 Tractor-feed mechanism in an impact printer

Local Lingo

Carbon copy Early multipart forms used a special carbon-backed piece of paper in between the top page and the blank page behind it. Striking the outer page had enough impact to imprint the carbon on the second page, giving it the name *carbon copy*.

Inkjet Printers

Inkjet printers create printouts by squirting ink out of special inkjet cartridges. They use both black and colored ink cartridges, and they can combine ink colors to create a wide range of hues. Inkjet printers use either liquid ink cartridges or solid, wax-based ink cartridges. Figure 11.3 shows a typical inkjet printer.

An inkjet printer is a *non-impact* printer because its print mechanism never actually touches the paper. Because an inkjet printer processes an entire page at a time before it starts to print it, it is referred to as a *page* printer. The inkjet printer uses a *friction-feed* mechanism (or *feeder*) to feed paper through the printer. Sheets of paper are stacked in the paper tray, where small rollers press down to create friction and pull a sheet of paper through the printer.

Most liquid inkjet printers and all solid inkjet printers use a thermal process to eject ink onto the paper. The printing element heats up, boiling the ink in the case of liquid inkjet printers, and melting it in the case of solid inkjet printers. A tiny bubble of ink forms on the end of the print nozzle. Once the bubble becomes sufficiently enlarged, it pops, at which point electrically charged plates

FIGURE 11.3 Typical inkjet printer

deflect the ink onto the paper. Sounds kind of messy, but it's actually precise. An inkjet print head contains between 300 and 600 nozzles, each about the diameter of a human hair. Figure 11.4 illustrates a typical inkjet print head. When the inkjet cartridge is not in use, pump pressure keeps the ink from leaking out the nozzle.

Epson printers use a different, proprietary inkjet technology featuring a special crystal at the back of the ink reservoir that flexes when an electric current is applied to it. When the crystal flexes, it forces a drop of ink out of the nozzle. The way it flexes determines the size and placement of the resulting drop.

Both types of inkjet printers place ink cartridges and print nozzles into a *carriage* attached to a *carriage belt*. An *electronic controller* uses the belt to move the carriage.

A common problem with inkjet printers is the tendency for the ink inside the jets to dry out when the printer is not used, even for a relatively short time. To counter this problem, all inkjet printers move the print head to a special park position that keeps the ink from drying. Except for replacing the inkjet cartridges and print heads, you don't need to do much maintenance. In some cases, you may need to replace the rubber paper rollers or tracking belts, but most serious repairs are simply not cost effective. The low cost of new liquid ink inkjet printers makes them candidates for replacement rather than repair. The solid ink printers, on the other hand, are very expensive and should be repaired rather than replaced.

| FIGURE 11.4 | Detail of an inkjet print head |

Dye-Sublimation Printers

The term *sublimation* means to cause something to change from a solid form into a vapor and then back into a solid. This is exactly the process behind dye-sublimation printing (sometimes called *thermal dye transfer* printing).

The dye-sublimation technique uses a roll of heat-sensitive plastic film embedded with page-sized sections of cyan, magenta, and yellow dye (some also have a section of black dye). A print head containing thousands of heating elements capable of precise temperature control moves across the film, vaporizing the dyes and causing them to soak into specially coated paper underneath before cooling and reverting to a solid form. The process requires one pass per page for each color. Some printers also utilize a final finishing pass that applies a protective laminate coating to the page. Figure 11.5 shows how a dye-sublimation printer functions.

Documents printed through dye-sublimation display *continuous tone* images, meaning that each pixel dot is a blend of the different dye colors. This is in

Dye-ribbon roll

Thermal print head

Vaporized dye

FIGURE 11.5 Dye-sublimation printing process

contrast to the *dithered* images of other print technologies, which use closely packed, single-color dots to simulate blended colors. Dye-sublimation printers produce high-quality color output that rivals professional photo lab processing. They are used mainly for photo printing, high-end desktop publishing, medical and scientific imaging, or other applications for which fine detail and rich color are more important than cost and speed.

Smaller, specialized printers called snapshot printers use dye-sublimation to print photos at a reduced cost (compared to their full-sized counterparts). Still, when you can get a high-end inkjet printer for the same price and have the versatility to print documents with speed and low expense *and* high-quality photographs, the snapshot printers become less desirable.

Thermal Printers

You'll see two kinds of thermal printers in use: the *direct thermal* printer and the *thermal wax transfer* printer.

Direct thermal printers use some kind of *heating element* —such as a heated print head—to burn dots into the surface of special heat-sensitive paper. A *feeding assembly* pulls the paper into the proper place. If you remember the first generation of fax machines, you're already familiar with this type of printer. You don't see many fax machines of the direct thermal type in the workplace anymore, but you will often see this type of printer used in retail point-of-sale areas as receipt printers.

Thermal wax transfer printers work similarly to dye-sublimation printers, except that instead of using rolls of dye-embedded film, the film is coated with colored wax. The thermal print head passes over the film ribbon and melts the wax onto the paper. Unlike dye-sublimation printers, however, thermal wax printers don't require special papers and so are more flexible and somewhat cheaper to use.

Also in contrast to dye-sublimation printers, thermal wax printers don't offer continuous tone output, using color dithering instead. This means that their output isn't as good as dye-sublimation printers, but it is still quite good.

Laser and LED Printers

Laser printers rely on the photoconductive properties of certain organic compounds. *Photoconductive* means that particles of these compounds, when exposed to light (that's the *photo* part), will conduct electricity. Laser printers use lasers as a light source because of their precision. LED printers work the same way as laser printers, except that they use tiny LEDs as a light source instead of lasers. Both types of printers are usually simply called a laser printer. Unlike inkjet printers, the relatively high initial cost of laser printers makes their repair a practical and popular option. Figure 11.6 shows a typical laser printer.

Like inkjet printers, laser printers are non-impact page printers—the print mechanism never touches the paper, and the entire page is imaged before being transferred to paper. Some laser printers support *duplex* printing, which enables printing on both sides of the paper, either through a built-in mechanism or an add-on duplexing tray device. Modern laser printers are capable of resolutions as high as 2400×2400 dots per inch (dpi).

Exam Tip	
Know that printer resolution is measured in dots per inch (dpi) and printer speed is typically measured by pages per minute (ppm).	

It used to be that color wasn't available in laser printers—at least, not without spending prohibitively big bucks! The price of laser printing in color has dropped dramatically, however, so you can expect to see full-color laser printers deployed in the workplace and referenced on the CompTIA A+ certification exams.

FIGURE 11.6 Typical laser printer

Laser Printer Parts

Laser printers have many components, and the CompTIA A+ certification exams expect you to know them. Here's the list.

Toner Cartridge Components Many manufacturers incorporate laser printer components such as the imaging drum and fuser assembly (both described in the text that follows) into the toner cartridge (see Figure 11.7). While this makes replacement of individual parts nearly impossible, it also greatly reduces maintenance costs. Those parts most likely to break are replaced every time you replace the toner cartridge.

Travel Advisory

If you're looking for a company that sells laser printer parts, try The Printer Works, a large mail-order outfit with knowledgeable sales folks. Like experts at an auto parts store, they can often help you determine the source of a problem and then sell you the necessary part to fix it. The Printer Works is on the Web at www.printerworks.com.

FIGURE 11.7 Laser printer's toner cartridge

Toner The *toner* in a laser printer is a fine powder that's made up of plastic particles bonded to iron particles. The reservoir in the toner cartridge where the toner is stored is called the *hopper*. The *toner cylinder* charges the toner with a negative charge of between ~200 and ~500 volts. Because that charge falls between the original uniform negative charge of the photosensitive imaging drum (~600 to ~1000 volts) and the charge of the particles on the drum's surface hit by the laser (~100 volts), particles of toner are attracted to the areas of the photosensitive drum that were hit by the laser—that is, they're attracted to the areas with a positive charge *relative to* the toner particles.

> ## Travel Advisory
>
> Watch out for toner spills; the super-fine toner particles make quite a mess. They'll stain your clothes as badly and as permanently as ink and, worse, can prove toxic if inhaled. Don't sniff any toner!

A monochrome laser printer has a single toner hopper, but color laser printers usually have four to accommodate the primary colors (cyan, magenta, yellow; or CMY) and black (K). That color scheme is called *CMYK*.

The Imaging Drum The *imaging drum* (sometimes called the *photosensitive drum*) is an aluminum cylinder coated with particles of photosensitive compounds (see Figure 11.8). The drum itself is grounded to the power supply, but the coating is not. When light hits these particles, whatever electrical charge they may have had drains out through the grounded cylinder.

FIGURE 11.8 Toner cartridge with imaging drum exposed

As noted, most printer component manufacturers incorporate the imaging drum into the toner cartridge so that both components are replaced when the cartridge runs out of toner. Some makers, such as Okidata, use long-life imaging drum components that are replaced separately from the toner cartridge.

The imaging drum is extremely light sensitive and should not be exposed to light for longer than a few seconds. Bright lights such as direct sunlight can permanently damage an imaging drum. Imaging drums sometimes become dirty from dust or spilled toner. In these cases, the drum can be wiped clean with a dry, lint-free cloth. Keep in mind, however, that if you scratch the drum, the scratch will appear on every page printed from that point on!

Travel Advisory

Most color laser printers have four drums, one for each color and one for black.

Transfer Belt To help keep the colors aligned properly on a printout, many color laser printers use a *transfer belt* in addition to the four imaging drums (Figure 11.9). The drums work the same way as a monochrome drum, but the transfer phase puts each color on the transfer belt rather than directly on the page. Once all the colors are on the transfer belt, the combined toner layers are placed on the page in one step.

Local Lingo

Registration The process of aligning colors in a color printer is called *registration*. A *registration error* means the colors are out of alignment and the printout will look bad.

FIGURE 11.9 Transfer belt on a color laser printer

Erase Lamp The *erase lamp* exposes the entire surface of the photosensitive imaging drum with light, making the photosensitive coating conductive. Any electrical charge present in the particles bleeds away into the grounded drum, leaving the surface particles electrically neutral.

Primary Corona Wire The *primary corona wire,* located close to the imaging drum, never touches the drum. When the wire is charged with an extremely high voltage, an electric field (or corona) forms, allowing voltage to pass to the drum and charge the photosensitive particles on its surface. The *primary grid* regulates the transfer of voltage, ensuring that the surface of the drum receives a uniform negative charge of between ~600 and ~1000 volts.

Transfer Corona Wire/Roller To transfer the image from the photosensitive drum to the paper, the paper must be given a charge that will attract the toner particles off the drum and onto the paper. The *transfer corona wire,* or *transfer corona roller,* applies a positive charge to the paper, drawing the negatively charged toner particles to the paper. The paper, with its positive charge, is also attracted to the negatively charged drum. To prevent the paper from wrapping around the drum, a *static charge eliminator* removes the charge from the paper.

Laser or LED The *laser* is the printer's writing mechanism. Any particle on the drum struck by the laser becomes conductive, allowing its charge to be drained away into the grounded core of the drum. In this way, the laser *writes* a positive image onto the drum. Particles struck by the laser are left with a ~100 volt negative charge, compared to the ~600 to ~1000 volt negative charge of the rest of the drum surface.

Some printers use an array of powerful LEDs in place of a laser beam to write the image onto the imaging drum. Otherwise, LED printers work identically to laser printers.

Fuser In most printers, the *fuser* assembly (sometimes called the *fuser pad*) is outside the toner cartridge, but it can be an integrated component. After the static charge eliminator has removed the paper's static charge, the toner is still merely resting on top of the paper. The toner must be fused to the paper to make the image permanent. Two rollers—a pressure roller and a heated roller—work together to fuse the toner to the paper. The pressure roller presses against the bottom of the page, while the heated roller presses down on the top of the page, melting the toner into the paper. The heated roller has a nonstick coating to prevent the toner from sticking to it.

> **Travel Advisory**
>
> Laser printers' fuser pad assemblies have probably been responsible for more burned fingers than any other PC components. Use caution when working around the fuser assembly of a laser printer.

Paper Handling Components Several components help the laser printer handle paper input. The *pickup rollers* pull sheets of paper into the laser printer. The *separator pads* help the printer pull a single sheet at a time. On better printers, the duplexing assembly flips a page so it can be printed on both sides.

The Laser Printing Process

You can put these steps together to see how a typical laser printer does its job. Remember that some brands of laser printers may depart from this exact process, although most do work in exactly this order. The printing process (imaging process) contains seven steps, in this order:

1. Processing
2. Charging
3. Exposing
4. Developing
5. Transferring
6. Fusing
7. Cleaning

> **Exam Tip**
>
> Know the order of a laser printer's printing/imaging process.

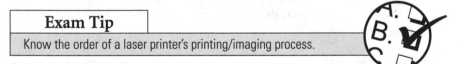

Step 1: Processing the Image Initially, the printer receives information about the queued image from the PC and the printer must process that image. Essentially, this means to respond to specific commands and get the rest of the device in motion.

Step 2: Charging the Drum Electrically charging the drum makes it receptive to new images. The corona wire applies a uniform negative charge to the entire surface of the drum, normally between ~600 and ~1000 volts.

Step 3: Exposing the Image Next the laser exposes or writes a positive image on the surface of the drum, as shown in Figure 11.10.

Step 4: Developing the Image Every particle on the drum hit by the laser will release most of its negative charge into the drum. Those particles are then positively charged relative to the toner particles and will attract them, creating a developed image on the drum.

Step 5: Transferring the Image To transfer the image from the drum onto the paper, the transfer corona charges the paper with a positive charge. Once in proximity to this positive charge, the negatively charged toner particles leap from the drum to the paper. Then the static charge eliminator removes the paper's positive charge, leaving the particles resting on the paper.

Step 6: Fusing the Image The fuser melts the toner onto the paper (see Figure 11.11). The printer then ejects the final printed copy, and the process of physical and electrical cleaning begins.

FIGURE 11.10 Exposing/writing the image

Static eliminator

Fuser rollers

Transfer corona

FIGURE 11.11 Fusing the image

Travel Advisory

The heated roller of the fuser produces enough heat to melt some types of plastic media, particularly overhead transparency materials. Never use transparencies in a laser printer unless they are specifically designed for use in laser printers. Use of nonapproved materials can seriously damage a laser printer and void the warranty!

Step 7: Cleaning the Drum Before printing each new page, the drum must be returned to a clean, fresh condition, so the printing process ends with the physical and electrical cleaning of the photosensitive drum. All residual toner left over from printing the previous page is removed, usually by a rubber cleaning blade that scrapes the surface of the drum. If residual particles remain on the drum, they appear as random black spots and streaks on the next page. The physical cleaning mechanism either deposits the residual toner in a debris cavity or recycles it by returning it to the toner cartridge hopper. Damage to the drum during the physical cleaning process causes a permanent mark to be printed on every page.

| **FIGURE 11.12** | Cleaning and erasing the drum |

The imaging drum must also be electrically cleaned, as shown in Figure 11.12. One or more erase lamps bombard the surface of the drum with the appropriate wavelengths of light, causing the surface particles to discharge into the grounded drum. After the cleaning process, the drum should be completely free of toner and have a neutral electrical charge.

Other Laser Printer Components

Although the majority of the printing activity takes place within the toner cartridge, many other parts of the laser printer are hard at work outside the cartridge, as you can see in Figure 11.13.

Power Supplies All laser printers have at least two separate power supplies. The first power supply is called the *primary power supply* or sometimes just the *power supply*. The primary power supply powers the motors that move the paper, the system electronics, the laser, and the transfer corona.

The second power supply is the *high-voltage* power supply. It usually powers only the primary corona. The extremely high voltage of this power supply makes it one of the most dangerous devices in the world of PCs. Therefore, it's imperative that—except when inserting a new toner cartridge or paper—you *always turn off* a laser printer before you open it.

Printer memory System board Toner cartridge High-voltage power supply

Gearbox/motors Fuser assembly Sublogic board Paper tray Primary power supply

FIGURE 11.13 Inside a laser printer

Turning Gears A laser printer performs many mechanical operations. The paper must be picked up, fed through, and kicked out of the printer. The photosensitive roller must be turned, and the laser, or a mirror, must be moved from left to right. The toner must be evenly distributed, and the fuser assembly must squish the toner into the paper. All these functions are performed by a complex system of gears. In most laser printers, these gear systems are packed together in discrete units powered by their own solenoid motors. These units are generically called *gear packs* or *gearboxes*. Most laser printers have two or three gearboxes. These are relatively easy to remove and replace in the rare case that one of them fails.

System Board Every laser printer has at least one electronic board containing the main processor, the printer's ROM, and the RAM it uses to store the image before it's printed. Many printers divide these functions among two or three boards dispersed around the printer. The printer may also have an extra ROM chip, or a slot where you can install an extra ROM chip, usually for special functions such as PostScript printing. When the printer doesn't have enough RAM to store the image before it prints, it generates a Memory Overflow error. Solve this condition by adding more RAM.

> ### Travel Advisory
>
> Adding RAM is usually a simple job—just snapping in a DIMM stick or two—but getting the *right* RAM is important. Call the printer manufacturer and ask what type of RAM it needs. Although most printer companies will happily sell you their expensive RAM, most printers can use generic dynamic RAM (DRAM) like the kind you use in your PC.

Status Screen Just about every laser and LED printer has a small display called generically a status screen, that enables the printer to communicate directly to the user. The status screen shows error messages and printer status (warming up, load letter, and so on). Various display technologies have been used over the years; current printer screens are standard LCDs.

Network Interface Recognizing that most offices share networked printers, many manufacturers include integrated network interface cards (NICs) on some printers. These printers have built-in print server software that enables them to be plugged directly into an available network plug instead of attached to a PC.

Ozone Filter The coronas inside laser printers generate *ozone* (O_3). While the amount generated isn't harmful to humans, high concentrations of ozone will damage printer components. To counter this problem, most laser printers have a special ozone filter that must be replaced periodically. The best time is when you replace the toner cartridge, and in fact, many toner cartridges come packaged with a new ozone filter.

Sensors and Switches Every laser printer contains a large array of sensors and switches. The sensors are used to detect a broad range of conditions such as paper jams, empty paper trays, or low toner levels. Many sensors are actually tiny switches that detect conditions such as open printer doors. Most of the time, these sensors and switches work reliably, but they can occasionally become dirty or broken and send a false signal to the printer. Simple inspection is usually sufficient to determine whether a problem is real or just the result of a faulty sensor or switch.

Finishers Some printers also include components called *finishers* that perform tasks such as collating, stapling, and binding printed documents. Typically, these functions are beyond the capabilities of all but high-end, commercial printers.

Exam Tip
Know and understand the various laser printer components.

Objective 11.02 Installing Printers

You need to take a moment to understand how Windows handles printing, and then you'll see how to install and configure printers for use with these operating systems.

To Windows, a "printer" is not a physical device; it is a *program* that controls one or more physical printers. The *physical* printer is called a "print device" to Windows (although I continue to use the term "printer" for most purposes, just like almost every tech on the planet). Printer drivers and a spooler are present, but in Windows they are integrated into the printer itself (Figure 11.14). This arrangement gives Windows amazing flexibility. For example, one printer can support multiple print devices, enabling a system to act as a print server. If one print device goes down, the printer software automatically redirects the output to a working print device.

| **FIGURE 11.14** | Printer driver and spooler in Windows |

Printer Languages

Printers are designed to accept predefined printer languages that handle both characters and graphics. Your software must use the proper language when communicating with your printer so that your printer can output documents onto a piece of paper. Most printers use the *graphical device interface (GDI)* component of Windows to handle print functions. Some might use the *Adobe PostScript* language, while others use the Hewlett-Packard–developed *Printer Control Language (PCL)*. The bottom line for installation purposes is that you need to install the proper drivers for the printer. That includes installing the drivers appropriate for a given operating system.

Physical Connection

Print devices connect through a multipurpose port, such as USB, FireWire, or parallel, or wirelessly through Bluetooth, Wi-Fi, or infrared (IR). You might encounter a dedicated serial printer or a SCSI (small computer systems interface) printer, but these are so rare as to be almost not worth mentioning. Some printers have a slot for an add-on Ethernet network card so you can connect them directly to a network switch, just like a PC. Finally, you can connect to a print server on a LAN and install a networked printer rather than a local printer.

Exam Tip
The most common wireless standard used with printers is *802.11x*. See Chapter 20 for the details on wireless networking.

Setting Up Printers

Setting up a printer is so easy that it's almost scary. Most printers are Plug and Play, so installation is as easy as plugging the printer in and loading the driver, if needed. If the system does not detect the printer or if the printer is not Plug and Play, choose Start | Printers and Faxes in Windows XP to open the Printers applet. For Windows Vista, you need to open up the Control Panel and find the Printer menu item—it is either by itself or, in the Category View, under Hardware. You can also find the icon for this applet in the Control Panel of Windows XP. In Windows 7, select Start | Devices and Printers to open the Devices and Printers applet (or open the applet directly from the Control Panel).

> **Exam Tip**
>
> If you're not logged in as a member of the Administrators group in Windows XP, you will be unable to install a printer. Switch user accounts and go through the installation process again.

As you might guess, you install a new printer by clicking the *Add a printer* link or icon. This starts the Add Printer Wizard. You must choose to install either a printer plugged directly into your system or a network printer (Figure 11.15). You can use the *Automatically detect and install my Plug and Play printer* option in many cases when installing a USB printer.

If you choose a local printer, the applet next asks you to select a port (Figure 11.16); select the port in which you installed the new printer. Once you select the port, Windows asks you to specify the type of printer, either by selecting the type from the list or using the Have Disk option, just as you would for any other device. When you click Next on this screen, Windows installs the printer.

🖶 Add Printer

What type of printer do you want to install?

➔ Add a local printer
Use this option only if you don't have a USB printer. (Windows automatically installs USB printers when you plug them in.)

➔ Add a network, wireless or Bluetooth printer
Make sure that your computer is connected to the network, or that your Bluetooth or wireless printer is turned on.

Next Cancel

FIGURE 11.15 Choosing a local or network printer in Windows 7

FIGURE 11.16 Selecting a port in Windows 7

Figure 11.17 shows a typical Windows 7 Devices and Printers screen on a system with several printers installed. Note the small check mark under the Samsung SCX-4623 Series icon; this shows that the device is the default printer. If you have multiple printers, you can change the default printer by right-clicking the printer's icon and selecting *Set as Default Printer*.

Exam Tip

In addition to the Devices and Printers applet, Windows 7 (excluding the Home Premium edition) also includes the Print Management console. This tool enables you to view and modify all the printers and drivers on your PC or connected to your network. You can also manage any Windows print servers connected to the network. Many of Print Management's advanced features go beyond the scope of the CompTIA A+ exams, but know that it centralizes (and in a few cases, enhances) the standard printer controls in Windows 7. You can find Print Management in Control Panel | Administrative Tools | Print Management.

FIGURE 11.17 Installed printers in the Devices and Printers applet

Optimizing Print Performance

Although a quality printer is the first step toward quality output, your output relies on factors other than the printer itself. What you see on the screen may not match what comes out of the printer, so calibration is important. Using the wrong type of paper can result in less-than-acceptable printed documents. Configuring the printer driver and spool settings can also affect your print jobs.

Calibration

If you've ever tweaked a digital photograph so it looks perfect on screen, only to discover that the final printout was darker than you had hoped, consider calibrating your monitor. *Calibration* matches the print output of your printer to the visual output on your monitor and governs that through software. All three parts need to be set up properly for you to print what you see consistently.

Computer monitors output in RGB—that is, they compose colors using red, green, and blue pixels—while printers mix their colors differently to arrive at

their output. The CMYK method, for example, composes colors from cyan (blue), magenta (red), yellow, and black.

The upshot of all this is that the printer tries to output using CMYK (or another technique) what you see on the screen that uses RGB. But because the two color modes do not create color the same way, you see color shifts and not-so-subtle differences between the onscreen image and the printed image. By calibrating your monitor, you can adjust the setting to match the output of your printer. This can be done manually through "eyeballing" it or automatically using calibration hardware.

To calibrate your monitor manually, obtain a test image from the Web (try sites such as www.DigitalDog.net) and print it out. If you have a good eye, you can compare this printout to what you see on the screen and make the adjustments manually through your monitor's controls or display settings.

You can (and should) calibrate a color inkjet if you're printing high-resolution photographs. Calibration tools align the cartridge nozzles properly to the paper. These tools aren't cheap, though, so you're unlikely to use them outside of a graphics company or professional photographer's shop.

Objective 11.03 Troubleshooting Printers

It's the rare business that has a dedicated printer technician on staff. As a CompTIA A+ certified PC tech, most businesses expect your problem-solving skills to extend beyond the computer to the printer. Printer-related errors come in a variety of forms, and troubleshooting them can range from pleasingly simple to headache-inducingly complex. When troubleshooting printers, try the obvious fix first, and then graduate to more advanced troubleshooting techniques. This section describes common printer errors and solutions.

Know that many manufacturers provide kits containing components that should be replaced on a regular schedule. These maintenance kits often include a fuser as well as one or more rollers or pads. Typically, you need to reset the page counter after installing a maintenance kit so the printer can remind you to perform maintenance again after a certain number of pages have been printed.

Exam Tip

Know the basic troubleshooting procedures for all printer types.

Feed and Output

Printers often develop problems with the paper-feed mechanism. When paper-feed problems occur, the paper can become jammed in the feed mechanism, halting the printing process.

Problems with Friction-Feed Mechanisms

The most common problem with friction-feed mechanisms is usually caused by user error: too much paper in the paper tray. This causes the feed mechanism to pick up several sheets of paper and try to send them through the printer at the same time, resulting in a paper jam. Most paper trays have a line or symbol on the edge to show the maximum allowed paper in the paper tray at one time.

Another cause of this type of error is static electricity. Static buildup in friction-feed mechanisms causes pages to stick together, which again results in several pages being fed through the printer at the same time. To prevent paper jams caused by static, fan the stack of papers on a desk or other surface before placing it in the paper feed tray. This loosens the pages and reduces the static cling.

Believe it or not, having too little paper in the paper tray also causes feed errors. If the paper level is too low, the rollers can have trouble catching hold of the top sheet. If sufficient paper seems to be in the tray, check to see whether you're using recycled paper, which can sometimes be thinner than normal paper and more difficult for the rollers to grab.

To fix a paper jam, turn off the printer, and then open it and gently extract the paper. Whenever possible, move the paper in the direction it would normally go. Remember your physics, and pull slowly and gently. This minimizes the likelihood that you'll rip off the exposed part of the paper. Also, pulling too hard can damage the rollers in the feed mechanism. Some printers won't continue printing after you fix the problem until you press the online or reset button.

Problems with Tractor-Feed Mechanisms

Impact printers' tractor-feed mechanisms require you to line up the spokes on the wheels with the holes in the paper. If the holes on either side of the paper aren't lined up evenly, the text might print diagonally on the page. If the holes are uneven, the paper will crease, wrinkle, and jam.

Because they use continuous-form paper, tractor-feed printers can require a bit of skill to position the paper properly. Each model of printer has its own special way of positioning the paper vertically, making trial and error an essential part of this process. If you get this wrong, your top and bottom margins will be off, and sometimes lines of text will even split across two sheets of paper.

Printer Errors

Printing errors centered on the printer itself can be a bit more complicated to troubleshoot than paper-feed errors. Sometimes, printer errors are accompanied by error messages from either the PC or the printer itself. Other times, you'll have to investigate a bit further to get to the root of the problem.

Sometimes, you'll need to do a Google search to interpret the error code displayed on the printer's LCD status screen so you can take appropriate action. An HP printer might show error code 20, but not include the accompanying "insufficient memory" text. A quick search will tell you it's a low memory error. You can decide at that point to either add more RAM to the printer or reduce the complexity of whatever it is you're trying to print.

Out-of-Paper Errors

The cause of a *paper out* error should be pretty obvious: no paper is in the printer. To correct this problem on a tractor-feed printer, lift the printer's lid and carefully feed the first sheet onto the tractor wheels. To fix this problem on a friction-feed printer, simply add paper to the paper tray.

Input/Output Errors

Input/output errors occur when the computer has no connectivity with the printer and thus cannot communicate. When troubleshooting an input/output error, start with these possibilities:

- Is the printer plugged in?
- Is the printer turned on?
- Are all cables firmly connected?
- Is the proper driver for your printer installed? If so, could it have become corrupted?
- If the PC connects wirelessly to the printer, is the Wi-Fi or Bluetooth network functional?

If all these check out, try restarting the printer, the PC, or both. Restart the wireless access point (WAP) for a wireless setup. Simply restarting can sometimes fix a multitude of problems. If the printer still produces the input/output error, connect the printer to another computer. If the printer does not work on the second computer, you know you have a printer problem. If it works fine on the other computer, you have a configuration problem.

Incorrect Port Mode Errors

An *incorrect port mode* error indicates the parallel port to which you connected the printer isn't using the correct port mode. If you receive this error, use the CMOS settings program to change the port mode to one that's compatible with your printer.

No Default Printer Errors

A *no default printer* error indicates that no printer has been installed or that you haven't set a default printer. To do so, open the Printers dialog box. Choose the printer you want to be used as the default printer, and then right-click it. Select *Set as Default Printer* from the menu. If there are no printers on that system, use the Add Printer Wizard and follow the instructions provided.

Toner Low and Ink Low Errors

When the toner cartridge in a laser printer runs low, it issues a warning before the cartridge runs out completely. Replace the cartridge as soon as you see the error to avoid half-finished or delayed print jobs. You should also replace inkjet cartridges promptly to prevent clogged print nozzles.

Consumable Refills Ink and toner refill kits are much less expensive than purchasing new cartridges and may seem like an economic solution to the consumable problem. Because you're reusing the original cartridge components, however, such as the pump and heating element, you risk damaging your printer. Purchasing new cartridges is more economical than fixing your laser printer because of damage caused by old cartridges.

Remanufactured laser toner cartridges, however, are usually safe to use and reliable. Many laser toner manufacturers even have their own recycling programs.

Access Denied

If you add a networked printer on a computer that requires authentication (a user name and password) and forget to select the check box to remember the password, you'll get an Access Denied error message when you try to print. This applies primarily to Windows XP Home edition.

Print Quality

Depending on the printer type you're using, several factors might affect print quality.

Impact Print Quality Issues

One downside to impact printers is the need for ongoing maintenance. Keep the *platen* (the roller or plate on which the pins impact) and the print head clean. Be sure to lubricate gears and pulleys according to the manufacturer's specifications. Never lubricate the print head, however, because the lubricant will smear and stain the paper.

White Bars on Text White bars through the text point to a dirty or damaged print head. Try cleaning the print head with a little denatured alcohol. If the problem persists, replace the print head. Print heads for most printers are readily available from the manufacturer.

Chopped Text If the characters look chopped off at the top or bottom, the print head probably needs to be adjusted. Follow the manufacturer's instructions for proper adjustment.

Pepper Look If the paper is covered with dots and small smudges—the "pepper look"—the platen is dirty. Clean the platen with a soft cloth.

Faded Image If the image is faded and you know the ribbon is good, try adjusting the print head closer to the platen.

Light to Dark If the image is okay on one side of the paper but fades on the other, the platen is out of adjustment. Platens are difficult to adjust, so your best plan is to send it to the manufacturer's local warranty/repair center. The money you'll spend will save you from the frustration of trying to do it yourself.

Inkjet Print Quality Issues

Inkjet printers are more complicated than impact printers, which also means more things can go wrong.

Unclear Images If an inkjet printer is producing unclear images, the ink cartridges are probably running low on ink and need to be replaced.

Blank Printouts If an inkjet printer is producing blank printouts, either the ink level is low or the nozzles have become clogged. First check the ink and replace the cartridge if it's low. If the ink is at an acceptable level, the nozzles have probably become clogged. To unclog the nozzles, dip a cotton swab in denatured alcohol and gently wipe away any dried ink.

Confetti Printouts Printouts with ink speckles, or *confetti,* always indicate an ink problem. Over time, ink can escape into the body of an inkjet printer, eventually finding its way onto subsequent printouts. To fix or prevent speckling, clean the insides of the printer with a damp cloth.

Wrong Colors in Printouts If an inkjet produces printouts using the wrong colors, check for low ink in one or more cartridges, or a dirty nozzle. First check the ink cartridges. If they're full, clean the nozzles with a cotton swab dipped in denatured alcohol.

Smudges on Printouts Smudges on printouts are most often caused by the user touching the printout before the ink has completely dried. Other causes include dirty printers and worn-out nozzles. Worn-out nozzles cannot be fixed. You must replace the ink cartridges if the nozzles have become worn out.

Laser Print Quality Issues

Laser printers usually manifest problems by creating poor output. One of the most important tests you can do on any printer—not only a laser printer—is called a *diagnostic print page* or an *engine test page.* You can print a test page by holding down the Online button as the printer is started or by selecting the menu option on the printer's operator panel. You can also open the Printers dialog box in Windows and issue the test page command from the printer's Properties dialog box.

> ### Exam Tip
>
> The CompTIA A+ certification exams are *very* concerned that you understand laser printer maintenance. Make sure you know the causes and solutions for various maintenance problems.

Blank Paper Blank sheets of paper usually mean the printer is out of toner. If the printer does have toner and nothing prints, print a diagnostic print page. If that's also blank, remove the toner cartridge and look at the imaging drum inside. If the image is still on the drum, you know the transfer corona or the high-voltage power supply has failed. Check the printer's maintenance guide to see how to zero in on the bad part and replace it.

Toner Not Fused If you get a printout with the toner not fused to the paper, check the fusing mechanism first. If it's dead, replace it.

Ghosting Sometimes ghost images appear at regular intervals on the printed page. Either the imaging drum hasn't fully discharged and is picking up toner from a previous image, or a previous image has used up so much toner that either the supply of charged toner is insufficient or the toner hasn't been adequately charged.

Light Ghosting vs. Dark Ghosting A variety of problems can cause both light and dark ghosting, but the most common source of light ghosting is *developer starvation*. If you ask a laser printer to print an extremely dark or complex image, it can use up so much toner that the toner cartridge won't be able to charge enough toner to print the next image. The proper solution is to use less toner by doing the following:

- Lowering the resolution of the page (print at 300 dpi instead of 600 dpi)
- Using a different pattern
- Avoiding 50 percent grayscale and dot-on/dot-off patterns
- Changing the layout so grayscale patterns don't follow black areas
- Making dark patterns lighter and light patterns darker
- Adjusting print density and Resolution Enhancement Technology (RET) settings
- Printing a completely blank page immediately prior to the page with the ghosting image and as part of the same print job

Low temperature and low humidity can aggravate ghosting problems. Check your users' manual for environmental recommendations.

Dark ghosting can sometimes be caused by a damaged drum. It can be fixed by replacing the toner cartridge. Light ghosting cannot be solved in this way. Switching other components usually won't fix ghosting problems because they're a side effect of the entire printing process.

Vertical White Lines Vertical white lines are usually caused by clogged toner. Clogs prevent the proper dispersion of toner on the drum. Try shaking the toner cartridge from side to side to dislodge the clog, or, if that doesn't work, replace the toner cartridge.

Blotchy Print This mostly results from the uneven dispersion of toner— especially if the toner is low. Try shaking the toner from side to side. Also, be sure the printer is level. Finally, make sure the paper isn't wet in spots. If the blotches are in a regular order, check the fusing rollers and the photosensitive drum for foreign objects.

Spotty Print If spots appear at regular intervals on the printout, the printer's drum may be damaged or toner may be stuck to the fuser rollers. Try wiping off the fuser rollers. Check the drum for damage. If the drum is damaged, you must get a new toner cartridge.

Embossed Effect If your prints have an embossed effect (like when you put a penny under a piece of paper and rub it with a pencil), a foreign object is almost certainly on a roller. Use regular water with a soft cloth to try to remove it. If the foreign object is on the photosensitive drum, you'll have to use a new toner cartridge.

Incomplete Characters Incompletely printed characters on laser-printed transparencies can sometimes be corrected by adjusting the print density. Remember to use only materials approved for use in laser printers.

Creased Pages Laser printers have up to four rollers. In addition to the heat and pressure rollers of the fusing assembly, rollers are designed to move the paper from the source tray to the output tray. These rollers crease the paper to avoid curling, which would cause paper jams in the printer. If the creases are noticeable, try using a different paper type. Cotton bond paper is usually more susceptible to noticeable creasing than other bonds. You might also try sending the output to the face-up tray, which eliminates one roller. No hardware solution exists for this problem. This is simply a side effect of the process.

Warped, Overprinted, or Poorly Formed Characters Poorly formed characters can indicate either a problem with the paper (or other media) or a problem with the hardware.

Incorrect media causes a number of problems. Avoid paper that is too rough or too smooth. Paper that's too rough interferes with the fusing of characters and their initial definition. If the paper is too smooth (like some coated papers, for example), it might feed improperly, causing distorted or overwritten characters. Although you can purchase laser printer–specific paper, all laser printers will run acceptably on standard photocopy paper. Because paper picks up humidity from the air, don't open a ream of paper until you're ready to load it into the printer. Always fan the paper before loading it into the printer—especially if the paper has been left out for more than a few days.

The durability of a well-maintained laser printer makes hardware a rare source of character-printing problems, but it is a possibility. Fortunately, checking the hardware is easy. Most laser printers have a self-test function, often combined with a diagnostic printout, that's quite handy to verify those "Is it the

printer or is it the computer?" questions. Run the self-test to check for connectivity and configuration problems. Following are possible solutions:

- Replace the toner cartridge, especially if you hear popping noises.
- Check the cabling.
- Replace the data cable, especially if bends or crimps exist or objects are resting on the cable.
- If you have a Front Menu Panel, turn off Advanced Functions and High Speed Settings to determine whether they aren't working properly or aren't supported by your current software configuration (check your manuals).

If these solutions don't work, the problem might not be user-serviceable. Contact an authorized service center.

General Print Quality Issues

Now that you understand some of the print quality issues that can affect the individual printer types, you need to understand the print quality issues that can affect all three types. Let's look at the most common print problems in Windows.

Print Job Never Prints If you click the Print button and nothing comes out of the printer, check the obvious things first. Is the printer turned on? Is it connected to the computer and to a power source? Is it online? Does it have paper? Assuming the printer is physically in good order, the next step is to check the print server's print *spooler* status.

The print spooler is the hard disk space reserved for channeling print jobs from the PC to the printer. You can see the spooler status either by double-clicking the printer's icon in the Printers applet or by clicking the tiny printer icon in the notification area if it's present (if you're having a problem, it's almost always there).

Print spoolers can overflow or become corrupt because of a lack of disk space or too many print jobs in the queue. The Printers window shows all the pending print jobs and enables you to delete, start, or pause jobs. The best answer is usually to delete the print jobs and try again or stop and start the Print Spooler service.

Exam Tip

You need administrator privileges to delete jobs from the print queue.

You can stop and start the Print Spooler service and flush print jobs in a couple of ways. The Services applet in Administrative Tools will do the job. Right-click the Print Spooler service and select Stop. Do the same thing to start it, only select Start. You can type the command-line command **net stop spooler** to stop the Print Spooler service. Typing **net start spooler** starts it back up.

You might also run into a situation where the print jobs seem to spool, but then just vanish, or "despool," as the jargon goes. The print spooler shows print jobs for a brief moment, but then nothing prints. Check the printer driver. An incorrect driver for the attached printer can cause this issue.

Incorrect Page Size A print job that comes out sized incorrectly usually points to a user mistake in setting up the job. Check the Print dialog box for incorrect print parameters. Also check the Page Setup option in the relevant application. Make sure the user is setting up the page properly.

If you know the page is set up correctly, recheck the printer drivers. If necessary, uninstall and reinstall the print drivers. If the problem persists, the printer's print engine may be causing the trouble, but that is a possibility only when you continually get the same strangely sized printouts using a number of different applications.

Garbled Characters in Printout Misaligned or garbled printouts invariably point to a corrupted or incorrect driver. Make sure you're using the appropriate printer driver and then uninstall and reinstall the driver. If the problem persists, it's possible that you're asking the printer to do something it cannot do. For example, you might be printing to a PostScript printer with a PCL driver. Check the printer type to verify you haven't installed the wrong type of driver for that printer. Try some of these diagnostic avenues:

- Make sure the printer cables are attached firmly and haven't become loose.
- Turn off the power to the printer, and then turn it on again.
- To check the basic communication between the PC and the printer, try printing a plain text file—Notepad is excellent for this.
- Restart your computer. Many Windows and application problems can be resolved simply by restarting your system.
- Reinstall your printer drivers. Drivers occasionally become corrupted and might need reinstalling.
- Check your resource settings for the parallel or USB port to verify no resource conflicts exist.

- Connect the printer to a different computer. If the printer continues producing garbage characters on the second computer, you know the problem lies within the printer.
- Try printing a smaller document. If you can print a smaller document, the problem may be insufficient memory in the printer. Insufficient memory can be remedied by adding more RAM to the printer.

Printer Not Responding If the printer isn't responding, check the easy things first. Make sure the printer is turned on and the cables are securely and correctly attached. Make sure the printer is online. Make sure the application you're printing from is sending the print job to the correct printer. Make sure you have the correct print driver installed for the printer. Try to print a test page. Try attaching the printer to a new computer. If nothing works, your printer might have to go to a printer repair facility.

> **Travel Advisory**
>
> As much as you might enjoy smacking an unresponsive printer, that's generally not the best idea, primarily because it rarely works.

Objective 11.04 Maintenance

Printers are more mechanical in nature than most PC components and so require regular maintenance to stay in top running form. Paper dust, toner, and ink deposits are the root of many printer problems. Paper dust can jam gears and causes electrostatic discharge (ESD). Excess ink or toner causes poor-quality printouts. Cleaning your printer regularly can prevent many problems from occurring.

On all types of printers, be sure to turn the power off and unplug all cables from the printer before servicing. You should also wait a few minutes after shutting down the printer to allow the print heads and fuser components to cool down and the onboard capacitor circuits to discharge.

Exam Tip
Know the proper cleaning procedures for all printer types.

Cleaning Impact Printers

Follow these steps to clean an impact printer:

1. Remove the plastic casing and carefully pull the print head away from the platen.
2. Inspect the ribbon and replace it, if necessary.
3. Loosen paper dust from the printer by using compressed air and remove it with an antistatic vacuum.
4. Clean the print head with denatured alcohol.
5. Remove paper from the platen.
6. Inspect the carriage belt and replace it if it's worn or cracked.

After you finish cleaning the printer, lubricate the gears and pulleys—*not* the print head itself! Never lubricate the print head, or your printouts will appear stained. Reassemble the printer in reverse order and run a test printout.

Cleaning Inkjet Printers

To clean liquid or solid inkjet printers, follow these steps:

1. Wear rubber or vinyl gloves to avoid contact with the ink in liquid inkjet printers. The ink won't hurt you, but it stains like crazy.
2. Remove the plastic housing and ink cartridges.
3. Loosen paper dust from the printer by using compressed air and remove it with an antistatic vacuum.
4. Wipe off the ink cartridges with a damp cloth.
5. Wipe excess ink from the inside of the printer with a damp cloth.
6. Clean the platen.
7. Inspect the carriage belt and replace it, if necessary.

Once you're finished, reassemble the printer and run a test printout.

Cleaning Thermal and Dye-Sublimation Printers

To clean thermal-based printers such as thermal wax and dye-sublimation printers, follow these steps:

1. Remove the wax or dye ribbon cartridge.

2. Loosen paper dust from the printer by using compressed air and remove it with an antistatic vacuum.

3. Wipe off the ribbon cartridges with a damp cloth.

4. Wipe excess ink residue from the inside of the printer with a damp cloth.

5. Use compressed air to loosen dust from the drive gears and remove it with an antistatic vacuum.

6. Be careful not to disturb the thermal print head!

Once you're finished, reassemble the printer and run a test printout.

Cleaning Laser Printers

To clean a laser printer, follow these steps:

1. Remove and wipe off the toner cartridges.

2. Loosen paper dust from the printer by using compressed air and remove it with an antistatic vacuum.

3. Use a special toner vacuum to clean up any toner. The particles are so fine that they'll go through a regular vacuum bag and slime the inside of the vacuum cleaner. Avoid getting any toner on your clothing, as it will create a permanent stain.

4. Use the special tool supplied with the printer to clean the transfer corona wire. You can also wipe the wire with a swab and denatured alcohol.

5. On LED printers, use a clean, lint-free cloth to clean the LED array. Many toner kits come with a special one-use cleaning pad for this purpose.

6. Clean the fusing rollers and replace the roller pad.

7. Replace the ozone filter.

8. Clean the rubber guide rollers with clean water.

When you finish, carefully reassemble and reconnect the printer and run a test printout.

Periodic Maintenance of Laser Printers

Although keeping the printer clean is critical to its health and well-being, every laser printer has certain components that you need to replace periodically. Your ultimate source for determining the parts that need to be replaced (and when to replace them) is the printer manufacturer. Following the manufacturer's maintenance guidelines will help to ensure years of trouble-free, dependable printing from your laser printer.

Many manufacturers provide kits that contain components that you should replace on a regular schedule. These *maintenance kits* often include a fuser as well as one or more rollers or pads. Typically, you need to reset the page counter after installing a maintenance kit so the printer can remind you to perform maintenance again after a certain number of pages have been printed.

Following these guidelines can help a laser printer last a very long time and thus provide more return on the initial investment.

CHECKPOINT

✔**Objective 11.01: Types of Printers**　Know the types of printers—impact, inkjet, dye-sublimation, thermal, and laser—and how each one works. Understand the laser printing process and know its seven discrete steps in the order they occur.

✔**Objective 11.02: Installing Printers**　Installing printers involves a few steps. First, you need to connect the print device to your system through parallel, USB, FireWire, NIC, or wirelessly. You need to install the proper driver, such as a GDI driver for Windows or a PCL driver for some HP printers.

✔**Objective 11.03: Troubleshooting Printers**　Common printer problems include paper jams and problems with paper-feed mechanisms, I/O errors, low toner/ink, a huge variety of print-quality issues, and nonresponsive printers.

✔**Objective 11.04: Maintenance**　The CompTIA A+ certification exams expect you to know the proper cleaning procedures for each printer type, including impact, inkjet, and laser. In general, you will vacuum up small particles; clean appropriate surfaces and mechanisms; and, where needed, replace certain parts such as ribbons, belts, pads, rollers, and filters.

REVIEW QUESTIONS

1. What are the seven steps of the laser printer process?

 A. Paper in, Cleaning, Charging, Developing, Transferring, Fusing, Paper out

 B. Processing, Charging, Exposing, Developing, Transferring, Fusing, Cleaning

 C. Charging, Cleaning, Exposing, Transferring, Printing, Fusing, Processing

 D. Cleaning, Processing, Charging, Developing, Transferring, Exposing, Fusing

2. What type of feed mechanism do impact printers use?

 A. Tractor feed

 B. Friction feed

 C. Paper feed

 D. Spoke feed

3. Which printer types use friction-feed mechanisms? (Select two.)

 A. Dot-matrix

 B. Laser

 C. Inkjet

 D. Impact

4. Garbled characters are appearing in a printout. What's the most likely problem?

 A. The printer is old and needs to be replaced.

 B. You have the wrong language set up for the printer.

 C. The printer needs to be cleaned.

 D. The computer isn't communicating correctly with the printer.

5. What does the primary corona wire in a laser printer do?

 A. Cleans the drum

 B. Charges the drum

 C. Creates the image on the drum

 D. Transfers the image from the drum to the paper

6. What do inkjet printers use to deflect ink onto a page?

 A. A print head

 B. Electrically charged plates

 C. Fusers

 D. Rollers

7. Dye-sublimation printers use what to transfer ink to the paper surface?

 A. Impact print head

 B. Thermal print head

 C. Electrically charged plates

 D. Print nozzles

8. Which part of an impact printer is most dangerous?

 A. The print head

 B. The ribbon

 C. The feed mechanism

 D. The wheels

9. Which part of a laser printer is the most dangerous?

 A. Laser

 B. Primary corona

 C. Fuser

 D. High-voltage power supply

10. Which type of printer can create carbon copies?

 A. Laser

 B. Inkjet

 C. USB

 D. Impact

11. What component of a laser printer transfers the image from the drum to the paper?

 A. Primary corona

 B. Fusing rollers

 C. Transfer corona

 D. Friction feed

REVIEW ANSWERS

1. **B** The steps of the laser printer process are Processing, Charging, Exposing, Developing, Transferring, Fusing, and Cleaning.

2. **A** Impact printers use a tractor-feed mechanism.

3. **B** **C** Both laser and inkjet printers use a friction-feed mechanism.

4. **D** Garbled characters in a printout mean the computer isn't communicating correctly with the printer. One possible reason for this is incorrect or corrupted drivers.

5. **B** The primary corona wire charges the drum.

6. **B** Electrically charged plates deflect ink onto the paper.

7. **B** Dye-sublimation printers use a thermal print head to vaporize dyes and transfer them to paper.

8. **A** The print head on an impact printer gets very hot and can burn you.

9. **D** The high-voltage power supply inside the laser printer can pack a lot of punch and give you a terrible shock. Be very careful inside a laser printer!

10. **D** Impact printers can create carbon copies.

11. **C** The transfer corona in laser printers transfers the image from the drum to the paper.

Portable Computers

ETA	NEWBIE	SOME EXPERIENCE	EXPERT
	3 hours	2 hours	1 hour

Portable computing devices come in all sorts of sizes these days, from the traditional clam-shell–style portable PC—usually called a *laptop* or *notebook*—to *tablets* like the Apple iPad and *smartphones* like the iPhone. Most users and techs refer to the latter as *mobile devices*. All of these portable computing devices enable you to do one thing—take the computing experience out of the office or house. Remarkably, the portable devices share similar hardware inside, with a motherboard, CPU, RAM, and mass storage. They differ more on the outside, on how we interact with them. They differ hugely on upgradeability. And they definitely differ in the operating system. This chapter covers portable PCs, that is, devices that run Windows. (Chapter 13 covers mobile devices.)

Local Lingo

Subnotebook Two very lightweight, long-battery-life portable computers not covered on the CompTIA A+ exams offer competing visions of the *subnotebook* market. *Netbooks* come in at the bottom of the stack, with power-sipping but a little anemic Intel Atom CPUs, small HDDs, and a 10- to 12-inch form factor. Battery life is outstanding, though, letting these little troopers keep going for eight or more hours on a single charge.

At the high end of the spectrum (price wise) are the *Ultrabooks*: super thin, super light, and smoking fast. They use high-end mobile CPUs from Intel and don't include an optical drive. They use solid-state drives (SSDs), and almost all models have a 13.3-inch screen; battery life ranges from five to nine hours. The kicker? Netbooks cost approximately $300; Ultrabooks start at $1000 and go way up from there.

Portable PCs use the same component types as desktop PCs, just smaller and more energy-efficient versions. There's no reason to go through each device, because you already know how they all work. This chapter, therefore, jumps right into the processes needed for upgrading and repairing portable PCs. You'll learn the quirks and names of laptop-specific parts along the way. The second section covers some features common to most laptops, such as attachment of peripherals and power management. The chapter wraps up with a discussion on maintaining and troubleshooting.

Objective 12.01 Upgrading and Repairing Laptop Computers

A competent tech can upgrade and repair portable computers to a degree, though true laptop techs are specialists. Upgrading the basics usually means breaking out the trusty screwdriver and avoiding electrostatic discharge (ESD). *Repairing* portables successfully, on the other hand, requires research, patience, organization, special tools, and documentation. Plus you need a ridiculously steady hand. This section provides an overview of the upgrade and repair process.

Disassembly Process

Disassembling a portable PC is pretty easy. Putting it back together in working condition is the hard part! After removing the battery and disconnecting the power cord, you need to follow a four-step process to succeed in disassembly/reassembly.

First, *document and label every cable and screw location.* Laptops don't use standard connectors or screws. Often you'll run into many tiny screws of varying threads.

Second, *organize any parts you extract from the laptop.* Seriously, put a big white piece of construction paper on your work surface, lay each extracted piece out in logical fashion, and clearly mark where each component connects and what it connects to as well.

Third, *refer to the manufacturer's documentation.* I can't stress this point enough. Unlike desktop PCs, portable PCs have no industry-wide standardization of internal structure. Everything in the portable is designed according to the manufacturer's best engineering efforts.

Finally, you need to *use the appropriate hand tools.* A portable PC, especially on the inside, will have a remarkable variety of tiny screws that you can't remove/reinsert without tiny-headed Phillips or torx drivers. You'll need tiny pry bars—metal and plastic—to open components. Figure 12.1 shows an entry-level toolkit for a laptop tech that you can order from iFixit.com (more on this site in a moment). Their professional version of the toolkit has 70 tools, plus there's an expansion kit! Like I said at the beginning of the chapter, portable techs are specialists.

FIGURE 12.1 Bare-minimum laptop repair tools

Exam Tip

Know the four-step disassembly process for the CompTIA A+ 220-802 exam:
1. Document and label cable and screw locations.
2. Organize parts.
3. Refer to the manufacturer's documentation.
4. Use appropriate hand tools.

Travel Advisory

Although the CompTIA 802 competencies lay out a four-step process for disassembly, they leave out an *absolutely essential* first step—remove all electricity from the laptop before you open it up. Unplug the power cable *and* remove the battery. Don't miss this step, because power kills!

Repairing Without the Manual

A lot of manufacturers don't provide documentation to just any tech, but only to authorized repair centers. So when faced with an unfamiliar laptop that a client brought in for repair, you have essentially three options. First, you can find a dedicated laptop tech and refer your client to that person. If the problem is exceptionally complicated and the portable in question is mission critical, that's often the best option.

Second, open up a Web browser and go to YouTube. Type in precisely what you want to do, such as "replace the keyboard on a Lenovo y530," and see what pops up (see Figure 12.2). You'll most likely be in shock and awe when you get the results back, especially if the laptop in question is a couple of years old. People all over the world have to deal with broken devices, so you're not alone.

Third, for general tools and parts and a lot of very detailed step-by-step instructions, I highly recommend *iFixit.com*. Billed as a "free repair manual you can edit," iFixit is built by techs like me and you who conquer a problem, document the steps, and post the details (see Figure 12.3). This means the next tech who runs into the same problem doesn't have to reinvent the wheel. Just go to iFixit.com. The proceeds from parts and tools they sell, by the way, go toward supporting the site. It's not a for-profit enterprise.

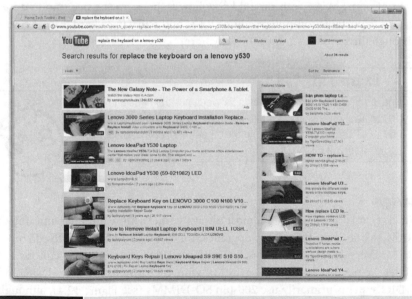

FIGURE 12.2 YouTube search result

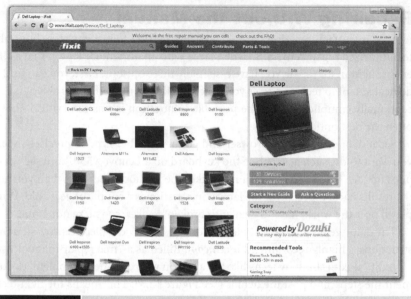

| **FIGURE 12.3** | Some of the Dell laptop repair walkthroughs at iFixit.com |

Standard Upgrades

Every CompTIA A+ tech should know how to perform the two standard upgrades to portable computers: adding RAM and replacing a hard drive. Let's go through the steps.

Exam Tip

One of the most striking contrasts between portable PCs and tablets and smartphones is in upgradability. You can and should upgrade portable PCs. Mobile devices, on the other hand, offer almost no upgradability at all.

RAM

Stock-factory portable PCs almost always come with a minimal amount of RAM, so one of the first laptop upgrades you'll be called on to do is to add more RAM. Every decent laptop has upgradeable RAM slots. Ancient laptops use either 72-pin or 144-pin SO-DIMMs with SDRAM technology. DDR and DDR2 systems primarily use 200-pin SO-DIMMs (see Figure 12.4), although some laptops use micro-DIMMs. DDR3 sticks are 204-pin SO-DIMMs and will not fit in 200-pin slots.

FIGURE 12.4 200-pin SO-DIMM stick (front and back)

Exam Tip

Just like with desktop PCs, you cannot upgrade to a newer RAM technology. If the laptop uses DDR2, for example, you must use DDR2 modules in it.

Travel Assistance

Revisit Chapter 6 to refresh your memory on RAM technologies and terminology.

How to Add or Replace RAM

Upgrading the RAM in a portable PC requires a couple of steps. First, you need to get the correct RAM. Many older portable PCs use proprietary RAM solutions, which means you need to order directly from Dell, HP, or Sony and pay exorbitant prices for the precious extra megabytes. Most manufacturers have taken pity on consumers in recent years and use standard SO-DIMMs or micro-DIMMs. Refer to the manufacturer's Web site or to the manual (if any) that came with the portable for the specific RAM needed.

Second, every portable PC offers a unique challenge to the tech who wants to upgrade the RAM, because there's no standard location for RAM placement in

portables. More often than not, you need to unscrew or pop open a panel on the underside of the portable (see Figure 12.5). Then you press out on the restraining clips and the RAM stick pops up (see Figure 12.6). Gently remove the old stick of RAM and insert the new one by reversing the steps.

Always remove all electrical power from the laptop before removing or inserting memory. Disconnect the AC cord from the wall outlet. Take out the battery! Failure to disconnect from power can result in a fried laptop.

Local Lingo

Shared memory Some laptops (and desktops) support *shared memory*. Shared memory reduces the cost of video cards by reducing the amount of memory on the video card itself. Instead of having 256 MB of RAM, the video card might have only 64 MB of RAM but be able to borrow 192 MB of RAM from the system. This equates to a 256 MB video card. The video card uses regular system RAM to make up for the loss.

Some systems give you control over the amount of shared memory, while others simply enable you to turn shared memory on or off. The settings are found in CMOS setup and only on systems that support shared memory. Shared memory is not reported to Windows, so don't panic if you have 1 GB of RAM in your laptop but Windows only sees 924 MB—the missing memory is used for video.

Adding more system RAM to a laptop with shared memory will improve laptop performance. Although it might appear to improve video performance, that doesn't tell the true story. It'll improve overall performance because the OS and CPU get more usable RAM.

HDD/SSD

You can replace a hard disk drive (HDD) or solid-state drive (SSD) in a portable PC fairly easily, especially if the laptop is only a few years old. SATA drives in the 2.5-inch drive format now rule in all laptops. Although much smaller than regular 3.5-inch hard drives, they use all the same features and configurations. These smaller hard drives have suffered, however, from diminished storage capacity as compared to their 3.5-inch brothers. Currently, large 2.5-inch hard drives hold up to 1 TB, while the 3.5-inch hard drives can hold more than 3 TB of data!

If you have a much older laptop, it might have a PATA drive, which means you need to pay more attention to cabling and jumpers. Some PATA drive manufacturers may require you to set the drive to use a cable-select setting as opposed to master or slave, so check with the laptop maker for any special issues. Otherwise, no difference exists between 2.5-inch drives and their larger 3.5-inch brethren (see Figure 12.7).

FIGURE 12.5 Removing a RAM panel

FIGURE 12.6 Releasing the RAM

FIGURE 12.7 The 2.5-inch and 3.5-inch drives are mostly the same.

Travel Assistance

Revisit Chapter 8 to refresh your memory on hard drive technologies and terminology.

One of the best upgrades you can make on a laptop is to go from an HDD to an SSD. Obviously, you'll get a lot less storage capacity for the money, but the trade-offs can be worth it. First, the SSD will use a lot less electricity than an HDD, thus extending battery life. Second, any SSD is rip-roaringly faster than an HDD and performance across the board will be boosted.

The process of replacing a hard drive mirrors that of replacing RAM. You find the hard drive hatch—either along one edge or in a compartment on the underside of the computer—and release the screws (see Figure 12.8). Remove the old drive and then slide the new drive into its place (see Figure 12.9). Reattach the hatch or cover and boot the computer. Grab a Windows disc and prepare to reinstall.

Hardware Replacement

Once you get beyond upgrading RAM and replacing a hard drive on a portable PC, you take the plunge into the laptop repair specialty. You can replace some

FIGURE 12.8 Removing the drive compartment cover

components by lifting them out, detaching a ribbon cable, and then reversing the steps with the replacement part. Other parts require a full teardown of the laptop to the bare bones, which presents a much greater magnitude of difficulty. Because every portable PC differs from every other one, this section provides guidance, but not concrete steps, for replacement.

FIGURE 12.9 Inserting a replacement drive

Components

Replaceable components require more work than the RAM or drive upgrades, but replacing them generally falls into the category of "doable." What I call *components* are the battery, keyboard, optical drive, internal speaker, and plastic parts.

Battery If a battery's performance falls below an acceptable level, you can replace it with a battery from the manufacturer or from an aftermarket vendor. Although this should be a simple swap replacement (and usually is), you might encounter a situation where the real problem wasn't the battery per se, but an inadequate or malfunctioning charging system. The new battery might not give you any better performance than the old one. Try it.

Keyboard Getting a keyboard off a laptop computer often requires little pry bars, but also look for screws, clips, and so on. Keyboards connect via a tiny, short, and very delicate cable, often held down by tape. Replacing one is tricky, but doable.

Optical Drive Replacing an optical drive can present a challenge. If the drive is part of a modular system, just pop out the old drive and pop in a new one. If the drive is part of the internal chassis of the portable, on the other hand, you're looking at a full dissection. (See the "Integral Parts" section for tips on dismantling the portable.)

Speaker Like the optical drive, replacing the internal speaker or speakers on a laptop can be simple or a total pain, depending on where the speakers connect. Some laptops have speakers mounted on the outside of the chassis. You pry off the covers, pull out the little speakers, disconnect the cable, and then reverse the process for replacement speakers. If the speakers are inside the chassis, on the other hand, you need to dismantle the portable to get to them. (See the "Integral Parts" section.)

Plastic Parts Laptops have a few plastic parts that can get lost or broken. These are slot covers or card blanks designed to keep dust out of the memory card and expansion slots (see Figure 12.10). If you need to replace one of these, simply get a spare from the manufacturer or an aftermarket vendor and replace it.

Expansion Cards Not to be confused with PC Cards, many portable PCs have one or more true expansion slots for add-on cards. The more modular varieties will have a hatch on the bottom of the case that opens like the RAM hatch that gives you access to the slot(s). This enables you to change out an 802.11g wireless

FIGURE 12.10 ExpressCard blank

card, for example, for an 802.11n card, thus greatly enhancing the Wi-Fi experience on this device. Figure 12.11 shows a wide-open laptop with the expansion slot exposed.

Just like when installing RAM in a portable, you must avoid ESD and remove all electricity before you take out or put in an expansion card. Failure to remove the battery and the AC adapter can, and probably will, result in a shorted-out laptop motherboard, and that just makes for a bad day.

The only other consideration with expansion cards applies specifically to wireless. Not only will you need to connect the card to the slot properly, but you must reattach the antenna connection and often a separate power cable. Pay attention when you remove the card as to the placement of these vital connections.

FIGURE 12.11 Mini-PCIe expansion slot on laptop

You'll find one of two types of expansion slots in a portable. The older ones (think 2005 and earlier) use *Mini-PCI*, because PCI dominated that time period. Just about every portable since then uses PCI Express, so the laptops come with *Mini-PCIe* slots.

CPU Replacing a CPU on a modern portable takes a lot more work than replacing RAM or a Mini-PCIe expansion card, but follows the same general steps. Many CPUs mount facing the bottom of the portable so that the venting goes away from your hands. When sitting properly on a flat surface, the heated air also goes to the back of the laptop and not toward the user. You access the CPU in this sort of system from the bottom of the portable.

As you can see in Figure 12.12, the CPU has an elaborate heat sink and fan assembly that includes both the CPU and the chipset. Each of the pieces screws down in multiple places, plus the fan has a power connection. Aside from the tiny screws, there's no difference here in process between replacing a mobile CPU and a desktop CPU that you learned way back in Chapter 5.

First, remove all power from the laptop, including the battery. Remove the hatch to expose the CPU. Remove the heat sink and fan assembly and lift out the CPU. Replace it with another CPU, apply thermal paste, and reattach the heat sink and fan assembly. Reconnect the fan power connector and you're good to go.

FIGURE 12.12 CPU heat sink and fan assembly exposed

Some older laptops use passive cooling and thus have the CPU pointed up rather than down. They have a heat sink beneath the keyboard that cools everything down. With that style laptop, you remove the keyboard and heat sink to expose the CPU.

Integral Parts

Some hardware replacements require you to get serious with the laptop, opening it fully to the outside, removing many delicate parts, and even stripping it down to the bare-metal chassis. I leave these repairs to the professional laptop repair folks, simply because they have the specific tools and expertise to do the job efficiently. CompTIA expects you to understand the process, though, so I've outlined it here. This pertains to four components: screen, DC jack, touchpad, and system board.

Portables open in two different ways, depending on the manufacturer. You either peel away layers from the top down, through the keyboard, or from the bottom up, through the base. Either direction requires careful attention to detail, part connectivity, and locations. You'll need a system to keep track of the dozens of tiny screws.

Every one of the replacements here requires you to detach the screen from the main chassis of the portable. Aside from finding the connection points and removing the proper screws, you need to pay attention to the connection points for the data stream to the monitor and the antenna that's in the frame of the display.

Once you have the portable stripped down, you replace whichever component you're in there to replace and then begin the process of building it back up into a coherent unit. Pay incredibly careful attention to getting data cables connected properly as you rebuild. I can't imagine a worse tech experience than replacing a touchpad and rebuilding a laptop only to have missed a connection and having to do it all over again.

Exam Tip

The DC jack requires extra-special love when you need to replace one. The part is soldered to the main board, so to replace it means you'll need to not only strip the laptop to the bare metal, but also unsolder the old part and solder the new part. Then you'll rebuild the laptop and hope you got everything right. CompTIA cannot expect a CompTIA A+ technician to know how to do this stuff. Expect a question that explores whether it *can* be done. Rest assured, specialized techs can replace *any* component on a laptop, even the DC jack.

Objective 12.02 Portable PC Features

P ortable PCs share many features that enable you to interact with input and output, plus add peripherals of all sorts. All use batteries and power management that require care and user attention. This section examines laptop-specific components and issues.

Keyboard Quirks

Laptop keyboards differ somewhat from those of desktop PCs, primarily because manufacturers have to cram all the keys onto a smaller form factor. They use the QWERTY format, but manufacturers make choices with key size and placement of the non-alphabet characters. Almost every portable keyboard uses a *Function (FN) key* to enable some keys to perform a third duty. Figure 12.13 compares a standard desktop keyboard with a large portable keyboard. You'll note that the latter has no separate number pad on the right. To use the number pad, you press the FN key (lower left in this case) to transform the (7, 8, 9), (U, I, O), (J, K, L), and (M) keys into the (7, 8, 9), (4, 5, 6), (1, 2, 3), and (0) keys.

Travel Advisory
The FN key also enables you to toggle other features specific to a portable, such as network connectivity and external displays. We'll examine these options shortly.

FIGURE 12.13 Keyboard comparison

In addition to the triple-purpose keys to accommodate the number pad options, most portables turn the traditionally single-purpose Function keys (F1–F12) into dual-function keys, activated by holding the FN key down and pressing a Function key to toggle a feature. The most common toggles enable or disable wireless features (use that when you go on an airplane), mute or unmute volume, and raise and lower the volume settings. Laptops offer a variety of features, though, so expect all sorts of options here. Laptops with a backlit keyboard, for example, will use one of the FN-Function key combinations to enable or disable the backlight. Similarly, laptops that support Bluetooth will use a FN-Function key combination for a toggle.

Travel Advisory

The CompTIA 801 exam only talks about Function keys for toggling features like wireless, volume settings, and Bluetooth, but real-world laptops can have any number of ways to get at these features. My primary laptop, for example, has a physical switch that enables or disables Wi-Fi and a slider for volume control. If you're working on a portable, keep looking if you don't find a function you expect.

Pointing Devices

Portables need a way to control your mouse pointer, but their smaller size requires manufacturers to come up with clever solutions. First, portables today have USB ports and can use every type of pointing device you'd see on a desktop. Second, early portables used *trackballs,* often plugged in like a mouse and clipped to the side of the case. Other models with trackballs placed them in front of the keyboard at the edge of the case nearest the user, or behind the keyboard at the edge nearest the screen.

The next wave to hit the laptop market was IBM's *TrackPoint* device, a joystick the size of a pencil eraser, situated in the center of the keyboard (see Figure 12.14). With the TrackPoint, you can move the pointer around without taking your fingers away from the "home" typing position. You use a forefinger to push the joystick around, and then click or right-click, using two buttons below the spacebar. This type of pointing device has since been licensed for use by other manufacturers, and it continues to appear on laptops today.

FIGURE 12.14 IBM TrackPoint

By far the most common laptop pointing device found today is the *touchpad* (see Figure 12.15)—a flat, touch-sensitive pad just in front of the keyboard. To operate a touchpad, you simply glide your finger across its surface to move the pointer, and tap the surface once or twice to single- or double-click. You can also click by using buttons just below the pad. Most people get the hang of this technique after just a few minutes of practice. The main advantage of the touchpad over previous laptop pointing devices is that it uses no moving parts—a fact that can really extend the life of a hard-working laptop.

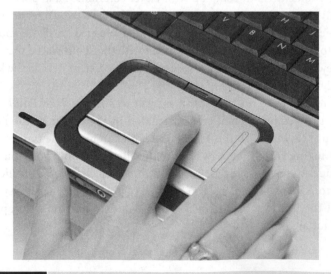

FIGURE 12.15 Touchpad on a laptop

Some manufacturers today include a *multitouch* touchpad that enables you to perform actions with multiple fingers, such as scrolling up and down or swiping to another screen or desktop.

Display Options

Laptops come in a variety of sizes and at varying costs. One major contributor to the overall cost of a laptop is the size of the LCD screen. Most laptops offer a range between 10.1-inch and 17.3-inch screens (measured diagonally), while a few offer just over 20-inch screens.

> ### Exam Tip
>
> Laptop LCDs are the same in almost every way as desktop LCDs with a TFT screen, an inverter (if using a CCFL backlight), and a backlight (CCFL or LED). You know all about these screens from Chapter 10. Expect questions about laptop displays, but know that they're pretty much the same as desktop displays. The only major difference is that they contain an antenna.

Many manufacturers are phasing out the standard 4:3 aspect ratio screen in favor of the widescreen format. *Aspect ratio* is the comparison of the screen width to the screen height, as you'll recall from Chapter 10. Depending on screen resolution, widescreens can have varying aspect ratios of 10:6, 16:9, 16:9.5, or 16:10.

Laptop LCD screens come in a variety of supported resolutions, described with acronyms such as XGA, WXGA, WSXGA, and more. The *W* in front of the letters indicates widescreen.

> ### Exam Tip
>
> The two most common resolutions are WXGA for the 14- to 15-inch models and HD 1080 for the 17.3-inch models.

Laptop screens typically come with one of two types of finish: *matte* or *high-gloss*. The matte finish was the industry standard for many years and offered a good trade-off between richness of colors and the reduction of glare. The better screens have a wide viewing angle and decent response time. The major drawback for matte-finished laptop screens is that they wash out a lot in bright

light. Using such a laptop at an outdoor café, for example, is almost hopeless during daylight.

Manufacturers released high-gloss laptop screens in 2006, and they rapidly took over many store shelves. The high-gloss finish offers sharper contrast, richer colors, and wider viewing angles when compared to the matte screens.

With the advent of LED backlighting for LCD panels, many manufacturers have switched back to an anti-glare screen, though they're not quite the matte screens of old. When the LED brightness is up high, these are lovely screens. (See the "Troubleshooting Portable Computers" section later in this chapter for issues specific to LED-backlit portables.)

What you will *not* find on portable PCs are two other display technologies: plasma and organic light-emitting diode (OLED). Plasma displays demand a lot more electricity than do LCDs and are completely inappropriate for portable PCs. OLED screens sip energy when compared to LCDs, but they're still so expensive that you'll only find them on a few smartphones today. Chapter 10 discussed OLED screen technology.

Almost every portable PC offers one or more connectors for attaching an external display. These include the standard video ports, such as VGA, DVI, HDMI, and DisplayPort. Most people use the video ports to attach the portable to a projector to facilitate some kind of presentation to an audience. Once you attach a monitor, you usually press and hold the FN key and then press one of the Function keys (my primary laptop uses F3, for example, but my netbook uses F9; it varies) to toggle among three *dual display* options: only the laptop, mirror display (same image on both laptop and projector screen), or external only.

Portable-Specific Expansion Slots

The makers of portable computers have developed methods for you to add features to a portable via specialized connections known generically as *expansion slots*. Once a common feature on laptops, these specialized expansion slots are quickly fading away due to the dominance of USB. Yet you'll still find laptops with these slots (and they're covered on the CompTIA A+ exams), so let's take a look at expansion slots over the years.

PCMCIA

For many years, the *Personal Computer Memory Card International Association* (*PCMCIA*) established standards involving portable computers, especially when it came to expansion cards, which are generically called PC Cards. *PC Cards* are roughly credit card–sized devices that enhance and extend the functions of a portable PC. PC Cards are easy to use, inexpensive, and convenient. Figure 12.16 shows a typical PC Card.

FIGURE 12.16 PC Card

> ### Exam Tip
> CompTIA uses the older term *PCMCIA cards* to describe PC Cards. Don't be shocked if you get that as an option on your exams! You'll hear many techs use the phrase as well.

Older portable PCs come with one or two PC Card slots, into which you insert a PC Card. Each card has at least one function, but many have two, three, or more! You can buy a PC Card that offers connections for removable media, for example, such as combination Secure Digital (SD) and CompactFlash (CF) card readers. You can also find PC Cards that enable you to plug into multiple types of networks. All PC Cards are hot-swappable, meaning you can plug them in without powering down the PC.

> ### Exam Tip
> Many manufacturers use the term *hot-pluggable* rather than hot-swappable to describe the ability to plug in and replace PC Cards on the fly. Look for either term on the exams.

The PCMCIA established two versions of PC Cards, one using a parallel bus and the other using a serial bus. Each version, in turn, offers two technology variations as well as several physical varieties. This might sound complicated at first, but here's the map to sort it all out.

TABLE 12.1	PC Card Types and Their Typical Uses			
Type	**Length**	**Width**	**Thickness**	**Typical Use**
Type I	85.6 mm	54.0 mm	3.3 mm	Flash memory
Type II	85.6 mm	54.0 mm	5.0 mm	I/O (modem, NIC, and so on)
Type III	85.6 mm	54.0 mm	10.5 mm	Hard drives

Parallel PC Cards

Parallel PC Cards come in two flavors, *16-bit* and *CardBus,* and each flavor comes in three physical sizes, called Type I, Type II, and Type III. The 16-bit PC Cards, as the name suggests, are 16-bit, 5-V cards that can have up to two distinct functions or devices, such as a modem/network card combination. CardBus PC Cards are 32-bit, 3.3-V cards that can have up to eight (!) functions on a single card. Regular PC Cards fit into and work in CardBus slots, but the reverse is not true. CardBus totally dominates the current PC Card landscape, but you might still run into older 16-bit PC Cards.

Type I, II, and III cards differ only in the thickness of the card (Type I being the thinnest, and Type III the thickest). All PC Cards share the same 68-pin interface, so any PC Card will work in any slot that accepts that card type. Type II cards are by far the most common of PC Cards. Therefore, most older laptops have two Type II slots, one above the other, so the computer can accept two Type I or II cards or one Type III card (see Figure 12.17).

Although PCMCIA doesn't require that certain sizes perform certain functions, most PC Cards follow their recommendations. Table 12.1 lists the sizes and typical uses of each type of PC Card.

| FIGURE 12.17 | PC Card slots |

ExpressCard

Slots for *ExpressCard,* the high-performance serial version of the PC Card, have replaced PC Card slots on laptop PCs over the last decade. ExpressCard comes in two widths: 34 mm and 54 mm, called *ExpressCard/34* and *ExpressCard/54.* Figure 12.18 shows both ExpressCard varieties. Both cards are 75 mm long and 5 mm thick, which makes them shorter than all previous PC Cards and the same thickness as a Type II PC Card.

ExpressCards connect to either the USB 2.0 bus or the PCI Express bus. These differ phenomenally in speed. The amazingly slow-in-comparison USB version has a maximum throughput of 480 Mbps. The PCIe version, in contrast, roars in at 2.5 Gbps in unidirectional communication.

Table 12.2 shows the throughput and variations for the parallel and serial PC Cards currently on the market.

PCMCIA announced ExpressCard 2.0 in 2009 with speeds up to 5 Gbps and support for SuperSpeed USB 3.0, and we expected to see devices roll out in 2010, but that's not what happened. PCMCIA has dissolved and shut its offices. The USB Implementer's Forum now manages all PC Card and ExpressCard standards, and there's not likely to be any further development.

FIGURE 12.18 34-mm and 54-mm ExpressCards

TABLE 12.2	PC Card Speeds
Standard	**Maximum Theoretical Throughput**
PC Card using 16-bit bus	160 Mbps
CardBus PC Card using PCI bus	1056 Mbps
ExpressCard using USB 2.0 bus	480 Mbps
ExpressCard using PCIe bus	2.5 Gbps

Travel Advisory

You can find ExpressCards that supposedly support USB 3.0. While technically these cards have USB 3.0 ports, they connect to the PCIe bus and therefore aren't capable of true USB 3.0 speeds of up to 5 Gbps.

Storage Card Slots

Many portable computers offer one or more flash-memory card slots to enable you to add storage to the portable. These slots also enable the fast transfer of data from the card to the portable, and vice versa. They come in the standard varieties that you already know from Chapter 9, such as SD, CompactFlash, and xD.

General-Purpose Ports

Laptops rarely come with all of the hardware you want. Today's laptops usually include at least USB ports to give you the option to add more hardware. Some laptops still provide legacy general-purpose expansion ports (PS/2, RS-232 serial ports, and so on) for installing peripheral hardware, while other portables focus on more modern ports like eSATA and FireWire. If you're lucky, you will have a docking station or port replicator so you don't have to plug in all of your peripheral devices one at a time.

Travel Advisory

Almost all handheld computing devices—such as iPod music players—connect to PCs through USB ports. Most come with a USB cable that has a standard connector on one end and a proprietary connector on the other. Don't lose the cable!

USB, FireWire, and eSATA

USB, FireWire (IEEE 1394), and eSATA enable users to connect a device while the PC is running—you won't have to reboot the system to install a new peripheral. With USB, FireWire, and eSATA, just plug the device in and go! Because portable PCs don't have a desktop's multiple internal expansion capabilities, USB, FireWire, and eSATA are three of the more popular methods for attaching peripherals to laptops (see Figure 12.19).

Exam Tip

The small device resting in a stand in Figure 12.19 is called a *personal digital assistant (PDA)*, a precursor to modern smartphones and tablets such as the Apple iPhone and iPad. You could view pictures, take notes, check a calendar, listen to music, and more on these devices. Expect PDA as an answer choice in exam questions, but most likely as one of the wrong answers. PDAs are rarely used today.

Port Replicators

A *port replicator* plugs into a single port on the portable computer—often a USB port but sometimes a proprietary port—and offers uncommon and common PC ports, such as serial, parallel, USB, network, and PS/2. By plugging the port replicator into your notebook computer, you can instantly connect the computer to nonportable components such as a printer, scanner, monitor, or a

FIGURE 12.19 Devices attached to USB on a portable PC

full-sized keyboard. Port replicators are typically used at home or in the office with the nonportable equipment already connected. Figure 12.20 shows a Dell Inspiron laptop connected to a port replicator.

The computer can access any devices attached to the port replicator; you don't need to connect each individual device to the PC. As a side bonus, port replicators enable you to attach legacy devices, such as parallel printers, to a new laptop that only has modern multifunction ports such as USB and FireWire and not parallel or serial ports.

Travel Assistance

Although portable PCs most often connect to port replicators via USB ports, some manufacturers have proprietary connections for proprietary port replicators. As long as such a portable PC has a USB port, you can use either the proprietary hardware or the more flexible USB devices.

Docking Stations

Docking stations resemble port replicators in many ways, offering legacy and modern single- and multifunction ports (see Figure 12.21). The typical docking station uses a proprietary connection but has extra features built in, such as a DVD drive or PC Card slot for extra enhancements. You can find docking

| **FIGURE 12.20** | Port replicator for a Dell portable computer |

FIGURE 12.21 Docking station

stations for many older small laptops. A docking station makes an excellent companion to such portables.

Batteries

Manufacturers have used three types of batteries for portable PCs: *Nickel-Cadmium (Ni-Cd)*, *Nickel-Metal Hydride (Ni-MH)*, and *Lithium-Ion (Li-Ion)*. Today, only Li-Ion is used because that battery chemistry provides the highest energy density for the weight and has few problems with external factors. Li-Ion batteries will explode if they are overcharged, so all Li-Ion batteries sold with PCs have built-in circuitry to prevent accidental overcharging. Lithium batteries can only be used on systems designed for them. Figure 12.22 shows a typical Li-Ion battery.

FIGURE 12.22 Li-Ion battery

Local Lingo

LiPO *Lithium polymer* (*LiPO*) batteries are a variation of Li-Ion that places the heart of the battery—the electrolyte—into a solid polymer shape rather than an organic solvent. This enables the batteries to take on unusual forms beyond the simple cylinder or rectangle shapes. LiPO batteries haven't replaced Li-Ion in most portable PCs (with the Apple MacBook the obvious exception), but they are widely used in smaller electronics such as tablets, smartphones, and portable media players.

The Care and Feeding of Batteries

In general, keep in mind the following basics. First, always store batteries in a cool place. Although a freezer is in concept an excellent storage place, the moisture, metal racks, and food make it a bad idea. Second, keep the battery charged, at least to 70 to 80 percent. Third, never drain a battery all the way down unless required to do so as part of a *battery calibration* (where you, in essence, reset the battery according to steps provided by the manufacturer). Rechargeable batteries have only a limited number of charge-discharge cycles before overall battery performance is reduced. Fourth, *never* handle a battery that has ruptured or broken; battery chemicals are very dangerous. Finally, always recycle old batteries.

Travel Advisory

Got an old portable PC battery lying around? Well, you need to get rid of it, and there are some pretty nasty chemicals in that battery, so you can't just throw it in the trash. Sooner or later, you'll probably need to deal with such a battery. Here are a few tips for disposing of old batteries:

- Do an online search to find the battery recycling center nearest to you.
- Sometimes, you can take old laptop batteries to an auto parts store that disposes of old car batteries—I know it sounds odd, but it's true! See if you can find one in your area that will do this.
- Many cities offer a hazardous materials disposal or recycling service. Check to see if and how your local government will help you dispose of your old batteries.

Power Management

Many different parts are included in the typical laptop, and each part uses power. The problem with early laptops was that every one of these parts used power continuously, whether or not the system needed that device at that time. The hard drive continued to spin even when it was not being accessed, for example, and the LCD panel continued to display even when the user walked away from the machine.

Local Lingo

APM/ACPI The power management standards for portable PCs have been in place for a very long time. Intel put forward the *Advanced Power Management (APM)* specification in 1992 and the *Advanced Configuration and Power Interface (ACPI)* standard in 1996. The only time you'll see the acronyms in use in modern systems is in CMOS labeling.

Power management settings can be found in the Control Panel applet Power Options. In Windows XP, the Power Options applet has several built-in *power schemes* such as Home/Office and Max Battery that put the system into Standby or Suspend after a certain interval (see Figure 12.23). You can also require the

FIGURE 12.23 The Windows XP Power Options applet's Power Schemes tab

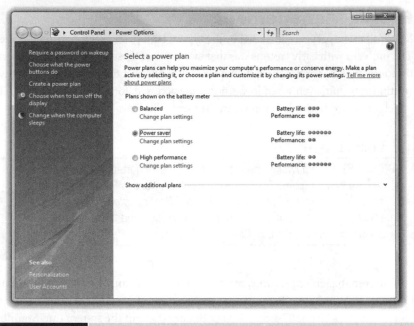

| FIGURE 12.24 | Windows Vista Balanced, Power Saver, and High Performance power plan options |

system to go into Standby after a set period of time or to turn off the monitor or hard drive after a time, thus creating your own custom power scheme. This is technically called adjusting the *sleep timers.*

Windows Vista and Windows 7 offer *power plans* that enable better control over power use by customizing a balanced, power-saver, or high-performance power plan (see Figure 12.24). You can customize a power-saver plan for your laptop, for example, and configure it to turn off the display at a certain time interval while on battery or plugged in and configure it to put the computer to sleep as desired (see Figure 12.25).

Another feature, Hibernate mode, takes everything in active memory and stores it on the hard drive just before the system powers down. When the PC comes out of hibernation, Windows reloads all the files and applications into RAM. Figure 12.26 shows the Power Options Properties applet in Windows XP.

FIGURE 12.25 Customizing a laptop power plan in Windows Vista

FIGURE 12.26 Windows XP hibernation settings in the Power Options applet

Exam Tip

Microsoft and ACPM don't quite use the same terminology for the various power-down modes, and the 802 exam reflects this disparity. Microsoft uses the term *standby* to mean that the drives and monitor are powered down, but the CPU and RAM remain active. ACPM calls this mode *S3*. Other vendors call this *Suspend to RAM*. The 802 objectives refer to this state as *Sleep/Suspend* and *Standby*. Go figure. It's all the same thing.

Manual Control over Power Use

Most portable PCs give you several manual options for reducing battery use in certain circumstances. We've already discussed using the on/off switch or keyboard combination for disabling the Wi-Fi antenna, for example, and shutting off Bluetooth. Laptops with backlit keyboards will have some way you can disable this feature when it's not needed, usually with a keyboard combination. You can also reduce the output of the LCD backlight using a combination of FN and another key to eke out a few more precious minutes of computing time before you have to shut down. Figure 12.27 shows a close-up of the FN-activated keys for adjusting screen brightness.

One of the best ways to conserve battery use is to plan ahead for times when you'll be unplugged. When I travel, for example, and know that I'm going to need a certain set of files stored on my file server at the office, I put those files on my laptop before I leave, while it's still plugged into the AC. It's tempting to throw the files on a thumb drive so I don't have to break out my laptop at the office, right? Or to let Dropbox do my syncing for me when I get to a Wi-Fi hotspot, but both USB and Wi-Fi use electricity.

Better than that even, Windows Vista and Windows 7 enable me to designate the files and folders I need as *offline files*, storing a local, duplicate copy of the files

FIGURE 12.27	Keys for adjusting screen brightness

and folders on my hard drive. When I connect my laptop into my office network, those offline files are automatically synced with the files and folders on the file server. Anything I changed on the laptop gets written to the server. Anything anyone changed in those folders on the server gets written to my laptop. (If changes were made on both sides, a sync conflict pops up automatically, enabling you to resolve problems without fear of overwriting anything important.)

To designate a folder and its contents as offline files, right-click the folder you want and select *Always available offline* from the menu (see Figure 12.28). The sync will occur and you're done. When you want to open the files offline, go to the Control Panel and open the Sync Center applet (see Figure 12.29). Click the *Manage offline files* link in the Tasks list to open the Offline Files dialog box (see Figure 12.30). Click the *View your offline files* button and you're in.

FIGURE 12.28 Setting up offline files

FIGURE 12.29 Sync Center applet

AC Adapters

AC adapters for portable devices offer the same function that power supplies offer desktop PCs: converting AC to DC so the devices can run properly. The typical laptop AC adapter has a big power brick in the middle—that's the transformer. Although many AC adapters offer similar connections, you have to use the proper adapter for your device. If you plug in a device that provides too much AC, for example, you could toast something on the portable. A device that provides insufficient AC can cause a perfectly good device to be a poorly functioning nightmare. (See Objective 12.03 for more details on AC adapters.)

Travel Advisory

Laptops have a charging circuit that takes power from the AC adapter to charge the battery. If this circuit fails, the laptop will run on AC power but will not charge the battery.

FIGURE 12.30 Offline Files dialog box

Objective 12.03 Maintaining and Troubleshooting Portables

Most portable PCs come from the factory solidly built and configured. Manufacturers know that few techs outside their factories know enough to work on them, so they don't cut corners. From a tech's standpoint, most maintenance involves taking care of the batteries and extending the battery life through proper power management, as discussed earlier. You also need to keep the machine clean, avoid excessive heat, and be careful about physical damage.

Everything you normally do to maintain a PC applies to portable PCs. You need to keep current on Windows patches and Service Packs, and use stable, recent drivers. Run Error-checking with some frequency, and definitely defragment the hard drive. Disk Cleanup is a must if the laptop runs Windows. That said, let's look at issues specifically involving portables.

For troubleshooting, portable PCs have distinctive issues regarding power and networking. You can run into issues with the screen and input devices, as well.

Cleaning

Most portable PCs take substantially more abuse than a corresponding desktop model, but constant handling, travel, food crumbled into the keyboard, and so on can radically shorten the life of a portable if you don't take action. One of the most important things you should do is clean the laptop regularly. Use an appropriate screen cleaner (not a glass cleaner!) to remove fingerprints and dust from the fragile LCD panel.

If you've had the laptop in a smoky or dusty environment where the air quality alone causes problems, try cleaning it with compressed air. Compressed air works great for blowing out the dust and crumbs from the keyboard and for keeping ExpressCard slots clear. Don't use water on your keyboard! Even a minor amount of moisture inside the portable can toast a component.

Heat

To manage and maintain a healthy portable PC, you need to deal with issues of heat. Every portable has a stack of electronic components crammed into a very small space. Unlike their desktop brethren, portables don't have lots of freely moving air space that enables fans to cool everything down. Even with lots of low-power-consumption devices inside, portable PCs still crank out a good deal of heat. Excessive heat can cause system lockups and hardware failures, so you should handle the issue wisely. Try this as a starter guide:

- Use power management, even when plugged into an AC outlet. This is especially important if you're working in a warm room (more than 80 degrees Fahrenheit).
- Keep air space between the bottom of the laptop and the surface on which it rests. Putting a laptop on a soft surface like a pillow on your lap, for example, creates a great heat retention system—not a good thing. Always use a hard, flat surface.
- Don't use a keyboard protector for extended amounts of time.

- Listen to your fan, assuming the laptop has one. If it's often running very fast—you can tell by the high-pitched whirring sound—examine your power management settings and your environment and change whatever is causing heat retention.

- Speaking of fans, be alert to a fan that suddenly goes silent. Fans do die on laptops, causing overheating and failure. All laptop fans can be replaced easily.

Protect the Machine

While prices continue to drop for basic laptops, a fully loaded system is still pricey. To protect your investment, you'll want to adhere to certain best practices. You've already read tips in this chapter to deal with cleaning and heat, so let's look at the "portable" part of portable computers.

Travel

If you are traveling with a laptop, take care to protect yourself from theft. If possible, use a case that doesn't look like a computer case. A well-padded backpack makes a great travel bag for a laptop and appears less tempting to would-be thieves. Don't forget to pack any accessories you might need, such as modular devices, spare batteries, and AC adapters. Make sure to remove any media, such as CDs/DVDs or floppies, from their drives, as well as removing any ExpressCards from their slots. Most important, back up any important data before you leave.

Make sure you have at least a little battery power available. Heightened security at airports means you might have to power on your system to prove it's really a computer and not a transport case for questionable materials. And never let your laptop out of your sight! If you're going through an x-ray machine, request a manual search. The x-ray won't harm your computer like a metal detector will, but if the laptop gets through the line at security before you do, someone else might walk away with it. If flying, keep your laptop out of the overhead bins and under the seat in front of you where you can keep an eye on it.

If you travel to a foreign country, be very careful about the electricity. North America uses ~115-V power outlets, but most of the world uses ~230-V outlets. Many portable computers have *auto-switching power supplies,* meaning they detect the voltage at the outlet and adjust accordingly. For these portables, a simple plug converter will do the trick. Other portable computers, however, have *fixed-input power supplies,* which means they run only on ~115-V or ~230-V power. For these portables, you need a full-blown electricity-converting device, either a step-down or step-up *transformer.* You can find converters and transformers at electrical parts stores, such as Radio Shack in the United States.

Shipping

Much of the preceding storage and travel advice can be applied to shipping. Remove batteries, discs, and ExpressCards from their drives. Pack the portable well and disguise the container as best you can. Back up any data and verify the warranty coverage. Ship with a reputable carrier and always request a tracking number and, if possible, delivery signature. It's also worth the extra couple of bucks to pay for the shipping insurance. And when the clerk asks what's in the box, it's safer to say "electronics" rather than "a brand-new 20-inch laptop."

Security

The fact is, if someone really wants to steal your laptop, they'll find a way. There are, however, some things you can do to make yourself, and your equipment, less desirable targets. As you've already learned, disguise is a good idea.

Another physical deterrent is a laptop lock. Similar to a steel bicycle cable, there is a loop on one end and a lock on the other. The idea is to loop the cable around a solid object, such as a bed frame, and secure the lock to the small security hole on the side of the laptop (see Figure 12.31). Again, if someone really wants to steal your computer, they'll find a way. They'll dismantle the bed frame if they're desperate. The best protection is to be vigilant and not let the computer out of your sight.

An alternative to securing a laptop physically with a lock is to use a software-tracking system. Software makers, such as Computer Security Products, Inc., offer tracking software that transmits a signal to a central office if the

FIGURE 12.31 Cable lock

computer is stolen and connected to a phone line or the Internet. Even LoJack, the company famous for recovering stolen automobiles via its tracking devices, lends its name to a tracking product sold by Absolute Software (see Figure 12.32). The location of the stolen PC can be tracked, and sensitive files can even be deleted automatically with the aid of the stealth signal.

Travel Assistance

If you're interested in more detail about tracking software, visit Computer Security Products here: www.computersecurity.com

FIGURE 12.32 LoJack

Troubleshooting Portable Computers

Many of the troubleshooting techniques you learned about with desktop systems can be applied to laptops. You can also try some laptop-specific procedures as well.

Laptop Won't Power On

- Verify AC power by plugging another electronic device into the wall outlet. If the other device receives power, the outlet is good.
- If the outlet is good, connect the laptop to the wall outlet and try to power on. If no LEDs light up, you may have a bad AC adapter. Swap it out with a known-good power adapter.
- A faulty peripheral device might keep the laptop from powering up. Remove any peripherals such as USB or FireWire devices.

Battery Won't Charge

- If you have a laptop with a battery that won't charge up, it could be one of two things: the battery might be cooked or the AC adapter isn't doing its job. To troubleshoot, replace the battery with a known-good battery. If the new battery works, you've found the problem. Just replace the battery. Alternatively, remove the battery and run the laptop on AC only. If that works, you know the AC adapter is good. If it doesn't, replace the AC adapter.

Screen Doesn't Come On Properly

- If the laptop is booting (you hear the beeps and the drives), first make sure the display is turned on. Press the FN key and the key to activate the screen a number of times until the laptop display comes on. If that doesn't work, check the LCD cutoff switch—on many laptops, this is the small nub somewhere near the screen hinge that shuts the monitor off when you close the laptop—and make sure it isn't stuck in the down position.
- If the laptop display is very dim, you may have lost an inverter. The clue here is that inverters never go quietly. They can make a nasty hum as they are about to die and an equally nasty popping noise when they actually fail. Failure often occurs when you plug in the laptop's AC adapter, as the inverters take power directly from the AC adapter. It's

also possible that the backlights in the LCD panel have died, though this is much less common than a bad inverter.

- If the screen won't come on or is cracked, most laptops have a port for plugging in an external monitor, which you can use to log into your laptop.

- If you plug a laptop into an external monitor and that monitor does not display, remember that you have both a hardware and an OS component to making dual displays successful. There's usually a combination of FN and another key to toggle among only portable, only external, and both displays, as described earlier in the chapter. Plus you have the Display applet in the Control Panel to mirror or extend the desktop to a second monitor.

- Many manufacturers have switched to LED displays on laptops, which has led to a phenomenon many techs thought long behind us: *flickering displays*. The LED backlights don't work quite the same as CCFL backlights, especially when you lower the brightness. This doesn't affect desktop LED displays, because they're usually so bright it doesn't matter. But portables need to be able to dim to save battery life. One technique for dimming LEDs is to have them turn on and off rapidly enough to keep the pixels lit, but slowly enough that there's a reduction in visible light and electricity use. With some of these panels, that flickering is not only noticeable, but headache and eyestrain inducing.

- There are two things you can do with a flickering LED display: crank up the brightness so that it goes away (and thus live with reduced battery life) or replace the laptop.

Wireless Doesn't Work or Works Intermittently

- If the wireless doesn't work at all, check along the front, rear, or side edges of the laptop for a physical switch that toggles the internal wireless adapter or Bluetooth adapter on and off.

- If a tech has recently replaced a component that required removal of the laptop display, dead wireless could mean simply a disconnected antenna. Most portables have the antenna built into the display panel, so check that connection.

- Try the special key combination for your laptop to toggle the wireless or Bluetooth adapter. You usually press the FN key in combination with another key.

- You might simply be out of range or, if the wireless works intermittently, then right at the edge of the range. Physically walk the laptop over to the wireless router or access point to ensure there are no out-of-range issues.
- With Bluetooth specifically, remember that the pairing process takes action or configuration on both devices to succeed. Turn on the Bluetooth device, actively seek it, and try again.

Input Problems

- If none of the keys work on your laptop, there's a good chance you've unseated the keypad connector. These connectors are quite fragile and are prone to unseating from any physical stress on the laptop. Check the manufacturer's disassembly procedures to locate and reseat the keypad.
- If you're getting numbers when you're expecting to get letters, the number lock (NUMLOCK) function key is turned on. There's usually a little NumLock indicator light/LED that tells you it's on, although that's not universal. Turn it off. (Press and hold the FN key and then press the NUMLOCK key to toggle it off.)
- Laptop keyboards take far more abuse than the typical desktop keyboard, because of all those lunch meetings and café brainstorm sessions. Eating and drinking while over or around a keyboard just begs for problems. If you have a portable with sticking keys, look for the obvious debris in the keys. Used compressed air to clean them out. If you have serious goo and need to use a cleaning solution, disconnect the keyboard from the portable first. Make sure it's fully dried out before you reconnect it, or you'll short it out.
- If the touchpad is having problems, a shot of compressed air does wonders for cleaning pet hair out of the touchpad sensors. You might get a cleaner shot if you remove the keyboard before using the compressed air. Remember to be gentle when lifting off the keyboard, and make sure to follow the manufacturer's instructions.
- The touchpad driver might need to be reconfigured. Try the various options in the Control Panel | Mouse applet.

Exam Tip

The troubleshooting issue known as a *ghost cursor* can mean one of two things. First, the display shows a trail of ghost cursors behind your real cursor as you move it. This might point to an aging display or an improperly configured refresh rate. Second, the cursor moves erratically, whether you are touching the touchpad or not. This probably means the touchpad has been damaged in some way and needs to be replaced.

CHECKPOINT

✔**Objective 12.01: Upgrading and Repairing Laptop Computers** Most portables are made up of fairly standard components that technicians can replace or upgrade. You can find modular replacement components. Follow standard laptop disassembly techniques when tearing apart a laptop so you can more easily put it back together again. Know how to replace or upgrade RAM, hard drives, modular CPUs, and video cards.

✔**Objective 12.02: Portable PC Features** Laptops have unique keyboards that rely on the FN key and other hot keys to enable the keyboards to do as much as a standard keyboard. Most use a touchpad for a pointing device. ExpressCard slots enable added functions. Docking stations enable laptops to maintain consistent connections to resources such as networks, printers, and mass storage drives. Port replicators are similar to docking stations, except that they simply duplicate the ports that exist on your laptop. The most common battery type used today is Li-Ion. Modern Li-Ion batteries provide about four hours of continuous use and can carry a charge for days or weeks when not in use. AC adapters transform AC electricity from the wall socket to DC electricity the portable device can use. They also recharge the battery.

✔**Objective 12.03: Maintaining and Troubleshooting Portables** You need to keep the machine clean, avoid excessive heat, and be careful about physical damage. Everything else you normally do to maintain a PC applies to portable PCs. For troubleshooting, portables have distinctive issues regarding power and networking. Plus, you can run into issues with the screen and input devices.

REVIEW QUESTIONS

1. What's the first thing you should do when disassembling a laptop after removing all electricity?

 A. Document and label every cable and screw location.

 B. Organize any parts you extract from the laptop.

 C. Install a fresh battery.

 D. Call a repair shop.

2. Rick wants to upgrade the memory in his laptop. He currently has a 1 GB stick of DDR2. Which of the following options would give him the best result?

 A. Replace the DDR2 RAM with DDR3.

 B. Replace the 200-pin SO-DIMM with a 204-pin SO-DIMM.

 C. Replace a 1-GB, 200-pin SO-DIMM with a 2-GB, 200-pin SO-DIMM.

 D. Replace a 1-GB, 200-pin SO-DIMM with a 2-GB, 204-pin SO-DIMM.

3. Which of the following is a standard internal expansion slot in portable PCs?

 A. AGP

 B. Mini-PCIe

 C. PCI

 D. PCIe

4. Which of the following display types show up on portable computers? (Select two.)

 A. LCD

 B. LED

 C. OLED

 D. Plasma

5. Which Control Panel applet enables you to change a laptop's power plan from balanced to power saver?

 A. Power Management

 B. Power Options

 C. Power Plans

 D. There isn't one. Windows shifts power plans automatically.

6. Aldo gets a tech call from a user who complains that his laptop keyboard is broken. Every time the user starts to type, some letters work but others come out as numbers. What should Aldo do?

 A. Tell the user to send in the laptop for a replacement keyboard.

 B. Tell the user that keyboards can't be replaced and he needs a new laptop.

 C. Tell the user to press and hold the FN key and toggle the NUMLOCK key.

 D. Escalate the problem to his supervisor.

7. What is the difference between a docking station and a port replicator?

 A. Port replicators can provide connections and devices that don't exist on the laptop; docking stations provide only connections that exist on the laptop.

 B. Docking stations can provide connections and devices that don't exist on the laptop; port replicators provide only connections that exist on the laptop.

 C. Docking stations work only on Windows laptops; port replicators work only on laptops running the Macintosh OS.

 D. There is no difference between docking stations and port replicators.

8. How can ExpressCards interface with portable computers? (Select two.)

 A. PCI

 B. ISA

 C. PCIe

 D. USB 2.0

9. What is the term used to describe a power supply that can adjust to the voltage detected?

 A. Auto-tuning

 B. Auto-switching

 C. Fixed-input

 D. Step-up transformer

10. If you encounter a laptop that doesn't seem to recharge, what might be the problem? (Select the best answer.)

 A. AC adapter

 B. CPU

 C. RAM

 D. Thermal process

REVIEW ANSWERS

1. **A** After removing the electricity, including the battery, document and label every cable and screw location before disassembling a laptop.

2. **C** Laptops that use DDR or DDR2 memory have one or more 200-pin SO-DIMM slots. You can't change memory technology types on laptops any more than you can on desktops (i.e., going from DDR or DDR2 to DDR3), nor can you put a 204-pin stick in a 200-pin slot.

3. **B** Most modern laptops have a Mini-PCIe expansion slot. Older laptops have a Mini-PCI slot.

4. **A B** Of the four listed here, LCD with a traditional CCFL backlight (LCD) and with an LED backlight (LED) are the two types of monitors you'll see on portable computers. Although CompTIA lists OLED and plasma as display types for portables, you'll only find the former on a very few smartphones, not on the larger devices.

5. **B** Use the Power Options applet to change power plans.

6. **C** The NUMLOCK key is toggled on. It happens. Have the user toggle it off.

7. **B** Docking stations enable the laptop to use connections and devices such as removable storage drives and network connections that may not exist on the laptop. Port replicators simply duplicate the existing ports.

8. **C D** ExpressCards use PCIe or USB 2.0 to interface with portable computers.

9. **B** Power supplies that can adjust for a detected voltage are called auto-switching power supplies.

10. **A** A laptop that doesn't recharge has a problem with either the AC adapter or the battery. The former is the logical choice for this question.

Mobile Devices

	NEWBIE	SOME EXPERIENCE	EXPERT
ETA	3 hours	2 hours	1 hour

Mobile devices have revolutionized the way we work and play in recent years. Devices such as smartphones and tablets enable people to access the Internet from just about anywhere and accomplish essential tasks on the go.

This chapter explores mobile devices in detail. We'll first look at the features and capabilities of devices that are common in the mobile market. The chapter then jumps into the details of configuring the devices for personal use, doing such things as setting up e-mail and adding productivity devices. The chapter wraps up with a discussion on securing mobile devices. I'm eager to jump into a topic new to this version of the CompTIA A+ certification, so let's get started.

Objective 13.01 Features and Capabilities of Smartphones and Tablets

Modern mobile devices fall into two categories, smartphones and tablets, and both types of devices have similar features and capabilities. The primary distinction between the types is that a *smartphone* is a cell phone enhanced to do things formerly reserved for fully grown PCs; a *tablet* embodies those enhanced computing features and capabilities on an expanded format and screen. Tablets generally do *not* have cellular phone capability.

Mobile Experience

Mobile devices might seem, at first description, like PCs scaled down to fit in a backpack, purse, or pocket, but they bring a unique experience to users that differs a lot from the standard PC experience. Mobile devices have a default screen—like the desktop in Windows—called the *home screen* and have icons for applications (*apps*) for accomplishing specific tasks. But the first thing that will strike you when you handle one of these devices is that it's *not* the same thing as a small PC (see Figure 13.1). The most obvious difference is the interface, so we'll start there.

Touch Interface

Mobile devices use a *touch interface,* meaning that to interact with them you touch the screen (see Figure 13.2). They don't come with a physical keyboard for typing or a mouse for clicking. (In fact, you can't add a mouse at all to most mobile devices.)

FIGURE 13.1 Small PC and tablet—cousins at best

Different gestures with your fingers accomplish different tasks. To start a program, or app as they're called, you *tap* its icon, which means to poke it with your finger. If you've opened an app with multiple screens, you hold your finger on the screen and slide it across the screen, either right to left or top to bottom, depending on the type of application (see Figure 13.3). This is called a *swipe*.

FIGURE 13.2 Mobile devices have a touch interface.

FIGURE 13.3 Swiping to move to the next screen

Holding a finger on the home screen or on an open app screen in many devices brings up a context menu for accomplishing things like changing the background picture (the *wallpaper*), bookmarking a page, or editing. Touching different parts of the screen when in an app can offer other options, such as closing the app or pushing the app to the background (see Figure 13.4).

FIGURE 13.4 Getting a context menu by touching and holding

FIGURE 13.5 Resizing and rotating an image using two fingers

Many mobile devices enable you to use multiple fingers to do tasks such as expand or shrink an image on the screen (see Figure 13.5). An open long document, such as a word processing document, for example, might give you two different responses when you scroll with one or two fingers, with one finger selecting text to edit, but two fingers scrolling the document up or down. Different vendors call this feature different things, but the common term is *multitouch*.

This multitouch interface enables you to expand or contract some content on the screen. You can *pinch* an image, for example, between two fingers and make that picture bigger or smaller according to the way your fingers move.

Screen Technology Current *capacitive* touch screens use electrical current in your body to determine movement of your fingers across the screen. They measure the difference between the electrical charge in your body and the static charge on the screen, which is quite cool when you think about it. Capacitive touch screens require physical contact, so gloved fingers won't work. Older technologies used *resistive* touch screens that responded to the pressure applied to the screen. Fingers worked, but best results came from using a special pointing stick called a *stylus* (see Figure 13.6).

> **Local Lingo**
>
> **Screen calibration** Resistive touch screen devices required periodic *screen calibration*, the resetting of the location of screen items to match where you needed to touch. Capacitive touch screens don't require calibration.

FIGURE 13.6 Older mobile device with stylus

Mobile devices use a variety of screen types. Most tablets use some type of LCD panel, just like portable PCs and desktop monitors. Some smaller devices, like the better smartphones, use a related but different technology called *organic light-emitting diode (OLED)* screens where an organic compound provides the light for the screen. Applying an electric current causes the organic layer to glow in the precise spots desired.

Exam Tip

OLED screens use an organic compound exposed to electrical current for lighting; they don't have a traditional backlight.

Orientation Mobile devices feature rectangular screens, just like desktop displays, but all of them rotate easily. Plus, the orientation of the screen rotates right along with the display, so by default, up is always up. The underlying technology, called an *accelerometer,* enables you to switch easily from portrait view to landscape view. If you want to switch from reading a book to watching a movie, just turn the device on its side (see Figure 13.7).

Some devices feature a *gyroscope* that can detect the position of the tablet or phone in 3-D space. This enables more intuitive control over onscreen devices,

FIGURE 13.7 Switching orientation

such as a plane's joystick. Tilting the device forward, for example, would have the effect of pushing the plane's nose down; tilting backward "pulls back" on the stick, easing the plane's nose up. Few applications (and those primarily games) use the gyroscope as of this writing.

Mobile Operating Systems

Two operating systems power the vast majority of mobile devices. Apple *iOS* runs on all Apple devices, such as the iPhone smartphone and the iPad tablet. Google *Android* runs almost every non-Apple product. Microsoft has a very small presence in the mobile devices market, but you'll find Windows Phone 7 on a few smartphones.

> **Local Lingo**
>
> **Metro** Microsoft Windows 8 (live right around press time for this book) offers an interface for both the desktop and mobile devices initially called *Metro* (although by launch they'd dropped the term). The interface looks similar to iOS and Android and functions similarly on mobile devices. CompTIA did not include Metro on the initial 801 and 802 exams, but check www.comptia.org for coverage if you're reading this after 2012.

Apps

An *app* enables you to accomplish a specific task on a mobile device, such as check e-mail, surf the Web, play games, and so on. (Apps are the same thing as applications. For some reason, it's more hip to use the short term when discussing mobile devices.) Programmers write apps for specific mobile platforms and sometimes for specific devices. So an app written for a Windows Phone 7 phone, for example, won't work on an Apple iPhone, even though both are smartphones. This applies somewhat to apps written for a specific operating system as well. Apps written for an Apple iPhone can run on an Apple iPad, because both devices use Apple iOS for an operating system, but the same app optimized for the iPad will look and run better than a scaled-up iPhone app.

Different apps bring out different features of the mobile device. An electronic book reader, for example, shows an interface that appears like a book. You swipe to change pages. A note-taking application, in contrast, will open a virtual keyboard that enables you to type as if you had a regular keyboard attached. Finally, a racing game will turn the entire mobile device into a steering wheel, relying on the accelerometer to provide accurate turning (see Figure 13.8).

Adding Apps

Mobile devices come from the manufacturer with a certain number of vital apps installed for accessing e-mail, surfing the Web, taking notes, making entries in a calendar, and so on. Almost all of them offer multimedia apps to enable you to listen to music, take pictures, watch YouTube videos, and view photos. You'll find instant messaging tools and, in the case of smartphones, telephone capabilities.

FIGURE 13.8 Racing

Travel Advisory

The one big gotcha about Apple is that none of their mobile devices support Adobe Flash, making a surprising number of Web sites not available. You simply cannot add an app that makes Flash work on an Apple iPhone or iPad.

Even when the prebundled tools offer great functionality, often other software developers will take an idea and run with it to create something wholly unexpectedly cool. All the smartphones and nearly every tablet, for example, include some sort map tool that also includes *positioning software*. This software taps into the *Global Positioning System (GPS)* network of satellites maintained by the U.S. government to pinpoint your current location on a map (see Figure 13.9). This helps you find how to get from where you are to where you want to be.

FIGURE 13.9 GPS app showing current location (an excellent café in the Montrose neighborhood of Houston, Texas, in this example)

Exam Tip

The GPS aspect of mobile devices goes both ways. Because mobile devices tap into the Internet or cellular phone networks, the devices have identifying numbers such as a MAC address. (See Chapter 19 for the scoop on networking features.) The cell phone companies and government agencies can use the ID or MAC address to pinpoint where you are at any given time. This feature, called *geotracking*, clearly has a lot of room for abuse of power, though nothing major has happened as of this writing.

The Internet has turned the concept of map viewing into something much more powerful, courtesy of tools like Google Earth. With Google Earth, you can zoom all over the world, seeing satellite images of cities, towns, and countryside. You can access embedded images of places (see Figure 13.10) and get information via Wikipedia. Adding Google Earth (or any other app) to a mobile device follows different patterns according to the operating system and manufacturer of a specific mobile device.

FIGURE 13.10 Image in Google Earth

Travel Advisory

Don't like the idea of Big Brother knowing where you are all the time? Turn off Location Services in iOS or GPS Services on your Android. Keep in mind that turning this off will keep all applications that need this information from working.

Apple and Closed Source

Apple makes the most popular mobile devices in the iPhone and the iPad (smartphone and tablet, respectively). Both devices use the iOS operating system. Unlike every other manufacturer, Apple tightly controls the user experience, insisting that all developers of apps for iOS follow the same guidelines.

Apple has created a *closed-source* or *single-source* system, meaning that if you want to get an app for your iPhone or iPad, you can only get it from the Apple App Store (see Figure 13.11). Apple must approve any app before it goes into the App Store, and Apple reserves the right to revoke permission on any app that fails to measure up.

FIGURE 13.11 App Store

FIGURE 13.12 Searching for Google Earth

To add an app, select the App Store icon from the home screen. You can select from featured apps or view by category. You can check out the top 25 paid or free apps or simply search for what you want (see Figure 13.12).

The first time you try to purchase an app through the App Store, you'll be prompted to set up an account. You can use an account that you created previously through the Apple iTunes music and video store or create a new account using the Apple iCloud service. Creating a new iCloud account takes a few steps and a lot of typing in of passwords and such (see Figure 13.13), but eventually you'll get the account figured out. You'll need a valid credit card to set up the account.

Android Experience

Google Android powers a majority of smartphones and a solid percentage of tablets, but Android differs greatly from Apple iOS in that Google gives the OS away and developers create versions suited to their devices. That means in practice that when you have a smartphone or tablet that uses Google Android for an OS, you have to amend that description to include the manufacturer as well. A Samsung tablet, in other words, uses an OS that differs somewhat from the OS an ASUS

New Account form screenshot:

smalll AT&T 1:21 PM 95%

Cancel **New Account**

Apple ID and Password

Email email@example.com

This will be your new Apple ID.

Password Required

Verify Retype your password

Passwords must be at least 8 characters, including a number, an uppercase letter, and a lowercase letter. Don't use spaces, the same character 3 times in a row, your Apple ID, or a password you've used in the last year.

Back Next

FIGURE 13.13 Creating an iCloud account

tablet uses. HTC, for example, uses a custom interface for its Android devices called HTC Sense that changes the look and feel of Android. When you want to get an app for an Android device, you have alternative sources for that app.

> ### Exam Tip
>
> The CompTIA A+ 220-802 objectives mention "touch flow" as if it were a standard feature of mobile operating systems. In fact, HTC's TouchFLO preceded HTC's Sense interface. TouchFLO is no longer used on HTC's Android phones.

Many vendors offer a store with apps developed or customized to work with their devices. These *vendor-specific* stores enable you to get apps that should work well with your Android smartphone or tablet.

You can also go to an *open-source* market for apps developed "for Android" that probably will work with your device, but there's no guarantee that they'll work on all Android devices. Google Play, for example, offers hundreds of thousands of apps. This Wild West approach to apps makes the Android experience vastly different from the iOS experience when it comes to smartphones and tablets.

Travel Advisory

Microsoft has a small but growing presence in the mobile devices market with Windows Phone 7 and Windows 8. Expect the market share to increase over the coming years. Microsoft embraces an app marketplace somewhere in between that of Apple and Google, with both Microsoft-created apps and those created by other developers available through the Windows Phone Marketplace and other venues.

Enhancing Hardware

A mobile device is a computer, just like your desktop PC or laptop, with the same basic components doing the same basic things. The construction centers on a primary circuit board, a *motherboard,* onto which every other component is attached. Each mobile device has a CPU and GPU, though not necessarily based on the same architecture as a portable PC. The Apple iPad uses an ARM processor, for example, rather than an Intel ×86 or ×64 processor. In contrast, the ASUS Transformer featured as the Android model in this chapter uses a processor called a Tegra from NVIDIA, billed as the first mobile super-processor. It features two to four CPU cores with integrated GPU, northbridge, southbridge, and memory controller for awesome power and serious 3-D capabilities.

Mobile devices use storage, though not usually a traditional hard disk drive (HDD) with spinning platters. More commonly, mobile devices use a *solid-state drive (SSD)* because SSDs use much less electricity than platter-based drives. Plus, they're cooler in general, just like you.

Mobile devices vary from their larger brethren in two very significant areas of importance to techs. First, none of them offer any field-serviceable parts. If something breaks, you send the device back to the manufacturer. Second, you can't upgrade them at all. Even a laptop enables you to upgrade RAM or a hard drive, for example, but the mobile device you buy is exactly what you get. You want something better? Buy a new one.

Exam Tip

Mobile devices have no field-replaceable units (FRUs) and no upgradability.

That said, every mobile device enables you to attach some kind of peripheral or external storage device. But every device offers different expansion capabilities, so it's hard to generalize about them.

FIGURE 13.14 Earbuds plugged into a smartphone

The one exception to the rule that you can't generalize about mobile devices relates to sound. Every mobile device has a single 3.5-mm audio jack for plugging in earbuds or speakers (see Figure 13.14). This applies to smartphones and tablets from all vendors.

Apple Expansion Options

Apple devices offer the least expansion capability of all the mobile devices, so even though they dominate the marketplace, there's not much to say about them. The iPhone and iPad use a single proprietary port that's used to recharge the device and to connect the few external devices available. Figure 13.15 shows the typical use for the port, a dongle that connects to a USB AC adapter for recharge.

Android Expansion Options

Devices that use Google Android come with a variety of connections and expansion capabilities. Many offer microSD slots for adding storage in the form of the tiny flash memory cards (see Figure 13.16). Some offer bigger slots, and a few feature Micro USB or even full-sized USB ports.

FIGURE 13.15 Recharger dongle

Many Android devices offer a proprietary socket that mimics the functions of Apple's dongle port, providing a way to recharge the tablet or smartphone and get data from a PC to the tablet and vice versa. Figure 13.17 shows a proprietary connector for power.

Finally, many tablets sport a connector for attaching the device to an external monitor, such as a big screen or projector. (Smartphones don't generally have this connector.) Figure 13.18 shows a Micro-HDMI port and connector.

FIGURE 13.16 MicroSD card and slot

FIGURE 13.17 ASUS proprietary power connector

Bluetooth

The last way that mobile devices expand their physical capabilities is wirelessly, most often using the Bluetooth standard for adding a keyboard (all) or mouse (not with Apple products). In theory, you could attach all sorts of Bluetooth devices to the mobile device, but the reality seems limited to keyboards. Figure 13.19 shows a diminutive Apple keyboard for the iPad and the iPad resting in a stand to make typing this chapter a little easier than using the virtual keyboard.

Travel Assistance
See the "Bluetooth" section of this chapter for the steps to set up a tablet with a Bluetooth keyboard.

FIGURE 13.18 Micro-HDMI port and connector

FIGURE 13.19 Keyboard associated with iPad

The Other Tablet

Microsoft started the *Tablet PC* initiative way back in 2001, defining the devices as fully featured portables running a tablet-aware version of Windows and using a stylus to interact directly with the screen. Many Tablet PCs have come to market since then, fulfilling the needs of specific professions, notably medicine.

> **Travel Assistance**
>
> *Tablet PC* is a Microsoft term and is *not* the equivalent of a tablet such as the Apple iPad or Samsung Galaxy Tab. The latter devices derive from the mobile phone market, as mentioned at the beginning of this chapter, so they're *not* PCs, but rather a unique class of mobile devices. According to Microsoft, a Tablet PC runs Windows.

Instead of (or in addition to) a keyboard and mouse, Tablet PCs provide a screen that doubles as an input device. With a special pen, called a *stylus,* you can actually write on the screen (see Figure 13.20). Unlike some touch screens, most

FIGURE 13.20 A Tablet PC

Tablet PC screens are not pressure sensitive—you have to use the stylus to write on the screen. Tablet PCs come in two main form factors: *convertibles,* which include a keyboard that you can fold out of the way, and *slates,* which do away with the keyboard entirely. The convertible Tablet PC in Figure 13.20, for example, looks and functions just like a typical clamshell laptop. But here it's shown with the screen rotated 180 degrees and snapped flat so it functions as a slate. Pretty slick!

Early Tablet PCs ran Windows XP Tablet edition. Windows Vista and Windows 7 support tablet features in all editions. Windows Vista, for example, has a dedicated Pen and Input Devices applet in Control Panel. Windows Vista and 7 also have a specific Tablet PC Settings applet (see Figure 13.21) that enables you to configure the tablet to recognize handwriting, place menus conveniently for right or left-handed users, and more.

Objective 13.02 Configuring Mobile Devices

Mobile devices require some setup and configuration to function seamlessly in your online life. That means you need to set up network connectivity, add Bluetooth devices, configure e-mail account(s), and enable the devices to synchronize with a PC. Let's look at all four options.

FIGURE 13.21 Tablet PC Settings applet

Network Connectivity

Mobile devices connect to the outside world through the cellular networks or through various 802.11 Wi-Fi standards. You'll learn specifics about the standards in Chapter 20, so I won't add specifics here. This section looks at standard configuration issues from the perspective of a mobile device.

When you want to connect to a Wi-Fi network, you need to turn Wi-Fi on and then actively connect to a network. If the network is properly configured with WPA or WPA2 encryption, then you also need to have the logon information to access the network. The most common way to connect is through the Settings app (see Figure 13.22). (This applies to all iOS and Android devices.)

Settings enables you to do the vast majority of configuration necessary for a mobile device. To join a network, for example, tap the Wi-Fi (or Networks) option to see available networks (see Figure 13.23). Simply select the one you want to join and type in the passphrase or passcode. Give the mobile device a moment to get IP and DNS information from the DHCP server, and you're on the network.

FIGURE 13.22 Selecting the Settings icon

FIGURE 13.23 Browsing available networks

After you connect to a network successfully, all mobile devices store that network access information automatically, creating a *profile* of that network based on the SSID (the name of the network). This works just like with any other device that connects to a Wi-Fi network. If the SSID of a network changes after you've connected to that network, your mobile device will fail to connect to the rechristened network. You need to delete the profile and reconnect. You do this through the Settings app by selecting the Wi-Fi network and selecting *Forget this network*.

Exam Tip
You can use the Settings app to turn Wi-Fi off or to go into Airplane Mode to stop the device from sending any signals out.

Data

Many mobile devices can use the cellular data services (discussed in Chapter 21) to access the Internet. This way, you can use your smartphone or tablet to get e-mail or browse the Web pretty much anywhere, even without a Wi-Fi hotspot.

By default, mobile devices that use cellular networks for Internet connectivity use *data roaming,* meaning they'll jump from cell tower to cell tower and from your provider to another provider without obvious notice. This is no big deal when you travel within your own country where competing providers have inexpensive roaming agreements.

Watch out for data roaming outside your country! If you travel outside of your country, your mobile device will also happily and seamlessly connect via some other available cell provider. This can lead to some shockingly huge bills from your cell phone company when you get back from that cruise or out-of-country trip. If you're going outside your cell provider's coverage area, get a plan that specifies that you're traveling. It'll still be more expensive than your regular plan, but not nearly as crazy as an accidental roaming charge.

If you don't need to connect when out of country, turn data roaming off. You'll find the feature in the Settings app, as you might expect. You can also turn off cellular data entirely or only turn off cellular services selectively, if your device can do more than one type. (You would want to turn off cellular data, for example, if you don't have an unlimited data plan and are getting near your limits.)

Bluetooth

Pairing a Bluetooth device with a mobile device follows a similar, simple pattern through the Settings icon. You turn on Bluetooth on the smartphone or tablet and then power on the Bluetooth device. Return to the mobile device to select to pair with the Bluetooth device, and then enter the appropriate personal identification number (PIN) code. For a keyboard, for example, the smartphone or tablet will display a set of characters for you to type on the keyboard (see Figure 13.24). Once you type in the PIN code, the devices connect.

Exam Tip
Not all Bluetooth pairings require a PIN code, but there's always some kind of pairing action to do on both devices to make a pairing. Note also that CompTIA uses the phrase *pin code* in lowercase to describe the pairing mechanism.

FIGURE 13.24 Prompting for PIN

Always test the connectivity between a mobile device and a newly added Bluetooth accessory. If you've added a keyboard, for example, open up a note-taking app and start typing to make sure it works.

Most mobile devices have Bluetooth discovery disabled by default to conserve battery life. Actively seeking pairing uses electricity, as does completed pairing, so use Bluetooth when you need to use it and be prepared for the battery hit.

E-mail

Setting up e-mail offers many levels of complexity with mobile devices, primarily because of the many different types of e-mail servers out there. The process is similar to that of setting up e-mail accounts on a desktop PC (discussed in Chapter 21). Apple devices go through the Settings app and then the Mail, Contacts, Calendars option (see Figure 13.25). Tap the Add Account option to bring up the default e-mail options (see Figure 13.26). If you want to connect to a Microsoft Exchange Server–based e-mail account, tap the appropriate option here and type in your e-mail address, domain, user name, password, and description.

FIGURE 13.25 Mail, Contacts, Calendars screen on iPhone

Mail... Add Account...

☁ **iCloud**

Microsoft®
Exchange

G🅼ail

YAHOO!

Aol.

Microsoft®
Hotmail

FIGURE 13.26	Default e-mail types on iPhone

If you want a more common POP3 or IMAP4 account set up, that's not one of Apple's default options, so you'd have to go through the Other option on the initial Add Account screen. Eventually, you'll get prompted as you would expect to choose POP3 or IMAP4 and type in addresses for the sending and receiving servers.

Android-based tablets assume you'll have a Gmail account as your primary account, so that option is offered as a distinctive icon on the home screen (see Figure 13.27). You'll also have an Email icon for setting up Exchange, POP3, or IMAP4 accounts. You configure them the same way as you would a desktop e-mail application, including putting in the port setting and security type, such as SSL or TLS (see Figure 13.28).

Synchronization

Smartphones and tablets can *synchronize*, or *sync*, with local machines or over the Internet with cloud-based servers to keep files and data up to date. Older devices, such as BlackBerrys and Palm Pilots, had a specialized sync program that installed onto your PC and that you could use to sync contacts, calendars, and so on. Today's devices either use a dedicated program or sync through the cloud.

FIGURE 13.27	Gmail account option

Most tablets and many smartphones use a proprietary dongle for syncing through a USB port on the computer. This is the same dongle used to recharge the battery. Some devices can sync through Wi-Fi connections. Many smartphones use a micro USB–to–regular USB cable to connect to the PC.

Account setup

Incoming server settings

Username	scottj@totalsem.com	
Password	••••••	**Previous**
IMAP server	imap.totalsem.com	
Security type	SSL/TLS	**Next**
Port	993	
IMAP path prefix	Optional	

FIGURE 13.28	Setting up a secure IMAP4 account

iTunes and iCloud

Apple iPhones and iPads synch through Apple iTunes installed on a Mac or PC, a free program that you download from Apple. Everything, such as music, videos, contacts, pictures, and so on, can be stored locally. You can choose to back up all the apps on your iPhone or iPad to iTunes as well. This single source for backup makes it easy to recover from something catastrophic happening to your Apple device. If you replace an Apple device, for example, you can simply sync that new device, and all your files, contact information, and apps copy to the new device.

Exam Tip

Apple iTunes will run on just about any Mac OS X machine. On Windows at the time of this writing, you need to be running Windows XP with Service Pack 2 or better or any later Windows OS.

The CompTIA A+ 802 competencies don't discuss hardware requirements. The only thing that's relevant to a tech is that hardware needs to scale up to play more complex media. You can play music with a 1-GHz CPU, for example, but need a 2.4-GHz CPU with two or more cores to play HD video.

In late 2011, Apple introduced a cloud-based storage solution called iCloud. With iCloud, you can have all your iPhone or iPad data backed up and thus accessible from anywhere. This includes any media purchased through iTunes and calendars, contacts, reminders, and so forth.

Android and Gmail

Android-based mobile devices don't have a central desktop application like Apple devices. Rather, they sync over the Internet—but only some data. Contacts, calendars, and e-mail (through Gmail) are all that sync by default. For every other type of data or media, you treat the Android device like a fat thumb drive—you drag and drop files into the appropriate folder on the smartphone or tablet.

Sync In, Sync Out

One of the radical differences between an Apple device and an Android device is in the direction of syncing (or even copying, for that matter). With Apple, you can sync files—especially media files—to the iPhone or iPad. You cannot take that Apple device, connect it to another computer, and copy files *from* it to the PC. It's a one-way street.

Android devices, in contrast, happily share like a thumb drive. You can drag and drop from an Android smartphone or tablet to any PC.

Objective 13.03 Securing Mobile Devices

Mobile devices almost long to roam freely, so you need to take active steps to secure them against damage, loss, or theft. Let's look at all three issues.

Preventing Damage

Mobile devices cost a fair amount of money and thus aren't disposable media for most people. That means you need to take steps to prevent damage, both physical and software based.

For physical damage, the first step you must take is to get a protective cover or sleeve for the mobile device. It doesn't help the HD camcorder in your new iPad if you get a scratch across the lens! You'll get a scratched, blurry movie even though the camcorder is capable of much, much more. Apple makes very nice covers for iPhones and iPads; plus, you can get many third-party covers and sleeves (see Figure 13.29).

FIGURE 13.29 Putting an Apple Smart cover on an iPad

Depending on the amount of money you're willing to spend, you can get covers that help protect your screen from scratches, impacts, and small amounts of water. Like to scuba with your Android device? There are waterproof cases (as opposed to a cover) that enable you to check your Facebook account from 40 feet underwater. (These are specialty devices and not very typical.)

Do the obvious to protect your devices. Don't get them anywhere near liquids. Don't run your smartphone through the wash in your trousers. Don't even think about placing heavy objects on that $600 tablet! Use common sense.

For software-based issues, you've got only a few options. At the time of this writing, for example, there is no antivirus software for smartphones or tablets. (Such software is unnecessary at this time.) About the only software protection you get is periodic *patching*, automatic updates and operating system patches from the device manufacturers.

Exam Tip

There's no antivirus solution for current mobile devices.

Dealing with Loss

Losing a mobile device creates a series of issues that you need to address. First, protect your data from access by putting a good *passcode lock* on the device, which requires you to type in a series of letters, numbers, or motion patterns to unlock the mobile device each time you press the power button. Don't assume that you'll never set the phone down in the lavatory at an airport and forget about it or lose it to a thief. Most mobile devices enable you to set a passcode lock or screen lock from the Settings icon (see Figure 13.30). Do it right now! Some devices enable you to encrypt the contents of the SSD, so even if a "finder" dismantles the device to access the drive, he or she will not get your documents.

Mobile devices also have a preset number of failed login attempt restrictions that, when exceeded, lock up the mobile device. This slows down someone trying to hack into a found mobile device while you use locator services or applications to try to recover it.

Both Apple and Google offer locator services for discovering the whereabouts of a misplaced mobile device. Google's service is okay, while Apple does a much better job with iCloud. Log in to your iCloud account and click the Find My iPhone button. (This works for both iPhones and iPads.) As soon as the device in question accesses the Internet (and thus receives an IP address and posts its MAC address), iCloud will pinpoint the location within a few yards (see Figure 13.31). Very slick!

| FIGURE 13.30 | Screen lock option in Settings |

| FIGURE 13.31 | Locating a device in iCloud |

Recovering from Theft

If your mobile device gets stolen and contains sensitive information, then you have a couple of options for dealing with it. Certainly the locator services help, but if you have credit card information or other very damaging information on your mobile device, you need to act quickly.

First, make sure you have your data backed up. You should have everything synced to a local machine and, if possible, backed up to one of the remote backup applications—like iCloud—to put your data beyond the reach of even a disaster that takes out your house. With iCloud, go into Settings and select iCloud. Tap the Storage & Backup option and turn iCloud Backup from OFF (the default) to ON (see Figure 13.32). Note that this will stop automatic backups to your local machine when you sync with iTunes.

Second, you can remotely wipe your mobile device. Apple makes it supremely easy through iCloud. Log in, locate, and nuke your device (see Figure 13.33). You may never get the device back, but at least the bad guys won't have your data.

FIGURE 13.32 Turning on remote backup

FIGURE 13.33 Remote wipe

CHECKPOINT

✔**Objective 13.01: Features and Capabilities of Smartphones and Tablets**
The primary distinction between the two mobile device types is that a smartphone is a cell phone enhanced to do things formerly reserved for fully grown PCs, whereas a tablet embodies those enhanced computing features and capabilities on an expanded format and screen. Apple uses a closed-source or single-source system, meaning that if you want to get an app for your iPhone or iPad, you can only get it from the Apple App Store. With Android devices, you get apps from vendor-specific stores or open-source markets for apps developed "for Android" that probably will work with your device. Finally, mobile devices offer no field-serviceable parts.

✔**Objective 13.02: Configuring Mobile Devices** Mobile devices connect to the outside world through the cellular networks or through various 802.11 Wi-Fi standards. When you want to connect to a Wi-Fi network, you need to turn Wi-Fi on and then actively connect to a network using proper authentication. To pair a Bluetooth device with a mobile device, turn on Bluetooth on the smartphone or tablet and then power on the Bluetooth device. Return to the mobile device to select to pair with the Bluetooth device, and then enter the appropriate PIN code.

The Settings icon enables you to set up all sorts of types of e-mail on both iOS and Android devices. You set up an Exchange, POP3, IMAP4, Gmail, or other types of e-mail accounts the same way you would on a desktop, with addresses for sending and receiving servers, login information, port settings, and security type, such as SSL or TLS. You can sync smartphones and tablets with local machines or over the Internet with cloud-based servers to keep files and data up to date. Apple devices use iTunes or iCloud. Android devices sync primarily with Gmail for mail and contacts.

✔**Objective 13.03: Securing Mobile Devices** For preventing physical damage, the first step you must take is to get a protective cover or sleeve for the mobile device. At the time of this writing, there is no antivirus software for smartphones or tablets. About the only software protection you get is periodic, automatic updates and operating system patches from the device manufacturers. Use passcode locks and device-finding services to protect and recover from losing your mobile device. Make sure you back up the device regularly. If the device is stolen and doesn't appear recoverable, you can wipe it from afar.

REVIEW QUESTIONS

1. Placing your phone in a typical protective cover will *not* protect the phone from:
 A. Scratches
 B. Impact
 C. Small amounts of water
 D. Immersion in water

2. Which type of display responds to the difference in electrical potential between you and the screen?
 A. Capacitive
 B. LCD
 C. OLED
 D. Resistive

3. John has a high-resolution image on his iPad of his two-year-old son and the family dog. The image initially displays smaller than the screen,

so he wants to zoom in to get the details of his son's expression. How can he accomplish this task?

A. Click the mouse in the middle of the picture to select it and then use the scroll wheel on the mouse to zoom in.

B. Tap the picture with his index finger on his son's face.

C. Right-click the picture with his index finger on his son's face.

D. Touch his son's face on the screen with his thumb and finger, pinching outward to scroll in.

4. Which mobile device screen technology uses no backlight?

A. CCFL

B. LCD

C. LED

D. OLED

5. What can a government use to determine your location at a specific time as long as you're using your mobile device?

A. Geocaching

B. Geotracking

C. Google Earth

D. Gyroscope

6. What are the steps involved in pairing a Bluetooth keyboard with a tablet?

A. Enable Bluetooth on the tablet; turn on the Bluetooth device; find the device with the tablet; enter a PIN code or other pairing sequence.

B. Turn on the Bluetooth device; find the device with the tablet; enter a PIN code or other pairing sequence.

C. Search for a Bluetooth device from the tablet; select pair from the options to enable the device.

D. Enable Bluetooth on the tablet; turn on the Bluetooth device; find the device with the tablet; select pair from the options to enable the device.

7. A client calls, wanting to copy his music from his iPhone to his new PC. How can he accomplish this task?

A. Connect the iPhone to the new PC. When it shows up as a new device, right-click it and select Properties. In the Properties dialog box, select Export Media Files.

B. Connect the iPhone to the new PC. Double-click it and go to the Media folder. Drag and drop the desired music to the Music library on his new PC.

 C. Access the iPhone wirelessly from the PC. Drag and drop the desired music to the Music library on his new PC.

 D. He can't.

8. A client calls and is upset that he's misplaced his iPad. The mobile device has literally thousands of client records, including business addresses, e-mail addresses, phone numbers, and, in some cases, credit card information. What should he do first?

 A. There's nothing he can do.

 B. He should call his ISP and have them track his iPad.

 C. He should access his iCloud account and reset his iPad to erase all personal data.

 D. He should purchase another iPad and sync with his iTunes account. This automatically erases the information on the old tablet.

9. Name the primary feature that separates a smartphone from a tablet.

 A. iTunes

 B. OLED screen

 C. Capacitive touch screen

 D. Capability to make telephone calls

10. What information do you need to connect an Android-based tablet to an IMAP4 account?

 A. POP3 server DNS name

 B. User name and password

 C. User name, password, sending and receiving server addresses

 D. Exchange server name, user name, and password

REVIEW ANSWERS

1. **D** A cover will not protect your phone from being immersed in water.

2. **A** A capacitive touch screen display responds to the difference in electrical potential between you and the screen.

3. **D** John can pinch outward with his fingers to zoom in on the image.

4. **D** OLED technology does not use a backlight.

5. **B** Geotracking can locate you and your GPS-equipped mobile device.

6. **A** To pair a Bluetooth keyboard with a tablet, enable Bluetooth on the tablet, turn on the Bluetooth device, find the Bluetooth device in the tablet's settings screen, and then enter a PIN code or finalize the pairing.

7. **D** You cannot copy music from an iPhone onto your PC.

8. **C** To protect his data, the client should log in to his iCloud account and reset the iPad and erase all personal data.

9. **D** A smartphone can make telephone calls, while a tablet cannot.

10. **C** To connect an Android-based tablet to an IMAP4 account, you'll need a user name and password and the sending and receiving server addresses.

Operating System Fundamentals

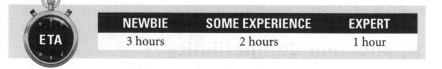

ETA	NEWBIE	SOME EXPERIENCE	EXPERT
	3 hours	2 hours	1 hour

An operating system (OS) brings a PC to life. It makes it a useful and essential tool for everyone from an actuary to a zoologist. Without an OS, even the most high-end computer would be reduced to a slick-looking cup holder.

This chapter examines the general functions of an OS and looks at how an OS manifests. You'll learn how to identify the characteristics of Windows and understand the features and functions common to all available versions of the OS.

Objective 14.01 Characteristics of the Operating System

All OSs share certain common characteristics. First, all have some degree of CPU specificity. Second, all OSs must have their own specifically written applications. Third, all take control of the PC after the POST and keep that control until you shut down the system.

CPU Specific

The OS must understand important aspects of the CPU, such as the amount of memory the CPU can handle, what modes of operation it is capable of performing, and the commands needed to perform any operation. For that reason, an OS works only with a particular type of processor. The Intel and AMD x86 and x64 lines of CPUs heavily dominate today's PCs, but other platforms have used different CPUs that were completely incompatible. The most obvious example of the latter is the jointly developed Apple-IBM-Motorola Power PC, the CPU used in older Macintosh computers.

Application Compatibility

Next, just as an OS has to be matched to a particular CPU, application programs have to be written for particular OSs. Manufacturers always provide a "rule book" that tells programmers how to write programs for their particular OS. These rule books are known as *application programming interfaces (APIs)*. Many applications are able to function on more than one OS through *porting*.

Local Lingo
Porting *Porting* means to rewrite an application to use another operating system's API. Many of today's development platforms, such as Microsoft C#, make porting easy to do.

PC Control

An OS takes control of the PC immediately following the POST process (described in Chapter 7) and controls all aspects of the PC operation. The OS continues running until you manually reboot or turn off the PC. You cannot exit from the OS unless you also turn off the PC.

Objective 14.02 Common Operating System Functions

All OSs are not created equal, but every OS provides certain functions:

- The OS must communicate, or provide a method for other programs to communicate, with the hardware of the PC.
- The OS must create a user interface—a visual representation of the computer on the monitor that makes sense to the people using the computer.
- The OS, via the user interface, must enable users to determine the available installed programs and run, use, and shut down the program of their choice.
- The OS should enable users to add, move, and delete the installed programs and data.

Those four tasks are common to any OS. Let's take a look at each of these in more detail.

Communicating with Hardware

It's up to the OS to access the hard drives, respond to the keyboard, and output data to the monitor. The OS works with the system BIOS to deal with these devices. If users want to access the hard drive to retrieve a program, the OS passes the request to the appropriate hard-drive BIOS instruction that tells the drive to send the program to RAM. Most recent OSs, including Windows, skip the system BIOS and talk directly to almost every piece of hardware.

Installing and configuring hardware devices was discussed in Chapter 10, so you should recall that hardware devices need their own programs to enable them to communicate with the OS—*device drivers*. OS makers provide development tools for hardware makers to create driver software for their products.

Creating a User Interface

Unless you happen to speak the binary language of computers fluently enough to keep up with the millions of calculation cycles per second that the CPU routinely handles, you need some other way to enter commands. The OS creates a way for you to do this through the *user interface (UI)*.

The UI might be a *command prompt* that enables you to use a keyboard to type simple instructions into the system, or it might be a graphical *desktop* with which you interact using a pointer device such as a mouse, trackball, touchpad, joystick, or even using handwriting or voice commands. Whatever the UI's manifestation, they all do the same thing—enable you to control the computer. The "Operating System Interfaces" section (Objective 14.03) of this chapter covers OS implementations in more detail.

Accessing and Supporting Programs

In addition to creating an environment for a user to interact with the PC, the OS creates the environment that enables users to interact with applications. In the old days, computers ran only one program at a time, but modern PCs are *multitasking* machines and must run two, three, ten, or any number of programs or processes concurrently. As with hardware, the OS must also determine the state of running programs and either correct the error states or alert the user when a program has stopped responding.

In addition, the OS enables you to install new programs and remove old ones with relative ease. Properly written programs should integrate with the OS seamlessly. You see problems when badly written or "buggy" programs are installed.

Organizing and Manipulating Programs and Data

For programs and data to be useful, the OS must organize them into a logical structure. Fortunately, all OSs share the same basic organization method. All programs and data are stored as files. A file is a discrete piece of data organized so that when the CPU loads it, the OS knows what to do with it. All files have two-part names: the first part, the *filename,* is the unique identifier (A+_Passport_Ch14), and the second part, the *extension,* defines the type of data (.docx is the universal extension for Microsoft Word files). You combine these to give the complete filename (A+_Passport_Ch14.docx). Other file extensions include .bat (batch files), .exe (executables), .jpg, .gif, .bmp (image files), .wav, .mp3 (sound files), and the list goes on.

Travel Advisory

Windows hides known file extensions by default, so A+_Passport_ Ch14.docx would actually look like A+_Passport_Ch14. Know that the file extension is still there and it defines the file type.

Files are useless if you can't organize them, so all OSs use a directory-tree organization. Each storage device has a name and an icon. You can subdivide each storage device into discrete folders or directories that contain related files. Windows creates a number of folders for the OS itself, but you can create others.

Exam Tip

All files have four special values, or *attributes,* that determine how programs treat the file in special situations. These can be added or removed through the file's properties or from the command prompt. With the hidden attribute, a file is not displayed when you issue the **dir** command. A file with a read-only attribute cannot be modified or deleted. The system attribute is used only for system files such as ntldr and boot.ini—in reality, it does nothing more than provide an easy identifier for those files. Finally, the archive attribute is used by backup software to identify files that have been changed since their last backup.

Speaking of creating folders, all these files and folders are *still* useless unless you can manipulate them. The OS enables users to create, manipulate, and arrange files on the storage devices. Common functions of this sort include copying, moving, and deleting data.

One of the greatest challenges to OS designers is making all of these functions comprehensible to users. Because of their inherent complexity, simply laying out every tool and function of an OS at once would be ugly and unusable. Instead, there needs to be something to guide the user through each function, enabling him or her to use the system productively. This is the goal of the user interface.

Objective 14.03 Operating System Interfaces

All OS user interfaces for the PC manifest in two ways: through a *command line interface* and through a *graphical user interface (GUI).* Undoubtedly, the GUI is more familiar to most users, but the command line has by no means become obsolete.

Command Line Interface

Mainframes and minicomputers of old all used the classic command line interface for many years before the advent of the GUI, and it is still used to this day. Although you won't find modern PCs that use a command line interface exclusively, all modern OSs—Windows, Mac, and the many flavors of Linux—enable users to "drop down" to a command prompt to enter instructions. In fact, many high-level functions and utilities can be run *only* from a command line environment; therefore, it's not only relevant but important for techs to understand how to talk to the PC from the command line.

Still considered by many to be an elegant OS, Microsoft's *MS-DOS* is the first OS that most old-school PC techs encountered. Many commands used in DOS, such as **copy**, **dir**, **attrib**, and others, are still used today. It's not uncommon for folks to refer (incorrectly) to the Windows command line interface as a *DOS window*.

Accessing the Command Line Interface

The command line interface program (also called the *command interpreter*) manifests as a simple text *prompt*—so-called because of the blinking text *cursor* character that prompts you for input. Anytime you've gone into one of the command line modes from the advanced Windows OS boot menu, you've seen the good old C:\> prompt.

You can also access a command line interface from within Windows. You can find the shortcut to the command line interface program in the Accessories folder, which is accessible from the Start menu (Start | All Programs | Accessories | Command Prompt). Most techs, however, simply start it by typing **cmd** in the Search or Run dialog (accessed by choosing Start | Search programs and files or Start | Run, as shown in Figure 14.1).

Issuing Instructions Using the Command Line

Working with the command line requires you to use commands recognized by the OS and to type in those commands correctly. Each OS has different commands. To see the contents of a folder in Windows, for example, you type the **dir** command. To see the contents of a folder in Linux, in contrast, you type the **ls** command.

In both instances, you must type the command properly, using what's called the proper *syntax*. To move the file beethoven.mp3 from the c:\temp folder to the c:\music folder, for example, you would type the **move** command followed by the target followed by the destination. Then press ENTER. It looks like this:

```
move c:\temp\beethoven.mp3 c:\music
```

FIGURE 14.1 Type **cmd** in the Search dialog box to open a command line interface in Windows 7.

If you reverse the target and destination folders or type something incorrectly, the command simply won't work. You might get an error message or you might not. Or you might accidentally delete a file or folder—it isn't very likely, but it's possible.

For a complete list of instructions, simply type **help** at the command prompt and press the ENTER key. For details on the various *switches* and *parameters* that apply to a particular command, type **help** followed by a space and the command name (for example, **help attrib**).

Exam Tip

You can get help for a specific command by typing the following at a command prompt:
[command name] /?

For the moment, concentrate on the handful of commands that you're most likely to use. Table 14.1 lists a few important commands that work in all versions of Windows command lines. Older forms of the commands are provided for reference. You might see these on the exams.

Navigating Using a Command Line Interface

The command prompt is always *focused* on a specific folder. This is important because any commands you issue are performed *on the files in the folder* on which the prompt is focused. If you see a prompt that looks like *C:\>*, for example, you know that the focus is on the root directory of the C: drive.

TABLE 14.1	Common Command Line Interface Commands
Command	**Description**
cd	Changes the focus of the command prompt from one folder (directory) to another. The older form of the command is **chdir**.
copy	Copies files from one folder to another.
copy /a	/a indicates an ASCII text file.
copy /v	/v verifies that the new files are written correctly.
copy /y	/y disables prompting to confirm you want to overwrite an existing file.
del	Permanently deletes files. The command **erase** works as well.
dir	Displays a listing of the files and folders (subdirectories) in a directory.
edit	Opens the text-editing program.
exit	Closes the command line interface program.
md	Creates a new folder. The older form of the command is **mkdir**.
move	Moves files from one folder to another.
rd	Deletes (removes) a folder. The older form of the command is **rmdir**.
regsvr32	Registers .dll files as command components in the Registry.
ren	Renames files. You can spell it out as well, using **rename** as the command.
robocopy	Enables you to copy files and folders across a network, fully replicating the structure on the destination system and deleting any extra files or folders.
shutdown	Enables you to shut down a local or remote computer.
tree	Graphically displays the structure of a path.
ver	Displays the version of Windows.
xcopy	Copies files and directories (including subdirectories).

As noted in Table 14.1, you change the command prompt's focus to another folder by typing **cd** followed by the target folder's name. To see which files are contained in a particular folder, use the **dir** command. Figure 14.2 shows the command prompt focused on the *Documents and Settings\scottj\Desktop* folder of the C: drive.

Exam Tip

Know the default command prompts in each version of Windows! In Windows XP, it's C:\Documents and Settings\Username. For Windows Vista and Windows 7, it's C:\Users\Username.

The **cd** command is *not* used to move between drives. To get the prompt to switch its focus to another hard drive, removable drive, or partition, just type the target drive letter followed by a colon. If, for example, the command prompt is focused at the *C:\Documents and Settings\scottj\Desktop* directory and you want to switch to the floppy drive (drive A:), just type **a:** and press the ENTER key and the command prompt will point to the floppy drive.

Travel Advisory

Windows navigation commands aren't case sensitive. Typing **c:** or **C:** followed by pressing the ENTER key gets you to the root drive.

Running Applications from the Command Prompt

Executing applications from the command line environment is done in the same way as running the built-in Windows command line utilities. Simply navigate to the folder containing the application, type the name of the executable

```
C:\WINDOWS\system32\cmd.exe

C:\Documents and Settings\scottj\Desktop>_
```

FIGURE 14.2 Command prompt indicating focus on *C:\Documents and Settings\scottj\Desktop*

file, and press ENTER. Valid executable files have an extension of .exe or .com, but typically you don't need to enter the file extension, just the filename.

Graphical User Interface

The GUI implementation of an OS is the most familiar interface for most users. Instead of using a character-based interface to run programs and administer files, you see files, folders, and programs represented as tiny graphics, called *icons,* arranged in a workspace called the *desktop.* You use a mouse or other pointing device to manipulate icons by selecting them with a *pointer.* Figure 14.3 shows the GUI for Windows Vista.

Modern versions of Windows are pure GUI-based OSs. Accessing vital OS functions and programs is, of course, possible through a command line interface in these OSs, but the command line interface is a function of the GUI, and not the GUI itself. The next section looks at the features of Windows that are common to all versions.

FIGURE 14.3 Windows Vista desktop

> ### Exam Tip
> You can start many graphical programs from the command line or Start | Run or Search interface. Try typing any of these at a command prompt: **notepad**, **mspaint**, **calc** …. Press **ENTER** to run the program.

Objective 14.04 Common Microsoft Windows Features

All versions of Windows share certain characteristics, configuration files, and that nebulous quality called *look and feel*. You'll find the same or similar utilities in almost all versions, and once you master one interface—both GUI and command line interface—you've pretty much got them all knocked.

Welcome/Login Screen

The Windows Welcome screen offers a high degree of security. In fact, you can't access Windows without logging in with a valid user account. Figure 14.4 shows a Windows 7 Welcome screen.

Windows XP offers the login procedure similarly to Windows Vista/7 in a simple workgroup environment. One version of the Windows XP login screen presents you with a list of user accounts stored on the PC, enabling you to choose one to log in with, as shown in Figure 14.5.

> ### Travel Advisory
> Windows XP Professional has two very different login methods. The one shown in Figure 14.5 shows Windows XP configured to log into a workgroup. If you log in to a Windows domain, you will see blanks for both a user name and a password. It doesn't give away the user name like with the workgroup version. See Chapter 19 for details on workgroups and domains.

Once you log into the system, you're presented with your user account's desktop, described in the next section.

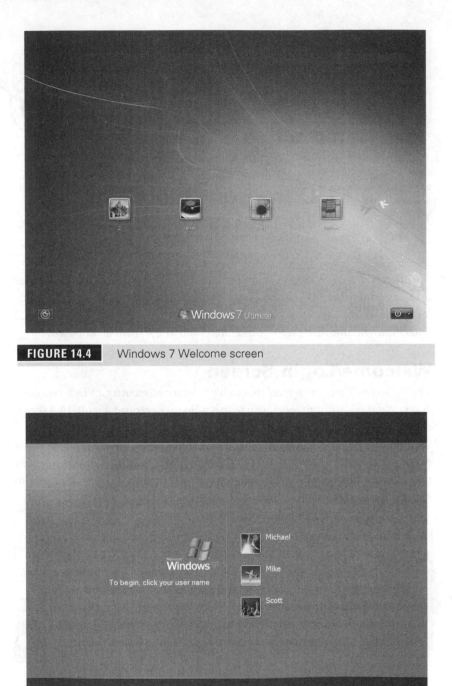

FIGURE 14.4 Windows 7 Welcome screen

FIGURE 14.5 Windows XP login screen

Desktop

The Windows desktop is your main interface to the OS. The desktop is the workspace where you launch applications, input and manipulate data, configure hardware, and, of course, watch videos and play games. Figure 14.6 shows a typical Windows XP Professional desktop.

The desktop is a highly customizable environment, in which you can personalize virtually every aspect, including such settings as the background wallpaper and default sound effects, screen resolution and color schemes, and language settings and accessibility options.

Windows systems enable different users to create different desktop environments (usually called *profiles*) that are loaded when a user logs onto the PC. Every Windows desktop, however, still shares a few common features, such as several default folder shortcut icons and the *taskbar*.

Windows Vista/7's *Aero* desktop adds a number of impressive aesthetic features to the desktop that Microsoft claims makes the user experience more enjoyable and productive. I'm not going to get into an argument on the value of the Aero desktop, but it is an important part of the Windows Vista/7 interface. Most of the Aero features are overly technical—even for the CompTIA A+ exams—but the end result is a faster, smoother desktop with two interesting features: transparency and

FIGURE 14.6 Windows XP Professional desktop

Flip 3D. *Transparency,* as the name implies, gives an adjustable amount of transparency to the edges of your windowed programs (Figure 14.7). *Flip 3D* enables you to view and select all of your open Windows in a 3-D format. It's actually very handy once you start using it.

> **Exam Tip**
>
> Windows Vista Home Basic and Windows 7 Starter do not support the Aero desktop.

My Computer/Computer

The folder called My Computer (or Computer, in Windows Vista/7) enables you to access all drives, folders, and files on the system. Windows XP and Vista/7 do not include My Computer/Computer on the desktop by default. You can readily access it through the Start menu. To open My Computer/Computer, simply double-click the icon on the desktop, or choose Start | My Computer/Computer. When opened, it shows you all the drives on the system, as shown in Figure 14.8.

My Computer/Computer is one view of a program called *Windows Explorer.* Windows Explorer enables you to view folders on your drives. It's flexible too and can change its interface in many ways.

> **Exam Tip**
>
> You can open a Windows Explorer interface with the Start | Run or Search option. Type **explorer** and press ENTER and it'll run. Try it!

FIGURE 14.7 Translucent windows in Windows 7

FIGURE 14.8 Computer in Windows 7

One part of the window, either on the left or along the bottom, provides details of whatever icon you currently have highlighted. For example, Figure 14.8 has the C: drive highlighted, so the left side provides details about that drive. We call this the *layout* for Windows Explorer and, as with so many other tools, you can change this pretty radically. Your basic Windows Explorer dialog box has the main window along with three other panes: navigation, preview, and details. You can't turn off the main windows, but you can turn any of these three panes on or off to suit your preferences. In Windows Vista, select Organize | Layout to change the interface.

Windows assigns different icons to different types of files according to their file type extensions, such as .exe or .jpg. As you look at these icons on your own screen, you might notice that you don't see any extensions—that's because current versions of Windows hides them by default.

To see the extensions in Windows XP, select Tools | Folder Options to open the Folder Options dialog box (Figure 14.9). Click the View tab and uncheck *Hide extensions for known file types*. In Vista/7, choose Organize | Folder And Search Options | View tab to see the same dialog box.

Exam Tip

You can use the Folder Options dialog box to view hidden files. Toggle hidden files on or off by selecting S*how hidden files and folders* or *Do not show hidden files and folders.*

FIGURE 14.9 Windows XP View tab

In every version of Windows prior to XP, Windows Explorer acted like a separate and distinct tool from My Computer. Windows XP and later have merged Explorer and My Computer/Computer into a single tool, but you can still get the Explorer-like interface by right-clicking a folder and choosing Explore from the pop-up options menu, or by holding down the WINDOWS key on your keyboard and pressing the E key.

My Documents, My [Whatever]

All versions of Windows provide a special folder structure for each user account so that they have their own places to store personal data. This folder grouping is called *My Documents* in Windows XP. Many Windows programs take advantage of My Documents and by default store their files in the folder or in a subfolder.

Windows XP installations do not show My Documents on the desktop by default. On Windows XP, you can access it readily through the Start menu, or you can add it to your desktop.

User's Files

Windows Vista/7 takes the equivalent of My Documents to a whole new level with the *User's Files* option. (Although a Documents folder is available, it's designed literally for documents, such as text files.) Click the Start menu and you'll

see a folder option with the user name of the account that's currently logged into the computer. With that option, not only can you get all the folders you get in Windows XP, but Vista and 7 also add a number of other folders, as well as interesting but important data such as your Internet Explorer favorites and copies of recent searches.

Exam Tip

In Windows XP, the default location of My Documents is C:\Documents and Settings\Username. In Windows Vista/7, the default location of Documents is C:\Users\Username.

My Network Places/Network

Systems tied to a network, whether via a network cable, modem, or wireless connection, have an icon for My Network Places (or Network, in Vista/7) on the desktop or in the Start menu. My Network Places/Network can be thought of as My Computer/Computer for the network. Use it to browse shared resources on the local network or on remote networks such as Web sites or *File Transfer Protocol (FTP)* servers. Figure 14.10 shows a typical Windows XP My Network Places folder.

FIGURE 14.10 Windows XP My Network Places folder

Recycle Bin

The Recycle Bin shows up on the desktop of all versions of Windows. Windows doesn't completely erase items when you delete them from your drives. Instead, the file, folder, icon, or what-have-you is moved into the Recycle Bin folder. From there, one of three things can occur:

- You manually empty the Recycle Bin.
- You restore the item.
- The Recycle Bin grows larger than a preset amount and the file is permanently deleted to make room for more recently deleted files.

Travel Advisory

These rules apply only when you're dealing with fixed disk drives. Files deleted from removable disks, such as floppy disks or USB thumb drives, don't go to the Recycle Bin when you delete them—once they're deleted, they're gone for good.

Configure Recycle Bin behavior by right-clicking its icon and selecting Properties from the pop-up menu. Figure 14.11 shows the Recycle Bin Properties dialog box.

FIGURE 14.11 Recycle Bin Properties dialog box

Travel Advisory

Everything in Windows has a properties setting. You can access these properties by right-clicking the object and selecting Properties. From here on, when I say "access properties," you know I mean to right-click and then choose Properties. You can also access properties by highlighting the object and pressing the ALT-ENTER key combination.

Important options include these:

- **Configure drives independently** This option lets you set limits on the amount of disk space reserved for the Recycle Bin for each hard drive or partition. The default setting is to reserve the same percentage of disk space for each drive or partition.

- **Do not move files to the Recycle Bin** This setting effectively disables the Recycle Bin, meaning that any deleted items are unrecoverable. Use this option with caution!

- **Maximum size of Recycle Bin** Displayed in percentage in Windows XP and megabytes in Windows Vista/7, this is the amount of disk or partition space reserved for deleted items.

Windows Sidebar

Windows Vista comes with a UI feature called the *Windows Sidebar*, a tool that sits on the desktop and enables small helper applications—called Microsoft Gadgets—to run. You can display a clock, for example, or a dynamic weather update, or even a CPU monitor that displays your CPU usage. Windows comes with a handful of Gadgets, but developers have gone crazy with them, enabling you to add all sorts of useful tools.

Taskbar and Start Menu

The *taskbar* runs along the bottom of all Windows desktops and includes up to four sections (depending on the version of Windows and your configuration). Starting at the left side, these are the Start button, the Quick Launch toolbar (in Windows XP and Windows Vista), the running programs area, and the notification area. Although the taskbar sits at the bottom of the desktop by default, you can move it to either side or to the top of the screen.

The taskbar contains the *Start button,* probably the most clicked button on all Windows systems. You can find the Start button on the far left end of the taskbar. Figure 14.12 shows the Start buttons for Windows XP, Windows Vista, and Windows 7 (in order from left to right). Click the Start button to open the Start menu, where you can see the applications installed on the system and start them.

FIGURE 14.12 Three different Windows Start buttons

Try moving your cursor onto the All Programs menu item. When the All Programs menu appears, move the cursor to Accessories. Locate the Notepad program and click it. By default, Windows XP hides lesser-used menu options, so if you don't see Notepad, click the double down arrows at the bottom of the Accessories menu to make Notepad appear.

Great! If you opened Notepad properly, you should see something like Figure 14.13, with Notepad displaying an untitled text page. Notice how Notepad shows up on the taskbar at the bottom of your screen. Most running programs appear on the taskbar in this way. Close the Notepad program by clicking the button with the X in the upper-right corner of the Notepad window. Look again at the taskbar to see that Notepad no longer appears there.

Now look all the way to the right end of the taskbar. This part of the taskbar is known officially as the *notification area,* though many techs and the CompTIA A+ certification exams call it the *system tray.* You will, at a minimum, see the current time displayed in the system tray, and on most Windows systems you'll also see a number of small icons there. Figure 14.14 shows the system tray on a Windows Vista PC.

> ### Exam Tip
>
> Microsoft calls the area at the far right of the taskbar the *notification area,* but you might see it referred to on the CompTIA A+ certification exams as the *system tray.*

These icons show programs running in the background. Most programs run in a window. Background programs function like any other program, except

FIGURE 14.13 Notepad application (note the buttons in the upper-right corner)

they do not use a window, simply because the nature of their particular jobs makes a window unnecessary. Thousands of programs like to run in the system tray: network status, volume controls, battery state (on laptops), and removable device status are just a few examples. What shows up on yours depends on your version of Windows, what hardware you use, and what background programs you have installed. Some of the icons in Figure 14.14, for example, include virtual machine software, a monitor calibration program, and my e-mail program.

On Windows XP and Vista systems, you'll find the *Quick Launch toolbar* near the left end of the taskbar (see Figure 14.15). Here, you can place often-used programs and open them with a single click. On Windows XP systems, the Quick Launch toolbar is not displayed on the taskbar by default, so before you can use this convenient feature, you must right-click the taskbar, select Properties, and check Show Quick Launch. To change the contents of the Quick Launch toolbar, simply drag icons onto or off of it.

Windows 7 takes the Quick Launch toolbar and marries it to the running program area thumbnails, creating *pinned applications* (see Figure 14.16). You can pin application icons directly onto the running application area. When you open one of these pinned applications, its icon changes to show that it is now open. If you open an application that isn't pinned to the taskbar, its icon still shows up, but will disappear when you close it. If you've ever used the Apple OS X dock (perish the thought!), then you've used this type of feature.

Microsoft introduced the *Jump List* with Windows 7 to show you context-sensitive information about whatever is on your taskbar (see Figure 14.17). If you look at the Jump List for Microsoft Word, for example, you'll see recently opened documents. The Jump List for iTunes enables you to skip forward and backward through the songs in your playlist. To open a Jump List, click and drag upward on the icon in the taskbar or right-click the icon.

OS Files and Folders

The modern versions of Windows organize essential files and folders in a relatively similar fashion. All have a primary system folder for storing most Windows internal tools and files. All have a set of folders for programs and user files.

FIGURE 14.16 Pinned applications

All use a special grouping of files called the Registry to keep track of all the hardware loaded and the drivers that enable you to use that hardware. Finally, every version has a RAM cache file, enabling more robust access to programs and utilities. Yet once you start to get into details, you'll find some very large differences among versions. It's very important for you to know in some detail the location and function of many common folders and their contents.

System Folder

Evidently, you can't simply go around calling the folder where Windows installs the operating system files "the folder where Windows installs the operating system files." Instead, *SystemRoot* is the tech name for the folder in which the latest versions of Windows is installed. The SystemRoot folder for Windows XP is named Windows by default, although you can change the folder name during installation. Windows Vista and Windows 7 also call the SystemRoot folder Windows and don't allow it to be named anything else.

It's handy to know about SystemRoot. You'll find it cropping up in many other tech publications, and it can also be specified when you're adjusting certain Windows settings to make sure that they work under all circumstances. When used as part of a Windows configuration setting, the term is often written as *%SystemRoot%* (the percent signs indicating that the SystemRoot is a variable parameter).

FIGURE 14.17 A Jump List

The system folder contains many subfolders, too numerous to mention here, but CompTIA wants you to know the names of a number of these subfolders as well as what goes in them. Let's run through the subfolders you should recognize and define (these folders are in all versions of Windows):

- **%SystemRoot%\Fonts** All the fonts installed in Windows live here.
- **%SystemRoot%\Offline Files** When you tell your Web browser to save Web pages for offline viewing, they are stored in this folder. Windows automatically deletes this folder if it needs the space.
- **%SystemRoot%\System32** This is the *real* Windows! All of the most critical programs that make Windows run are stored here.
- **%SystemRoot%\Temp** Any time Windows or an application running in Windows needs to create temporary files, they are placed here. Windows deletes these files automatically as needed, so never place an important file in this folder.

> **Travel Advisory**
>
> Here's a handy trick. If you don't know where Windows was installed on a particular system, go to a command prompt, type **cd %systemroot%**, and press the ENTER key. The prompt will change focus to the folder in which the Windows OS files are stored.

Registry

The Registry is a database that stores everything about your PC, including information on all the hardware in the PC, network information, user preferences, file types, and virtually anything else you might run into with Windows. Almost any form of configuration done to a Windows system involves editing the Registry. In fact, the Control Panel applets that you know and love are simply user-friendly Registry-editing tools.

The Registry in Windows is composed of many files. The numerous Registry files (called *hives*) are stored in the *%SystemRoot%\System32\config* folder.

Accessing the Registry All good techs should know how to access, navigate, and when necessary, edit the system Registry. Microsoft provides a tool for doing this—the *Registry Editor*.

Launch the Registry Editor by choosing Start | Run/Search and typing **regedit** or **regedt32** (Figure 14.18).

FIGURE 14.18 Registry Editor in Windows Vista

Exam Tip

The Registry files are binary. You cannot edit the Registry with Edit, Notepad, or any other text editor. You must use the Registry Editor tool.

Registry Components The Registry is a *hierarchical* database, organized in a tree structure similar to the folders in the PC. Open the Registry Editor, and you'll see five main subgroups or root keys:

- HKEY_CLASSES_ROOT
- HKEY_CURRENT_USER
- HKEY_LOCAL_MACHINE
- HKEY_USERS
- HKEY_CURRENT_CONFIG

Try opening one of these root keys. Note that more subkeys are listed underneath them. Many subkeys also have other subkeys or values. The secret to understanding the Registry is to understand the function of the five root keys first. Each of these root keys has a specific function, so let's take a look at them individually:

- **HKEY_CLASSES_ROOT** This root key defines the standard *class objects* used by Windows. A class object is a named group of functions. Pretty much everything that has to do with files on the system is defined by a class object.

- **HKEY_USERS and HKEY_CURRENT_USER** Windows can be configured to support more than one user on the same PC, storing personalized information such as colors, screen savers, and the contents of the desktop. HKEY_USERS stores all of the personalization information for all users on a PC. HKEY_CURRENT_USER stores the current user settings, such as fonts, icons, and colors, on systems that are set up to support multiple users.

- **HKEY_LOCAL_MACHINE** This root key contains all the data for a system's non–user-specific configurations. This includes every device in your PC, including devices that you have removed.

- **HKEY_CURRENT_CONFIG** If values in HKEY_LOCAL_MACHINE have more than one option, such as two different monitors, this root key defines which one is currently being used. Because most people have only one type of monitor and similar equipment, this area is almost never touched.

Exam Tip	
Make sure you know the default root keys of the Windows Registry.	

Virtual Memory/Page File

Windows uses a portion of the hard drive as an extension of system RAM, through what's called a *RAM cache*. A RAM cache is a block of cylinders on a hard drive set aside as what's called a *page file, swap file,* or *virtual memory.* When the PC starts running out of real RAM because you've loaded too many programs, the system swaps programs from RAM to the page file, opening more space for programs currently active.

> **Local Lingo**
>
> **Virtual memory, swapfile, pagefile** All these terms refer to the same thing: space on the hard drive reserved as temporary storage for running programs.

Swapping programs between RAM and virtual memory takes time, because compared to RAM, the hard drive is painfully slow. You may notice a reduction in performance if a lot of "paging" activity is occurring. To counter this performance hit, you can do the following:

- Because virtual memory is brought heavily into play only when there's insufficient RAM to accommodate running programs, you can decrease paging by adding more RAM to the system.
- You can change the location of the pagefile. If you have more than one hard drive, you can increase performance by moving the pagefile from the system disk—the disk that has Windows installed on it—to another hard drive.

We'll talk more about how to increase system performance later in this book.

> **Exam Tip**
>
> Windows 7 offers a caching tool called ReadyBoost that enables you to use flash memory devices—like USB thumb drives—to speed up performance of a computer. With ReadyBoost, Windows gets access to a smart caching tool that preloads common program files, very much complimenting the standard cache.

To turn a flash device into a ReadyBoost device, right-click it in Computer and select Properties. Click the ReadyBoost tab and select the radio button next to either *Dedicate this device to ReadyBoost* or *Use this device*. Click Apply to enhance your system's performance.

Program Files

By default, most programs install some or all of their essential files into a subfolder of the C:\Program Files folder. If you installed a program, it should have its own folder in here. Individual companies decide how to label their subfolders. Installing Photoshop made by Adobe, for example, creates the Adobe subfolder and then

an Adobe Photoshop subfolder within it. Installing Silverlight from Microsoft, on the other hand, creates only a Microsoft Silverlight folder with the program files within it. (Some programmers choose to create a folder at the root of the C: drive, bypassing All Programs altogether, but that's becoming increasingly rare.)

The 64-bit versions of Windows Vista and Windows 7 create two directory structures for program files. The 64-bit applications go into the C:\Program Files folder. The 32-bit applications, in contrast, go into the C:\Program Files (x86) folder. The separation makes it easier to find the proper version of whatever application you seek.

Hot Keys

Windows has a number of key combinations—called *hot keys*—that enable you to go directly to different programs and places. Here's a list of general-purpose commands for Windows. Be aware that some applications may change the use of these commands.

Function Keys

- F1 Help
- F2 Rename
- F3 Search menu
- F4 Open the Address Bar options
- F5 Refresh the current window
- F6 Move among selections in current windows
- F10 Activate menu bar options

Popular Hot Keys

- CTRL-ESC Open the Start menu
- ALT-TAB Switch among open programs
- ALT-F4 Quit program
- CTRL-Z Undo the last command
- CTRL-A Select all the items in the current window
- SHIFT-DELETE Delete item permanently
- SHIFT-F10 Open a shortcut menu for the selected item (same as right-clicking an object)
- SHIFT Bypass the automatic-run feature for optical media (by pressing and holding down the SHIFT key while you insert optical media)
- ALT-SPACE Display the main window's System menu (where you can restore, move, resize, minimize, maximize, or close the window)
- ALT-ENTER Open the properties for the selected object

Working with Text

- CTRL-C Copy
- CTRL-X Cut
- CTRL-V Paste
- CTRL-Z Undo
- CTRL-B Bold
- CTRL-U Underline
- CTRL-I Italic

Windows Key Shortcuts These shortcuts use the special Windows key:

- WINDOWS key Start menu
- WINDOWS key-D Show desktop
- WINDOWS key-E Windows Explorer
- WINDOWS key-F Search menu
- WINDOWS key-L Log off or lock Windows
- WINDOWS key-R Run dialog box
- WINDOWS key-CTRL-F Find computer
- WINDOWS key-TAB Cycle through taskbar buttons
- WINDOWS key-BREAK System Properties dialog box

Exam Tip

Only the most basic parts of the Windows desktop are covered in this chapter. The typical Windows desktop will include many other parts, but for techs and for the CompTIA A+ certification exams, what you've learned here about the desktop is more than enough!

CHECKPOINT

✔ **Objective 14.01: Characteristics of the Operating System** Operating systems are made to work on a particular type of CPU platform. Microsoft Windows runs on the Intel and AMD x86 and x64 CPU families. Software applications are likewise made to work on one type of OS (although some are ported to operate on more than one OS). The OS takes over control of the PC after POST and continues to run until you exit the OS or shut down the system. An OS must be flexible enough to enable you to install new hardware and software.

✔**Objective 14.02: Common Operating System Functions** Functions that are common to any OS include communicating with hardware, creating a user interface (a means for the user to issue instructions to the PC and retrieve information from it), enabling users to access application programs, and enabling users to create and manipulate data.

✔**Objective 14.03: Operating System Interfaces** The user interface manifests in two ways: a text-only command line interface, and an icon-driven graphical user interface (GUI). Microsoft DOS is an example of a text-only command line interface OS, and modern versions of Microsoft Windows are GUI-based OSs. GUI versions of Windows also offer command line interface access to the OS.

✔**Objective 14.04: Common Microsoft Windows Features** Different versions of Windows offer different features, but all versions have a common feature set. The Windows user interface is the same or similar in all versions of Windows; it includes the login screen, the desktop, and the taskbar. On networked systems, Windows places the My Network Places/Network icon on the desktop or in the Start menu. All versions of Windows use common OS files and folders, such as the system folder (the folder where the Windows OS files are stored), the Registry, and the virtual memory pagefile.

REVIEW QUESTIONS

1. What is the best way to access the Registry Editor in Windows XP?

 A. Start | All Programs | DOS prompt icon. Type **edit**.

 B. Start | All Programs | Registry Editor.

 C. Start | Run. Type **regeditor** and click OK.

 D. Start | Run. Type **regedt32** and click OK.

2. Which of the following is *not* a Registry root key in current versions of Windows?

 A. HKEY_CURRENT_MACHINE

 B. HKEY_CLASSES_ROOT

 C. HKEY_CURRENT_USER

 D. HKEY_DYN_DATA

3. An employee reports that he accidentally deleted a file from his USB thumb drive and cannot find it in the Recycle Bin. What can you do to correct this?

 A. Tell the employee to open My Computer or Computer and choose Tools | Folder Options. Then click the View tab and select the *View hidden files and folders* radio button.

 B. Tell the employee to open My Computer or Computer, and choose View | Options to open the Options menu. Click the View tab and uncheck the *Hide MS-DOS file extensions for file types that are registered* check box.

 C. Right-click the Recycle Bin icon and select Properties from the pop-up menu. Select the *Do not move files to the Recycle Bin* check box.

 D. You cannot correct this.

4. Which of the following commands entered in the Start | Run/Search dialog box will start the Command Prompt? (Select two.)

 A. CMD

 B. COMMAND

 C. WINNT32

 D. CMD32

5. What is the default location of Documents in Windows Vista and Windows 7?

 A. C:\Users

 B. C:\Users and Settings\Username

 C. C:\Users\Username

 D. C:\Documents and Settings\Username

6. What are the major functions of an operating system (OS)?

 A. An OS provides a method by which other programs can communicate.

 B. An OS creates a user interface.

 C. An OS enables users to add, move, and delete installed programs and data.

 D. All of the above.

7. Which of the following is a typical command prompt?

 A. A:\\

 B. D:/>

 C. C:\>

 D. C://

8. Which of the following best describes the operating system's user interface?

 A. It enables the system to communicate with peripheral devices.

 B. It provides a means for the user to enter commands and retrieve data.

 C. It provides a display of the system hardware to the user.

 D. It provides error handling or notification displays when communicating with hardware.

9. To manipulate and organize data and programs, which of the following must the OS do? (Select two.)

 A. Identify all the data and programs on the system and organize them in a binary-code format.

 B. Provide a method to identify data according to the type of program that uses that particular data.

 C. Provide a naming system for each drive.

 D. Give the user an interface to assign drive letters to drives.

10. What type of memory stores running programs in a pagefile on a hard drive?

 A. Extended memory

 B. Flash memory

 C. Virtual memory

 D. Random access memory

REVIEW ANSWERS

1. **D** Go to Start | Run, and then type **regedt32** and click OK to start the Registry Editor in Windows XP.

2. **D** HKEY_DYN_DATA is not a valid Registry root key in Windows.

3. **D** Files deleted from removable drives are not stored in the Recycle Bin and cannot be retrieved.

4. **A B** Typing **cmd** or **command** at the Start | Run/Search dialog box starts the command line interface.

5. **C** The default location of Documents in Windows Vista and Windows 7 is C:\Users\Username.

6. **D** All of the above are the major functions of an operating system.

7. **C** C:\> is a typical command prompt.

8. **B** The user interface enables users to input commands and retrieve data.

9. **B** **C** The user must have some method to know which data files are used by particular programs. Further, the OS must provide a naming system for every drive.

10. **C** Virtual memory holds the pagefile (or swapfile).

Windows in Detail

	NEWBIE	SOME EXPERIENCE	EXPERT
ETA	3 hours	2 hours	1 hour

This chapter picks up where Chapter 14 left off. You've had the overview and user-level tour of Windows. Now it's time to look at the tools and features of Windows a tech needs to know. You'll learn about tech utilities, the boot process, and the structure of Windows. The chapter wraps with a round-up of the current versions of Windows and all the editions within each version, from Windows XP Professional to Windows 7 Enterprise Edition. Although Windows 8 is available, Windows 7 is the latest version of Windows covered by the current CompTIA A+ certification exams.

Objective 15.01 Essential Tech Utilities

Windows offers a huge number of utilities that enable techs to configure the OS, optimize and tweak settings, install hardware, and more. The trick is to know where to go to find them. This section shows some of the most common locations in Windows where you can go to access utilities, including right-click, the Control Panel, System Tools, Administrative Tools, the Microsoft Management Console, and more.

Travel Advisory

You know about one other great location for tech utilities from Chapter 14, and that's the command line. The command line offers all kinds of great tools and quick access to stuff you'll rely on for troubleshooting and maintaining Windows.

Right-Click

Any single thing you see on your desktop is called an *object*. If you want to open any object in Windows, you double-click it. If you want to change something about an object, you right-click it.

Right-clicking an object brings up a small pop-up, or *context*, menu, and it works on almost everything in Windows. What you see when you right-click varies dramatically, depending on the item you click. If you right-click a data file icon on the desktop, for example, you'll see options relevant to that file, such as Open, Print, Share with, and so on (Figure 15.1). Right-clicking directly on the desktop, in contrast, presents you with options for adjusting the look and feel of the desktop.

Pop-up menu that appears when you right-click a data file icon

One menu item you'll see almost anywhere you right-click is Properties. Every object in Windows has properties. When you right-click an item and can't find what you're looking for, choose Properties to open the Properties window. Figure 15.2 shows the screen that appears after right-clicking My Computer in Windows XP and selecting Properties.

Control Panel

The *Control Panel* handles most of the maintenance, upgrade, and configuration aspects of Windows. As such, the Control Panel is the first set of tools for every tech to explore. In Windows XP, Vista, and 7, a Control Panel button appears directly on the Start menu by default.

The Control Panel opens in the Category view, in which all the icons are grouped into broad categories such as "Printers and Other Hardware." This view requires an additional click (and sometimes a guess about which category includes the icon you need), so most techs use the Switch to Classic View link in Windows XP or Vista to get back to the icons. In Windows 7, you can switch from Category to Large or Small icons view. Figure 15.3 shows the Windows 7 Control Panel in both Category (left) and Large icons (right) views.

FIGURE 15.2 System Properties window

Exam Tip

The CompTIA A+ 220-802 exam assumes you have Control Panel set to Classic View or Large icons view depending on the OS you are using.

A large number of programs, called *applets*, populate the Control Panel. The names and selection of applets vary depending on the version of Windows and whether any installed programs have added applets. But all versions of Windows share many of the same applets, including Display/Personalization, Add or Remove Programs/Programs and Features, and System (all versions)—what I call the *Big Three* applets for techs. With Display/Personalization, you can make changes to the look and feel of your Windows desktop and tweak your video settings. Add or Remove Programs/Programs and Features enables you to add or remove programs. The System applet gives you access to essential system information and tools, such as the Device Manager, although Microsoft wisely added Device Manager directly on the Control Panel starting with Vista.

FIGURE 15.3 Windows 7 Control Panel—two views

Exam Tip

Even common applets vary slightly among Windows versions. The CompTIA A+ certification exams do not test you on every little variance among the same applets in different versions—but you should know what each applet does.

Device Manager

The *Device Manager* enables techs to examine and configure the hardware and drivers in a Windows PC. You've seen it at work in several earlier chapters, and you'll work with the Device Manager many more times during the course of your career as a PC tech.

You can access the Device Manager in many ways—make sure you know all of them! The first way is to open the Control Panel and double-click the System applet icon. This brings up the System Properties dialog box. In XP, you access the Device Manager by selecting the Hardware tab and then clicking the Device Manager button. Figure 15.4 shows the Hardware tab of the System Properties dialog box in Windows XP. In Vista/7, the System dialog box has a direct connection to Device Manager.

Travel Advisory

Holding down the WINDOWS key and pressing the PAUSE key is yet another way to access the System Properties dialog box. Keyboard shortcuts are cool!

FIGURE 15.4 Windows XP System applet with the Hardware tab selected

FIGURE 15.5 Right-click My Computer/Computer and choose Manage

The second (and more streamlined) method is to right-click My Computer/Computer and choose Manage (Figure 15.5). This opens the Computer Management window, where you'll see Device Manager listed on the left side, under System Tools (Figure 15.6). Click Device Manager and it will open. You can also access Computer Management by opening the Administrative Tools applet in the Control Panel and then choosing Computer Management.

FIGURE 15.6 Device Manager in Computer Management

Why so many ways to open Device Manager? Remember that you're looking only at locations in Windows from which to open utilities, not at the actual utilities themselves. Microsoft wants you to get to the tools you need when you need them; it's better to have multiple paths to a utility rather than just one.

The Device Manager displays every device that Windows recognizes, organized in special groups called *types*. All devices of the same type are grouped under the same type heading. To see the devices of a particular type, you must open that type's group. Figure 15.7 shows a Device Manager screen with all installed devices in good order—which makes us techs happy. If Windows detects a problem, it shows a red X next to the device or a black exclamation point on a yellow field, as is the case with the USB controllers in Figure 15.8.

| FIGURE 15.7 | Happy Device Manager |

FIGURE 15.8 Sad Device Manager

The Device Manager isn't used only for dealing with problems. It also enables you to update drivers with a simple click of the mouse (assuming you have a driver downloaded or on disc). Right-click a device and select Update Driver Software to get the process started. Figure 15.9 shows the options in Windows 7.

By double-clicking a device (or by selecting the device and clicking the Properties button) and then clicking the Driver tab, you can see the driver information, such as date and version. Figure 15.10 shows the Driver tab for an ATI Radeon video card.

Make sure you can get to Device Manager. You will return to it again and again in subsequent chapters, because it is the first tool you should access when you experience a hardware problem.

FIGURE 15.9 Selecting Update Driver Software in the Windows 7 Device Manager

System Tools

The Start menu offers a variety of tech utilities in one place: choose Start | All Programs | Accessories | System Tools. In the *System Tools* menu, you'll find commonly accessed tools, such as System Information and Disk Defragmenter (Figure 15.11).

Many techs fail to memorize how to find the appropriate Windows tool to diagnose problems, but nothing hurts your credibility with a client like fumbling around, clicking a variety of menus and applets, mumbling, "I know it's around here somewhere." The CompTIA A+ certification exams, therefore, test you on a variety of paths to appropriate tools. One of those paths is Start | All Programs | Accessories | System Tools. Windows Vista has all the same tools as Windows XP, plus a few more, and 7 adds a few beyond Vista. I'll mention what version of Windows has the particular system tool in the following sections.

FIGURE 15.10 Driver information displayed in the Windows 7 Device Manager

FIGURE 15.11 System Tools menu options

Activate Windows (All)

Windows XP unveiled a copy-protection scheme called *activation,* a process by which your computer sends Microsoft a unique code generated on your machine based on the Install CD/DVD's product key and a number of hardware features, such as the amount of RAM, the CPU model, and other ones and zeroes in your PC. Normally, activation occurs at install time, but if you choose not to activate at install, or if you make "substantial" changes to the hardware, you'll need to use the Activate Windows utility.

Backup (XP)

The Backup utility enables you to back up selected files and folders to removable media such as tape drives. Backing up is an important function that Chapter 17 covers in detail.

Travel Advisory

Neither Windows XP Home nor Windows Media Center automatically includes Backup. You must install the Backup program from the Windows Install CD by running the *\Valueadd\MSFT\Ntbackup\NTbackup.msi* program.

Backup Status and Configuration (Vista)

Vista and 7 do not enable you to back up files on your computer selectively. You can only back up personal data with the Backup Status and Configuration Tool, or, if you have Vista Business, Ultimate, or Enterprise, you can perform a complete PC backup by using Windows Complete PC Backup. Windows 7 does not have a backup tool in the System Tools. You need to access the Backup and Restore applet in the Control Panel for backup options.

Character Map (All)

Have you ever been using a program only to discover you need to enter a strange character such as the euro character (€), but your word processor doesn't support it? That's when you need the Character Map. It enables you to copy any Unicode character into the clipboard (Figure 15.12).

Disk Cleanup (All)

Disk Cleanup looks for unneeded files on your computer, which is handy when your hard drive starts to get full and you need space. Windows XP, Vista, and 7 start this program whenever your hard drive gets below 200 MB of free disk space.

FIGURE 15.12 Character Map in Windows Vista

Disk Defragmenter (All)

Disk Defragmenter was discussed in Chapter 8. You can access this utility in the same way you access the Device Manager: from the Computer Management Console. A simpler method is to choose Start | All Programs | Accessories | System Tools—you'll find Disk Defragmenter listed there.

Files and Settings Transfer Wizard (XP)

Suppose you have an old computer full of files and settings, and you just got yourself a brand-new computer. You want to copy everything from your old computer onto your new computer—what to do? Microsoft touts the *Files and Settings Transfer Wizard* (Figure 15.13) as just the tool you need. This utility copies your desktop files and folders, and most conveniently, your settings from Internet Explorer (IE) and Outlook Express; however, it won't copy over your programs—not even the Microsoft apps—and it won't copy settings for any programs other than IE and Outlook Express. If you need to copy everything from an old computer to a new one, you'll probably want to use a disk imaging tool such as Norton Ghost.

| **FIGURE 15.13** | Files and Settings Transfer Wizard in Windows XP |

Windows Easy Transfer (Vista, 7)

Windows Easy Transfer is an aggressively updated version of the Files and Settings Transfer Wizard. It does everything the older version does and adds the ability to copy user accounts and other settings (Figure 15.14). Windows 7 adds a Windows Easy Transfer Reports tool also that provides details on transfers made.

Scheduled Tasks/Task Scheduler (All)

The Scheduled Tasks/Task Scheduler utility enables you to schedule any program to start and stop any time you want. The only trick to this utility is that you must enter the program you want to run as a command on the command line, with all the proper switches. Figure 15.15 shows the configuration line for running the Disk Defragmenter program.

Security Center (XP, Vista)

The Security Center is the one-stop location for configuring many security features on your computer. This tool is also in the Control Panel. Vista removed Security Center from System Tools. All these security features, and many more, are discussed in detail in their related chapters.

| FIGURE 15.14 | Windows Easy Transfer in Windows Vista |

Resource Monitor (7)

Windows 7 has a link to the Resource Monitor in System Tools that provides a quick overview of allocated resources. This shows you immediately which programs are running and the CPU, memory, hard drive, and network usage for each.

System Information (All)

System Information is one of those tools that everyone (including the CompTIA A+ certification exams) likes to talk about, but it's uncommon to meet techs who say they actually use this tool. System Information shows tons of information about the hardware and software on your PC (Figure 15.16). In Windows XP, you can also use it as a launch point for a number of programs by clicking the Tools menu, but this feature was removed in Vista.

FIGURE 15.15 Task Scheduler

> **Exam Tip**
>
> The CompTIA A+ exam objectives refer to System Information by the file name of its executable, *msinfo32*. You also need to know that you can run the utility by typing **msinfo32** at the Start | Run or Search dialog and pressing ENTER.

System Restore (All)

System Restore is not only handy; it's also arguably the most important single utility you'll ever use in Windows when it comes to fixing a broken system. *System Restore* enables you to take a "snapshot"—a copy of a number of critical files and settings—and return to that state (Figure 15.17). System Restore holds multiple snapshots, any of which you may restore to in the future.

Imagine you're installing some new device in your PC, or maybe a piece of software. Before you actually install it, you take a snapshot and call it "Before Install." If something starts acting weird after it is installed, you can go back into System Restore and reload the previous snapshot; the problem goes away. Windows takes some of these snapshots automatically, such as when you install unsigned drivers or apply a major patch to Windows through Windows Update.

FIGURE 15.16 System Information in Windows Vista

FIGURE 15.17 System Restore in Windows XP

System Restore isn't perfect. It backs up only a few critical items, and it's useless if the computer won't boot, but it's usually the first thing to try when something goes wrong—assuming, of course, that you already made a snapshot.

BitLocker (Vista and 7 Enterprise and Ultimate)

BitLocker is a tool to encrypt files, folders, or entire hard drives. It's a great way to make sure other people can't read your stuff, but it also makes data recovery risky. If you really want security, use BitLocker. To implement BitLocker requires the correct version of Windows and a hardware chip on the motherboard called a *Trusted Platform Module* (*TPM*). Many newer, better motherboards have a TPM chip. Windows 7 Ultimate and Enterprise editions include BitLocker To Go that enables you to encrypt removable drives.

Microsoft Management Console

One of the biggest complaints about earlier versions of Windows was the wide dispersal of the many utilities needed for administration and troubleshooting. Despite years of research, Microsoft could never find a place for all the utilities that would please even a minority of support people. In a moment of sheer genius, Microsoft determined that the ultimate utility was one that the support person made for himself or herself. This brought on the creation of the amazing *Microsoft Management Console* (*MMC*).

Exam Tip

The CompTIA A+ certification exams expect you to know about the MMC and other tools discussed in the rest of this chapter, so don't skip it!

The MMC is simply a shell program in Windows that holds individual utilities called *snap-ins*. You can start the MMC by choosing Start | Run or Start | Search, typing **mmc**, and pressing ENTER to get a blank MMC. Blank MMCs aren't much to look at (Figure 15.18).

You make a blank MMC console useful by adding snap-ins. Most of the utilities you use in Windows are actually snap-ins—even the good old Device Manager is a snap-in. You can add as many snap-ins as you like, and you have many from which to choose. Many companies sell third-party utilities as MMC snap-ins.

FIGURE 15.18 Blank MMC

For example, to add the Device Manager snap-in, open the blank MMC, choose File | Add/Remove Snap-in to open the Add or Remove Snap-in dialog box, and then click the Add button to open the Add Standalone Snap-in dialog box. Here you will see a list of available snap-ins (Figure 15.19). Select Device Manager, and click the Add button to open a dialog box that prompts you to choose whether you want the snap-in to work on the local PC or a remote PC. Choose *Local computer* for this exercise, and click the Finish button. Click OK to close the Add/Remove Snap-in dialog box.

You should see Device Manager listed in the console. Click it. Hey, that looks kind of familiar, doesn't it? (See Figure 15.20.)

Once you've added the snap-ins you want, save the console under any name, anywhere you want. If you saved this console as Device Manager, for example, and dropped it on your desktop, you'd be just a double-click away from the Device Manager.

Administrative Tools

Windows combines the most popular snap-ins into the Administrative Tools applet in the Control Panel. Open the Control Panel and double-click Administrative Tools to open it (Figure 15.21).

FIGURE 15.19 Available snap-ins

FIGURE 15.20 Device Manager as a snap-in

Control Panel ▸ Administrative Tools ▸ Search

Organize ▾ Views ▾

Favorite Links
- Documents
- Recently Changed
- Searches
- TOTALFS2
- TERA
- Dev (TOTALFS2) (Y)
- Research (TOTALFS2) (W)
- Users (TOTALFS2)
- Miscellaneous (TERA)
- A+ 7th Edition

Name	Date modified	Type	Size

Computer Management · Data Sources (ODBC) · Event Viewer · iSCSI Initiator · Local Securi... · Memory Diagnosti...

Print Management · Reliability and Perfor... · Services · System Configurat... · Task Scheduler · Windows Firewall wi...

Folders ∧

12 items

FIGURE 15.21 Administrative Tools

Administrative Tools is a folder that stores a number of premade consoles. As you poke through these, you'll notice that many of the consoles share some of the same snap-ins. Of the consoles in a standard Administrative Tools collection, those with which you'll spend the most time are Computer Management, Event Viewer, Performance, and Services.

> **Exam Tip**
>
> The CompTIA A+ certification exams have little interest in some of these snap-ins, so this book won't cover them all. If it's not mentioned here, it's almost certainly not on the exams.

Computer Management

The *Computer Management* applet is a tech's best buddy, or at least a place where you'll spend a lot of time when building or maintaining a system (Figure 15.22). You've already spent considerable time with two of its components: System Tools and Storage. Depending on the version of Windows, System Tools also offers System Information, Performance Logs and Alerts, Reliability and Performance, Device Manager, and more. Storage is where you'll find Disk Management. Each of these tools is of particular interest to techs, as you've seen earlier and will see again in Chapter 17.

FIGURE 15.22 Computer Management applet

Event Viewer Event Viewer enables you to see what has happened in the last day, week, or more, including when people logged in and when the PC had problems. You'll see more of Event Viewer in Chapters 18 and 22.

Performance (Windows XP) The Performance console consists of two snap-ins: System Monitor and Performance Logs and Alerts. You can use these for reading *logs*—files that record information over time. The System Monitor can also monitor real-time data (Figure 15.23).

Suppose you installed a new cable modem and you want to know how fast you can download data. Click the plus sign (+) on the toolbar to add a counter. Click the *Use local computer counters* radio button, and then choose *Network Interface* from the Performance object pull-down menu. Make sure the *Select counters from list* radio button is selected. Last, select *Bytes Received/sec*. The Add Counters dialog box should look like Figure 15.24.

Click Add, and then click Close—probably not much is happening. Go to a Web site, preferably one where you can download a huge file. Start downloading and watch the chart jump; that's the real throughput (Figure 15.25).

Reliability and Performance Monitor (Vista) The *Reliability and Performance Monitor* in Windows Vista offers just about everything you can find in the Performance applet of older versions of Windows—although everything is monitored by default, so there's no need to add anything. In addition, it includes the

FIGURE 15.23 System Monitor in action

Reliability Monitor. The Reliability Monitor shows what's been done to the computer over a period of time, including software installations and uninstallations, failures of hardware or applications, and general uptime (Figure 15.26). It's a nice starting tool for checking a Vista machine that's new to you.

FIGURE 15.24 Setting up a throughput test

FIGURE 15.25 Downloading with blazing speed

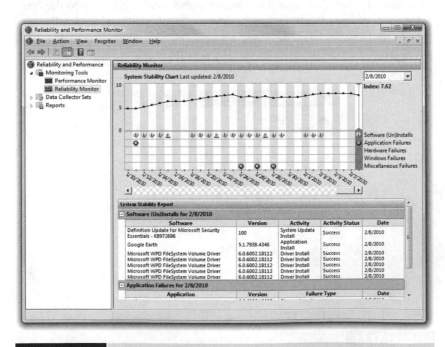

FIGURE 15.26 Reliability Monitor in Windows Vista

> ## Travel Assistance
>
> You'll learn more about the Performance/Reliability and
> Performance Monitor console in Chapter 17.

Performance (7) Microsoft split off the Reliability Monitor into its own tool in Windows 7, simplifying the Performance Monitor portion of the applet. Otherwise, it's similar to the Windows Vista tool. You can still find Reliability Monitor in Windows 7 by searching for it in the Search bar.

Services

Windows runs a large number of separate programs called *services*. The best way to visualize a service is to think of it as something that runs, yet is invisible. Windows comes with about 100 services by default, and they handle a huge number of tasks, from application support to network functions. The Services applet shows the status of all services on the system, including services that are not running (Figure 15.27).

FIGURE 15.27 Services applet

Right-click a service and choose Properties to modify its settings. Figure 15.28 shows the properties for the Bluetooth Support service. See the Startup Type pull-down menu? It shows three options in Windows XP and four in Windows Vista/7: Automatic, Manual, Disabled, and Windows Vista/7 adds Automatic (Delayed Start). *Automatic* means it starts when the system starts, *Manual* means you have to come to this tab to start it, and *Disabled* prevents anything from starting it. *Automatic (Delayed Start)* starts the service after Windows has finished booting and starting up other programs and services. Make sure you know these settings, and also make sure you understand how to start, stop, pause, and resume services (note the four buttons underneath Startup Type).

Exam Tip

You don't need to memorize all of these services for the CompTIA A+ certification exams—just make sure you can manipulate them.

FIGURE 15.28 Bluetooth Support Service properties

Action Center (Unique to Windows 7)

Sometimes, you just want to glance at your system and know that nothing has gone terribly wrong. Previous versions of Windows lacked a single "peephole" to view the status of your computer. *Action Center* fills that gap, providing a one-page aggregation of event messages, warnings, and maintenance messages that, for many techs, might quickly replace Event Viewer as the first place to look for problems. Unlike Event Viewer, Action Center separates issues into two sections, Security and Maintenance, making it easier to scan a system quickly (see Figure 15.29).

Action Center only compiles the information, taking data from well-known utilities such as Event Viewer, Windows Update, Windows Firewall, and User Account Control (UAC) and placing it into an easy-to-read format. If you wish, you can tell Action Center where to look for information by selecting *Change Action Center settings* (see Figure 15.30).

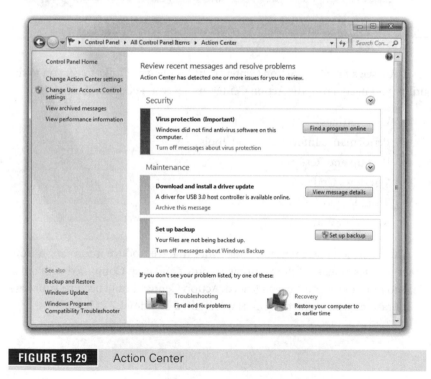

FIGURE 15.29 Action Center

FIGURE 15.30 Change Action Center settings

If you see a problem, Action Center includes plenty of links to get you to the utility you need. From the Action Center applet, you get direct links to

- UAC settings
- Performance Information and Tools
- Backup and Restore
- Windows Update
- Troubleshooting Wizard
- System Restore

Although Action Center does little more than reproduce information from other utilities, it makes finding problems quick and easy. Combined with quick links to most of the utilities you'll need, Action Center should become your base of operations when something goes wrong on a Windows 7 PC.

Objective 15.02 Windows Structure

Microsoft Windows is a stable, high-performance OS that offers scalability and security. Each version of Windows shares the same core structure, files, and features, so the discussion that follows applies to all Windows versions. Each is covered in detail, followed by a discussion of the differences among them.

NT File System (NTFS)

From the beginning, Microsoft designed and optimized every aspect of Windows 2000 and later for multi-user, networked environments. Whereas all previous Microsoft OSs used either FAT16 or FAT32, modern versions of Windows use a far more powerful and robust file system called *New Technology File System (NTFS)*.

Chapter 8 offers a good basic description of NTFS, but let's go into a bit more detail here. NTFS offers the following excellent features:

- Long filenames (LFNs)
- Redundancy
- Backward compatibility
- Recoverability
- Security

Long Filenames

NTFS supported LFNs long before FAT32 even existed. NTFS filenames can be up to 255 characters.

Redundancy

NTFS has an advanced FAT called the *master file table (MFT)*. An NTFS partition keeps a backup copy of the most critical parts of the MFT in the middle of the disk, reducing the chances that a serious drive error can wipe out both the MFT and the MFT copy. Whenever you defrag an NTFS partition, you'll see a small, immovable "chunk" in the middle of the drive; that's the backup MFT.

Backward Compatibility

For all its power, NTFS is amazingly backward compatible. You can copy DOS or Windows 9*x* programs to an NTFS partition—Windows will even keep the LFNs.

Recoverability

Accidental system shutdowns, reboots, and lockups in the midst of a file save or retrieval wreak havoc on most systems. NTFS avoids this with *transaction logging*. Transaction logging identifies incomplete file transactions and restores the file to the original format automatically and invisibly.

Security

NTFS truly shines with its powerful security functions. When most people hear the term *security*, they tend to think about networks, and NTFS security works perfectly in a networked environment, but it works equally well on single systems that support multiple users. Let's look at three major features of NTFS security: accounts, groups, and permissions.

Accounts To use a Windows system, you must have a valid account (and, frequently, a password). Without an account, you cannot use the system (Figure 15.31).

Every Windows system has a "super" account called *administrator*. Remember when you saw the installation of Windows and it prompted you for a password for the administrator account? As you might imagine, this account has access to everything—a dangerous thing in the wrong hands!

Groups The administrator creates user accounts with a special program called User Accounts in Windows XP, Vista, and 7 (Figure 15.32). The simplest version of the User Accounts tool is the applet with the same name in the Control Panel. You can access a more fully featured version in Computer Management.

FIGURE 15.31 Login failure

FIGURE 15.32 User Accounts dialog box in Windows 7

Each user account is labeled in two ways: the *user name* defines an account for the person who has access to the PC; the *group* is simply the collection of accounts that share the same access capabilities. A single account can be a member of multiple groups.

Groups make Windows administration much easier in two ways. First, you can assign a certain level of access for a file or folder to a group, instead of just to a single user account. For example, you can make a group called Accounting and put all the accounting users' accounts in that group. If a user quits, you don't need to worry about assigning all the proper access levels when you create a new account for that user's replacement. After you make the new account, you simply add it to the appropriate group.

Second, Windows provides several built-in groups, depending on your version of Windows, including Administrators, Power Users, Users, Backup Operators, Replicator, Everyone, and Guests. For example, Windows Vista/7 do not include the Everyone group, but they do include other special groups such as Remote Desktop Users. These built-in groups have a number of preset abilities. You cannot delete these groups, although they can be renamed.

- **Administrators** Any account that is a member of this group has complete administrator privileges. It is common for the primary user of a Windows system to have his or her account in the Administrators group.

- **Power Users** Power users are almost as powerful as administrators, but they cannot install new devices or access other users' files or folders unless the files or folders specifically grant them access.

- **Users (or Standard Users)** Users cannot edit the Registry or access critical system files. They can create groups but can manage only those groups they create.

- **Backup Operators** Backup operators have the same rights as users, except that they can run backup programs that access any file or folder—for backup purposes only.

- **Replicator** Members of the Replicator group can replicate files and folders in a domain.

- **Everyone** This group applies to any user who can log onto the system. You cannot edit this group.

- **Guests** Someone who does not have an account on the system can log on using a Guest account if the system has this option enabled. This group is useful in certain network situations.

Exam Tip

CompTIA targets the Administrator, Power User, Guest, and Standard User account types. Make sure you understand their abilities.

Travel Advisory

A Windows system running simple file sharing has only three account types: Computer Administrator, Limited or Standard User, and Guest. Computer Administrators can do anything, as you might suspect. Limited or Standard Users and Guests can access only certain things and have limits on where they can save files on the PC.

NTFS Permissions In Windows, every folder and file on an NTFS partition has a list that contains two sets of data. First, the list details every user and group that has access to that file or folder. Second, the list specifies the level of access that each user or group has to that file or folder. The level of access is defined by a set of restrictions called *NTFS permissions*.

NTFS permissions define exactly what a particular account can or cannot do to the file or folder and are thus quite detailed and powerful. You can make it

possible, for example, for a person to edit a file but not delete it. You can let someone create a folder and not allow other people to make subfolders. NTFS file and folder permissions are so complicated that entire books have been written on them! Fortunately, the CompTIA A+ certification exams test your understanding of only a few basic concepts of NTFS permissions: Ownership, Take Ownership permission, Change permission, Folder permissions, and File permissions:

- **Ownership** When you create a new file or folder on an NTFS partition, you become the *owner* of that file or folder. A newly created file or folder by default gives everyone full permission to access, delete, and otherwise manipulate that file or folder. Owners can do anything they want to the files or folders they own, including changing the permissions to prevent anybody, even administrators, from accessing them.

- **Take Ownership permission** With the *Take Ownership* special permission, anyone with the permission can seize control of a file or folder. Administrator accounts have Take Ownership permission for everything. Note the difference here between owning a file and accessing a file. If you own a file, you can prevent anyone from accessing that file. An administrator whom you have blocked, however, can take that ownership away from you and *then* access that file!

- **Change permission** This is another important permission for all NTFS files and folders. An account with this permission can give or take away permissions for other accounts.

- **Folder permissions** Let's look at a typical folder in my Windows XP system to see how this one works. My E: drive is formatted as NTFS, and on it I created a folder called E:\MIKE. I can set the permissions for the E:\MIKE folder by right-clicking the folder, selecting Properties, and clicking the Security tab (see Figure 15.33).

- **File permissions** File permissions are similar to Folder permissions. I'll talk about File permissions shortly.

Exam Tip

As displayed in Figure 15.33, you can Allow or Deny certain permissions for groups or users. Be sure you know where and how to do this for the exams.

FIGURE 15.33 Set permissions in the Security tab.

Local Lingo

Permission propagation Inherited permissions are used to ease the administration of permissions and are propagated to an object from a parent object. Applying the same permission of a parent folder to all subfolders is called permission propagation.

In Windows, just about everything in the computer has a Security tab in its properties, and every Security tab contains two main areas. The top area shows the list of accounts that have permissions for that resource. The lower area shows exactly what permissions have been assigned to the selected account.

Here are the standard permissions for a folder:

- **Full Control** Enables you to do anything you want.
- **Modify** Enables you to do anything except delete files or subfolders.
- **Read & Execute** Enables you to see the contents of the folder and any subfolders.

- **List Folder Contents** Enables you to see the contents of the folder and any subfolders. (This permission seems the same as the Read & Execute permission, but it is only inherited by folders.)
- **Read** Enables you to read any file in the folder.
- **Write** Enables you to write to files and create new files and folders.

File permissions are quite similar to folder permissions, with the main difference being the Special Permissions option, which I'll talk about a bit later in the chapter.

- **Full Control** Enables you to do anything you want!
- **Modify** Enables you to do anything except take ownership or change permissions on the file.
- **Read & Execute** If the file is a program, you can run it.
- **Read** If the file is data, you can read it.
- **Write** Enables you to write to the file.

Take some time to think about these permissions. Why would Microsoft create them? Think of situations for which you might want to give a group the Modify permission. You can even assign more than one permission. In many situations, you might give users both Read and Write permissions.

Permissions are cumulative. If you have Full Control on a folder and only Read permission on a file in the folder, you get Full Control permission on the file. This is called *inheriting* permission.

Travel Advisory

Windows versions for home use have only a limited set of permissions you can assign. As far as folder permissions go, you can assign only one: Make This Folder Private. To see this in action, right-click a file or folder and select Sharing and Security from the options. Note that you can't just select the properties and see a Security tab as you can in the professional-oriented versions of Windows. Windows Home versions do not have file-level permissions.

Techs and Permissions Techs, as a rule, hate NTFS permissions. You must have administrative privileges to do almost anything on a Windows machine, and most administrators hate giving out administrative permissions (for obvious reasons). If a tech does give you administrative permission for a PC and something goes wrong with that system while you're working on it, you immediately become the primary suspect.

If you're working on a Windows system administered by someone else, make sure he or she understands what you are doing and how long you think it will take. Have the administrator create a new account for you with administrator privileges. Never ask for the password for a permanent administrator account. That way, you won't be blamed if anything goes wrong on that system: "Well, I told Janet the password when she installed the new hard drive—maybe she did it!" When you have fixed the system, make sure that the administrator deletes the account you used.

> ### Travel Advisory
>
> This "protect yourself from passwords" attitude transcends Windows. PC support folks get lots of passwords, scan cards, keys, and ID tags. Most newer techs tend to get an "I can go anywhere and access anything" attitude, and this is dangerous. I've seen many jobs lost and friendships ruined when a tape backup suddenly disappears or a critical file gets erased. Everybody points to the support tech in these situations. In physical security situations, make other people unlock doors for you. In some cases, I've asked the administrator or system owner to sit directly behind me so that they can jump up and punch in passwords as needed. What you don't have access to can't hurt you.

Objective 15.03 Booting Windows

While much of Windows remains relatively the same from iteration to iteration, the boot process that loads the OS has seen a major change from the boot.ini and ntldr days of Windows XP, to the bootmgr of Windows Vista/7. That's a lot of nonsensical-looking letter combinations (without many vowels), so I'll cover each boot process in great detail.

Booting Windows XP

Windows XP distinguishes between the files that start the OS (called the *system files*) and the rest of the OS files (usually in the \Windows folder). The system files consist of three required files: ntldr, boot.ini, and ntdetect.com. If you're using a SCSI hard drive, there is a fourth file called ntbootdd.sys. The ntldr (pronounced *NT loader*) file begins the boot process.

You know from earlier chapters that making a drive bootable requires an active, primary partition, right? Let's look at the process in a PC with a hard drive partitioned as C: and D:.

Exam Tip

Memorize the Windows XP system files: ntldr, boot.ini, ntdetect.com, and, if you're using a SCSI hard drive, ntbootdd.sys.

The Boot Process

The CPU wakes up and runs the system BIOS, and then the BIOS sends out a routine looking for a valid OS in the boot sector of the primary, master hard drive. The MFT lives in the boot sector of the C: partition. It points to the location of the Windows XP system files, also on the C: drive, because that's the bootable drive. Windows calls the primary, active partition the *system partition* or the *system volume* (if it's a dynamic disk).

The Windows XP *boot files* consist of ntoskrnl.exe (the Windows kernel), the \Windows\system32\config\system file (which controls the loading of device drivers), and the device drivers. Even though these files are the core of the Windows XP OS, they are not capable of booting, or starting, the system. For that feat, they require ntldr, ntdetect.com, and boot.ini—the system files.

The system files start the PC and then, at the end of that process, point the CPU to the location of the boot files. The CPU goes over and chats with ntoskrnl, and the GUI starts to load. The OS is then up and running, and you're able to do work.

The odd part about all this is that Microsoft decided to make the OS files mobile; the Windows OS files can reside on any partition or volume in the PC. The \WINDOWS folder, for example, could very well be on drive D:, not drive C:. Whichever drive holds the core OS files is called the *boot partition*. This can lead to a little confusion when you say, "The system files are on my C: drive, but Windows is on my D: drive," but that's just the way it is. The vast majority of Windows XP systems have the system partition and the boot partition both on the same big C: partition.

You've got the process now in general, so let's look more specifically at the makeup and function of the individual files involved in the boot process.

Exam Tip

The Windows XP boot process can be broken down into four phases, so remember the following for your exam: The system files (ntldr, boot.ini, etc.) make up the first phase, called the *Boot Loader Phase*. The second phase is the *Kernel Loading Phase*, which loads ntoskrnl.exe, the registry, and device drivers. After that comes the *Session Manager*, which loads the GUI. Finally, the *Winlogon Phase* loads the Login screen.

System Partition Files

Windows XP requires the three system files in the root directory of the system partition:

- ntldr
- boot.ini
- ntdetect.com

To see these files, go into My Computer and open the C: drive. Then open Folder Options, as shown in the "My Computer/Computer" section of Chapter 14. Click the *Show hidden files and folders* radio button, uncheck the *Hide protected operating system files (Recommended)* option, and click OK. When you return to viewing the folder in My Computer, you will see certain critical files that Windows otherwise hides from you so you don't accidentally move, delete, or change them in some unintended way (Figure 15.34).

ntldr When the system boots, the master boot record (MBR) or MFT on the hard drive starts the *ntldr* program. The ntldr program then launches Windows XP or another OS. To find the available OSs, the ntldr program must read the boot.ini configuration file, and to do so it loads its own minimal file system, which enables it to read the boot.ini file off the system partition.

boot.ini The boot.ini text file lists the OSs available to ntldr and tells ntldr where to find the boot partition (where the OS is stored) for each of them. The boot.ini file has sections defined by headings enclosed in brackets. A basic boot.ini in Windows XP looks like this:

```
[boot loader]
timeout=30
default=multi(0)disk(0)rdisk(0)partition(1)\WINDOWS
[operating systems]
multi(0)disk(0)rdisk(0)partition(1)\WINDOWS="Microsoft Windows
XP Professional" /fastdetect
```

My Computer showing the system files residing in a local disk

A more complex boot.ini may look like this:

```
[boot loader]
timeout=30
default=multi(0)disk(0)rdisk(0)partition(1)\WINDOWS
[operating systems]
multi(0)disk(0)rdisk(0)partition(1)\WINDOWS="Microsoft Windows
XP Professional" /fastdetect
multi(0)disk(0)rdisk(0)partition(1)\WINNT="Microsoft Windows
2000 Professional" /fastdetect
```

Such a boot.ini would result in the boot menu that appears in Figure 15.35.

If you want to boot to a SCSI drive, Windows will add a fourth file to your system files called ntbootdd.sys. Most people don't boot to a SCSI, so don't worry if you don't see this file with the other three system files.

On rare occasions, you might find yourself needing to edit the boot.ini file. Any text editor handily edits this file, but most prefer to edit boot.ini via the System Startup dialog box. In Windows XP, open the System applet from the Control Panel. Click the Advanced tab and then click the Startup and Recovery button. The boot.ini options show up at the top (Figure 15.36). Click the Edit button to edit startup options manually.

```
Please select the operating system to start:

    Microsoft Windows XP Professional
    Microsoft Windows 2000 Professional

Use the up and down arrow keys to move the highlight to your choice.
Press ENTER to choose.
Seconds until highlighted choice will be started automatically: 29

For troubleshooting and advanced startup options for Windows, press F8.
```

FIGURE 15.35 Boot loader in Windows XP

FIGURE 15.36 boot.ini

The boot.ini file has some interesting switches that give special instructions on how the OS should boot. Sometimes Windows puts these in automatically, and sometimes you will add them manually for troubleshooting. Here are a few of the more common ones:

- **/bootlog** Tells Windows to create a log of the boot process and write it to a file called Ntbtlog.txt.
- **/cmdcons** Tells Windows to start the Recovery Console (see Chapter 18).
- **/lastknowngood** Tells Windows to boot the Last Known Good set of files (see Chapter 18).
- **/noexecute** Newer CPUs come with Data Execute Protection (DEP) to prevent unruly programs from causing system lockups. The setting for this, **/noexecute=optin**, is the default on Windows systems.

ntdetect.com If the ntldr determines that you have chosen to start Windows XP, it boots the system into protected mode and then calls on *ntdetect.com* to detect the installed hardware on the system. ntldr then refers to the boot.ini file to locate the Windows boot files.

Critical Boot Files Naming all the critical boot files for Windows XP is akin to naming every muscle in the human body—completely possible, but time-consuming and without any real benefit. A few of the *most* important files, however, certainly deserve a short mention.

Once ntldr finishes detections, it loads ntoskrnl.exe, hal.dll, some of the Registry, and some basic device drivers; then it passes control to the ntoskrnl.exe file. ntoskrnl.exe completes the Registry loading, initializes all device drivers, and starts the winlogon.exe program, which displays the Windows XP logon screen (Figure 15.37).

FIGURE 15.37 Where do you want to go today?

Take the time to memorize the primary boot files and the boot process for Windows XP. Most boot errors are easily repaired if you know which files are used for booting and in which order they load.

Booting Windows Vista/7

Windows Vista and Windows 7 have a very different boot process from previous versions of Windows. Instead of having a unified Windows Vista/7 boot process, it actually uses two slightly different boot processes: one for systems using BIOS and one for systems with UEFI, or Unified Extensible Firmware Interface.

The first thing that happens when you power on a system with Windows Vista or Windows 7 is that either the BIOS or the UEFI starts up. In a BIOS-based system, the BIOS uses its boot order to scan partitions, one by one, for an MBR. The MBR holds a small bit of file-system boot code that scans the system's partition table for the system partition and then loads its boot sector. The boot sector in turn contains code that does nothing but point the boot process toward a file called bootmgr (pronounced "boot manager," or "boot mugger" if you're trying to make nerds laugh).

On a UEFI system, on the other hand, neither the MBR nor the file system boot code is run and UEFI simply loads up bootmgr directly. When the bootmgr starts, it reads data from a Boot Configuration Data (BCD) file that contains information about the various OSs installed on the system as well as instructions for how to load (bootstrap) them.

Once an OS is selected (or immediately if only one is present), bootmgr loads a program called winload.exe, which readies your system to load the OS kernel itself, rather like the way you clean up your house before Aunt Edna comes to visit. It does this by loading into memory the hardware abstraction layer, the system Registry, and the drivers for any boot devices before the OS itself takes over.

Travel Advisory

bootmgr is also responsible for bringing Windows out of hibernation, so if your computer refuses to wake up, blame bootmgr!

Once the OS process (called ntoskrnl.exe) takes over, it loads up all the various processes and systems that make up Windows, the Windows Vista or Windows 7 logo comes up, and you're happily computing, completely oblivious to all of the complex electronic communication that just took place inside your computer.

Here's a look at some important changes that have been made to the Windows Vista/7 boot process, compared to Windows XP:

- ntldr has been replaced with bootmgr.exe, winload.exe, and winresume.exe.
- boot.ini has been replaced with the BCD.
- Boot options are now edited using the built-in tool bcdedit.exe.

Objective 15.04 Windows Versions and Editions

Up to this point, you've read about a few different versions of Windows, focusing on Windows XP, Windows Vista, and Windows 7. This section looks at the differences in more detail, discussing the many editions within each version.

Windows XP

Windows XP was designed to be the one-stop OS for everyone. And because Microsoft sees three types of users—professionals, home users, and media junkies—Windows XP comes in three different editions: Windows XP Professional, Windows XP Home, and Windows XP Media Center. There is no official server edition of Windows XP.

Windows XP Professional

Microsoft Windows XP Professional offers a complete computing solution, tuned for office environments that support multiple users. It provides full-blown data security, and it is the only edition of Windows XP with the ability to log into a special Windows Server–controlled network called a *domain*. (Windows domains are discussed in detail in Chapter 19.)

Windows XP Home

As its name implies, Windows XP Home is designed for the home and small office user. The best way to describe Windows XP Home is to list the Windows XP Professional features that Windows XP Home lacks. Windows XP Home does *not* have these features:

- **The ability to log on to a Windows domain** A Windows Home PC may log into any single Windows server, but you must have a user name and password on every single server. With a domain, you can have one user name and password that works on all computers that are members of the domain.

- **Encrypting File System** With Windows XP Professional, you can encrypt a file so that only you can read it.

- **Support for multiple processors** Windows XP Home does not support more than one CPU. Surprisingly, it does support dual-core CPUs.

- **Support for Remote Desktop** A Windows XP Professional PC may be remotely accessed from another computer using the Remote Desktop (Figure 15.38). You cannot access a Windows XP Home system in this fashion.

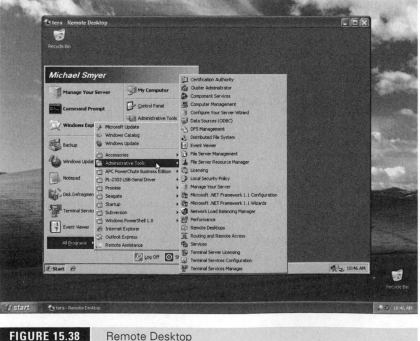

FIGURE 15.38 Remote Desktop

- **Support for NTFS access control** Remember all those excellent NTFS permissions like Full Control, Modify, and Read & Execute? Windows XP Home doesn't give you the ability to control these NTFS permissions individually. When you look at the properties of a file or folder in Windows XP Home, you won't see a Security tab. Instead, Windows XP Home's Sharing tab (Figure 15.39) shows that only one folder, the Shared Documents folder, is open for sharing—very different from XP Professional. This is called *Simple File Sharing*.

- **Support for group policies** Do you need to keep users from using a certain program? Do you want to prevent them from changing the screensaver? What do you want to do if they try to log in three times unsuccessfully? That's the job of group policies. If you want this level of control on your system, get Windows XP Professional, since XP Home doesn't support them.

Windows XP Professional and XP Home have a few more differences, but you're most likely to encounter these. If you want serious control of the folders, files, users, and network, you need XP Professional.

FIGURE 15.39 Windows XP Home Sharing tab

Windows XP Media Center

Microsoft Media Center is a specialized XP edition that includes the very handy Windows Media Center program (Figure 15.40). Media Center is a Personal Video Recorder (PVR) program that enables you to watch and record television (you'll need a TV tuner card) and organize all of your media, from photos to music.

Windows Vista

It's important that you recognize Vista and know what choices you had when deciding which edition you needed for a particular PC. Microsoft issued a number of Vista editions, each geared toward a particular market segment. Let's look at the most common editions.

Windows Vista Home Basic

Windows Vista Home Basic is roughly equivalent to Windows XP Home. Microsoft geared it to home users who didn't need advanced multimedia support.

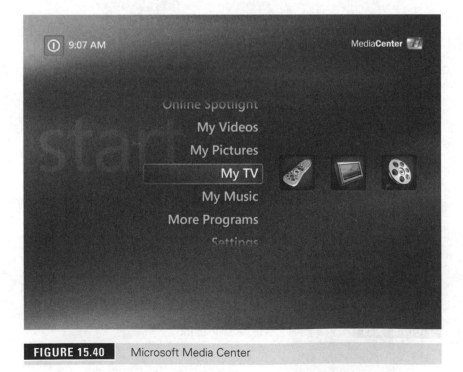

FIGURE 15.40 Microsoft Media Center

Windows Vista Home Premium

Windows Vista Home Premium is the same as Windows Vista Home Basic, but it adds an upgraded Windows Media Center PVR application, similar to the one found in Windows XP Media Center (Figure 15.41).

Windows Vista Business

Windows Vista Business is the basic business edition and has all the security, file-sharing, and access controls seen in Windows XP Professional.

Windows Vista Ultimate

Windows Vista Ultimate combines all the features of every other Vista edition and includes some other features, such as a game performance tweaker, DVD ripping capability, and BitLocker Drive Encryption (Figure 15.42).

Windows Vista Enterprise

Windows Vista Enterprise is an enhanced edition of Windows Vista Business and includes extra features like BitLocker Drive Encryption and support for two physical CPUs. This edition cannot be purchased through normal stores. You'll have to go through Microsoft directly to purchase it.

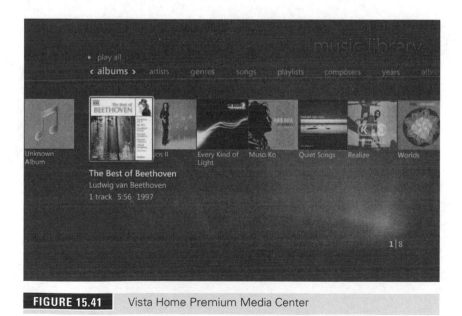

FIGURE 15.41 Vista Home Premium Media Center

FIGURE 15.42 Vista Ultimate

Exam Tip

Remember that you can determine your Windows version and edition by right-clicking My Computer in Windows XP or Computer in Windows Vista and Windows 7, and selecting Properties.

Windows 7

Comparing the look and feel of Windows Vista to Windows 7 might make you think that the two operating systems are far more alike than different—and you'd be right. So if Windows Vista and Windows 7 look and act so much alike, why didn't Microsoft just call Windows 7 "Windows Vista: The Fixed Version"? By the time Microsoft "fixed" Windows Vista, nobody wanted anything to do with it—people were reinstalling Windows XP! Microsoft didn't have a choice; it had to call this "fixed" Vista something new. Enter Windows 7 (see Figure 15.43).

FIGURE 15.43 The Windows 7 desktop

Microsoft created several editions of Windows 7, closely following Windows Vista's release model. Let's look at each edition of Windows 7 and see how they compare.

Windows 7 Starter

Around the time of Windows 7's release, netbooks (super-lightweight laptops, mostly used for Web browsing) were incredibly popular. Windows 7 Starter is a stripped-down edition of the OS designed to complement the limited role of the netbook. Windows 7 Starter lacks many of the advanced networking, media, and graphics capabilities of other editions of Windows, focusing instead on easy Internet access.

Windows 7 Home Premium

Windows 7 Home Premium is the most basic and most widely released edition of Windows 7. Roughly comparable to Windows Vista Home Premium, this edition of Windows 7 includes a lot of media functionality and some advanced network functions.

Windows 7 Professional

Stepping up from Windows 7 Home Premium, Windows 7 Professional adds support for joining domains, as well as support for powerful features like Windows XP Mode (enabling you to run Windows XP programs inside Windows 7) and Remote Desktop Connection (enabling you to connect to another computer over a network and see that computer's desktop as if it were your own).

Exam Tip

You should know which tools are available in the various editions of Windows for the CompTIA exam. For example, Windows XP Mode works only with Windows 7 Professional, Ultimate, and Enterprise. It comes as a separate download and requires virtualization software such as Windows Virtual PC.

Windows 7 Ultimate

Windows 7 Ultimate includes, as the name implies, everything that Windows 7 has to offer. You'll find advanced networking, backup, and security tools to complete your ultimate OS experience.

Windows 7 Enterprise

Windows 7 Enterprise is very similar to Windows Vista Enterprise and can only be purchased directly from Microsoft. Based on Windows 7 Professional, Enterprise includes extra features designed for large businesses, such as enhanced network searches, increased application security, and data protection using BitLocker.

Windows 64-Bit Editions

The 64-bit-only edition of Windows XP was called Windows XP 64-bit Edition (apparently Microsoft decided not to get cute when naming that one). Since it worked only on Intel Itanium processors, the chance of your seeing this OS was (and is) pretty slim unless you decided to work in a place with powerful server needs. The Windows XP Professional x64 Edition is a little more common, as it runs on any AMD or Intel processor that supports both 32 and 64 bits (Figure 15.44).

Windows XP 64-bit editions have had some impact, because they were the first stable Windows versions that truly supported 64-bit processing, but it was the introduction of Microsoft Vista that really started the move into the 64-bit world.

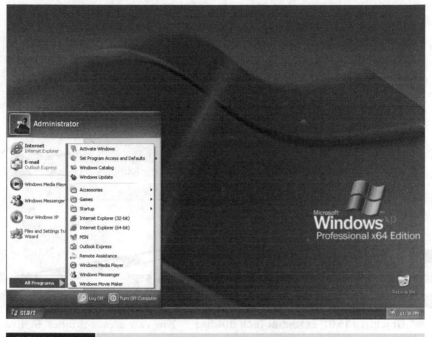

FIGURE 15.44 Windows XP Professional x64 Edition

Every one of the Vista editions comes in both a 32-bit and 64-bit version. Microsoft similarly released every version of Windows 7 in both. As PCs with more than four gigabytes of RAM become commonplace, it's important for you to make sure your version of Windows is a 64-bit version.

Transitioning to 64-bit Windows

The transition from 32-bit versions to 64-bit versions of Windows requires a certain update in terminology. Intel originally used numbers, such as 8086, 80286, 80386, and so on, to name its CPUs. To talk about them collectively, the industry replaced the leading numbers with an *x* and kept the numbers that stayed consistent for all the processors—thus *x86* describes the Intel CPU architecture for PCs. All the 32-bit versions of Windows were designed to run on x86 architecture.

The move to 64-bit CPUs and, equally importantly, to 64-bit versions of Windows, required some sort of change in terminology. Microsoft and others picked up the *x#* terminology and changed it to market 64-bit-only versions of

their software, branding the 64-bit software as *x64*. A consumer, therefore, could look at a product such as Windows XP Professional x64 Edition and very quickly know that the software was designed for 64-bit CPUs rather than 32-bit CPUs.

Most of the 64-bit processors run either 32-bit or 64-bit versions of Windows without missing a beat. The 64-bit versions of Windows require a 64-bit CPU. Many companies have produced 64-bit versions of application software that work only with 64-bit Windows running with a 64-bit CPU.

> **Travel Advisory**
>
> Review Chapter 5 for more information on 32-bit versus 64-bit computing.

CHECKPOINT

✔**Objective 15.01: Essential Tech Utilities** You can access utilities in five common locations in Windows: a pop-up menu (right-click), the Control Panel, System Tools, Administrative Tools, and the Microsoft Management Console. Throw in the command line, and you've got a sixth.

✔**Objective 15.02: Windows Structure** Windows is robust and scalable. It can handle multiple processors and implement NTFS on hard drives for serious data security. You can enhance security and make user management far more streamlined by using user accounts and groups. These plus NTFS enable you to set permissions of various levels on just about everything in the PC.

✔**Objective 15.03: Booting Windows** In Windows XP, the CPU wakes up and runs the system BIOS, and then the BIOS sends out a routine looking for a valid OS in the boot sector of the primary master hard drive. The MFT lives in the boot sector of the C: partition. It points to the location of the Windows XP system files, also on the C: drive, because that's the bootable drive. In Windows Vista/7, either the BIOS or UEFI starts up. The BIOS then finds the MBR, which then looks for the boot sector. bootmgr runs and loads Windows. UEFI skips straight to the bootmgr and loads Windows.

✔**Objective 15.04: Windows Versions and Editions** Windows comes in three versions covered on the CompTIA A+ exams, and each version has multiple editions: Windows XP has Home, Professional, Media Center, and 64-bit editions. Windows Vista comes in Home Basic, Home Premium, Business, Enterprise, and Ultimate, with both 32-bit and 64-bit editions of each. Windows 7 comes in Starter, Home Basic, Home Premium, Professional, Ultimate, and Enterprise editions—all of which support both 32-bit and 64-bit architecture, except Starter, which is only available in 32-bit.

REVIEW QUESTIONS

1. What's the easiest way to access the properties of an object in Windows?

 A. Right-click and select Properties.

 B. Left-click and select Properties.

 C. Double-click and select Properties.

 D. In the Control Panel, select the Properties applet.

2. Which Control Panel applet enables you to access essential system information and tools, such as Device Manager?

 A. Add or Remove Programs

 B. Display

 C. Program Options

 D. System

3. Which keyboard shortcut opens the System Properties dialog box?

 A. WINDOWS-PAUSE

 B. WINDOWS-ENTER

 C. CTRL-PAUSE

 D. CTRL-ENTER

4. What Windows XP tool would you use to migrate a coworker's essential files and folders to a new computer?

 A. Character Map

 B. Disk Cleanup

 C. Files and Settings Transfer Wizard

 D. Migrate Wizard

5. How do you open the Microsoft Management Console?

 A. Start | All Programs | System Tools | MMC

 B. Start | Control Panel | Manage applet

 C. Start | Run/Search and then type **mmc**

 D. Start | Run/Search and then type **manage**

6. Which tool enables you to view logs and monitor real-time data?

 A. Device Manager

 B. Log console

 C. Performance console

 D. System applet

7. Which of the following runs first after a Windows Vista/7 system is turned on?

 A. bootmgr

 B. BIOS

 C. boot.ini

 D. mbr

8. Which of the following are advantages of NTFS over FAT32? (Select two.)

 A. Long filenames

 B. Support for Windows 9x files

 C. Security through user accounts

 D. Transaction logging

9. What account type can access anything on a Windows system?

 A. Administrator

 B. Power User

 C. Super User

 D. User

10. Which files are the Windows XP system files?

 A. ntoskrnl.exe, system

 B. ntoskrnl.exe, ntldr, boot.ini

 C. ntldr, ntdetect.com, boot.ini

 D. system, ntdetect.com, boot.ini

REVIEW ANSWERS

1. **A** Right-click any object in Windows and select Properties from the pop-up menu to see the properties for that object.

2. **D** The System applet enables you to access essential system information and tools, such as Device Manager.

3. **A** Use the WINDOWS-PAUSE keyboard combination to open the System Properties applet.

4. **C** Windows XP's Files and Settings Transfer Wizard can assist in migrating from one computer to another.

5. **C** You can open a blank MMC by choosing Start | Run/Search, typing **mmc**, and pressing ENTER.

6. **C** The Performance console offers the System Monitor and Performance Logs and Alerts snap-ins. These enable you to view logs and monitor real-time data.

7. **B** After a Windows Vista/7 system loads, either the BIOS or UEFI runs first.

8. **C D** Among other things, NTFS offers better security through user accounts and recoverability through transaction logging.

9. **A** The Administrator account can access any object on a Windows system.

10. **C** The three Windows XP system files are ntldr, ntdetect.com, and boot.ini.

Installing and Upgrading Windows

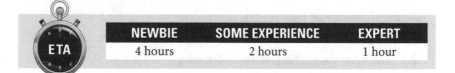

	NEWBIE	SOME EXPERIENCE	EXPERT
ETA	4 hours	2 hours	1 hour

523

This chapter details installing and upgrading Windows, starting with steps you should take before installing the operating system (OS). It also covers both generic installation and the specifics of installing and upgrading Windows XP, Windows Vista, and Windows 7. The third section covers the steps for installing Windows into a virtual machine. The chapter wraps with a discussion on troubleshooting installations and upgrades.

Objective 16.01 Preparing for Installation or Upgrade

Because installing an OS can be a time-consuming task, even when everything goes right, the Windows installation process holds great potential for lost time. Nothing sets your teeth to grinding as much as encountering an indecipherable or ambiguous error message, or the infamous Blue Screen of Death, 25 minutes into a 45-minute-long system installation.

These preparation tasks help minimize such problems. They go pretty fast, and skipping them can cause you a lot of grief later. You need to complete the following nine tasks *before* you insert the installation media:

1. Identify hardware requirements.
2. Verify hardware and software compatibility.
3. Decide whether to perform a clean installation or an upgrade.
4. Determine how to back up and restore existing data, if necessary.
5. Select an installation method.
6. Determine how to partition the hard drive and what file system to use.
7. Determine your computer's network role.
8. Decide on your computer's language and locale settings.
9. Plan for post-installation tasks.

Identify Hardware Requirements

Hardware requirements help you decide whether a computer system is a reasonable host for a particular OS. Requirements include the CPU model; the amount of RAM; the amount of free hard disk space; and the video adapter, display, and

storage devices that may be required to install and run the OS. They are stated as minimums or, more recently, as recommended minimums. Although you could install an OS on a computer with the old minimums that Microsoft published, they were not realistic if you wanted to actually accomplish work. With the last few versions of Windows, Microsoft has published recommended minimums that are much more realistic.

Travel Assistance
You will find the published minimums for each OS on the packaging and at Microsoft's Web site (www.microsoft.com).

Verify Hardware and Software Compatibility

Assuming your system meets the requirements, you next need to find out how well Windows supports the brand and model of hardware and the application software you intend to use under Windows. You have two basic sources for this information: Microsoft and the manufacturer of the device or software. How do you access this information? Use the Web!

When you install Windows, the Setup Wizard automatically checks your hardware and software and reports any potential conflicts. But please don't wait until you are all ready to install to check this out. With any flavor of Windows, *first do your homework!* To help, Windows also provides a utility called Upgrade Advisor (see Figure 16.1) on the installation media (also downloadable) that you run before you attempt to install the software.

Web Sites and Lists

To ensure that your PC works well with Windows, Microsoft has put a lot of hardware and software through a series of certification programs to create a list of devices that work with Windows. The challenge is that Microsoft seems to change the name of the list with every version of Windows.

Local Lingo
HCL alternatives You'll occasionally hear the HCL or Windows Logo'd Products List referred to as the Windows Catalog. The Windows Catalog was a list of supported hardware Microsoft would add to the Windows XP installation media. The Windows 7 Compatibility Center Web site is the modern tech's best source, so use that rather than any printed resources.

```
┌──────────────────────────────────────────────────────────────────────┐
│  Windows 7 Upgrade Advisor                                   ─  □  ✕   │
├──────────────────────────────────────────────────────────────────────┤
│  [ 32-bit report ] [ 64-bit report ]                                   │
│                                                                        │
│  Your computer can run Windows 7                  💾 Save Report  🖶 Print │
│                                                                        │
│  System                              Details                           │
│  ✓ Upgrade options available         You can upgrade to 32-bit Windows 7 Ultimate. │
│                                      Go online to get detailed instructions on how to │
│                                      upgrade                           │
│  ⓘ Windows Mail, Parental Controls   These features are no longer included in Windows 7. │
│    (Web Filtering), and Ultimate     You can get similar programs for Windows 7 from │
│    Extras                            other software manufacturers.    │
│                                      Go to the Microsoft website to learn more │
│  ✓ 4 system requirements passed                                       │
│    See all system requirements                                         │
│                                                                        │
│  Devices               Status        Details                           │
│  ? VMware VMCI Bus Device  Unknown   We don't have compatibility information about this │
│    VMware, Inc.                      device.                           │
│  ✓ VMware VMaudio (VMAUDIO) Check Windows  Check Windows Update after installing Windows 7 to │
│                                                                        │
│                                           [ Start again ]   [ Close ]  │
└──────────────────────────────────────────────────────────────────────┘
```

FIGURE 16.1 Upgrade Advisor

It all began back with Windows 95 when Microsoft produced a list of known hardware that would work with their OS, called the Hardware Compatibility List (HCL). Every version of Windows up to Windows Vista contained an HCL. This list was originally simply a text file found on the install disc or download-able from Microsoft's Web site.

Over time, Microsoft created specialized Web sites where you could look up a piece of hardware or software to determine whether or not it worked with Windows. These Web sites have gone through a number of names. Microsoft's current Web site acknowledging what hardware and software work with Windows is the *Windows 7 Compatibility Center,* formerly known as the Windows Logo'd Products List (for Windows Vista) and the Windows Catalog (for Windows XP). Now the magic words are Windows 7 Compatibility Center, as shown in Figure 16.2. Here you can find information on compatible components for Windows 7.

Travel Advisory

If you go looking for the Windows Catalog or Windows Logo'd Products List, you won't find them. You'll be redirected to the Windows 7 Compatibility Center (or a Web page explaining why you should upgrade to Windows 7).

FIGURE 16.2 Windows Compatibility Center

When you install a device that hasn't been tested by Microsoft, a rather scary screen appears (see Figure 16.3). This doesn't mean the component won't work; only that it hasn't been tested by Microsoft. Not all component makers go through the rather painful process of getting the Microsoft approval that allows them to list their component in the Windows Compatibility Center. As a general rule, unless the device is more than five years old, go ahead and install it. If it still doesn't work, you can simply uninstall it later.

Exam Tip

The CompTIA A+ 802 exam expects you to know the different *compatibility tools* available for each OS covered. Windows XP offered the Upgrade Advisor and the HCL. Windows Vista added the online Windows Vista Compatibility Center. Every online tool (with the exception of ftp.microsoft.com where you can find old HCLs in text format) now just points to the Windows 7 Compatibility Center.

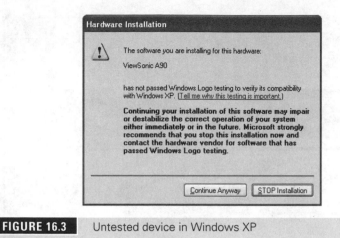

FIGURE 16.3 Untested device in Windows XP

Manufacturer Resources

Don't panic if you don't see your device on the official Microsoft list; many supported devices aren't on it. Check the optical disc that came with your hardware for proper drivers. Better yet, check the manufacturer's Web site for the most up-to-date drivers. Even when the Windows Compatibility Center lists a piece of hardware, I still make a point of checking the manufacturer's Web site for newer drivers.

When preparing to upgrade, check with the Web sites of the manufacturers of the applications already installed on the previous OS. If there are software compatibility problems with the versions you have, the manufacturer should provide upgrades or patches to fix the problem.

Perform a Clean Installation or an Upgrade

A *clean installation* of an OS involves installing it onto an empty hard drive with no previous OS installed. An *upgrade installation* is an installation of an OS on top of an earlier installed version, thus inheriting all previous hardware and software settings.

Clean Installation

A clean installation usually begins with a completely empty hard disk. The advantage of doing a clean installation is that you don't carry over problems from the old OS to the new one, but the disadvantage is that all applications have to be reinstalled and the desktop and each application reconfigured to the user's preferences. You perform a clean installation by setting your CMOS to tell the

system to boot from the optical drive before booting from your hard drive. You then boot off a Windows installation disc; it will give you the opportunity to partition and format the hard drive and then install Windows.

Upgrade Installation

In an upgrade installation, the new OS installs into the same folders as the old OS, or, in tech speak, the new installs *on top of* the old. The new OS replaces the old OS but retains all saved data and inherits all the previous settings (such as font styles, desktop colors and background, and so on), hardware, and applications—you don't have to reinstall your favorite programs!

> ### Local Lingo
>
> **In-place upgrade** Microsoft uses the term *in-place upgrade* to define an upgrade installation, so expect to see it on the 802 exam. On the other hand, Microsoft documentation also uses the term for a completely different process, called a *repair installation,* so read whatever question you get on the exam carefully for context.

To begin the upgrade of Windows, you must run the appropriate program from the optical disc. This usually means inserting a Windows installation disc into your system while your old OS is running, which will start the installation program. Then, to do an upgrade, you indicate that the new version of Windows should install into a directory that already contains an installation of Windows (it will do this by default). You will be asked whether it is an upgrade or a new installation; if you select new installation, it will remove the existing OS before installing.

If, for some reason, the Windows XP installation program doesn't start automatically, go to My Computer, open the installation disc, and locate winnt32.exe. This program starts an upgrade to Windows XP. For a Windows Vista or Windows 7 upgrade, open the disc in Windows Explorer and run Setup.exe in the disc's root directory, which starts the upgrade for those versions of Windows.

Multiboot Installation

A third option that you need to be aware of is the dual-boot or multiboot installation. Windows XP can install in a separate folder from an existing copy of Windows, enabling you to put two operating systems on the same partition. Neither Windows Vista nor Windows 7 allows you to define the install folder, so multibooting using Windows Vista or 7 requires you to put each installation on a different partition.

Travel Advisory

When configuring a computer for multibooting, there are two basic rules: first, you must format the system partition in a file system that is common to all installed operating systems, and second, you must install the operating systems in order from oldest to newest.

Other Installation Methods

In medium to large organizations, more advanced installation methods are often employed, especially when many computers need to be configured identically. A common method is to place the source files in a shared directory on a network server. Then, whenever a tech needs to install a new OS, he can boot up the computer, connect to the source location on the network, and start the installation from there. This is called generically a *remote network installation*. This method alone has many variations and can be automated with special scripts that automatically select the options and components needed. The scripts can even install extra applications at the end of the OS installation, all without user intervention once the installation has been started. This type of installation is called an *unattended installation*.

Another type of installation that is very popular for re-creating standard configurations is an *image deployment*. An image is a complete copy of a hard disk volume on which an operating system and, usually, all required applications have been preinstalled. Images can be stored on optical discs, in which case the tech runs special software on the computer that copies the image onto the local hard drive. Images can also be stored on special network servers, in which case the tech connects to the image server by using special software that copies the image from the server to the local hard drive. A leader in this technology has been Norton Ghost, which is available from Symantec. Other similar programs are Clonezilla and Acronis's True Image.

Beginning with Windows 2000 Server, Microsoft added *Remote Installation Services* (*RIS*), which can be used to initiate either a scripted installation or an installation of an image. With Windows Server 2008 and 2008 R2, Microsoft implemented *Windows Deployment Services* (*WDS*) to replace RIS. Though they are two different systems, they work very similarly from a tech's viewpoint. These tools help with big rollouts of new systems and operating system upgrades.

Travel Advisory

Scripting OS and application installations is a full-time job in many organizations. Many scripting tools and methods are available from both Microsoft and third-party sources.

Back Up and Restore Existing Data, If Necessary

Whether you are installing or upgrading, you may need to back up existing user data first, because things can go wrong either way, and the data on the hard drive might be damaged. You'll need to find out where the user is currently saving data files. If files are being saved onto the local hard drive, it must be backed up before the installation or replacement takes place to preserve the data. If all data has been saved to a network location, however, you are in luck, because the data is safe from damage during installation.

If the user saves data locally, and the computer is connected to a network, save the data, at least temporarily, to a network location until after the upgrade or installation has taken place. If the computer is not connected to a network, but the computer has a burnable optical drive, copy the data to optical media. You can also use an external hard drive or USB thumb drive, which are handy devices for any tech to have.

Wherever you save the data, you will need to copy or restore any lost or damaged data back to the local hard disk after the installation. If you plan to migrate a user from one system to another, here's where you might start the process by running the Files and Settings Transfer Wizard (Windows XP) or Windows Easy Transfer (Windows Vista and 7).

Select an Installation Method

Once you've backed up everything important, you need to select an installation method. You have two basic choices: insert the installation disc into the drive and go, or install over a network.

Partition the Hard Drive and Choose a System

If you are performing a clean installation, you need to decide ahead of time how to partition the disk space on your hard disk drive, including the number and size of partitions and the file system (or systems) you will use. Actually, in the decision process, the file system comes first and the space issue follows, as you will see.

This was a much bigger issue back in the days when older OSs couldn't use newer file systems, but now that every Windows OS that you could reasonably want to install supports NTFS, there's really no reason to use anything else. You still might have a reason to partition your drive, but as for choosing a file system, your work is done for you.

Your Computer's Network Role

The question of your computer's network role comes up in one form or another during a Windows installation. A Windows computer can have one of several roles relative to a network (in Microsoft terms). One role, called *standalone,* is actually a non-network role, and it simply means that the computer does not participate on a network. You can install any version of Windows on a standalone computer. A standalone computer belongs to a workgroup by default, even though that workgroup contains only one member.

In a network environment, a computer must be a member of either a workgroup or a domain. If you're using Windows 7 in a workgroup on a home network, it can also belong to a homegroup.

Your Computer's Language and Locale Settings

These settings are especially important for Windows OSs because these versions have greatly increased support for various spoken languages and locale conventions. The locale settings determine how date and time information is displayed and which math separators and currency symbols are used for various locations.

Post-Installation Tasks

After installing Windows, you will need to install the latest service pack and updates. You may also need to install updated drivers and reconfigure any settings, such as network settings, that were found not to work. You will also need to install any applications (word processor, spreadsheet, database, and so on) required by the user of the computer. Finally, don't forget to restore any data backed up before the installation or upgrade.

Objective 16.02 Installing and Upgrading Windows XP, Vista, and 7

Installing a modern OS follows pretty standardized steps: insert disc, click when prompted, reboot a few times, and then run through essential post-installation steps. At the same time, there are nuances between installing Windows XP or upgrading to Windows 7 that every CompTIA A+ certified tech must know, so this section goes through many installation processes in some detail.

During the Installation

When performing a Windows XP installation (also called setup), you'll notice that the screen progresses from simple textual information on a plain background to a full graphical interface. Windows Vista and 7, on the other hand, begin with a graphical interface. The first few steps of the installation include inspecting the hardware and reading through the *End User License Agreement (EULA)*, which you must accept for setup to continue. It is during the text display portion of a Windows XP installation that you can partition your hard disk. Also during this time, the computer copies files to the local hard disk, including a base set of files for running the graphical portion of the XP setup.

You will eventually be prompted to enter the *product key*, which is invariably located on the installation disc's case. Most techs learn the hard way that these covers tend to disappear when you need them most, and they write the product code directly on the disc itself. (Just don't use a ballpoint pen; it'll scratch the surface of the disc.) See Figure 16.4.

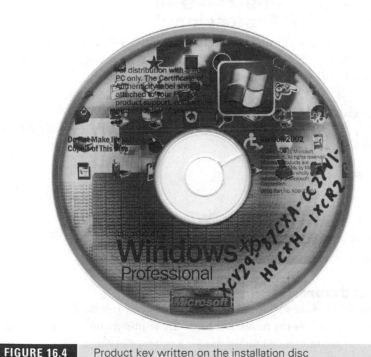

FIGURE 16.4 Product key written on the installation disc

Most of the XP installation process (and the entire Vista/7 installation) takes place in the graphical portion. This is where you select configuration options and choose optional Windows components.

No matter your version of Windows, the installation process always gets to the point where Windows begins to install itself on the system. I call this "The Big Copy" and use this time to catch up on my reading, eat a sandwich, or count ceiling tiles.

Travel Advisory

Windows comes in both upgrade and full versions. Make sure you use the correct disc. Some systems, particularly laptops, require a special OEM disc made just for that system. Don't bother trying to use an upgrade disc to install on a blank drive unless you also possess a disc with a full earlier version of Windows.

Installing or Upgrading to Windows XP Professional

Windows XP has been around for a long time with a well-established upgrade and installation process. This is the one part of the CompTIA A+ exams where older versions of Windows may be mentioned, so be warned!

Upgrade Paths

You can upgrade to Windows XP Professional from all of the following versions of Windows:

- Windows 98 (all versions)
- Windows Me
- Windows NT 4.0 Workstation (Service Pack 5 and later)
- Windows 2000 Professional
- Windows XP Home Edition

XP Hardware Requirements

Windows XP runs on a wide range of computers, but you need to be sure that your computer meets the minimum hardware requirements shown here. Also shown is my recommended minimum for a system running a typical selection of business productivity software.

Component	Minimum for a Windows XP Computer	Recommended for a Windows XP Computer
CPU	Any Intel or AMD 233 MHz or higher processor	Any Intel or AMD 300 MHz or higher processor
Memory	64 MB of RAM (though Microsoft admits XP will be somewhat crippled with only this amount)	512 MB of RAM or higher
Hard disk	1.5 GB of available hard drive space	4 GB of available hard drive space
Network	None	Modern network card
Display	Video card that supports SVGA with at least 800×600 resolution	Video card that supports DirectX with at least 1024×768 resolution
Optical drive	Any CD- or DVD-media drive	Any CD- or DVD-media drive

Hardware and Software Compatibility

You'll need to check hardware and software compatibility before installing Windows XP Professional as either an upgrade or a new installation. Of course, if you purchase a computer with Windows XP preinstalled, you're spared this task, but you'll still need to verify that the application software you plan to add to the computer will be compatible. Luckily, Microsoft includes the Upgrade Advisor on the Windows XP disc.

Upgrade Advisor The Upgrade Advisor is the first process that runs on the XP installation disc. It examines your hardware and installed software (in the case of an upgrade) and provides a list of devices and software that are known to have issues with XP. You can also run the Upgrade Advisor separately from the Windows XP installation disc.

Booting into Windows XP Setup

The Windows XP discs are bootable, and Microsoft no longer includes a program to create a set of setup boot disks. This should not be an issue, because PCs manufactured in the past several years can boot from the optical drive. This system BIOS setting, usually described as boot order, is controlled through a PC's CMOS Setup program.

Registration vs. Activation

During setup, you will be prompted to register your product and activate it. Registration tells Microsoft who is the official owner or user of the product, providing contact information such as name, address, company, phone number, and e-mail address. Registration is still entirely optional. Activation is a way to combat software piracy, meaning that Microsoft wants to ensure that each license for Windows XP is used solely on a single computer. It's more formally called *Microsoft Product Activation* (*MPA*). Activation is mandatory, but you can skip this step during installation. You have 30 days in which to activate the product, during which time it works normally. If you don't activate it within that time frame, it will be disabled.

Activation Mechanics Here's how product activation works. When you choose to activate, either during setup or later when XP reminds you to do it, an installation ID code is created from the product ID code that you entered during installation and a 50-digit value that identifies your key hardware components. You must send this code to Microsoft, either automatically if you have an Internet connection or verbally via a phone call to Microsoft. Microsoft then returns a 42-digit product activation code. If you are activating online, you don't have to enter the activation code; it happens automatically. If you are activating over the phone, you must read the installation ID to a representative and enter the resulting 42-digit activation code into the Activate Windows by Phone dialog box.

No personal information about you is sent as part of the activation process. Figure 16.5 shows the dialog box that opens when you start activation by clicking the reminder message balloon.

Installing or Upgrading to Windows Vista

Preparing for a Windows Vista installation is not much different from preparing for a Windows XP installation. There are, of course, a few things to consider before installing or upgrading your system to Vista. (The most obvious one, though it's not on the exam, is: *why?* There's no reason to use Windows Vista in the current computing environment.)

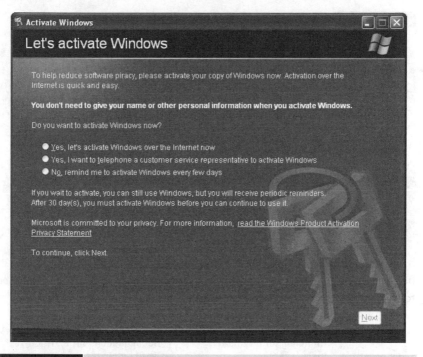

FIGURE 16.5 Activation takes just seconds with an Internet connection.

Upgrade Paths

Windows Vista is persnickety about doing upgrade installs with different editions; although you can upgrade to any edition of Vista from any edition of Windows XP, many upgrade paths will require you to do a clean installation of the Vista OS. Vista's upgrade paths are so complicated that the only way to really explain them is using a grid showing the OS you're trying to upgrade from and the edition of Vista you're upgrading to. Fortunately for you, Microsoft provides such a grid, which I've re-created in Table 16.1.

Hardware Requirements

Windows Vista requires a substantially more powerful computer to run than Windows XP. Make sure your computer meets at least the following minimum

TABLE 16.1	Vista's Labyrinthine Upgrade Paths			
	Vista Home Basic	**Vista Home Premium**	**Vista Business**	**Vista Ultimate**
XP Professional	Clean Installation	Clean Installation	Upgrade Installation	Upgrade Installation
XP Home	Upgrade Installation	Upgrade Installation	Upgrade Installation	Upgrade Installation
XP Media Center	Clean Installation	Upgrade Installation	Clean Installation	Upgrade Installation
XP Tablet PC	Clean Installation	Clean Installation	Upgrade Installation	Upgrade Installation
XP Professional x64	Clean Installation	Clean Installation	Clean Installation	Clean Installation

hardware requirements suggested by Microsoft, although it would be far better to meet my recommended requirements.

Component	Minimum for a Windows Vista Computer	Recommended for a Windows Vista Computer
CPU	1 GHz 32-bit (x86) or 64-bit (x64) processor	Any dual-core Intel or AMD processor or better
Memory	512 MB of RAM for Vista Basic (for all other editions, 1 GB of RAM)	2 GB of RAM or higher
Hard disk	20-GB hard drive with 15 GB of available hard drive space for Vista Basic (for all other editions, 40-GB hard drive with 15 GB of free space)	100-GB hard drive or greater
Network	Modern network card with Internet access	Modern network card with Internet access
Display	Support for DirectX 9 graphics and 32 MB of graphics memory for Vista Basic (for all other editions, 128 MB of graphics memory, plus Pixel Shader 2.0 support, the WDDM driver, and 32 bits per pixel)	DirectX 10–capable graphics card with at least 512 MB of graphics memory
Optical drive	Any DVD-media drive	Any DVD-media drive

If you're uncertain about whether your computer will run Vista, you can download and run the Windows Vista Upgrade Advisor from www. microsoft.com/windows/windows-vista/get/upgrade-advisor.aspx, which will tell you whether your computer meets Microsoft's minimum requirements.

Exam Tip
The CompTIA exams are likely to test your knowledge regarding the minimum installation requirements for Windows Vista Home Basic, Home Premium, Business, and Ultimate. Know them well!

Hardware and Software Compatibility

Windows Vista is markedly different from Windows XP in many basic, fundamental ways, and this causes all sorts of difficulty with programs and device drivers designed for Windows XP. When Vista was released, you probably heard a lot of people grumbling about it, and likely they were grumbling about hardware and software incompatibility. Simply put, a lot of old programs and devices don't work in Windows Vista, which is bad news for people who are still running Microsoft Word 97.

Most programs developed since Microsoft released Windows Vista in 2007 should work, but check compatibility if you need to run something important. Because the tools for checking compatibility with Windows Vista have disappeared in favor of tools for Windows 7 (or Windows 8, depending on when you're reading this book), you'll need to check with the developers or manufacturers of the software and devices.

Travel Advisory
Software incompatibility in Vista was such a problem for many corporate customers and end users that Microsoft includes a Windows XP Mode in the higher-end editions of Windows 7, enabling most Windows XP programs to be run despite the different OS.

Installing or Upgrading to Windows 7

Windows 7 did not add anything new in terms of installation types. You still need to decide between a clean installation and an upgrade installation, but that's easy to do because you can only upgrade to Windows 7 from Windows

Vista—and that's only if you have the same bit edition. In other words, you can upgrade 32-bit Vista to 32-bit Windows 7, but you can't upgrade 32-bit Windows Vista to 64-bit Windows 7. All other Windows editions, including Windows XP Home and Professional, require a clean installation to get Windows 7. Table 16.2 outlines the upgrade paths.

If you have Windows 7 and you want to upgrade to a higher edition with more features—from Windows 7 Home Premium to Windows 7 Ultimate, for example—you can use the built-in Windows Anytime Upgrade feature. You can find this option pinned to the Start menu. Don't forget your credit card!

Hardware Requirements for Windows 7

With Windows 7, Microsoft released a single list of system requirements, broken down into 32-bit and 64-bit editions. Quoting directly from Microsoft's Windows 7 Web site, the requirements are as follows:

- 1 gigahertz (GHz) or faster 32-bit (x86) or 64-bit (x64) processor
- 1 gigabyte (GB) RAM (32-bit) or 2 GB RAM (64-bit)
- 16 GB available hard disk space (32-bit) or 20 GB (64-bit)
- DirectX 9 graphics device with WDDM 1.0 or higher driver

> **Note**
>
> Windows 7 has incredibly humble minimum requirements. Today, a low-end desktop computer will have 4 GB of RAM, a processor around 2 GHz, approximately a terabyte of hard drive space, and a DirectX 11 video card with 256 or even 512 MB of graphics memory.

TABLE 16.2	Installing or Upgrading to Windows 7	
Existing OS	**Can Upgrade To...**	**Can Clean Install To...**
32-bit Vista (any edition)	32-bit Windows 7 only	Any edition of Windows 7
64-bit Vista (any edition)	64-bit Windows 7 only	Any edition of Windows 7
Any pre-Vista Windows	Not allowed	Any edition of Windows 7

Make sure you memorize the list of requirements. Microsoft also added a fairly extensive list of additional requirements that vary based on the edition of Windows 7 you use. From the same Web site, they include (author's comments in brackets):

- Internet access (fees may apply). [You need Internet access to activate, register, and update the system easily.]
- Depending on resolution, video playback may require additional memory and advanced graphics hardware.
- Some games and programs might require a graphics card compatible with DirectX 10 or higher for optimal performance. [Video has improved dramatically over the years, and DirectX 9 dates back to 2004. Many games and high-definition videos need more than DirectX 9. Also, Windows Aero Desktop (aka Aero Glass) adds amazing beauty and functionality to your desktop. You must have a video card with 128 MB of graphics memory for Aero to work.]
- For some Windows Media Center functionality, a TV tuner and additional hardware may be required. [Windows Media Center works fine without a TV tuner. You can still use it to play Blu-ray Disc and DVD movies as well as video files and music. If you want to watch live TV, however, you'll need a tuner.]
- HomeGroup requires a network and PCs running Windows 7.
- DVD/CD authoring requires a compatible optical drive. [If you want to burn something to an optical disc, you need a drive that can burn discs.]
- Windows XP Mode requires an additional 1 GB of RAM and an additional 15 GB of available hard disk space.

Windows 7 is also designed to handle multiple CPU cores and multiple CPUs. Many, if not most, modern computers use multicore processors. The 32-bit editions of Windows 7 can handle up to 32 processor cores, making it an easy fact to remember for the exams. The 64-bit editions of Windows 7 support up to 256 processor cores.

In terms of multiple physical processors (found on high-end PCs), Windows 7 Professional, Ultimate, and Enterprise can handle two CPUs, whereas Windows 7 Starter and Home Premium support only one CPU.

> **Exam Tip**
>
> In this chapter, you've learned some of the different installation procedures for Windows XP, Windows Vista, and Windows 7. Keeping them straight can be hard, but if you want to avoid being tricked on the CompTIA A+ exams, you must be able to. Review the procedures and then make sure you can identify the points of similarity and, more importantly, the differences among the three.

Upgrading Issues

A few extra steps before you pop in that installation disc are worth your time. If you plan to upgrade rather than perform a clean installation, follow these steps first.

1. Remember to check hardware and software compatibility as explained earlier in the chapter.

2. Have an up-to-date backup of your data and configuration files handy.

3. Perform a "spring cleaning" on your system by uninstalling unused or unnecessary applications and deleting old files.

4. Perform a disk scan (error-checking) and a disk defragmentation.

5. Uncompress all files, folders, and partitions.

6. Perform a virus scan, and then remove or disable all virus-checking software.

7. Disable virus checking in your system CMOS.

8. Keep in mind that if worse comes to worst, you may have to start over and do a clean installation anyway. This makes step 2 exceedingly important. Back up your data!

The Windows XP Clean Installation Process

A clean installation begins with your system set to boot to your optical drive and the Windows installation disc in the drive. You start your PC, and assuming you have the boot order correct, the installation program starts booting (Figure 16.6). Note at the bottom that it says to press F6 if you need to install a third-party SCSI or RAID driver. You do this only if you want to install Windows onto a strange drive and Windows does not already have the driver for that drive.

```
Windows Setup

Press F6 if you need to install a third party SCSI or RAID driver...
```

FIGURE 16.6 Windows Setup text screen

Don't worry about this; Windows has a huge assortment of drivers for just about every hard drive ever made, and for the rare situation in which you need a third-party driver, the folks who sell you the SCSI or RAID array will tell you ahead of time.

After the system copies a number of files, you'll see the Welcome to Setup screen (Figure 16.7). This is an important screen! As you'll see in later chapters,

```
Windows XP Professional Setup

    Welcome to Setup.
    This portion of the Setup program prepares Microsoft(R)
    Windows(R) XP to run on your computer.

        • To set up Windows XP now, press ENTER.
        • To repair a Windows XP installation using
          Recovery Console, press R.
        • To quit Setup without installing Windows XP, press F3.

    ENTER=Continue   R=Repair   F3=Quit
```

FIGURE 16.7 Welcome to Setup text screen

techs often use the Windows installation disc as a repair tool, and this screen enables you to choose between installing Windows and repairing an existing installation. Because you're making a new installation, just press ENTER.

Next, you're prompted to read and accept the EULA. Nobody ever reads this—it gives you a stomachache when you see what you're really agreeing to—so just press F8 and move to the next screen to start partitioning the drive (Figure 16.8).

If your hard disk is unpartitioned, you need to create a new partition when prompted. Follow the instructions. In most cases, you can make a single partition, although you can easily make as many partitions as you want. You can also delete partitions if you're using a hard drive that was partitioned in the past (or if you mess up your partitioning). Note that there is no option to make a primary or extended partition; this tool makes the first partition primary and the rest extended.

After you've made the partition(s), you must select the partition on which to install XP (sort of trivial if you have only one partition), and then you need to decide which file system format to use for the new partition. Unless you have some weird need to support FAT or FAT32, format the partition by using NTFS (Figure 16.9).

Setup now formats the drive and copies some basic installation files to the newly formatted partition, displaying another progress bar. Go get a book to read while you wait.

```
Windows XP Professional Setup

    The following list shows the existing partitions and
    unpartitioned space on this computer.

    Use the UP and DOWN ARROW keys to select an item in the list.

        •  To set up Windows XP on the selected item, press ENTER.

        •  To create a partition in the unpartitioned space, press C.

        •  To delete the selected partition, press D.

    8190 MB Disk 0 at Id 0 on bus 0 on atapi [MBR]

         Unpartitioned space                    8189 MB

    ENTER=Install   C=Create Partition   F3=Quit
```

FIGURE 16.8 Partitioning text screen

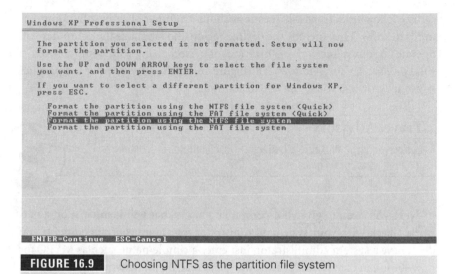

FIGURE 16.9 Choosing NTFS as the partition file system

After it completes copying the base set of files to the hard drive, your computer reboots, and the graphical mode of Windows Setup begins.

You will see a generic screen during the installation that looks like Figure 16.10.

FIGURE 16.10 Beginning of graphical mode

The following screens ask questions about a number of things the computer needs to know. They include the desired region and language the computer will operate in, your name and organization for personalizing your computer, and a valid *product key* for Windows XP (Figure 16.11). Be sure to enter the product key exactly, or you will be unable to continue.

> **Travel Advisory**
>
> Losing your product key is a bad idea! Document it—at least write it on the installation disc.

Next, you need to give your computer a name that will identify it on a network. Check with your system administrator for an appropriate name. If you don't have a system administrator, just enter a simple name such as MYPC for now—you can change this at any time—and read up on networking later in this book. You also need to create and confirm a password for the Administrator user account (Figure 16.12). Every Windows system has an Administrator user account that has permission to do anything on the computer. Techs will need this account to modify and fix the computer in the future.

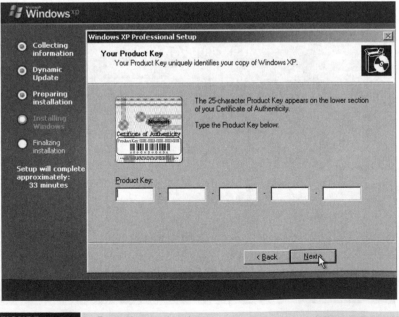

FIGURE 16.11 Enter the product key.

![Windows XP Professional Setup - Computer Name and Administrator Password dialog showing the setup progress on the left (Collecting information, Dynamic Update, Preparing installation, Installing Windows, Finalizing installation, Setup will complete approximately: 33 minutes) and fields for Computer name: MYPC, Administrator password, and Confirm password]

FIGURE 16.12	Computer name and administrator password

Last, you're asked for the correct date, time, and time zone. Then Windows tries to detect a network card. If a network card is detected, the network components will be installed and you'll have an opportunity to configure the network settings. Unless you know you need special settings for your network, just select the *Typical settings* option (Figure 16.13). Relax; XP will do most of the work for you. Plus you can easily change network settings after the installation.

Travel Advisory
Even experienced techs usually select the *Typical settings* option. Installation is not the time to be messing with network details (found under *Custom settings*) unless you need to do so.

The Big Copy of files now begins from the CD-ROM to your hard drive. This is a good time to pick your book up again, because watching the ads is boring (Figure 16.14).

After the files required for the final configuration are copied, XP reboots again. During this reboot, XP determines your screen size and applies the appropriate resolution. This reboot can take several minutes to complete, so be patient.

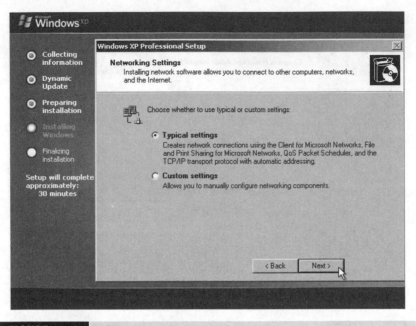

FIGURE 16.13 Selecting typical network settings

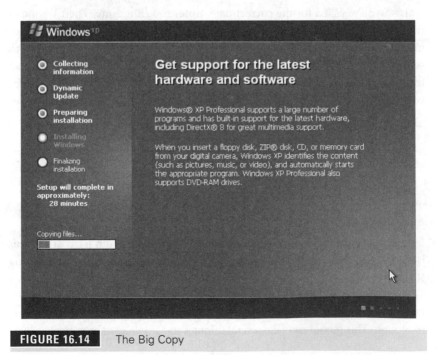

FIGURE 16.14 The Big Copy

FIGURE 16.15 Windows XP desktop with Bliss background

Once the reboot is complete, you can log on as the Administrator. Balloon messages may appear over the tray area of the taskbar—a common message concerns the display resolution. Click the balloon and allow Windows XP to adjust the display settings automatically.

The final message in the installation process reminds you that you have 30 days left for activation. Go ahead and activate now over the Internet or by telephone. That's it! You have successfully installed Windows XP and should have a desktop with the default Bliss background, as shown in Figure 16.15.

The Windows Vista/7 Clean Installation Process

The installation methods for Windows Vista and Windows 7 are so close to identical that it would be silly to address them as separate entries in this book (see Figure 16.16). Only the splash screens and the product-key entry dialog box have changed between Windows Vista and Windows 7! Because of this trivial difference, showing the installation process for both operating systems would waste paper. This walkthrough uses the Windows Vista screenshots just because you might never see them anywhere else.

FIGURE 16.16 Windows 7 and Vista splash screens

Just as when installing Windows XP, you need to boot your computer from some sort of Windows installation media. Usually, you'll use a DVD, though you can also install Vista or 7 from a USB drive, over a network, or even from several CD-ROMs (for those who have only a CD-ROM drive) that you must specially order from Microsoft. When you've booted into the installer, the first screen you see asks you to set your language, time/currency, and keyboard settings, as shown in Figure 16.17.

The next screen in the installation process is somewhat akin to the Windows XP Welcome screen, in that it enables techs to use the installation disc's repair tools (Figure 16.18). Just like the completely revamped installer, the Vista and 7 repair tools are markedly different from those in Microsoft's previous OS versions. Because you're just installing Windows in this chapter, click *Install now*.

The next screen shows just how wildly different the Vista installation order is. When installing Vista, you enter your product key before you do anything else, as you can see in Figure 16.19. With Windows XP, this didn't come until much, much later in the process, and there's a very interesting reason for this change.

FIGURE 16.17 Windows Vista language settings screen

FIGURE 16.18 The Windows Vista setup Welcome screen

FIGURE 16.19 The Windows Vista product key screen

Instead of having different discs for each edition of Windows Vista or Windows 7, every installation disc contains all of the available editions. In Windows XP, your product key did very little besides let the installation disc know that you had legitimately purchased the OS. In Windows Vista and Windows 7, your product key not only verifies the legitimacy of your purchase; it also tells the installer which edition you purchased, which, when you think about it, is a lot to ask of a randomly generated string of numbers and letters.

If you leave the product key blank and click the Next button, a new screen will ask you which edition of Vista you would like to install (Figure 16.20). (Windows 7, however, disables this option—while every version is on the disc, you can only install the edition named on the box or disc label.) Lest you start to think that you've discovered a way to install Windows without paying for it, you should know that doing this simply installs a 30-day trial of the OS. After 30 days, you will no longer be able to boot to the desktop without entering a valid product key that matches the edition of Vista/7 you installed.

After the product key screen, you'll find Microsoft's new and improved EULA (Figure 16.21), which you can skip unless you're interested in seeing what's changed in the world of obtuse legalese since the release of Windows XP.

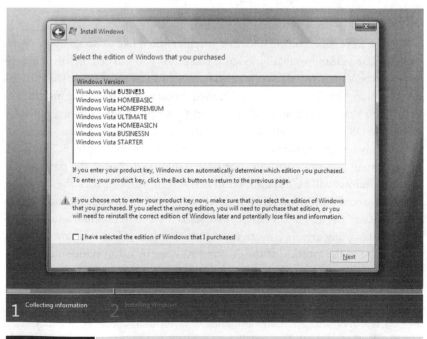

FIGURE 16.20 Choose the edition of Vista you want to install.

FIGURE 16.21 The Vista EULA

On the next page, you get to decide whether you'd like to do an upgrade installation or a clean installation (Figure 16.22). As you learned earlier, you have to begin the Vista/7 installation process from within an older OS to use the Upgrade option, so this option will be dimmed if you've booted off the installation disc. To do a clean installation of Vista/7, edit your partitions, and just generally install the OS like a pro, you choose the Custom (advanced) option.

You may remember the next screen (Figure 16.23) from Chapter 8. This is the screen where you can partition your hard drives and choose the partition to which Windows will be installed. From this screen, you can click the *Drive options (advanced)* button to display a variety of partitioning options, and you can click the *Load Driver* button to, well, load hard drive drivers (Figure 16.24). The process of loading drivers is much more intuitive than it is in Windows XP: you just browse to the location of the drivers you want by using Windows' familiar browsing window.

Once you've partitioned your drives and selected a partition for the Vista/7 installation, the installation process takes over, copying files, expanding files, installing features, and generally doing lots of computerish things. When Vista/7 has finished unpacking and installing itself, it asks you to choose a user name

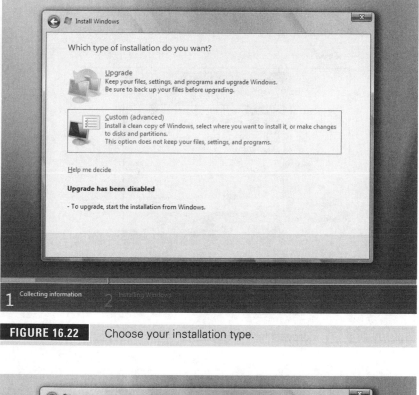

FIGURE 16.22 Choose your installation type.

FIGURE 16.23 The partitioning screen

FIGURE 16.24 Browse for drivers.

and picture (Figure 16.25). This screen also asks you to set up a password for your main user account, which is definitely a good idea if multiple people will be using the computer.

After picking your user name and password, and letting Windows know how much you like pictures of kitties, you're taken to a screen where you can type in a computer name (Figure 16.26). By default, Windows makes your computer name the same as your user name but with -*PC* appended to it, which in most cases is fine.

This is also the screen where you can change the desktop background that Windows will start up with. You can change this easily later on, so pick whatever you like and click the Next button.

At this point, Windows 7 will ask for your product key. On Windows Vista, you did this at the beginning of the installation.

The next page asks you how you want to set up Windows Automatic Updates (Figure 16.27). Most users want to choose the top option, *Use recommended settings,* because it provides the most hassle-free method for updating your computer. The middle option, *Install important updates only,* installs only the most critical security fixes and updates and leaves the rest of the updates up to you.

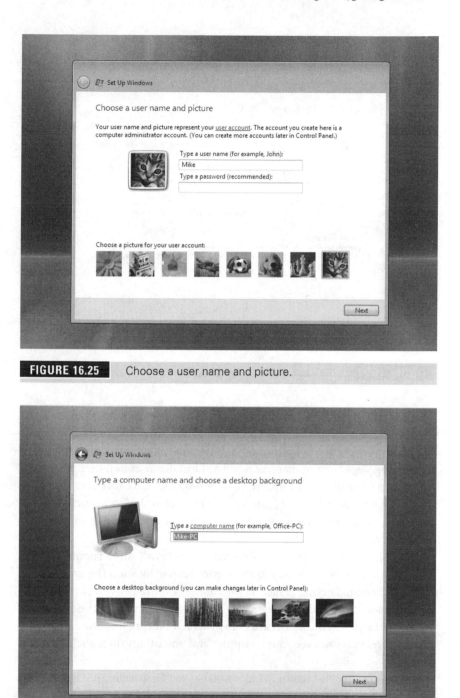

FIGURE 16.25 Choose a user name and picture.

FIGURE 16.26 Choose your computer name.

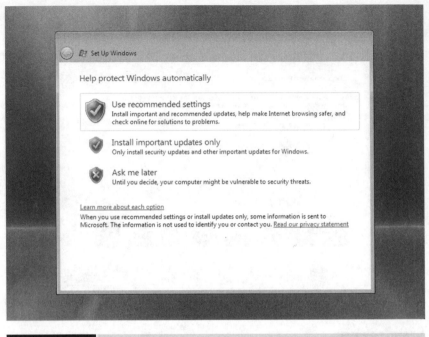

FIGURE 16.27 The automatic updates screen

This is useful when setting up computers for businesses, as many companies' IT departments like to test any updates before rolling them out to the employees. You should select the last option, *Ask me later,* only if you can dedicate yourself to checking weekly for updates, as it will not install any automatically.

Next up is the time and date screen, where you can make sure your OS knows what time it is, as shown in Figure 16.28. This screen should be pretty self-explanatory, so set the correct time zone, the correct date, and the correct time, and move to the next screen.

If you have your computer connected to a network while running the installer, the next screen will ask you about your current location (Figure 16.29). If you're on a trusted network, such as your home or office network, make the appropriate selection, and your computer will be discoverable on the network. If you're on, say, a Starbucks' network, choose *Public location* so the caffeine addicts around you can't see your computer and potentially do malicious things to it.

Once you're past that screen, Windows thanks you for installing it (Figure 16.30), which is awfully polite for a piece of software, don't you think?

FIGURE 16.28 Windows pities the fool who doesn't know what time it is.

FIGURE 16.29 Tell Windows what kind of network you're on.

FIGURE 16.30 Aw, shucks, Windows. Don't mention it.

Lest you think you're completely through the woods, Windows will run some tests on your computer to give it a performance rating, which, in theory, will tell you how well programs will run on your computer. You'll sometimes see minimum performance ratings on the sides of game boxes, but even then, you're more likely to need plain, old-fashioned minimum system requirements. This process can take anywhere from 5 to 20 minutes, so this is another one of those coffee-break moments in the installation process.

Once the performance test finishes, Windows Vista or Windows 7 boots up and you have 30 days to activate your new OS.

Travel Advisory

When it comes right down to it, you don't really need a performance rating on your computer. If you don't want to waste your time, you can use the ALT-F4 keyboard shortcut to skip this step.

Automating the Installation

As you can see, you may have to sit around for quite a while when installing Windows. Instead of sitting there answering questions and typing in product keys, wouldn't it be nice just to boot up the machine and have the installation process finish without any intervention on your part—especially if you have 30 PCs that need to be ready to go tomorrow morning? Fortunately, Windows offers two good options for automating the installation process: scripted installations and disk cloning.

Scripting Windows XP Installations with Setup Manager

For automating a Windows XP install, Microsoft provides *Setup Manager* to help you create a text file—called an *answer file*—containing all of your answers to the installation questions. This enables you to do an *unattended installation,* which means you don't have to sit in front of each computer throughout the installation process.

You can find Setup Manager on the Windows installation disc in the \Support\Tools folder. Double-click the DEPLOY cabinet file, and then right-click setupmgr.cab and select Extract (see Figure 16.31). Choose a location for the file.

FIGURE 16.31 Extracting Setup Manager from the DEPLOY cabinet file

Setup Manager supports creating answer files for three types of setups: Unattended, Sysprep, and Remote Installation Services (see Figure 16-32). The latest version of the tool can create answer files for Windows XP Home Edition, Windows XP Professional, and Windows .NET (Standard, Enterprise, or Web Server).

Automating a Windows Vista or Windows 7 Installation with the Automated Installation Kit

As of Windows Vista and Windows 7, Setup Manager is history—as is any method of automating an installation that isn't extremely complicated and intimidating. Microsoft has replaced Setup Manager with the Windows Automated Installation Kit (AIK), a set of tools that, although quite powerful, seems to have made something of a Faustian deal to obtain that power at the expense of usability (see Figure 16.33).

Exam Tip

Writing a step-by-step guide to creating an answer file in the AIK would almost warrant its own chapter, and as the CompTIA A+ exams don't cover it at all, I'm not going to cover it here either.

FIGURE 16.32 Setup Manager can create answer files for three types of setups.

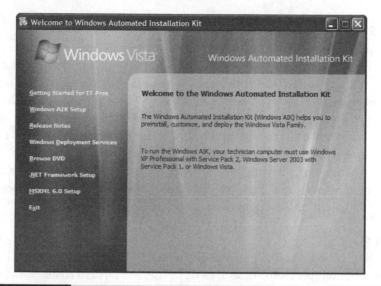

FIGURE 16.33 The Automated Installation Kit

Disk Cloning

Disk cloning simply takes an existing PC and makes a full copy of the drive, including all data, software, and configuration files. You can then transfer that copy to as many machines as you like, essentially creating clones of the original machine. In the old days, making a clone was pretty simple. You just hooked up two hard drives and copied the files from the original to the clone by using something like the venerable XCOPY program (as long as the hard drive was formatted with FAT or FAT32). Today, you'll want to use a more sophisticated program, such as Norton Ghost, to make an image file that contains a copy of an entire hard drive and then lets you copy that image either locally or over the network.

Local Lingo

Ghosting Norton Ghost is not the only disk-imaging software out there, but it is so widely used that techs often refer to disk cloning as "ghosting the drive."

Installing Windows over a Network

The phrase "network installation" can involve many different tools depending on which version of Windows you use. Most importantly, the machines that receive the installations (the clients) need to be connected to a server. That server might be another copy of Windows XP, Vista, or 7; or it might be a fully fledged server running Windows Server 2003, 2008, or 2008 R2. The serving PC needs to host an image, which can be either the default installation of Windows or a custom image, often created by the network administrator.

All of the server-side issues should be handled by a network administrator—setting up a server to deploy Windows installations and images goes beyond what the CompTIA A+ exams cover.

PXE

On the client side, you'll need to use the Preboot Execution Environment (PXE). PXE uses multiple protocols such as IP, DHCP, and DNS to enable your computer to boot from a network location. That means the PC needs no installation disc or USB drive. Just plug your computer into the network and go! Okay, it's a little more complicated than that.

To enable PXE, you'll need to enter your BIOS System Setup. Find the screen that configures your NIC, which changes depending on your particular BIOS. If there is a PXE setting there, enable it. You'll also need to change the boot order so that the PC boots from a network location first.

Note

Not every NIC supports PXE. To boot from a network location without PXE, you can create boot media that forces your PC to boot from a network location.

When you reboot the PC, you'll see the familiar first screens of the boot process. At some point, you should also see an instruction to "Press F12 for network boot." (It's almost always F12.) The PC will attempt to find a server on the network to which it can connect. When it does, you'll be asked to press F12 again to continue booting from the network, as you can see in Figure 16.34.

Depending on how many images are prepared on the server, you'll either be taken directly to the Windows installation screen or be asked to pick from multiple images. Pick the option you need, and everything else should proceed as if you were installing Windows from the local optical drive.

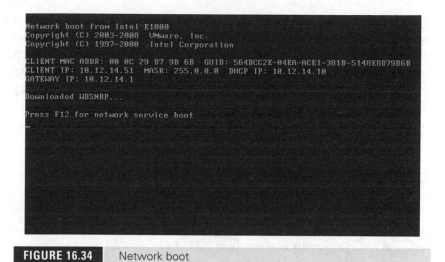

```
Network boot from Intel E1000
Copyright (C) 2003-2008  VMware, Inc.
Copyright (C) 1997-2000  Intel Corporation

CLIENT MAC ADDR: 00 0C 29 D7 9B 6B   GUID: 564DCC2E-04EA-ACE1-381B-5148E8D79B6B
CLIENT IP: 10.12.14.51   MASK: 255.0.0.0   DHCP IP: 10.12.14.10
GATEWAY IP: 10.12.14.1

Downloaded WDSNBP...

Press F12 for network service boot
_
```

FIGURE 16.34 Network boot

Post-Installation Tasks

You might think that's enough work for one day, but a few more tasks remain on
your list. They include identifying installation problems (if they occur), updating
the OS with patches and service packs, upgrading drivers, and restoring user
data files.

Identifying Installation Problems

After you install or upgrade Windows, you need to use your powers of observa-
tion to check whether you've had a serious installation problem. The worst prob-
lems show up early in the installation process, but others may show up later as you
work in Windows. If your installation wasn't successful, check out Objective 16.04,
"Troubleshooting Installations and Upgrades," for information and help.

Patches, Service Packs, and Updates

Someone once described an airliner as consisting of millions of parts flying in
close formation. I think that's also a good description for an OS. And we can
even carry that analogy further by thinking about all the maintenance required
to keep an airliner and an OS safely flying. Like an airliner, the parts (program-
ming code) of your OS were created by different people, and some parts may
have been manufactured by contractors rather than by the company that makes
the OS. Although each component is tested as much as possible, and the assem-
bled OS is also tested, it's not possible to test for every possible combination of
events. Sometimes a piece of the OS is defective. The fix for such a problem is a
corrective program called a *patch*.

In the past, Microsoft would provide patches for individual problems. It would also accumulate patches until they reached some sort of "critical mass" and then bundle them together as a *service pack*. Microsoft still does this, but it also combines appropriate patches and service packs into *updates* to make the process easier for you. These updates are available at Microsoft's Web site. Many organizations make the updates available for distribution from network servers. Immediately after installing Windows, install the latest updates on the computer. Chapter 17 covers this process fully.

Upgrading Drivers

Even if you completed all your pre-installation tasks, you may decide to go with the default drivers that come with Windows and then upgrade them to the latest drivers after the fact. This is a good strategy, because installation is a complicated task, and you can simplify it by installing old but adequate drivers. Maybe those newest drivers are just a week old—waiting until after the Windows installation to install new drivers will give you a usable driver to go back to if the new driver turns out to be a lemon.

Restoring User Data Files (If Applicable)

Remember when you backed up the user data files before installation? You don't? Well, check again, because now is the time to restore that data. Your method of restoring will depend on how you backed up the files in the first place.

Files and Settings Transfer Wizard

When migrating to a new system, you would run the Files and Settings Transfer Wizard on the newer computer (assuming the newer computer is running Windows XP, but more on Vista's and 7's migration options later), which would then use the wizard to pull files off the older one. You start the wizard by going to Accessories | System Tools from Windows XP's All Programs menu.

User State Migration Tool

If you're the sort of computer user who demands maximum functionality and power from your OS, you'll probably want to use the *User State Migration Tool (USMT)*. The USMT has all of the same features as the Files and Settings Transfer Wizard, but with much more control over advanced configurations for the new computer. Its primary use is in businesses, because it has to be run in a Windows Server domain. In practice, if you're migrating a single user, use the Files and Settings Transfer Wizard. If you need to migrate multiple users, the User State Migration Tool is the tool.

Exam Tip

The CompTIA A+ exam competencies mention that the very old Windows NT (that's the version before Windows 2000, which in turn preceded Windows XP) came with the *User Data Migration Tool* (*UDMT*) that facilitated migrating users from an earlier version, just like the USMT. This tool *does not exist* on current OSs, but it might show up as a wrong answer choice.

Windows Easy Transfer

With Windows Vista and 7, Microsoft has upgraded the Files and Settings Transfer Wizard, calling it *Windows Easy Transfer*. Windows Easy Transfer comes native in Vista/7 and can be downloaded and installed on Windows XP as well. Windows Easy Transfer is located in the System Tools subfolder of the Accessories folder in your All Programs menu.

Migration Practices

When talking about migration or retirement in terms of security, you need to answer one question: What do you do with the old system or drive?

All but the most vanilla new installations have sensitive data on them, even if it's simply e-mail messages or notes-to-self that would cause embarrassment if discovered. Most PCs, especially in a work environment, contain a lot of sensitive data. You can't just format C: and hand over the drive.

Follow three principles when migrating or retiring a computer. First, migrate your users and data information in a secure environment. Until you get passwords properly in place and test the security of the new system, you can't consider that system secure. Second, remove data remnants from hard drives that you store or give to charity. Third, recycle the older equipment; don't throw it in the trash. PC recyclers go through a process of deconstructing hardware, breaking system units, keyboards, printers, and even monitors into their basic plastics, metals, and glass for reuse.

The easiest way for someone to compromise or access sensitive data is to simply walk up and take it when you're not looking. This is especially true when you are in the process of copying information to a new, unprotected system. Don't set a copy to run while you go out to lunch, but rather be there to supervise and remove any remnant data that might still reside on any mass storage devices, especially hard drives.

Data Destruction

You might think that, as easy as it seems to be to lose data, you could readily get rid of data if you tried. That's not the case with magnetic media, though, such as hard drives and flash memory. When you delete something in Windows, or even empty the Recycle Bin, the "deleted" data remains on your storage device until new data overwrites it, or replaces it. (This "deleted" data is also what you see as free space in Windows.) This can be a big security hole when you dispose of a drive.

Cleaning a drive completely is very difficult. You can either physically destroy the hard drive or *sanitize* it using a software utility. Physical destruction isn't complicated—you bust up the drive into tiny little bits. Tools to accomplish this include drive shredders, drills, electromagnets, and degaussing tools (which reduce or remove the magnetic fields that store data on HDDs). Keep in mind that as hard drives advance and pack more data into smaller spaces, you'll need to break the hard drive into smaller pieces to prevent anyone from recovering your data.

Sanitizing your drive means that the hard drive will still function once the data has been destroyed. There are several more or less effective ways to do this.

The CompTIA A+ exams want you to know the difference between a standard format and a *low-level format*. You already learned about standard formatting back in Chapter 8, so how is low-level formatting different? With older drives (pre-1990s), low-level formatting would create the physical marks on the disk surface so that the drive knew where to store data; in the process, it erases the data from the drive. This was initially done at the factory, but utilities existed to repeat this operation later. As drives became more complex, hard drive manufacturers disabled the ability to perform low-level formats outside the factory.

Today, the term "low-level formatting" is often used to describe a *zero-fill* or *overwrite* operation. This process returns the drive to a state as close to like-new as possible by writing zeros to every location on the disk.

You can also use a *drive wiping* utility to erase any old, deleted data that hasn't been overwritten yet. Piriform's CCleaner is a data-sanitizing utility that can erase your Web browsing history, erase your recent activity in Windows (such as what programs you ran), and even scrub your hard drive's free space to make deleted files unrecoverable (see Figure 16.35).

Recycle

An important and relatively easy way to be an environmentally conscious computer user is to *recycle*. Recycling products such as paper and printer cartridges not only keeps them out of overcrowded landfills, but also ensures that the more

FIGURE 16.35 Piriform's CCleaner showing files to be removed

toxic products are disposed of in the right way. Safely disposing of hardware containing hazardous materials, such as computer monitors, protects both people and the environment.

Anyone who's ever tried to sell a computer more than three or four years old learns a hard lesson: they're not worth much, if anything at all. It's a real temptation to take that old computer and just toss it in the garbage, but never do that!

First of all, many parts of your computer—such as your computer monitor—contain hazardous materials that pollute the environment. Luckily, thousands of companies now specialize in computer recycling and will gladly accept your old computer. If you have enough computers, they might even pick them up. If you can't find a recycler, call your local municipality's waste authority to see where to drop off your system.

An even better alternative for your old computer is donation. Many organizations actively look for old computers to refurbish and to donate to schools and other organizations. Just keep in mind that the computer can be too old—not even a school wants a computer more than five or six years old.

Objective 16.03 Installing Windows into a Virtual Machine

The power of today's PC hardware enables you to install multiple operating systems that can function simultaneously on a single physical machine through a process called virtualization. In the simplest terms, *virtualization* is the process of using special software—a class of programs called *hypervisors* or *virtual machine managers (VMMs)*—to create a complete environment in which a guest operating system can function as though it were installed on its own computer. That guest environment is called a *virtual machine (VM)*.

There are two basic types of computers that handle virtual machines: hosted and bare metal. A hosted VM is installed on a computer that runs an operating system, such as Windows 7. I mentioned "Windows XP mode" earlier, right? That's a VM that runs on top of Windows 7 that in turn runs a fully functional version of Windows XP. Other typical hosted solutions include installing Oracle VirtualBox or VMWare Workstation.

A bare-metal VM manager doesn't really have an OS installed. It's a machine with all the tools for installing multiple VMs that you access over a network.

Purposes and Benefits of VMs

Going virtual enables companies to combine multiple servers onto fewer machines than in traditional computing. This offers tremendous savings in hardware purchases, electricity use, and the space used for computing.

Because a VM is only a single file or two, a hacked or corrupted server can rapidly be replaced with a snapshot (a backup) taken of the properly working server. This provides better uptime than in a traditional server setup. Likewise, the minimal file numbers makes it easy to duplicate a VM.

The capability to run many operating systems on a single physical machine makes multiplatform testing and research much easier and less costly than with traditional setups.

> **Exam Tip**
>
> Virtualized operating systems use the same security features as real operating systems. For each virtual machine user account, you'll need to keep track of user names, passwords, permissions, and so on, just like on a normal PC.

Emulation vs. Virtualization

Virtualization takes the hardware of the host system and segments it into individual virtual machines. If you have an Intel system, a hypervisor creates a virtual machine that acts exactly like the host Intel system. It cannot act like any other type of computer. For example, you cannot create on an Intel system a virtual machine that acts like a Sony PlayStation 3. Hypervisors simply pass the code from the virtual machine to the actual CPU.

Emulation is very different from virtualization. An *emulator* is software or hardware that converts the commands to and from the host machine into an entirely different platform. Figure 16.36 shows a Super Nintendo Entertainment System emulator, Snes9X, running a game called *Donkey Kong Country* on a Windows system.

FIGURE 16.36 Super Nintendo emulator running on Windows

Exam Tip

While the CompTIA A+ 220-802 exam objectives include emulation as a part of virtualization, the concepts are not the same. For the sake of completeness, however, know that emulating another platform (using a PC to run Sony PlayStation 3 games, for example) requires hardware several times more powerful than the platform being emulated.

Installation Process

Installing Windows in a virtual machine takes essentially only a few steps. First, you need to have the proper hardware to support the VM. Second, you boot to the hypervisor (on a bare-metal machine) or host OS. Third, on a hosted solution, you install and run virtual machine manager software, such as VMware Workstation. Fourth, you set up the virtual machine parameters. Finally, you install Windows into the VM, a process that almost precisely matches the installation process of Windows into a standalone machine.

Hardware

If you're going with a bare-metal solution—which is probably not covered on the CompTIA A+ 802 exam—you need to drop some serious cash on a dedicated VM server.

More likely, you're going to go with a hosted solution. That means you need a standard PC, though one with some serious resource muscle. You're about to add one or more "Windows machines" into a single PC, after all! Make sure the computer has a lot of RAM, a fast CPU (multicore is best), and enough hard drive space for however many VMs you're going to create. Because the VMs will share a network connection, you'll most likely want to go with Gigabit Ethernet rather than settle for a slower or wireless solution.

Boot to the Host and Load the VM Manager Software

In a bare-metal solution, both steps are the same thing. You'll usually power up the server with the hypervisor stored on something other than the server hard drives. VMWare's ESX, for example, is a tiny operating system/hypervisor that's usually installed on something like a USB-based drive. Figure 16.37 shows how I loaded my copy of ESX: via a small USB thumb drive. Power up the server; the server loads ESX off the thumb drive; and in short order, a very rudimentary

FIGURE 16.37 USB drive on server system

interface appears where I can input essential information, such as a master password and a static IP address.

On a standard hosted solution, you press the power button and let Windows load normally. Then you load the VMM like any other installed application—double-click the icon for the program.

Set Up VM Parameters

Once you're in the hypervisor or VMM, you can set the parameters for the VM. Since we're installing Windows here, check the requirements for a Windows machine and set up the VM accordingly. You'll determine how much RAM to use, HDD or SSD space to allocate, and more (see Figure 16.38).

Install the OS into the VM

Once you have a VM set up properly, you start the VM. Have an appropriate Windows setup media prepared. This can be a disc, a USB drive, or a network solution. All work fine in this scenario. The VM will go through POST like a standard computer does when starting up and then prompt for the installation media. Point the way and let Windows install. Slick!

New Virtual Machine Wizard x

Specify Disk Capacity
How large do you want this disk to be?

The virtual machine's hard disk is stored as one or more files on the host computer's physical disk. These file(s) start small and become larger as you add applications, files, and data to your virtual machine.

Maximum disk size (GB): 20

Recommended size for Ubuntu: 20 GB

◉ Store virtual disk as a single file

○ Split virtual disk into multiple files

 Splitting the disk makes it easier to move the virtual machine to another computer but may reduce performance with very large disks.

Pocket ACE size calculator

Help < Back Next > Cancel

FIGURE 16.38 Setting the virtual drive size

Objective 16.04 # Troubleshooting Installations and Upgrades

Y ou may be asking, "Troubleshooting installations? You mean I have to start troubleshooting Windows before I even have it installed?" Actually, the installation process itself almost never fails. Usually, something else fails during the process and is generally interpreted as an "installation failure." Let's look at some typical installation problems and how to correct them.

Text Mode Errors

If you're going to have an installation problem, this is the place to get one. It's always better to have the error right off the bat, as opposed to when the

installation is nearly complete. Text mode errors most often take place during clean installations and usually point to one of the following problems:

RAID Array Not Detected If Windows fails to detect a RAID array during the text mode portion of the Windows XP installation, this could be caused by Windows not having the proper driver for the hard drive or RAID controller. If the hard drives show up properly in the RAID controller setup utility, then it's almost certainly a driver issue. Get the driver disc from the manufacturer and run setup again. Press F6 when prompted very early in the Windows XP installation process. Nothing happens right away when you push F6, but later in the process you'll be prompted to install drivers.

No Boot Device Present when Booting Off the Startup Disk Either the startup disk is bad or the CMOS is not set to look at that disk drive first.

Windows Setup Requires XXXX Amount of Available Drive Space You forgot to format the C: drive, or there's a bunch of stuff on the drive already.

Not Ready Error on Optical Drive You probably just need to give the optical drive a moment to catch up. Press R for retry a few times. You may also have a damaged installation disc, or the optical drive may be too slow for the system.

A Stop Error (Blue Screen of Death) after the Reboot at the End of Text Mode This may mean you didn't do your homework in checking hardware compatibility, especially the BIOS. You'll read more about stop errors in Chapter 18, but if you encounter one of these errors during installation, check out the Microsoft Knowledge Base.

Graphical Mode Errors

Once the installation passes the text mode and moves into graphical mode, a whole new crop of problems may arise.

Hardware Detection Errors

Failure to detect hardware properly by any version of Windows Setup can be avoided by simply researching compatibility beforehand. Or, if you decided to skip that step, you might be lucky and have a hardware detection error involving only a noncritical hardware device. You can troubleshoot this problem at your leisure. In a sense, you are handing in your homework late, checking out compatibility and finding a proper driver after Windows is installed.

Every Windows installation depends on Windows Setup properly detecting the computer type (motherboard and BIOS stuff, in particular) and installing the correct hardware support. Microsoft designed Windows to run on several hardware platforms using a layer of software tailored specifically for the hardware, called the *hardware abstraction layer (HAL)*.

Can't Read CAB Files (Windows XP only)

This is probably the most common of all installation errors. *CAB (as in cabinet) files* are special compressed files, recognizable by the .cab file extension, that Microsoft uses to distribute copies of Windows (before Vista). If your system can't read them, first check the installation disc for scratches. Then try copying all the files from the source directory on the disc (\i386) into a directory on your local hard drive. Then run Windows Setup from there, remembering to use the correct program (winnt32.exe). If you can't read any of the files on the installation disc, you may have a defective drive.

Lockups During Installation

Lockups are one of the most challenging problems that can take place during installation because they don't give you a clue as to what's causing the problem. Following are a few things to check if you get a lockup during installation.

Smart Recovery, Repair Installation

Most system lockups occur when Windows Setup queries the hardware. If a system locks up once during setup, turn off the computer—literally. *Unplug the system.* Do *not* press CTRL-ALT-DEL. Do *not* click Reset. *Unplug it.* Then plug it back in, turn the system on, boot into Setup, and rerun the setup program. Windows will see the partial installation and either restart the installation process automatically (Smart Recovery) or prompt you for a "Repair Installation." Both of these look at the installation progress and complete the installation.

Optical Drive, Hard Drive

Bad optical discs, optical drives, or hard drives may cause lockups. Check the optical disc for scratches or dirt, and clean it up or replace it. Try a known good disc in the drive. If you get the same error, you may need to replace the drive.

Log Files

Windows generates a number of special text files called *log files* that track the progress of certain processes. While Windows creates a number of different log files for different purposes, only a few files most interest us:

- Setuplog.txt tracks the complete installation process, logging the success or failure of file copying, Registry updates, reboots, and so on.
- Setupapi.log tracks each piece of hardware as it is installed. This is not an easy log file to read, as it uses Plug and Play code, but it will show you the last device installed before Windows locked up.

Windows Vista and Windows 7 create about 20 log files each, organized by the phase of the installation. Each phase, however, creates a setuperr.log file to track any errors during that phase of the installation.

Windows stores these log files in the WINNT or Windows directory (the location in which the OS is installed). These OSs have powerful recovery options, so, honestly, the chances of you ever actually having to read a log file, understand it, and then get something fixed as a result of that understanding are pretty small. What makes log files handy is when you call Microsoft or a hardware manufacturer. They *love* to read these files, and they have people on staff who understand them. Don't worry about trying to understand log files for the CompTIA A+ certification exams; just make sure you know the names of the log files and their locations. Leave the details to the übergeeks.

No Installation Is Perfect

Even when the installation seems smooth, issues may slowly surface, especially in the case of upgrades. Be prepared to reinstall applications or deal with new functions that were absent in the previous OS. If things really fall apart, you can always go back to the previous OS.

The procedures laid out in this chapter may seem like a lot of work—how bad could it be to grab an installation disc, fling a copy of Windows onto a system, and, as the saying goes, let the chips fall where they may? Plenty bad, is how bad. Not only is it important that you understand these procedures for the CompTIA A+ certification exams, but they can save your hide once you're a working PC tech and you're tasked to install the latest version of Windows on the boss's new computer!

CHECKPOINT

✔**Objective 16.01: Preparing for Installation or Upgrade** Identify hardware requirements, making sure that your computer meets the recommended minimums for CPU, RAM, free hard disk space, video adapter, display, and other components. Check the Windows 7 Compatibility Center or use the Upgrade Advisor at the Microsoft Web site to verify that the Windows edition you're installing supports the hardware and application software you will run.

✔**Objective 16.02: Installing and Upgrading Windows XP, Vista, and 7**
Installing a modern OS follows standardized steps: insert disc, click at prompts, reboot a few times, and then run through essential post-installation steps, such as patching Windows and upgrading drivers.

✔**Objective 16.03: Installing Windows into a Virtual Machine** To install Windows into a virtual machine, you first create that virtual machine using some sort of hypervisor or virtual machine manager software, such as VMWare Workstation. If installed on a typical PC, the PC needs sufficient resources to handle the multiple operating systems simultaneously, so lots of RAM, hard drive space, CPU power, and network bandwidth. The benefits of virtualization are many: saving money, using less electricity, taking up less server space, and so on.

✔**Objective 16.04: Troubleshooting Installations and Upgrades** While the installation process itself rarely fails, you may encounter an installation failure caused by something else. Text mode errors during a clean installation may range from "No Boot Device Present" to a Stop Error (BSoD). Graphical mode errors indicate a different set of problems, such as a hardware detection error. If the system locks up during installation, do *not* press CTRL-ALT-DEL or the Reset button to restart the installation. Instead, unplug the system and then turn it back on; Windows will recover.

REVIEW QUESTIONS

1. Mary's Windows installation has failed. What file should she check to see what files failed to copy?

 A. install.log

 B. setup.log

 C. setup.txt

 D. setuplog.txt

2. If you do not complete the activation process for Windows 7, what will happen to your computer?

 A. Nothing. Activation is optional.

 B. The computer will work fine for 30 days and then Windows will be disabled.

 C. Microsoft will not know how to contact you to provide upgrade information.

 D. It will revert to Windows XP.

3. After you have completed a Windows installation and verified that the system starts and runs okay, what should you do next?

 A. Do nothing. You're through.

 B. Install *World of Warcraft* and enjoy.

 C. Install productivity applications and restore data.

 D. Install the latest service pack or updates along with any updated drivers.

4. If Windows locks up during the installation, what should you do?

 A. Press CTRL-ALT-DEL to restart the installation process.

 B. Push the Reset button to restart the installation process.

 C. Press the ESC key to cancel the installation process.

 D. Unplug the computer and restart the installation process.

5. When upgrading to Windows Vista Home Basic, from which edition of Windows can you perform an upgrade installation?

 A. Windows XP Professional

 B. Windows XP Home

 C. Windows 98

 D. Windows 2000

6. If you get an error message saying that the Setup program cannot read the CAB files, what should you do?

 A. Copy the CAB files from the Windows installation disc to your local hard drive and run the Setup program from there.

 B. Skip this step since the CAB files are not necessary to install Windows successfully.

 C. Go to the Microsoft Web site and download the latest version of the CAB file wizard.

 D. Cancel the installation process and keep your old operating system, since your hardware does not meet the minimum requirements.

7. If you are not sure your system can support Windows 7, what should you do?

 A. Consult the Windows Catalog.

 B. Use XP Mode instead.

 C. Run the Windows 7 Upgrade Advisor.

 D. Install Windows 7 and hope for the best, since it will probably work.

8. What is the minimum amount of RAM needed to run Windows Vista Business?

 A. 256 MB

 B. 512 MB

 C. 1 GB

 D. 4 GB

9. Which of the following processes provides Microsoft with contact information for the owner of a Windows license?

 A. EULA

 B. Microsoft Product Activation

 C. Registration

 D. Upgrade Advisor

10. If you plan a single-boot installation, which file system should you use?

 A. FAT

 B. FAT16

 C. FAT32

 D. NTFS

11. What priorities should be considered for a single PC supporting multiple VMs?

 A. High-end GPU, sound, cooling, media streaming

 B. RAM, hard drive space, CPU cores, Gigabit NIC

 C. Surround-sound audio, HDMI output, cooling, RAM

 D. Hard drive space, RAID array, file sharing, GPU

12. What process returns the drive to a state as close to like-new as possible by writing zeros to every location on the disk?

 A. Low-level format

 B. Degaussing

 C. Standard format

 D. Disk cloning

REVIEW ANSWERS

1. **D** Mary should check setuplog.txt.

2. **B** If you do not complete the activation process for Windows, the computer will work fine for 30 days and then Windows will be disabled. This is true for all versions of the OS covered in the CompTIA A+ exams.

3. **D** After you have completed a Windows installation and verified that the system starts and runs okay, you should install the latest service pack or updates along with any updated drivers.

4. **D** If Windows locks up during the installation, you should unplug the computer and restart the installation process.

5. **B** When upgrading to Windows Vista Home Basic, you can perform an upgrade installation only from Windows XP Home.

6. **A** If you get an error message that the Setup program cannot read the CAB files, you should copy the CAB files from the Windows installation disc to your local hard drive and run the Setup program from there.

7. **C** If you are not sure your system can support Windows 7, you should run the Windows 7 Upgrade Advisor.

8. **C** Windows Vista Business can install and run on a computer with 1 GB of RAM.

9. **C** Registration, rather than activation, provides Microsoft with personal details.

10. **D** NTFS is the logical answer here. None of the others provide any kind of local security.

11. **B** A PC running multiple VMs needs lots of RAM, hard drive space, CPU power, and network bandwidth.

12. **A** The term "low-level formatting" is often used to describe a zero-fill or overwrite operation.

Maintaining and Optimizing Windows

	NEWBIE	SOME EXPERIENCE	EXPERT
ETA	5 hours	3 hours	1.5 hours

You finally buy that shiny new convertible you always wanted, only to drive it through a puddle and get it covered in mud. But that's okay—all you need is a carwash. Likewise, an installed Windows operating system (OS) gets dirty once in a while, so it needs occasional maintenance and optimization. Microsoft has done such a good job with the latest versions of Windows that, out of the box, they are easy to optimize and maintain.

Objective 17.01 Maintaining Windows

To maintain Windows properly, you need to run various utilities periodically. This includes utilities for patching, managing users, cleaning up hard drives and the Registry, and keeping your security settings up to date.

Patches, Updates, and Service Packs

You must keep Windows patched and polished. All OSs have flaws, and Windows is no exception. The Internet has enabled Microsoft to make updates available, and the *Windows Update* program can grab those updates and patch user systems easily and automatically. Microsoft provides the Windows Update utility for all versions of Windows.

> ### Local Lingo
>
> **Patch management, service packs** The CompTIA A+ exams typically use the phrase *patch management* to describe the process of keeping a computer up to date on patches and service packs. A *service pack* is Microsoft's term for a group of patches collected into a single executable.

You can also start Windows Update manually. When your computer is connected to the Internet, start the utility at Start | All Programs | Windows Update. This either connects to the Microsoft Web site (XP) or opens the Windows Update Control Panel applet (Vista/7) and scans your computer to determine what updates may be needed. Within a few seconds or minutes, depending on your connection speed, you'll see a straightforward screen, like the one shown in Figure 17.1.

FIGURE 17.1 Microsoft Windows Update screen

You have several choices now. If in XP, you can click the Express button; Windows Update will grab any high-priority updates—these are security patches—and install them on your computer. If you click the Custom button, you can select from a list of optional updates (Figure 17.2). In Vista/7, click the important or optional updates link to install the two types of updates, respectively.

Automatic Updates

Updates are so important that Microsoft gives you the option of updating Windows automatically through the *Automatic Updates* feature. Actually, it nags you about it! Soon after installing Windows (a day or two, in my experience), a message balloon will pop up from the taskbar suggesting that you automate updates. If you click this balloon, the Automatic Updates Setup Wizard will run, enabling you to configure the update program.

In Windows XP, you can also right-click My Computer, choose Properties, click the Automatic Updates tab, and select Automatic Update options. In Vista/7 click the *Change settings* link in the Windows Update applet for options. Then, whenever your computer connects to the Web, it checks the

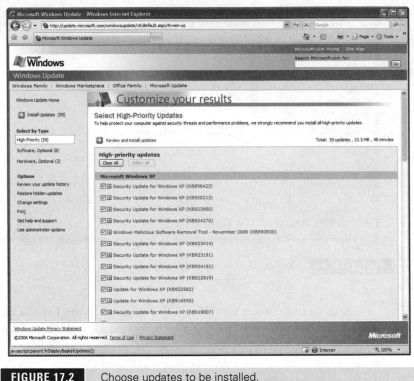

FIGURE 17.2 Choose updates to be installed.

Windows Update page. What happens next depends on the setting you choose. You have four choices:

- **Automatic (recommended)** Windows Update will keep your computer patched up and ready to go. This is the best option for most users, although it's not necessarily good for portable computer users. Nobody wants to log onto a slow hotel dial-up connection and have most of their bandwidth sucked away by Automatic Update downloading hot fixes!

- **Download updates for me** Windows Update downloads all patches in the background, and then, when they're complete, it tells you about them. You have the option at that point to install or not install.

- **Notify me** Windows Update simply flashes you a dialog box that tells you updates are available but it does not download anything until you say go. This is the best option for users of portable computers. You can download files when it's convenient for you, such as when you're home rather than traveling on business.

- **Turn off Automatic Updates** This does precisely what is advertised. You get neither automatic patches nor notifications that patches are available. Use this option only on a system that does not or cannot connect to the Internet. If you're online, your computer needs to be patched!

When Windows Update works the way Microsoft wants it to work, it scans the Microsoft Web site periodically, downloads patches as they appear, and then installs them on your computer. If you opt for the download but don't install option, Windows Update simply notifies you when updates are downloaded and ready to install (Figure 17.3).

Managing User Accounts and Groups

The most basic element of Windows security is the *user account*. Each user must present a valid user name and password to log on to a Windows computer. You can make this logon highly simplified, even invisible in some cases, but there is no exception to this rule. Each user is also a member of one or more *groups* of users. Groups enable the system administrator to assign the same rights and permissions to all members of the group without the need to set those rights and permissions individually.

Windows creates several built-in groups and user accounts during installation, including the Administrator and Guest accounts. When you install Windows, you supply the password for the Administrator account. This is the only usable account you have for logging on to the computer, unless you join the computer to a domain or create a new user account.

You can manage users and groups using the Local Users and Groups node in the Computer Management console, accessed by right-clicking My Computer/Computer and choosing Manage. Local Users and Groups can also be used on stand-alone computers, but there are simpler GUI tools for that purpose.

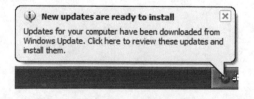

FIGURE 17.3 Windows Update balloon message

Managing Users in Windows XP

Windows XP provides the *User Accounts applet* in the Control Panel for basic user and group management, as mentioned in Chapter 15. Here you can create new users, delete users, change passwords, and so forth.

User Accounts hides the complete list of users, using a simplistic reference to account types that is actually a reference to its group membership. An account that is a member of the local Administrators group is said to be a Computer Administrator; an account that belongs only to the Local Users group is said to be a Limited account. Which users the applet displays depends on which type of user is currently logged on (see Figure 17.4). When an Administrator is logged on, she will see both types of accounts and the Guest account. A Limited user will see only his own account in User Accounts.

Windows XP requires you to create a second account that is a member of the Administrator's group during the initial Windows installation. This is for simple redundancy—if one administrator is not available or is unable to log on to the computer, another one can.

To create users, you need to provide a user name (a password can be added later), and you need to know which type of account to create: Computer Administrator or Limited. To create a new user in Windows XP, open the User Accounts applet from the Control Panel and click *Create a new account*. On the *Pick an account type* page (Figure 17.5), you can create either type of account. Simply

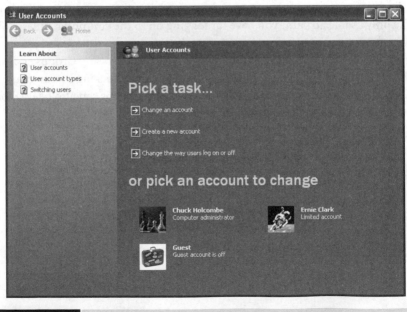

| **FIGURE 17.4** | User Accounts dialog box showing a Computer Administrator, a Limited account, and the Guest account (disabled) |

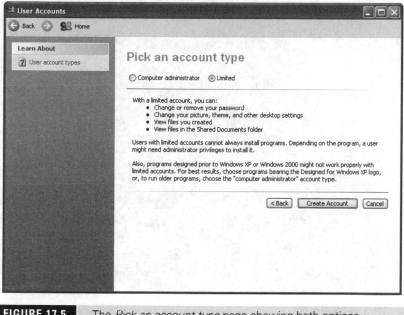

FIGURE 17.5 The *Pick an account type* page showing both options available

follow the prompts on the screen. After you have created your local accounts, you'll see them listed when you open the User Accounts applet. It will look something like Figure 17.6.

Head back to the User Accounts applet and look at the *Change the way users log on and off* option. Select it; you will see two check boxes (Figure 17.7). If you select the *Use the Welcome screen* check box, Windows will bring up the friendly Welcome screen shown in Figure 17.8 each time users log in. If this box is unchecked, you'll have to enter a user name and password.

The second option, *Use Fast User Switching,* enables you to switch to another user without logging off the currently running user. This is a handy option when two people actively share a system, or when someone wants to borrow your system for a moment but you don't want to close all your programs. This option is active only if you have the *Use the Welcome screen* check box enabled. If *Fast User Switching* is enabled, when you click the Log Off button on the Start menu, you get the option to switch users, as shown in Figure 17.9.

Managing Users in Windows Vista

Windows Vista changes user accounts and the applet used to create and modify them. Just as with Windows XP, you create three accounts when you set up a

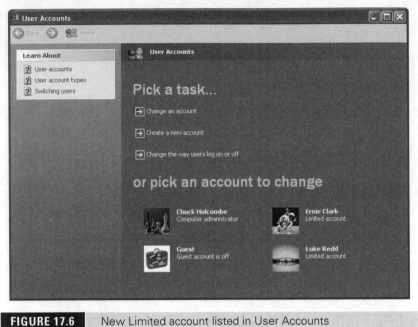

FIGURE 17.6 New Limited account listed in User Accounts

FIGURE 17.7 Select logon and logoff options.

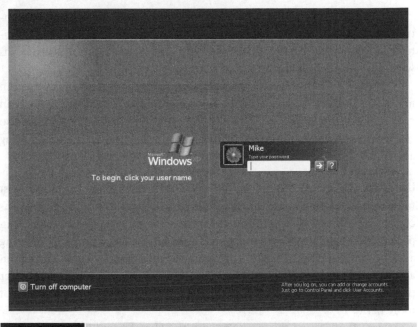

Single account logon screen

computer: guest, administrator, and a local account that's a member of the Administrators group. That's about where the similarities end.

To add or modify a user account, you have numerous options, depending on which Control Panel view you select and which edition and update of Vista you have installed. Most techs almost immediately change the Control Panel view to Classic, but even there the different versions of Windows—and whether you're logged into a workgroup or a domain—give you different versions of the User Accounts applet.

Switch User option

The Tasks options on the left are similar, with the addition of Parental Controls in the Home Premium edition, but the main options differ a lot. This chapter assumes a stand-alone machine, so we'll look more closely at the options with Vista Home Premium.

Windows Vista Home Premium uses Vista's version of the Welcome screen for logging in, so each user account has a picture associated with it. You can change the picture from the User Accounts applet (Figure 17.10). You can also change the name of the user account here and alter the account type, demoting an account from administrator to standard user, for example.

User Account Control　Windows XP made it too easy—and, in fact, almost necessary—to make your primary account on a computer an administrator account. Because limited users can't do common tasks, such as running certain programs, installing applications, installing devices such as printers, updating applications, updating Windows, and so on, most users simply created an administrator-level account and logged on. Such accounts have full control over the computer, so any malware that slipped in with the account could do a lot more harm.

Microsoft addressed this problem with the *User Account Control (UAC)*, a feature that enables standard users to do common tasks and provides a permissions dialog box when standard users *and* administrators do certain things that could potentially harm the computer (such as attempt to install a program). We'll discuss UAC in detail at the end of this chapter.

Parental Controls　With *Parental Controls,* an administrator account can monitor and limit the activities of any standard user in Windows Vista (and Windows 7), a feature that gives parents and managers an excellent level of control over the

FIGURE 17.10　User Accounts applet in Windows Vista

content their children and employees can access (see Figure 17.11). Activity Reporting logs applications run or attempted to run, Web sites visited or attempted to visit, any kind of files downloaded, and more. You can block various Web sites by typing a specific URL, or you can allow only certain Web sites, a far more powerful option.

Parental Controls enable you to limit the time that standard users can spend logged on. You can specify acceptable and unacceptable times of day when standard users can log on. You can restrict access both to types of games and to specific applications. If you like playing rather gruesome games filled with monsters and blood that you don't want your kids to play, for example, you can simply block any games with certain ESRB (Entertainment Software Rating Board) ratings, such as E for Everyone, T for Teen, or M for Mature or Mature 17+.

Managing Users in Windows 7

Windows 7 handles user creation in a manner very similar to Windows Vista, continuing the use of the User Accounts Control Panel applet. The Windows 7 applet is virtually identical to the one used in Windows Vista.

To create a user account, open the User Accounts applet and select *Manage another account* to see something like Figure 17.12.

FIGURE 17.11 Parental Controls

FIGURE 17.12 Manage Accounts

Click *Create a new account* to see your options for making a new account (see Figure 17.13). Note that this applet only enables you to make administrator accounts (in the Administrators group) or standard users (in the Users group).

FIGURE 17.13 Adding a new user

While smaller, less sophisticated systems can get away with putting all their users into one of these two groups, you'll need to turn to Local Users and Groups to take full advantage of the power of Windows' users and groups.

Passwords

Passwords are the ultimate key to protecting your computers. A user account with a valid password will get you into any system. Even if the user account has only limited permissions, you can still experience a security breach. Remember that, for a hacker, just getting into the network is half the battle.

Protect your passwords. Never give out passwords over the phone. If a user loses a password, an administrator should reset the password to a complex combination of letters and numbers, and then allow the user to change the password to something else. All of the stronger OSs have this capability.

Make your users choose good passwords. I once attended a security seminar where the speaker had everyone stand up. She then began to ask questions about our passwords—if we responded yes to the question, we were to sit down. She began to ask questions such as "Do you use the name of your spouse as a password?" and "Do you use your pet's name?" By the time she was done asking about 15 questions, only 6 out of some 300 people were still standing! The reality is that most of us choose passwords that are amazingly easy to hack. Make sure you use strong passwords: at least eight characters in length, including letters, numbers, and punctuation symbols.

Exam Tip

Keep in mind that using nonalphanumeric characters makes any password much more difficult to crack for two reasons. First, adding nonalphanumeric characters forces the hacker to consider many more possible characters than just letters and numbers. Second, most password crackers use combinations of common words and numbers to try to hack a password.

Because nonalphanumeric characters don't fit into common words or numbers, including a character such as an exclamation point will defeat these common-word hacks. Not all serving systems allow you to use characters such as $, %, or \, however, so you need to experiment to see if a particular server will accept them.

Resetting Forgotten Passwords in Windows Windows XP, Windows Vista, and Windows 7 enable currently logged-on users to create a *password reset disk* they can use if they forget a password. This is very important to have. If an administrator resets the password by using User Accounts or Local Users and

Groups, and you then log on with the new password, you will discover that you cannot access some items, including files you encrypted when logged on with the forgotten password. When you reset a password with a password reset disk, you can log on with the new password and still have access to files encrypted previously.

Best of all, with the password reset disk, users have the power to fix their own passwords. Encourage your users to create this disk; they have this power only if they create a password reset disk *before* they forget the password! If you need to create a password reset disk for a computer on a network (domain), search the Help system for "password reset disk" and follow the instructions for password reset disks for a computer on a domain.

Hard Drive Tools and Tasks

Keeping drives healthy and happy is a key task for every tech. Three tools help you accomplish this task: Error-checking, Disk Defragmenter, and Disk Cleanup. You learned about all three tools back in Chapter 8, so there's no need to recap here how to run them. Just run them regularly!

Registry Maintenance

Your Registry is a huge database that Windows updates every time you add a new application or hardware or make changes to existing applications or hardware. As a result, the Registry tends to be clogged with entries that are no longer valid. These usually don't cause any problems directly, but they can slow down your system. Interestingly, Microsoft does not provide a utility to clean up the Registry, but you can turn to a third-party utility. Quite a few Registry cleaner programs are out there, but my favorite is the freeware CCleaner by Piriform (Figure 17.14).

> **Travel Assistance**
>
> You can download the latest copy of CCleaner here: www.piriform.com/ccleaner.

Before you start cleaning your Registry with wild abandon, keep in mind that all Registry cleaners are risky because they may delete something you want in the Registry. Microsoft makes changes to the Registry for every version of Windows, so make sure your utility supports the Windows version you're running. This is especially true for any 64-bit version of Windows! I've used CCleaner for a while, and it has worked well for me—your experience may differ.

FIGURE 17.14 CCleaner

Travel Advisory

Remember to back up your Registry *before* you run any software that might modify (or break) something in it.

Security: Spyware/Antivirus/Firewall

You simply cannot run a computer today without having a large number of security programs installed to protect you from malicious attacks by spyware, malware, viruses, and hacking. In fact, the installation, monitoring, and updating of these programs (and possibly even hardware) are so important that they get their own chapter. Head to Chapter 22 for a complete discussion of how to keep your computer safe.

Objective 17.02 Optimizing Windows

Maintenance is about keeping Windows' performance from degrading with time and use. Of course, we don't just want to keep trouble at bay—we want to make our systems better, stronger, faster! Anything you do that improves

Windows, such as adding a piece of software or hardware to make something run better, is called an *optimization*.

Installing and Removing Software

The most common optimization performed on any PC is probably adding and removing applications. Installing and removing software is part of the normal life of any PC. Each time you add or remove software, you make changes and decisions that can affect the system beyond whatever the program does, so it pays to know how to do it correctly.

System Information

As you'll recall from Chapter 15, Windows comes with a handy built-in utility called *System Information* that collects information about hardware resources, components, and the software environment. When it finishes doing that, it provides a nice and tidy little report, helping you troubleshoot and diagnose any issues and conflicts. As they do regarding the many other tools you can access from the Start | Run or Start | Search dialog box, the CompTIA A+ certification exams refer to System Information by its executable, *msinfo32*.

Installing Software

Most application programs are distributed on optical discs (although this is slowly changing). Windows supports *Autorun,* a feature that enables the OS to look for and read a special file called—wait for it—autorun.inf. Immediately after a removable media device (optical disc or thumb drive) is inserted into your computer, whatever program is listed in autorun.inf runs automatically. Most application programs distributed on removable media have an Autorun file that calls up the installation program.

Sometimes, however, you need to institute the installation sequence yourself. Perhaps the installation disc lacks an Autorun installation program, or perhaps Windows is configured so that you must start programs on optical discs manually. In some cases, a disc may contain more than one program, and you must choose which of them to install. Regardless of the reason, a manual installation is a simple and straightforward process of using the Add or Remove Programs applet in the Control Panel in Windows XP.

Exam Tip
Windows 2000 called the applet *Add/Remove Programs.* The 802 competencies use that phrase, even though Windows 2000 is no longer covered. Don't be surprised by the old term on the exam.

Click the Add New Programs button (Figure 17.15), follow the prompts, and provide the media or location of the files. In Windows Vista and 7, Microsoft has replaced the Add or Remove Programs applet with Programs and Features, which does not have the Add New Programs feature.

If you have sufficient permissions to install an application—your account is an administrator account in Windows XP and up—the application will begin its installation routine. If you don't have sufficient permissions to install an application, Windows UAC (in Vista/7) will stop the installation.

Removing Software

Each installed application program takes up space on your computer's hard drive, and programs that you no longer need simply waste space that could be used for other purposes. Removing unnecessary programs can be an important piece of optimization.

You remove a program from a Windows PC in much the same way that you install it. That is, you use the application's own uninstall program when possible. You normally find the uninstall program listed under the application's icon on the Start menu, as shown in Figure 17.16.

If an uninstall program is not available, use the appropriate Windows Control Panel applet to remove the software. Figure 17.17 shows this applet in Windows Vista. You select the program you want to remove and click the Uninstall/Change button or Change/Remove button. Windows displays a message

FIGURE 17.15 Add new programs

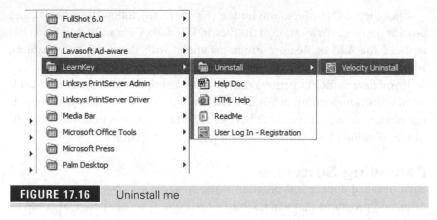

Uninstall me

warning you that the program will be permanently removed from your PC. If you're certain you want to continue, click Yes.

You may then see a message telling you that a shared file that appears to no longer be in use is about to be deleted and asking your approval. Generally speaking, it's safe to delete such files. If you do not delete them, they will likely be orphaned and remain unused on your hard drive forever. In some cases, clicking the Change/Remove button will start the application's install program (the one you couldn't find before) so that you can modify the installed features. This is a function of the program you're attempting to remove. The end result should be

Programs and Features applet

the removal of the application and all of its pieces and parts, including files and Registry entries.

Adding or Removing Windows Components

When you installed Windows, it tried to guess which optional Windows components you would need. It installed Notepad, modem support, and games on your computer. You can remove these Windows components from your system and add other components as well. If you're adding components, you'll need a copy of your Windows disc or another location where the Windows source files are stored. This task really hasn't changed from previous versions of Windows.

To add or remove a Windows XP component, open the Add or Remove Programs applet in the Control Panel. From here, select Add/Remove Windows Components, which opens the Windows Components Wizard (Figure 17.18). You can select an installed program, see how frequently it is used, how much disk space it uses, and (sometimes) the last time it was used.

In Windows Vista/7, open the Programs and Features applet in the Control Panel, and then click the *Turn Windows features on or off* option on the Tasks list. Click Continue if you're prompted by UAC, and you will be presented with the Windows Features dialog box. To toggle a feature on or off, simply click its check box. Unlike previous versions of Windows, you no longer need to have the installation disc to turn on features.

FIGURE 17.18 Windows Components Wizard in Windows XP

Installing/Optimizing a Device

The processes for optimizing hardware in each version of Windows are all very similar. The installation process is covered in every chapter of this book that deals with one type of device or another, so this section concentrates on the issues that fit best under optimization.

Exam Tip
Both CompTIA A+ certification exams test you on installing and optimizing devices.

Driver Updates

Device manufacturers occasionally update their device drivers. Most of these updates are intended to fix problems, but many updates incorporate new features. Whatever the case, when one of your devices gets an updated driver, it's your job to install it. Many devices have software that will ping the manufacturer periodically to see if new drivers are available. This is especially true about video cards. When you run Windows Update, Microsoft will also make some drivers available. Barring both those options, just check the manufacturers' Web sites for updates.

Any new device is also a good candidate for an update. When you buy that new cool toy for your system, make a point to head over to the manufacturer's Web site and see if any updates have come out since it was packaged for sale. That happens more often than you might think!

Driver Signing

Device drivers become part of the OS and thus have the potential to cause lots of problems if they're poorly written. To protect Windows systems from bad device drivers, Microsoft uses *driver signing,* which means that each driver has a digital signature. Any drivers included on the Windows installation media or at the Windows Update Web site are digitally signed. Once you have installed a driver, you can look at its Properties to confirm that it was digitally signed. Figure 17.19 shows a digitally signed network card driver.

When an unsigned driver is detected during hardware installation, you'll see the message shown in Figure 17.20, offering you the choice to stop or continue the installation. Signed drivers are more or less a sure thing, but that doesn't mean unsigned drivers are a problem—just consider the source of the driver and ensure that your device works properly after installation.

FIGURE 17.19 A digitally signed driver

You can control how Windows behaves when drivers are being installed. Click the Driver Signing button on the Hardware tab of the System Properties dialog box to display the Driver Signing Options dialog box shown in Figure 17.21. If you select Ignore, Windows will install an unsigned driver

FIGURE 17.20 Stop or continue installation of an unsigned driver

FIGURE 17.21 Driver Signing Options dialog box

without warning you. If you select Warn, you will be prompted when Windows detects an unsigned driver during driver installation, and you will be given the opportunity either to stop or continue the installation. Choosing Block will prevent the installation of unsigned drivers.

The default Driver Signing setting is Warn. This is also the default setting during installation, so you will always be warned when Windows detects an unsigned driver. This is no problem for a standard installation, when you are sitting at the computer, responding to all prompts—but it is a problem for automated, unattended installations. This is a good reason to check out all your device drivers before installing Windows. In 64-bit versions of Windows, all drivers must be signed. No exceptions. Microsoft wants to keep tight controls on the drivers to improve stability.

Device Manager

You've worked with Device Manager in other chapters when installing and troubleshooting devices; it's also the tool to use when you're optimizing device drivers. Right-click a device in Device Manager to display the context menu. From here you can update or uninstall the driver, disable the device, scan for hardware changes, or display the Properties dialog box. When you open the Properties dialog box, you'll see several tabs that vary according to the specific device. Most have General, Driver, Details, and Resources. The tab that matters most for optimization is the Driver tab.

The Driver tab has buttons labeled Driver Details, Update Driver, Roll Back Driver, and Uninstall. Driver Details lists the driver files and their locations on disk. Update Driver opens the Hardware Update Wizard—not very useful given

FIGURE 17.22 Rollback dialog

that the install programs for almost all drivers do this automatically. The Roll Back Driver option is a different story. It enables you to remove an updated driver, thus rolling back to the previous driver version. Rollback (Figure 17.22) is a lifesaver when you install a new driver and suddenly discover it's worse than the driver it replaced! Uninstall removes the driver.

> **Exam Tip**
>
> You can also use Device Manager to disable a troublesome device. Simply right-click the device and select *Disable*. To enable it again, select *Enable* from the same menu.

Adding a New Device

Windows should automatically detect any new device you install in your system. If Windows does not detect a newly connected device, use the Add Hardware Wizard (Figure 17.23) to get Windows to recognize the device and install drivers. You'll find it on the Hardware tab of the System Properties dialog box.

FIGURE 17.23 Add Hardware Wizard

Click Next on the Welcome screen, and the wizard will search for hardware that has been connected but does not yet have a driver installed. If it detects the device, select the device, and the wizard will install the driver. You may have to point to the source location for the driver files. If it does not detect the device, which is likely, it will ask you if the hardware is connected. When you answer yes and click Next, it will give you a list of installed hardware, similar to Figure 17.24.

If the device is in the list, select it and click Next. If not, scroll to the bottom and select Add a New Hardware Device, and then click Next. If the device is a printer, network card, or modem, select *Search for and install the hardware automatically* and click Next. In that case, once it detects the device and installs the driver, you're done. If you do see your device on the list, your best hope is to select *Install the hardware that I manually select from a list*. In the subsequent screens, select the appropriate device category, select the device manufacturer and the correct model, and respond to the prompts from the Add Hardware Wizard to complete the installation.

Performance Options in the System Applet

One optimization you can perform on all versions of Windows is setting *Performance Options*, which are used to configure CPU, RAM, and virtual memory (page file) settings. To access these options in Windows XP, right-click My Computer and select Properties, click the Advanced tab, and click the Settings button (Windows XP) in the Performance section of that tab. In Windows Vista/7, right-click Computer and select Properties; then click the *Advanced system settings*

FIGURE 17.24 List of installed hardware

option in the Tasks list. Click the Advanced tab and click the Settings button in the Performance section of that tab.

Exam Tip

You can also access the Performance Options through the Control Panel. Select the System applet and drill down as described in the preceding paragraph.

The Performance Options dialog box has three tabs: Visual Effects, Advanced, and Data Execution Prevention (Figure 17.25). In the Visual Effects tab, you can adjust visual effects that impact performance. Try clicking the top three choices in turn and watch the list of settings. Notice the tiny difference between the first two choices. The third choice, *Adjust for best performance,* turns off all

FIGURE 17.25 Windows Vista Performance Options dialog box

visual effects, and the fourth option is an invitation to make your own adjustments. If you're on a computer that barely supports Windows, turning off visual effects can make a huge difference in the responsiveness of the computer. For the most part, though, you should leave these settings alone.

The Advanced tab, shown in Figure 17.26, has three sections: Processor scheduling, Memory usage (Windows XP only), and Virtual memory. Under the Processor scheduling section, you can choose to adjust for best performance of either Programs or Background services. The Memory usage settings enable you to allocate a greater share of memory to programs or to the system cache. The Virtual memory section of this tab enables you to modify the size and location of the page file. Microsoft dropped the Memory usage settings option in Windows Vista and Windows 7.

Microsoft introduced *Data Execution Prevention (DEP)* with Windows XP Service Pack 2. DEP works in the background to stop viruses and other malware from taking over programs loaded in system memory. It doesn't prevent viruses from being installed on your computer, but it does make them less effective. By default, DEP monitors only critical OS files in RAM, but the Data Execution Prevention tab enables you to have DEP monitor all running programs. It works, but you'll take a performance hit. Like other options in the Performance Options dialog box, leaving the DEP settings as default is the best option most of the time.

FIGURE 17.26 Advanced tab of Performance Options dialog box

Hardware Profiles

Windows XP *hardware profiles* enable you to have Windows know when your portable PC is a stand-alone device or is connected to a docking station. In the latter circumstance, you'd want Windows to know immediately about all the extra hardware features available.

You can inspect hardware profiles by going to the System applet in the Control Panel, selecting the Hardware tab, and then clicking Hardware Profiles (see Figure 17.27). All Windows XP systems have one hardware profile by default.

There was a tremendous uproar from a small group of impassioned hardware profile fans when Microsoft decided to drop the feature from Windows Vista and Windows 7.

Resource Tracking

One big issue with optimization is knowing when something needs to be optimized. Let's say your Windows computer seems to be running slowly. Resource tracking is important for identifying the performance problem. You can use the Task Manager and Performance Console to figure out what (if anything) has become a bottleneck.

FIGURE 17.27 Default Hardware Profiles

Task Manager

The *Task Manager* has many uses. Most users are aware of only the Applications tab, which is used to shut down a troublesome program. For optimization purposes, Task Manager is a great tool for investigating how hard your RAM and CPU are working at any given moment and why. The quickest way to open the Task Manager is to press CTRL-SHIFT-ESC. Click the Performance tab to reveal a handy screen with the most commonly used information: CPU usage, available physical memory, the size of the disk cache, commit charge (memory for programs), and kernel memory (memory used by Windows). Figure 17.28 shows a system with a dual-core processor, which is why you see two screens under CPU Usage History. A system with a single-core processor would have a single screen.

Not only does Task Manager tell you how much CPU and RAM usage is occurring, but it also tells you what program is using those resources. Let's say your system is running slowly. You open Task Manager and see that your CPU usage is at 100 percent. You then click the Processes tab to see all the processes running on your system. Click the CPU column to sort all processes by CPU usage to see who's hogging the CPU (Figure 17.29). To shut off a process, just right-click the process and choose End Process. Many times, a single process will open many other processes. If you want to be thorough, click End Process Tree to turn off not only the one process, but also any other processes it started. You can also set the

FIGURE 17.28 Task Manager Performance tab

Windows Task Manager

File Options View Help

| Applications | Processes | Performance | Networking |

Image Name	User Name	CPU	Mem Usage
hl2.exe	michaels	99	8,096 K
WINWORD.EXE	michaels	00	17,172 K
Bridge.exe	michaels	00	86,072 K
Adobelm_Cleanup...	michaels	00	1,916 K
taskmgr.exe	michaels	00	5,336 K
dfrgntfs.exe	michaels	00	82,792 K
explorer.exe	michaels	00	17,584 K
iPodService.exe	SYSTEM	00	3,748 K
dfrgntfs.exe	michaels	00	19,508 K
Adobelmsvc.exe	SYSTEM	00	1,208 K
wcescomm.exe	michaels	00	3,752 K
ctfmon.exe	michaels	00	4,656 K
Adobelm_Cleanup...	michaels	00	1,908 K
Steam.exe	michaels	00	26,188 K
sapisvr.exe	michaels	00	6,656 K
wmiprvse.exe	NETWORK SERVICE	00	5,780 K
explorer.exe	michaels	00	16,784 K
mmc.exe	michaels	00	9,592 K
Adobelm_Cleanup...	michaels	00	1,912 K
iTunesHelper.exe	michaels	00	4,096 K

Processes: 52 CPU Usage: 50% Commit Charge: 762M / 6500M

FIGURE 17.29 CPU Usage

process priority by right-clicking the process and selecting from the Set Priority submenu. If you raise the priority of a process, Windows will allocate more resources to help improve its performance. If you lower its priority, performance for that process will worsen.

Local Lingo

Processes Every program that runs on your system is composed of one or more processes.

Task Manager Tabs Details The 802 exam will ask questions on various aspects of the Task Manager beyond just resource monitoring, especially on the more complex tool available in Windows Vista/7. This seems a good spot for some details. The Vista/7 Task Manager has six tabs. Each enables you to control or view running tasks:

- The *Applications* tab shows all the running applications on your system. If you're having trouble getting an application to close normally, this is the place to go.

- The *Processes* tab shows you every running process and, as mentioned earlier, enables you to kill those processes.

- The *Services* tab enables you to work directly with services, the small programs that control various components of Windows (such as printing, sharing files, and so on). Here, services can be stopped or started, and you can go to the associated process.

- You already know what the *Performance* tab enables you to see.

- The other two tabs in the Task Manager, *Networking* and *Users,* enable you to see network use at a glance and see which users' accounts are currently logged on to the local machine. The Networking tab is a good first spot to look if you think the computer is running slowly on the network.

The tasklist and taskkill Commands The two command line utilities *tasklist* and *taskkill* enable you to work with tasks, similarly to what you can do with the Task Manager. The tasklist command enables you to view running processes on a local or remote system. Open up a command prompt and type **tasklist**. The following is a partial example of the output:

```
C:\Users\mike>tasklist

Image Name                   PID Session Name       Session#    Mem Usage
=====================  =====  ============  ==========  ===========
System Idle Process            0 Services                    0         24 K
System                         4 Services                    0        940 K
smss.exe                     268 Services                    0        340 K
csrss.exe                    372 Services                    0      2,388 K
wininit.exe                  444 Services                    0        968 K
csrss.exe                    452 Console                     1      9,788 K
winlogon.exe                 500 Console                     1      2,420 K
services.exe                 544 Services                    0      4,536 K
svchost.exe                  756 Services                    0      4,320 K
MsMpEng.exe                  828 Services                    0     42,164 K
atiesrxx.exe                 904 Services                    0        824 K
notepad.exe                 3932 Console                     0      6,612 K
```

Exam Tip

The CompTIA A+ 802 exam objectives mention a command line utility called *tlist*. Tasklist replaced tlist back in Windows XP, but for some reason CompTIA included it anyway.

You can kill a process using the taskkill command. See the notepad.exe listing in the preceding tasklist output? You can kill the process using either the name or the process ID (PID), as shown here:

```
C:\>taskkill /pid 3932
SUCCESS: Sent termination signal to the process with PID 3932.
```

> ### Exam Tip
>
> You can use the *kill* command in the Windows PowerShell command line environment to stop a running process. The kill command is actually an alias for the Stop-Process cmdlet, although you don't need to know that for the exam.

Performance Console

Task Manager is good for identifying current problems, but what about problems that happen when you're not around? What if your system is always running at a CPU utilization of 20 percent—is that good or bad? Windows XP provides a tool called the *Performance console* that is used to log resource usage so that you can track items such as CPU and RAM usage over time. The Performance console is a Microsoft Management Console (MMC) file, *perfmon.msc*, so you start it from Start | Run or through the Performance icon in Administrative Tools. Figure 17.30 shows two nodes: System Monitor and Performance Logs and Alerts.

Objects and Counters To begin working with the Performance console, you need to understand two terms: *object* and *counter*. An *object* is a system component that is given a set of characteristics and can be managed by the OS as a single entity. A *counter* tracks specific information about an object. For example, the Processor object has a counter, %Processor Time, that tracks the

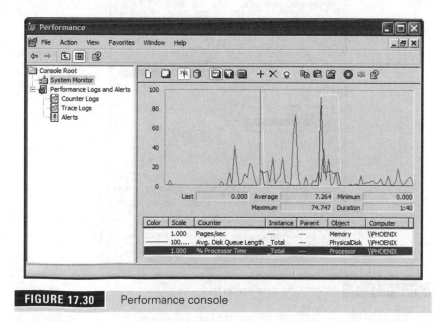

FIGURE 17.30 Performance console

percentage of elapsed time the processor uses to execute a nonidle thread. Many counters can be associated with an object.

System Monitor *System Monitor* gathers real-time data on objects such as memory, physical disk, processor, and network and displays this data as a graph (line graph), histogram (bar graph), or a simple report. Think of System Monitor as a more detailed, customizable Task Manager. When you first open the Performance console, the System Monitor shows data in graph form. The data displayed is from the set of three counters listed below the chart. If you want to add counters, click the Add button (the one that looks like a plus sign) or press CTRL-I to open the Add Counters dialog box. Click the Performance object drop-down list and select one of the many different objects you can monitor. The Add Counters dialog box includes a helpful feature: you can select a counter and click the Explain button to learn about the counter (see Figure 17.31). Try that now.

Even with just three counters selected, the graph can get a little busy. That's where one of my favorite System Monitor features shines. If you want the line of charted data from just one counter to stand out, select the counter in the list below the graph and then press CTRL-H. See how this trick makes the %Processor

FIGURE 17.31 Add Counters dialog box

FIGURE 17.32 Pressing CTRL-H makes one set of data stand out.

Time line stand out in Figure 17.32? Imagine how useful that would be when you are monitoring a dozen counters.

Performance Logs and Alerts The *Performance Logs and Alerts* snap-in enables Windows to create a written record of just about anything that happens on your system. Do you want to know if someone is trying to log onto your system when you're not around? The following procedure works in Windows XP.

To create the new event log, right-click Counter Logs and select New Log Settings. Give the new log a name—in this example, "Unauthorized Accesses." Click OK, and a Properties box for the new log will open, similar to that shown in Figure 17.33.

To select counters for the log, click Add Counters and then select the *Use local computer counters* radio button. Select Server from the Performance object pull-down menu, and then select Errors Logon from the list of counters; click Add and then Close.

Back in the Properties box for your new log, click the Schedule tab and set up when you want this thing to start running—probably at the end of the workday today. Then select when it should stop logging—probably tomorrow morning when you start work. Click the Log Files tab to see where the log file will be saved—probably C:\PerfLogs—and make a note of the filename. The filename

FIGURE 17.33 Creating a new performance log

will consist of the name you gave the log and a number. In this example I named the new performance log "Unauthorized Accesses," so the filename is *Unauthorized Accesses_000001.blg*.

When you come back in the morning, open the Performance console, select Performance Logs and Alerts, and then select Counter Logs. Your log should be listed on the right. The icon by the log name will be green if the log is still running or red if it has stopped. If it has not stopped, select it and click the stop button (the one with the black square). See Figure 17.34.

To view the log, open the Performance console, select System Monitor, change to Report view, and load the file as a new source using the properties box.

Performance Tools in Windows Vista and Windows 7

Microsoft improved on the Performance console dramatically with Reliability and Performance Monitor in Windows Vista and yet again with Performance Monitor in Windows 7. *Reliability and Performance Monitor* still has a complete Performance console with all the objects and counters you see in Windows XP, but it adds an excellent Resource Overview, a Reliability Monitor tool, and a much more flexible way to use counters with Data Collector Sets and Reports.

FIGURE 17.34 Stopping the performance log

Performance Monitor in Windows 7 functions almost identically to Reliability and Performance Monitor in Windows Vista, but Microsoft pulled out the Reliability tool to make the remaining tool smaller and tighter.

You can open Reliability and Performance Monitor/Performance Monitor by starting the Performance Information and Tools applet in Control Panel. The initial screen is the *Rate and improve your computer's performance* screen (see Figure 17.35), which shows how your computer's hardware stacks up in the Windows Experience Index. Click the Advanced tools link in the left task area. Then click Open Reliability and Performance Monitor or Open Performance Monitor, depending on the Windows version. You can also open the tool by going to Start | Search bar, typing **perfmon.msc**, and pressing ENTER.

FIGURE 17.35 Performance Information and Tools showing the computer's rating on the Windows Experience Index

Reliability and Performance Monitor in Windows Vista opens to a Resource Overview screen (see Figure 17.36). Think of the Resource Overview as an advanced Task Manager, giving details on CPU, hard drive, network, and memory usage.

When you click one of the four bars, you get details on exactly which processes are using those resources—a powerful tool when you suspect a program might be hogging something! Figure 17.37 shows the Network bar opened to reveal the processes using the network and how much data each is sending.

Travel Advisory

The Reliability Monitor tool gives you an overview of how a PC has behaved over time, showing important events such as application or OS crashes. You can find the tool in Windows 7 as part of the Action Center Control Panel applet.

Performance Monitor in Windows 7 opens to a more modest screen that displays some text about Performance Monitor and a System Summary (see Figure 17.38). You can get to the Overview screen by clicking the Open

FIGURE 17.36 Resource Overview in Windows Vista

FIGURE 17.37 Network bar in Resource Overview

FIGURE 17.38 Initial Performance Monitor screen in Windows 7

Resource Monitor link on the main screen. Aside from orienting the graphical screens on the right rather than on the top, the tool is the same as the Resource Overview in Windows Vista (see Figure 17.39).

The Performance Monitor option you can select under Monitoring Tools in either version of the OS is simply a re-creation of the Performance console and works as described earlier for Windows XP (see Figure 17.40). This is a great tool for quick checks on specific counters.

Microsoft included *Data Collector Sets* in Reliability and Performance Monitor and Performance Monitor, groupings of counters you can use to make reports. You can make your own Data Collector Sets (User Defined) or you can just grab one of the predefined system sets. Once you start a Data Collector Set, you can use the Reports option to see the results (see Figure 17.41). Data Collector Sets not only enable you to choose counter objects to track, but also enable you to schedule when you want them to run.

FIGURE 17.39 Resource Monitor displaying CPU usage

FIGURE 17.40 Reliability and Performance Monitor

Exam Tip

The CompTIA A+ exams aren't going to ask too many detailed questions on either Performance Monitor or Reliability and Performance Monitor. That doesn't mean you can ignore these amazing tools! Make sure you understand that these tools give you the power to inspect anything happening on your system to help you diagnose problems.

Tools for Programmers

Earlier in the book, I discussed many of the tools available under Administrative Tools in Control Panel. I left out two applets that I want to discuss now for two reasons: first, because they're covered on the CompTIA A+ 220-802 exam, and second, because they deal with some low-level functionality in Windows that affects how a lot of applications are programmed. Read on to find out more about the Component Services and Data Sources (ODBC) applets.

FIGURE 17.41 Sample report

Component Services

To understand all that *Component Services* can do would require a huge amount of information—far greater than the scope of CompTIA's A+ exams. Simply put, as long as Windows has existed, Microsoft has come up with many tools (with names like COM, DCOM, and COM+) to enable programmers to share data objects (an element of programs) between applications on a single computer. Over time, this sharing was extended so that you could share objects among computers on a network.

In almost all cases, this object sharing doesn't require you to do anything more than install an application that uses these features. Component Services is there, however, for those very rare times when something's either wrong or a programmer needs you to make manual changes (see Figure 17.42). If you have

FIGURE 17.42 Component Services in Windows 7

a company that creates in-house applications or buys custom applications, there's a better-than-good chance that you'll be firing up Component Services and working with programmers, manually installing programs, and tweaking those programs to get them to work the way you wish. Professional, third-party applications (the kind you buy in stores) should automatically configure any of these programs during the installation process, making it extremely rare that you'll need to go into Component Services.

Every version of Windows has Component Services, but there's no ready-to-go icon in Windows XP or Windows Vista. You'll need to make a custom MMC and load Component Services from there.

Data Sources

One of the oldest and most common motivations to make networks is the idea of a number of computers accessing one or more shared databases. These computers might not all be running the same operating system, nor will they always use the same application to access those databases. That's where Open Database Connectivity (ODBC) really shines. ODBC is a coding standard that enables programmers to write databases and the applications that use them in a way that

they can query ODBC to see how to locate and access a database without any concern about what application or operating system is used.

Microsoft's tool to configure ODBC is called *ODBC Data Source Administrator* (see Figure 17.43). Data Source Administrator enables you to create and manage entries called Data Source Names (DSNs) that point ODBC to a database. DSNs are used by ODBC-aware applications to query ODBC to find their databases. Keep in mind that you'll rarely go into Data Source Administrator unless you're making your own shared databases.

Preparing for Problems

As part of optimizing Windows, techs need to prepare for problems. You must have critical system files and data backed up and tools in place for the inevitable glitches. Different versions of Windows enable you to prepare for problems differently. Microsoft seems to separate backups into certain types: backing up personal data, backing up local copies of critical system state information, backing up a small amount of very critical system information on some form of removable media, and providing some way to use backups if your system won't boot. Let's look at all of these.

FIGURE 17.43 Data Source Administrator in Windows 7

Back Up Personal Data

The most important data on your computer is personal data: your documents, e-mail messages and contacts, Web favorites, photographs, and other files. To handle backing up personal data, every version of Windows comes with some form of backup utility. There are big differences between the backup that comes with Windows XP compared to the backup utility that comes with Vista (and the one that comes with Windows 7 is different still), so let's break up the idea of backing up personal data between Windows versions.

Backup Utility for Windows XP (ntbackup)

Windows XP's *Backup Utility* (popularly known by the name of the executable program, *ntbackup*) provides almost all the tools you need to back up files and folders. It has come a long way from its origins in Windows NT. The ntbackup program supports a greater variety of devices, enabling you to back up to network drives, local drives, tape, and removable disks (but not optical discs). Most folks, however, still turn to third-party utilities to create system, e-mail, browser, and personal data backups.

Travel Advisory

The Backup Utility is not included in the default installation of Windows XP Home. You must install it manually from the Windows disc.

You can start ntbackup by navigating from the Start menu to Accessories | System Tools, or by clicking the Backup Now button on the Tools page of the local disk Properties box. I prefer to start it from Start | Run with the command **ntbackup**. Click the Backup Wizard button to run the Backup Wizard. To use the Windows XP version in Advanced Mode, click Advanced Mode on the opening screen (Figure 17.44). To have it always open in Advanced Mode, deselect the *Always start in wizard mode* check box. If the program is in Advanced Mode and you want to run it as a wizard, click the Wizard Mode link to open the Backup or Restore Wizard.

To create a backup, start the Backup Utility, click Advanced Mode, and choose the Backup tab.

1. Check the boxes next to the drives and files you want to include in the backup.

2. To include your system state information, such as Registry and boot files (which you should do), click the *System State* check box.

FIGURE 17.44 The opening screen of the Backup or Restore Wizard

3. To specify where to put the backup file you're creating, either type the path and filename in the *Backup media or file name* box or click Browse, select a location, type the filename, and click Save.

4. Click Start Backup.

5. Choose whether you want to append this backup to a previous one or overwrite it.

6. Click Advanced to open the Advanced Backup Options dialog box, select *Verify data after backup,* and click OK.

7. Click Start Backup again. A dialog box shows you the utility's progress.

8. When it finishes, click Close and then close the Backup Utility.

The Backup Utility gives you three choices after you click Advanced Mode: Backup Wizard (Advanced), Restore Wizard (Advanced), and a third choice that is very important. The third option in Windows XP is the *Automated System Recovery Wizard* (Figure 17.45).

Tape Backup The odd fact that Microsoft did not update Windows XP's Backup or Restore Wizard to enable you to back up to optical discs of any sort kept alive the practice of tape backups. Tape drives connect to the Advanced Technologies Attachment (ATA) or small computer systems interface (SCSI) bus, just like optical drives, but rather than using a shiny optical media disc, you have to back up to magnetic tape (Figure 17.46).

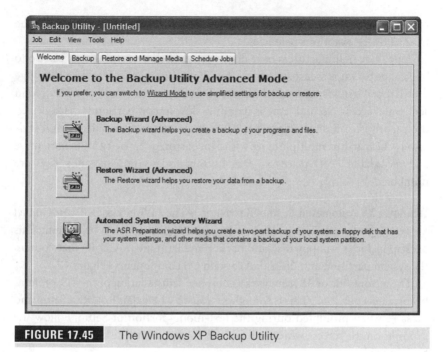

FIGURE 17.45 The Windows XP Backup Utility

There are a large number of different tape formats, but CompTIA lists only one technology, Digital Linear Tape (DLT), in the CompTIA A+ Acronyms list. DLT was a popular tape format from the 1980s up to the early 2000s, with capacities from 10 MB in the early versions up to (arguably) around 800 GB. DLT is

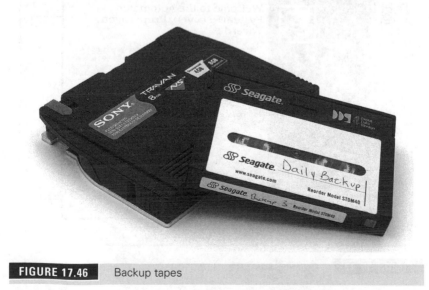

FIGURE 17.46 Backup tapes

rarely used anymore, and CompTIA should have removed this from the CompTIA A+ exam competencies.

Tape drive manufacturers have done pretty much everything they can do to make tape backups as fast as possible, but the technology suffers from two huge drawbacks: First, it's tape, which means all data must be stored and restored in sequential access. Second, tape is painfully slow in comparison to hard drives, optical drives, or flash-media drives. The only great benefit to tape is that it's relatively cheap to buy multiple tapes with a lot of storage capacity. With hard drive and recordable DVD prices at rock bottom today, though, tape's days are numbered.

Windows XP Automated System Recovery The Windows XP *Automated System Recovery (ASR)* enables you to create a backup of your system. This backup includes a floppy disk and backup media (tape or CD-R) that contain the system partition and disks that contain OS components (Figure 17.47).

The restore side of ASR involves a complete reinstallation of the OS, preferably on a new partition. This is something you do when all is lost. Run Setup and press F2 when prompted during the text-mode portion of Setup. Follow the prompts on the screen, which will first ask for the floppy disk and then for the backup media.

FIGURE 17.47 Creating an ASR backup

Travel Advisory

Restoring an ASR backup will format your boot and system partition(s). Make sure you have a recent backup before proceeding with this worst-case scenario.

Backup and Restore Center for Vista/7

One of the many changes between XP and Vista was the replacement of ntbackup with the Windows Backup and Restore Center. If you open this program, you'll notice that you have four options: back up some files, back up everything, restore the files you backed up, or restore everything (Figure 17.48).

You can back up your files in two ways: back up specific files or back up the entire computer. *Back up files* gives you a choice of the file types you want to back up (Figure 17.49). *Back up computer* backs up the entire computer—every single file and folder. Vista doesn't support tape backups, and you cannot choose between differential or incremental backups. If you want these options, you need to buy a third-party backup tool.

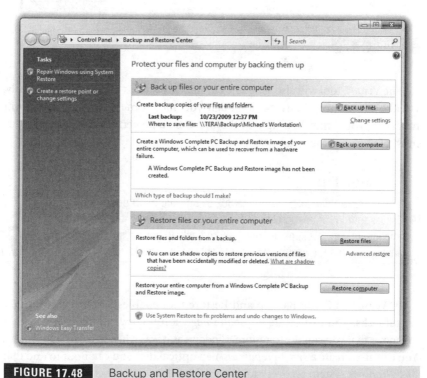

FIGURE 17.48 Backup and Restore Center

FIGURE 17.49 Back Up Files dialog box

The Vista/7 tool will also schedule automatic backups of your files on a daily, weekly, or monthly basis. So although you lose some of the options from ntbackup, you'll find Backup and Restore to be a powerful tool that works for most of your backup needs.

Exam Tip

Look for *scheduled backups* on the 802 exam. Microsoft doesn't discuss timing for best practices for scheduling backups, but does recommend full backups. I would say to back up your system at least once a month. Weekly would probably be appropriate too.

In Windows 7, the Backup and Restore tool enables you to do two other useful tasks. You can create a *system image*, a full copy of the drives used in Windows that you can use to restore Windows as it was when you made the image. You can also create a *system repair disk*, an optical disc you can boot to and that has Windows system recovery tools on it. You should make one right now.

System Restore

Every technician has war stories about the user who likes to add the latest gadget and cool software to his computer. Then he's amazed when things go very, very wrong: the system locks up, refuses to boot, or simply acts weird. This guy also can't remember what he added or when. All he knows is that you should be able to fix it—fast.

This is not news to the folks at Microsoft, and they have a solution to this problem. It's called *System Restore,* and they first introduced it in Windows Me, with further refinements in Windows XP. The System Restore tool enables you to create a *restore point,* a copy of your computer's configuration at a specific point in time. If you later crash or have a corrupted OS, you can restore the system to its previous state.

Here's how to create a restore point:

1. Go to Start | All Programs | Accessories | System Tools | System Restore.

2. When the tool opens, select *Create a restore point* and then click Next (Figure 17.50).

3. Type in a description on the next screen. There's no need to include the date and time because the System Restore adds them automatically.

4. Click Create and you're finished.

FIGURE 17.50 Create a restore point

System Restore in Windows Vista/7 is much more automatic, with the OS making a number of restore points automatically. To make your own restore point, go to System Properties, select System Protection, and then click the Create button, as shown in Figure 17.51.

If you click the System Restore button, you might be surprised at how many system restore points are already made for you (Figure 17.52). In most cases, one of these is all you'll need to return your system to an earlier point.

The System Restore tool creates some of the restore points in time automatically. For instance, by default, every time you install new software, XP creates a restore point. Thus, if installation of a program causes your computer to malfunction, simply restore the system to a point in time prior to that installation, and the computer should work again.

During the restore process, only settings and programs are changed. No data is lost. Your computer includes all programs and settings as of the restore date. This feature is absolutely invaluable for overworked techs. A simple restore fixes many user-generated problems.

FIGURE 17.51 Creating a manual System Restore in Windows 7

System Restore

Restore your computer to the state it was in before the selected event

How do I choose a restore point?

Current time zone: Central Daylight Time

Date and Time	Description	Type
4/10/2012 4:53:15 PM	Windows Update	Critical Update
4/9/2012 8:46:32 AM	Windows Update	Critical Update
4/5/2012 11:32:53 AM	Windows Update	Critical Update
4/2/2012 9:25:32 AM	Installed Raw Therapee V4.0.7.1 x64	Install
4/2/2012 8:51:22 AM	Windows Update	Critical Update
3/26/2012 9:23:14 AM	Windows Update	Critical Update

☑ Show more restore points

Scan for affected programs

< Back Next > Cancel

FIGURE 17.52 Restore points in Windows 7

Here's how to restore to a previous time point:

1. Start the System Restore Wizard by choosing Start | All Programs |
 Accessories | System Tools | System Restore.

2. Select the first radio button, *Restore my computer to an earlier time,* and
 click Next. Figure 17.53 shows a calendar with restore points. Any day
 with a boldface date has at least one restore point. These points are
 created after you add or remove software or install Windows updates
 and during the normal shutdown of your computer.

3. Select a date on the calendar; then select a restore point from the list on
 the right and click Next.

FIGURE 17.53 Calendar of restore points

The last screen before the system is restored shows a warning. It advises you to close all open programs and reminds you that Windows will shut down during the restore process. It also states that the restore operation is completely reversible. Thus, if you go too far back in time, you can restore to a more recent date.

You don't have to count on the automatic creation of restore points. You can open System Restore at any time and simply select *Create a restore point.* Consider doing this before making changes that might not trigger an automatic restore point, such as directly editing the Registry.

System Restore is turned on by default and uses some of your disk space to save information on restore points. To turn System Restore off or change the disk space usage, open the System Properties applet in Control Panel and select the System Restore tab. Then click Settings to open the Settings dialog box (Figure 17.54).

System Properties ? X

General	Computer Name	Hardware	Advanced
System Restore		Automatic Updates	Remote

System Restore can track and reverse harmful changes to your computer.

☐ Turn off System Restore on all drives

Drive settings

To change the status of System Restore or the maximum amount of disk space available to System Restore on a drive, select the drive, and then click Settings.

Available drives:

Drive	Status	
(C:)	Monitoring	Settings...
(D:)	Monitoring	

Drive (C:) Settings ? X

(C:) Monitoring

(C:) is the system drive. You cannot turn off System Restore on this drive without turning it off on all drives. To do this, click OK or Cancel to return to the System Restore tab.

Disk space usage

Move the slider to the right to increase or to the left to decrease the amount of disk space for System Restore. Decreasing the disk space may reduce the number of available restore points.

Disk space to use:

Min ━━━━━━━━━━━━⬤━━━━ Max

12% (1835 MB)

[OK] [Cancel]

FIGURE 17.54 System Restore tab in System Properties applet

CHECKPOINT

✔**Objective 17.01: Maintaining Windows** It is important that you keep Windows updated with the latest security patches from Microsoft. Each Windows computer user must log on with a valid user name and password. User accounts enable a system administrator to set permissions for users and to audit their access to files and network resources. Keep the hard drive running properly by regularly running Error-checking, Disk Defragmenter, and Disk Cleanup.

✔**Objective 17.02: Optimizing Windows** Removing applications that are no longer needed is an important part of housekeeping. When possible, use the uninstall program that came with the application. You can add or remove Windows components as needed. Installing the proper driver for a hardware device is essential. You can find the driver on the discs that come with the device, at Microsoft's Web site, or at the Web site of the device manufacturer. To protect Windows systems from bad device drivers, Microsoft uses *driver signing*. The Device Manager is one of the most important tools for checking hardware, drivers, and resources. Resource tracking can help solve performance problems. The Task Manager and Performance tools help identify bottlenecks. Several tools enable you to prepare for possible problems: System Restore, the Backup Utility, and the Automated System Recovery (Windows XP only).

REVIEW QUESTIONS

1. Which tool in Windows Vista would you use to back up your essential system files?

 A. System Restore

 B. Backup and Restore Center

 C. Windows Update

 D. Automated System Recovery

2. Phil tried to install a printer on his Windows machine, but found he didn't have permission. What could be the problem? (Select two.)

 A. Phil is logged on with a Limited account.

 B. Phil is logged on as a Standard User.

 C. Phil is logged on as a Local Administrator.

 D. Phil is logged on as Guest.

3. Mary wants to get a quick snapshot of her System Resources on a Windows XP Home machine. How does she get to the appropriate tool?

 A. Start | Run | Perfmon

 B. Start | Control Panel | Administrative Tools | Performance

 C. Start | All Programs | Accessories | System Resources

 D. Press CTRL-ALT-DEL once and click the Performance tab

4. What tool should Bill use to put his computer's configuration back to a specific point in time?

 A. System Restore

 B. Performance console

 C. System Resource Meter

 D. Task Manager

5. Sven loaded a new video card on his system, but now everything looks very bad. What should he do first?

 A. Go to Event Viewer and check the log.

 B. Go to Device Manager.

 C. Go to the printed manual.

 D. Call tech support.

6. Which of the following passwords will probably be the most secure?

 A. MaryEllen

 B. MEO2144

 C. M-21e44w

 D. MikeM

7. Which of the following should be your first choice to remove an application that you no longer need?

 A. Delete the program files.

 B. Use the uninstall program that came with the application.

 C. Use the Add or Remove Programs applet or the Programs and Features applet.

 D. Use the Registry Editor to remove references to the application.

8. Diane complains that her system seems sluggish and she keeps running out of disk space. What tool can you use to get rid of unnecessary files and compress older files? Select the best answer.

 A. Disk Cleanup

 B. Disk Doctor

 C. File Manager

 D. Registry Cleaner

9. Which of the following commands opens the System Information tool?

 A. msconfig

 B. msinfo

 C. msinfo32

 D. mscnfg32

10. When performing automatic updates, Windows uses which feature to download additional updates for other Microsoft products?

 A. Software notifications

 B. msinfo32

 C. Windows Update

 D. Registry

REVIEW ANSWERS

1. **B** The Backup and Restore Center in Windows Vista is used for backing up essential files (or all files).

2. **A D** Phil needs to be logged on as an Administrator or Standard User, not a Limited account or Guest.

3. **D** Mary should press CTRL-ALT-DEL once and click the Performance tab.

4. **A** System Restore is the tool Bill needs.

5. **B** Always go to Device Manager first when hardware goes awry.

6. **C** The combination of letters, numbers, and nonalphanumeric characters, along with a length of eight characters, makes M-21e44w the strongest password.

7. **B** Use the uninstall program that came with the application.

8. **A** Diane can use Disk Cleanup to get rid of unnecessary files and compress older files.

9. **C** Type **msinfo32** at the Start | Run or Start | Search box to open the System Information tool.

10. **C** When performing automatic updates, Windows uses Windows Update to download additional updates for other Microsoft products.

Troubleshooting Windows

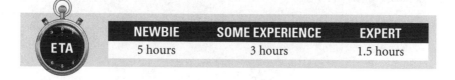
	NEWBIE	SOME EXPERIENCE	EXPERT
ETA	5 hours	3 hours	1.5 hours

You know about Disk Management, Device Manager, Event Viewer, and more. You've spent countless hours preparing systems for disaster with Windows Backup and System Restore. While learning about the tools, you also learned how to use them. This section puts it all together and shows you a plan to deal with potential disasters for a Windows computer.

This section looks at Windows problems from the ground up. It starts with catastrophic failure—a PC that won't boot—and then discusses ways to get past that problem. The next section covers the causes and workarounds when the Windows GUI fails to load. Once you can access the GUI, the world of Windows diagnostic and troubleshooting tools that you've spent so much time learning about is at your fingertips. First, though, you have to get there.

Objective 18.01 Troubleshooting Windows Boot Problems

When Windows fails to boot, you need to determine whether the problem relates to hardware or software. You'll recall from Chapter 8 that a hard drive needs proper connectivity and power, and that CMOS must be configured correctly. If not, you'll get an error like the one in Figure 18.1. We'll look more closely at these sorts of scenarios in the first part of this section as a refresher.

```
Operating System not found
-
```

FIGURE 18.1 If you see this screen, the problem is with hardware. Windows hasn't even started trying to boot.

But after the drive powers on and the POST completes successfully, the computer tries to boot to an OS. Failure at *this* point gives you an entirely different set of errors, such as *NTLDR is missing* or *BOOTMGR is missing* (see Figure 18.2). You need a totally different set of tools from the ones used to troubleshoot hardware or CMOS issues. Windows XP and Windows Vista/7 boot differently, so to troubleshoot these failures to boot, you need to know both the processes and the tools available. We'll look at this type of scenario in the second part of this section.

Failure to Boot: Hardware or Configuration

Most failed boot scenarios require you to determine where the fault occurred: with the hardware and configuration, or in Windows. This is a pretty straightforward problem. Imagine that a user calls and says, "My PC won't boot" or "My computer is dead." At this point, your best tools are knowledge of the boot process and asking lots of questions. Here are some I use regularly:

"What displays on the screen—if anything—after you press the power button on the case?"

"What do you hear—if anything—after you press the power button on the case?"

"Is the PC plugged in?"

"Do you smell anything weird?"

```
BOOTMGR is missing
Press Ctrl+Alt+Del to restart
_
```

FIGURE 18.2 Scary error

Hardware problems can give you a blank screen on bootup, so follow the tried and true troubleshooting methodology for hardware. Make sure everything is plugged in and turned on. If the PC is new, as in less than 30 days old, you know it might have suffered a burn-in failure. If the customer smells something, one of the components might have fried. Try replacing with known good devices: RAM, power supply, CPU, hard drive, motherboard.

If the user says that the screen says "No boot device detected" and the system worked fine before, it *could* mean something as simple as the computer has attempted to boot to an incorrect device, such as to something other than the primary hard drive. This scenario happens all the time. Someone plugs a thumb drive into a USB port and CMOS is configured to boot to removable media before hard drives. The first few times it happened to me, I nearly took my machine apart before experiencing that head-slapping moment. I removed the thumb drive and then watched Windows boot normally.

Exam Tip

The CompTIA A+ 802 exam objectives list "Invalid boot disk" as a symptom of a Windows problem, but it's more typical of a CMOS or hardware issue.

Failure to Boot: Windows XP

Windows boot errors take place in those short moments between the time POST ends and the *Loading Windows* screen begins. For Windows XP to start loading the main operating system, the critical system files ntldr, ntdetect.com, and boot.ini must reside in the root directory of the C: drive, and boot.ini must point to the Windows boot files. In a scenario where any of these requirements isn't in place, the system won't get past this step. Here are some of the common error messages you see at this point:

- No Boot Device Present
- NTLDR Bad or Missing
- Invalid BOOT.INI

Notice that these text errors take place early in the startup process. That's your big clue that you have a boot issue. If you get to the Windows splash screen and then it locks up, that's a whole different ballgame, so know the difference.

> **Exam Tip**
>
> The 802 exam uses three generic error options that require almost identical steps to troubleshoot and repair: missing NTLDR, missing Boot.ini, and missing operating system. Follow the steps outlined in this section and in the Windows Vista/7 failure to boot section if you run into one of these scenarios.

If you get one of the catastrophic error messages and you're running Windows XP, it takes a three-level process to get back up and running.

1. You first should attempt to repair the installation.

2. If that fails, attempt to restore from a backup copy of Windows.

3. If restore is either not available or fails, your only recourse is to rebuild. You will lose data at the restore and rebuild phases, so you definitely want to spend a lot of energy on the repair effort first!

If you're running Vista or 7, the repair process for boot failures is exactly the same as a failure to load the GUI. Read about the System Recovery Options in the next section to see what you need to do.

Attempt to Repair Using a Repair Installation

Windows XP has a repair option included with the installation CD, called a *repair installation*, that will overwrite critical system files with clean versions and leave your data, Registry, and programs intact. It doesn't always work, but it's worth the shot.

Boot to the CD and get to the Welcome to Setup screen (see Chapter 16 for the screens). Windows will have detected that you have a version of Windows installed already and prompt you to either set up or repair through the Recovery Console. Press ENTER on this screen to begin the setup process; don't press R for the Recovery Console. Keep going, accepting the EULA. You'll get to another screen that shows the existing Windows partition and prompts you to repair. Let Windows do its installation thing (45 to 60 minutes) and hope for the best. If that doesn't work, move on to the Recovery Console.

Attempt to Repair Using Recovery Console

The *Recovery Console* is a text-based startup of Windows that gets you to a command prompt similar to the Windows command prompt. It has all sorts of tools for repairing Windows.

Boot to the Windows XP CD-ROM. You can start the Recovery Console by running Setup, selecting Repair, and then selecting Recovery Console. You will see a message about ntdetect, another one that the Recovery Console is starting up, and then you will be greeted with the following message and command prompt:

```
Microsoft Windows XP<TM> Recovery Console.
The Recovery Console provides system repair and recovery functionality.
Type Exit to quit the Recovery Console and restart the computer.

1: C:\WINDOWS
Which Windows XP installation would you like to log onto
<To cancel, press ENTER>?
```

The cursor is a small, white rectangle sitting to the right of the question mark on the last line. If you are not accustomed to working at the command prompt, this may be disorienting. If only one installation of Windows XP is on your computer, type the number 1 at the prompt and press the ENTER key. If you press ENTER before typing in a valid selection, the Recovery Console will cancel and the computer will reboot. The only choice you can make in this example is 1. Having made that choice, the only change to the screen is a new line, followed by the cursor:

```
Type the Administrator password:
```

Enter the Administrator password for that computer and press ENTER. The password does not display on the screen; you will see asterisks in place of the password. The screen still shows everything that has happened so far, unless something has happened to cause an error message. It now looks like this:

```
Microsoft Windows XP<TM> Recovery Console.
The Recovery Console provides system repair and recovery functionality.
Type Exit to quit the Recovery Console and restart the computer.

1: C:\WINDOWS
Which Windows XP installation would you like to log onto
<To cancel, press ENTER>? 1
Type the Administrator password: ********
C:\Windows>
```

By now, you've caught on and know that a rectangular prompt is located immediately after the last line. Now what do you do? Use the Recovery Console commands, of course. Recovery Console uses many of the commands that work in the Windows command line interface, as well as some uniquely its own. Table 18.1 lists the common Recovery Console commands.

TABLE 18.1	Common Recovery Console Commands
Command	**Description**
attrib	Changes attributes of selected file or folder
cd (or chdir)	Displays current directory or changes directories
chkdsk	Runs CheckDisk utility
cls	Clears screen
copy	Copies from removable media to system folders on hard disk; no wildcards
del (or delete)	Deletes service or folder
dir	Lists contents of selected directory on system partition only
disable	Disables service or driver
diskpart	Replaces FDISK—creates/deletes partitions
enable	Enables service or driver
extract	Extracts components from CAB files
fixboot	Writes new partition boot sector on system partition
fixmbr	Writes new master boot record for partition boot sector
format	Formats selected disk
listsvc	Lists all services on system
logon	Enables you to choose which Windows installation to log on to if more than one
map	Displays current drive letter mappings
md (or mkdir)	Creates a directory
more (or type)	Displays contents of text file
rd (or rmdir)	Removes a directory
ren (or rename)	Renames a single file
systemroot	Makes current directory system root of drive into which you're logged
type	Displays a text file

The Recovery Console shines in the business of manually restoring Registries, stopping problem services, rebuilding partitions (other than the system partition), and extracting copies of corrupted files from a CD-ROM or floppy disk.

Using the Recovery Console, you can reconfigure a service so that it starts with different settings, format drives on the hard disk, read and write on local FAT or NTFS volumes, and copy replacement files from a floppy or CD-ROM. The Recovery Console enables you to access the file system and is still constrained by the file and folder security of NTFS, which makes it a more secure tool to use than some third-party solutions.

The Recovery Console is best at fixing three items: repairing the MBR, reinstalling the boot files, and rebuilding boot.ini. Let's look at each of these.

A bad boot sector usually shows up as a No Boot Device error. If it turns out that this isn't the problem, the Recovery Console command to fix it won't hurt anything. At the Recovery Console prompt, type **fixmbr**. This fixes the MBR.

The second problem the Recovery Console is best at fixing is missing system files, usually indicated by the error NTLDR Bad or Missing. Odds are good that if ntdlr is missing, so are the rest of the system files. To fix this, get to the root directory and type the following line: **copy d:\i386\ntldr**. Then type this line: **copy d:\i386\ntdetect.com**.

This takes care of two of the big three and leads us to the last issue, rebuilding boot.ini. If the boot.ini file is gone or corrupted, run this command from the Recovery Console: **bootcfg /rebuild**. The Recovery Console will then try to locate all installed copies of Windows and ask if you want to add them to the new boot.ini file it's about to create. Say yes to the ones you want.

If all goes well with the Recovery Console, do a thorough backup as soon as possible (just in case something else goes wrong). If the Recovery Console does not do the trick, the next step is to restore Windows XP.

Attempt to Restore

If you've been diligent about backing up, you can attempt to restore to an earlier, working copy of Windows. Assuming you made an Automated System Recovery (ASR) backup, this will restore your system to a previously installed state, but you should use it as a last resort. You lose everything on the system that was installed or added after you created the ASR disk. If that's the best option, though, follow the steps outlined earlier in the chapter.

Local Lingo

Restore To use the Windows XP System Restore, you need to be able to get into Windows. *Restore* in the context used here means to give you an option to get into Windows.

Exam Tip

Windows 2000 offered a version of the repair tool that had you create an Emergency Repair Disk (ERD) floppy disk. For some reason, CompTIA included this term/item in the 802 competencies, even though it no longer exists.

Rebuild

If you're faced with a full system rebuild, you have several options, depending on the particular system. You could simply reboot to the Windows CD-ROM and install right on top of the existing system, but that's usually not the optimal solution. To avoid losing anything important, you'd be better off swapping the C: drive for a blank hard drive and installing a clean version of Windows.

Most OEM systems come with a misleadingly named *Recover CD* or *factory recovery partition*. The Recover CD is a CD-ROM that you boot to and run. The factory recovery partition is a hidden partition on the hard drive that you activate at boot by holding down a key combination specific to the manufacturer of that system. (See the motherboard manual or users' guide for the key combination and other details.) Both "recover" options do the same thing—restore your computer to the factory-installed state. If you run one of these tools, you will wipe everything off your system—all personal files, folders, and programs will go away! Before running either tool, make sure all important files and folders are backed up on an optical disc or spare hard drive.

Failure to Boot: Windows Vista and Windows 7

Two critical boot files risk corruption in Windows Vista and Windows 7, bootmgr and bcd, both of which you can fix with one tool, bcdedit. You can use this tool in the Windows Recovery Environment.

WinPE and the Death of the Recovery Console

With Windows Vista, Microsoft upgraded the installation environment from the 16-bit text mode environment used in every previous version of Windows to 32- and 64-bit. This upgrade enabled the Windows installation process to go graphical and support features such as a mouse pointer and clickable elements, rather than relying on command line tools. Microsoft calls the installation environment the *Windows Preinstallation Environment* (*WinPE* or *Windows PE*).

With Windows PE, you can boot directly to the Windows DVD. This loads a limited-function graphical operating system that contains both troubleshooting and diagnostic tools, along with installation options. The Windows installation media is called a *Live DVD* because WinPE loads directly from disc into memory and doesn't access or modify the hard drive.

> **Travel Advisory**
>
> Although here I discuss only how WinPE helps boot repair, know that WinPE goes much further. WinPE can assist unattended installations, network installations, and even booting diskless workstations on a network.

When you access Windows PE and opt for the troubleshooting and repair features, you open a special set of tools called the *Windows Recovery Environment* (*WinRE* or *Windows RE*). The terms can get a little confusing because of the similarity of letters, so mark this: Windows RE is the repair tools that run within Windows PE. WinPE powers WinRE. Got it? Let's tackle WinRE.

> **Exam Tip**
>
> Microsoft also refers to the Windows Recovery Environment as the *System Recovery Options menu*. It's unclear as of this writing which label CompTIA will use.

Enter Windows RE

It would be unfair to say that the Windows Recovery Environment only replaces the Recovery Console. WinRE includes an impressive, powerful set of both automated and manual utilities that collectively diagnose and fix all but the most serious of Windows boot problems. Although WinRE does all the hard work for you, you still need to know how to access and use it. When faced with a failure-to-boot scenario in Windows Vista or Windows 7, WinRE is one of your primary tools.

Getting to Windows RE

In Windows 7, you can access WinRE in three ways. (See the Exam Tip for Windows Vista options.) First, you can boot from the Windows installation media and select *Repair*. Second, you can use the *Repair Your Computer* option on the Advanced Boot Options (F8) menu (see Figure 18.3). Third, you can create a system repair disc before you have problems. Go to Control Panel | System and Security | Backup and Restore and select *Create a system repair disc*, which opens the dialog box shown in Figure 18.4.

```
                    Advanced Boot Options

Choose Advanced Options for: Windows 7
(Use the arrow keys to highlight your choice.)

    Repair Your Computer

    Safe Mode
    Safe Mode with Networking
    Safe Mode with Command Prompt

    Enable Boot Logging
    Enable low-resolution video (640x480)
    Last Known Good Configuration (advanced)
    Directory Services Restore Mode
    Debugging Mode
    Disable automatic restart on system failure
    Disable Driver Signature Enforcement

    Start Windows Normally

Description: View a list of system recovery tools you can use to repair
             startup problems, run diagnostics, or restore your system.

ENTER=Choose                                                ESC=Cancel
```

FIGURE 18.3 Selecting Repair Your Computer in the Advanced Boot Options menu

FIGURE 18.4 Making a system repair disc in Windows 7 (using a Blu-ray Disc combo drive)

> ### Exam Tip
>
> Windows Vista does not have the Repair Your Computer option on the Advanced Boot Options menu. You can either use a Windows installation media or, if you have SP1 or later, make a bootable system repair disc.

Although any of these methods works fine, I recommend that you access WinRE from the Windows installation media for three reasons:

- The hard drive can be so messed up that you won't make it to the Advanced Boot Options menu.
- Accessing WinRE using the Repair Your Computer option in the Advanced Boot Options menu requires a local administrator password.
- Using a bootable disc enables you to avoid any malware that might be on the system.

Using Windows RE

No matter how you choose to access the Windows Recovery Environment, the main menu looks the same (see Figure 18.5). You have five options in WinRE:

- Startup Repair
- System Restore
- System Image Recovery (Windows 7) or Windows Complete PC Restore (Vista)
- Windows Memory Diagnostic (Tool) (only Vista includes "Tool" in the name)
- Command Prompt

The name of the third option differs between Windows 7 and Windows Vista, though the intent—rebuilding from a backup—is the same. I'll talk about how these options differ a little later in the chapter.

> ### Exam Tip
>
> Make sure you know how to access the Windows Recovery Environment and what each of the available tools does.

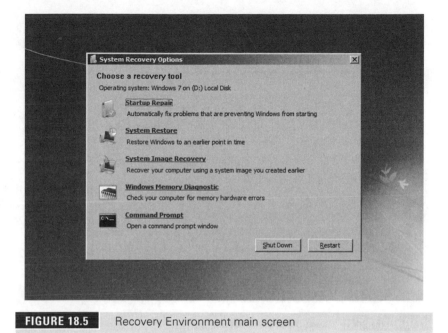

FIGURE 18.5 Recovery Environment main screen

Startup Repair The *Startup Repair* utility serves as a one-stop, do-it-all option (see Figure 18.6). When run, it performs a number of repairs, including the following:

- Repairs a corrupted Registry by accessing the backup copy on your hard drive
- Restores critical system and driver files
- Runs the equivalent of the Recovery Console's fixboot and fixmbr
- Rolls back any nonworking drivers
- Uninstalls any incompatible service packs and patches
- Runs chkdsk
- Runs a memory test to check your RAM

Startup Repair fixes almost any Windows boot problem. In fact, if you have a system with one hard drive containing a single partition with Windows Vista or Windows 7 installed, you'd have trouble finding something it *couldn't* fix. Upon completion, Startup Repair shows the screen shown in Figure 18.7.

Note the link in Figure 18.7 that says *View diagnostic and repair details*. This opens a text file called srttrail.txt that lists exactly what the program found,

FIGURE 18.6 Startup Repair in action

FIGURE 18.7 Startup Repair complete; no problems found

what it fixed, and what it failed to do. It may look cryptic, but you can type anything you find into Google for more information. I've reproduced the beginning of the (very long) srttrail.txt file here:

```
Startup Repair diagnosis and repair log
---------------------------
Last successful boot time: 7/14/2012 2:37:43 AM (GMT)
Number of repair attempts: 6

Session details
---------------------------
System Disk = \Device\Harddisk0
Windows directory = C:\Windows
AutoChk Run = 0
Number of root causes = 1

Test Performed:
---------------------------
Name: Check for updates
Result: Completed successfully. Error code =  0x0
Time taken = 32 ms

Test Performed:
---------------------------
Name: System disk test
Result: Completed successfully. Error code =  0x0
Time taken = 0 ms
```

Travel Advisory

The *View advanced options for system recovery and support* link simply returns you to the main screen.

In Windows 7, Startup Repair starts automatically if your system detects a boot problem. If you power up a Windows system and see the screen shown in Figure 18.8, Windows has detected a problem in the startup process.

Personally, I think this menu pops up way too often. If you fail to shut down your computer properly, for example, this menu appears. In this case, you can save time by booting normally. When in doubt, however, go ahead and run Startup Repair. It can't hurt anything.

A powerful tool like Startup Repair still doesn't cover everything. You may have specific needs that require more finesse than a single, do-it-all approach. In many cases, you've already discovered the problem and simply want to make a single fix. You might want to perform a system restoration or check the memory. For this, we'll need to explore the other four options available in WinRE.

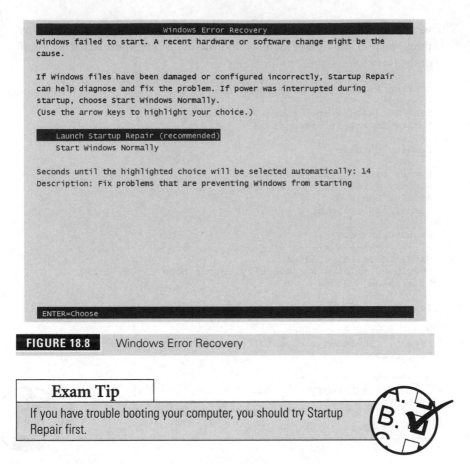

```
                        Windows Error Recovery
Windows failed to start. A recent hardware or software change might be the
cause.

If Windows files have been damaged or configured incorrectly, Startup Repair
can help diagnose and fix the problem. If power was interrupted during
startup, choose Start Windows Normally.
(Use the arrow keys to highlight your choice.)

     Launch Startup Repair (recommended)
       Start Windows Normally

Seconds until the highlighted choice will be selected automatically: 14
Description: Fix problems that are preventing Windows from starting

ENTER=Choose
```

FIGURE 18.8 Windows Error Recovery

Exam Tip

If you have trouble booting your computer, you should try Startup Repair first.

System Restore As you'll recall from Chapter 17, *System Restore* does the same job here it has done since Microsoft first introduced it in Windows Me, enabling you to go back to a time when your computer worked properly. Placing this option in Windows RE gives those of us who make many *restore points*—snapshots of a system at a given point of time—a quick and handy way to return our systems to a previous state (see Figure 18.9).

System Image Recovery/Windows Complete PC Restore Windows 7's backup tools differ from Windows Vista's. Note Figure 18.10, which shows the Windows Vista Recovery Environment menu on the left next to the Windows 7 Recovery Environment on the right. The third WinRE option differs. Windows Vista uses the Windows Complete PC Restore utility, whereas Windows 7 includes the System Image Recovery tool.

With an image in hand, you can use the Windows Complete PC Restore/ System Image Recovery tool to restore your system after a catastrophe.

System Restore

Restore your computer to the state it was in before the selected event

How do I choose a restore point?

Current time zone: GMT-8:00

Date and Time ▼	Description	Type
2/19/2010 11:37:54 AM	Automatic Restore Point	System
11/10/2009 7:59:00 PM	Installed VMware Tools	Install
11/10/2009 2:06:08 PM	Windows Update	Critical Update

☐ Show more restore points Scan for affected programs

< Back Next > Cancel

FIGURE 18.9 System Restore points

If you have the drive containing the system image plugged in when you first run the wizard, it should detect your latest backup and present you with the dialog box shown in Figure 18.11. If it doesn't list a system image or it lists the wrong one, you can select an image from another date on the same disk or even a remote network share.

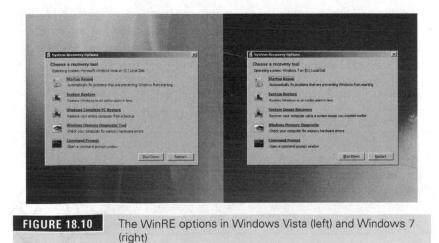

FIGURE 18.10 The WinRE options in Windows Vista (left) and Windows 7 (right)

FIGURE 18.11 Selecting a system image

After you select the image you want to restore, the utility presents you with a few more options, as shown in Figure 18.12. Most importantly, you can choose to format and repartition disks. With this option selected, the utility wipes out the existing partitions and data on all disks so the restored system will get the same partitions that the backed-up system had.

After you click Finish on the confirmation screen (see Figure 18.13), which also contains a final warning, the restore process begins (see Figure 18.14). The utility removes the old system data and then copies the backed-up system image to the hard drive(s). Once the process completes, your system reboots and should start up again with all of your data and programs just where you left them when you last backed up.

Exam Tip

The CompTIA A+ 802 exam objectives use the phrase *recovery image,* which conflates separate tools in Windows 7. You can use Backup and Restore to create a system image and a system repair disc. You can use the system repair disc to get to the System Image Recovery that uses the system image on the second disc to write a "fixed" or previously working version of Windows 7 to the hard drive. Got all that?

FIGURE 18.12 Additional restore options

FIGURE 18.13 Confirming your settings

FIGURE 18.14 Restoring your computer

Windows Memory Diagnostic (Tool) Bad RAM causes huge problems for any operating system, creating scenarios where computers get Blue Screens of Death (BSoDs), system lockups, and continuous reboots. Starting with Windows Vista, Microsoft added a memory tester to the Windows Recovery Environment. When you click the Windows Memory Diagnostic (Tool) link from the main WinRE screen, it prompts you to *Restart now and check for problems (recommended)* or *Check for problems the next time I start my computer* (see Figure 18.15). It doesn't really matter which option you choose, but if you think you need to test the system's RAM, that probably means you should do it now.

Once you restart, your system immediately starts running the Windows Memory Diagnostics Tool, as shown in Figure 18.16. While the program runs, you can press F1 to see the Memory Tester options (see Figure 18.17).

The tool lists three important Test Mix options at the top of the screen: Basic, Standard, and Extended. *Basic* runs quickly (about one minute) but performs only light testing. *Standard,* the default choice, takes a few minutes and tests more aggressively. *Extended* takes hours (you should let it run overnight), but it will very aggressively test your RAM.

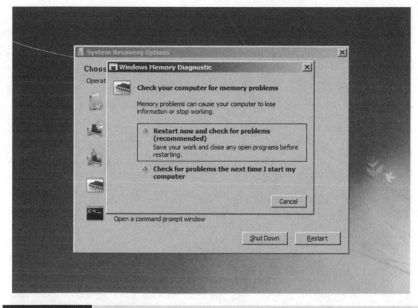

FIGURE 18.15 Windows Memory Diagnostic screen

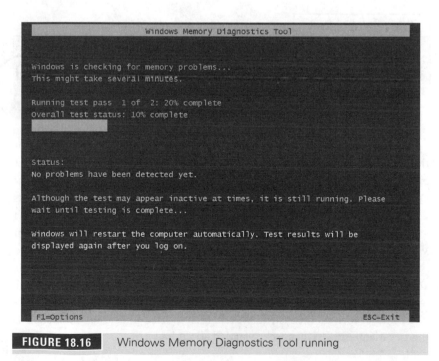

FIGURE 18.16 Windows Memory Diagnostics Tool running

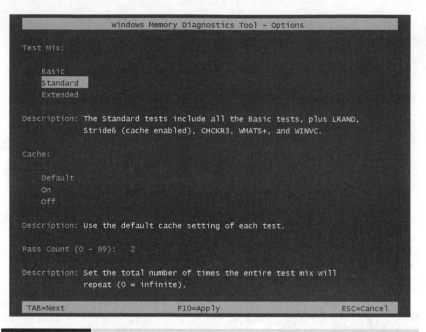

```
                  Windows Memory Diagnostics Tool - Options

Test Mix:

    Basic
    Standard
    Extended

Description: The Standard tests include all the Basic tests, plus LRAND,
             Stride6 (cache enabled), CHCKR3, WMATS+, and WINVC.

Cache:

    Default
    On
    Off

Description: Use the default cache setting of each test.

Pass Count (0 - 99):   2

Description: Set the total number of times the entire test mix will
             repeat (0 = infinite).

 TAB=Next                    F10=Apply                    ESC=Cancel
```

FIGURE 18.17 Windows Memory Diagnostics Tool options

Travel Advisory

You can also find the Windows Memory Diagnostic Tool in the Control Panel under System and Security | Administrative Tools, or start it from an administrative command prompt using the **mdsched** command.

This tool includes two other options: Cache and Pass Count. The *Cache* option enables you to set whether the tests use the CPU's built-in cache as well as override the default cache settings for each test type. Simply leave Cache set at Default and never touch it. *Pass Count* sets the number of times each set of tests will run. This option defaults to 2.

After the tool runs, your computer reboots normally. You can open Event Viewer to see the results (see Figure 18.18).

Sadly, I've had rather poor results with the Windows Memory Diagnostic Tool. We keep lots of bad RAM around the labs here at Total Seminars, and, when put to the test, we were unable to get this tool do anything other than give us a BSoD or lock up the system. We still turn to tried-and-tested tools such as the free Memtest86+ when we're worried about bad RAM.

FIGURE 18.18 Event Viewer results

Travel Assistance

You can find out more about Memtest86+ at www.memtest.org.

Command Prompt The last, most interesting, and easily nerdiest option in the WinRE menu is Command Prompt. Unlike the Recovery Console, the WinRE command prompt is a true 32- or 64-bit prompt that functions similarly to the regular command prompt. WinRE's command prompt, however, includes an important utility (bootrec) that you can't find in the regular command prompt. The WinRE command prompt also lacks a large number of the command prompt tools you'd have in a regular Windows command prompt (though all the important ones remain). Let's begin by looking at the bootrec command. After that, we'll look at some other utilities that the WinRE command prompt offers.

Travel Advisory

The Startup Repair tool runs many of these command prompt utilities automatically. You need to use the WinRE command prompt only for unique situations where the Startup Repair tool fails.

It's important for you to understand that the CompTIA A+ exams do not expect you to know everything about all these command prompt utilities. The CompTIA A+ exams expect that you do know these things, however:

- Which utilities are available and their names
- How to access these utilities (WinRE, regular command prompt)
- What these utilities basically do
- Some of the basic switches used for these utilities
- That with higher-level support, you can fix computers using these tools (being led by a specialist tech over the phone, for example)

The *bootrec* command is a Windows Recovery Environment troubleshooting and repair tool that repairs the master boot record, boot sector, or BCD store. It replaces the old fixboot and fixmbr Recovery Console commands and adds two more repair features:

- **bootrec /fixboot** Rebuilds the boot sector for the active system partition
- **bootrec /fixmbr** Rebuilds the master boot record for the system partition
- **bootrec /scanos** Looks for Windows installations not currently in the BCD store and shows you the results without doing anything
- **bootrec /rebuildmbr** Looks for Windows installations not currently in the BCD store and gives you the choice to add them to the BCD store

Local Lingo

BCD Boot configuration data (BCD) files contain information about operating systems installed on a computer. In Microsoft speak, that information is called a *store* or *BCD store*. This applies to Windows Vista and Windows 7 only.

With ntldr, you could access the boot.ini text file to see the Windows boot order. With boot.ini replaced by the BCD store, you can use a tool called *bcdedit* to see how Windows boots. Running bcdedit by itself (without switches) shows the boot options. The following boot information comes from a system with a single copy of Windows installed. Note there are two sections: the *Windows Boot Manager* section describes the location of bootmgr, and the *Windows Boot Loader* section describes the location of the winload.exe file.

Exam Tip

Instead of editing the boot.ini text file, Windows Vista/7 includes the bcdedit program for editing the BCD store.

```
Windows Boot Manager
--------------------
identifier              {bootmgr}
device                  partition=\Device\HarddiskVolume1
description             Windows Boot Manager
locale                  en-US
inherit                 {globalsettings}
default                 {current}
resumeobject            {d4539c9b-481a-11df-a981-a17cb98be35c}
displayorder            {current}
toolsdisplayorder       {memdiag}
timeout                 30

Windows Boot Loader
-------------------
identifier              {current}
device                  partition=C:
path                    \Windows\system32\winload.exe
description             Windows 7
locale                  en-US
inherit                 {bootloadersettings}
recoverysequence        {d4539c9d-481a-11df-a981-a17cb98be35c}
recoveryenabled         Yes
osdevice                partition=C:
systemroot              \Windows
resumeobject            {d4539c9b-481a-11df-a981-a17cb98be35c}
nx                      OptIn
```

To make changes to the BCD store, you need to use switches:

- **bcdedit /export** <filename> exports a copy of the BCD store to a file. This is a very good idea whenever you use bcdedit!

- **bcdedit /import** <filename> imports a copy of the BCD store back into the store.

If you look carefully at the previous bcdedit output, you'll notice that each section has an identifier such as {bootmgr} or {current}. You can use these identifiers to make changes to the BCD store using the /set switch. Here's an example:

```
BCDEDIT /SET {current} path \BackupWindows\system32\winload.exe
```

This changes the path of the {current} identifier to point to an alternative winload.exe.

The bcdedit command supports multiple OSs. Notice how this BCD store has three identifiers: {bootmgr}, {current}, and {ntldr}—a fairly common dual-boot scenario.

```
Windows Boot Manager
--------------------
identifier              {bootmgr}
device                  partition=D:
description             Windows Boot Manager
locale                  en-US
inherit                 {globalsettings}
default                 {current}
resumeobject            {60b80a52-8267-11e0-ad8a-bdb414c1bf84}
displayorder            {ntldr}
                        {current}
toolsdisplayorder       {memdiag}
timeout                 30

Windows Legacy OS Loader
------------------------
identifier              {ntldr}
device                  partition=D:
path                    \ntldr
description             Earlier Version of Windows

Windows Boot Loader
-------------------
identifier              {current}
device                  partition=C:
path                    \Windows\system32\winload.exe
description             Windows 7
locale                  en-US
inherit                 {bootloadersettings}
recoverysequence        {60b80a54-8267-11e0-ad8a-bdb414c1bf84}
recoveryenabled         Yes
osdevice                partition=C:
systemroot              \Windows
resumeobject            {60b80a52-8267-11e0-ad8a-bdb414c1bf84}
nx                      OptIn
```

A BCD store like this will cause the following menu to pop up at boot (see Figure 18.19).

You can use the bcdedit command to change the display order of the menu. If you wanted to add Windows XP to the beginning of the list, type this command:

```
bcdedit /displayorder [WindowsXP} /addfirst
```

You can also use bcdedit to set the default OS:

```
bcdedit /default {current}
```

You can even remove one of the identifiers, preventing others from booting to that OS:

```
bcdedit /delete {WindowsXP}
```

```
                      Windows Boot Manager

Choose an operating system to start, or press TAB to select a tool:
(Use the arrow keys to highlight your choice, then press ENTER.)

    Earlier Version of Windows
    Windows 7                                                        >

To specify an advanced option for this choice, press F8.

Tools:

   Windows Memory Diagnostic

  ENTER=Choose              TAB=Menu                    ESC=Cancel
```

FIGURE 18.19 bootmgr showing available versions of Windows

The bcdedit command is a tricky tool to use. To make your life easier, consider using the popular EasyBCD program from NeoSmart Technologies. You can run EasyBCD only from within a normal Windows boot, not the WinRE, but it provides more power and safety than bcdedit (see Figure 18.20).

| Travel Advisory |
You can find EasyBCD at www.neosmart.net.

The command prompt also includes *diskpart,* a fully featured partitioning tool. This tool lacks many of the safety features built into Disk Management, so proceed with caution. You can, for example, delete any partition of any type at any time. Starting diskpart opens a special command prompt as shown here:

```
C:\Windows\system32>diskpart
Microsoft DiskPart version 6.1.7600
Copyright (C) 1999-2008 Microsoft Corporation.
On computer: MIKESPC
DISKPART>
```

EasyBCD at work

You can list volumes (or partitions on basic disks):

```
DISKPART> list volume
  Volume ### Ltr Label        Fs     Type      Size    Status    Info
  ---------- --- --------     ---    -------   -----   ------    ------
  Volume 0   D                       DVD-ROM   0 B     No Media
  Volume 1   C   New Volume   NTFS   Partition 1397 GB Healthy   System

DISKPART>
```

Select a volume to manipulate (you may also select an entire drive):

```
DISKPART> select volume 1
Volume 1 is the selected volume.
DISKPART>
```

You can run commands at the diskpart prompt to add, change, or delete volumes and partitions on drives; mount or dismount volumes; and even manipulate software-level RAID arrays.

Run the **clean** command at the diskpart prompt to wipe all partition and volume information off the currently selected disk. This tool handles nasty corruptions that simply won't let Windows boot and serves as my last-ditch step before I toss a drive.

Commands available at the diskpart prompt handle volumes and partitions, but you still need a tool for handling file systems. Both WinRE and the regular command prompt provide all of the typical utilities such as copy, move, del, and format. One tool, however—fsutil—does a few more interesting jobs:

- Typing **fsinfo** provides a detailed query about the drives and volumes.
- Typing **fsutil dirty** <drivename> tells you if Windows considers the drive to be "dirty"—meaning you need to run autochk at the next reboot. When Windows detects an error in the file system for a drive, it flags that drive as a *dirty drive* or *dirty volume.* The disk-checking utility autochk runs after a reboot and before Windows loads and will correct errors in the file system of a drive.
- Typing **fsutil repair initiate** <drive letter> runs a basic version of chkdsk without rebooting.

Objective 18.02 Troubleshooting Windows GUI Problems

Assuming that Windows gets past the boot part of the startup, it will then begin to load the real Windows OS. You will see the Windows startup image on the screen (Figure 18.21), hiding everything until Windows loads the desktop.

Several issues can cause Windows to hang during the GUI-loading phase, such as buggy device drivers or Registry problems. Even autoloading programs can cause the GUI to hang on load. The first step in troubleshooting these issues is to use one of the Advanced Startup options (covered later in the chapter) to try to get past the hang spot and into Windows.

Exam Tip

The 802 competencies differentiate between "Graphical Interface fails to load" and "Missing Graphical Interface." This section covers the former phrase. The latter phrase points to a catastrophic failure, like a hard drive death or serious file corruption. To cope with such disastrous scenarios (and exam questions on such), follow the "Failure to Boot" options outlined earlier in the chapter.

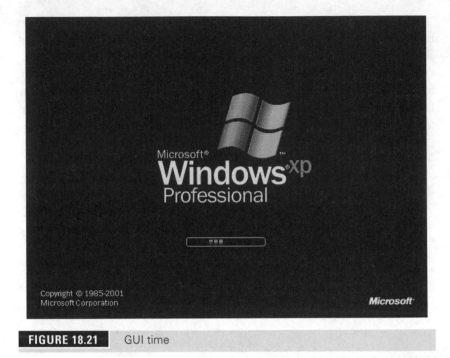

FIGURE 18.21 GUI time

Device Drivers

Device driver problems that stop the Windows GUI from loading look pretty scary. Figure 18.22 shows the infamous Windows *Stop error,* better known as the *Blue Screen of Death (BSoD).* The BSoD appears only when something causes an error from which Windows cannot recover. The BSoD is not limited to device driver problems, but bad device drivers can cause you to see the BSoD.

Whenever you get a BSoD, take a moment and read what it says. Windows BSoDs tell you the name of the file that caused the problem and usually suggest a recommended action. Once in a while these are helpful—but not often.

BSoD problems due to device drivers almost always take place immediately after you've installed a new device and rebooted. Take out the device and reboot. If Windows loads properly, head over to the manufacturer's Web site. A new device producing this type of problem is a serious issue that should have been caught before the device was released. In many cases, the manufacturer will have updated drivers available for download or will recommend a replacement device.

```
A problem has been detected and windows has been shut down to prevent damage
to your computer.

NO_MORE_IRP_STACK_LOCATIONS

If this is the first time you've seen this Stop error screen,
restart your computer. If this screen appears again, follow
these steps:

Check to make sure that any new hardware or software is properly installed.
If this is a new installation, ask your hardware or software manufacturer
for any windows updates you might need.

If problems continue, disable or remove any newly installed hardware
or software. Disable BIOS memory options such as caching or shadowing.
If you need to use Safe Mode to remove or disable components, restart
your computer, press F8 to select Advanced Startup Options, and then
select Safe Mode.

Technical information:

*** STOP: 0x00000035 (0x00000000,0xF7E562B2,0x00000008,0xC00000000)

***    wdmaud.sys - Address F7E562B2 base at F7E56000, DateStamp 36B047A5
```

FIGURE 18.22 BSoD

The second indication of a device problem that shows up during the GUI part of startup is a freeze-up: The Windows startup screen just stays there and you never get a chance to log on. If this happens, try one of the Advanced Startup Options, covered shortly.

Registry

The Registry files load every time the computer boots. Windows does a pretty good job of protecting your Registry files from corruption, but from time to time something may slip by Windows and it will attempt to load a bad Registry. These errors may show up as BSoDs that say "Registry File Failure" or text errors that say "Windows could not start." Whatever the case, when you run into these sorts of scenarios, you need to restore a good Registry copy. The best way to do this is the Last Known Good Configuration boot option (see the upcoming section). If that fails, you can restore an earlier version of the Registry through the Recovery Console in Windows XP or through Windows RE in Windows Vista/7.

Replacing the Registry in Windows XP

Boot to the Windows installation CD-ROM, get to the Recovery Console, and type these commands to restore a Registry. Notice I didn't say "your" Registry in the previous sentence. Your Registry is corrupted and gone, so you need to rebuild.

```
delete c:\windows\system32\config\system
delete c:\windows\system32\config\software
delete c:\windows\system32\config\sam
delete c:\windows\system32\config\security
delete c:\windows\system32\config\default

copy c:\windows\repair\system c:\windows\system32\config\system
copy c:\windows\repair\software c:\windows\system32\config\software
copy c:\windows\repair\sam c:\windows\system32\config\sam
copy c:\windows\repair\security c:\windows\system32\config\security
copy c:\windows\repair\default c:\windows\system32\config\default
```

Replacing the Registry in Windows Vista/7

Windows Vista and Windows 7 keep a regular backup of the Registry handy in case you need to overwrite a corrupted Registry. By default, the RegIdleBackup task runs every ten days, so that's as far back as you would lose if you replaced the current Registry with the automatically backed-up files. Of course, it would be better if you kept regular backups too, but at least the damage would be limited. You can find the backed-up Registry files in \Windows\System32\config\RegBack (see Figure 18.23).

To replace the Registry, boot to the Windows DVD to access Windows RE and get to the command prompt shell. Run the **reg** command to get to a reg prompt. From there, you have numerous commands to deal with the Registry. The simplest is probably the *copy* command. You know the location of the backed-up Registry files. Just copy the files to the location of the main Registry files—up one level in the tree under the \config folder.

Advanced Startup Options

If Windows fails to start up, use the Windows *Advanced Startup Options* menu to discover the cause. To get to this menu, restart the computer and press F8 after the POST messages but before the Windows logo screen appears. Windows XP's Startup options are a tad different from Windows Vista's and Windows 7's. Central to these advanced options are Safe Mode and Last Known Good Configuration. Here's a rundown of the menu options.

FIGURE 18.23 The backed-up Registry files located in the RegBack folder

Exam Tip

Windows 9x had an option for step-by-step confirmation, but that is not a choice in Windows XP/Vista/7. Look for it as a wrong answer on the exams!

Safe Mode (All Versions)

Safe Mode starts up Windows but loads only very basic, non–vendor-specific drivers for mouse, 640×480 resolution monitor (in XP) and 800×600 resolution monitor (Vista and 7), keyboard, mass storage, and system services (see Figure 18.24).

Exam Tip

The 802 objectives mention a scenario where a computer boots to Safe Mode. That's not really what happens. When the computer crashes, you'll usually get an option to boot to Safe Mode, but it won't automatically boot to it. You need to select that option from the Advanced Startup Options menu.

Once in Safe Mode, you can use tools such as Device Manager to locate and correct the source of the problem. When you use Device Manager in Safe Mode, you can access the properties for all the devices, even those that are not working in Safe Mode. The status displayed for the device is the status for a normal startup. Even the network card will show as enabled. You can disable any suspect device or perform other tasks, such as removing or updating drivers. If a problem with a device driver is preventing the operating system from starting normally, check Device Manager for warning icons that indicate an unknown device.

FIGURE 18.24 Safe Mode

There is no safety or repair feature in any version of Windows that makes the OS boot to Safe Mode automatically. In most cases, Windows automatically booting to Safe Mode indicates that someone has set the System Configuration utility to force Windows to do so. Type **msconfig** at the Start | Search or Start | Run option and press ENTER to open the System Configuration utility, and then deselect the Safe boot or Boot to Safe Mode check box (see Figure 18.25).

Exam Tip

For Windows to boot directly to Safe Mode, a tech must make a change in the System Configuration utility.

Safe Mode with Networking (All Versions)

This mode is identical to plain Safe Mode except that you get network support. I use this mode to test for a problem with network drivers. If Windows won't start up normally but does start up in Safe Mode, I reboot into Safe Mode with

FIGURE 18.25 Uncheck Safe boot

Networking. If it fails to start up with Networking, the problem is a network driver. I reboot back to Safe Mode, open Device Manager, and start disabling network components, beginning with the network adapter.

Safe Mode with Command Prompt (All Versions)

When you start Windows in this mode, rather than loading the GUI desktop, it loads the command prompt (cmd.exe) as the shell to the operating system after you log on, as shown in Figure 18.26. From here you can run any of the commands you learned about in Chapter 14, plus a lot of utilities as well. Error-checking runs fine as **chkdsk**, for example. Disk Defragmenter probably runs even faster when you type **defrag** followed by a drive letter at the command prompt than it does from the graphical version of the tool.

Safe Mode with Command Prompt is a handy option to remember if the desktop does not display at all, which, after you have eliminated video drivers, can be caused by corruption of the explorer.exe program. From the command prompt, you can delete the corrupted version of explorer.exe and copy in an un-damaged version. This requires knowing the command line commands for navigating the directory structure, as well as knowing the location of the file you are replacing. Although Explorer is not loaded, you can load other GUI tools that don't depend on Explorer. All you have to do is enter the correct command. For instance, to load Event Viewer, type **eventvwr.msc** at the command line and press ENTER.

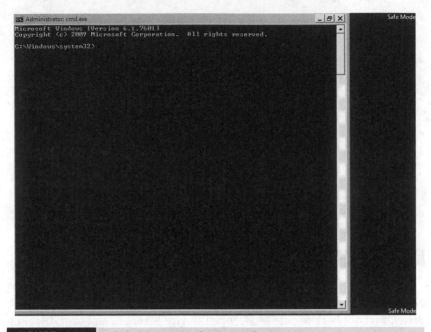

FIGURE 18.26 Safe Mode with Command Prompt

Enable Boot Logging (All Versions)

This option starts Windows normally and creates a log file of the drivers as they load into memory. The file is named ntbtlog.txt and is saved in the %SystemRoot% folder. If the startup failed because of a bad driver, the last entry in this file may be the driver the OS was initializing when it failed.

Reboot and go into the Recovery Console or WinRE. Use the tools there to read the boot log (type **ntbtlog.txt**) and disable or enable problematic devices or services.

Enable VGA Mode (XP)/Enable Low-Resolution Mode (Vista and 7)

Enable VGA Mode/Enable Low-Resolution Mode starts Windows normally, but only loads a default VGA driver. If this mode works, it may mean you have a bad driver, or it may mean you are using the correct video driver but it is configured incorrectly (perhaps with the wrong refresh rate and/or resolution). Whereas Safe Mode loads a generic VGA driver, this mode loads the driver Windows is configured to use, but starts it up in standard VGA mode rather than using the settings for which it is configured. After successfully starting in this mode, open the Display applet and change the settings.

Last Known Good Configuration (All Versions)

When Windows' startup fails immediately after installing a new driver but before you have logged on again, try the *Last Known Good Configuration* option. This option applies specifically to new device drivers that cause failures on reboot.

Directory Services Restore Mode (All Versions)

The title says it all here; this option only applies to Active Directory domain controllers, and only Windows Server versions can be domain controllers. I have no idea why Microsoft includes this option. If you choose it, you simply boot into Safe Mode.

Debugging Mode (All Versions)

If you select this choice, Windows starts in kernel debug mode. It's a super-techie thing to do, and I doubt that even über techs do debug mode anymore. To do this, you have to connect the computer you are debugging to another computer via a serial connection, and as Windows starts up, a debug of the kernel is sent to the second computer, which must also be running a debugger program.

Disable Automatic Restart on System Failure (All Versions)

Sometimes a BSoD will appear at startup, causing your computer to spontaneously reboot. That's all well and good, but if it happens too quickly, you might not be able to read the BSoD to see what caused the problem. Selecting *Disable automatic restart on system failure* from the Advanced Startup Options menu stops the computer from rebooting on Stop errors. This gives you the opportunity to write down the error and hopefully find a fix.

Disable Driver Signature Enforcement (Vista and 7)

Windows Vista and 7 require that all very low-level drivers (kernel drivers) must have a Microsoft driver signature. If you are using an older driver to connect to your hard drive controller or some other low-level feature, you must use this option to get Windows to load the driver. Hopefully you will always check your motherboard and hard drives for Windows compatibility and never have to use this option.

Start Windows Normally (All Versions)

This choice will simply start Windows normally, without rebooting. You already rebooted to get to this menu. Select this if you changed your mind about using any of the other exotic choices.

Reboot (All Versions)

This choice will actually do a soft reboot of the computer.

Return to OS Choices Menu (All Versions)

On computers with multiple operating systems, you get an OS Choices menu to select which OS to load. If you load Windows and press F8 to get the Advanced Startup Options menu, you'll see this option. Choosing it returns you to the OS Choices menu, from which you can select the operating system to load.

Troubleshooting Tools in the GUI

Once you're able to load into Windows, whether through Safe Mode or one of the other options, the whole gamut of Windows tools is available for you. If a bad device driver caused the startup problems, for example, you can open Device Manager and begin troubleshooting, just as you've learned in previous chapters. If you suspect some service or Registry issue caused the problem, head on over to Event Viewer and see what sort of logon events have happened recently.

Event Viewer

Event Viewer enables you to examine logs kept by Windows about important events, such as application failures and OS errors. If you've just had to recover from a catastrophic error, fire up Event Viewer as soon as you can access the GUI.

Travel Advisory

This discussion covers Event Viewer in Windows XP, the simplest of the three OS tools. Windows Vista/7 go into a lot more detail, though most is well beyond the scope of the CompTIA A+ exams.

You can start Event Viewer from Administrative Tools in Control Panel. The Event Viewer will display events from several log files depending on the version of the OS, such as Application, Security, System, and Internet Explorer. Figure 18.27 shows the contents of a System event log in Event Viewer.

Types of Events Event Viewer displays five types of events. The System and Application logs have Error, Warning, and Information events, while the Security log displays Success Audit and Failure Audit events. Figure 18.28 shows an Application log with two types of events displayed.

FIGURE 18.27 System event log in Event Viewer

FIGURE 18.28 Application log showing two types of events

An Error event is bad news—something's broken or data has been lost. In the Application log, this can mean an entire application hung up or an operation failed. In the System log, this can mean that a service failed. A *service* is a special program that provides specific functionality to the OS. A warning is something that isn't critical but may mean there is trouble to come. For instance, if disk space is low, a Warning event is logged. An Information event is the only good news, because it means an application, driver, or service successfully completed an operation.

Travel Advisory

Real techs don't waste time slogging through the menus for tools they use frequently. A quicker way is to start up the console by typing its name in the Run dialog box. For example, start Event Viewer by selecting Start | Run or Start | Search and typing the filename of the console: **eventvwr**.

Autoloading Programs

Windows loves to autoload programs so they start at boot. Most of the time, this is an incredibly handy option, used by every Windows PC in existence. The problem with autoloading programs is that when one of them starts behaving badly—you need to shut off that program!

At least five different locations in folders, files, and the Registry are accessed by Windows to autoload programs. To help you, Windows XP and later versions include the handy *System Configuration utility*, a one-stop spot to see and maintain every program (and service) that autoloads at startup. Let's look at services and then examine the System Configuration utility in detail.

Services

Windows loads a number of *services* (small, background helper programs) as it starts. If any critical service fails to load, Windows will tell you at this point with an error message. The important word here is *critical*. Windows will not report *all* service failures at this point. If a service that is less than critical in Windows' eyes doesn't start, Windows usually waits until you actually try to use a program that needs that service before it prompts you with an error message (Figure 18.29).

To work with your system's services, go to Control Panel | Administrative Tools | Services (alternately, right-click My Computer/Computer, select Manage, and then select Services) and verify that the service you need is running. If it's not, right-click it and select Start to turn it on. Also notice that each service has a Startup Type—Automatic, Manual, or Disabled—that defines when it starts.

FIGURE 18.29 Service error

It's common to find that a service has been set to Manual when it needs to be set to Automatic so that it starts when Windows boots (Figure 18.30).

> ### Exam Tip
>
> You can open the Services applet from the Start | Run or Search text area by typing **services.msc** and pressing **ENTER**.

FIGURE 18.30 Autostarting a service

System Configuration

The System Configuration utility enables techs to view many things happening behind the scenes in Windows and modify how those features (programs, services, and more) act. Moreover, the utility provides a gateway to many other tools. System Configuration has at least five tabs (seven in Windows XP); the CompTIA A+ exams care about the five in Windows 7, so let's go through each one. First off, you need to start the program. Go to Start | Run or Search, type **msconfig** and press ENTER. This is the only way to start System Configuration in Windows XP. Windows Vista/7 have a System Configuration applet in Administrative tools.

Exam Tip

Many seasoned techs call System Configuration *msconfig,* probably because originally you could only access the tool from the Start | Run dialog. Look for msconfig on the 802 exam as well.

The General tab (Figure 18.31) shows the current state of the tool, such as whether it's set for Normal startup (where everything installed loads), Diagnostic startup (only basic stuff loads), or Selective startup (startup options are manually selected by a tech). If you want to reset the utility after making changes, selecting Normal startup on the General tab and rebooting will do it in one shot. It's very handy!

FIGURE 18.31 The General tab of System Configuration

The Boot tab (Figure 18.32) shows currently installed operating systems and enables you to do some very fine-tuned troubleshooting. You can enable a boot log, for example, to track each thing that loads (or fails to load) at startup. You can tell Windows to use basic video settings on reboot, handy for working with hard-to-trace video issues. Most of these tools go well beyond the typical tech needs, but they're there if you need them.

The Services tab (Figure 18.33) shows all the installed services and their current status (running or stopped). You cannot start, stop, or restart a service here, but you can enable or disable services to take effect at reboot. You can even enable or disable all services at one shot, again an effect that occurs at reboot.

The Startup tab (Figure 18.34) is the tab you will use the most as a tech. This tab enables you to select which programs will start or not start automatically at reboot. This is hugely important for troubleshooting. Disabling potentially troublesome programs simply stops them from starting; it does *not* uninstall anything. That way, you can nondestructively see if an autostarting program is truly a problem. If you accidentally turn off something vital, just go back into System Configuration, enable it, and reboot.

Finally, the Tools tab (Figure 18.35) is like a one-stop shop for every important troubleshooting tool built into Windows. Everything is there except for Device Manager, and even that's accessible with a second click by choosing Computer Management. It doesn't get much better than this in Windows!

FIGURE 18.32 The Boot tab of System Configuration

FIGURE 18.33 The Services tab of System Configuration

FIGURE 18.34 The Startup tab of System Configuration

FIGURE 18.35 The Tools tab of System Configuration

System Files

Windows lives on dynamic link library (DLL) files. Almost every program used by Windows—and certainly all of the important ones—call to DLL files to do most of the heavy lifting that makes Windows work. Windows protects all of the critical DLL files carefully, but once in a while you may get an error saying Windows can't load a particular DLL.

Although rare, the core system files that make up Windows itself may become corrupted, preventing Windows from starting properly. You usually see something like "Error loading XXXX.DLL," or sometimes a program you need simply won't start when you double-click its icon. In these cases, the tool you need is the System File Checker.

The System File Checker is a command prompt program (sfc.exe) that is used to check a number of critical files, including the ever-important DLL cache. sfc takes a number of switches, but by far the most important is /scannow. Go to a command prompt and type **sfc /scannow** to start the program. sfc will automatically check all critical files and replace any it sees as corrupted. During this process, it may ask for the Windows installation disc, so keep it handy.

> ### Exam Tip
>
> The command line tool Regsvr32 can be used to register .dll files as command components in the registry. The proper syntax is
>
> ```
> regsvr32 [/u] [/s] [/n] [/i[:cmdline]] dllname
> ```

System Restore

With Windows XP and Vista/7 systems, you can recover from a bad device or application installation by using System Restore to load a restore point. Follow the process explained earlier in the chapter. System Restore is the final step in recovering from a major Windows meltdown.

Troubleshooting Tools in Windows Vista and Windows 7

Windows Vista and Windows 7 include amazing utilities designed to help you support your system. Many of these tools first appeared in Windows Vista, but Windows 7 either refined them or made them easily accessible. These Control Panel tools perform a number of different jobs, from telling you what's happening on the system to showing you how well a system's performance stacks up to other computers.

Problem Reports and Solutions (Windows Vista) and Action Center (Windows 7) centralize a lot of useful information about the status of your computer. The Performance and Information Tools applet tells you just how powerful your computer really is. Let's take a look at this crazy mixture of utilities in alphabetical order and explore the scenarios appropriate for their use.

Problem Reports and Solutions

If a computer is having a problem, wouldn't it be great to tell the people who are in charge of the program you're having that problem so they can fix it? That's the idea behind *Windows Error Reporting*. There's a good chance that, like many users, you've run into errors that look something like Figure 18.36.

The problem with these errors is that, while they might help Microsoft, they traditionally do little to help us fix the computer. Windows Error Reporting was a one-way tool, until Microsoft upgraded it with Vista to a much more powerful, two-way tool that gives developers a way to give you ways to fix computers.

FIGURE 18.36 Crash.exe has stopped working.

The *Problem Reports and Solutions* Control Panel applet in Windows Vista lists all Windows Error Reporting issues (plus a few easy-to-check items like firewall and antimalware status), as shown in Figure 18.37. You click the solution and, in many cases, the problem is fixed.

Product	Problem	Date	Status
Desktop Window Manager			
Desktop Window Manager	Stopped working	4/12/2012 10:26 AM	Not Reported
Driver software installation (2)			
Driver software installation	Installed generic driver software	8/31/2010 11:59 AM	Not Reported
Driver software installation	Could not find driver software	8/31/2010 11:59 AM	Not Reported
Host Process for Windows Services			
Host Process for Windows Servi...	Windows Update installation problem	5/4/2011 10:59 AM	Not Reported
VMware SVGA 3D (Microsoft Corporation - WDDM) (2)			
VMware SVGA 3D (Microsoft Co...	Could not load driver software	8/31/2010 10:32 AM	Not Reported
VMware SVGA 3D (Microsoft Co...	Could not load driver software	8/31/2010 11:31 AM	Not Reported

Problems Windows has identified

FIGURE 18.37 Problem Reports and Solutions

Action Center

Problem Reports and Solutions is a good tool, but lacks some refinements. For example, once you fix a problem, you have to delete the problem from the list manually. Also, there are a number of issues that don't have anything to do with Windows Error Reporting that just make sense to combine, such as Microsoft Troubleshooter and System Restore. Microsoft realized that they could organize the solutions to make it easier for you to choose what you wanted to do. *Action Center* in Windows 7 provides a one-page aggregation of event messages, warnings, and maintenance messages that, for many techs, might quickly replace Event Viewer as the first place to look for problems. Unlike Event Viewer, Action Center separates issues into two sections, Security and Maintenance, making it easier to scan a system quickly (see Figure 18.38).

Action Center only compiles the information, taking data from well-known utilities such as Event Viewer, Windows Update, Windows Firewall, and UAC and placing it into an easy-to-read format. If you wish, you can tell Action Center where to look for information by selecting *Change Action Center settings* (see Figure 18.39).

FIGURE 18.38 Action Center

FIGURE 18.39 Change Action Center settings

If you see a problem, Action Center includes plenty of links to get you to the utility you need. From the Action Center applet, you get direct links to the following tools:

- UAC settings
- Performance Information and Tools
- Backup and Restore
- Windows Update
- Troubleshooting Wizard
- System Restore

Although Action Center does little more than reproduce information from other utilities, it makes finding problems quick and easy. Combined with quick links to most of the utilities you'll need, Action Center should become your base of operations when something goes wrong on your Windows 7 PC.

Performance Information and Tools

Techs must often answer difficult questions like, "Why is my machine running so slowly?" Before Windows Vista, we could only use Performance Monitor baselines or third-party tools. Neither of these options worked very well.

Baselines required you to choose the right counters—choosing the wrong counters made useless and sometimes even distracting logs. Third-party tools often measured one aspect of a system (like video quality) very well but didn't help much when you wanted an overview of your system.

This changed with Microsoft's introduction of the Performance Information and Tools Control Panel applet (see Figure 18.40).

The *Performance Information and Tools* applet doesn't fix anything. It just provides a relative feel for how your computer stacks up against other systems using the Windows Experience Index. Windows bases this on five components:

- **Processor** Calculations per second
- **Memory (RAM)** Memory operations per second
- **Graphics** Desktop performance for Windows Aero
- **Gaming graphics** 3-D business and gaming graphics performance
- **Primary hard disk** Disk data transfer rate

Each component generates a subscore. These values range from 1 to 5.9 for Windows Vista and 1 to 7.9 for Windows 7. Microsoft determines the calculations that generate these numbers, so I don't know exactly what it takes to give, for example, a CPU a score of 6.1. Your system's base score is based on the lowest subscore.

Control Panel Home	Rate and improve your computer's performance			
Adjust visual effects	The Windows Experience Index assesses key system components on a scale of 1.0 to 7.9.			
Adjust indexing options				
Adjust power settings	**Component**	What is rated	Subscore	Base score
Open disk cleanup	**Processor:**	Calculations per second	7.4	
Advanced tools	**Memory (RAM):**	Memory operations per second	7.4	
	Graphics:	Desktop performance for Windows Aero	7.2	**5.9**
	Gaming graphics:	3D business and gaming graphics performance	7.2	Determined by lowest subscore
	Primary hard disk:	Disk data transfer rate	5.9	

Rate and improve your computer's performance

What do these numbers mean?

Tips for improving your computer's performance.

Learn more about scores and software online

Your scores are current
Last update: 6/7/2011 2:35:12 PM

Re-run the assessment

See also
Action Center

FIGURE 18.40 Performance Information and Tools

The Performance Information and Tools applet won't fix anything, but tells you which component is the weakest link in overall performance.

Exam Tip

You can't change a subscore in the Windows Experience Index without making some kind of hardware change.

Objective 18.03 Troubleshooting Windows Application Problems

Programmers want to write applications that work well, enable you to accomplish a specific task, and be good enough to earn your money. But PCs are complicated, and programmers can't get it right every time with every combination of hardware and software.

Application problems show up in several ways. The typical scenario has the application failing to install or uninstall. Operating system version issues can cause compatibility problems. Another typical scenario is where an application tries to access a file and that file is either missing or won't open. The least common problems come from sloppy or poorly written code that causes the application or the operating system to crash. Finally, corrupted applications can corrupt data too, but Windows has tools for recovering previous versions of files and folders.

Exam Tip

Every once in a while you'll get an application that reports an error if the clock settings in Windows don't match. This can cause the application not to run. Likewise, if a computer has a failing battery and is offline for a while, the BIOS time and settings will be off. You'll get a brief "error" noting the change when you connect that computer to a network timeserver. This is both a hardware issue (failing battery) and an application issue. When the Windows clock resets, so do the BIOS time and settings.

Application Installation Problems

Almost all Windows programs come with some form of handy installer. When you insert the disc, Windows knows to look for a text file called autorun.inf that tells it which file to run off the disc, usually setup.exe. If you download the application, you'll need to double-click it to start the installation. Either way, you run the installer and the program runs. It almost couldn't be simpler.

> **Exam Tip**
>
> The fact that Windows looks for the autorun.inf file by default when you insert a disc creates a security issue. Someone could put a malicious program on a disc and write an autorun.inf file to point to the virus. Insert the disc and boom! There goes your clean PC.

Of course, if someone has access to your computer and is fully logged on with administrator privileges, then you've already lost everything, with or without a disc-born program, so this "big" security issue is pretty much not an issue at all. Nevertheless, you should know that to turn off this behavior in Windows requires opening the Registry Editor and changing up to six different settings.

A well-behaved program should always make itself easy to uninstall as well. In most cases, you should see an uninstallation option in the program's Start menu area; and in all cases (unless you have an application with a badly configured installer), the application should appear in either the Add/Remove Programs applet or the Programs and Features applet (see Figure 18.41) in the Control Panel.

> **Exam Tip**
>
> Remember that you need local administrator privileges to install applications in all versions of Windows.

Programs that fail to install usually aren't to blame in and of themselves. In most cases, a problem with Windows prevents them from installing, most notably the lack of some other program that the application needs so it can operate. One of the best examples of this is the popular Microsoft .NET Framework. .NET is an extension to the Windows operating system that includes support for a number of features, particularly powerful interface tools and flexible database access. If a program is written to take advantage of .NET, .NET must itself be

FIGURE 18.41 Programs and Features Control Panel applet

installed. In most cases, if .NET is missing, the application should try to install it at the same time it is installed, but you can't count on this. If .NET is missing or if the version of .NET you are using is too old (there have been a number of .NET versions since it came out in 2002), you can get some of the most indecipherable errors in the history of Windows applications.

Figure 18.42 shows one such example in Windows 7 where the VMware vSphere client fails due to the wrong .NET version. Too bad the error doesn't give you any clues!

These types of errors invariably require you to go online and do Web searches, using the application name and the error. No matter how bad the error, someone else has already suffered from the same problem. The trick is to find out what they did to get around it.

Problems with Uninstalling

The single biggest problem with uninstalling is that people try to uninstall without administrator privileges. If you try to uninstall and get an error, log back on as an administrator and you should be fine. Don't forget you can right-click most uninstallation menu options on the Programs menu and select *Run as administrator* to switch to administrator privileges (see Figure 18.43).

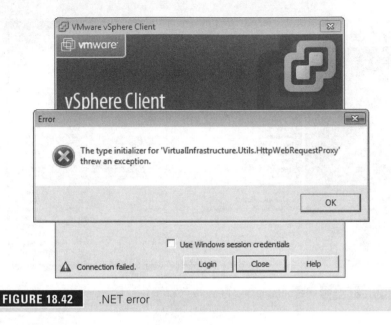

FIGURE 18.42 .NET error

Compatibility

Most applications are written with the most recent version of Windows in mind, but as Windows versions change over time, older programs have difficulty running in more recent Windows versions. In some cases, such as the jump from Windows Vista to Windows 7, the changes are generally minor enough to cause few, if any, compatibility problems. In other cases—say, a program written back when Windows 98 was around—the underpinnings of the OS differ so much that you have to perform certain steps to ensure that the older programs run. Windows XP, Windows Vista, and Windows 7 provide different forms of *compatibility modes* to support older applications.

Windows XP handles compatibility using the aptly named Compatibility tab (see Figure 18.44) in every executable program's Properties dialog box (right-click the executable file and click Properties). Select the version of Windows you want Windows XP to emulate, and in many cases, that is all you need to do to make that older program work (see Figure 18.45).

You can also set other settings on the Compatibility tab, such as the following located under Display settings:

- **Run in 256 colors** Many old Windows programs were designed to run in 256 colors. Later versions of Windows that support more colors can confuse these older programs.

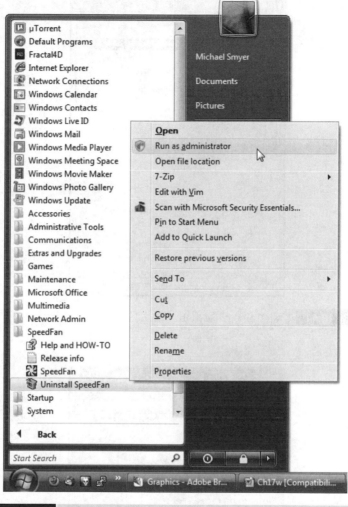

FIGURE 18.43 Selecting *Run as administrator* from the context menu

- **Run in 640×480 screen resolution** A few (badly written) older programs assume the screen to be at 640×480 resolution. This setting enables them to work.
- **Disable visual themes** Windows themes change a program window's title bar, fonts, and menus, which might make problems for some programs.

Windows Vista and Windows 7 add some important improvements to the Compatibility tab. Both add more recent OS options to the Compatibility mode drop-down menu. Figure 18.46 shows the many options available in Windows 7.

FIGURE 18.44 XP Compatibility tab

FIGURE 18.45 Compatibility mode options in Windows XP

FIGURE 18.46 Compatibility mode options in Windows 7

The newer Compatibility tab also adds some new options (see Figure 18.47) to help older programs run:

- **Disable desktop composition** Disables all display features such as Aero. More advanced Windows display features often bog down older programs.

- **Disable display scaling on high DPI settings** Turns off automatic resizing of a program's windows if you're using any high DPI (dots per inch) font. This was added because many programs with large fonts would look bizarre if resized.

- **Run this program as an administrator** As stated, enables you to run the program as an administrator. If this option isn't available, log on as an administrator to see it.

- **Change settings for all users** Clicking this button applies compatibility changes made to a program to every user account on the machine. Otherwise, the settings are only for the current user.

FIGURE 18.47 Windows 7 Compatibility tab

If you need to make things 100 percent compatible with Windows XP and you have Windows 7 (Professional, Ultimate, and Enterprise only) installed on your system, you can download Windows XP Mode. *Windows XP Mode* is nothing more than a premade Windows XP SP3 virtual machine that runs under Microsoft's popular (and free) virtualization program, Windows Virtual PC (see Figure 18.48).

The secret to using compatibility mode isn't much of a secret at all: if the program doesn't run, try a compatibility mode. If you want to be really careful, do a Web search on your application before you try to run it. Compatibility mode is a handy tool to get older applications running.

Missing File or Incorrect File Version

An application may rely on other files, in particular, DLL files. Sometimes the application installer will bring specially formatted versions of common DLL or other files to Windows, overwriting the previous versions. Later applications might look for the earlier version of the DLL and fail when it's not found.

FIGURE 18.48 Windows XP Mode

You'll experience this sort of scenario with error messages such as "missing DLL" or "cannot open file *xyz.*" The usual fix for either issue is to perform an Internet search for the missing DLL or file that fails to open, along with the name of the program you're trying to use.

Crashing Programs

Occasionally, a program gets released that isn't ready for prime time and the error-prone code causes the application to crash or even causes the operating system to crash. I've seen this most often with games rushed to market near the winter holidays. The results of this rushed code can be pretty spectacular. You're right in the middle of a thrilling fight with the bad guy and then what happens? A crash to desktop (CTD).

Poorly written or buggy programs can have awful effects on you and your clients. Some of the scenarios caused by such programs are the computer locking up or unexpectedly shutting down. The system might spontaneously shut down and restart. That kind of improper shutdown can cause problems, especially to open files and folders.

The problem here is that all this crashing can be caused by hardware and driver problems, not just application problems. You've got to keep in mind all of these things as you approach troubleshooting a crash.

Here's a typical scenario where you need to troubleshoot broadly first. If you're playing a graphically intensive game that happens to be huge and takes up a lot of RAM, what could the problem be if the screen locks up and Windows locks up too? It could be that the program ran a routine that clashed with some other application or used a Windows feature improperly. It could be that the video card was marginal and failed when taxed too much. It could be that the system accessed a section of RAM that had gone bad.

In that same scenario, though, where the game runs but degrades the overall performance of Windows, what could cause that problem? That points more squarely at the application side of things rather than the hardware or drivers, especially if the computer successfully runs other programs. The bottom line with crash issues is to keep an open mind and not rule out anything without testing it first.

Exam Tip

One error common on older systems, still mentioned on the CompTIA A+ exams but largely absent or invisible on modern systems, is a *general protection fault* (*GPF*). A GPF occurs when a program tries to do something not permitted, like writing to protected memory or something else Windows doesn't like. This can cause an error message to appear or can even crash the computer. You are very unlikely to encounter a GPF today.

Volume Shadow Copy Service and System Protection

One of the big headaches to a failure with an application isn't so much the application itself, but any data it may have corrupted. Sure, a good backup or a restore point might save you, but these can be a hassle. Unless the data was specifically saved (in the backup), there's a chance you don't have a backup in the first place. Microsoft came to your rescue in Windows Vista (Business, Ultimate, and Enterprise only) and Windows 7 (all editions) with a feature called System Protection.

This amazing feature is powered by Volume Shadow Copy Service (VSS), a feature introduced in Windows XP and used by ntbackup. VSS enables the operating system to make backups of any file, even one that is in use. In Windows Vista and 7, VSS is also used by *System Protection,* enabling you to access previous versions of any data file or folder. Try right-clicking any data file and selecting *Restore previous versions,* which opens the file's Properties dialog box with the Previous Versions tab displayed, as shown in Figure 18.49.

FIGURE 18.49 Previous Versions tab

If any of the following criteria is met, you will have at least one previous version in the list:

- The file or folder was backed up using the backup program.
- You created a restore point.
- The file or folder was changed.

You must make sure System Protection is enabled as well. Go to the System Protection tab in the System Properties dialog box (see Figure 18.50) to see if the feature is enabled (it should be running by default).

Travel Advisory

Keep in mind that System Protection doesn't have to be only for recovery of corrupted data files caused by bad applications. It's also a great tool to recover previous versions of files that users accidentally overwrite.

The System Protection tab also enables you to load a restore point and to create restore points manually—very handy features.

System Protection falls in the category generically called *file recovery software*, and does an outstanding job. You can also get many third-party utilities that accomplish general file recovery. I've used Recuva from Piriform many times, for example, to get "deleted" data off a hard drive or RAID array.

Troubleshooting (Windows 7 Only)

Windows 7 has a nice troubleshooting tool in the Control Panel called, appropriately, *Troubleshooting* (Figure 18.51). It offers a variety of unrelated issues that fall into the category of "doesn't work right." When you run into problems where an application fails to load or a device fails to start, try this tool. Heck, try it if you can't record audio or connect to the Internet. It's worth a shot!

FIGURE 18.50 System Protection tab

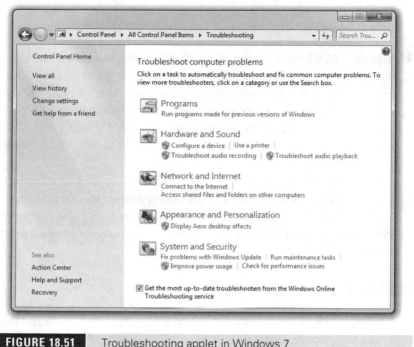

FIGURE 18.51 Troubleshooting applet in Windows 7

CHECKPOINT

✔ **Objective 18.01: Troubleshooting Windows Boot Problems** If you see an "NTLDR is Missing" or "BOOTMGR is missing" error, you first want to check your hardware configuration. Check the screen—what do you see? Is the PC plugged in? These are all common problems. If that doesn't work, you should use either Windows XP's Recovery Console or Windows Vista/7's Recovery Environment (also known as the System Recovery Options menu). From Windows RE, you can access Startup Repair, System Restore, System Image Recovery/Windows Complete PC Restore, Windows Memory Diagnostic (Tool), and the Command Prompt.

✔ **Objective 18.02: Troubleshooting Windows GUI Problems** Several issues can cause Windows to hang during the GUI-loading phase, such as buggy device drivers, Registry problems, and even autoloading programs. Event Viewer in Windows shows you all sorts of interesting happenings on the system. You can record application events, security events, and system events. The System

Configuration utility enables you to keep individual programs and services from autoloading, but it does not actually remove the programs/services.

✔ **Objective 18.03: Troubleshooting Windows Application Problems** Programs that fail to install usually aren't to blame in and of themselves. In most cases, a problem with Windows prevents them from installing, most notably the lack of some other program that the application needs so it can operate. If you get an error while trying to uninstall a program, log back on as an administrator and try again. You can use compatibility modes to emulate older versions of Windows.

Windows Vista Business, Ultimate, and Enterprise and all editions of Windows 7 use Volume Shadow Copy Service, which enables the OS to make backups of any files, even one that is in use. Windows Vista/7 also use System Protection, which enables you to access previous versions of any data file or folder.

REVIEW QUESTIONS

1. Your Windows XP Professional system fails to boot up. You suspect that the boot sector has become corrupted. You start the system using the set of boot disks and then launch the Recovery Console. Which command should you use to write a new boot sector into the system partition?

 A. chkdsk

 B. fdisk

 C. fixmbr

 D. fixboot

2. You've just installed a software update, rebooted, and now your system experiences random crashes. Which utility should you use first to try to fix the problem?

 A. Automated System Restore

 B. Device Manager

 C. System Restore

 D. Recovery Console

3. You suspect your system is failing to boot because of a corrupt master boot record. Which utility is the best to fix this?

 A. Automated System Restore

 B. Device Manager

 C. System Restore

 D. Recovery Console

4. What command should you run to check and fix corrupt system files, DLLs, and other critical files?

 A. cmdcons /fixboot

 B. sfc /scannow

 C. chkdsk /r

 D. defrag –a

5. You get a tech call from a distraught Windows 7 user who can't get into Windows. He says he has a Recovery CD from the manufacturer and plans to run it. What would you suggest?

 A. Run the Recovery CD to restore the system.

 B. Run the Recovery CD to return the system to the factory-installed state.

 C. Try to get the computer to boot into Safe Mode.

 D. Reinstall Windows by using a Windows 7 disc.

6. Which of the following points to a hardware or CMOS problem rather than an OS problem with a PC that won't boot?

 A. A black screen with the error message "invalid boot disk"

 B. A black screen with the error message "NTLDR Bad or Missing"

 C. A black screen with the error message "Invalid BOOT.INI"

 D. A black screen with the error message "Invalid BCD"

7. John's computer has an error that says bootmgr is corrupted. What tool can he use to fix this problem?

 A. bcdedit

 B. chkdsk

 C. config.sys

 D. regedit

8. What does Microsoft call the 32- or 64-bit installation environment in Windows 7?

 A. WinEE

 B. WinPE

 C. WinRE

 D. Recovery Console

9. Ralph suspects a bad RAM stick is causing Windows to fail to boot. What default Windows tool can he use to check the RAM?

 A. MEMMAKER

 B. Memtest86+

 C. Windows RAM Diagnostic Tool

 D. Windows Memory Diagnostic Tool

10. Ellen tries to boot into Windows, but the computer crashes at the logon screen. What tool should she use first to try to fix the problem?

 A. Boot to the Windows DVD, get to WinRE, and type **clean** at the diskpart prompt.

 B. Boot to the Windows DVD, get to WinRE, and run Startup Repair.

 C. Reboot the PC, press F8 to open the Advanced Startup Options menu, and select Safe Mode.

 D. Reboot the PC, press F8 to open WinRE, and select Safe Mode.

REVIEW ANSWERS

1. **D** The Recovery Console command **fixboot** writes a new partition boot sector to the system partition. The Recovery Console command **chkdsk** runs the CheckDisk utility; **fdisk** is not a valid command for the Recovery Console; and **fixmbr** writes a new master boot record for the partition boot sector.

2. **C** You should first try to fix the problem with a System Restore.

3. **D** Of the options available, the best tool to fix a corrupt MBR is Recovery Console. Use the **fixmbr** command.

4. **B** Run the **sfc /scannow** command to fix corrupt system files, DLLs, and other critical files.

5. **C** Ack! Tell him to try Safe Mode first!

6. **A** A black screen with the error message "invalid boot disk" points to a hardware or CMOS problem rather than an OS problem with a PC that won't boot.

7. **A** John can use the bcdedit tool to fix an error that says bootmgr is corrupted.

8. **B** Microsoft calls the 32- or 64-bit installation environment in Windows 7 the WinPE.

9. **D** Ralph should run the Windows Memory Diagnostic Tool if he suspects that a bad RAM stick is causing Windows to fail to boot.

10. **C** Ellen should reboot the PC, press F8 to open the Advanced Startup Options menu, and select Safe Mode first.

Networking

	NEWBIE	SOME EXPERIENCE	EXPERT
ETA	5 hours	4 hours	2 hours

Few PCs are islands unto themselves. To experience the full power of computers, you have to hook them up to other computers. Networking is the name of the game, and Windows PCs play the game very well indeed! Networking enables different users on different computers to share resources such as printers, scanners, files, and Internet connections.

Networks range in size from the smallest and simplest network—two computers connected together—to the largest and most complex network of all—the Internet. As a CompTIA A+ certified PC tech, you'll have many opportunities to put your networking knowledge to use. This chapter runs through the basics of networking hardware, topologies, and protocols, and then covers the software side of things with network operating systems and installing and configuring a LAN. Finally, you'll learn a few new ways to think about network organization and troubleshooting.

Objective 19.01 Networking Components for the PC

Networks need hardware to move data between computers. The network adapter, or *network interface card (NIC)*, links the PC to the rest of the networking hardware. NICs come in wired and wireless varieties, meaning that they use either physical network cabling (such as Ethernet) or some sort of wireless technology (such as infrared or radio waves) to transfer data. Next, you must install appropriate networking software—a network *client* and one or more protocols. These enable your PC to access network services and resources.

Installing Network Adapters and Drivers

Installing a NIC into any version of Windows is usually a no-brainer, because most NICs today are completely Plug and Play (PnP) or built into the motherboard. It is simply a matter of turning off the PC, installing the card into an available expansion bus slot, and turning the system on again. If you use a USB or ExpressCard NIC, you don't even need to turn the system off! Simply insert the NIC into the slot and wait for Windows PnP to do its thing.

After Windows detects the NIC, you supply the appropriate driver, and you're ready to go. The only trick is to remember that you should use the driver disc that comes with the NIC, even if Windows offers to use its own drivers.

Vendor-supplied NIC drivers are usually more up to date than the versions that ship with Windows.

All the issues discussed with respect to installing devices also hold true for NICs. If the NIC shows up in the Device Manager, you're done with this step. If it doesn't, you follow the normal hardware troubleshooting steps to resolve the problem. Figure 19.1 shows an installed network adapter in Windows XP Device Manager.

The Link Between Networking Hardware and Data Frames

At this point, you've got all the hardware in place that you need to access a network. There's more to it, of course, but we'll save the rest of this discussion for Chapter 20. Before moving on, however, you need to understand the link between networking hardware and the data packets that they send out.

Every NIC in the world has a built-in identifier called a *media access control (MAC)* address. The MAC address is a binary address that is unique for every network card. The MAC address is 48 bits long, providing more than 281 *trillion* individual MAC addresses, so there are plenty of MAC addresses to go around. Note that the MAC is hard-coded to the card's circuitry and can't be reset. Some (very few) NICs permit you to configure this value in the card properties.

 FIGURE 19.1 Windows XP Device Manager showing NICs installed

Local Lingo

Frame A container for data that includes the MAC address of the sending NIC.

Each variety of data frame shares certain features:

- All frames contain the MAC address of the network card to which the data is being sent.
- All frames have the MAC address of the network card that sent the data.
- The data itself (no matter what type) can vary in size depending on the type of frame.
- Some type of data check (such as Cyclic Redundancy Check, or CRC) is in place to enable the receiving network card to indicate whether the data was received in good order (see Figure 19.2).

Exam Tip

A detailed understanding of how data frames (and packets) are assembled, addressed, sent out over the network, and then retrieved and reassembled at the other end isn't necessary for the CompTIA A+ certification exams. These topics are part of the CompTIA Network+ certification exam. You should, however, understand that each data frame is "tagged" with the physical MAC address of the hardware from which it originates.

FIGURE 19.2 Generic frame

At this point, you're ready to plug a piece of network cable into the PC and connect to the network, right? But how does the PC communicate with another PC? You need software for that, specifically client services and software protocols.

Client Service

The *client service* is the component that enables your computer to see and be seen on the network. All modern versions of Windows install the *Client Service for Microsoft Networks* by default.

Software Protocols

Protocols handle the details of data transfer, such as making sure that the sending PC packages the data properly and in uniformly understood *packets*— containers specific to the network protocol used—and that the receiving PC knows how to put the data back together. Each protocol uses its own unique "language" for a packet, so packets created with one protocol cannot be read by another machine that does not have that protocol installed.

Local Lingo

Packet and frame The terms *packet* and *frame* get used interchangeably quite often, but they actually mean different things. A *frame* is used in Ethernet networks, and a *packet* is used in TCP/IP networks. When you get to the "OSI Seven-Layer Model" section of this chapter, remember that a frame is at Layer 2 and a packet is at Layer 3.

All modern operating systems and networks use *Transmission Control Protocol/ Internet Protocol (TCP/IP)*. That includes the Internet. TCP/IP is technically not a single protocol, but a group of protocols that networking devices use to communicate in many ways. A simple example will suffice here, though we'll look at other pieces of the TCP/IP protocol suite in Chapter 21.

When moving data from one system to another, the TCP/IP protocol suite needs to know if the communication is connection oriented or connectionless. When you want to be positive that the data moving between two systems gets there in good order, use a connection-oriented application. If it's not a big deal for data to miss a bit or two, then connectionless is the way to go. The connection-oriented protocol used with TCP/IP is called the *Transmission Control Protocol (TCP)*. The connectionless one is called the *User Datagram Protocol (UDP)*.

Over 95 percent of all TCP/IP applications use TCP—that's why we call the protocol suite "TCP/IP" and not "UDP/IP." TCP gets an application's data from one machine to another reliably and completely. As a result, TCP comes with communication rules that require both the sending and receiving machines to acknowledge the other's presence and readiness to send and receive data.

UDP is the "fire and forget" missile of the TCP/IP protocol suite. It doesn't possess any of the extras you see in TCP to make sure the data is received intact. UDP works best when you have a lot of data to send that doesn't need to be perfect or when the systems are so close to each other that the chances of a problem occurring are too small to bother worrying about. A few dropped frames on a Voice over IP call, for example, won't make much difference in the communication between two people. So there's a good reason to use UDP: it's smoking fast compared to TCP.

Objective 19.02 Types of Networks

Networks come in a variety of types today. We differentiate among local networks and bigger networks, for example. Plus, there are names for how the computers connect and send data. Let's take a look.

LANs, Routing, and WANs

A *local area network (LAN)* is a group of computers that are located physically close to each other—no more than a few hundred meters apart at most. A LAN might be in a single room, on a single floor, or in a single building. But I'm going to add that a LAN is almost always a group of computers that are able to "hear" each other when one of them sends a broadcast. A group of computers connected by one or more switches is a broadcast domain (see Figure 19.3).

Exam Tip
For the CompTIA A+ exams, remember that a LAN is a group of networked computers that are close to each other. Also, remember that a LAN is almost always a broadcast domain.

A *wide area network (WAN)* is a widespread group of computers connected using long-distance technologies. You connect LANs into a WAN with a magical box called a *router* (see Figure 19.4). The best example of a WAN is the Internet.

FIGURE 19.3 Two broadcast domains—two separate LANs

Topologies

Even though most networks share the same basic look and feel, the way the data moves around inside those wires may be quite different from one network to the next. The *topology* of a network describes these different configurations of the cabling between computers.

The most common network topologies are called *bus, ring, star,* and *mesh*. Each of these topologies has advantages and disadvantages. *Hybrid topologies,* such as star bus or star ring, combine aspects of the other topologies to capitalize on their strengths and minimize their weaknesses. The best topology for a specific situation depends on a variety of factors, including cost, speed, ease of installation, the physical position of the PCs, and the number of PCs in the network. We'll look at the most important hybrid topology, star bus, in a moment, but for now, make sure you know the four main topologies!

FIGURE 19.4 Two broadcast domains connected by a router—a WAN

In a *bus topology*, all computers connect to the network via a main line called a *bus cable*. In a *ring topology*, all computers on the network attach to a central ring of cable. In a *star topology*, the computers on the network connect to a central wiring box. Finally, in a *mesh topology*, each computer has a dedicated line to every other computer—the mesh topology is most often used in wireless networks. Figure 19.5 shows the four topologies.

Most techs make a clear distinction between the *logical topology* of a network—how the network is laid out on paper, with nice straight lines and boxes—and the physical topology. The *physical topology* describes the typically messy computer network, with cables running diagonally through the ceiling space or snaking their way through walls. If someone describes the topology of a particular network, make sure you understand whether they're talking about the logical or physical topology.

FIGURE 19.5 Bus, ring, mesh, and star topologies

Star Bus

Imagine shrinking the bus in a bus network so it will fit inside a box. Then, instead of attaching each PC directly to the wire, you attach it via cables to special ports on the box (Figure 19.6). The box with the bus takes care of all of the tedious details required by a bus network. The bus topology would look a lot like a star topology, wouldn't it?

The central box with the bus is called a switch. The switch provides a common point for connection for network devices. Switches can have a wide variety of ports. Most consumer-level switches have 4 or 8, but business-level switches can have 32 or more ports.

Local Lingo

Hub Early networks used a central box called a *hub* because switches hadn't been invented yet. With hubs, all connected devices or nodes shared the network bandwidth and could see all the traffic, so traffic on a 10-Mbps network with 30 devices would run at a fraction of that 10-Mbps speed. Switches make every port its own separate network. Traffic between devices runs at the full speed of the network.

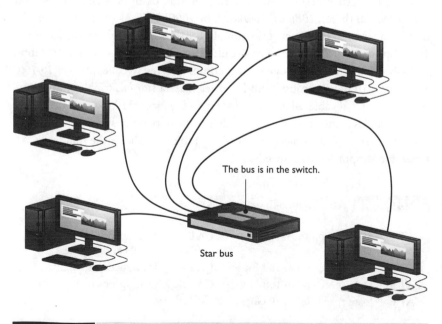

The bus is in the switch.

Star bus

FIGURE 19.6 Star bus topology

Objective 19.03 Network Cabling Standards

In the vast majority of networks, physical network cabling is the medium by which data packets are moved from one PC to the other. Wireless alternatives exist, as you'll see in Chapter 20, but at some point, even wireless networks connect to a wired network "backbone."

Wired (and even wireless) networking hardware—the cabling, switches, routers, and patch panels—must conform to standards defined by the IEEE (Institute of Electrical and Electronics Engineers, pronounced "I-triple-E"). The predominant standard is called *Ethernet*.

Ethernet

The Ethernet standard—controlled by the 802 committee of the IEEE standards body—has appeared in several physical forms, such as 10BaseT, 100BaseT, 1000BaseT, and 802.11x wireless. Significant differences exist among the forms, mainly in terms of cabling media and data throughput, but it's all Ethernet. This means that with the appropriate hardware, you can mix and match without losing the ability to communicate.

Most modern Ethernet networks employ one of three technologies (and sometimes all three), *10BaseT, 100BaseT,* or *1000BaseT.* As the numbers in the names suggest, 10BaseT networks run at 10 Mbps, 100BaseT networks run at 100 Mbps, and 1000BaseT networks—called Gigabit Ethernet—run at 1000 Mbps, or 1 Gbps. All three technologies—sometimes referred to collectively as *10/100/1000BaseT,* 10*BaseT, or just plain Ethernet—use a *star bus* topology and connect via a type of cable called *unshielded twisted pair (UTP).*

UTP cables come in categories that define the maximum speed at which data can be transferred (also called *bandwidth*). Table 19.1 shows the standard CAT types and supporting data speeds.

TABLE 19.1	Standard CAT Types		
CAT 1	Standard phone line	CAT 2	Data speeds up to 4 Mbps (ISDN and T1 lines)
CAT 3	Data speeds up to 16 Mbps	CAT 4	Data speeds up to 20 Mbps
CAT 5	Data speeds up to 100 Mbps	CAT 5e	Data speeds up to 1 Gbps
CAT 6	Data speeds up to 10 Gbps		

The *Telecommunication Industry Association/Electronics Industries Alliance* (*TIA/EIA*) establishes the UTP categories, which fall under the TIA/EIA 568 specification. Currently, most installers use CAT 5e or CAT 6 cable. Although many networks run at 10 Mbps, the industry standard has shifted to networks designed to run at 100 Mbps and faster. Because only CAT 5 or better handles these speeds, just about everyone is installing the higher-rated cabling, even if they are running at speeds that CAT 3 or CAT 4 would accommodate. Consequently, it is becoming more difficult to get anything but CAT 5e or CAT 6 cables.

Local Lingo

CAT 1–6 levels Experienced network techs refer to the different types of cabling as "*CAT x*," as opposed to "*Category x*," as in, "Yo, Frankie! Toss me that coil o' CAT 5e, alright?"

Shielded Twisted Pair

Shielded twisted pair (STP), as its name implies, consists of twisted pairs of wires surrounded by shielding to protect them from electromagnetic interference (EMI). STP really matters only in locations with excessive electronic noise, such as a shop floor area with lots of lights, electric motors, or other machinery that could cause problems for other cables. It's far cheaper than any other solution to handle noise. (See the section on fiber networks later in the chapter for the only competition to STP.)

Implementing 10/100/1000BaseT

The 10/100/1000BaseT cabling standard requires two pairs of wires: a pair for sending and a pair for receiving. 10/100/1000BaseT cables use a connector called an *RJ (Registered Jack)* connector. The RJ designation was invented by Ma Bell years ago and is still used today. Currently, you see only two types of RJ connectors: *RJ-11* and *RJ-45,* as shown in Figure 19.7.

The RJ-11 connector is the connector that hooks a telephone to the telephone jack. It supports up to two pairs of wires, although most phone lines use only one pair (the other pair is used to support a second phone line). RJ-11 connectors aren't used in any common network installation, although some proprietary "out-of-the-box" network solutions use the telephone lines already installed in a building to transmit data. These types of networks aren't very popular, however.

RJ-45 is the standard for UTP connectors. RJ-45 has connections for up to four pairs of wires and is visibly much wider than RJ-11. The #1 pin on an RJ-45 jack is the first one on the *left* when pointing the jack away from you with the clip facing *down.*

FIGURE 19.7 RJ-11 (left) and RJ-45 (right)

Exam Tip

Know the 10'BaseT numbers and names—10-, 100-, and 1000-Mbps data transfers; 100-meter segment length; RJ-45 connectors; and UTP cabling.

Two standards exist for CAT 5/5e/6 cabling: the TIA/EIA *568A* and the TIA/EIA *568B*. Both are acceptable. The only truly critical thing is to use the *same* standard on each end of the cable, but your life will be much simpler if you choose one standard and stick with it. The wires in UTP cabling are color-coded to make standardization easy. Table 19.2 shows the official TIA/EIA standard colors as they correspond to the wire number.

TABLE 19.2 UTP Cabling Color Chart

Pin	568A	568B	Pin	568A	568B
1	White/Green	White/Orange	5	White/Blue	White/Blue
2	Green	Orange	6	Orange	Green
3	White/Orange	White/Green	7	White/Brown	White/Brown
4	Blue	Blue	8	Brown	Brown

Exam Tip

Memorize the TIA/EIA 568 wiring colors for the CompTIA A+ certification exams. The 801 exam refers to the wiring standards by shorthand names, T568A and T568B.

Plenum vs. PVC Cabling

Most workplace installations of network cable go up above the ceiling and then drop down through the walls to present a nice port in the wall. The space in the ceiling, under the floors, and in the walls through which cable runs is called the *plenum* space. The potential problem with cabling running through the plenum space is that the protective sheathing for networking cables, called the *jacket*, is made from plastic, and if you get any plastic hot enough, it creates smoke and noxious fumes. Standard network cables usually use PVC (polyvinyl chloride) for the jacket, but PVC produces noxious fumes when burned. Fumes from cables burning in the plenum space can quickly spread throughout the building, so you want to use a more fire-retardant cable in the plenum space. Plenum-grade cable is simply network cabling with a fire-retardant jacket and is required for cables that go in the plenum space. Plenum-grade cable costs about three to five times more than PVC, but you should use it whenever you install cable in a plenum space.

Exam Tip

The only two types of coaxial cable you need to know for the CompTIA A+ exams are RG-59 and RG-6. Both of these coax cables are used by your cable television, but RG-59 is thinner and doesn't carry data quite as far as RG-6.

Link Lights

All NICs made today have some type of light-emitting diode (LED) *status indicator* that gives information about the state of the NIC's link to whatever's on the other end of the connection. Even though you know the lights are actually LEDs, get used to calling them *link lights*, because that's the term all network techs use. NICs can have between one and four different link lights, and the LEDs can be any color. These lights give you clues about what's happening with the link and are one of the first items to check whenever you think a system is disconnected from the network (Figure 19.8).

FIGURE 19.8 Mmmm, pretty lights!

Switches also have link lights enabling you to check the connectivity at both ends of the cable. If a PC can't access a network, always check the link lights first. A properly functioning link light is steady on when the NIC is connected to another device. No flickering, no on and off, just on. A link light that is off or flickering shows a connection problem.

Another light is the *activity light*. This little guy turns on when the card detects network traffic, so it makes an intermittent flickering when operating properly. The activity light is a lifesaver for detecting problems, because in the real world, the connection light sometimes lies to you.

No standard governs how NIC manufacturers use their lights; as a result, they come in an amazing array of colors and layouts. When you encounter a NIC with a number of LEDs, take a moment to try to figure out what each one means. Although different NICs have different ways of arranging and using their LEDs, the functions are always the same: link, activity, and speed.

> ### Exam Tip
>
> Although no real standard exists for NIC LEDs, CompTIA will test you on some more or less *de facto* LED meanings. You should know that a solid green light means connectivity, a flashing green light means intermittent connectivity, no green light means no connectivity, and a flashing amber light means there are collisions on the network (which is sometimes okay). Also, know that the first things you should check when having connectivity issues are your NIC's LEDs.

Fiber-Optic Ethernet

Fiber-optic cable is an attractive networking solution for a number of reasons. First, because it uses light instead of electricity, fiber-optic cable is immune to electrical interference and "crosstalk." Second, fiber-optic signals travel much farther than copper cabling signals: up to 2000 meters (compared with 100 meters on UTP). Third, fiber-optic cabling and hardware have become quite affordable in recent years. Last, fiber-optic technology is only slightly more difficult to work with than standard Ethernet, and in some cases it's even easier.

Most fiber Ethernet networks use *62.5/125 multimode* fiber-optic cable. All fiber Ethernet networks that use these cables require two cables. Figure 19.9 shows three of the more common connectors used in fiber-optic networks. Square *SC* connectors are shown in the middle and on the right, and the round *ST* connector is on the left.

Local Lingo

Single-mode vs. multimode Fiber networks use either lasers or LEDs for light sources. Single-mode fiber uses lasers to pulse single bursts over long distances and incredible speeds. Multimode fiber transmits multiple LED signals at the same time, each using a different reflection angle within the core of the cable. The multiple reflection angles tend to disperse over long distances, so multimode fiber-optic cables are used for relatively short distances.

FIGURE 19.9 Typical fiber-optic cables with connectors

Like many other fiber-optic connectors, the SC and ST connectors are half-duplex, meaning data flows only one way—hence, the need for two cables in a fiber installation. Other half-duplex connectors you might run into are FC/PC, SMA, D4, MU, and LC. They look similar to SC and ST connectors, but offer variations in size and connection. Newer and higher-end fiber installations use full-duplex connectors, such as the MT-RJ connectors.

> ### Exam Tip
>
> When setting up an Ethernet network, there are times where you need to transfer the medium from, for example, UTP to fiber or maybe UTP to wireless. In these cases you need a device called a bridge. A *bridge* is distinct in that it will always have two interfaces, one interface for each of the different mediums.

The two most common fiber-optic standards are called *1000BaseSX* and *100GBaseSR*. As you can guess by the names, the biggest difference is the speed of the network (some important differences occur in the way switches are interconnected, and so on).

> ### Exam Tip
>
> You might see two older fiber-optic standards on the CompTIA A+ certification exams, 10BaseFL (10 Mbps transfers up to 2 kilometers) and 100BaseFX (100 Mbps transfers up to 100 meters).

Switches

In a 10/100/1000BaseT network, each PC connects to a 10/100/1000BaseT switch. These devices have multiple connections called *ports,* one per connected device. To add a device to the network, you simply plug another cable into the switch, shown in Figure 19.10.

Networks running 10ˣBaseT use the star bus topology. The switch holds the actual bus and allows access to the bus through the ports. Using a star bus topology creates a robust network: the failure of a single node will not bring down the entire network.

The maximum distance from the switch to any device is 100 meters. No more than one PC can be hooked to each segment, and the maximum number of PCs that can be hooked up to any one hub or switch is 1024. You'll be hard pressed,

FIGURE 19.10 Typical switch with several cables connected

though, to find a switch with that many connectors. Most switches come with 4, 8, 16, 32, or 64 ports. 10xBaseT switches act as repeaters, resending the signals between devices hooked into the network.

Although just about every 10xBaseT network worth its salt uses a switch of sorts to connect the PCs, in a desperate pinch you can hook two 10xBaseT network cards together without a switch. Just connect the two PCs together with a *crossover cable!* Crossover cables provide a quick way to network two PCs. You can make a crossover cable by using a TIA/EIA 586A on one end and TIA/EIA 568B on the other.

Local Lingo

Patch cable A specific length (usually short, but can be up to 100 feet) of cable terminated at each end with a plug or socket. Also called a patch cord.

Travel Advisory

To expand a network, technically called *scaling,* you simply add more switches. Switches are connected together by a normal patch cable through an integrated port called an *uplink port,* which performs the same action as a crossover cable.

Objective 19.04 Network Operating Systems

It's time to move to the software side of things—you could have all the computers of the world connected by cables and wires, but it won't be very helpful until those computers have the correct software to tell them what to do, beginning with an OS. In a classic sense, a *network operating system (NOS)* is a portion of your OS that communicates with the PC hardware and makes the connections among multiple machines on a network. The NOS enables one or more PCs to act as server machines and share data and services over a network—to share *resources,* in other words. You then need to run software on client computers so those computers can access the shared resources on the server machine.

Every Windows OS is an NOS and enables the PC to share resources and access shared resources. But it doesn't come out of the box ready to work on all networks. You need to configure Windows to handle all three tasks to make all this work: install a network protocol to communicate with hardware, enable server software to share resources, and install client software to enable the PC to access shared resources.

All NOSs are not alike, even among Windows versions. Before you can share resources across a network, you must answer a number of questions. How do you make a resource available to share? Can everyone share his or her hard drive with everyone else? Should you place limits on sharing? If everyone needs access to a particular file, where will it be stored? What about security? How are backups to be handled? Different versions of Windows answer these questions differently.

Network Organization

All NOSs can be divided into four basic organizational groups: client/server, peer-to-peer, domain-based, and homegroups. Let's take a look at network organization.

Client/Server

In a *client/server network,* one machine is dedicated as a resource to be shared over the network. This machine will have a dedicated NOS, optimized for sharing files. This special OS includes powerful caching software that enables high-speed file access. It will have extremely high levels of protection and an organization that permits extensive control of the data. This machine is called a

dedicated server. All the other machines that use the data are called *clients* (because it's what they usually are) or *workstations*.

The client/server system dedicates one machine to act as a server. Its only function is to serve up resources to the other machines on the network. These servers do not run Windows XP, Vista, or 7. They use highly sophisticated and expensive NOSs that are optimized for the sharing and administration of network resources. Dedicated server OSs include Windows Server 2008, big UNIX systems such as IBM AIX and HP-UX, and some versions of Linux.

Travel Advisory

The terms *client* and *server* are, to say the least, freely used in computing. Keep in mind that a client generally refers to any process (or in this context, computer system) that can request a resource or service, and a server is any process (or system) that can fulfill the request.

Peer-to-Peer

Some networks do not require dedicated servers—every computer can perform both server and client functions. A *peer-to-peer network* enables any or all of the machines on the network to act as a server. Peer-to-peer networks are much cheaper than client/server networks, because the software costs less and does not require that you purchase a high-end machine to act as the dedicated server. The most popular peer-to-peer network OSs today are the various versions of Windows and Mac OS X.

The biggest limiting factor to peer-to-peer networking is that it's simply not designed for a large number of computers. Windows has a built-in limit (ten) on the number of users who can concurrently access a shared file or folder. Microsoft recommends that peer-to-peer *workgroups*—that's what such networks are called in Windows—not exceed 15 PCs. Beyond that, creating a domain-based network makes more sense. Security is the other big weakness of peer-to-peer networks. Each system on a peer-to-peer network maintains its own security.

With the Windows Professional/Business/Ultimate/Enterprise versions, you can tighten security by setting NTFS permissions locally, but you are still required to place a local account on every system for any user who's going to access resources. So even though you get better security in a Windows Professional/Business/Ultimate peer-to-peer network, system administration entails a lot of running around to individual systems to create and delete local users every time someone joins or leaves the workgroup.

Peer-to-peer workgroups are little more than a pretty way to organize systems to make navigating through Windows networks a little easier (Figure 19.11). In reality, workgroups have no security value. Still, if your networking needs are limited—such as a small home network—peer-to-peer networking is an easy and cheap solution.

> **Exam Tip**
>
> Know the difference between client/server and peer-to-peer networks.

Domain-Based

One of the similarities between the client/server network model and peer-to-peer networks is that each PC in the network maintains its own list of user accounts. If you want to access a server, you must log on. When only one server exists, the logon process takes only a second and works very well. The

FIGURE 19.11 Multiple workgroups in a network

trouble comes when your network contains multiple servers. In that case, every time you access a different server, you must repeat the logon process (Figure 19.12). In larger networks containing many servers, this becomes a time-consuming nightmare not only for the user, but also for the network administrator.

A domain-based network provides an excellent solution for the problem of multiple logins. In a domain-based environment, one or more dedicated servers, called *domain controllers*, hold the security database for all systems. This database includes a list of all users and passwords in the domain. When you log on to your computer, or to any computer, the logon request goes to an available domain controller to verify the account and password.

Local Lingo

Single sign-on In a domain-based network with centrally stored security, users only need to log on to the domain, not individual machines. This is called *single sign-on*.

Modern domain-based networks use what is called a *directory service* to store user and computer account information. Large Microsoft-based networks use the *Active Directory* (*AD*) directory service. Think of a directory service as a big, centralized index, similar to a telephone book, that each PC accesses to locate resources in the domain.

| **FIGURE 19.12** | Multiple logins |

Every Windows system contains a special account called the *administrator account.* This one account has complete and absolute power over the entire system. When you install Windows, you must create a password for the administrator account. Anyone who knows the administrator password can install/delete any program, read/change/delete any file, run any program, and change any system setting. As you might imagine, you should protect the administrator password carefully. Without it, you cannot create additional accounts (including additional accounts with administrative privileges) or change system settings. If you lose the administrator password (and no other account with administrative privileges exists), you have to reinstall Windows completely to create a new administrator account—so don't lose it!

In Windows XP, open the Properties window for My Computer, and select the Computer Name tab, as shown in Figure 19.13. This shows your current selection. Windows Vista and 7 show the computer name in the System Properties dialog box and give you a link to the XP-style dialog box (Figure 19.14). Clicking the Network ID button opens the Network Identification Wizard, but most techs just click the Change button, which brings up the Computer Name/

FIGURE 19.13 Computer Name tab in Windows XP

FIGURE 19.14 System Properties dialog box in Windows Vista

Domain Changes dialog box (Figure 19.15). Clicking the Change button does the same thing as clicking the Network ID button, except that the wizard does a lot of explaining that you don't need if you know what you want to do. Make sure you have a valid domain account, or you won't be able to log into a domain.

Homegroups

The problem with workgroups is that they provide almost no security and require lots of signing on to access resources. Domains provide single sign-on and lots of security, but require special servers and lots of administration. To address this, Microsoft introduced a new feature in Windows 7 called *HomeGroup*.

> **Travel Advisory**
>
> Homegroups are not available in Windows XP or Windows Vista. Windows 8 computers can create a homegroup and join a Windows 7 homegroup.

FIGURE 19.15 Computer Name/Domain Changes dialog box

HomeGroup uses the idea that people want to connect data, not folders. Most people just want to share their music, not their My Music folder. So homegroups skip folders completely and share your Windows 7 libraries.

A homegroup connects a group of computers using a common password—no special user names required. Each computer can be a member of only one homegroup at a time.

Exam Tip

Microsoft refers to the technology as HomeGroup, but drops the capitalization to homegroup when talking about the groups themselves. Look for it to appear either way on the CompTIA A+ exams.

By sharing libraries with homegroups, Microsoft hides folders for most users, helping users share their stuff (documents, pictures, music, and videos) instead of folders. Homegroups fit a very specific world: smaller, nondomain home networks, but within that realm, they work wonderfully.

Objective 19.05 Installing and Configuring a LAN

You've got the basics, so now let's install a network. To have network connectivity, you need to have four things in place:

- **Network infrastructure** This is the cabling in the walls, the switch for the LAN, and other devices.
- **NIC** The physical hardware that connects the computer system to the network media.
- **Protocol** The language that the computer systems use to communicate.
- **Network client** The interface that allows the computer system to speak to the protocol.

If you want to share resources on your PC with other network users, you also need to enable Microsoft's File and Printer Sharing. Plus, of course, you need to connect the PC to the network switch via some sort of cable. When you install a NIC, by default, Windows installs TCP/IP, the Client for Microsoft Networks, and File and Printer Sharing for Microsoft Networks upon setup.

Network Infrastructure

A typical office network has cables running from a central wiring closet or room filled with networking gear (such as switches, patch panels, and so forth) above the drop ceiling, down the walls, and terminating at the wall outlet. This *structured cabling* is the playground of CompTIA Network+ techs and specialized cable installers.

Almost every networking thing a CompTIA A+ tech does happens on the outside of the Ethernet wall jack. As far as structured cabling goes, all you need to know for the CompTIA A+ exams is the basic layout and a few tools to help support CompTIA Network+ techs with basic tasks. We'll cover those tools in the "Troubleshooting Networks" section of this chapter.

Installing a NIC

The NIC is your computer system's link to the network, and installing one is the first step required to connect to a network. Follow the manufacturer's instructions for installation. If your NIC is of recent vintage, it will be detected, installed, and configured automatically by Windows.

You almost never need to configure a NIC manually, but you're expected to know some options for the 802 exam. You can adjust NIC properties for half-duplex, full-duplex, or autosensing connections. You can change the default speed and, on some NICs, adjust WoL, PoE, and QoS settings. To get to any of these settings, open the Network Connections applet | right-click the Local Area Connection and select Properties | click the Configure button just below the NIC listing in the Local Area Connections Properties dialog box.

- All modern NICs can run in *full-duplex* mode, meaning they can send and receive data at the same time. The vast majority of NICs and switches use a feature called *autosensing* to accommodate very old devices that might attach to the network and need to run in half-duplex mode. *Half-duplex* means that the device can send and receive, but not at the same time.

- For backward compatibility with slower and older networks, you can manually reduce the speed of the NIC. You usually do this when you have to change the duplexity of it as well. Figure 19.16 shows the Link Speed tab of a typical NIC's Properties dialog box.

- *Wake on LAN (WoL)* settings enable you to tell a NIC to respond to certain network events, such as waking up the computer when the NIC receives a Magic Packet. (A Magic Packet is essentially a wake-up packet wrapped in a broadcast frame.)

- *Power over Ethernet (PoE)* usually applies to network devices like wireless access points (see Chapter 20) and security cameras. They get their electrical power directly from the Ethernet cable rather than an AC or DC power source. The 802 exam mentions this setting for a NIC, but it's more common as a setting on a switch.

- *Quality of Service (QoS)* enables you to specify the priority given to a particular kind of network traffic. This is usually done at the switch or router level, but can apply specifically to a NIC. You'll find options to tag packets in the Advanced tab of the NIC's properties.

Travel Advisory

If you have the option, you should save yourself potential headaches and troubleshooting woes by acquiring new, name-brand NICs for your Windows installation.

FIGURE 19.16 Options for changing link speed and duplex settings

Configuring a Network Client

To establish network connectivity, you need a network client installed and configured properly. You need a client for every type of server NOS to which you plan to connect on the network. Let's look at Microsoft's client.

Client for Microsoft Networks

Installed as part of the OS installation, the Client for Microsoft Networks rarely needs configuration, and, in fact, few configuration options are available:

- To start it in Windows Vista/7, click Start; then right-click Network and select Properties. Then click *Manage network connections* on the left.
- In Windows XP, click Start, and then right-click My Network Places and select Properties.

In all versions of Windows, your next step is to double-click the Local Area Connection icon, click the Properties button, highlight Client for Microsoft Networks, and click the Properties button. There's not much to do here. Unless you're told to do something particular by a network administrator, just leave this alone.

Configuring TCP/IP

Before a PC can access the Internet, it must have TCP/IP loaded and configured properly. TCP/IP has become so predominant that most network folks use it even on networks that do not connect to the Internet. TCP/IP is powerful and quite complex. So whether you are installing a modem for a dial-up connection to the Internet or setting up 500 computers on their own private *intranet,* you must understand some TCP/IP basics. We'll go through the following basic sections of the protocol and then look at specific steps to install and configure TCP/IP.

Exam Tip

Modems enable computers to talk to each other via standard commercial telephone lines by converting analog signals to digital signals, and vice versa. The term *modem* is short for modulator/demodulator, a description of transforming the signals.

Network Addressing

Any network address must provide two pieces of information: it must uniquely identify the machine, and it must locate that machine within the larger network. In a TCP/IP network, the *IP address* identifies the PC and the network on which it resides.

Exam Tip

Windows XP includes a tool called the Network Setup Wizard that enables you to configure a simple home network easily.

IP Addresses In a TCP/IP network, every system has a unique IP address. An *IP address* consists of four sets of eight binary numbers (octets) separated by periods. This is called *dotted-octet notation.* Here's a typical IP address:

```
202.34.16.11
```

Written in binary form, you'd get an address like this:

```
11001010.00100010.00010000.00001011
```

But the TCP/IP folks decided to write the decimal equivalents:

```
00000000 = 0
00000001 = 1
00000010 = 2
...
11111111 = 255
```

The IP address is the unique identification number for your system on the network. Part of the address (the network ID) identifies the network, and another part (the host ID) identifies the local computer (host) address on the network. For example, my computer's IP address is 192.168.4.23. On my network (these are usually different on all networks), my network ID is 192.168.4 and my host ID is 23. A traditional TCP/IP network divides IP addresses into classes, which correspond to the potential size of the network: Class A, Class B, and Class C. Class A addresses were intended for huge organizations, such as major multinational corporations. Class C networks were targeted for LANs. The crushing need for more IP addresses for the Internet pretty much blew the class structure out of the water, but here it is to satisfy your curiosity:

- Class A networks use the first octet to identify the network address and the remaining three octets to identify the host.
- Class B networks use the first two octets to identify the network address and the remaining two octets to identify the host.
- Class C networks use the first three octets to identify the network address and the last octet to identify the host.

Table 19.3 lists range (class) assignments.

TABLE 19.3 Class A, B, and C Addresses

Network Class	Address Range of First Octet	Number of Network Addresses Available	Number of Host Nodes (Computers) Supported
A	1–126	126	16,777,214
B	128–191	16,384	65,534
C	192–223	2,097,152	254

> **Travel Advisory**
>
> The 127 address range (i.e., 127.0.0.1) is reserved for network testing (loopback) operations.

> **Local Lingo**
>
> **Localhost** The address 127.0.0.1 is known as the *localhost,* meaning the local machine.

The IP addresses shown here are technically IP version 4, or IPv4 addresses, but this type of addressing has a bit of a problem—namely that we're running out of possible IP addresses, and in a few years, none will be available. No big deal. Now, before you go running out into the streets shouting about the impending demise of the Internet or start hoarding canned food in your basement, let me tell you about the solution.

IP version 6, the newest version of the Internet Protocol, which will save us all from an Internetless world, uses a 128-bit address instead of IPv4's 32-bit address. What this means is that more addresses are possible than with IPv4. A lot more. My favorite illustration is to think of all of the molecules that make up the Earth and divide them by seven. That's how many possible IPv6 addresses exist. The drawback is that IPv6 addresses are not quite as svelte and easy to remember as IPv4 addresses. For example, an IPv6 address looks like this: 2001:0db8:85a3:0000:0000:8a2e:0370:7334. Not quite as easy to work with as 192.168.1.1, eh?

IPv6 also handles routing and various other things differently than IPv4, but the main things to know are that the IP addresses look remarkably different and there are enough of them to last for a while. The switch to IPv6 is happening as I type these words. Windows 7/8 homegroups, for example, require IPv6 to function. Many organizations have an IPv6 Web server as well.

Subnet Mask The *subnet mask* is a value that distinguishes which part of the IP address is the network address and which part of the address is the host address. The subnet mask blocks out (or masks) the network portions (octets) of an IP address. Certain subnet masks are applied by default. The default subnet mask for Class A addresses is 255.0.0.0; for Class B, it's 255.255.0.0; and for Class C, 255.255.255.0. For example, in the Class B IP address 131.190.4.121 with a subnet mask of 255.255.0.0, the first two octets (131.190) make up the network address, and the last two (4.121) make up the host address.

Exam Tip

The CompTIA A+ exams do not require you to configure IP addresses and subnet masks, but you should know what they are and how to find them on a PC.

TCP/IP Services

TCP/IP is a different type of protocol. Although it supports File and Printer Sharing, it adds a number of special sharing functions unique only to it, lumped together under the umbrella term *TCP/IP services*. The most famous TCP/IP service is called *Hypertext Transfer Protocol (HTTP)*, the language of the World Wide Web. If you want to surf the Web, you must have TCP/IP. But TCP/IP supplies many other services beyond just HTTP. By using a service called Telnet, for example, you can access a remote system as though you were actually sitting in front of that machine.

The goal of TCP/IP is to link any two hosts (remember, a host is just a computer in TCP/IP lingo), whether the two computers are on the same LAN or on some other network within the WAN. The LANs within the WAN are linked together with a variety of connections, ranging from basic dial-ups to dedicated high-speed (and expensive) data lines. To move traffic between networks, you use routers. Each host sends traffic to the router only when that data is destined for a remote network, cutting down on traffic across the more expensive WAN links. The host makes these decisions based on the destination IP address of each packet.

TCP/IP Settings

TCP/IP has a number of unique settings that you must set up correctly to ensure proper network functioning. Unfortunately, these settings can be quite confusing, and there are quite a few of them. Not all settings are used for every type of TCP/IP network, and it's not always obvious where you go to set them.

Windows makes this fairly easy by letting you configure both dial-up and network connections by using the Network Connections window (Figure 19.17). To get there, right-click My Network Places (Windows XP) or Network (Windows Vista/7) and select Properties. In Vista/7, you have to click the *Manage network connections* button, but in XP, you simply select the connection you want to configure and then set its TCP/IP properties.

| FIGURE 19.17 | Network Connections window showing dial-up and LAN connections |

Exam Tip

The CompTIA A+ certification exams have a rather strange view of what you should know about networking. Take a lot of time practicing how to get to certain network configuration screens. Be ready for questions that ask, "Which of the following steps will enable you to change a particular value?"

The CompTIA A+ exams assume that someone else, such as a tech support person or some network guru, will tell you the correct TCP/IP settings for the network. Your only job is to understand roughly what they do and to know where to enter them so the system works. Following are some of the most common TCP/IP settings.

Default Gateway A computer that wants to send data to another machine outside its LAN is not expected to know all the IP addresses of all the computers on the Internet. Instead, all IP hosts know the IP address of one computer, to which they pass all the data they need to send outside the LAN. This machine is called the *default gateway*, which is just another way of saying "the local router" (Figure 19.18).

FIGURE 19.18 Setting a default gateway

Domain Name Service Knowing that users could not remember lots of IP addresses, early Internet pioneers came up with a way to correlate those numbers with more human-friendly computer designations. Special computers, called *Domain Name Service (DNS)* servers, keep databases of IP addresses and their corresponding names. For example, a machine called TOTALSEMINAR1 will be listed in a DNS directory with a corresponding IP address, such as 209.34.45.163. So instead of accessing the \\209.34.45.163\FREDC share to copy a file, you can ask to see \\TOTALSEMINAR1\FREDC. Your system will then query the DNS server to get TOTALSEMINAR1's IP address and use that to find the right machine.

Unless you want to type in IP addresses all of the time, a TCP/IP network will need at least one DNS server (Figure 19.19). You can manually set DNS settings on PCs in a network—what CompTIA calls *client-side DNS*—or you can use automatic settings (see "DHCP" next).

FIGURE 19.19 Adding two DNS servers in Windows

The Internet has regulated domain names. If you want a domain name that others can access on the Internet, you must register your domain name and pay a small yearly fee. In most cases, your ISP can handle this for you. Originally, DNS names all ended with one of the following seven domain name qualifiers, called *top-level domains (TLDs)*:

.com	General business	**.org**	Nonprofit organizations
.edu	Educational organizations	**.gov**	Government organizations
.mil	Military organizations	**.net**	Internet organizations
.int	International		

As more and more countries joined the Internet, an entire new level of domains was added to the original seven to indicate a DNS name in a particular country, such as *.uk* for the United Kingdom. It's common to see DNS names such as *www.bbc.co.uk* or *www.louvre.fr.* The Internet Corporation for Assigned Names and Numbers (ICANN) has announced the creation of several more new domains, including *.name, .info,* and others. Given the explosive growth of the Internet, these are unlikely to be the last ones!

Local Lingo

WINS The *Windows Internet Name Service (WINS)* enabled Windows NetBIOS network names such as SERVER1 to be correlated to IP addresses on ancient Windows systems. Modern Windows networks don't use WINS; they use an improved "dynamic" DNS (DDNS) that supports both Internet names and Windows names.

DHCP Every machine in a TCP/IP network must have an IP address. This can be added manually using the TCP/IP Properties dialog box. A permanent IP address assigned to a machine is known as a *static* IP address.

Dynamic Host Configuration Protocol (DHCP) enables you to create a pool of IP addresses that are given temporarily to machines. DHCP is especially handy for networks with a lot of laptops that join and leave the network on a regular basis—why give a machine that is on the network for only a few hours a day a static IP address? For that reason, DHCP is quite popular. If you add a NIC to a Windows system, the default TCP/IP settings are set to use DHCP. When you accept those automatic settings, you're really telling the machine to use DHCP (Figure 19.20).

FIGURE 19.20 Obtain an IP address automatically.

A typical DHCP server hands out an IP address, subnet mask, default gateway address, and DNS server addresses.

TCP/IP Tools

All versions of Windows come with handy tools to test TCP/IP networks. Those that you're most likely to use in the field are ping, ipconfig, nslookup, and tracert. All of these programs are command prompt utilities—you must open a command prompt to run them.

ping The *ping* command is a great way to determine whether your system can talk to another system. Here's how it works. Get to a command prompt and type **ping** followed by an IP address or by a DNS name, such as **ping www.chivalry.com**. Press the ENTER key on your keyboard and away it goes. Figure 19.21 shows the common syntax for ping.

The ping command has a few options beyond the basics that CompTIA wants you to know about. The first option is –*t*. By using the –*t* switch, ping continuously sends ping packets until you stop it with the break command (CTRL-C). The second option is the –*l* switch, which enables you to specify how big a ping packet to send. This helps in diagnosing specific problems with the routers between your computer and the computer you ping.

```
Administrator: C:\Windows\system32\cmd.exe

C:\>ping /?

Usage: ping [-t] [-a] [-n count] [-l size] [-f] [-i TTL] [-v TOS]
            [-r count] [-s count] [[-j host-list] | [-k host-list]]
            [-w timeout] [-R] [-S srcaddr] [-4] [-6] target_name

Options:
    -t             Ping the specified host until stopped.
                   To see statistics and continue - type Control-Break;
                   To stop - type Control-C.
    -a             Resolve addresses to hostnames.
    -n count       Number of echo requests to send.
    -l size        Send buffer size.
    -f             Set Don't Fragment flag in packet (IPv4-only).
    -i TTL         Time To Live.
    -v TOS         Type Of Service (IPv4-only).
    -r count       Record route for count hops (IPv4-only).
    -s count       Timestamp for count hops (IPv4-only).
    -j host-list   Loose source route along host-list (IPv4-only).
    -k host-list   Strict source route along host-list (IPv4-only).
    -w timeout     Timeout in milliseconds to wait for each reply.
    -R             Use routing header to test reverse route also (IPv6-only).
    -S srcaddr     Source address to use.
    -4             Force using IPv4.
    -6             Force using IPv6.

C:\>
```

FIGURE 19.21 The ping command's syntax

ipconfig The Windows command line tool *ipconfig* gives you a quick glance at a computer's network settings. Choose Start | Run or Search and type **cmd** to get a command prompt. From the prompt, type **ipconfig /all** (note the space before the slash) to see all of your TCP/IP settings (Figure 19.22).

When you have a static IP address, ipconfig does little beyond reporting your current IP settings, including your IP address, subnet mask, default gateway, DNS servers, and WINS servers. It'll also show whether or not a computer has DHCP enabled, as long as you use the /all switch. When using DHCP, ipconfig is also the primary tool for releasing and renewing your IP address. Type **ipconfig /renew** to get a new IP address or **ipconfig /release** to give up the IP address you currently have.

nslookup The *nslookup* command is a powerful command line program that enables you to determine exactly what information the DNS server is giving you about a specific host name. Every version of Windows makes nslookup available when you install TCP/IP. To run the program, type **nslookup** from the command line and press the ENTER key (Figure 19.23). Notice that this gives you a little information, but the prompt has changed—that's because you're running the application. Type **exit** and press the ENTER key to return to the command prompt.

```
Administrator: C:\Windows\system32\cmd.exe

C:\>ipconfig /all

Windows IP Configuration

    Host Name . . . . . . . . . . . . : michaels
    Primary Dns Suffix  . . . . . . . : totalhome
    Node Type . . . . . . . . . . . . : Hybrid
    IP Routing Enabled. . . . . . . . : No
    WINS Proxy Enabled. . . . . . . . : No
    DNS Suffix Search List. . . . . . : totalhome

Ethernet adapter Intel Nic:

    Media State . . . . . . . . . . . : Media disconnected
    Connection-specific DNS Suffix  . :
    Description . . . . . . . . . . . : Intel(R) PRO/100 S Desktop Adapter
    Physical Address. . . . . . . . . : 00-02-B3-41-6F-07
    DHCP Enabled. . . . . . . . . . . : Yes
    Autoconfiguration Enabled . . . . : Yes

Ethernet adapter Gigabit NIC:

    Connection-specific DNS Suffix  . :
    Description . . . . . . . . . . . : Realtek RTL8169/8110 Family PCI Gigabit E
thernet NIC (NDIS 6.0)
    Physical Address. . . . . . . . . : 00-0D-61-52-4D-8F
    DHCP Enabled. . . . . . . . . . . : Yes
    Autoconfiguration Enabled . . . . : Yes
    Link-local IPv6 Address . . . . . : fe80::c547:4dd3:86a3:739d%8(Preferred)
    IPv4 Address. . . . . . . . . . . : 192.168.4.49(Preferred)
    Subnet Mask . . . . . . . . . . . : 255.255.255.0
    Lease Obtained. . . . . . . . . . : Thursday, September 25, 2008 8:27:19 AM
    Lease Expires . . . . . . . . . . : Friday, October 03, 2008 8:27:19 AM
    Default Gateway . . . . . . . . . : fe80::213:10ff:fee8:263d%8
                                        192.168.4.1
    DHCP Server . . . . . . . . . . . : 192.168.4.11
    DNS Servers . . . . . . . . . . . : 192.168.4.11
    NetBIOS over Tcpip. . . . . . . . : Enabled
```

FIGURE 19.22 An ipconfig /all command on Windows 7

Travel Advisory

You can do some cool stuff with nslookup, and consequently some techs love the tool. It's way outside the scope of CompTIA A+ certification, but if you want to play with it, type **help** at the nslookup prompt and press ENTER to see a list of common commands and syntax.

tracert The *tracert* utility shows the route that a packet takes to get to its destination. From a command line, type **tracert** followed by a space and an IP address or DNS name. The output describes the route from your machine to the destination machine, including all devices it passes through and how long each hop takes (Figure 19.24). The tracert command can come in handy when you have to troubleshoot bottlenecks. When users complain that it's difficult to reach a particular destination using TCP/IP, you can run this utility to determine whether the problem exists on a machine or connection over which you have control, or if it is a problem on another machine or router.

```
Administrator: C:\Windows\system32\cmd.exe

C:\>tracert www.chivalry.com

Tracing route to www.chivalry.com [69.94.71.175]
over a maximum of 30 hops:

  1     1 ms     1 ms     1 ms  Router.totalhome [192.168.4.1]
  2     8 ms     8 ms    16 ms  adsl-208-190-121-38.dsl.hstntx.swbell.net [208.1
90.121.38]
  3     8 ms     8 ms     8 ms  dist2-vlan50.hstntx.sbcglobal.net [151.164.11.12
5]
  4     8 ms     8 ms     8 ms  bb2-g14-0.hstntx.sbcglobal.net [151.164.92.206]

  5    75 ms    61 ms    61 ms  12.83.63.165
  6    61 ms    61 ms    61 ms  ded1-g2-3-0.mrdnct.sbcglobal.net [151.164.42.55]

  7    90 ms    67 ms    62 ms  orm-llc-1123020.cust.snet.net [69.183.190.38]
  8    70 ms    66 ms   102 ms  69.94.1.69
  9    61 ms    61 ms    62 ms  chivalry.com [69.94.71.175]

Trace complete.

C:\>_
```

Exam Tip

Although there are other tools that will do this, the *netstat* command shows active TCP/IP connections to a computer. You can use netstat as a quick check when you think a computer has some sort of virus, for example, and has excessive network traffic.

Steps for Configuring TCP/IP

By default, TCP/IP is configured to receive an IP address automatically from a DHCP server on the network (and automatically assign a corresponding subnet mask). To configure an alternative IP address means to input the address settings manually. As far as the CompTIA A+ certification exams are concerned, CompTIA Network+ techs and administrators give you the IP address, subnet mask, and default gateway information, and then you plug them into the PC. That's about it—so here's how to do it manually:

1. In Windows XP, open the Control Panel and double-click the Network Connections applet. Double-click the Local Area Connection icon.

 In Windows Vista, right-click Network and then click *Manage network connections*. After that, double-click the Local Area Network icon. In Windows 7, right-click Network and select Properties. Then select *Change adapter settings* and right-click Local Area Connection.

2. Click the Properties button, highlight Internet Protocol (TCP/IP), and click the Properties button. In Windows Vista/7, you should highlight Internet Protocol Version 4 (TCP/IPv4) because Vista and 7 both have IPv4 and IPv6 installed by default.

3. In the dialog box, click the radio button next to *Use the following IP address*.

4. Enter the IP address in the appropriate fields.

5. Press the TAB key to skip down to the Subnet mask field. Note that the subnet mask is entered automatically, although you can type over this if you want to enter a different subnet mask. See Figure 19.25.

6. Optionally, enter the IP address for a default gateway (a router or another computer system that will forward transmissions beyond your network).

7. Optionally, enter the IP addresses of a primary and a secondary DNS server.

FIGURE 19.25 Internet Protocol (TCP/IP) Properties

8. Click the OK button to close the dialog box.

9. Click the Close button to exit the Local Area Connection Status dialog box.

10. Windows will alert you that you must restart the system for the changes to take effect.

Automatic Private IP Addressing

Windows supports a feature called *Automatic Private IP Addressing (APIPA)* that automatically assigns an IP address to the system when the client cannot obtain an IP address automatically. The Internet Assigned Numbers Authority (IANA), the nonprofit corporation responsible for assigning IP addresses and managing root servers, has set aside the range of addresses from 169.254.0.1 to 169.254.255.254 for this purpose.

If the computer system cannot contact a DHCP server, the computer randomly chooses an address in the form of 169.254.*x.y* (where *x.y* is the computer's identifier) and a 16-bit subnet mask (255.255.0.0) and broadcasts it on the network segment (subnet). If no other computer responds to the address,

the system assigns this address to itself. When using APIPA, the system can communicate only with other computers on the same subnet that also use the 169.254.*x.y* range with a 16-bit mask. APIPA is enabled by default if your system is configured to obtain an IP address automatically.

Exam Tip
A computer system on a network with an active DHCP server that has an IP address in this range (169.254.0.1 to 169.254.255.254) usually indicates a problem connecting to the DHCP server.

Sharing and Security

Windows systems can share all kinds of resources: files, folders, entire drives, printers, faxes, Internet connections, and much more. Conveniently for you, the CompTIA A+ certification exams limit their interests to folders, printers, and Internet connections. Let's see how to share folders and printers now; we'll save Internet connection sharing for Chapter 21.

Simple File Sharing

With *simple file sharing,* you essentially have one local sharing option: to put anything you want to share into the Shared Documents. To share a folder over a network, you have only a couple of options as well—to share or not to share, and if you share, whether to give full control to everybody. It's pretty much all or nothing.

Windows XP Home and Media Center provide only simple file sharing, so the sharing of files and folders is straightforward. Windows XP Professional, on the other hand, enables you to turn off simple file sharing and unlock the true power of NTFS and permissions. To turn off simple file sharing, in some form of Windows Explorer, such as My Documents, go to Tools | Folder Options and select the View tab. The very last option on the View tab is *Use simple file sharing (recommended).* Deselect that option and then click OK. Windows Vista and 7 do not allow simple file sharing.

Sharing Drives and Folders

All versions of Windows share drives and folders in basically the same manner. Simply right-click any drive or folder and choose Properties. Select the Sharing tab (Figure 19.26). Select *Share this folder,* add something in the *Comment* or *User limit* field if you want (neither is required), and click Permissions to open the Permissions dialog box (Figure 19.27).

FIGURE 19.26 Windows Sharing tab on NTFS volume

FIGURE 19.27 Network permissions

Hey! Doesn't NTFS have all those wild permissions such as Read, Execute, Take Ownership, and all that? Yes, it does, but NTFS permissions and network permissions are totally separate beasties. Microsoft wanted Windows to support many different file systems (NTFS, FAT16, FAT32), old and new. Network permissions are Microsoft's way of enabling you to administer file sharing on any type of partition supported by Windows, no matter how ancient. Sure, your options will be pretty limited if you are working with an older partition type, but you *can* do it.

NTFS is where the power lies, but power always comes with a price: you must configure two separate sets of permissions. If you share a folder on an NTFS drive, you must set *both* the network permissions and the NTFS permissions to enable others to access your shared resources. Just set the network permissions to give everyone full control, and then use the NTFS permissions to exercise more precise control over *who* accesses the shared resources and *how* they access them. Open the Security tab to set the NTFS permissions.

Travel Advisory

In Windows, you can set security on files and folders in two places: share permissions, which apply security to the folder that is designated to be a connection point to the files and folders within that folder, and NTFS security on files and folders. Share permissions affect only network users who access the files and folders from across a network, while NTFS security affects both network and local users. Share permissions is another term for network permissions.

Setting Up a Homegroup

We talked about homegroups earlier, so now let's look at how to set one up. To make a homegroup, open the HomeGroup Control Panel applet. Assuming you currently connect to a workgroup and haven't already created a homegroup, you'll see a dialog box like the one shown in Figure 19.28.

Click the *Create a homegroup* button to create a homegroup. You'll then see the Create a Homegroup dialog box shown in Figure 19.29.

Notice the five options: Pictures, Music, Videos, Documents, and Printers. The Documents check box is probably not checked, but go ahead and check it to share all five things. Click Next to see the homegroup's password (see Figure 19.30).

Travel Advisory

Interestingly, all homegroup data is encrypted between systems.

FIGURE 19.28 Default HomeGroup dialog box

Perhaps you've heard that you shouldn't write down passwords? Well, this password is so long that you might *need* to write it down. The dialog box even gives you a way to print it out! Click Next one more time to see the dialog box shown in Figure 19.31. This is the dialog box you will now see every time you click the HomeGroup applet in the Control Panel.

FIGURE 19.29 Create a Homegroup dialog box

FIGURE 19.30 The homegroup's password

FIGURE 19.31 Homegroup configured

FIGURE 19.32 HomeGroup showing an existing homegroup

Once you've created a homegroup, go to another computer on the network and open the HomeGroup Control Panel applet. Assuming all the factors stated earlier, you will see a dialog box like Figure 19.32.

Click the Join now button, enter the password, choose which libraries you want to share with everyone else, and the new computer is in the homegroup!

Accessing Shared Drives/Directories

Once you have set up a drive or directory to be shared, the final step is to access that shared drive or directory from another machine. Windows XP uses My Network Places and Windows Vista/7 use Network, although you'll need to do a little clicking to get to the shared resources (Figure 19.33).

Network resources can also be "mapped" to a local resource name. For example, the FREDC share can be mapped to be a local hard drive letter such as V: or W:. From within any Explorer window (such as My Documents or Documents), choose Tools | Map Network Drive to open the Map Network Drive dialog box (Figure 19.34). In Windows Vista/7, you'll need to press the ALT key once to see the menu bar. Click the Browse button to check out the neighborhood and find a shared drive or folder (Figure 19.35).

FIGURE 19.33 Shared resources in Network

FIGURE 19.34 Map Network Drive dialog box in Windows Vista

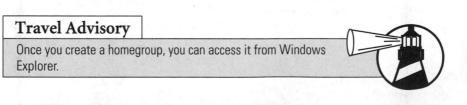

FIGURE 19.35 Browsing for shared folders

With homegroups, accessing shared files is a snap. Access the files shared through a homegroup by opening Windows Explorer, as shown in Figure 19.36. To see what others are sharing, select the corresponding computer name. You can then open those libraries to see the shared folders.

> **Travel Advisory**
>
> Once you create a homegroup, you can access it from Windows Explorer.

Issues with NTFS vs. Share Permissions

Due to the overlapping nature of permissions when using NTFS, several issues can trip up the unsuspecting tech or user when trying to access resources shared on a network. First, deny trumps allow. In other words, if user Bob has full-control access to a share, but that share locally has NTFS set to deny Bob access, Bob will get nothing.

FIGURE 19.36 Using homegroups

Exam Tip

If a file or folder has the encryption attribute set to on, it can't be copied or moved over a network. Encryption is tied to local user accounts.

Second, moving and copying folders and files differ in the level of permission required. Moving is essentially two steps: copying the folder or file to the new location and then deleting it from the old location. With read-only permission, a user could copy but not delete, and thus not move a folder or file.

Third, by default, subfolders and files in them inherit the permissions of the folder that holds them. In Windows 7, if you access a folder's Properties dialog box, click the Security tab, and then click the Advanced button, you'll see a little check box that says *Include inheritable permissions from this object's parent.* In other words, a user receives the parent folder's permissions for any files or subfolders created in that folder—a feature called *inheritance.* All versions of Windows have inheritance turned on by default, which most of the time is a good idea.

Inheritance also affects files and folders that you move or copy. With permission propagation, when you place an item in a folder, it gets the permissions of that folder. If you had a read-only file in one folder, but then copied it to a folder with read/write permissions set, that copy becomes read/write too!

> **Exam Tip**
>
> Windows automatically protects system files and folders accessible over a network.

Administrative Shares

Every version of Windows since Windows NT comes with several default shares, notably all hard drives (such as the C: drive, *C$*)—not optical drives or removable devices, such as thumb drives—plus the *%systemroot%* folder—usually C:\Windows (labeled *admin$*)—and a couple of others, depending on the system. These *administrative shares* give local administrators administrative access to these resources, whether they log in locally or remotely. (In contrast, shares added manually are called *local shares.*)

Administrative shares are odd ducks. You cannot change the default permissions on them. You can delete them, but Windows will re-create them automatically every time you reboot. They're hidden, so they don't appear when you browse a machine over the network, although you can map them by name. Keep the administrator password safe, and these default shares won't affect the overall security of the computer.

> **Travel Advisory**
>
> Administrative shares have been exploited by malware programs, especially because many users who set up their computers never give the administrator account a password. Starting with Windows XP Home, Microsoft changed the remote access permissions for such machines. If you log into a computer remotely as administrator with no password, you get guest access rather than administrator access. That neatly nips potential exploits in the bud.

Universal Naming Convention

All computers that share must have a network name, and all of the resources they share must also have network names. Any resource on a network can be described by combining the names of the resource being shared and the system that's sharing it. So, for example, if a machine called SERVER1 is sharing its C: drive as FREDC, the complete name would be described like this:

```
\\SERVER1\FREDC
```

This is called the *universal naming convention (UNC)*. The UNC is distinguished by its use of double backslashes in front of the sharing system's name and a single backslash in front of the shared resource's name.

net

Windows enables you to view a network quickly from the command line through the *net command*. This works great when you plug into a network for the first time and, naturally, don't know the names of the other computers on that network. To see the many options that net offers, type **net** at a command prompt and press ENTER. The view and use options offer excellent network tools.

You can think of net view as the command line version of My Network Places/Network. When run, net view returns a list of Windows computers on the network:

```
C:\Users\Mike>net view
Server Name            Remark
-------------------------------------------------------
\\SABERTOOTH
\\UBERBOX
\\SERVER1
```

The command completed successfully.

```
C:\Users\Mike>
```

Once you know the names of the computers, you type **net view** followed by the computer name. The net view command will show any shares on that machine and whether they are mapped drives:

```
C:\>net view server1
Shared resources at SERVER1
Share name   Type   Used as   Comment
-------------------------------------------------------
FREDC        Disk
Research     Disk   W:
The command completed successfully.
```

The net use command is a command line method for mapping network shares. For example, if you wanted to map the Research share shown in the previous example to the X: drive, you simply type

```
C:\>net use x: \\server1\research
```

This will map drive X: to the Research share on the SERVER1 computer.

nbtstat

The nbtstat command is an old command line utility that goes back to before Windows. It stands for NetBIOS over TCP/IP Statistics. Even though NetBIOS is long gone, it's still a great tool for learning anything "Windowsy" you want to know about your network, such as "What other workgroups or domains are on this network?" It's also a great tool to answer the question, "Who am I connected to right now?" Try running **nbtstat –s** to see all your connections:

```
C:\>nbtstat -s
Local Area Connection:
Node IpAddress: [192.168.15.102] Scope Id: []
                    NetBIOS Connection Table

    Local Name         State     In/Out  Remote Host     Input   Output

    ----------------------------------------------------------------------

    UBERBOX     <00>   Connected  Out     SABERTOOTH      <20>    1KB
        769B
    UBERBOX     <00>   Connected  Out     AARONV          <20>    760B
        606B
    UBERBOX     <00>   Connected  Out     AARONV          <20>    950B
        695B
    UBERBOX     <00>   Connected  Out     THEATER         <20>    620B
        659B
    UBERBOX            Connected  In      SABERTOOTH      <00>    649KB
        791KB
C:\>
```

Note that nbtstat –s shows every connection, even if two computers have multiple connections. You can also use nbtstat with the –c switch for a more abbreviated list:

```
C:\>nbtstat -c
Local Area Connection:
Node IpAddress: [192.168.15.102] Scope Id: []

                    NetBIOS Remote Cache Name Table
        Name              Type       Host Address      Life [sec]
    -----------------------------------------------------------------
    AARONV      <20>  UNIQUE     192.168.15.100          327
    SABERTOOTH  <20>  UNIQUE     192.168.15.101          485
    THEATER     <20>  UNIQUE     192.168.15.201          380
C:\>
```

Sharing Printers

Sharing printers in Windows is just as easy as sharing drives and directories. Assuming that the system has printer sharing services loaded, just go to the Printers/Devices and Printers folder in the Control Panel or Start menu and right-click the printer you want to share. Select Sharing and then click *Share this*

printer and give it a name (see Figure 19.37). In Windows 7, there is no *Share this printer* button, so you have to right-click the printer, select *Printer properties*, and then go to the Sharing tab to do this.

To access a shared printer in any version of Windows, simply click the Add Printer icon in the Printers folder. When asked if the printer is Local or Network, select Network; browse the network for the printer you want to access, and Windows takes care of the rest. In almost all cases, Windows will copy the printer driver from the sharing machine. In the rare case where it doesn't, it will prompt you for drivers.

To add a printer via TCP/IP, do the following:

1. Re-open the Add Printer Wizard.

2. Select Local Printer and uncheck *Automatically detect and install my plug-and-play printer* if needed. Click Next.

FIGURE 19.37 Naming a shared printer in Windows XP

3. On the next screen, select *Create a new port* and choose Standard TCP/IP Port. Click Next.

4. When prompted, enter the printer name or IP address for the printer you are trying to connect to.

5. Click Next, and Windows will attempt to connect to that printer. If needed, you will be prompted to install drivers.

6. Finish the wizard as instructed by the Add Printer Wizard.

One of the most pleasant aspects of configuring a system for networking under all versions of Microsoft Windows is the amazing amount of the process that is automated. For example, if Windows detects a NIC in a system, it will automatically install the NIC driver, a network protocol (TCP/IP), and Client for Microsoft Networks (the NetBIOS part of the Microsoft networking software). So if you want to share a resource, everything you need is automatically installed.

Objective 19.06 Troubleshooting Networks

After you go beyond a single PC and enter the realm of networked computers, your troubleshooting skills need to take a giant leap up in quality. Think of the complexity added with networks. Suddenly you have multiple PCs with multiple users who could, at the drop of a hat, do all kinds of inadvertent damage to a fully functional PC. Networked PCs have a layer of networked hardware and resource sharing that adds a completely new dimension to a user's cry for help, "I can't print!"

CompTIA likes to ask questions that deal with "no connectivity." There are two ways to look at connectivity issues, and CompTIA A+ exam objectives don't specify which type is covered on the exams. The first type of connectivity issue (and probably the one CompTIA means) is when your computer loses physical connectivity. The second type is when you're on the network and can't access a particular resource (you can access other resources, just not the one you want right now). Let's consider both.

OSI Seven-Layer Model

A lot of people think about networks and troubleshoot networking issues using the Open System Interconnection (OSI) seven-layer model. Using this model (or my four-layer model, described in the next section) helps you isolate problems and then implement solutions. Here are the seven layers of the OSI model:

- **Layer 1** Physical
- **Layer 2** Data Link
- **Layer 3** Network
- **Layer 4** Transport
- **Layer 5** Session
- **Layer 6** Presentation
- **Layer 7** Application

The *Physical layer* defines the physical form taken by data when it travels across a cable. Devices that work at the Physical layer include NICs, hubs, and switches. Figure 19.38 shows a sending NIC turning a string of 1's and 0's into an electrical signal and a receiving NIC turning it back into the same 1's and 0's.

The *Data Link layer* defines the rules for accessing and using the Physical layer. MAC addresses and Ethernet's CSMA/CD operate at the Data Link layer.

The *Network layer* defines the rules for adding information to the data packet that controls how routers move it from its source on one network to its destination on a different network. The IP protocol that handles IP addressing works on Layer 3.

| **FIGURE 19.38** | The Physical layer turns binary code into a physical signal and back into 1's and 0's. |

The *Transport layer,* Layer 4, breaks up data it receives from the upper layers (that is, Layers 5–7) into smaller pieces for transport within the data packets created at the lower layers. In TCP/IP networks, the protocols that typically handle this transition between upper and lower layers are TCP and UDP.

The *Session layer* manages the connections between machines on the network. Protocols such as NetBIOS and sockets enable a computer to connect to a server, for example, and send and receive e-mail or download a file. Each different task you can perform on a server would require a different kind of session.

The *Presentation layer* presents data from the sending system in a form that a receiving system can understand. Most Layer 6 functions are handled by the same software that handles Layer 7 functions.

The *Application layer* is where you (or a user) get to interact with the computers. These are programs that make networking happen, such as Web browsers and e-mail applications.

The key to using the OSI seven-layer model is to ask the traditional troubleshooting question: What can the problem be? If Jill can't browse a Web site, for example, could this be a Layer 7 issue? Sure: If her browser software was messed up, this could stop her from browsing. It could also be a lower-level problem, though, and you need to run through the questions. Can she do anything over the network? If her NIC doesn't show flashing link lights, that could point all the way down to the Physical layer and a bad NIC, cable, hub, or switch. If she has good connectivity to the overall network but can't ping the Web server, that could point to a different problem altogether.

Figure 19.39 shows the OSI seven-layer model graphically.

Exam Tip

Although the 801/802 exam objectives do not mention the OSI seven-layer model, expect to see questions on it on the exams. The questions we've seen focus primarily on the Physical and Data Link layers.

Repairing Physical Cabling

Networks fail for many reasons, and the first thing to know is that good-quality, professionally installed cabling rarely goes bad, but when it does, you need to know what to do. A PC tech needs to know how to help a network tech analyze and fix network problems.

FIGURE 19.39 The OSI seven-layer model

Symptoms

Losing physical connectivity is pretty obvious in Windows. Windows XP gives you a nice pop-up message warning you that you have lost a connection, along with a red X over the network icon (see Figure 19.40). Windows Vista and Windows 7 aren't quite as obvious, displaying only the red X over the network icon in the system tray to show you're not connected (see Figure 19.41).

If you encounter this problem, first check the obvious: Is the cable unplugged at your system? At the wall outlet? Then go for the less obvious: Is the NIC disabled in Device Manager? If these checks don't solve the problem, take a peek on the other side of the cable. If you're not connected to a running switch, you're going to get the disconnect errors.

FIGURE 19.40 Windows XP pop-up message and red X error icon

FIGURE 19.41 Windows 7 red X error icon

Diagnosing Physical Problems

Look for errors that point to physical disconnection. A key clue that the computer may have a physical problem is that a user gets a "No server is found" error, or tries to use the operating system's network explorer utility (like Network in Windows 7) and doesn't see any systems besides his or her own.

Multiple systems failing to access the network often points to hardware problems. This is where knowledge of your network cabling helps. If all the systems connected to one switch suddenly no longer see the network but all the other systems in your network still function, you not only have a probable hardware problem, but also have a suspect: the switch.

Check the Lights

If you suspect a hardware problem, first check the link lights on the NIC and switch. If they're not lit, you know the cable isn't connected somewhere. If you're not physically at the system in question (if you're on a tech call, for example), you can have the user check his or her connection status through the link lights or through software.

If the problem system clearly cannot connect, eliminate the possibility of a failed switch or other larger problem by checking to make sure other people can access the network and that other systems can access the shared resource (server) that the problem system can't see. Inspect the cable running from the back of the PC to the outlet. Finally, if you can, plug the system into a known good outlet and see if it works. A veteran network tech keeps a long patch cable for just this purpose. If you get connectivity with the second outlet, you should begin to suspect the structured cable running from the first outlet to the switch. Assuming the cable is installed properly and has been working correctly before this event, a simple continuity test will confirm your suspicion in most cases.

Check the NIC

Be warned that a bad NIC can also generate a "can't see the network" problem. Use the utility provided by the OS to verify that the NIC works. If you've got a NIC with diagnostic software, run it—this software will check the NIC's circuitry. The NIC's female connector is a common failure point, so NICs that come with diagnostic software often include a special test called a *loopback test*.

FIGURE 19.42 Loopback plug

A loopback test sends data out of the NIC and checks to see if it comes back. Some NICs perform only an internal loopback, which tests the circuitry that sends and receives, but not the actual connecting pins. A true external loopback requires a *loopback plug* inserted into the NIC's port (see Figure 19.42). If a NIC is bad, replace it.

| Travel Advisory |

Onboard NICs on laptops are especially notorious for breaking due to frequent plugging and unplugging. On some laptops, the NICs are easy to replace; others require a motherboard replacement.

Cable Testing

You can test cable at all levels of networking, assuming you have the right tools. In the most basic network, with two computers connected to a switch, where there are cables exposed (i.e., not running through the walls), you need physical tools, such as a wire stripper, crimper, multimeter, and cable tester.

If you're making your own network cables, the first tool you'd use is a *wire stripper* to clear off the end of the protective cover on the UTP cable. Save it for CompTIA Network+.

A *crimper* or *crimping tool* tightens an RJ-45 jack onto a twisted pair cable. If you're working with homemade cables and the RJ-45 jack didn't get tightened on properly, you can try a crimper to squeeze it more.

You can use a *multimeter*—like the ones used to test power supplies—to test continuity and see if the send wire on one RJ-45 connects to the proper wire on the other RJ-45. *You will never do this,* but it shows up on the 801 exam. Far more commonly, you'd use a simple cable tester.

A *cable tester* checks continuity and to see if the proper wiring standards were followed. You press both ends of a cable into the two sockets on the cable tester, press the button, and the lights or LEDs tell you whether you have a T568A or B on both ends or if one or more wires didn't connect properly on the homemade cable (see Figure 19.43).

In a SOHO environment, the vast majority of network disconnection problems occur at the *work area.* (That's where you'll find the RJ-45 wall jack.) If you've tested those connections, though, and the work area seems fine, it's time to consider deeper issues.

With the right equipment, diagnosing a bad cabling run is easy. Anyone with a full-blown office network should own a *time domain reflectometer (TDR)* such as the Fluke MicroScanner. A TDR measures impedance in network cabling. If the tester measures any impedance, something is wrong with the cable. With a little practice, you can easily determine not only whether a cable is disconnected but also where the disconnection takes place. Sometimes patience is required, especially if you've failed to label your cable runs, but you will find the problem.

FIGURE 19.43 A cable tester in action

Toners

It would be nice to say that all cable installations are perfect and that over the years they won't tend to grow into horrific piles of spaghetti-like, unlabeled cables. In the real world, though, you might eventually find yourself having to locate, or *trace,* cables. Even in the best-planned networks, labels fall off ports and outlets, mystery cables appear behind walls, new cable runs are added, and mistakes are made counting rows and columns on patch panels. Sooner or later, most network techs will have to be able to pick out one particular cable or port from a stack.

When the time comes to trace cables, network techs turn to a device called a toner for help. *Toner* is the generic term for two separate devices that are used together: a tone generator and a tone probe. The *tone generator* connects to the cable using alligator clips, tiny hooks, or a network jack, and it sends an electrical signal along the wire at a certain frequency. The *tone probe* emits a sound when it is placed near a cable connected to the tone generator. These two devices are often referred to by the brand-name Fox and Hound, a popular model of toner made by the Triplett Corporation (see Figure 19.44).

| FIGURE 19.44 | Fox and Hound |

> **Exam Tip**
>
> You'll see a tone probe referred to on the CompTIA A+ exam as a *toner probe*.

To trace a cable, connect the tone generator to the known end of the cable in question, and then position the tone probe next to the other end of each of the cables that might be the right one. The tone probe makes a sound when it's placed next to the right cable. Some toners have one tone probe that works with multiple tone generators. Each generator emits a separate frequency, and the probe sounds a different tone for each one. Even good toners are relatively inexpensive ($75); although inexpensive toners can cost less than $25, they don't tend to work well, so spending a little more is worthwhile. Just keep in mind that if you have to support a network, you'd do best to own a decent toner.

> **Local Lingo**
>
> **Punchdown tool** For some unknown reason, the 801 exam insists that you know that you would use a *punchdown tool* in the rare instance where you needed to go into the wiring closet, access the rack, and connect the end of a cable run to the punchdown block. That's a job for a network tech or cable installer, not a CompTIA A+ tech, but don't be shocked if you see it on your exam.

Other No Connectivity Problems

If you have an APIPA address (an IP address that starts 169.154.*x.y* with a Class B subnet mask), that clearly points to no connectivity to a DHCP server. This could point to a physical problem (dead cable, broken switch) or a configuration error. If the network has no DHCP server, for example, you'd need to reconfigure the disconnected PC to use a static IP address.

If you've previously connected a portable PC to a static network and then plug it into a different network—one that uses statically or dynamically assigned IPs—you could get an IP conflict error. Since no two devices on a network can share an IP address, the second one to join would get no connectivity.

Fixing Common Problems

Let's go back and look at the second possible meaning for a loss in connectivity. It's very common to try to connect to a shared resource and either fail or find that a shared resource you've used time and again has suddenly disappeared.

Failing to Connect to a New Resource

When you can't connect to a resource on the first try, it often points to a configuration issue. In most cases, a quick double-check of the sharing system will reveal one of the following problems (and call for the associated solution):

- You don't have the right share name? Go check at the serving system.
- You don't have the required user name/password? Ask someone who might have this knowledge, or double-check that your account has access.
- You don't have permission to use/access/connect to the shared resource? Make sure you have the correct permissions.
- You're not on the right homegroup/domain/workgroup? Check your system and the sharing system to verify which workgroup/domain name to use. On a homegroup, make sure you've used the proper password.
- The folder or printer isn't shared? Share it!
- The folder or printer doesn't exist? Make sure the serving system still hosts the folder you want. Install the network printer if you haven't yet.

Failing to Connect to a Previously Used Resource

If you suddenly can't connect to a resource that you've used many times before, go with the easy answers first:

- Verify that you are not already connected by using **nbtstat –s**.
- Check that you can see the resource using My Network Places/Network or **net view**.
- Check that the serving system is on.
- Check that the computer is physically connected to the serving system.

CHECKPOINT

✔ **Objective 19.01: Networking Components for the PC** Network interface cards (NICs) send data on to the network cabling as discrete chunks called data packets, or frames. Every NIC has a unique 48-bit MAC address. PCs also need a client service and a common protocol. The most popular protocol is TCP/IP. The connection-oriented protocol used with TCP/IP is called the *Transmission Control Protocol* (*TCP*). The connectionless one is called the *User Datagram Protocol* (*UDP*).

✔**Objective 19.02: Types of Networks** A *local area network (LAN)* is a group of computers that are located physically close to each other. A *wide area network (WAN)* is a widespread group of computers connected using long-distance technologies.

Bus topology refers to a network in which all computers are physically connected by a single length of cable. Each end of the cable must be terminated. Ring topology also refers to a network in which a single length of cable connects all computers, except the ends are joined, thus making, appropriately, a ring. Star topology uses a switch at its center, with each computer connecting to it directly. Mesh topology involves each computer directly connecting to every other computer in the network. Star bus topology involves a bus network inside the switch at the center of a star topology.

✔**Objective 19.03: Network Cabling Standards** Ethernet (10BaseT, 100BaseT, 1000BaseT) uses UTP cabling (usually CAT 5e or CAT 6) with RJ-45 connectors. The maximum distance from an Ethernet switch to any device is 100 meters. Cables come in UTP, STP, and fiber-optic varieties.

Plenum-grade cable is simply network cabling with a fire-retardant jacket and is required for cables that go in the plenum space.

✔**Objective 19.04: Network Operating Systems** Network OSs enable PCs to share resources and access shared resources across a network. They provide a network organization, such as client/server or peer-to-peer. You can make a PC a member of a workgroup or, in high-end settings, a member of a domain.

Domains provide single sign-on and lots of security, but require special servers and lots of administration. To address this, Microsoft introduced a new feature in Windows 7 called *HomeGroup*.

✔**Objective 19.05: Installing and Configuring a LAN** It takes at least four components to have a functional network: NIC, client software, protocol, and server software. First, you need to install a NIC, including proper drivers. Then you must install client software so that the PC can see and be seen on the network. Windows installs the Client for Microsoft Networks by default when you install a NIC. Third, the NIC needs to run a properly configured network protocol that matches that of other machines. The most common protocol in use is TCP/IP, the protocol of the Internet. DHCP sets up your IP address, subnet mask, default gateway, and more, automatically. Any manual settings you'll get from a network administrator. Finally, you must enable File and Printer Sharing to turn the PC into a server and make its resources

available for other users across the network. Sharing resources is a matter of selecting the properties for a folder or device and coming up with a share name. You use My Network Places/Network to access shared resources on a LAN.

✔**Objective 19.06: Troubleshooting Networks** Look for errors that point to physical disconnection. Check the link lights on the NIC and switch. A loopback test sends data out of the NIC and checks to see if it comes back. A true external loopback requires a loopback plug inserted into the NIC's port. Tools for testing cables and connectivity include cable testers and tone probes. Look for DHCP or static IP problems if a system has an APIPA address or IP address conflict, respectively.

REVIEW QUESTIONS

1. To provide a physical and electronic connection from a computer to a network, what must be installed?

 A. A switch

 B. A router

 C. A NIC

 D. A crossover cable

2. What is the maximum distance for a 10/100/1000BaseT segment?

 A. 1000 meters

 B. 330 meters

 C. 185 meters

 D. 100 meters

3. Brad has three Windows 7 computers that he wants to use to share media libraries, such as movies and pictures. One is in the upstairs study; one is in his bedroom; the third is a laptop that he'll use primarily in the kitchen. His house is professionally wired, so it has RJ-45 jacks available in the appropriate places. How should he set up his network to share most easily?

 A. Turn one of the computers into a domain controller and join the other two to the same domain.

 B. Have all three computers join the same workgroup.

 C. Have all three computers join the same homegroup.

 D. Replace his Windows PCs with Mac OS X computers.

4. Which command line tool enables you to see the computers connected to a workgroup or domain?

 A. net use

 B. net view

 C. net see

 D. net scan

5. Richard sets up a small LAN composed of five Windows computers to a router that connects to a DSL connection. What kind of network has he set up?

 A. Client/server

 B. Domain-based

 C. Peer-to-peer

 D. Not enough information

6. Simon's Windows system can't contact a DHCP server to obtain an IP address automatically, but he can still communicate with other systems on his subnet. What feature of Windows makes this possible?

 A. Subnet masking

 B. Windows Internet Naming Service

 C. Automatic Private IP Addressing

 D. Client for Microsoft Networks

7. Everything worked fine on your 10/100/1000BaseT star bus topology network yesterday, but today, no one can connect to the server. The server seems to be in good running order. Which of the following is the most likely problem?

 A. A switch is malfunctioning.

 B. Someone changed all the passwords for server access.

 C. Someone's NIC LED is flashing amber.

 D. The server's cable is wired as TIA/EIA 568A, and all the others are wired as TIA/EIA 568B.

8. How far apart can two PCs that share the same 10/100/1000BaseT switch be placed?

 A. 1000 meters

 B. 330 meters

 C. 200 meters

 D. 100 meters

9. In a TCP/IP network, the two parts of an IP address are the
 _____ and the _____.

 A. Network ID, host ID

 B. IP address, subnet mask

 C. Client, server

 D. TCP address, IP address

10. What is special about plenum-grade network cabling?

 A. Plenum-grade cabling doubles the bandwidth throughput speed.

 B. Plenum-grade cabling increases the maximum length of Ethernet network segments from 100 meters to 185 meters.

 C. Plenum-grade cabling does not give off toxic fumes when burned.

 D. Plenum-grade cabling has no special qualities: it is simply a marketing term.

11. You need to check the status of the local area connection of a Windows XP machine on your Microsoft network. How do you get to the screen where you can perform this task? (Select two.)

 A. Start | right-click My Network Places | Properties | Local Area Connection

 B. Start | Settings | Network and Dial-up Connections | Local Area Connection

 C. Start | Control Panel | Network Connections | Local Area Connection

 D. Right-click My Computer | Properties | Network Connections | Local Area Connection

REVIEW ANSWERS

1. **C** A system must have a network interface card (NIC) to participate in any type of network.

2. **D** 10/100/1000BaseT has a maximum segment distance of 100 meters.

3. **C** Because all three computers run Windows 7, putting them in the same homegroup is the easiest way to share libraries. A workgroup would work, of course, but require that he also create user accounts on each computer and share folders with those specific user accounts.

4. **B** The net view command quickly shows computers connected to a workgroup or domain.

5. **C**　Because no server is involved, Richard must have set up a peer-to-peer network.

6. **C**　Automatic Private IP Addressing is the Windows feature that makes it possible for Simon's system to communicate with other systems on his subnet even though he can't contact a DHCP server to obtain an IP address.

7. **A**　Although someone might have changed all the passwords or the cables during the night, a bad switch is the most probable answer.

8. **C**　As each system can be 100 meters from the switch, any two systems can be up to 200 meters apart.

9. **A**　The two parts of an IP address are the network ID and the host ID.

10. **C**　Unlike normal network cabling, plenum-grade cabling doesn't give off toxic fumes when burned. It is usually required by law when stringing cable into a building's plenum space.

11. **A C**　To check the status of the local area connection of a Windows XP machine on your Microsoft network, you can select either Start | right-click My Network Places | Properties | Local Area Connection, or Start | Control Panel | Network Connections | Local Area Connection.

Wireless Networking

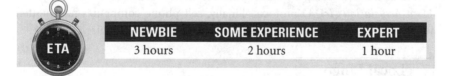

	NEWBIE	SOME EXPERIENCE	EXPERT
ETA	3 hours	2 hours	1 hour

773

Some of the biggest hurdles to setting up a wired network are the wires. Most businesses frown on having CAT 6 cabling running down every hall and along every wall, so wiring a building for networking means installing cabling up into ceiling crawl spaces and down behind walls and paneling. Any tech who's had to do this more than a few times can tell you that "pulling cable" is a tough job even under the best conditions. In many cases, installing network cabling is impractical, and in some cases it may even be prohibited, such as in a building that's been designated a historical landmark. Thankfully, developments in wireless technology give you several alternatives to traditional wired networks.

Objective 20.01 Wireless Networking Basics

A wireless network eliminates the need for the network cabling that connects PCs to one another in a typical wired network. Instead of a physical set of wires running between networked PCs, servers, printers, or other *nodes,* wireless networks use either radio waves or beams of infrared light to communicate with one another.

Various kinds of wireless networking solutions have come and gone. The types of wireless radio wave networks you'll be supporting these days are those based on the most common implementation of the IEEE 802.11 wireless Ethernet standard—*Wi-Fi*—and those based on the *Bluetooth* technology. Wireless networks using infrared light are limited to those that use the *Infrared Data Association (IrDA)* protocol. Finally, cell phone companies have gotten into the mix and now offer access to the Internet through cellular networks.

Local Lingo

Wi-Fi Many folks think that Wi-Fi stands for *wireless fidelity*, a play on high fidelity audio signal, but Wi-Fi is simply a trademark of the Wi-Fi Alliance, the organization that determines the Wi-Fi specifications.

Wireless devices use the same networking protocols and clients that their wired counterparts use, but the basic networking scheme differs. Ethernet bus devices use *carrier sense multiple access/collision detection (CSMA/CD)* to communicate on the same network media without stepping on each other's data

packets; wireless devices use a variation called *carrier sense multiple access/ collision avoidance (CSMA/CA)*.

If two networked systems in a CSMA/CD network attempt to transmit data at the same time, the two packets collide, thereby canceling each other out. This collision is detected by each network node, which responds by generating a random timeout period. When the timeout period expires, the nodes then retransmit the data packet, counting on the randomness of their respective timeouts to prevent another collision. It's not very elegant, but it gets the job done.

Wireless devices use the CSMA/CA networking scheme so that, instead of dealing with collisions after they occur, they proactively take steps to avoid collisions in the first place. Wireless nodes listen in on the wireless medium to see if another node is currently broadcasting data. If so, it waits a random amount of time before retrying.

Exam Tip
Wireless networks use the CSMA/CA media access contention method to transmit data.

Wireless Ethernet offers the option of using the *Request to Send/Clear to Send (RTS/CTS)* protocol. When enabled, a transmitting node that determines whether the wireless medium is clear to use sends an RTS frame to the receiving node. The receiving node responds with a CTS frame, telling the sending node that it's okay to transmit. Then, once the data is sent, the transmitting node waits for an acknowledgment (ACK) from the receiving node before sending the next data packet. It's very elegant, but keep in mind that using RTS/CTS introduces significant overhead to the process and can impede performance.

Exam Tip
Wireless local area networks are called WLANs.

Let's look at the components you need for a wireless network.

Wireless Networking Components

Wireless networking capabilities of one form or another are built into many modern computing devices. Though their popularity may have waned, infrared *transceiver* ports were standard issue on portable computers, personal digital assistants (PDAs), and high-end printers for years. Figure 20.1 shows the infrared transceiver ports on a laptop computer and a PDA.

FIGURE 20.1 Infrared transceiver ports on a laptop and PDA

Wireless Ethernet and Bluetooth capabilities are practically ubiquitous as integrated components, or they can easily be added using USB, PCI, PCI Express, or PC Card adapters. Figure 20.2 shows a PCI card that handles 802.11g.

You can also add wireless network capabilities using an external USB wireless NIC, as shown in Figure 20.3.

FIGURE 20.2 802.11g PCI card

FIGURE 20.3 External USB wireless NIC

Wireless NICs aren't limited to PCs. Many tablets and smartphones have wireless built in or available as add-on options. Figure 20.4 shows a smartphone accessing the Internet wirelessly.

To extend the capabilities of a wireless Ethernet network, such as by connecting to a wired network or by sharing a high-speed Internet connection, you need a *wireless access point (WAP)*. A WAP centrally connects wireless network nodes in the same way that a network switch connects wired PCs. Many WAPs also act as high-speed switches and Internet routers, such as the Linksys device shown in Figure 20.5.

| **FIGURE 20.4** | Smartphone with wireless capability |

Exam Tip

You'll see a WAP referred to as an *access point (AP)* on the exams.

Wireless Networking Software

In terms of configuring wireless networking software, you need to do very little. Wireless network adapters are Plug and Play, so any modern version of Windows will immediately recognize one when installed into a PCI, PCIe, or

Linksys device that acts as wireless access point, switch, and router

PC Card slot, or into a USB port, prompting you to load any needed hardware drivers.

You will, however, need a utility to set your network name. Windows includes built-in tools for configuring these settings, or you can use one from the wireless network adapter vendor. Figure 20.6 shows a typical wireless network adapter configuration utility.

Using this utility, you can determine your link state and signal strength, configure your wireless networking *mode* (discussed in the next section), set security encryption and power-saving options, and perform other networking tasks.

Wireless Network Modes

The simplest wireless network consists of two or more PCs communicating directly with each other without cabling or any other intermediary hardware. More complicated wireless networks use a WAP to centralize wireless communication and bridge wireless network segments to wired network segments. These two different methods, or *modes,* are called *ad hoc* mode and *infrastructure* mode.

Dell Wireless WLAN Card Utility

Wireless Networks | Link Status | Statistics | Site Monitor | Diagnostics | Information

Network status

Connection status:	Connected
Encryption type:	TKIP
Network name (SSID):	CorpHQ_WiFi
Connection type:	Infrastructure
Speed:	54.0 Mbps
Channel:	8 (2447 Mhz)
Radio streams:	1
AP MAC address:	00:1C:10:F4:ED:19
Gateway IP address:	192.168.1.1
Client MAC address:	00:1B:FC:53:C7:B2
Client IP address:	192.168.1.101
Client IPv6 address:	Not available

Signal & noise history

Signal & noise

-31 dBm -92 dBm

OK Cancel Apply Help

FIGURE 20.6 Wireless configuration utility

Ad Hoc Mode

In ad hoc mode, sometimes called peer-to-peer mode, each wireless node is in direct contact with every other node in a decentralized free-for-all, as shown in Figure 20.7. Two or more wireless nodes communicating in ad hoc mode form an *Independent Basic Service Set (IBSS)*.

Ad hoc mode networks are easier to configure than infrastructure mode networks and are suited for small groups of computers (less than a dozen or so) that need to transfer files or share printers. Ad hoc networks are also good for temporary networks such as study groups or business meetings.

Infrastructure Mode

Wireless networks running in infrastructure mode use one or more WAPs to connect the wireless network nodes to a wired network segment, as shown in Figure 20.8. If you plan on setting up a wireless network for a large number of PCs or need to have centralized control over the wireless network, you need to use infrastructure mode.

FIGURE 20.7 Wireless ad hoc mode network

Exam Tip

Wireless networks in infrastructure mode use WAPs, while ad hoc wireless networks do not.

A Wi-Fi network with a single WAP is called a *Basic Service Set (BSS)*. The service area can be extended by adding more WAPs. A bigger network with more than one WAP is called, appropriately, an *Extended Basic Service Set (EBSS)*.

Wireless networks running in infrastructure mode require more planning and are more complicated to configure than ad hoc mode networks, but they also give you finer control over how the network operates. Infrastructure mode

FIGURE 20.8 Wireless infrastructure mode network

is better suited to business networks or networks that need to share dedicated resources such as Internet connections and centralized databases.

Securing a SOHO Wireless Network

One of the major complaints about wireless networking, especially in the small office/home office (SOHO) implementations, is that it offers weak security. In many cases, the only thing you need to do to access a wireless network is walk into an unsecured WAP's coverage area and turn on your wireless device! Further, data packets float through the air instead of traveling safely wrapped up inside network cabling. What's to stop an unscrupulous PC tech with the right equipment from grabbing those packets out of the air and reading that data?

Wireless networks use four methods to secure access to the network itself and secure the data that's being transferred. Changing the *Service Set Identifier (SSID)* parameter—also called the *network name*—and default administrator password is the first step. Better WAPs enable you to change the administrator's user name too. You can tighten security even further by employing *MAC filtering* to create a list of the machines that are permitted to access a network or are denied access to a network. Enabling wireless encryption through *Wired Equivalent Privacy (WEP)*, *Wi-Fi Protected Access (WPA)*, or *WPA2* ensures that the data packets themselves are secure while in transit.

SSID and Administrator User Name and Password

One of the main security weaknesses with wireless networks is that out of the box, *no* security is configured at all! Wireless devices *want* to be heard, and WAPs are usually configured to broadcast their presence to their maximum range, welcoming all other wireless devices that respond.

Always change the default SSID to something unique, and change the administrator password on the WAP right away. If you have the option to change the administrator user name, do that as well. Configuring a unique SSID name and password is the first step you should do to set up a wireless network. The default SSID names and passwords are well known and widely available online. This is intended to make setting up a wireless network as easy as possible, but can cause problems in places with a lot of overlapping wireless networks. Each wireless network node and access point needs to be configured with the same unique SSID name. This SSID name is then included in the header of every data packet broadcast in the wireless network's coverage area. Data packets that lack the correct SSID name in the header are rejected.

If you don't change the default SSID and password, as soon as a potential hacker picks up the "Linksys" network that's broadcasting madly, he'll try to access the WAP using the default password.

MAC Filtering

Most WAPs support MAC address filtering, a method that enables you to limit access to your wireless network using the physical, hard-wired address of the units' wireless network adapters. MAC filtering is a handy way to create a type of "accepted users" or "denied users" list to limit access to your wireless network. A table stored in the WAP—the *access control list (ACL)*—lists the MAC addresses that are permitted to participate or that are excluded from participating in that wireless network. An inclusive list is called a *white list*; a list of excluded MAC addresses is called a *black list*. Any data packets that don't contain the MAC address of a node listed in the white list table are rejected. The reverse is true for a black list.

WEP

The next step up in wireless security is enabling WEP encryption. WEP encryption was meant to secure data being wirelessly transmitted. WEP encryption uses a standard 40-bit encryption to scramble data packets. Many vendors also support 104-bit encryption.

WEP sounds secure, but its implementation contains some serious security flaws. Shortly after it was released, hackers demonstrated that WEP could be cracked in a matter of minutes using software readily available off the Internet. WEP is better than nothing, but it only stops casual prying into a network. It will not deter any serious hacker. The industry quickly came out with a replacement for WEP called WPA.

WPA

WPA was designed to address the weaknesses of WEP, and it functions as a sort of security protocol upgrade to WEP-enabled devices. WPA uses the *Temporal Key Integrity Protocol (TKIP)*, which provides a new encryption key for every sent packet. This protects WPA from many of the attacks that make WEP vulnerable. WPA also offers security enhancements such as an encryption key integrity-checking feature and user authentication through the industry-standard *Extensible Authentication Protocol (EAP)*. The use of EAP is a huge security improvement over WEP. User names and passwords are encrypted and therefore much more secure.

Even with these enhancements, WPA was intended only as an interim security solution until the IEEE 802.11i security standard was finalized.

WPA2

Recent versions of Mac OS X and Microsoft Windows support the full IEEE 802.11i standard, WPA2, to lock down wireless networks. WPA2 uses the Advanced Encryption Standard (AES), among other improvements, to provide a secure wireless environment. If you haven't upgraded to WPA2, you should.

WPS

While most techs can configure wireless networks blindfolded, the thought of passwords and encryption might intimidate the average user. If anything, most people plug in their wireless router and go on their merry way. Because everyone should secure their wireless network, the developers of Wi-Fi created *Wi-Fi Protected Setup (WPS),* a standard included on most WAPs and clients to make secure connections easier to configure.

WPS works in one of two ways. Some devices use a push button, such as the one shown in Figure 20.9, and others use a password or code.

Let's say you want to connect a WPS-capable wireless printer to a WPS-capable WAP. First, you would press the button on the printer for a short moment (usually two seconds). You then have a set time (usually two minutes) to press the button on the WAP. This should automatically configure a secure connection.

Some devices enable you to use a code. A WPS-capable WAP will have an eight-digit numeric code printed on the device. To access the WAP, just enter the code in Windows as you would a WPA/WPA2 password. Now you're on the network.

Sadly, WPS has a security flaw. A hacker can use a program to repeatedly guess the eight-digit code. Because of how the code is set up, it's very easy to guess. As long you have WPS enabled on your WAP, you are vulnerable. The only way to stop this hack is to shut down WPS. Check the WAP manufacturer's Web site for instructions on turning off WPS.

FIGURE 20.9 WPS button on an e2500 router

Access Point Placement and Radio Power

When setting up your wireless network, keep your space in mind. While encryption can protect your network from intruders, you can also limit your risk by hiding your network from outsiders altogether. When using an omnidirectional antenna, keep it near the center of your home or office. The closer you place it to a wall, the farther away someone outside your home or office can be and still detect your wireless network.

Your wireless access point might also enable you to adjust the radio power levels of your antenna. Decrease the radio power until you can get reception at the furthest point *inside* your home or office, but not outside. This will take some trial and error.

Exam Tip

Don't forget to protect the WAP physically, too. Most WAPs have physical Ethernet ports in addition to their wireless capabilities. These ports are not password-protected or encrypted. Keep the WAP in a location where unscrupulous folk can't get to it.

Wireless Networking Speed

Wireless networking data throughput speeds depend on several factors. Foremost is the standard used by the networked wireless devices. Depending on the standard used, wireless throughput speeds range from a measly 2 Mbps to a snappy 100+ Mbps.

Another factor affecting speed is the distance between wireless nodes (or between wireless nodes and centralized WAPs). Wireless devices dynamically negotiate the top speed at which they can communicate without dropping too many data packets. Speed decreases as distance increases, so the maximum throughput speed is achieved only at an extremely close range (less than about 25 feet). At the outer reaches of a device's effective range, speed may decrease to around 1 Mbps before it drops out altogether.

Finally, throughput speed can be affected by interference from other wireless devices operating in the same frequency range, such as cordless phones and baby monitors, as well as by solid objects. So-called *dead spots* occur when something capable of blocking the radio signal comes between wireless network nodes. Large electrical appliances (and some smaller ones, such as microwaves) are *very* effective at blocking wireless network signals. Other culprits include electrical fuse boxes, metal plumbing, and air conditioning units.

Wireless Networking Range

Wireless networking range is hard to define, and you'll see most descriptions listed with qualifiers such as "*around* 150 feet" or "*about* 300 feet." This is simply because, like throughput speed, range is greatly affected by outside factors. Interference from other wireless devices affects range, as does interference from solid objects. The maximum ranges listed in the next section are presented by wireless manufacturers as the theoretical maximum ranges. In the real world, you'll see these ranges only under the most ideal circumstances. The true effective range is probably about half what you see listed.

Range can be increased in a couple of ways. First, you can install multiple WAPs to permit "roaming" between one WAP's coverage area and another's—this is the EBSS described earlier in this chapter. Second, on some models, you can install a higher-gain antenna that increases a single WAP's range.

Objective 20.02 Wireless Networking Standards

To help you gain a better understanding of wireless network technology, here is a brief look at the standards that they use. We'll look at 802.11-based wireless networking and then talk about infrared and Bluetooth networking.

IEEE 802.11–Based Wireless Networking

The IEEE 802.11 wireless Ethernet standard defines methods by which devices can communicate using spread-spectrum radio waves. *Spread-spectrum* broadcasts data in small, discrete chunks over the different frequencies available within a certain frequency range. The 802.11-based wireless technologies broadcast and receive on one of two license-free industrial, scientific, and medical (ISM) *radio frequency (RF)* bands: 2.4 GHz and 5.8 GHz. Even though the ISM band is 5.8 GHz, we just say "5 GHz" for some reason.

The original 802.11 standard has been extended to the 802.11a, 802.11b, 802.11g, and 802.11n variations used in Wi-Fi wireless networks.

Wi-Fi Wireless Networking Standards

Currently, Wi-Fi is by far the most widely adopted type of wireless networking. Not only do thousands of private businesses and homes have wireless networks,

but many public places such as coffee shops and libraries also offer Internet access through wireless networks.

Technically, only wireless devices that conform to the extended versions of the 802.11 standard—802.11a, 802.11b, 802.11g, and 802.11n—are Wi-Fi certified. Wi-Fi certification comes from the Wi-Fi Alliance (formerly the Wireless Ethernet Compatibility Alliance, or WECA), a nonprofit industry group made up of more than 175 member companies that design and manufacture wireless networking products.

Newer wireless devices can communicate with older wireless devices, so if you are using an 802.11n WAP, all of your 802.11g devices can use it. The exception to this is 802.11a, which requires that all the equipment directly support it. The following paragraphs describe the important specifications of each of the popular 802.11-based wireless networking standards.

802.11a Despite the "a" designation of this extension to the 802.11 standard, 802.11a was actually developed *after* 802.11b. 802.11a differs from the other 802.11-based standards in significant ways. Foremost is that it operates in a different frequency range, 5 GHz. This less-popular frequency range means that 802.11a devices are less prone to interference from other devices. 802.11a also offers considerably greater throughput than 802.11 and 802.11b, reaching speeds up to 54 Mbps. Range, however, suffers somewhat, topping out at about 150 feet. Despite the superior speed of 802.11a, it isn't widely adopted in the PC world.

802.11b 802.11b was the first standard to take off in wireless networking. The 802.11b standard supports data throughput of up to 11 Mbps (with actual throughput averaging 4 to 6 Mbps)—on par with older wired 10BaseT networks—and a maximum range of 300 feet under ideal conditions. In a typical office environment, its maximum range is lower. The main downside to using 802.11b is, in fact, that it uses a very popular frequency. The 2.4-GHz band is already crowded with baby monitors, garage door openers, microwaves, and wireless phones, so you're likely to run into interference from other wireless devices.

802.11g 802.11g came out in 2003, taking the best of 802.11a and b and rolling them into a single standard. 802.11g offers data transfer speeds equivalent to 802.11a, up to 54 Mbps, with the wider 300-foot range of 802.11b. More important, 802.11g runs in the 2.4-GHz band so it is backward-compatible with 802.11b, meaning that the same 802.11g WAP can service both 802.11b and 802.11g wireless nodes. 802.11g was incredibly popular, but has pretty much given way to the newest version, 802.11n.

802.11n The 802.11n standard brings several improvements to Wi-Fi networking, including faster speeds and new antenna technology implementations. The 802.11n specification requires all but handheld devices to use multiple antennae to implement a feature called *multiple in/multiple out (MIMO)*, which enables the devices to make multiple simultaneous connections. With up to four antennae, 802.11n devices can achieve amazing speeds. (The official standard supports throughput of up to 600 Mbps, although practical implementation drops that down substantially.)

Like 802.11g, 802.11n WAPs can run in the 2.4-GHz band, supporting earlier, slower 802.11b/g devices. However, 802.11n also has a more powerful, so-called *dual-band*. To use dual-band 802.11n, you need a more advanced (and more expensive) WAP that runs at both 5 GHz and 2.4 GHz simultaneously; some support 802.11a devices as well as 802.11b/g devices. Nice!

Table 20.1 compares the important differences between the versions of the 802.11 standards.

Travel Advisory

Most Wi-Fi devices you can buy right now support WPA2, but what about the millions of older Wi-Fi devices out there working for a living? You can update some devices to support WPA2 with a firmware upgrade or driver update. You'll also need to patch earlier versions of Mac OS X and Windows. Windows Vista/7/8 support WPA2 out of the box.

Infrared Wireless Networking

Wireless networking using infrared technology is largely overlooked these days, probably as a result of the explosion of interest in the newer and faster wireless standards. This is a shame, because infrared provides an easy and reasonably fast way to transfer data, often without the need to purchase or install any additional hardware or software on your PC.

Infrared Data Association Standard

Communication through infrared devices is enabled via the *Infrared Data Association (IrDA)* protocol. The IrDA protocol stack is a widely supported industry standard and has been included in all versions of Windows since Windows 95. Apple computers also support IrDA, as do Linux computers.

Speed- and range-wise, infrared isn't impressive. Infrared devices are capable of transferring data at speeds ranging from about 115 Kbps up to 4 Mbps.

TABLE 20.1	Comparison of 802.11 Standards			
Standard	**802.11a**	**802.11b**	**802.11g**	**802.11n**
Max. throughput	54 Mbps	11 Mbps	54 Mbps	100+ Mbps
Max. range	150 feet	300 feet	300 feet	300+ feet
Frequency	5 GHz	2.4 GHz	2.4 GHz	2.4 and 5 GHz
Security	SSID and password, MAC filtering, WEP, WPA, WPA2	SSID and password, MAC filtering, WEP, WPA, WPA2	SSID and password, MAC filtering, WEP, WPA, WPA2	SSID and password, MAC filtering, WEP, WPA, WPA2
Communication mode	Ad hoc or infrastructure	Ad hoc or infrastructure	Ad hoc or infrastructure	Ad hoc or infrastructure
Description	Products that adhere to this standard are considered Wi-Fi Certified. Eight available channels. Less prone to interference than 802.11b and 802.11g.	Products that adhere to this standard are considered Wi-Fi Certified. Fourteen channels available in the 2.4 GHz band (only 11 of which can be used in the United States due to FCC regulations). Three nonoverlapping channels.	Products that adhere to this standard are considered Wi-Fi Certified. Improved security enhancements. Fourteen channels available in the 2.4 GHz band (only 11 of which can be used in the United States due to FCC regulations). Three nonoverlapping channels.	Same as 802.11g but adds the 5-GHz band that 802.11a uses. 802.11n can also make use of multiple antennae (MIMO) to increase its range and speed.

Not too shabby, but hardly stellar. The maximum distance between infrared devices is limited—only one meter. Infrared links work on a direct line-of-sight basis and is susceptible to interference. An infrared link can be disrupted by anything that breaks the beam of light—a badly placed can of soda, a coworker passing between desks, or even bright sunlight hitting the infrared transceiver can cause interference.

Infrared is designed to make a point-to-point connection between two devices in ad hoc mode only. No infrastructure mode is available. You can, however, use an infrared access point device to enable Ethernet network communication using IrDA. Infrared devices operate at half-duplex, meaning that while one is talking, the other is listening—they can't talk and listen at the same time. IrDA has a mode that emulates full-duplex communication, but it's still just half-duplex.

Security-wise, the IrDA protocol offers exactly nothing in the way of encryption or authentication. Infrared's main security feature is the fact that you have to be literally within arm's reach to establish a link.

Clearly, infrared is not the best solution for a dedicated network connection, but for doing a quick file transfer or print job without getting your hands dirty, it'll do in a pinch. Table 20.2 lists infrared's important specifications.

Bluetooth

Bluetooth wireless technology, named for a tenth-century Danish king (see the Travel Advisory), is designed to create small wireless networks preconfigured to do very specific jobs. Some great examples are audio devices such as headsets that connect to your smartphones, *personal area networks (PANs)* that link two PCs for a quick-and-dirty wireless network, and input devices such as keyboards and mice. Bluetooth is *not* designed to be a full-function networking solution, nor is it meant to compete with Wi-Fi.

Bluetooth, like any technology, has been upgraded over the years to make it faster and more secure. Two major versions of Bluetooth are widespread today. The first generation (versions 1.1 and 1.2) supports speeds around 1 Mbps. The second generation (2.0 and 2.1) is backward-compatible with its first-generation cousins and adds support for more speed by introducing Enhanced Data Rate (EDR), which pushes top speeds to around 3 Mbps.

The IEEE organization has made first-generation Bluetooth the basis for its 802.15 standard for wireless PANs. Bluetooth uses the FHSS spread-spectrum broadcasting method, switching between any of the 79 frequencies available in the 2.45-GHz range. Bluetooth hops frequencies some 1600 times per second, making it highly resistant to interference.

Generally, the faster and farther a device sends data, the more power it needs to do so, and the Bluetooth designers understood a long time ago that some devices (such as a Bluetooth headset) could save power by not sending data as

TABLE 20.2	Infrared Specs
Standard	**Infrared (IrDA)**
Max. throughput	Up to 4 Mbps
Max. range	One meter (39 inches)
Security	None
Compatibility	IrDA
Communication mode	Point-to-point ad hoc
Description	IrDA is good for short-range data transfers between devices.

quickly or as far as other Bluetooth devices may need to. To address this, all Bluetooth devices are configured for one of three classes that define maximum power usage in milliwatts (mW) and maximum distance:

- Class 1 100 mW, 100 meters
- Class 2 2.5 mW, 10 meters
- Class 3 1 mW, 1 meter

Travel Advisory

Bluetooth wireless technology is named for Harald Blåtand (Bluetooth in English), a tenth-century Danish king. Special Interest Group (SIG) representatives used *Bluetooth* as a code name for the budding technology, since the king had been instrumental in uniting warring factions in parts of what are now Norway, Sweden, and Denmark, and the technology promised to allow collaboration among different industries. The name stuck. This information does not appear on the CompTIA A+ certification exams, but it's a pretty common question in the real world, so now you can sound knowledgeable when some user asks you.

Travel Assistance

Another wireless networking method employs the cellular telephone network infrastructure. You'll learn about those methods in Chapter 21.

Objective 20.03 # Configuring, Connecting, and Troubleshooting Wireless Networking

The mechanics of setting up a wireless network don't differ much from those for a wired network. Physically installing a wireless network adapter is the same as installing a wired NIC, whether it's an internal PCI or PCIe card, a PC Card, or an external USB device. Simply install the device and let Plug and Play

handle detection and resource allocation. Install the device's supplied driver when prompted, and you're practically done. Unless you're using Windows XP or later, you also need to install the wireless network configuration utility supplied with your wireless network adapter so that you can set your communication mode, SSID, and so on.

Exam Tip

The wireless configuration utility in Windows XP is called Wireless Zero Configuration (WZC). In Windows Vista/7 it is called WLAN AutoConfig.

As mentioned, wireless devices want to talk to each other, so communicating with an available wireless network is usually a no-brainer. The trick is to configure the wireless network so that specific wireless nodes can connect and secure the data that's being sent through the air.

Configuring Wi-Fi

Wi-Fi networks support both ad hoc and infrastructure operation modes. Which mode you choose depends on the number of wireless nodes you need to support, the type of data sharing they'll perform, and your management requirements.

Ad Hoc Mode

The only requirements in an ad hoc mode wireless network are that each wireless node be configured with the same SSID and that no two nodes use the same IP address. You may also have to select a common channel for all ad hoc nodes and ensure that the File and Printer Sharing service is running. Figure 20.10 shows a wireless network configuration utility with ad hoc mode selected.

Travel Advisory

Wi-Fi networks (in the Americas) running on the 2.4-MHz band use one of 11 channels within that frequency range, numbered 1–11. This is true of both ad hoc and infrastructure mode networks. That sounds like a lot of choices, but only three of those bands don't overlap in a given area: 1, 6, and 11. If you're getting a poor signal in a crowded space, try changing to one of the other nonoverlapping channels.

FIGURE 20.10 Selecting ad hoc mode in a wireless configuration utility

Infrastructure Mode

Infrastructure mode wireless networks require one or more WAPs and typically connect to a wired network segment, a corporate intranet or the Internet, or both. As with ad hoc mode wireless networks, infrastructure mode networks require that the same SSID be configured on all nodes and access points. Figure 20.11 shows a wireless network access point configuration utility set to infrastructure mode. Depending on the capabilities of your WAP, you may also configure DHCP options, filtering, and so on.

Access Point SSID Configuration WAPs have an integrated Web server, and you configure them through a browser-based setup utility. Typically, you connect a PC to a WAP with an Ethernet cable, then fire up a Web browser. If the WAP also has a DHCP server built in, set your PC to use DHCP and enter the WAP's default IP address, such as 192.168.1.1, to bring up the configuration page. You will need to supply an administrative password, included with your WAP's documentation, to log in (see Figure 20.12).

FIGURE 20.11 Selecting infrastructure mode in a wireless configuration utility

On WAPs that don't have DHCP or that have it disabled, you need to set the PC to a static IP that matches the same network as the WAP. If the WAP is set to 192.168.0.1, for example, set your PC to 192.168.0.2 and then use the browser interface to connect.

Exam Tip

Using a range of static IP addresses for the devices connected to a WAP—and turning DHCP off, of course—adds a small layer of security to a Wi-Fi network.

FIGURE 20.12 Security login for Linksys WAP

Setup screens vary from vendor to vendor and from model to model. Figure 20.13 shows the initial setup screen for a popular Linksys WAP router.

Configure the SSID option where indicated, and you're in business. Channel selection is usually automatic, but you can reconfigure this option if you have particular needs in your organization (such as if multiple wireless networks are operating in the same area). Remember that it's always more secure to configure a unique SSID and change the password than it is to accept the well-known default one.

Travel Advisory

Some techs advise disabling SSID broadcast as a way to make it harder for someone unauthorized to access your Wi-Fi network. Although this can have a chilling effect on casual surfers, even a semi-decent hacker can find a nonbroadcasting network, run sniffing software, and then get the SSID. Windows Vista/7/8 make it easy as well, showing Wi-Fi networks that don't broadcast as Unnamed or Hidden Network, pretty much begging hacker wannabes to try to access the network. Plus, not broadcasting the SSID can make it more difficult for legitimate users to access the network. It's not a great security option, though you'll see it listed as such on the 802 exam.

FIGURE 20.13 Linksys WAP setup screen

MAC Filtering Using MAC filtering to increase security is pretty straightforward. Figure 20.14 shows the MAC filtering configuration screen on a Linksys WAP. Simply enter the MAC address of a wireless node that you want to allow (or deny) access to your wireless network. You can create a white list of approved nodes or a black list of denied nodes.

Encryption Set up encryption by turning it on at the WAP and then generating a unique security key. Then configure all connected wireless nodes on the network with the same key information. Figure 20.15 shows the WPA2 encryption key configuration dialog box for a Linksys WAP.

When setting up WEP you have the option of automatically generating a set of encryption keys or doing it manually—save yourself a headache and use the automatic method. Select an encryption level—the usual choices are either 64-bit or 128-bit—and then enter a unique passphrase and click Generate (or whatever the equivalent button is called on your WAP). Then select a default key and save the settings.

FIGURE 20.14 MAC filtering configuration screen for a Linksys wireless access point

Security Settings

Select SSID: ciscosb ▼

Wireless Isolation (between SSID w/o VLAN): ◉ Enable ○ Disable

Security Mode: WPA2-Personal ▼

Wireless Isolation (within SSID): ○ Enable ◉ Disable

Encryption: AES

Shared Secret: secret_password

Key Renewal: 3600 seconds

Save Cancel

FIGURE 20.15 WPA2 encryption key configuration screen on Linksys WAP

The encryption level, key, and passphrase must match on the wireless client node, or communication will fail. Many WAPs let you export the encryption key data onto a floppy disk for easy transfer to a client workstation. You can also manually configure encryption using the vendor-supplied configuration utility, as shown in Figure 20.16.

WPA and WPA2 encryption are configured in much the same way. You may be required to input a valid user name and password to configure encryption using WPA/WPA2 on the WAP. On the client side, you often only need to type in a passphrase to get in, making either much easier than WEP. I highly recommend that you use WPA2, or WPA at least, if your equipment supports it. WEP is a very insecure protocol that can be cracked at the push of a button.

Disabling DHCP If you add a multifunction Wi-Fi box (one of the WAP + switch + router varieties) to a small office network, the router's built-in DHCP server might conflict with the DHCP server on your network. These conflicts, although not dangerous, can cause a lot of frustration and shouting when network connections stop working. To avoid this blow to interoffice relations, you should disable the DHCP server in the router before you plug it into the network. To do this, use a separate computer such as a laptop, or unplug your computer from the wall and plug it into the new router to log in.

FIGURE 20.16 WEP encryption screen on client wireless network adapter configuration utility

Once the DHCP server is disabled, the router will no longer hand out IP addresses, so you must make sure that the router's IP address is in the correct subnet of your office's LAN. If it isn't, you need to change it before you disable DHCP. On my router, all that I need to do is enter the new address and subnet. If you are unsure what address you need, ask your network administrator or CompTIA Network+ tech. Once you have the router's IP address taken care of, you can simply disable DHCP and save the settings. Then you can safely plug your router into the LAN without risking the ire of Internet-less coworkers.

Setting Static IP Addresses Now let's look at setting up the router to use a static IP address for the Internet or WAN connection. In most cases, when you plug in the router's Internet connection, it receives an IP address using DHCP just like any other computer. Of course, this means that your Internet IP address will change from time to time, which can be a bit of a downside. This does not affect most people, but for some home users and businesses, it can present a problem. To solve this problem, most ISPs let you order a static IP address. Once your ISP has allocated you a static IP address, you must manually enter it into

your router. You do this in the same way you entered all the preceding changes you've just read about. My router has a WAN configuration tab where I can enter all the settings that my ISP has provided. Remember that you must change your connection type from Automatic/DHCP to Static IP to enter the new addresses.

Updating Firmware WAP routers are just like any other computer in that they run software—and software has bugs, vulnerabilities, and other issues that sometimes require updating. The router manufacturers call these "firmware updates" and make them available on their Web sites for easy download. To update a modern router, you simply download the latest firmware from the manufacturer's Web site to your computer. Then you enter the router's configuration Web page and find the firmware update screen. From here, follow the directions and click Update. A quick word of caution: Unlike a Windows update, a firmware update gone bad can *brick* your router. In other words, it can destroy the hardware and make it as useful as a brick sitting on your desk. This rarely happens, but you should keep it in mind when doing a firmware update.

Connecting to a Wi-Fi Network

Most typically, available Wi-Fi connections manifest in a small icon in the notification area that displays the networks on a mouseover. This icon can be the Network and Sharing Center or proprietary vendor software. Left-click to select the detectable Wi-Fi networks and then left-click one to access. If the network is protected with WEP, WPA, or WPA2, you'll be prompted for a passphrase or passcode. Unsecured networks will often just let you on right away.

Local Lingo

Wireless locator If you want to know whether your local café, bookstore, airport, or other public place has a Wi-Fi access point (otherwise known as a *hotspot*), you can use a *Wi-Fi* or *wireless locator*. The locator is usually the size of a car remote and lights up or otherwise signals you whenever you are in range of a Wi-Fi access point.

Troubleshooting Wi-Fi

Properly configured wireless clients should automatically and quickly connect to the desired SSID. If this isn't taking place, it's time for some troubleshooting. Most wireless connectivity problems come down to either an incorrect

configuration (such as an incorrect password) or low signal strength. Without a strong signal, even a properly configured wireless client isn't going to work or you'll get glacially slow data transfer speeds. Wireless clients use a multibar graph (usually five bars) to give an idea of signal strength: zero bars indicates no signal and five bars indicates maximum signal.

The link state defines the wireless NIC's connection status to a wireless network: connected or disconnected. If your link state indicates that your computer is currently disconnected, you may have a problem with your WAP. If your signal is too weak to receive a signal (referred to on the CompTIA A+ exams as a "low RF signal"), you may be out of range of your access point, or there may be a device causing interference. Sometimes, you'll get just enough signal to connect, but the signal will drop irregularly, a state of intermittent connectivity.

You can fix these problems in a number of ways. Because Wi-Fi signals bounce off of objects, you can try small adjustments to your antennas to see if the signal improves. You can swap out the standard antenna for one or more higher-gain antennas. You can relocate the PC or access point, or locate and move the device causing interference.

Two other connectivity issues point to swamped access points rather than anything wrong with signal, range, or channel: limited connectivity and local connectivity. Both manifest with messages or icons in the notification area (Figure 20.17).

If you're connecting in a busy place, such as a hotel or airport, sometimes the WAPs used (or more technically, the DHCP portion of the wireless routers) are simply overwhelmed with the number of users. You'll connect, but then get no Internet access. Keep trying and you'll get in eventually.

If you get a limited or local connectivity notification on a local network, on the other hand, that usually points to a router that needs to be reset. Unplug the power for ten seconds or a little longer, then plug it back in. Try to connect at that point and you should be good.

FIGURE 20.17 What, no Internet? Waaaa!

CHECKPOINT

✔**Objective 20.01: Wireless Networking Basics** Wireless networks operate much like their wired counterparts, except they eliminate the network cabling by using either radio waves or infrared light as a network medium. Wireless NICs usually require configuration software supplied by the manufacturer. Windows XP, Windows Vista, and Windows 7 have wireless NIC configuration software built in. Wireless networks operate in ad hoc (decentralized) or infrastructure (centralized) fashion. Security is enabled by changing the SSID and password and by employing MAC filtering and WEP, WPA, or WPA2 encryption. Speeds range from 2 Mbps to 100+ Mbps.

✔**Objective 20.02: Wireless Networking Standards** Wireless networks are based around several standards: IEEE 802.11x, Infrared Data Association (IrDA), Bluetooth, and cellular. Of these, 802.11n (100+ Mbps throughput) is the fastest. Infrared is line-of-sight only and tops out at 4 Mbps. Bluetooth is not a true networking standard, due to its limited range (30 feet) and slow speed (1 Mbps). Bluetooth enables you to connect a PC wirelessly to its peripheral devices and synchronize the PC with tablets and smartphones.

✔**Objective 20.03: Configuring, Connecting, and Troubleshooting Wireless Networking** Ad hoc mode is the simplest way to network wireless computers, but offers no fine control over shared resources. Infrastructure mode requires more planning and wireless access point (WAP) hardware. Wi-Fi networks in the Americas running on the 2.4-MHz band use one of 11 channels within that frequency range, numbered 1–11. Wireless access points are configured using built-in browser-based utilities. You can employ various security measures, disable or enable DHCP, and set up a static IP through that interface. The firmware on a WAP or multifunction box can be updated if necessary.

REVIEW QUESTIONS

1. Which of these wireless networking technologies uses the 5-GHz frequency range?

 A. 802.11

 B. 802.11a

 C. 802.11b

 D. 802.11g

2. The 802.11b wireless specification enables what maximum throughput speed?

 A. 2 Mbps

 B. 11 Mbps

 C. 54 Mbps

 D. 4 Mbps

3. The 802.11g wireless specification enables what maximum throughput speed?

 A. 2 Mbps

 B. 11 Mbps

 C. 54 Mbps

 D. 4 Mbps

4. What is the maximum range of a Class III Bluetooth device?

 A. 1 meter

 B. 30 feet

 C. 10 meters

 D. 300 feet

5. What function does CSMA/CA provide that CSMA/CD does not?

 A. Data packet collision detection

 B. End-to-end data packet encryption

 C. Data packet collision avoidance

 D. Data packet error checking

6. How can you increase the range of a wireless network? (Select two.)

 A. Replace the stock antenna with a higher-gain antenna.

 B. Replace the 802.11b WAP with an 802.11g WAP.

 C. Change the SSID channel.

 D. Add another WAP to the network.

7. What is the maximum speed of IrDA?

 A. 115 Kbps

 B. 2 Mbps

 C. 4 Mbps

 D. 11 Mbps

8. Which encryption method offers the best security?

 A. SSID

 B. WEP

 C. WPA

 D. WPA2

9. What hardware do you need to enable wireless PCs to connect to resources on a wired network segment in infrastructure mode?

 A. A wireless access point

 B. A wired router

 C. A wireless hub

 D. A wireless bridge

10. What do you call a wireless Ethernet network in infrastructure mode with more than one access point?

 A. BSS

 B. EBSS

 C. PAN

 D. PICONET

REVIEW ANSWERS

1. **B** 802.11a operates in the 5-GHz frequency range.

2. **B** The 802.11b wireless networks run at a maximum of 11 Mbps.

3. **C** The 802.11g wireless networks run at a maximum of 54 Mbps.

4. **A** A Class III Bluetooth device has a maximum range of 1 meter (~3 feet).

5. **C** CSMA/CA uses the RTS/CTS protocol to provide data packet collision avoidance.

6. **A D** Replacing the stock antenna or adding another WAP will increase the overall range of a wireless network.

7. **C** 4 Mbps is the maximum data throughput speed of IrDA.

8. **D** No contest! WPA2 offers the best security.

9. **A** A wireless access point enables you to connect wireless PCs to a wired network segment.

10. **B** A wireless network with more than one access point is called EBSS, Extended Basic Service Set.

The Internet

ETA	NEWBIE	SOME EXPERIENCE	EXPERT
	3 hours	2 hours	1 hour

How great would it be if you could connect your computer or local area network (LAN) to other computers and other LANs? And not just to one other network, but to every other network in the country? Or the *world?* You could share data back and forth, spreading news and information, music, and pictures, across the planet almost instantaneously! An entirely new culture could form around it, bringing about new platforms for media and business, not to mention changing forever the term "multiplayer gaming"—it would probably be the greatest thing since the invention of the paperclip. I'm just glad I thought of it first. Wait, that idea's taken? Well, of course it is—it's the Internet!

This chapter covers the various methods of connecting to the Internet, as well as the software, such as browsers and e-mail clients, you'll use to interact with it.

Objective 21.01 Connecting to the Internet

To use the Internet successfully, you need to connect properly and then run special applications that work with TCP/IP, such as HTTP for Web browsing. Let's start with connections and then hit Internet software.

PCs commonly connect to an Internet service provider (ISP) using one of several technologies that fit into four categories: dial-up, analog, and Integrated Services Digital Network (ISDN); dedicated, such as digital subscriber line (DSL), cable, and fiber; wireless; and satellite. Analog dial-up is the slowest of the bunch and requires a telephone line and a special networking device called a *modem.* ISDN uses digital dial-up and has much greater speed. All the others use a regular wired or wireless Ethernet network interface card (NIC), discussed in Chapter 19. Satellite is the odd one out here; it may use either a modem or a NIC, depending on the particular configuration you have, although most folks will use a NIC. Let's take a look at all these various connection options.

Dial-up Networking

A dial-up connection to the Internet requires two pieces to work: hardware, such as a modem or ISDN terminal adapter (TA), to dial the ISP, and software, such as Microsoft's Dial-up Networking (DUN), to govern the connection. Modems and TAs install similarly to any other expansion card or device, into a PCI or PCIe slot on the motherboard or to an external expansion connection such as USB. Install the drivers and you're pretty much done with the hardware side of things.

Modems

Modems enable computers to talk to each other via standard commercial telephone lines by converting analog signals to digital signals, and vice versa (Figure 21.1). The individual serial bits of data are converted into 8-bit parallel data that the PC can understand through the *universal asynchronous receiver/transmitter (UART)* chip (Figure 21.2).

The fastest data transfer speed a modem can handle is based on its implementation of one of the *V standards*. Set by the International Telecommunication Union (ITU-T), the current top standards are V.90 and V.92. Both standards offer download speeds of just a hair under 56 Kbps, but they differ in upload speeds: up to 33.6 Kbps for V.90, and up to 48 Kbps for V.92 modems.

The software side of dial-up networks requires configuration within Windows to include information provided by your ISP: a dial-up telephone number or numbers, as well as your user name and initial password. In addition, the ISP will tell you about any special configuration options you need to specify in the software setup. The full configuration of dial-up networking is beyond the scope of this book, but you should at least know where to go to follow instructions from your ISP. Let's look at how it's done in Windows XP as an example.

Network and Internet Connections

To start configuring a dial-up connection in Windows XP, open the Control Panel. In Category View, select Network and Internet Connections from the *Pick a category* menu, and then choose *Set up or change your Internet connection* from the *Pick a task* menu The Internet Properties dialog box opens with the Connections tab displayed (Figure 21.3). All your work will proceed from here.

FIGURE 21.1 Modem converting digital signal to analog signal

FIGURE 21.2 The UART chip converts serial data to parallel data that the CPU can read.

Click the Setup button to run the New Connection Wizard, and then work through the screens (Figure 21.4). At this point, you're going to need information provided by your ISP to configure your connection properly.

When you finish the configuration, you'll see a new Connect To option on the Start menu. Choose Start | Connect To | Show All Connections to see something similar to Figure 21.5, which shows the option to connect to a fictitious ISP, Cool-Rides.com.

FIGURE 21.3 The Connections tab in the Internet Properties dialog box

FIGURE 21.4 The New Connection Wizard

FIGURE 21.5 Connections in Windows XP

PPP Dial-up links to the Internet have their own special hardware protocol called the *Point-to-Point Protocol (PPP)*. PPP is a streaming protocol developed especially for dial-up Internet access. To Windows, a modem is nothing more than a special type of network adapter. Modems have their own configuration entry in the Network Connections applet.

Most dial-up "I can't connect to the Internet"–type problems are user errors. Your first line of defense is the modem itself. Use the modem's properties to make sure the volume is turned up. Have the user listen to the connection. Does she hear a dial tone? If she doesn't, make sure the modem's line is plugged into a good phone jack. Does she hear the modem dial and then hear someone saying, "Hello? Hello?" If so, she probably dialed the wrong number. Wrong password error messages are fairly straightforward—remember that the password may be correct, but the user name may be wrong. If the user still fails to connect, it's time to call the network folks to see what is not properly configured in the Dial-up Networking settings.

ISDN

A standard telephone connection has many pieces. First, the phone line runs from your phone out to a network interface box (the little box on the side of your house) and into a central switch belonging to the telephone company. Standard metropolitan areas have a large number of central offices, each with a central switch. These central switches connect to one another through high-capacity *trunk lines*. Before 1970, the entire phone system was analog. To-day, the entire telephone system, with the exception of the line from your phone to the central office, is digital.

By adding special equipment at the central office and the user's location, phone companies can now achieve a throughput of up to 64 K per line over the same copper wires already used by telephone lines. This process of sending telephone transmission across fully digital lines end to end is called *integrated services digital network (ISDN) service*.

ISDN service consists of two types of channels: Bearer, or B, channels and Delta, or D, channels. B channels carry data and voice information at 64 Kbps. D channels carry setup and configuration information and data at 16 Kbps. Most providers of ISDN allow the user to choose either one or two B channels. The more common setup uses two B channels and one D channel, usually called a *basic rate interface (BRI)* setup. A BRI setup uses only one physical line, but each B channel sends 64 Kbps, doubling the throughput total to 128 Kbps. The big limitation is that you usually need to be within about 18,000 feet of a central office to use ISDN.

The physical connections for ISDN bear some similarity to analog modems. An ISDN wall socket usually looks something like a standard RJ-45 network jack. The most common interface for your computer is a device called a *terminal adapter (TA)*. TAs look much like regular modems, and like modems, they come in external and internal variants.

Travel Advisory

Another type of ISDN, called a primary rate interface (PRI), uses twenty-three 64-Kbps B channels and one 64-Kbps D channel, giving it a total throughput of 1.5 Mbps. PRI ISDN lines are rarely used as dial-up connections—they are far more common on dedicated lines.

Dedicated Connections

Increasingly, consumers and businesses are using dedicated high-speed connections such as DSL, cable, or fiber to link their LANs to the Internet. Almost all of these dedicated connections use 10'BaseT Ethernet to connect a single PC or a switch to a special box called a modem or receiver.

DSL

Digital subscriber line (DSL) connections to ISPs use a standard telephone line but special equipment on each end to create always-on Internet connections at blindingly fast speeds, especially when compared with analog dial-up connections. Service levels vary around the United States, but the typical upload speed is ~768 Kbps, while download speed comes in at ~3+ Mbps.

Local Lingo

ADSL and **SDSL** The two most common forms of DSL you'll find are *asynchronous (ADSL)* and *synchronous (SDSL)*. ADSL lines differ between slow upload speed (such as 384, 512, or 768 Kbps) and faster download speed (such as 1.5, 3, or 6 Mbps). SDSL has the same upload and download speeds, but telecom companies charge a lot more for the privilege. DSL encompasses many such variations, so you'll often see it referred to as *x*DSL.

DSL requires little setup from a user standpoint. A tech comes to your house to install a NIC in the Internet-bound PC and drop off a DSL receiver (often called a DSL modem; see Figure 21.6). The receiver connects to the telephone

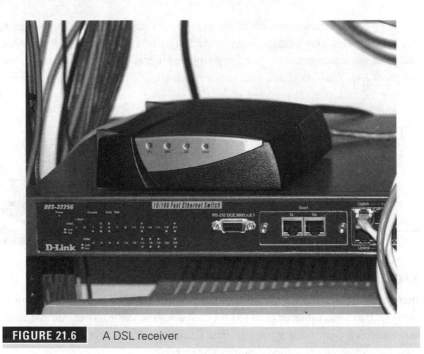

FIGURE 21.6 A DSL receiver

line and the PC (Figure 21.7). The tech (or the user, if knowledgeable) then configures the TCP/IP options for the NIC to match the settings demanded by the DSL provider, and that's about it. Within moments, you're surfing at blazing speeds. You don't need a second telephone line. You don't need to wear a special propeller hat or anything. The only kicker is that your house has to be within a fairly short distance from a main phone service switching center, something like 18,000 feet. This pretty much stops everybody but inner-city dwellers from having access to DSL service.

FIGURE 21.7 DSL connections

Cable

Cable offers a different approach to high-speed Internet access, using regular cable TV cables to serve up lightning-fast speeds. It offers service that's often faster than DSL with a 1–10 Mbps upload and 6–50+ Mbps download. Cable Internet connections are theoretically available anywhere you can get cable TV.

Cable Internet connections start with an RG-6 or RG-59 cable coming into your house. The cable connects to a cable modem that then connects to a NIC in your PC via UTP Ethernet cable. Figure 21.8 shows a typical cable setup. Both DSL and cable modem Internet connections can be used by two or more computers if they are part of a LAN.

Local Lingo

F connector The screw-on coaxial connector used in cable television is called an *F connector.* The 801 competencies mention it as a networking standard. That definition applies only to cable modems for Internet connectivity.

Fiber

Until recently, high costs meant that only those with money to burn could enjoy the super-fast speeds of a fiber connection. Now DSL providers have developed very popular fiber-to-the-node (FTTN) and fiber-to-the-premises (FTTP) services that provide Internet (and more), making them head-to-head competitors with the cable companies.

With FTTN, the fiber connection runs from the provider to a box somewhere in your neighborhood. This box is connected to your home or office using normal coaxial or Ethernet cabling. FTTP runs from the provider straight to a home or office, using fiber the whole way. Once inside the home or office, you can use any standard cabling (or wireless) to connect your PCs to the Internet.

FIGURE 21.8 Cable connections

One popular FTTN service is AT&T's U-verse, which offers speeds up to 24 Mbps for downloads and 3 Mbps for uploads (see Figure 21.9). Verizon's FiOS service is the most popular and widely available FTTP service in the United States, providing download speeds up to 150 Mbps and upload speeds up to 50 Mbps (if you can afford it, of course).

LAN

Most businesses (and many homes) connect their LAN to an ISP via some hardware solution like a router. Figure 21.10 shows a typical small-business wiring closet with routers that connect the LAN to the ISP. You learned all about wiring up a LAN in Chapter 19, so there's no need to go through any basics here.

802.11 Wireless

Every once in a while a technology comes along that, once the kinks are smoothed out, works flawlessly, creating a magical computing experience. Unfortunately, the various wireless networking technologies out there today aren't quite *magical*, at least not all the time. When they work, it's like magic. You walk into a coffee shop, sit down, and flip open your laptop computer. After firing up your Internet browser, suddenly you're quaffing lattes and surfing Web sites—with no wires or setup at all.

802.11 Wireless is so prevalent that for many of us it's the way we get to the Internet. Wireless access points (WAPs) designed to serve the public abound in coffee shops, airports, fast-food chains, and bars. Even some cities provide partial to full 802.11 coverage.

We covered 802.11 in detail in Chapter 20, so there's no reason to repeat the process of connecting to a hotspot. However, do remember that most hotspots do not provide any level of encryption, meaning it's an easy task for a bad guy to monitor your connection and read everything you send or receive.

FIGURE 21.9 U-verse gateway

FIGURE 21.10 A wiring closet

Travel Advisory

Secure your public hotspot Web browsing using HTTPS-secured
sites. It's surprisingly easy to do. Instead of typing facebook.com,
for example, type in https://facebook.com or use a service like the
Electronic Freedom Federation's *HTTPS Everywhere*.

802.11 works well as an Internet access option for densely populated areas,
but 802.11's short range makes it impractical in areas where it's not easy to place
new access points.

Local Lingo

MAN An 802.11 network that covers a single city is an excellent
example of a *metropolitan area network (MAN)*.

Cellular

Who needs computers when you can get online with any number of mobile devices? Okay, there are plenty of things a smartphone or tablet can't do, but with the latest advances in cellular data services, your mobile Internet experience will feel a lot more like your home Internet experience than it ever has before.

Cellular data services have gone through a number of names over the years, so many that trying to keep track of them and place them in any order is extremely challenging. In an attempt to make organization somewhat clearer, the cellular industry developed a string of marketing terms using the idea of generations: first-generation devices are called 1G, second generation are 2G, followed by 3G and 4G. On top of that, many technologies use G-names such as 2.5G to show they're not 2G but not quite 3G. You'll see these terms all over the place, especially on your phones (see Figure 21.11). Marketing folks tend to bend and flex the definition of these terms in advertisements, so you should always read more about the device and not just its generation.

FIGURE 21.11 iPhone with 4G showing

Exam Tip

The CompTIA A+ exams will not ask you to define a G level for a particular cellular technology.

The first generation (1G) of cell phone data services was analog and not at all designed to carry packetized data. It wasn't until the early 1990s that two fully digital technologies called the Global System for Mobile Communications (GSM) and code division multiple access (CDMA) came into wide acceptance. GSM evolved into GPRS and EDGE, while CDMA introduced EV-DO. GPRS and EDGE were 2.5G technologies, while EV-DO was true 3G. Current standards, with names like UTMS, HSPA+, and HSDPA, have brought GSM-based networks into the world of 3G and 3.5G. Current mobile data services provide real-world download speeds around 3 or 4 Mbps.

The current cutting-edge set of cellular technologies use the term 4G. The two biggest 4G technologies currently available are called *Worldwide Interoperability for Microwave Access (WiMAX)* and *3GPP Long Term Evolution (LTE)*. With these networks, you'll see download speeds closer to 10 Mbps, though WiMAX lags behind LTE in the speed department.

In fact, while the CompTIA A+ 220-801 exam objectives specifically cover WiMAX, the wireless technology has already been replaced as the 4G frontrunner. The only major U.S. WiMAX carrier, Clearwire, Inc., has declared its intention to adopt LTE, along with every other major mobile phone network in the United States. But since CompTIA asked, and there are still some WiMAX users (for now), I'm more than happy to tell you a little more about WiMAX.

Exam Tip

You can share your smartphone's or tablet's connection to a cellular network using a process called *tethering*. You'll need to turn on the service on your device and then connect your phone to your computer, either wirelessly as a *mobile hotspot* or directly using a USB connection. Most carriers charge extra to enable tethering on your smartphone or tablet. Check with your carrier to see if your service plan supports tethering.

WiMAX runs at (depending on distance from a tower) a maximum speed of around 10 Mbps. The maximum range is 30 miles. There are two versions of WiMAX.

Line-of-sight (LoS) WiMAX uses fixed antennas that point directly at a WiMAX transceiver. Non-LoS WiMAX uses base stations that are not visible to the WiMAX tower. As you might imagine, LoS WiMAX is far faster than non-LoS WiMAX.

Exam Tip

Just like LANs and WANs, we also have WLANs and WWANs. A wireless wide area network (WWAN) works similar to a WLAN, except it connects multiple networks like a WAN. WiMAX is an excellent example of a WWAN.

Satellite

Of all the possible connections to the Internet, satellite is the most unique. Satellite connections to the Internet get the data beamed to a satellite dish on your house or office; a receiver handles the flow of data, eventually sending it through an Ethernet cable to the NIC in your PC. I can already sense people's eyebrows raising. "Yeah, that's the download connection. But what about the upload connection?"

The early days of satellite required you to connect via a modem. You would upload at the slow 26- to 48-Kbps modem speed, but then get much faster downloads from the dish. It worked, so why complain? Newer technology still requires that the initial setup be done via modem, but the download and the upload go through the dish. You can relax on a farm in Africa to write the great Kenyan novel and get high-speed Internet connectivity. The only significant issue to satellite is that the distance the signal must travel creates a small delay called *satellite latency*. This latency is usually unnoticeable unless the signal degrades in foul weather such as rain and snow.

Satellite setup consists of a dish, professionally installed with line of sight to the satellite. A coaxial cable runs from the dish to your satellite modem. The satellite modem has an RJ-45 connection, which you may then connect directly to your computer or to a router.

Internet Connection Sharing

Internet Connection Sharing (ICS) enables one system to share its Internet connection with other systems on the network, providing a quick and easy method for multiple systems to use one Internet connection. Figure 21.12 shows a

FIGURE 21.12 Typical ICS setup

typical setup for ICS. Note the terminology used here. The PC that connects to the Internet and then shares via ICS that connection with machines on a LAN is called the *ICS host* computer. PCs that connect via LAN to the ICS host computer are simply called *client* computers.

To connect multiple computers to a single ICS host computer requires that several things be in place. First, the ICS host computer has to have a NIC dedicated to the internal connections. If you connect via dial-up, for example, the ICS host computer uses a modem to connect to the Internet. It will also have a NIC that plugs into a hub, switch, or router. Other PCs on the LAN likewise connect to the hub, switch, or router. If you connect via some faster service, such as DSL that uses a NIC cabled to the DSL receiver, you'll need a second NIC in the ICS host machine to connect to the LAN and the client computers.

Setting up ICS in Windows is very simple. If you are using Windows XP, open the Properties dialog for My Network Places. If you are using Windows Vista or 7, open the Network and Sharing Center and click *Manage network connections* (Windows Vista) or *Change adapter settings* (Windows 7) in the task list on the left. Now access the properties of the connection you want to share.

Click the Sharing tab (Windows Vista and 7) or the Advanced tab (Windows XP), and select *Allow other network users to connect through this computer's Internet connection* (Figure 21.13). Clients don't need any special configuration but should simply be set to use DHCP for their IP address and other configurations.

FIGURE 21.13 Enabling Internet Connection Sharing in Windows

Objective 21.02 Internet Software Tools

After you've established a connection between the PC and the ISP, you can do nothing on the Internet without applications designed to use one or more TCP/IP services, such as Web browsing and e-mail. Here are several commonly used TCP/IP services:

- The World Wide Web (HTTP and HTTPS)
- E-mail (POP3, IMAP4, and SMTP)
- FTP and SFTP
- Telnet and SSH
- Remote Desktop (RDP)
- VoIP
- VPN
- Various support applications (LDAP, SNMP, SMB)

Each of these services (sometimes referred to by the overused term *TCP/IP protocols*) requires a special application, and each of those applications has special settings. Let's look at all these services and see how to configure them. As a quick reference, Table 21.1 shows some common port numbers the CompTIA A+ exams expect you to know.

> **Exam Tip**
>
> You know about DNS from Chapter 19, so there's no need to cover it again. Definitely memorize the port number DNS uses!

The World Wide Web

The Web provides a graphical face for the Internet. *Web servers* (servers running specialized software) provide Web sites that you access by using HTTP on port 80 and thus get more or less useful information. Using Web browser software, such as Internet Explorer or Mozilla Firefox, you can click a link on a Web page and be instantly transported not just to some Web server in your home town, but to anywhere in the world. Figure 21.14 shows Firefox at the home page of my company's Web site, www.totalsem.com. Where is the server located? Does it matter? It could be in a closet in my office or in a massive data center in Houston, Texas. The great part about the Web is that you can get from here to there and access the information you need with a click or two of the mouse.

Although the Web is the most popular part of the Internet, setting up a Web browser takes almost no effort. As long as the Internet connection is working, Web browsers work automatically. This is not to say you can't make plenty of

TABLE 21.1	TCP/IP Service Port Numbers

TCP/IP Service	Port Number
DNS	53
HTTP	80
HTTPS	443
FTP	20, 21
POP3	110
IMAP4	143
SMTP	25
Telnet	23
SSH	22
RDP	3389

FIGURE 21.14 Mozilla Firefox showing a Web page

custom settings, but the default browser settings work almost every time. If you type in a Web address, such as that of the best search engine on the planet—www.google.com—and it doesn't work, check the line and your network settings and you'll figure out where the problem is.

Configuring Internet Explorer

Web browsers are highly configurable. On most Web browsers, you can set the default font size, choose whether to display graphics, and adjust several other settings. Although all Web browsers support these settings, where you go to make these changes varies dramatically. If you are using the popular Internet Explorer that comes with Windows, you will find configuration tools in the Internet Options Control Panel applet or under the Tools menu in Internet Explorer (see Figure 21.15). Note that the applet is called Internet Options, but the window it launches is labeled Internet Properties.

Internet Properties

General | Security | Privacy | Content | Connections | Programs | Advanced

Home page

To create home page tabs, type each address on its own line.

http://www.google.com/

Use current | Use default | Use blank

Browsing history

Delete temporary files, history, cookies, saved passwords, and web form information.

☐ Delete browsing history on exit

Delete... | Settings

Search

Change search defaults.

Settings

Tabs

Change how webpages are displayed in tabs.

Settings

Appearance

Colors | Languages | Fonts | Accessibility

OK | Cancel | Apply

FIGURE 21.15 Internet Options applet

I find it bizarre that CompTIA specifically lists Internet Options as an objective on the CompTIA A+ 220-802 exam. It's just so…Microsofty. There are obviously more browsers than just Internet Explorer, so I'll begin by explaining the options available to you in Internet Explorer, and then show you some of the common options found in other browsers, too.

When you open the Internet Options applet, you'll see seven tabs along the top. Here are the basics of each tab:

- **General** Controls the most basic features of Internet Explorer, such as the home page, browsing history, searching, and other appearance controls.
- **Security** Enables you to set how severely Internet Explorer safeguards your Web browsing (see Figure 21.16). Each setting can be adjusted for a particular zone, such as the Internet, your local intranet, trusted sites, and restricted sites.
- **Privacy** Controls privacy matters, such as cookies and pop-ups. There is a slider that enables you to control what is blocked—everything is blocked on the highest setting; nothing is blocked on the lowest.

FIGURE 21.16 The Security tab in Internet Options

- **Content** Filters content using certificates and a tool called the Content Advisor, which uses ratings that consider language, gambling, substance abuse, and more. The Content tab also enables you to adjust the AutoComplete feature that fills in Web addresses for you, as well as control settings for RSS feeds and Web Slices.

- **Connections** Enables you to set up your connection to the Internet, via broadband or dial-up, connect to a virtual private network (VPN), configure a proxy server connection, or adjust some LAN settings (which you probably won't need to deal with). Because they're a little complicated and CompTIA wants you to know about them, let's quickly talk about proxy servers.

Many corporations use a proxy server to filter employee Internet access, and when you're on their corporate network, you need to set your proxy settings within the Web browser (and any other Internet software you want to use). A *proxy server* is software that enables multiple connections to the Internet to go through one protected PC. Applications that want to access Internet resources send requests to the proxy server instead of trying to access the Internet directly, which both protects the client PCs and enables the network administrator to monitor and restrict Internet access. Each application must therefore be configured to use the proxy server.

- **Programs** Contains settings for the default Web browser, any add-ons you use (like Java), and how other programs deal with HTML files and e-mail messages.

- **Advanced** Lists a bunch of advanced options that you can turn on and off with the check of a box (see Figure 21.17). The available options include accessibility, browsing, international, and, most importantly, security settings. From here, you can control how Internet Explorer checks Web site certificates, among many other settings.

Configuring Other Web Browsers

I don't want to stomp all over Internet Explorer and tell you how bad it is—okay, yes I do. You can download several other Web browsers that run faster and support more Web standards. Two of the big browser heavyweights that fit this description are Mozilla Firefox and Google Chrome.

You control their settings just like you do in Internet Explorer, though you won't find an applet tucked away in Control Panel. In Google Chrome, you can

FIGURE 21.17 The Advanced tab in Internet Options

click the wrench icon in the upper-right corner of the browser and select Settings. In Mozilla Firefox, click the Firefox button in the upper-left corner and click Options.

In these menus, you'll find a lot of settings very similar to the ones you find in Internet Options. In fact, Firefox's controls are laid out almost exactly the same, though you won't find everything in the same place (see Figure 21.18). Google Chrome's controls look more like a Web page, but it still controls the same features: home page, security, font size, cookies, and all your old favorites (see Figure 21.19). Take some time to use these browsers and explore their settings. You'll be surprised how your knowledge of one browser helps you set up another.

FIGURE 21.18 Mozilla Firefox options

Exam Tip

The term *Internet appliance* enjoyed some popularity in the 1990s to describe the first wave of consumer devices accessible via TCP/IP. You could use a Web browser to check on the status of an Internet-connected refrigerator, for example, or check to see if you'd left the stove on (and if so, shut it off remotely). Although the term is no longer in use, it might show up on the 220-801 exam.

Web Security with HTTPS

People don't like to enter credit card information, home phone numbers, or other personal information for fear this information might be intercepted by hackers. Fortunately, there are methods of encrypting this information, the most common being HTTP over Secure Sockets Layer (HTTP over SSL or

FIGURE 21.19 Google Chrome settings

simply HTTPS) Web sites. It's easy to tell if your Web site is using HTTPS because the Web address will start with HTTPS instead of just HTTP, and you'll usually see a tiny lock to the right of the status bar or in the lower-right corner of the browser window.

There's one security risk that no computer can completely defend against: you. In particular, be careful when downloading programs from the Internet. The watchword here is *common sense.* Download programs only from reliable sources. Take time to read the online documentation so that you're sure you're downloading a version of the program that works on your OS. Finally, always run a good antivirus program, preferably one that checks incoming programs for viruses before you install them. Failure to do this can lead to lockups, file corruption, and boot problems that you simply should not have to deal with.

E-mail

You can use an e-mail program to access e-mail. The most popular client by far is Microsoft Outlook. E-mail clients need a little more setup. First, you must provide your e-mail address and password. All e-mail addresses come in the now-famous *accountname@Internet domain* format.

The second things you must add are the names of the Post Office Protocol version 3 (POP3) or Internet Message Access Protocol version 4 (IMAP4) server and the Simple Mail Transfer Protocol (SMTP) server. The POP3 or IMAP4 server is the computer that handles incoming (to you) e-mail. POP3 is by far the most widely used standard, although IMAP4 supports some features POP3 doesn't. For example, IMAP4 enables you to search through messages on the mail server to find specific keywords and select the messages you want to download onto your machine. Even with the advantages of IMAP4 over POP3, the vast majority of incoming mail servers use POP3.

> **Exam Tip**
>
> The CompTIA A+ exams always refer to POP as POP3, but IMAP as IMAP, without the version number.

The SMTP server handles your outgoing e-mail. These two systems (POP3 or IMAP4, plus SMTP) may often have the same name, or close to the same name, as shown in Figure 21.20. All these settings should be provided to you by your ISP. If they are not, you should be comfortable knowing what to ask for. If one of these names is incorrect, either you will not get your e-mail or you will not be able to send e-mail. If an e-mail setup that has been working well for a while suddenly encounters errors, it is likely that either the POP3/IMAP4 or SMTP server is down, or the DNS server has quit working.

> **Exam Tip**
>
> Assuming you have an active Internet connection—if you can't receive incoming mail, you should ensure you have the correct incoming POP3 or IMAP4 mail server settings. If you can't send mail, you should check your SMTP outgoing mail server settings.

E-mail Security

If you have a serious need for secure e-mail, you can set up a mail client to use a *digital signature,* something embedded in the body of the e-mail message that confirms the identity of the sender. The concepts of digital signatures are simple,

FIGURE 21.20 POP3 and SMTP information

but the implementation is more complex. To use a digital signature, you need to get a certificate from an *issuing authority* (the same folks who create certificates for secure e-commerce). Then you must add the certificate to your e-mail application. Finally, you need to be on the Web of Trust for the issuing authority.

Implementing digital signatures falls well outside the scope of the CompTIA A+ exams. You should know that they can be used to create more secure e-mail.

Travel Advisory

It's actually quite easy to send an e-mail message to someone and make it look like it came not from you, but from someone else entirely. This is called *spoofing*. You don't have to worry about spoofing for the most part, though, as long as you're careful. If you get a suspect message from a friend, for example, just call them or forward the message to them asking for confirmation that they sent it.

Web Mail

Increasingly users have turned to one or more of the many free Web mail clients available for their e-mail needs. Web mail uses an Internet connection and a Web browser to provide standard e-mail services. Web mail has some distinct advantages over client-based mail. It's available anywhere you have Internet access, so you can check your e-mail from any computer connected to the Internet. Most services offer lots of storage, searchable messages, flagging of messages for later, and more. And did I mention the price? Popular Web mail applications include Gmail, Hotmail, and Yahoo! Mail.

File Transfer Protocol

File Transfer Protocol (FTP), using ports 20 and 21, is a great way to share files between systems. FTP server software exists for most operating systems, so you can use FTP to transfer data between any two systems, regardless of the OS. To access an FTP site, you must use an FTP client such as FileZilla, although older versions of most Web browsers provided at least download support for FTP. Just type in the name of the FTP site. Figure 21.21 shows Firefox accessing ftp.kernel.org.

FIGURE 21.21 Accessing an FTP site in Firefox

Although some folks still use a Web browser, all FTP sites require you to log on. Most FTP clients will assume that you want to log in as "anonymous." If you want to log on as a specific user, you have to add your user name to the URL. (So, for example, instead of typing **ftp://ftp.example.com**, you would type **ftp://mikem@ftp.example.com**.) An anonymous logon works fine for most public FTP sites. Many techs prefer to use third-party programs such as FileZilla (Figure 21.22) for FTP access because these third-party applications can store user name and password settings. This enables you to access the FTP site more easily later.

Telnet and SSH

Telnet is a terminal emulation program for TCP/IP networks that uses port 23 and enables you to connect to a server or fancy router and run commands on that machine as if you were sitting in front of it. This way, you can remotely administer a server and communicate with other servers on your network.

As you can imagine, this is rather risky. If *you* can remotely control a computer, what's to stop others from doing the same? Of course, Telnet does not allow just *anyone* to log on and wreak havoc with your network. You must enter a special user name and password to run Telnet. Unfortunately, Telnet shares FTP's bad habit of sending passwords and user names as clear text, so you should generally use it only within your own LAN.

FIGURE 21.22 The FileZilla program

If you need a remote terminal that works securely across the Internet, you need *Secure Shell (SSH)*. In fact, SSH has replaced Telnet in almost all places Telnet used to be popular. To the user, SSH works just like Telnet. Behind the scenes, SSH uses port 22, and the entire connection is encrypted, preventing any eavesdroppers from reading your data. SSH has one other trick up its sleeve: it can move files or any type of TCP/IP network traffic through its secure connection. In networking parlance, this is called *tunneling*, and it is the core of a technology called *virtual private networks (VPN)*, which is discussed later.

> ### Exam Tip
>
> The CompTIA A+ certification exams test your knowledge of a few networking tools, such as Telnet, but you need to know only enough to support a CompTIA Network+ tech or network administrator. If you need to run Telnet (or its more secure cousin, SSH), you will get the details from a network administrator. Implementation of Telnet falls well beyond the CompTIA A+ exams.

SFTP

Secure FTP is nothing more than FTP running through an SSH tunnel. This can be done in a number of ways. You can, for example, start an SSH session between two computers. Then, through a moderately painful process, start an FTP server on one machine and an FTP client on the other and redirect the input and output of the FTP data to go through the tunnel. You can also get a dedicated SFTP server and client. Figure 21.23 shows OpenSSH, a popular SSH server with a built-in SFTP feature as well.

Remote Applications

Telnet and SSH are excellent tools for accessing and controlling remote computers, but they're so *command line*. Wouldn't it be nice to have a tool that made a distant computer appear on your screen in all its graphical glory?

Remote Desktop

Windows comes with *Remote Desktop*, a tool that enables you to log into a remote computer and have that computer's screen appear on your screen, as if you were sitting in front of the remote computer. Network administrators commonly use Remote Desktop to log into *headless servers*, powerful computers

FIGURE 21.23 OpenSSH

connected to a network that have no peripherals, such as a monitor and keyboard. Here's how to get there:

Start | Run or Start Search | mstsc

Start | All Programs | Accessories | Communications | Remote Desktop

Remote Assistance

Wouldn't it be cool if, when you're called about a technical support issue, you could see what the client sees from your own computer? When the client says that something doesn't work, it would be great if you could transfer yourself from your desk to your client's desk to see precisely what the client sees. This would dramatically cut down on the miscommunication that can make a tech's life so tedious. Windows Remote Assistance does just that. *Remote Assistance* enables a user to give someone control of his desktop. If a user has a problem, he can request support directly from you. Figure 21.24 shows Remote Assistance in action.

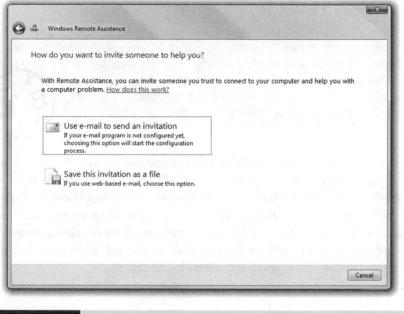

FIGURE 21.24 Remote Assistance in action

With Remote Assistance, you can do anything remotely that you would do from the actual computer. You can troubleshoot some hardware configuration or driver problem. You can install drivers, roll back drivers, download new ones, and so forth. You're in command of the remote machine as long as the client allows you to be. The client sees everything you do, by the way, and can stop you cold if you get out of line or do something that makes the client nervous!

Using Remote Assistance, you can teach someone how to use a particular application. You can log on to a user's PC and fire up Outlook, for example, and then walk through the steps to configure it while the user watches. The user can then take over the machine and walk through the steps while you watch, while the two of you chat with each other the whole time. Sweet!

System Applet Options

Remote desktop applications provide everything you need to access one system from another. They are common, especially now that Microsoft provides Remote Desktop for free. Whichever application you use, remember that you will always need both a server and a client program. The server goes on the system you want to access and the client goes on the system you use to access the server. On many solutions, the server and client software are integrated into a single product.

Exam Tip

Know the difference between Remote Assistance and Remote Desktop. With Remote Assistance you can help a user in trouble by remotely viewing the user's computer screen and controlling the computer at the user's request. Remote Desktop enables a user to connect to a remote Windows system, giving him access to his data and applications. Also, Remote Desktop does not require an invitation or a password.

In Windows, you can turn Remote Assistance and Remote Desktop on and off and configure other settings. Go to the System Control Panel applet. In Windows XP, click the Remote tab. In Windows Vista and Windows 7, click *Remote settings.* You will see check boxes for both Remote Assistance and Remote Desktop, along with buttons to configure more detailed settings. (In Windows XP, you'll only see Remote Desktop controls if you installed the Remote Desktop client, which is not installed by default.)

Exam Tip

Windows 7 (and Windows Vista with the appropriate update) is capable of running specific applications hosted on a Windows Server 2008/2008 R2 machine. Think of it as Remote Desktop without the desktop—a single application run on one machine (a server) and appearing on another desktop (a client). You can set up your connection to the Windows Server machine using the *RemoteApp and Desktop Connections* applet in Control Panel.

Voice over IP

You can use *Voice over IP (VoIP)* to make voice calls over your computer network. Why have two sets of wires, one for voice and one for data, going to every desk? Why not just use the extra capacity on the data network for your phone calls? That's exactly what VoIP does for you. VoIP works with every type of high-speed Internet connection, from DSL to cable to satellite.

VoIP doesn't refer to a single protocol, but rather to a collection of protocols that make phone calls over the data network possible. Vendors such as Skype and Vonage offer popular VoIP solutions, and many corporations use VoIP for their internal phone networks. A key to remember when installing and trouble-shooting VoIP is that low network latency is more important than high network speed. *Latency* is the amount of time a packet takes to get to its destination and is measured in milliseconds. The higher the latency, the more problems there are, such as noticeable delays during your VoIP call.

Local Lingo

QoS Better routers can enable a technology called *Quality of Service (QoS)* to optimize the flow of data for specific applications. Done properly, QoS can greatly improve the performance of a VPN or VoIP connection. Check your router to see if it has the capability and give it a try, especially if you have jittery VoIP sessions.

VoIP isn't confined to your computer, either. It can completely replace your old copper phone line. Two popular ways to set up a VoIP system are to either use dedicated *VoIP phones*, like the ones that Cisco makes, or use a small VoIP phone adapter (see Figure 21.25) that can interface with your existing analog phones.

True VoIP phones have RJ-45 connections that plug directly into the network and offer advanced features such as HD-quality audio and video calling. Unfortunately, these phones require a complex and expensive network to function, which puts them out of reach of most home users.

For home users, it's much more common to use a VoIP phone adapter to connect your old-school analog phones. These little boxes are very simple to set up: just connect it to your network, plug in a phone, and then check for a dial tone. With the VoIP service provided by cable companies, the adapter is often built right into the cable modem itself, making setup a breeze.

Virtual Private Networks

Remote connections have been around for a long time, long before the Internet existed. The biggest drawback with remote connections was the cost to connect.

FIGURE 21.25 Vonage Box VoIP phone adapter

If you were on one side of the continent and had to connect to your LAN on the other side of the continent, the only connection option was a telephone. Or, if you needed to connect two LANs across the continent, you ended up paying outrageous monthly charges for a private connection. The introduction of the Internet gave people wishing to connect to their home networks a very cheap connection option, but with one problem: the whole Internet is open to the public. People wanted to stop using dial-up and expensive private connections and use the Internet instead, but they wanted to do it securely.

Those clever network engineers worked long and hard and came up with several solutions to this problem. Standards have been created that use encrypted tunnels between a computer (or a remote network) to create a private network through the Internet (see Figure 21.26), resulting in what is called a *virtual private network (VPN)*.

An encrypted tunnel requires endpoints—the ends of the tunnel where the data is encrypted and decrypted. In the SSH tunnel you've seen thus far, the client for the application sits on one end and the server sits on the other. VPNs do the same thing. Either some software running on a computer or, in some cases, a dedicated box must act as an endpoint for a VPN (see Figure 21.27).

To make VPNs work requires a protocol that uses one of the many tunneling protocols available and adds the capability to ask for an IP address from a local DHCP server to give the tunnel an IP address that matches the subnet of the local LAN. The connection keeps the IP address to connect to the Internet, but the tunnel endpoints must act like NICs (see Figure 21.28). Let's look at one of the protocols, PPTP.

Los Angeles Office

New York Office

VPN

Internet

VPN

FIGURE 21.26 VPN connecting computers across the United States

Los Angeles Office

FIGURE 21.27 Typical tunnel

PPTP VPNs

So how do we make IP addresses appear out of thin air? Microsoft got the ball rolling with the *Point-to-Point Tunneling Protocol (PPTP),* an advanced version of a protocol used for dial-up Internet called PPP that handles all of this right out of the box. The only trick is the endpoints. In Microsoft's view, a VPN is intended for individual clients (think employees on the road) to connect back to the office network, so Microsoft places the PPTP endpoints on the client and a special remote access server program called Routing and Remote Access Service (RRAS), available on Server versions of Windows, on the server (see Figure 21.29).

FIGURE 21.28 Endpoints must have their own IP addresses.

FIGURE 21.29 RRAS in action

On the Windows client side, you right-click My Network Places and click Create a New Connection (Windows XP) or type **VPN** into the Start Search bar (Windows Vista and 7) and press ENTER. This presents you with a dialog box where you can enter all your VPN server information. Your network administrator will most likely provide this to you. The result is a virtual network card that, like any other NIC, gets an IP address from the DHCP server back at the office (see Figure 21.30).

Exam Tip

A system connected to a VPN looks as though it's on the local network but often performs much slower than if the system were connected directly back at the office.

When your computer connects to the RRAS server on the private network, PPTP creates a secure tunnel through the Internet back to the private LAN. Your client takes on an IP address of that network as if your computer were plugged into the LAN back at the office. Even your Internet traffic will go through your office first. If you open your Web browser, your client will go across the Internet to the office LAN and then use the LAN's Internet connection! Because of this, Web browsing is very slow over a VPN.

FIGURE 21.30 VPN connection in Windows

Support Applications (Internet Utilities)

The CompTIA A+ 220-801 objectives list three rather unique protocols. Personally, I doubt you'll ever deal directly with two of them, and the other is more common to LANs, not the Internet, but you should know a little bit about all three anyway.

LDAP

The *Lightweight Directory Access Protocol (LDAP)* enables operating systems and applications to access directories. If you've got a Windows Server system running Active Directory, for example, Windows uses LDAP to do anything with Active Directory. If you're sitting at a computer and add it to an Active Directory domain, Windows uses LDAP commands to update the Active Directory with the computer's information. You don't see LDAP, but it works hard to keep networks running smoothly.

SNMP

The *Simple Network Management Protocol (SNMP)* enables remote query and remote configuration of just about anything on a network. Assuming all your computers, switches, routers, and so on are SNMP-capable, you can use programs

to query the network for an unimaginable amount of data. SNMP is a popular tool to check on your network, but you'll need to take the CompTIA Network+ exam to see SNMP in action.

SMB

The *Server Message Block (SMB)* protocol isn't even an application but rather proof as to the power of Microsoft. SMBs date back to the old NetBIOS naming service and were the tools that tossed a PC's name around a network. NetBIOS names are gone, but SMBs are the reason that tools like Network can show you all the computers on your network. SMB is so powerful that other operating systems copy it using a popular program called SAMBA. SAMBA emulates SMB—it makes non-SMB operating systems on a network look like Windows.

CHECKPOINT

✔ **Objective 21.01: Connecting to the Internet** To use the Internet successfully, you need to connect properly and then run special applications that work with TCP/IP services. Many users connect to an ISP using a modem and Dial-up Networking (DUN), which uses PPP to enable access to remote resources. Other users connect via a dedicated solution, such as DSL, cable, or fiber, or wirelessly through a LAN or cellular connection. Windows offers Internet Connection Sharing to enable computers on a LAN to connect to the Internet through a single machine.

✔ **Objective 21.02: Internet Software Tools** The TCP/IP services used commonly on the Internet are HTTP for Web browsing, POP3 and SMTP for e-mail, FTP for transferring files, and Telnet or SSH for controlling remote computers. Other tools include VoIP, VPN, Remote Desktop, and Remote Assistance.

REVIEW QUESTIONS

1. What is the port number for the HTTPS service?

 A. 440

 B. 101

 C. 3

 D. 443

2. The delay caused by the distance a signal must travel to a satellite dish is called the satellite _____.

 A. Slow down

 B. Latency

 C. Interdiction

 D. Proxy

3. Ethan connects to the Internet through a dial-up connection. He has multiple computers and wants to be able to get online from each of them. Which Windows solution would help him the most?

 A. Windows Firewall

 B. Internet Explorer

 C. Device Manager

 D. Internet Connection Sharing

4. In terms of dial-up connections, what does PPP stand for?

 A. Portal-to-Portal Protocol

 B. Point-to-Point Protocol

 C. Person-to-Person Protocol

 D. Place-to-Place Protocol

5. A more secure alternative to the Telnet remote terminal is

 _____.

 A. PPP

 B. TCP/IP

 C. HTTP

 D. SSH

6. John wants to log into a server remotely and take full control over the remote machine without an invitation, but he wants to have graphical control, not command line only. What tool should he use?

 A. Remote Assistance

 B. Remote Desktop

 C. SSH

 D. Telnet

7. To configure dial-up networks with Windows XP, use the _____ applet.

 A. Network and Internet Connections

 B. Network Neighborhood

 C. Internet Connection Sharing

 D. Remote Assistance

8. What are encrypted tunnels created between computers or networks through the Internet called?

 A. RDPs

 B. Internet appliances

 C. WiMAX

 D. VPNs

9. What can be implemented to greatly improve the performance of a VPN or VoIP connection?

 A. 4G

 B. SNMP

 C. QoS

 D. LDAP

10. Liz can receive her e-mail, but she cannot send e-mail. Which of the following is most likely causing her problem?

 A. POP3

 B. SMTP

 C. IMAP4

 D. UART

REVIEW ANSWERS

1. **D** HTTPS uses port 443.

2. **B** The delay caused by the distance a signal must travel to a satellite dish is called satellite latency.

3. **D** Ethan could use Internet Connection Sharing to share his connection with the other computers.

4. **B** In terms of dial-up connections, PPP stands for Point-to-Point Protocol.

5. **D** The more secure remote terminal is called SSH, or Secure Shell.

6. **B** All four choices enable you to control a remote computer, but Remote Desktop is the best answer here. Remote Desktop gives you full graphical control and doesn't require an invitation.

7. **A** To configure dial-up networks with Windows XP, use the Network and Internet Connections applet.

8. **D** Encrypted tunnels between computers or networks through the Internet are called virtual private networks (VPNs).

9. **C** Quality of Service (QoS) can greatly improve the performance of a VPN or VoIP connection.

10. **B** Liz can receive her e-mail, but she cannot send e-mail. SMTP is the most likely cause of her problem. Remember that SMTP is used to send e-mail, while POP3 and IMAP4 are used to receive e-mail.

Securing Computers

	NEWBIE	SOME EXPERIENCE	EXPERT
ETA	3 hours	2 hours	1 hour

Your PC is under siege. Through your PC, a malicious person can gain valuable information about you and your habits. He can steal your files. He can run programs that log your keystrokes and thus gain account names and passwords, credit card information, and more. He can run software that takes over much of your computer processing time and use it to send spam or steal from others. The threat is real and right now. Worse, he's doing one or more of these things to your clients as I write these words. You need to secure your computer and your users' computers from these attacks.

This chapter explains essentials of security. We'll look at threats first and then explore key security concepts and techniques. The chapter finishes with a discussion about securing computers in a networked environment.

Objective 22.01 Analyzing Security Threats

Threats to your data and PC come from two directions: accidents and malicious people. All sorts of things can go wrong with your computer, from users getting access to folders they shouldn't see to a virus striking and deleting folders. Files can be deleted, renamed, or simply lost. Hard drives can die, and optical discs get scratched and rendered unreadable. Accidents happen, and even well-meaning people can make mistakes.

Unfortunately, a lot of people out there intend to do you harm. Add that intent together with a talent for computers, and you have a deadly combination. Let's look at the following issues:

- Unauthorized access
- Data destruction, accidental or deliberate
- Administrative access
- Catastrophic hardware failures
- Malware

Unauthorized Access

Unauthorized access occurs when a person accesses resources without permission. Resources in this case mean data, applications, and hardware. A user can alter or delete data; access sensitive information, such as financial data,

personnel files, or e-mail messages; or use a computer for purposes the owner did not intend.

Not all unauthorized access is malicious—often this problem arises when users who are randomly poking around in a computer discover that they can access resources in a fashion the primary user did not intend. Unauthorized access becomes malicious when outsiders knowingly and intentionally take advantage of weaknesses in your security to gain information, use resources, or destroy data!

One of the ways to gain unauthorized access is through intrusion. You might imagine someone kicking in a door and hacking into a computer, but more often than not it's someone sitting at a home computer, trying various passwords over the Internet. Not quite as glamorous, but still….With *shoulder surfing*, a more active option, a would-be intruder observes someone's screen or keyboard to get information, often passwords. Watch for prying eyes when working at your local café!

Local Lingo

Dumpster diving *Dumpster diving* is the generic term for anytime a hacker goes through your refuse, looking for information. This is also a form of intrusion.

Social Engineering

Although you're more likely to lose data through accident, the acts of malicious users get the vast majority of headlines. Most of these attacks come under the heading of *social engineering*—the process of using or manipulating people inside the networking environment to gain access to that network from the outside— which covers the many ways humans can use other humans to gain unauthorized information. This unauthorized information may be a network login, a credit card number, company customer data—almost anything you might imagine that one person or organization may not want a person outside of that organization to access.

Social engineering attacks aren't hacking—at least in the classic sense of the word—although the goals are the same. Social engineering means people attacking an organization through the people in the organization or physically accessing the organization to get the information they need. Following are a few of the more classic types of social engineering attacks.

Travel Advisory

It's common for social engineering attacks to be used together, so if you discover one of them being used against your organization, it's a good idea to look for others.

Infiltration

Hackers can physically enter your building under the guise of someone who might have a legitimate reason for being there, such as cleaning personnel, repair technicians, or messengers. They then snoop around desks, looking for whatever they can find. They might talk with people inside the organization, gathering names, office numbers, department names—little things in and of themselves but powerful tools when combined later with other social engineering attacks.

Local Lingo

Tailgating Dressing the part of a legitimate user—with fake badge and everything—enables malicious people to gain access to locations and thus potentially your data. Following someone through the door, for example, as if you belong, is called *tailgating*. Tailgating is a common form of infiltration.

Telephone Scams

With *telephone scams,* an attacker makes a phone call to someone in the organization to gain information. The attacker attempts to come across as someone inside the organization and uses this to get the desired information. Probably the most famous of these scams is the "I forgot my user name and password" scam. In this gambit, the attacker first learns the account name of a legitimate person in the organization, often using an infiltration method. The attacker then calls someone in the organization, usually the help desk, in an attempt to gather information, in this case a password.

Phishing

Phishing is the act of trying to get people to give their user names, passwords, or other security information by pretending to be someone else electronically. A classic example is when a bad guy sends you an e-mail that's supposed to be from your local credit card company asking you to send them your user name and password. Phishing is by far the most common form of social engineering done today.

Data Destruction

Often an extension of unauthorized access, data destruction means more than just intentionally or accidentally erasing or corrupting data. It's easy to imagine some evil hacker accessing your network and deleting all your important files, but authorized users may also access certain data and then use that data beyond what they are authorized to do. A good example is the person who legitimately accesses a Microsoft Access product database to modify the product descriptions, only to discover that she can change the prices of the products, too.

This type of threat is particularly dangerous when users are not clearly informed about the extent to which they are authorized to make changes. A fellow tech once told me about a user who managed to mangle an important database when someone gave him incorrect access. When confronted, the user said: "If I wasn't allowed to change it, the system wouldn't let me do it!" Many users believe that systems are configured in a paternalistic way that wouldn't allow them to do anything inappropriate. As a result, users often assume they're authorized to make any changes they believe are necessary when working on a piece of data they know they're authorized to access.

Administrative Access

Every operating system enables you to create user accounts and grant those accounts a certain level of access to files and folders in that computer. As an administrator, supervisor, or root user, you have full control over just about every aspect of the computer. Windows XP, in particular, makes it entirely too easy to give users administrative access to the computer, especially Windows XP Home, which has only two kinds of users: administrators and limited users. Because you can't do much as a limited user, most home and small office systems simply use multiple administrator accounts. If you need to control access, you need to use non-Home versions of Windows.

System Crash/Hardware Failure

As with any technology, computers can and will fail—usually when you can least afford for it to happen. Hard drives crash, the power fails—it's all part of the joy of working in the computing business. You need to create redundancy in areas prone to failure (such as installing backup power in case of electrical failure) and perform those all-important data backups. Chapter 17 goes into detail about using backups and other issues involved in creating a stable and reliable system.

Physical Theft

Thieves use social engineering to gain access to sensitive areas and physically steal data and equipment. Not very elegant, perhaps, but you can certainly lose a lot that way. Never forget that the best software security measures can be rendered useless if you fail to protect your systems physically.

Malware

Networks are without a doubt the fastest and most efficient vehicles for transferring computer viruses among systems. News reports focus attention on the many malicious software attacks from the Internet, but a huge number of such attacks still come from users who bring in programs on optical discs and USB drives. The "Protecting Computers from Network Threats" section of this chapter describes the various methods of virus infection and other malware and what you need to do to prevent such attacks from damaging your networked systems.

Objective 22.02 Security Concepts and Technologies

O nce you've assessed the threats to your computers and networks, you need to take steps to protect those valuable resources. Depending on the complexity of your organization, this can be a small job encompassing some basic security concepts and procedures, or it can be exceedingly complex. The security needs for a three-person desktop publishing firm, for example, would differ wildly from those of a defense contractor supplying top-secret toys to the Pentagon. Let's look at three concept and technology areas: access control, data classification and compliance, and reporting.

Access Control

Access is the key. If you can control access to the data, programs, and other computing resources, you've secured your systems. *Access control* is composed of four interlinked areas that a good security-minded tech should think about: physical security, authentication, users and groups, and security policies. Much of this you know from previous chapters, but this section should help tie it all together as a security topic.

Secure Physical Area and Lock Down Systems

The first order of security is to block access to the physical hardware from people who shouldn't have access. This isn't rocket science. Lock the door to your workspace. Don't leave a PC unattended when logged in. In fact, don't ever leave a system logged in, even as a limited user. God help you if you walk away from a server still logged in as an administrator. You're tempting fate.

> ### Exam Tip
>
> In a small network, you can use static IP addresses as a failsafe in case of a physical security breach. If someone gets access to your office, for example, and has a portable computer to plug into a wall jack, without DHCP running, his machine would get no IP information. If DHCP was running, on the other hand, his machine will immediately have an IP address, subnet mask, DNS server, and default gateway.

Employee ID badges are now so common that even relatively small organizations use them. Badges are a great way not only to control building access but also to store authentication tools such as radio frequency identification (RFID) or smart cards (see "Authentication" later in this chapter). Figure 22.1 shows a typical badge.

Be aware of the risk of shoulder surfing. One handy tool to prevent this is a privacy filter. A privacy filter is little more than a framed sheet or film that you apply to the front of your monitor. Privacy filters reduce the viewing angle, making it impossible to see the contents on the screen for anyone except those directly in front of the screen (see Figure 22.2).

Security is more of an issue when users walk away from their computers, even for a moment. When you see a user's computer logged in and unattended, do the user and your company a huge favor and lock the computer. Just walk up and press WINDOWS LOGO KEY-L on the keyboard to lock the system. It works in all versions of Windows. Better yet, make a point to make users aware of this issue so they understand the risk and can take the precaution themselves. You should also instruct them how to password-protect their screensaver. When the password feature is enabled, a user won't be able to return to the desktop until he or she has entered the proper password. It's a little like locking the computer, and good for those who like using screensavers.

| FIGURE 22.1 | Typical employee badge/smart card |

| FIGURE 22.2 | Privacy filter |

While you're looking at a user's monitor, examine around his or her desk. Is the user writing down passwords and putting them in plain sight? If so, tell the user to get rid of them! Teach users to create easy-to-remember passwords. Are critical, personal, or sensitive documents also lying about in plain sight? The user should put them in a closed, secure place. Documents no longer needed should be shredded immediately.

Authentication

Security requires properly implemented *authentication,* which means in essence how the computer determines who can or should access it and, once accessed, what that user can do. A computer can authenticate users through software, hardware, or a combination of both.

You can categorize ways to authenticate into three broad areas: knowledge factors, ownership factors, and inherent factors. A *knowledge factor* is something the user knows, like a password or personal identification number (PIN). An *ownership factor* is something the user has, like an ID card or security token. An *inherent factor* (also called a biometric) is something that is part of the user, like a fingerprint or retinal pattern.

Exam Tip

A popular way to remember authentication factors is to think of them as something you know (passwords), something about you (biometric), and something you have (badge, key fob, or security token).

Multifactor authentication provides the best authentication, where a user must use two or more factors to prove his or her identity. Note that multifactor means more than one factor, not just more than one *thing.* Logging in with a user name and password is two things, for example, but because both fall into the category of what a user knows, it's not multifactor authentication.

Many organizations use *two-factor authentication.* An example is a key fob that generates a numeric key. A user authenticates by entering a user name and password (something you know) and is then prompted to enter the key (something you have).

Exam Tip

Remember the concept of single sign-on from Chapter 19? You can log on to any computer in a domain using one set of credentials. In addition to being a time-saver, this is a great security feature that helps network administrators better control who can gain access to the network.

FIGURE 22.3 CMOS access password request

Software Authentication: Proper Passwords Whenever I power up a friend's computer and go straight to her desktop without being prompted for a password, I find it shocking. This is just wrong! I'm always tempted to assign a password right then and there (without saying anything, of course) so that my friend might learn the error of her ways. I don't do it, but I always try to explain gently the importance of passwords. Make sure you and your users use *strong passwords* of at least eight characters in length, including letters, numbers, and punctuation symbols.

You know about passwords from Chapter 17, so I won't belabor the point here. Suffice it to say that you must require that your users have proper passwords. Don't let them write passwords down or tape them to the underside of their mouse pads either!

It's not just access to Windows that you need to think about. There's always the temptation for people to do other mean things, such as changing CMOS settings, opening up the case, and even stealing hard drives. Any of these actions renders the computer inoperable to the casual user until a tech can undo the damage or replace components. All modern CMOS setup utilities come with a number of tools to protect your computer, such as drive lock, intrusion detection, and, of course, system access passwords such as the one shown in Figure 22.3. Refer to Chapter 7 to refresh yourself on what you can do at a BIOS level to protect your computer.

Hardware Authentication Smart cards and biometric devices enable modern systems to authenticate users with more authority than mere passwords. *Smart cards* are credit card–sized cards with circuitry that can identify the bearer of the card. Smart cards are relatively common for such tasks as authenticating users for mass transit systems, for example, but are fairly uncommon in computers. Figure 22.4 shows a smart card and keyboard combination.

Security tokens are devices that store some unique information that the user carries on their person. They may be digital certificates, passwords, or biometric data. They may also store an RSA token. *RSA tokens* are random-number generators that are used with user names and passwords to ensure extra security. Most security tokens come in the form of key fobs, as shown in Figure 22.5.

You can also get many types of security tokens as software. Anyone who plays *World of Warcraft* knows that there's an entire illegal industry known as "gold

FIGURE 22.4 Keyboard-mounted smart card reader being used for a commercial application (photo courtesy of Cherry Corp.)

farmers" who like to hack accounts and steal all the hard-earned loot your character collects. It's a terrible feeling to log in to the game only to find your character cleaned out (see Figure 22.6).

To counter this problem, Blizzard Entertainment, the folks who own *World of Warcraft,* provide free security tokens. Most folks think "hardware" in the form of key fobs when they hear the words "security tokens," but you can also download a security token as software—Blizzard offers an app for your smartphone, as shown in Figure 22.7.

People can guess or discover passwords, but it's a lot harder to forge someone's fingerprints. The keyboard in Figure 22.8 authenticates users on a local machine by using fingerprints. Other devices that will do the trick are key fobs and retinal scanners. Devices that require some sort of physical, flesh-and-blood authentication are called *biometric devices.*

FIGURE 22.5 RSA key fob (photo courtesy of EMC Corp.)

| FIGURE 22.6 | I've been robbed! My fine armor is gone, my bags are empty, and my bank account only has a few copper pieces! |

Clever manufacturers have developed key fobs and smart cards that use RFID to transmit authentication information so users don't have to insert something into a computer or card reader. The Privaris plusID combines, for example, a biometric fingerprint fob with an RFID tag that makes security as easy as opening a garage door remotely! Figure 22.9 shows a plusID device.

| FIGURE 22.7 | Blizzard Software security token for iPhone |

FIGURE 22.8	Microsoft keyboard with fingerprint accessibility

For some reason, CompTIA lists *retinal scanners* as a form of biometric security. While retinal scanners do exist, I have been in hundreds of high-security facilities and have only seen one retinal scanner in operation in almost 30 years as a tech. CompTIA should remove this silly objective, but until they do, Figure 22.10 shows about the only image of a retinal scanner in operation you'll ever encounter.

FIGURE 22.9	plusID (photo courtesy of Privaris, Inc.)

FIGURE 22.10 Retinal scanner in *Half-Life 2*

NTFS, not FAT32!

The file system on a hard drive matters a lot when it comes to security. On a Windows machine with multiple users, you simply must use NTFS or you have no security at all. Not just primary drives but also any secondary drives in computers in your care should be formatted as NTFS, with the exception of removable drives such as the one you use to back up your system.

When you run into a multiple-drive system that has a second or third drive formatted as FAT32, you can use the *convert* command line utility to go from FAT to NTFS. The syntax is pretty straightforward. To convert a D: drive from FAT or FAT32 to NTFS, for example, you'd type the following:

```
convert d: /fs:ntfs
```

You can substitute a mount name in place of the drive letter in case you have a mounted volume. The command has a few extra switches as well, so at the command prompt, type /? after the convert command to see all of your options.

Users and Groups

Windows uses user accounts and groups as the bedrock of access control. A user account is assigned to a group, such as Users, Power Users, or Administrators, and by association gets certain permissions on the computer. Using NTFS enables the highest level of control over data resources.

Assigning users to groups is a great first step in controlling a local machine, but this feature really shines once you go to a networked environment. Let's go there now.

User Account Management Through Groups

Access to user accounts should be restricted to the assigned individuals, and those who configure the permissions to those accounts should follow the *Principle of Least Privilege:* Accounts should have permission to access only the resources they need and no more. Tight control of user accounts is critical to preventing unauthorized access. Disabling unused accounts is an important part of this strategy, but good user account management goes far deeper than that.

Exam Tip

The 802 exam insists that you should restrict *directory* permissions according to the PoLP, by which, of course, it means *Principle of Least Privilege.*

Groups are a great way to achieve increased complexity without increasing the administrative burden on network administrators, because all operating systems combine permissions. When a user is a member of more than one group, which permissions does that user have with respect to any particular resource? In all operating systems, the permissions of the groups are *combined,* and the result is what you call the *effective permissions* the user has to access the resource. As an example, if Rita is a member of the Sales group, which has List Folder Contents permission to a folder, and she is also a member of the Managers group, which has Read and Execute permissions to the same folder, Rita will have both List Folder Contents *and* Read and Execute permissions to that folder.

Watch out for *default* user accounts and groups—they can become secret backdoors to your network! All network operating systems have a default Everyone group that can be used to sneak into shared resources easily. This Everyone group, as its name implies, literally includes anyone who connects to that resource. Windows gives full control to the Everyone group by default, for example, so make sure you know to lock this down! The other scary one is the Guest account. The Guest account is the only way to access a system without a user name and password. Unless you have a compelling reason to provide guest access, you should always make sure the Guest account is disabled.

All of the default groups—Everyone, Guest, Users—define broad groups of users. Never use them unless you intend to permit all of those folks access to a resource. If you use one of the default groups, remember to configure them with the proper permissions to prevent users from doing things you don't want them to do with a shared resource!

Exam Tip

The 802 exam suggests changing the default user names as one of the "best practices to secure a workstation." More commonly, though, you'd disable the Guest account and give the Administrator account a particularly strong password. Watch out for this one on the exam.

Security Policies

Although permissions control how users access shared resources, there are other functions you should control that are outside the scope of resources. For example, do you want users to be able to access a command prompt on their Windows system? Do you want users to be able to install software? Would you like to control what systems a user can log on to or at what time of day a user can log on? All network operating systems provide you with some capability to control these and literally hundreds of other security parameters, under what Windows calls *policies*. I like to think of policies as permissions for activities, as opposed to true permissions, which control access to resources.

A policy is usually applied to a user account, a computer, or a group. Every Windows system has its own local policies program, which enables policies to be placed on that system only. To access the program, double-click the Local Security Policies applet in the Administrative Tools folder. Figure 22.11 shows the tool you use to set local policies on an individual system, called *Local Security Policy*, being used to set a minimum password length.

Travel Advisory

When you open the Local Security Policy tool in Windows XP, note that the program is labeled "Local Security Settings," even though the icon is labeled "Local Security Policy." In Windows Vista and Windows 7, it is always called Local Security Policy.

Local policies work great for individual systems, but they can be a pain to configure if you want to apply the same settings to more than one PC on your

FIGURE 22.11 Local Security Policy

network. If you want to apply policy settings en masse, you need to step up to Windows Active Directory domain-based *Group Policy.* By using Group Policy, you can exercise deity-like—Microsoft prefers to use the term *granular*—control over your network clients.

Want to set default wallpaper for every PC in your domain? Group Policy can do that. Want to make certain tools inaccessible to everyone except authorized users? Group Policy can do that, too. Want to control access to the Internet, redirect home folders, run scripts, deploy software, or just remind folks that unauthorized access to the network will get them nowhere fast? Group Policy is the answer. Figure 22.12 shows Group Policy; I'm about to change the default title on every instance of Internet Explorer on every computer in my domain!

That's just one simple example of the settings you can configure by using Group Policy. You can apply literally hundreds of tweaks through Group Policy, from the great to the small, but don't worry too much about familiarizing yourself with each and every one. Group Policy settings are a big topic on most of the Microsoft certification tracks, but for the purposes of the CompTIA A+ exams, you simply have to be comfortable with the concept behind Group Policy.

FIGURE 22.12 Using Group Policy to make IE title say "provided by Mike!"

Although I could never list every possible policy you can enable on a Windows system, here's a list of some commonly used ones:

- **Prevent Registry Edits** If you try to edit the Registry, you get a failure message.
- **Prevent Access to the Command Prompt** Keeps users from getting to the command prompt by turning off the Run command and the Command Prompt shortcut.
- **Log on Locally** Defines who may log on to the system locally.
- **Shut Down System** Defines who may shut down the system.
- **Minimum Password Length** Forces a minimum password length.
- **Account Lockout Threshold** Sets the maximum number of logon attempts a person can make before being locked out of the account.
- **Disable Windows Installer** Prevents users from installing software.
- **Printer Browsing** Enables users to browse for printers on the network, as opposed to using only assigned printers.

Although the CompTIA A+ exams don't expect you to know how to implement policies on any type of network, you are expected to understand that

policies exist, especially on Windows networks, and that they can do amazing things to control what users can do on their systems. If you ever try to get to a command prompt on a Windows system only to discover the Run command is dimmed, blame it on a policy, not the computer!

Travel Assistance

Another "best practice" mentioned for securing a workstation is to "disable Autorun," the feature where Windows either executes or queries what you want to do with a disc or USB flash drive when inserted. To disable it, you need to change the Local Security Policy option. Go to this Microsoft Knowledge Base article for the steps in each version of Windows: http://support.microsoft.com/kb/967715.

Data Classification and Compliance

Larger organizations, such as government entities, benefit greatly from organizing their data according to its sensitivity—what's called *data classification*—and making certain that computer hardware and software stay as uniform as possible. In addition, many government and internal regulations apply fairly rigorously to the organizations.

Data classification systems vary by the organization, but a common scheme classifies documents as public, internal use only, highly confidential, top secret, and so on. Using a classification scheme enables employees such as techs to know very quickly what to do with documents, the drives containing documents, and more. Your strategy for recycling a computer system left from a migrated user, for example, will differ a lot if the data on the drive was classified as internal use only or top secret.

Compliance means, in a nutshell, that members of an organization or company must abide by or comply with all of the rules that apply to the organization or company. Statutes with funny names such as Sarbanes-Oxley impose certain behaviors or prohibitions on what people can and cannot do in the workplace.

From a technician's point of view, the most common compliance issue revolves around software, such as what sort of software users can be allowed to install on their computers or, conversely, why you have to tell a user that he can't install the latest application that may help him do the job more effectively because that software isn't on the approved list. This can lead to some uncomfortable confrontations, but it's part of a tech's job.

The concepts behind compliance in IT are not, as some might imagine at first blush, to stop you from being able to work effectively. Rather, they're designed to

stop users with not quite enough technical skill or knowledge from installing malicious programs or applications that will destabilize their systems. This keeps technical support calls down and enables techs to focus on more serious problems.

Reporting

As a final weapon in your security arsenal, you need to report any security issues so a network administrator or technician can take steps to make them go away. You can set up auditing within Windows so that the OS reports problems to you. *Event Viewer* enables you to read the logs created by auditing. You can then do your work and report those problems. Let's take a look.

Auditing

The Security section of Event Viewer doesn't show you anything by default. To unlock the full potential of Event Viewer, you need to set up auditing. *Auditing* in the security sense means to tell Windows to create an entry in the Security Log when certain events happen, such as when a user logs on—called *event auditing*—or tries to access a certain file or folder—called *object access auditing*. Figure 22.13 shows Event Viewer tracking logon and logoff events.

The CompTIA A+ certification exams don't test you on creating a brilliant auditing policy for your office—that's what network administrators do. You simply need to know what auditing does and how to turn it on or off so you can provide support for the network administrators in the field. To turn on auditing at a local level, go to Local Security Policy in Administrative Tools. Select Local Policies and then click Audit Policy. Double-click one of the policy options and select one or both of the check boxes in the Properties dialog box that opens. Figure 22.14 shows the Audit object access Properties dialog box.

Exam Tip

Event Viewer stores log files in %SystemRoot%\System32\Config.

Incidence Reporting

Once you've gathered data about a particular system or you've dealt with a computer or network problem, you need to complete the mission by telling your supervisor. This is called *incidence reporting*. Many companies have premade forms that you simply fill out and submit. Other places are less formal. Regardless, you need to do this!

FIGURE 22.13 Event Viewer displaying security alerts

Incidence reporting does a couple of things for you. First, it provides a record of work you've accomplished. Second, it provides a piece of information that, when combined with other information you might or might not know, reveals a pattern or bigger problem to someone higher up the chain. A seemingly innocuous security audit report, for example, might match other such events in numerous places in the building at the same time and thus show that conscious, coordinated action rather than a glitch was at work.

Evidence Handling

As a tech, you'll need to deal with people who use company computers in prohibited ways. In most cases, you're not paid to be the police and should not get involved. There are times, however, where something bad—really bad—takes place on one of the systems you support, and if you're the first tech person there, everyone is going to turn to you for action.

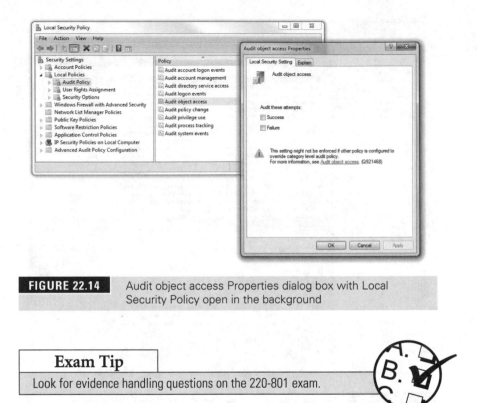

FIGURE 22.14 Audit object access Properties dialog box with Local Security Policy open in the background

Exam Tip

Look for evidence handling questions on the 220-801 exam.

A technician should ignore personal information in and around a person's computer. As mentioned back in Chapter 1, you should treat anything said to you and anything you see as a personal confidence, not to be repeated to customers, coworkers, or bosses.

But what about the scary stuff? Obvious espionage? Pornography? People passing out personal information? Hacking? In these cases, you've just become the first line of defense and you need to act accordingly. Let's address the objectives as listed by CompTIA for the 220-801 exam.

Identify the Action or Content as Prohibited Use common sense, but keep in mind that most organizations have an acceptable-use policy that employees must sign. The acceptable-use policy defines what actions employees may or may not perform on company equipment. Remember that these polices aren't just for obvious issues such as using a computer for personal use. These policies cover computers, phones, printers, and even the network itself. This policy will define the handling of passwords, e-mail, and many other issues.

Report Through Proper Channels In most cases, you'll report any prohibited actions or content directly to your supervisor. There's also a chance your company will have a security officer or incident response leader who you'll contact instead. Do *not* speak to the person making the infraction unless your supervisor approves that contact.

Data/Device Preservation You might end up in a situation serious enough that a computer or other device becomes evidence. In these cases, the location of the system and who has touched it may come into question, so you need to establish a *chain of custody:* a documented history of who has been in possession of the system. You'll hopefully have a legal expert to guide you, but the following are fairly common rules:

1. Isolate the system. Shut down the system and store it in a place where no one else can access it.

2. Document when you took control of the system and the actions you took: shutting it down, unplugging it, moving it, and so on. Don't worry about too much detail, but you must track its location.

3. If another person takes control of the system, document the transfer of custody.

Objective 22.03 **Protecting Computers from Network Threats**

Networks are under threat from the outside as well, so this section looks at issues involving Internet-borne attacks, firewalls, and wireless networking. This content is the security bread and butter for a CompTIA A+ technician, so you need to understand the concepts and procedures and be able to implement them properly.

Malicious Software

The beauty of the Internet is the ease of accessing resources just about anywhere on the globe, all from the comfort of your favorite chair. This connection, however, runs both ways, and people from all over the world can potentially access your computer from the comfort of their evil lairs. The Internet is awash with malicious software that is, even at this moment, trying to infect your systems.

The term *malware* defines any program or code (macro, script, and so on) that's designed to do something on a system or network that you don't want done. Malware comes in quite a variety of guises, such as grayware, spam, viruses, worms, macros, Trojan horses, and rootkits. Let's examine all these malware flavors and then explore how to deal with them.

Grayware

Programs that intrude unwanted into your computing experience but don't actually do any damage to your systems or data—what's called *grayware*—can make that computing experience less than perfect. On most systems, the Internet Web browser client is the most often used piece of software.

There are basically two irritating grayware types: pop-ups and spyware. *Pop-ups* are those surprise browser windows that appear automatically when you visit a Web site, proving themselves irritating and unwanted and nothing else. *Spyware,* meanwhile, defines a family of programs that run in the background on your PC, sending information about your browsing habits to the company that installed it on your system. Of the two, spyware is much less noticeable but far more nefarious.

Local Lingo

Adware The term *adware* generally refers to programs that support themselves using revenue from ads, like all those "free" Internet game sites. Every once in a while those ads can lead to spyware installing on a system, making many authors lump adware into the grayware category.

Pop-ups Getting rid of pop-ups is actually rather tricky. You've probably noticed that most of these pop-up browser windows don't look like browser windows at all. They have no menu bar, button bar, or address window, yet they are separate browser windows. HTML coding permits Web site and advertising designers to remove the usual navigation aids from a browser window so all you're left with is the content. In fact, as I'll describe in a minute, some pop-up browser windows are deliberately designed to mimic similar pop-up alerts from the

Windows OS. They might even have buttons similar to Windows' own exit buttons, but you might find that when you click them, you wind up with more pop-up windows instead! What to do?

The first thing you need to know when dealing with pop-ups is how to close them without actually having to risk clicking them. Right-click the browser window's taskbar icon to generate a pop-up menu of your own. Select Close, and the window should go away. You can also press ALT-TAB to bring the browser window in question to the forefront and then press ALT-F4 to close it.

Spyware Some types of spyware go considerably beyond grayware's level of intrusion. They can use your computer's resources to run *distributed computing* applications, capture your keystrokes to steal passwords, reconfigure your dial-up settings to use a different phone number at a much higher connection charge, or even use your Internet connection and e-mail address list to propagate itself to other computers in a virus-like fashion! Are you concerned yet?

Setting aside the legal and ethical issues—and there are many—you should at least appreciate that spyware can seriously impact your PC's performance and cause problems with your Internet connection. The threat is real, so what practical steps can you take to protect yourself? Let's look at how to prevent spyware installation and how to detect and remove any installed spyware.

How does this spyware get into your system in the first place? Obviously, sensible people don't download and install something that they know is going to compromise their computers. Makers of spyware know this, so they bundle their software with some other program or utility that purports to give you some benefit.

Another popular spyware method is to use pop-up browser windows crudely disguised as Windows' own system warnings (see Figure 22.15). When clicked, these may trigger a flood of other browser windows, or may even start a file download.

The lesson here is simple: *Don't install these programs,* at least not without researching the program first. Careful reading of the software's license agreement before you install a program is a good idea, but realistically, it does little to protect your PC. With that in mind, here are a couple of preventive measures you can take to keep parasitic software off your system.

If you visit a Web site that prompts you to install a third-party application or plug-in that you've never heard of, *don't install it.* Well-known and reputable plug-ins, such as Adobe's Shockwave or Flash, are safe, but be suspicious of any others. Don't click *anywhere* inside of a pop-up browser window, even if it looks just like a Windows alert window or DOS command-line prompt—as I just mentioned, it's probably fake and the Close button is likely a hyperlink. Instead,

FIGURE 22.15 A spyware pop-up browser window, disguised as a Windows alert

use other means to close the window, such as pressing ALT-F4 or right-clicking the browser window's icon on the taskbar and selecting Close.

You can also install spyware detection and removal software on your system and run it regularly. Let's look at how to do that.

Windows comes with Windows Defender, a fine tool for catching most spyware, but it's not perfect. The better solution is to back up Windows Defender with a second spyware removal program. There are several on the market, but two that I highly recommend are Lavasoft's Ad-Aware (see Figure 22.16) and Safer Networking's Spybot Search & Destroy.

Both of these applications work exactly as advertised. They detect and delete spyware of all sorts—hidden files and folders, cookies, Registry keys and values, you name it. Ad-Aware is free for personal use, while Spybot Search & Destroy is shareware (see Figure 22.17). Many times I've used both programs at the same time because one tends to catch what the other misses.

Travel Assistance

If you haven't done this already, do it now. Go to www.safer-networking .org and download the latest copy of Spybot Search & Destroy. Install it on your computer and run it. Did it find any spyware that slipped in past your defenses?

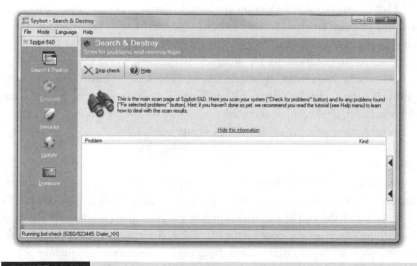

FIGURE 22.16 Lavasoft's Ad-Aware

FIGURE 22.17 Spybot Search & Destroy

Spam

E-mail that comes into your Inbox from a source that's not a friend, family member, or colleague, and that you didn't ask for, can create huge problems for your computer and you. This unsolicited e-mail, called *spam,* accounts for a huge percentage of traffic on the Internet. Spam comes in many flavors, from legitimate businesses trying to sell you products, to scammers who just want to take your money. Hoaxes, pornography, and get-rich-quick schemes pour into the Inboxes of most e-mail users. They waste your time and can easily offend.

You can use several options to cope with the flood of spam. The first option is defense. Never post your e-mail address on the Internet. One study tested this theory and found that *over 97 percent* of the spam received during the study went to e-mail addresses they had posted on the public Internet.

Filters and filtering software can block spam at your mail server and at your computer. Google Mail has powerful blocking schemes, for example, that drop the average spam received by its subscribers by a large percentage, usually more than 90 percent. You can set most e-mail programs to block e-mail from specific people—good to use if someone is harassing you—or to specific people. You can block by subject line or keywords. Most people use a third-party antispam program instead of using the filters in their e-mail program.

A lot of spam contains malware or points to dangerous Web sites. Never click any link or open an e-mail from someone you don't know! You might just save your computer.

Spam is also notorious for phishing scams. Phishing works by sending you an e-mail message that looks legitimate, like a bill or account information, hoping you will enter important personal information. If you receive an e-mail from Amazon.com, ebay.com, or some other site (like your bank), don't click it! Like Admiral Ackbar said in *Star Wars,* "It's a trap!"

Virus

A *virus* is a program that has two jobs: to replicate and to activate. *Replication* means it makes copies of itself, often as code stored in boot sectors or as extra code added to the end of executable programs. *Activation* is when a virus does something like erase the boot sector of a drive. A virus only replicates to other drives, such as thumb drives or optical media. It does not replicate across networks. Plus, a virus needs human action to spread.

Worm

A *worm* functions similarly to a virus, though it replicates exclusively through networks. A worm, unlike a virus, doesn't have to wait for someone to use a removable drive to replicate. If the infected computer is on a network, a worm will

immediately start sending copies of itself to any other computers on the network it can locate. Worms can exploit inherent flaws in program code like *buffer overflows,* where a buffer cannot hold all the data sent to it.

Macro

A *macro* is any type of virus that exploits application macros to replicate and activate. A *macro* is also programming within an application that enables you to control aspects of the application. Macros exist in any application that has a built-in macro language, such as Microsoft Excel, that users can program to handle repetitive tasks (among other things).

Trojan Horse

A *Trojan horse* is a piece of malware that looks or pretends to do one thing while, at the same time, doing something evil. A Trojan horse may be a game, like poker, or a free screensaver. The sky is the limit. The more "popular" Trojan horses turn an infected computer into a server and then open TCP or UDP ports so a remote user can control the infected computer. Trojan horses can be used to capture keystrokes, passwords, files, credit card information, and more. Trojan horses do not replicate.

Rootkit

For a virus or Trojan horse to succeed, it needs to come up with some method to hide itself. As awareness of malware has grown, antimalware programs make it harder to find new locations on a computer to hide malware. A *rootkit* is a Trojan horse that takes advantage of very low-level operating system functions to hide itself from all but the most aggressive of antimalware tools. Worse, a rootkit, by definition, gains privileged access to the computer. Rootkits can strike operating systems, hypervisors, and even firmware.

The most infamous rootkit appeared a few years ago as an antipiracy attempt by Sony on its music CDs. Unfortunately for the media giant, the rootkit software installed when you played a music CD and opened a backdoor that could be used for malicious intent.

Malware Signs and Symptoms

If your PC has been infected by malware, you'll bump into some strange things before you can even run an antimalware scan. Like a medical condition, malware causes unusual symptoms that should stand out from your everyday computer use. You need to become a PC physician and understand what each of these symptoms means.

Malware's biggest strength is its flexibility: it can look like anything. In fact, a lot of malware attacks can feel like normal PC "wonkiness"—momentary slow-downs, random one-time crashes, and so on. Knowing when a weird application crash is actually a malware attack is half the battle.

A slow PC can mean you're running too many applications at once or you've been hit with malware. How do you tell the difference? In this case, it's the fre-quency. If it's happening a lot, even when all of your applications are closed, you've got a problem. This goes for frequent lockups, too. If Windows starts mis-behaving (more than usual), run your antimalware application right away.

Malware, however, doesn't always jump out at you with big system crashes. Some malware tries to rename system files, change file permissions, or hide files completely so that they disappear. Most of these issues are easily caught by a reg-ular antimalware scan, so as long as you remain vigilant, you'll be okay.

Exam Tip

While it's not necessarily a malware attack, watch out for hijacked e-mail accounts, too, belonging either to you or to someone you know. Hackers can hit both e-mail clients and Web mail users. If you start receiving some fishy (or phishy) e-mail messages, change your Web mail user name and password or scan your PC for malware.

Some malware even fights back, defending itself from your many attempts to remove it. If your Windows Update feature stops working, preventing you from patching your PC, you've got malware. If other tools and utilities throw up an "Access Denied" road block, you've got malware. If you lose all Internet connec-tivity, either the malware is stopping you or removing the malware broke your connection. In this case, you might need to reconfigure your Internet connec-tion: reinstall your NIC and its drivers, reboot your router, and so on.

Even your browser and antimalware applications can turn against you. If you type in one Web address and end up at a different site than you anticipated, a malware infection might have overwritten your *hosts* file. The *hosts* file overrules any DNS settings and can redirect your browser to whatever site the malware adds to the file. Most browser redirections point you to phishing scams or Web sites full of free downloads (that are, of course, covered in malware). In fact, some free antimalware applications are actually malware—what techs call a *rogue antimalware* program. You can avoid these rogue applications by sticking to the recommended lists of antimalware software found online.

Watch for security alerts in Windows, either from Windows' built-in security tools or from your third-party antimalware program. Windows XP (SP2 and later) and Windows Vista include the Security Center, a Control Panel applet that monitors your software firewall, automatic updates, malware protection, and more. Windows 7 includes a similar tool, but calls it the Action Center, which you learned about back in Chapter 18 (see Figure 22.18). You don't actually configure much using these applets; they just tell you whether or not you are protected. Both of these tools place an icon and pop up a notification in the notification area whenever Windows detects a problem. Windows XP and Vista use a red shield with a white X to notify you, while Windows 7 uses a white flag.

Malware Prevention and Recovery

The only way to protect your PC permanently from getting malware is to disconnect it from the Internet and never permit any potentially infected software to touch your precious computer. Because neither scenario is likely these days, you need to use specialized antimalware programs to help stave off the inevitable assaults. Even with the best antimalware tools, there are times when malware still manages to strike your computer. When you discover infected systems, you need to know how to stop the spread of the malware to other computers, how to fix infected computers, and how to remediate (restore) the system as close to its original state as possible.

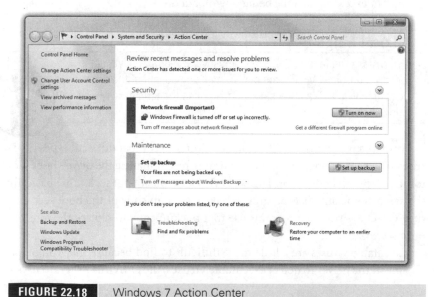

FIGURE 22.18 Windows 7 Action Center

Dealing with Malware

You can deal with malware in several ways: antimalware programs, training and awareness, patch management, and remediation. A good tech maintains proper incident response records to see if any pattern to attacks emerges. He or she can then adjust policies and procedures to mitigate these attacks.

> ### Exam Tip
>
> One of the most important malware mitigation procedures is to keep systems under your control patched and up to date through proper *patch management*. Microsoft does a very good job of putting out bug fixes and patches as soon as problems occur. If your systems aren't set up to update automatically, then perform manual updates regularly.

Antimalware Programs

An *antimalware program* such as a classic *antivirus* program protects your PC in two ways. It can be both sword and shield, working in an active seek-and-destroy mode and in a passive sentry mode. When ordered to seek and destroy, the program scans the computer's boot sector and files for viruses and, if it finds any, presents you with the available options for removing or disabling them. Antivirus programs can also operate as *virus shields* that passively monitor a computer's activity, checking for viruses only when certain events occur, such as a program executing or a file being downloaded.

> ### Local Lingo
>
> **Antivirus** The term *antivirus* (and antispyware, or anti-anything) is becoming obsolete. Viruses are only a small component of the many types of malware. Many people continue to use the term as a synonym for antimalware.

Antivirus programs use different techniques to combat different types of viruses. They detect boot sector viruses simply by comparing the drive's boot sector to a standard boot sector. This works because most boot sectors are basically the same. Some antivirus programs make a backup copy of the boot sector. If they detect a virus, the programs use that backup copy to replace the infected boot sector.

Executable viruses are a little more difficult to find because they can be on any file in the drive. To detect executable viruses, the antivirus program uses a

library of signatures. A *signature* is the code pattern of a known virus. The antivirus program compares an executable file to its library of signatures. There have been instances where a perfectly clean program coincidentally held a virus signature. Usually the antivirus program's creator provides a patch to prevent further alarms. Now that you understand the types of viruses and how antivirus programs try to protect against them, let's review a few terms that are often used when describing certain traits of viruses.

Polymorphic/Polymorphs A *polymorphic virus* attempts to change its signature to prevent detection by antivirus programs, usually by continually scrambling a bit of useless code. Fortunately, the scrambling code itself can be identified and used as the signature—once the antivirus makers become aware of the virus. One technique used to combat unknown polymorphs is to have the antivirus program create a checksum on every file in the drive. A *checksum* in this context is a number generated by the software based on the contents of the file rather than the name, date, or size of that file. The algorithms for creating these checksums vary among different antivirus programs (they are also usually kept secret to help prevent virus makers from coming up with ways to beat them). Every time a program is run, the antivirus program calculates a new checksum and compares it with the earlier calculation. If the checksums are different, it is a sure sign of a virus.

Stealth The term "stealth" is more of a concept than an actual virus function. Most *stealth virus* programs are boot sector viruses that use various methods to hide from antivirus software. The AntiEXE stealth virus hooks on to a little-known but often-used software interrupt, for example, running only when that interrupt runs. Others make copies of innocent-looking files.

Recommended Antimalware Programs You can download many excellent antimalware programs for free, either for extended trial periods or for indefinite use. Since you need these programs to keep your systems happy, download one or more antimalware programs, such as the following:

- **Windows Defender** Windows Defender is a good antispyware program, but it won't protect you against any other form of malware. It's free with Windows, however, and better than nothing.
- **Microsoft Security Essentials** Recognizing the shortcomings of Windows Defender and no longer willing to count on users to download and install third-party programs, Microsoft offers a complete antimalware solution called Microsoft Security Essentials. You can download this

program for free from Microsoft (search for Microsoft Security Essentials). This program automatically shuts off Windows Defender when installed.

- **Malwarebytes Anti-Malware (www.malwarebytes.org)** Malwarebytes' Anti-Malware program rocks the house in terms of dealing with malicious software. They offer both a free version that scans your computer for malware and quarantines it and a pro version that actively protects against any incoming malware. Anti-Malware is my first choice in dealing with malware on a client's computer.

- **Lavasoft Ad-Aware (www.lavasoft.com)** Ad-Aware is an excellent antispyware program. Ad-Aware will root out all sorts of files and programs that can cause your computer to run slowly (or worse).

- **Spybot Search & Destroy (www.safer-networking.org)** Spybot Search & Destroy from Safer Networking Ltd. is another superb antispyware program. Many folks use both Ad-Aware and Spybot—though sometimes the two programs detect each other as spyware!

- **AVG Anti-Virus (http://free.avg.com)** AVG offers a free version of their antivirus software for noncommercial use. Updated regularly to add the latest virus signatures, the software will keep your system clean and bug free.

User Education

A powerful tool to prevent malware attacks and to reduce the impact of malware attacks when they happen is to educate your users. Teach users to be cautious of incoming e-mail they don't clearly recognize and to never click an attachment or URL in an e-mail message unless they are 100 percent certain of the source.

Explain to users the dangers of going to questionable Web sites and teach them how to react when they see questionable actions take place. Let's look at a few of the more evil ones. All Web browsers have built-in attack site warnings like the one shown in Figure 22.19.

Travel Advisory

Mozilla provides a sample Web site that displays the attack site sign—a great way to show users what it looks like: www.mozilla .org/firefox/its-an-attack.html.

Nobody wants their systems infected with malware. Users are motivated and happy when you give them the skills necessary to protect themselves. The bottom line is that educated and aware users will make your life a lot easier.

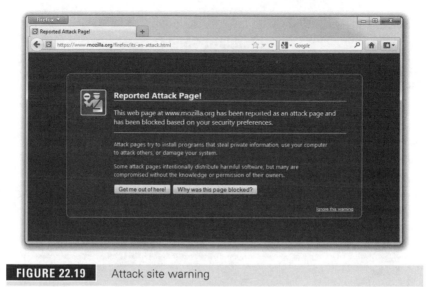

FIGURE 22.19 Attack site warning

Malware Prevention Tips

The secret to preventing damage from a malicious software attack is to keep from getting malware on your system in the first place. As discussed earlier, for example, all good antivirus programs include a virus shield that scans e-mail, downloads, running programs, and so on automatically (see Figure 22.20).

Use your antivirus shield. It is also a good idea to scan PCs daily for possible virus attacks. All antivirus programs include terminate-and-stay resident programs (TSRs) that run every time the PC is booted. Last but not least, know the source of any software before you load it. Although the chance of commercial, shrink-wrapped software having a virus is virtually nil (there have been a couple of well-publicized exceptions), that copy of *Call of Duty: Modern Warfare 3* you borrowed from a local hacker should definitely be inspected with care.

Keep your antivirus and antimalware programs updated. New viruses and other malware appear daily, and your programs need to know about them. The list of virus signatures your antivirus program can recognize, for example, is called the *definition file,* and you must keep that definition file up to date so your antivirus software has the latest signatures. Fortunately, most antivirus programs update themselves automatically. Further, you should periodically update the core antimalware software programming—called the *engine*—to employ the latest refinements the developers have included.

FIGURE 22.20 A virus shield in action

Boot CD Antimalware Tools

If you run antimalware software and your computer still gets infected, especially after a reboot, you need a more serious antimalware tool. Many antimalware companies provide bootable CDs or flash drives (or show you how to make one) that enable you to boot from a known-clean OS and run the same antimalware software, but this time not corrupted by the malware on your system.

Malware Recovery Tips

When the inevitable happens and either your computer or one of your user's computers gets infected by malware such as a computer virus, you need to follow certain steps to stop the problem from spreading and get the computer back up safely into service. Try this five-step process.

1. Recognize
2. Quarantine
3. Search and destroy
4. Remediate
5. Educate

Recognize and Quarantine The first step is to identify and recognize that a potential malware outbreak has occurred. If you're monitoring network traffic and one computer starts spewing e-mail, that's a good sign. Or users might complain that a computer that was running snappily the day before seems very sluggish.

Many networks employ software such as the open-source PacketFence that automatically monitors network traffic and can cut a machine off the network if that machine starts sending suspicious packets. You can also quarantine a computer manually by disconnecting the network cable. Once you're sure the machine isn't capable of infecting others, you're ready to find the virus or other malware and get rid of it.

At this point, you should disable System Restore. If you make any changes going forward, you don't want the virus to be included in any saved restore points. To turn off System Restore in Windows XP, open the Start menu, right-click My Computer, and select Properties. Switch to the System Restore tab and select Turn off System Restore. On the dialog box that pops up, confirm your selection by clicking Yes. To turn off System Restore in Windows Vista/7, open the Start menu, right-click Computer, and select Properties. Click the *System protection* link. In the Protection Settings section, select a drive and click Configure. In the System Protection dialog box that opens, select *Turn off system protection*. Repeat the procedure for each hard drive on your Windows Vista/7 system.

Exam Tip

Windows 7 also enables you to jump to the Protection Settings described earlier by using the System applet, System Protection tab.

Search and Destroy Once you've isolated the infected computer (or computers), you need to get to a safe boot environment and run antimalware software. You can try Windows Safe Mode first, because it doesn't require anything but a reboot. If that doesn't work, or if you suspect a boot sector virus, you need to turn to an external bootable source, such as a bootable CD or flash memory drive.

Get into the habit of keeping around a bootable antimalware flash drive or optical media. If you suspect a virus or other malware, use the disc, even if your antimalware program claims to have eliminated the problem. Turn off the PC and reboot it from the antimalware disc. (You might have to change CMOS settings to boot to optical media.) This will put you in a clean boot environment that you know is free from any boot sector viruses. If you only support fairly recent computers, most have an option to boot to a USB flash drive, so you can put a boot environment on a thumb drive for even faster start-up speeds.

You have several options for creating the bootable optical disc or flash drive. First, some antivirus software comes in a bootable version, such as the avast! Virus Cleaner Tool (see Figure 22.21).

Second, you can download a copy of Linux that offers a live CD option such as Ubuntu. With a live CD, you boot to the CD and install a complete working copy of the operating system into RAM, never touching or accessing the hard drive, to give you full Internet-ready access to many online antimalware sites. (You'll obviously need Internet access for those tools.) Kaspersky Labs provides a nice option at www.kaspersky.com.

FIGURE 22.21 avast! Virus Cleaner Tool

Finally, you can download and burn a copy of the Ultimate Boot CD. It comes stocked with several antivirus and antimalware programs, so you wouldn't need any other tool. Find it at www.ultimatebootcd.com. The only downside is that the antimalware engines will quickly be out of date, as will their malware libraries.

Once you get to a boot environment, run your antimalware program's most comprehensive scan. (Make sure you have all the latest updates for the software.) Then check all removable media that were exposed to the system and any other machine that might have received data from the system or that is networked to the cleaned machine. A virus or other malicious program can often lie dormant for months before anyone knows of its presence.

E-mail is still a common source of viruses, and opening infected e-mails is a common way to get infected. Viewing an e-mail in a preview window opens the e-mail message and exposes your computer to some viruses. Download files only from sites you know to be safe and avoid the less reputable corners of the Internet, the most likely places to pick up computer infections.

Exam Tip

CompTIA considers the process of removing a virus part of the remediation step. Since you can't remediate a PC until after a virus is gone, I've laid out the steps as you see here.

Remediate Malware infections can do a lot of damage to a system, especially to sensitive files needed to load Windows, so you might need to remediate formerly infected systems after cleaning off the drive or drives. *Remediation* simply means that you fix things the virus or other malware harmed. This can mean replacing corrupted Windows Registry files or even startup files.

If you can't start Windows after the malware scan is finished, you need to follow the steps outlined in Chapter 18 to boot to the Recovery Console in Windows XP, or boot from the Windows Preinstallation Environment into the Windows Recovery Environment in Windows Vista or Windows 7.

In the Windows XP Recovery Console, you'll have access to tools to repair the boot sector (or *boot blocks,* as CompTIA calls them) through the fixmbr and fixboot commands. You can run bootcfg to rebuild a corrupted boot.ini file.

With the Windows Vista/7 Recovery Environment, you have access to more repair tools, such as Startup Repair, System Restore, Windows Complete PC Restore (System Image Recovery in Windows 7), and the command prompt (see Figure 22.22). Run the appropriate option for the situation and you should have the machine properly remediated in a jiffy.

FIGURE 22.22 System Recovery options in Windows Vista

Exam Tip

Remember to re-enable System Restore and create a new restore point once the system has been repaired.

Educate The best way to keep from having to deal with malware and grayware is education. It's your job as the IT person to talk to users, especially the ones whose systems you've just spent the last hour cleaning of nasties, about how to avoid these programs. Show them samples of dangerous e-mails they should not open, Web sites to avoid, and the types of programs they should not install and use on the network. Any user who understands the risks of questionable actions on their computers will usually do the right thing and stay away from malware.

Finally, have your users run antivirus and antispyware programs regularly. Schedule them while interfacing with the user so you know it will happen.

Firewalls

Firewalls are an essential tool in the fight against malicious programs on the Internet. *Firewalls* are devices or software that protect an internal network from unauthorized access to and from the Internet at large. Firewalls use a number of methods to protect networks, such as hiding IP addresses and blocking TCP/IP ports.

A typical network uses one of two types of firewalls: *hardware firewalls,* often built into routers, and *software firewalls* that run on your computers. Both types of firewalls protect your computer and your network. You also run them at the same time. Let's look at both a typical SOHO router's firewall features and your computer's software firewall to see how they protect your network and your computers.

Hardware Firewall Settings

Most SOHO networks use a hardware firewall, often as a feature built into a router (Figure 22.23). A hardware firewall hides and separates an internal LAN from outside connections like the Internet by using *Network Address Translation (NAT).* NAT presents an entire LAN of computers to the Internet as a single machine. It effectively hides all of your computers and makes them appear invisible to other computers on the Internet. All anyone on the Internet sees is your *public* IP address. This is the address your ISP gives you, while all the computers in your LAN use private addresses that are invisible to the world.

FIGURE 22.23 A router often comes with a firewall

FIGURE 22.24 Default Web interface

Routers, however, have a few other tricks up their sleeves. From the router's browser-based settings screen, you can configure a hardware firewall (see Figure 22.24). Let's walk through a few of the available settings.

A hardware firewall watches for and stops many common threats—all you have to do is turn it on (see Figure 22.25). Hardware firewalls use *Stateful Packet Inspection* (*SPI*) to inspect each incoming packet individually. SPI also blocks any incoming traffic that isn't in response to your outgoing traffic. You can even disable ports entirely, blocking all traffic in or out. But what if you want to allow outside users access to a Web server on the LAN? Because NAT hides the true IP address of that system, you'll need a way to allow incoming traffic past the router/firewall and a way to redirect that traffic to the right PC.

Port forwarding enables you to open a port in the firewall and direct incoming traffic on that port to a specific IP address on your LAN. In the case of the Web server referenced in the previous paragraph, you would open port 80 (for HTTP packets) and instruct the router to send all incoming traffic to the server machine. Figure 22.26 shows port forwarding configured to send all HTTP packets to an internal Web server.

FIGURE 22.25 SPI firewall settings

Port forwarding isn't the only way to open ports on a firewall. *Port triggering* enables you to open an incoming connection to one computer automatically based on a specific outgoing connection. The *trigger port* defines the outgoing connection, and the *destination port* defines the incoming connection. If you set the trigger port to 3434 and the destination port to 1234, for example, any outgoing traffic on port 3434 will trigger the router to open port 1234 and send any received data back to the PC with the original outgoing traffic. Figure 22.27 shows a router set up for port triggering of an Internet Relay Chat (IRC) server.

If you want to go beyond port forwarding and port triggering and open every port on a machine, you need a demilitarized zone (DMZ). A DMZ puts systems with the specified IP addresses outside the protection of the firewall, opening all ports and enabling all incoming traffic (see Figure 22.28). If you think this sounds incredibly dangerous, you are right! Any PC inside the DMZ will be completely exposed to outside attacks. Don't use it!

FIGURE 22.26 Port forwarding

Exam Tip

The 802 exam suggests enabling media access control (MAC) filtering as a way to secure a SOHO wired network. You'll recall MAC filtering from Chapter 20, where you create a whitelist of approved MAC addresses for accessing your network. This is great for wireless networks. Although you *can* do this for wired networks, in practice it's a pain in the you-know-what. Every time you add a computer to the network, including allowing a guest to connect, you have to go to the router and manually update the whitelist. Ugh!

FIGURE 22.27 Port triggering

FIGURE 22.28 DMZ set up on a SOHO router

Software Firewalls

While a hardware firewall does a lot to protect you from outside intruders, you should also use a software firewall, such as the firewalls built into each version of Windows, called (appropriately) Windows Firewall. Windows Firewall handles the heavy lifting of port blocking, security logging, and more.

You can access Windows Firewall in Windows XP by opening the Windows Firewall applet in the Control Panel. The Windows XP's Windows Firewall applet (see Figure 22.29) looks a lot different from the one available in Windows 7 (see Figure 22.30), though their primary function remains the same. Configuring Windows Firewall involves turning it on or off and choosing which programs and services can pass through the firewall, known as *exceptions*. If you wanted to play *Starcraft 2* (a PC game that requires an Internet connection), for example, it would need to be on the list of exceptions for your firewall—most programs you install add themselves to this list automatically; otherwise,

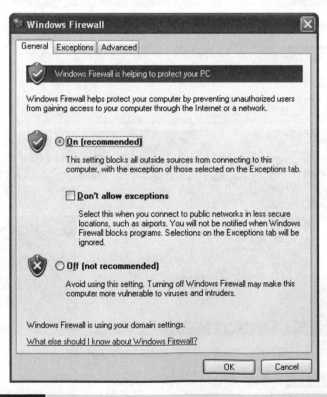

FIGURE 22.29 Windows XP's Firewall applet

FIGURE 22.30 Windows 7 Firewall applet

Windows Firewall prompts you the first time you run it and asks if you want to add the program as an exception.

> **Exam Tip**
>
> To disable Windows Firewall (which I don't recommend doing), open the Windows Firewall applet. In Windows XP, click the *Off (not recommended)* radio button. In Windows Vista, click *Turn Windows Firewall on or off* and then select *Off (not recommended)*. In Windows 7, select *Turn Windows Firewall on or off* and then select *Turn off Windows Firewall (not recommended)* for each network type you use. Reverse these steps to enable the Windows Firewall.

The Windows XP firewall's biggest shortcoming is that it fails to consider that a single PC, especially a portable, might connect to multiple networks. You don't necessarily want the same firewall settings used for both public and private networks. Microsoft needed to develop a way for you to separate trustworthy networks (like the one in your house or at the office) from nontrustworthy

networks (like a public Wi-Fi Internet connection at the airport). To accomplish this, Microsoft included three network types in Windows Vista/7: Domain, Private, and Public:

- A *Domain* network is a Windows network controlled by a Windows domain controller. In this case, the domain controller itself tells your machine what it can and cannot share. You don't need to do anything when your computer joins a domain.
- A *Private* network enables you to share resources, discover other devices, and allow other devices to discover your computer safely.
- A *Public* network prevents your computer from sharing and disables all discovery protocols.

When your computer connects to a network for the first time, Windows Vista and 7 will prompt you to choose the network type: Home, Work, or Public location (see Figure 22.31).

Set Network Location

Select a location for the 'Network 2' network

Windows will automatically apply the correct network settings for the location.

Home
Choose this for a home or similar location. Your computer is discoverable and you can see other computers and devices.

Work
Choose this for a workplace or similar location. Your computer is discoverable and you can see other computers and devices.

Public location
Choose this for airports, coffee shops, and other public places or if you are directly connected to the Internet. Discovery of other computers and devices is limited.

Customize the name, location type, and icon for the network
Help me choose

Cancel

FIGURE 22.31 Set Network Location in Vista

First, notice that Domain is not an option. There's a good reason for this: If your computer is on a domain, you won't see the dialog box in Figure 22.31. When your computer joins a domain, Windows automatically sets your network location to Domain (unless your domain controller chooses something different, which is unlikely).

So what exactly does Windows do when you select Home, Work, or Public location? Windows configures Windows Firewall to block or unblock discovery and sharing services. When running on a Private (Home or Work) network, Windows enables Network Discovery and File and Printer Sharing as exceptions. When running on a Public network, Windows disables these exceptions.

Exam Tip

The Network Discovery setting dictates whether a computer can find other computers or devices on a network and vice versa. Even with Network Discovery activated, several firewall settings can overrule certain connections.

In Windows Vista, Microsoft cleverly used Windows Firewall and the network type to turn services on and off, but Microsoft made one mistake: the firewall configuration and network type remain the same for every connection. If your Windows machine never changes networks, you won't have a problem. But what about machines (mainly laptops) that hop from one network to another (see Figure 22.32)? In that case, you need different firewall settings for each network the system might encounter.

In this regard, Windows 7 makes a big departure from Windows Vista. In Windows 7, the Set Network Location dialog box appears every time you connect to a new network. Windows 7 even includes three different firewall settings: one for Domains, one for Private networks (Home or Work), and one for Public networks.

Once you've picked a network type, you might want to customize the firewall settings further. If you click the Advanced Settings option in Windows Vista/7's Firewall applet, you'll discover a much deeper level of firewall configuration, one very different from the settings found in Windows XP (see Figure 22.33). In fact, it's an entirely different tool called Windows Firewall with Advanced Security.

One firewall is good enough for me.

I need different firewalls depending on where I am.

FIGURE 22.32 Many machines need more than one network setting.

Exam Tip

You can find the *Windows Firewall with Advanced Security* applet in Administrative tools. For some reason, the 802 exam lists this as two tools, *Windows Firewall* and *Advanced Security*.

Microsoft enhanced how Windows Vista/7 treat exceptions. In Windows XP, you can only choose a program and make it an exception, giving it permission to pass through the firewall. But programs both send and receive network data;

FIGURE 22.33 Windows Firewall with Advanced Security

Windows Firewall with Advanced Security

File Action View Help

Windows Firewall with Advance
 Inbound Rules
 Outbound Rules
 Connection Security Rules
 Monitoring

Outbound Rules

Name	Group	Profile	Enabled	Action	Program
BranchCache Content Retrieval (HTTP-O...	BranchCache - Content Retr...	All	No	Allow	SYSTEM
BranchCache Hosted Cache Client (HTT...	BranchCache - Hosted Cach...	All	No	Allow	SYSTEM
BranchCache Hosted Cache Server(HTTP...	BranchCache - Hosted Cach...	All	No	Allow	SYSTEM
BranchCache Peer Discovery (WSD-Out)	BranchCache - Peer Discove...	All	No	Allow	%System...
Connect to a Network Projector (TCP-Out)	Connect to a Network Proje...	Domain	No	Allow	%System...
Connect to a Network Projector (TCP-Out)	Connect to a Network Proje...	Private...	No	Allow	%System...
Connect to a Network Projector (WSD Ev...	Connect to a Network Proje...	Private...	No	Allow	System
Connect to a Network Projector (WSD Ev...	Connect to a Network Proje...	Domain	No	Allow	System
Connect to a Network Projector (WSD Ev...	Connect to a Network Proje...	Private...	No	Allow	System
Connect to a Network Projector (WSD Ev...	Connect to a Network Proje...	Domain	No	Allow	System
Connect to a Network Projector (WSD-O...	Connect to a Network Proje...	All	No	Allow	%System...
Core Networking - DNS (UDP-Out)	Core Networking	All	Yes	Allow	%System...
Core Networking - Dynamic Host Config...	Core Networking	All	Yes	Allow	%System...
Core Networking - Dynamic Host Config...	Core Networking	All	Yes	Allow	%System...
Core Networking - Group Policy (LSASS-...	Core Networking	Domain	Yes	Allow	%System...
Core Networking - Group Policy (NP-Out)	Core Networking	Domain	Yes	Allow	System
Core Networking - Group Policy (TCP-O...	Core Networking	Domain	Yes	Allow	%System...
Core Networking - Internet Group Mana...	Core Networking	All	Yes	Allow	System
Core Networking - IPHTTPS (TCP-Out)	Core Networking	All	Yes	Allow	%System...
Core Networking - IPv6 (IPv6-Out)	Core Networking	All	Yes	Allow	System
Core Networking - Multicast Listener Do...	Core Networking	All	Yes	Allow	Any
Core Networking - Multicast Listener Qu...	Core Networking	All	Yes	Allow	Any
Core Networking - Multicast Listener Rep...	Core Networking	All	Yes	Allow	Any
Core Networking - Multicast Listener Rep...	Core Networking	All	Yes	Allow	Any
Core Networking - Neighbor Discovery A...	Core Networking	All	Yes	Allow	Any
Core Networking - Neighbor Discovery S...	Core Networking	All	Yes	Allow	Any
Core Networking - Packet Too Big (ICMP...	Core Networking	All	Yes	Allow	Any
Core Networking - Parameter Problem (I...	Core Networking	All	Yes	Allow	Any
Core Networking - Router Advertisement...	Core Networking	All	Yes	Allow	Any
Core Networking - Router Solicitation (IC...	Core Networking	All	Yes	Allow	Any
Core Networking - Teredo (UDP-Out)	Core Networking	All	Yes	Allow	%System...
Core Networking - Time Exceeded (ICMP...	Core Networking	All	Yes	Allow	Any

Actions

Outbound Rules
 New Rule...
 Filter by Profile
 Filter by State
 Filter by Group
 View
 Refresh
 Export List...
 Help

FIGURE 22.34 Outbound Rules list

Windows XP ignores the "inbound" and "outbound" aspect of firewalls. Windows Vista/7 take the exceptions concept and expand it to include custom rules for both inbound and outbound data. Figure 22.34 shows the outbound rules for a typical Windows Vista/7 system.

A rule always includes at least the following:

- The name of the program
- Group: an organizational group that helps sort all the rules
- The associated profile (All, Domain, Public, Private)
- Enabled/disabled status
- Remote and local address
- Remote and local port number

You can add, remove, and customize any rule to your liking. It quickly gets complicated, so unless you need to set a lot of custom rules, stick to the standard Windows Firewall applet.

Authentication and Encryption

You know from earlier in the chapter that the first step in securing data is authentication, through a user name and password. But when you throw in networking, you're suddenly not just a single user sitting in front of a computer and typing. You're accessing a remote resource and sending login information over the Internet. What's to stop someone from intercepting your user name and password?

Firewalls do a great job of controlling traffic coming into a network from the Internet and going out of a network to the Internet, but they do nothing to stop interceptor hackers who monitor traffic on the public Internet looking for vulnerabilities. Worse, once a packet is on the Internet itself, anyone with the right equipment can intercept and inspect it. Inspected packets are a cornucopia of passwords, account names, and other tidbits that hackers can use to intrude into your network. Because we can't stop hackers from inspecting these packets, we must turn to *encryption* to make them unreadable.

Network encryption occurs at many levels and is in no way limited to Internet-based activities. Not only are there many levels of network encryption, but each encryption level also provides multiple standards and options, making encryption one of the most complicated of all networking issues. You need to understand where encryption comes into play, what options are available, and what you can use to protect your network.

Network Authentication

Have you ever considered the process that takes place each time a person types in a user name and password to access a network rather than just a local machine? What happens when this *network* authentication is requested? If you're thinking that when a user types in a user name and password, that information is sent to a server of some sort to be authenticated, you're right—but do you know how the user name and password get to the serving system? That's where encryption becomes important in authentication.

In a local network, authentication and encryption are usually handled by the OS. In today's increasingly interconnected and diverse networking environment, there is a motivation to enable different operating systems to authenticate any client system from any other OS. Modern operating systems such as Windows and Mac OS X use standard authentication encryptions such as Massachusetts Institute of Technology's (MIT's) *Kerberos,* enabling multiple brands of servers to authenticate multiple brands of clients. These LAN authentication methods are usually transparent and work quite nicely, even in mixed networks.

Data Encryption

Encryption methods don't stop at the authentication level. There are a number of ways to encrypt network *data* as well. The choice of encryption method is dictated to a large degree by the method used by the communicating systems to connect. Many networks consist of multiple networks linked together by some sort of private connection, usually some kind of WAN connection such as DSL or T1. Microsoft's encryption method of choice for this type of network is called *IPsec* (derived from *IP security*). IPsec provides transparent encryption between the server and the client. IPsec also works in VPNs, but other encryption methods are more commonly used in those situations.

Application Encryption

When it comes to encryption, even TCP/IP applications can get into the swing of things. The most famous of all application encryptions is Netscape's *Secure Sockets Layer (SSL)* security protocol, which is used to create secure Web sites. Microsoft incorporates SSL into its more far-reaching *HTTPS* (HTTP over SSL) protocol. These protocols make it possible to create the secure Web sites people use to make purchases over the Internet. As mentioned in Chapter 20, you can identify HTTPS Web sites by the *https://* (rather than http://) included in the URL (see Figure 22.35).

FIGURE 22.35 A secure Web site

To make a secure connection, your Web browser and the Web server must encrypt their data. That means there must be a way for both the Web server and your browser to encrypt and decrypt each other's data. To do this, the server sends a public key to your Web browser so the browser knows how to decrypt the incoming data. These public keys are sent in the form of a *digital certificate*. This certificate is signed by a trusted authority that guarantees that the public key you are about to get is actually from the Web server and not from some evil person trying to pretend to be the Web server. A number of companies issue digital certificates to Web sites, probably the most famous being VeriSign, Inc.

Your Web browser has a built-in list of trusted authorities. If a certificate comes in from a Web site that uses one of these highly respected companies, you won't see anything happen in your browser; you'll just go to the secure Web page, where a small lock will appear in the corner of your browser. Figure 22.36 shows the list of trusted authorities built into the Firefox Web browser.

FIGURE 22.36 Trusted authorities

If you receive a certificate from someone *not* listed in your browser, however, the browser will warn you and ask you if you wish to accept the certificate, as shown in Figure 22.37.

What you do here is up to you. Do you wish to trust this certificate? In most cases, you simply say yes, and this certificate is added to your SSL cache of certificates. An accepted certificate may become invalid, however, usually because of something boring; for instance, it may go out of date or the public key may change. This never happens with the "big name" certificates built into your browser—you'll see this more often when a certificate is used, for example, in-house on a company intranet and the administrator forgets to update the certificates. If a certificate goes bad, your browser issues a warning the next time

FIGURE 22.37 Incoming certificate

Internet Options

General | Security | Privacy | **Content** | Connections | Programs | Advanced

Content Advisor

Ratings help you control the Internet content that can be viewed on this computer.

Enable... | Settings

Certificates

Use certificates for encrypted connections and identification.

Clear SSL state | Certificates | Publishers

AutoComplete

AutoComplete stores previous entries on webpages and suggests matches for you. | Settings

Feeds and Web Slices

Feeds and Web Slices provide updated content from websites that can be read in Internet Explorer and other programs. | Settings

OK | Cancel | Apply

FIGURE 22.38 Internet Options Content tab in Internet Explorer

you visit that site. To clear invalid certificates, you need to clear the SSL cache. The process varies in every browser, but in Internet Explorer, go to the Content tab under Internet Options and click the *Clear SSL state* button (see Figure 22.38).

Exam Tip

The 802 exam uses the term *digital security* to refer to the many tools covered in this chapter, such as antivirus and antispyware software, firewalls, user authentication, strong passwords, and directory/folder permissions.

CHECKPOINT

✔**Objective 22.01: Analyzing Security Threats** Threats to your data come from two sources: accidents and malicious people. Unauthorized access occurs when a user accesses resources in an unauthorized way. Most computer attacks are accomplished through social engineering—infiltration, telephone scams, phishing—rather than hacking. Computers, hard drives, and power all fail. As a tech, you need to plan for redundancy in these areas. You also need to protect your computers against viruses distributed through the network and removable media. You should implement good access policies and implement methods for tracking computer usage.

✔**Objective 22.02: Security Concepts and Technologies** Controlling access to programs, data, and other computing resources is the key to securing your system. Access control includes four interlinked areas requiring your attention: physical security, authentication, users and groups, and security policies. Accounts should be given permissions to access only what they need and no more. Unused accounts should be disabled. Use the Local Security Policy tool to manage policies for an individual computer.

Incidence reporting means telling your supervisor about the data you've gathered regarding a computer or network problem. This provides a record of what you've done and accomplished. It also provides information that, when combined with other information you may or may not know, may reveal a pattern or bigger problem to someone higher up the chain.

Try to avoid any personal information on a PC. If you find something private (that isn't illegal), ignore it and forget about it. If you find something illegal, you must follow the proper procedures. If a device you work on becomes evidence in legal proceedings, isolate the system and document everything that happens going forward. Pay special attention to the chain of custody, or whoever is currently in control of the machine.

✔**Objective 22.03: Protecting Computers from Network Threats** Malware includes grayware, spam, viruses, worms, macros, Trojan horses, and rootkits, all of which can wreak havoc on your system. To help protect a computer from malware, make sure to run up-to-date antivirus software, use a firewall, and apply all security patches for your software and operating system. Some of the common symptoms of a malware infection include browser redirections, crashes, unresponsiveness, changed file permissions, hidden files, missing system files, and so on.

When the inevitable happens and either your computer or one of your user's computers is infected by a computer virus or other malware, you need to follow a process to stop the problem from spreading and get the computer back up safely into service: recognize, quarantine, search and destroy, remediate, educate.

Hardware firewalls protect networks by hiding IP addresses and blocking TCP/IP ports. Port forwarding and port triggering enable traffic to pass through the firewall on specific ports to specific machines. Windows firewall also enables strong protection against network attacks.

REVIEW QUESTIONS

1. What is the process of using or manipulating people to gain access to network resources?

 A. Cracking

 B. Hacking

 C. Network engineering

 D. Social engineering

2. Which of the following might offer good hardware authentication?

 A. Strong password

 B. Encrypted password

 C. NTFS

 D. Smart card

3. Randall needs to change the file system on his second hard drive (currently the D: drive) from FAT32 to NTFS. Which of the following commands would do the trick?

 A. convert d: /fs:ntfs

 B. convert d: ntfs

 C. ntfs d:

 D. ntfs d: /fat32

4. Which of the following tools would enable you to require a minimum password length for all users of a workstation?

 A. AD Policy

 B. Group Policy

 C. Local Security Policy

 D. User Settings

5. Which of the following offers the best file system security?

 A. NTFS

 B. FAT32

 C. Privacy filter

 D. Security-minded tech

6. Which of the following are the best examples of remediation? (Select two.)

 A. Boot to the Recovery Console in Windows XP and run fixmbr or fixboot to repair boot sector damage.

 B. Boot to the Windows Recovery Environment in Windows Vista/7 and run System Restore.

 C. Boot to a safe environment and run antivirus software.

 D. Remove a computer suspected of having a virus from the network, effectively quarantining the computer.

7. A user account is a member of several groups, and the groups have conflicting rights and permissions to several network resources. The culminating permissions that ultimately affect the user's access are referred to as what?

 A. Effective permissions

 B. Culminating rights

 C. Last rights

 D. Persistent permissions

8. What is true about virus shields?

 A. They automatically scan e-mails, downloads, and running programs.

 B. They protect against spyware and adware.

 C. They are effective in stopping pop-ups.

 D. They can reduce the amount of spam by 97 percent.

9. Which threats are categorized as social engineering? (Select two.)

 A. Telephone scams

 B. Dumpster diving

 C. Trojans

 D. Spyware

10. A user calls to complain that his computer seems awfully sluggish. All he's done so far is open his e-mail. What should the tech do first?

 A. Educate the user about the dangers of opening e-mail.

 B. Quarantine the computer so the suspected virus does not spread.

 C. Run antivirus software on the computer.

 D. Remediate the infected system.

REVIEW ANSWERS

1. **D** Social engineering is the process of using or manipulating people to gain access to network resources.

2. **D** A smart card might offer good hardware authentication.

3. **A** The convert d: /fs:ntfs command will change the file system on the D: drive from FAT32 to NTFS.

4. **C** Local Security Policy enables you to require a minimum password length for all user accounts on a workstation.

5. **A** NTFS offers the best file system security through encryption.

6. **A B** Booting to the Recovery Console (XP) or WinRE (Vista/7) enables you to run tools for remediation, such as fixboot and System Restore.

7. **A** Effective permissions are the result of combined permissions, and determine access to resources.

8. **A** Virus shields automatically scan e-mails, downloads, and running programs.

9. **A B** Telephone scams and dumpster diving are forms of social engineering.

10. **B** The user should quarantine the computer immediately.

Career Flight Path

CompTIA A+ certification generally serves as the foundation for any number of career paths. Most IT companies, big and small, see CompTIA A+ certification as the entry point to IT. From CompTIA A+, you have a number of certification options, depending on whether you want to focus more on hardware or on network administration (although these are not mutually exclusive goals). Take a look at these four options in particular:

- CompTIA Network+ certification
- CompTIA Security+ certification
- Microsoft Technical Series certifications
- Cisco certification

CompTIA Network+ Certification

If you haven't already taken the CompTIA Network+ exam, make it your next certification. Just as CompTIA A+ certification shows you have solid competency as a PC technician, CompTIA Network+ certification demonstrates your skill as a network technician, including your understanding of network hardware, installation, and troubleshooting. CompTIA's Network+ certification is a natural fit for continuing toward your Microsoft or Cisco certifications.

CompTIA Security+ Certification

Like CompTIA Network+ certification, CompTIA Security+ certification is a more in-depth testing of your knowledge of PC and server-specific hardware and operating systems. It's the first step into a lucrative career in keeping data safe. Security is top on the list of priorities for many companies, so demonstrating that you know how to protect systems and data by becoming CompTIA Security+ certified will make you more competitive in the job market.

Microsoft Technical Series Certifications

Microsoft provides a series of certifications geared for computer specialists. Most new techs start with one or more Microsoft Certified Technology Specialist (MCTS) certification exams, such as Exam 70-680, MCTS: Windows 7, Configuration, to get deeper information on supporting Windows operating systems. After a couple of MCTS certifications, your next step is to get one of the Microsoft Certified IT Professional (MCITP) certifications. These provide you with the knowledge to administer and support Windows in higher-end business and home environments. MCITP certifications are composed of two or more MCTS certification exams and are the next logical certification step.

If you plan a career focused more on networking at an enterprise level, you can pursue Microsoft's cloud-focused Microsoft Certified Solutions Associate (MCSA) and Microsoft Certified Solutions Expert (MCSE) certifications. These deal with virtual machines, remote access, Windows Server in the enterprise, and more.

Cisco Certification

Cisco routers pretty much run the Internet, and most intranets in the world, so Cisco provides several levels and paths of certification for folks who want to show their skills at handling Cisco products. Most everyone interested in Cisco certification starts with the Certified Cisco Network Associate (CCNA). The CCNA is only one exam (640-802) and a darn easy way to slap the word *Cisco* on your resume! After attaining CCNA, you should consider the CCNP (Certified Cisco Networking Professional) certification.

As with the Microsoft certifications, each level of certification offers different career paths. You can specialize in routing and switching, for example, or network security. Either path would take you first to CCNA and then to CCNP.

See the Cisco certification Web site for more details: www.cisco.com/en/US/learning/le3/learning_career_certifications_and_learning_paths_home.html

About the CD-ROM

APPENDIX B

The disc included with this book comes with:

- A video introduction to CompTIA A+ exams from the author, Mike Meyers
- Digital copies of the CompTIA A+ 220-801 and 220-802 exam objectives
- A copy of the Glossary for the book
- Total Tester practice exam software with hundreds of practice exam questions
- Links to a collection of Mike's current favorite tools and utilities for PC troubleshooting
- A link to more than one hour of Mike Meyers video training
- A PDF copy of the book

The software can be installed on any Windows XP/Windows Vista/Windows 7/Windows 8 computer and must be installed to access the Total Tester practice exam software.

Playing the Mike Meyers Introduction Video

If your computer's optical drive is configured to auto-run, the menu will automatically start up upon inserting the disc. If the auto-run feature did not launch the disc, browse to the disc and click the Launch.exe icon.

From the opening screen you can launch the video message from Mike by clicking the Mike Meyers Introduction Video button. This launches the video file using your system's default video player.

Viewing the Glossary and the CompTIA Exam Objectives

To view the Glossary or the CompTIA A+ exam objectives, select the CompTIA Exam Objectives and Glossary button from the main menu of the disc. On the next page, click the Glossary button, the CompTIA A+ (220–801) Objectives button, or the CompTIA A+ (220–802) Objectives button to open a PDF of the appropriate file. The objectives are the actual exam objectives from CompTIA as of the date of publication. Please visit the CompTIA Web site for the most up-to-date exam objectives. Adobe Acrobat Reader must be installed to view the Glossary or objectives lists. Adobe Acrobat Reader is available from www.acrobat.com. The Glossary is also included in the free eBook download available with this CD.

System Requirements

The software requires Windows XP or higher, Internet Explorer 7 or higher, Firefox with Flash Player, or any version of Chrome, and 30 MB of hard disk space for full installation.

Installing and Running Total Tester

From the main screen of the CD you may install the Total Tester by clicking the Software and Videos button and then selecting the Total Tester A+ Practice Exams button. This will begin the installation process and place an icon on your desktop and in your Start menu. To run Total Tester, navigate to Start | (All) Programs | Total Seminars or double-click the icon on your desktop.

To uninstall the Total Tester software, go to Start | Settings | Control Panel | Add/Remove Programs (XP) or Programs and Features (Vista/7/8), and then select the A+ Total Tester program. Select Remove and Windows will completely uninstall the software.

Total Tester

Total Tester provides you with a simulation of the CompTIA A+ exams. You may select practice exams for CompTIA A+ Exam 801 or CompTIA A+ Exam 802. The exams can be taken in either Practice mode or Exam Simulation mode. Practice mode provides an assistance window with hints, an explanation of the answer, and the option to check your answer as you take the test. Both Practice mode and Exam Simulation mode provide an overall grade and a grade broken down by certification objective. To take a test, launch the program and select CompTIA A+ from the Installed Question Packs menu. Next select either the 801 exam or the 802 exam from the dropdown menu. Finally select Practice Exam or Exam Simulation mode and then select Start Exam to begin your test.

Mike's Cool Tools

Mike loves freeware/open source PC tools! Most of the utilities mentioned in the text can be downloaded from the Internet using URLs provided on the disc on the Mike's Cool Tools page. You can access the menu by clicking on the Software and Videos button on the main page of the disc and then selecting the Access Mike's Cool Tools link.

Please read the Cool Tools page for a description of the utilities.

Travel Advisory

While all of the tools are "Mike Meyers Approved," there is no guarantee they will work for you. Read any and all documentation that comes with each utility before downloading and using that program.

Mike's Video Training

Your disc comes with a link to hours of free PC video training starring Mike Meyers. On the main page of the disc, click the Software and Videos link and then select Access Mike Meyers Video Training. You'll have access to several training segments, with an option to purchase even more of Mike's instructional videos.

Electronic Book

The contents of this book are provided in PDF format on the CD. This file is viewable on your computer and many portable devices.

To view the file on your computer, Adobe's Acrobat Reader is required and has been included on the CD.

Note
For more information on Adobe Reader and to check for the most recent version of the software, visit Adobe's Web site at www.adobe.com and search for the free Adobe Reader or look for Adobe Reader on the product page.

To view the electronic book on a portable device, copy the PDF file to your computer from the CD, and then copy the file to your portable device using a USB or other connection. Adobe offers a mobile version of Adobe Reader, the Adobe Reader mobile app, which currently supports iOS and Android. The Adobe Web site also has a list of recommended applications.

Technical Support

For questions regarding the Total Tester software, the video, Mike's Cool Tools, or operation of the CD, visit www.totalsem.com or e-mail support@totalsem.com.

For questions regarding the PDF book or video, e-mail techsolutions@mhedu .com or visit http://mhp.softwareassist.com.

For questions regarding book content, please e-mail customer.service @mheducation.com. For customers outside the United States, e-mail international_ cs@mcgraw-hill.com.

Index